The Sec

The Secular Revolution

Power, Interests, and Conflict in the Secularization of American Public Life

Edited by
Christian Smith

UNIVERSITY OF CALIFORNIA PRESS
Berkeley   Los Angeles   London

University of California Press
Berkeley and Los Angeles, California

University of California Press, Ltd.
London, England

© 2003 by the Regents of the University of California

A version of chapter 5, P. C. Kemeny's "Power, Ridicule, and the
Destruction of Religious Moral Reform Politics in the 1920s," was
published as "Banned in Boston: Commercial Culture and the
Decline of Protestant Moral Reform Political Action in Boston in
the 1920s," in *Faith in the Market: Religion and Urban Commercial
Culture in North America, 1889–1990,* ed. Diane Winston and John
Gigge, © 2002 by P. C. Kemeny. Reprinted by permission of Rutgers
University Press.

Library of Congress Cataloging-in-Publication Data

The secular revolution : power, interests, and conflict in the
secularization of American public life / edited by Christian Smith.
    p.   cm.
Includes bibliographical references and index.
  ISBN 0-520-23000-0 (alk. paper) — ISBN 0-520-23561-4 (pbk. :
alk. paper)
1. United States—Church history. 2. Secularism—United
States—History. 3. Church and state—United States—History.
4. Protestant churches—United States—History. I. Smith,
Christian (Christian Stephen), 1960–

BR517.S36 1003
261'.0973—dc21

2002015442

Manufactured in the United States of America

11 10 09 08 07 06 05 04 03
10 9 8 7 6 5 4 3 2 1

The paper used in this publication is both acid-free and totally
chlorine-free (TCF). It meets the minimum requirements of
ANSI/NISO Z39.48-1992 (R 1997) (*Permanence of Paper*).♾

CONTENTS

PREFACE

The central claim of this book is that the historical secularization of the institutions of American public life was not a natural, inevitable, and abstract by-product of modernization; rather it was the outcome of a struggle between contending groups with conflicting interests seeking to control social knowledge and institutions. My intent is to move agency, interests, power, resources, mobilization, strategy, and conflict to the foreground in our understanding of macrosocial secularization—a topic until now largely framed by abstract and agentless terms like *differentiation* and *rationalization*. By suggesting revolution as the central analytical image, I mean to highlight issues of power and authority, mobilization, and cultural and institutional transformation.

I must make a few brief comments on two key terms and this book's analytical boundaries. By *religion* I mean the distinctive way of life of communities of followers shaped by their particular system of beliefs and practices that are oriented toward the supernatural. Religion thus conceived is not merely a set of cognitive beliefs, emotional dispositions, or ethical imperatives, but is expressed fully as a way of life practiced by communities of people. This particularistic, substantive definition intentionally excludes implicit religions, "civil religion," "quasi-religions," and "secular religions" from consideration. In my use of *public life*, I follow Habermas broadly in meaning those fields of social life in which culturally different groups of people must live together with common normative and institutional arrangements that govern or influence important dimensions of their lives. These include the areas of law, education, science, medicine, the mass media, and so on. As to analytical boundaries, this project will generally focus on the proximate causes of the secularization of American public life, not on its ultimate causes and long historical context. Ancient Israelite monotheism, ancient Greek philosophies, the Renaissance, the Protestant Reformation, the Enlightenment, and so on helped to create a certain background for macrosocial secularization in America. But my concern here is not primarily with how long-term forces may have created a general context, but with the proximate whos, whys, and hows of the secular revolution that were played out within that context. I should also state explicitly that while the arguments that follow intend to address the question of secularization broadly, I proceed in that direction by analyzing a set of specific, concrete, historical events surrounding the loss by American Protestant establishment elites of their public institutional influence in the United States. While the former hopefully will illuminate the latter, the two should not be conflated in a way that suggests that secularization generally equals the demise of Protestant elite control.

This project has been formed by some theoretical influences worth noting. First, it is obviously shaped by the sociology of revolutions and social movements, which insists that students of intentional social change pay attention to the interests and benefits, political opportunities, organizations, resources, grievances, ideologies, and issue-framing work of contending actors. More specifically, this project has taken a cue from Chaves (1994) and Dobbelaere (1981), who have suggested shifting the focus of secularization theory from questions of belief to issues of authority. This project has also been influenced by William Sewell's (1992) theory of structure, which demonstrates the culturally constituted nature of all social structures. Sewell's approach leads us to attend to how cultural schemas both form and legitimate particular distributions of resources within and among institutions, and also to ways that historical shifts in available resources have altered the viability of certain cultural schemas. Moreover, this project has been shaped by social constructionism. Taking human social reality not as an objectively fixed, external fact, but rather as significantly constructed through processes of social interaction—which draw on culturally available cognitive categories and unevenly distributed resources—this project problematizes the facts about American religion and public life and inquires into the historical social processes by which that reality has been produced.[1] The analysis here also picks up the central insight of recent "social studies of science" that science and related forms of knowledge-production are profoundly social and political activities that merit critical analysis. Furthermore, this project has been influenced by certain postmodernist sensibilities. It takes seriously the postmodern critique of Enlightenment universalism as the imperialistic absolutization of one historically situated narrative, the exposing of which can open up possibilities for more genuine intellectual and social pluralism. It also takes seriously postmodernism's claim that discourse is power-laden, sensitizing our analysis to the ways that historical debates which redefined languages and vocabularies functioned to redistribute power and authority.

In these ways, this project indulges somewhat in the postmodern penchant for unmasking misrecognized relations of domination—though without fully embracing what I think are the overstated intellectual programs of Foucault, Derrida, Bourdieu, Fish, and the like. Readers may also detect in this work the influences of Andrew Abbott (1988) on professions, Robert Wuthnow (1987, 1989) on moral order and communities of discourse, and Raymond Boudon (1981) on what I think is a sensible version of methodological individualism.

This book's argument raises important political issues. By analytically problematizing what *did* happen to religion in American public life, it inevitably prompts the normative question of what *ought to* have happened and should today happen when it comes to religion in the public square. That is part of my intention. However, my historical analysis does not itself imply or underwrite any specific political position on the matter. Both strict separationists and religious accommodationists (i.e., those who want the state to advantage one or all religions in public life because of the benefits for democracy and civic life that religion is said to provide), as different as they are, might equally be persuaded by the analytical approach here. The separationists will simply celebrate the secular revolution, while accommodationists will lament it.[2] Thus, the reader's own normative position on the proper role of religion in public life per se should not determine whether he or she finds this book convincing.

That said, however, I disclose that my own normative approach to these matters is structural pluralism. I understand and am sympathetic to the claims of both religious accommodationism and strict separationism. But in the end I can embrace neither. Particularly in a society as pluralistic as the United States, I believe it is unjust to privilege one religion over other religions, or to privilege all religions over nonreligion, as accommodationism tends to do. But I also believe, particularly with a people as religious as Americans are, that it is unjust to privilege the secular over the religious by excluding religion from whole spheres of public life, as strict separationism tends to do. In addition, both accommodationism and separationism are problematic because they tend to generate ongoing social strife, as groups—religious and secular—who feel excluded or dominated by others in winner-take-all situations recurrently mobilize for battles to protect their values and autonomy.

A more just and socially peaceable approach, I believe, is some version of structural pluralism. This approach affirms cultural and religious pluralism as a positive social good, and believes that pluralism should be able to find significant expression in public life. Structural pluralism views the state as called to establish justice, by which it means, among other things, acting with nonpreferential neutrality or impartiality (rather than separationist exclusionism or accommodationist preferentialism) toward different religious and nonreligious groups—when financing public education, funding social service programs, and so on. It thus charges the state in its dealings not to privilege or disadvantage any religious or nonreligious tradition or perspective over any other. Structural pluralism recognizes the existence, validity, and potential civic value of diverse religious communities (and not simply the individuals and their religious beliefs), and their right to live out their religious ways of life not only in private but also significantly in public life. In these ways, it represents a notable step institutionally in the direction of affirming and protecting diversity, and away from winner-take-all uniformity. Structural pluralism is no panacea. But it has the potential to protect the rights of minority religions and secularists, without excluding religion from public deliberation and practice (see, e.g., Monsma 1993; Monsma and Soper 1997, 1998; Wolterstorff 1997; Skillen and McCarthy 1991; also see Rescher 1993).

My normative commitments have undoubtedly shaped my approach to my work. Whose do not? Structural pluralism, for example, causes me to consider the old Protestant establishment as oppressive, unjust, and deserving of challenge by the groups it excluded. I have no great love for nineteenth-century Christian America, and do not bemoan its passing. But structural pluralism also leads me to believe that political liberalism's strict separationism—the view of church-state relations that reigned in the United States for the second half of the twentieth century—was also oppressive and unjust, especially for religious believers whose faith cannot be privatized without violation, and needs rethinking. Still, this book is not for structural pluralists particularly. The analysis here can and I hope will be persuasive and useful to readers who hold a whole range of other normative commitments about religion and public life.

This project was a collaborative effort by a terrific team of scholars, not all of whom share my analytical approach. Participants were not chosen primarily for their assent to my way of thinking about either secularization or church-state relations. The consequent diversity among the project's scholars—practicing, perhaps, a form of academic structural pluralism—and the critical discussions that resulted proved a valuable asset to the project. In any case, do not assume that all of the contributors to this volume are uncritical advocates of the secular revolution thesis that I lay out in the introduction.

Thanks go first of all to Luis Lugo, Kimon Sargeant, and Susan Harper of The Pew Charitable Trusts for the resources which made this research project possible. Needless to say, the positions in this book are those of the authors and do not necessarily reflect those of The Pew Charitable Trusts. Thanks also to Ruby Massey, Bev Wiggins, Gretchen McCoy, and Charif Soubra of the Odum Institute for Research in Social Science at the University of North Carolina for their administrative support of this project from start to finish. I am also grateful to Craig Calhoun, Robert Wuthnow, Diane Winston, and George Marsden for constituting an advisory board that helped to launch this project. Thanks go to Ginger Strickland, Erin Lunsford, Natalia Deeb-Sossa, Karen Benjamin, Stephanie Barber, Jenny MacArthur, Melinda Lundquist, Heather Kane, Stephen Lippman, Kate Joyce, Bob Woodberry, Chris Eberle, Nick Wolterstorff, Randy Heinig, Bob Faris, Mark Noll, Roger Finke, Michael Young, Tom Tyson, Charlie Kurzman, and Mark Chaves for various forms of research assistance and critical readings of previous drafts of chapters of this book. Kelly Moore was a tremendous help in working out the collective thinking of this project. Finally, thanks go to the participants in a conference held in Chapel Hill on June 1–2, 2001, whose comments and criticisms were helpful in refining the argument of this book: David Baker, John Bartkowski, Michael Beaty, Margaret Bendroth, Lis Clemens, Sally Gallagher, Phil Gorski, Michael Hamilton, Daryl Hart, Brooks Holifield, Heather Kane, Phil Kim, Charlie Kurzman, Frank Lechner, Michael Lienesch, Stephen Lippmann, Larry Lyon, Kelly Moore, Warren Nord, Ronald Numbers, Alison Parker, Mark Regnerus, Martin Ruef, Jon Roberts, John Schmalzbauer, Jim Skillen, Pamela Walters, James Wellman, Rhys Williams, Nicholas Wolterstorff, Richard Wood, Robert D. Woodberry, David Yamane, and Michael Young.

NOTES

1. To be clear, I do not espouse a strong neo-Kantian, antirealist social constructionism that denies the existence of any external reality apart from human consciousness and ordering of it. Rather, I adopt what might be called a "perspectivalist realism," or what Sismondo (1996) calls a "deflationary" or "minimal and piecemeal realism." Things are not of human construction and interpretation all the way down; there does exist an ordered reality objective of human consciousness of it, which provides the materials which humans then interpret to construct what for them is reality.

2. David Hollinger (1996: 29) makes a parallel point in explaining why the important role of Jews in secularizing American universities in the twentieth century has been neglected: "Perhaps this dimension has been avoided because many who have thought about the transition from Protestant culture to religious pluralism have continued to honor an old suspicion that America would be better off today were it somehow more Christian than it is. Given this presumption, any account of how Jews contributed to the diminution of Christianity's influence could be construed as a criticism of Jews. . . . But this historiographical inhibition disappears if we believe, instead, that whatever may be wrong with American universities, and with America, it is not that they are insufficiently Christian."

REFERENCES

Abbott, Andrew. 1988. *The System of Professions*. Chicago: University of Chicago Press.
Boudon, Raymond. 1981. *The Logic of Social Action*. London: Routledge & Kegan Paul.

Chaves, Mark. 1994. "Secularization as Declining Religious Authority." *Social Forces* 72, no. 3: 749–74.

Dobbelaere, Karel. 1981. "Secularization: A Multi-Dimensional Concept." *Current Sociology* 29: 1–216.

Hollinger, David. 1996. *Science, Jews, and Secular Culture*. Princeton, NJ: Princeton University Press.

Monsma, Stephen. 1992. *Positive Neutrality*. Westport, CT: Greenwood Press.

Monsma, Stephen, and J. Christopher Soper. 1997. *The Challenge of Pluralism*. Lanham, MD: Rowman and Littlefield.

———. 1998. *Equal Treatment of Religion in a Pluralistic Society*. Grand Rapids, MI: Eerdmans.

Rescher, Nicholas. 1993. *Pluralism*. Oxford: Oxford University Press.

Sewell, William H. 1992. "A Theory of Structure: Duality, Agency, and Transformation." *American Journal of Sociology* 98, no.1: 1–29.

Sismondo, Sergio. 1996. *Science without Myth*. Albany: State University of New York Press.

Skillen, James, and Rockne McCarthy, eds. 1991. *Political Order and the Plural Structure of Society*. Atlanta, GA: Scholars Press.

Wolterstorff, Nicholas. 1997. "The Role of Religion in Decision and Discussion of Political Issues." In *Religion in the Public Square,* ed. Robert Audi and Nicholas Wolterstorff. Lanham, MD: Rowman and Littlefield.

Wuthnow, Robert. 1987. *Meaning and Moral Order*. Berkeley, CA: University of California Press.

———. 1989. *Communities of Discourse*. Cambridge, MA: Harvard University Press.

Introduction

Rethinking the Secularization
of American Public Life

Christian Smith

WHY RETHINK SECULARIZATION?

Secularization is not a zeitgeist but a process of conflict.
RANDALL COLLINS, *The Sociology of Philosophies*

A Secular Revolution?

History is written by the victors. And for this reason, perhaps, we are not accustomed to thinking about the secularization of American public life as the
successful outcome of an intentional political struggle by secularizing activists to overthrow a religious establishment's control over socially legitimate knowledge. Rather, we have been taught to think of secularization as
the natural and inevitable by-product of "modernization." But this standard
modernization account of secularization is moribund. In hopes of offering
a more interesting and insightful explanation for the profound changes
that altered American institutions between 1870 and 1930, this book ex-
plores the possibility that the secularization of American public life was in
fact something much more like a contested revolutionary struggle than a
natural evolutionary progression.

Thinking through the revolution analogy in the American context, we
should understand the overthrown regime in this secular revolution as what
we commonly think of as the nineteenth century's mainline Protestant establishment. The rebel insurgency consisted of waves of networks of activists
who were largely skeptical, freethinking, agnostic, atheist, or theologically
liberal; who were well educated and socially located mainly in knowledge-
production occupations; and who generally espoused materialism, naturalism, positivism, and the privatization or extinction of religion. They were

motivated by a complex mix of antipathy toward the Protestant establishment's exclusivity and perceived outdatedness; by their own quasi-religious visions of secular progress, prosperity, and higher civilization; and often by the material gain that secularization promised them, for example, with the professionalization of a field that seemed to require the exclusion of religion. In different times, places, and ways, these insurgents enjoyed limited alliances with activist Protestant liberals and certain other excluded religious groups, including Roman Catholics, Mormons, Adventists, and separationist Baptists. As with most successful political insurgencies, the secular revolution was decisively abetted by a complex of distracting and debilitating internal divisions within mainline Protestantism and by other unintentionally facilitating structural forces and historical events, such as expanding capitalism, state expansion, and so on. It was also aided by the intellectually thin character of mainstream nineteenth-century Protestantism, which tended to emphasize populist common sense, subjective experience, and mass-based emotional revivalism and so failed to develop a defensible theological approach to knowledge and society that could withstand the attacks of elite challengers in the late nineteenth and early twentieth centuries.

To be more precise, the secularization of American public life might be helpfully thought of as a kind of revolution in several ways. First, before the revolution, there existed an established regime whose institutional privilege and dominance provoked increasing grievances among excluded groups. Second, in response, these aggrieved groups mobilized movements to depose the established regime from its positions of control. Third, aided by a set of facilitating forces and events, these insurgent activists managed to overthrow the established regime in most quarters and to transform the institutions which it had previously dominated. Fourth, in the process of transferring power and control from the old to the new regime, this insurgency effected a profound cultural revolution which transformed cultural codes and structures of thought, expectations, and practices. In sum, macrosocial secularization in America was revolutionary in that (1) it fundamentally concerned questions of power and authority; (2) an identifiable network of insurgents intentionally and successfully struggled to displace an established power, largely against its will; and (3) the triumphant regime fundamentally transformed in many areas the cultural and institutional structures that governed the public life of the nation.

Thus, for example, the secular revolution transformed the social construction of science and its production of new knowledge from an enterprise thought compatible with and, to some extent, at the service of theism into one which considered religion to be irrelevant and often an obscuring impediment to true knowledge. The secular revolution transformed higher education from college institutions promoting a general Protestant world view and morality into universities where religious concerns were marginalized in favor of the "objective," a-religious and irreligious pursuit and transmission of knowledge and credentializing of new professions. The secular revolution transformed mass primary and secondary education from a mainline Protestant program to homogenize dissimilar social groups—that is, to "Protestantize" Catholics, Jews, and others—into a "neutral," "nonsectarian," secular enterprise in which religious discourse and practice are assiduously excluded through legal mandate. In public philosophy, the secular revolution deposed the mainline Protestant custodianship of public culture, with its emphasis on Christian America and moral integration, supplanting it with the liberal political theory's "procedural republic," in which religion is privatized and made irrelevant to public deliberations. In the judicial sphere, the secular revolution replaced the old Protestant legal supposition that religion is and should be an integral part of normal social relations which involve the state with the liberal legal doctrine that things religious are "sectarian," that they belong exclusively to the private sphere, and that the courts must maintain a strict "wall of separation" between church and state. The secular revolution transformed the basic cultural understanding of the human self and its care, displacing the established spiritually and morally framed Protestant conception of the "care of souls" (over which the church and its agencies held jurisdiction), and establishing instead a naturalistic, psychologized model of human personhood (over which therapists and psychologists are the authorities). In the sphere of print and broadcast media, the secular revolution (aided by the interests of corporate capitalism) replaced rather pluralistic and religion-friendly modes of public discourse with a centrally owned system involving "objective" and "neutral" reporting practices, which marginalized the particularities of religious and other explicitly value-committed perspectives.

But does the revolution image really work? Misunderstandings of political revolutions and how they happen might raise concerns about political revolution as an appropriate analytical image for macrosocial secularization. Revolutions are popularly thought of as the result of explosive emotional grievances reacting against an established regime; as sudden and dramatic events that result from people's losing patience with the old system and finally deciding to mobilize to take power; as involving a unitary, well-organized cadre of insurgents who struggle together to topple an old government; as propelled by the extraordinary efforts of history-making leaders (like Lenin, Mao Tse-tung, George Washington); as always accomplished through armed violence, in which members of the overthrown regime are executed, imprisoned, or physically exiled; and as complete overthrows of established regimes and comprehensive transformations of sociopolitical systems. These images make it difficult to think of secularization as revolution, since most secularizing agents cannot be fairly characterized as emotionally explosive actors; since the secularization of American public life was not a sudden event, but an extended process; since the process of secularization certainly must be explained by structural factors and unintended consequences in addition to the intentional actions of certain actors; since the activists propelling secularization were many, diverse, and sometimes at best loosely networked; since secularization was not clearly the result of the actions of only a few identifiable leaders; since secularization did not involve guns and bombs, nor were leaders of the Protestant establishment physically executed[1]; and since the deposing of the Protestant establishment was a less than complete accomplishment, varying in extent in different areas of public life.

However, studies of political revolutions tell us that these popular images are often misinformed. Revolutions certainly involve emotional grievances, but they also entail dispassionate, rational, strategic actions by revolutionaries. Political revolutions are seldom won by unitary, consolidated organizations of insurgents, but usually by conglomerations of diverse, often disconnected, and typically competing opposition groups. No revolution succeeds merely by the efforts of famous individual leaders, or even by the intentional actions of rebel groups, however important they may be; success requires multilayered complexities of partisans, allies, facilitating resources, mobilizing organizations, structured political opportunities, and so on, which often operate with irony and unintended consequences. Furthermore, not all political revolutions are accomplished through armed violence; some—such as the overthrow of Filipino dictator Ferdinand Marcos in 1986 and Czechoslovakia's "Velvet Revolution" of 1991—are achieved without violence and bloodshed. In addition, not all revolutions execute, imprison, or exile their deposed enemies, who are sometimes merely deprived of power and forced to live marginal lives. Moreover, not all political revolutions are complete and comprehensive—some never entirely displace elements of the old regime from positions of influence and thus fail to consolidate fully their revolutionary programs. Finally, it is wrong to view revolutions as happening suddenly and dramatically; they are usually aided by long-term structural and organizational shifts and sometimes take years and even decades to come to fruition.

The secularization of American public life might be thought of as a kind of revolution insofar as it fundamentally concerned questions of power and authority. An identifiable network of insurgents intentionally and largely successfully struggled to displace an established power; and the triumphant regime significantly transformed the cultural and institutional structures that governed the public life of the nation. Even so, if we are to think about secularization as a kind of revolution, we must consider it as accomplished in uneven stages over decades in a series of ongoing "campaigns" by a loosely connected network of activists. It was intentional, rational, and strategic, but simultaneously made successful through the facilitation of propitious external structural forces and unintended effects. This secular revolution was achieved in part by well-known leaders, but also by a multitude of unrenowned partisans and allies. And, although its success was decisive, it was not absolute and entirely complete. Thus, we might argue that the secular revolution was a *distinctive kind* of revolution, but a real political, cultural, and institutional revolution nonetheless.

Again, we are not used to thinking about the secularization of modern public life as a kind of political revolution. But that may be partly because most of those who have theorized and narrated secularization for us, frequently like the historians of "real" political revolutions, are themselves socially situated vis-à-vis that secular revolution. Their stories are told from a particular perspective—one which encourages us to think about secularization not as a revolution, but instead as a natural and inevitable historical process.

Why Even Think about Secularization?

Many scholars have become bored with or frustrated by secularization theory. They say, often with good reason, that it is too broad and analytically unhelpful to be worth paying much attention to. Some are even prepared to drop the concept from sociological vocabulary altogether. So why might attention to secularization now be worth the effort?

Certain considerations suggest that a rethinking of secularization in fact might prove rewarding. For one thing, the idea of secularization still persists in the sociological conceptual repertoire, however much in the backwaters, and emerges recurrently—sometimes ritualistically—in everything from introductory sociology textbooks to sophisticated sociological analyses that touch only tangentially on religious change. Moreover, scholars from other fields, such as history, continue to rely with varying degrees of explicitness on sociological secularization theory in their work. Between 1985 and 1999 alone, for example, 51 American Ph.D. students wrote dissertations about secularization specifically, and 314 wrote dissertations using secularization as a central analytical concept.[2] But if conventional secularization theory is defective, as its critics suggest, then it does no good to sociology—or any other discipline which employs the idea—passively to allow it to linger, like some embarrassingly eccentric uncle that nobody in the family will ask to leave. Better to revise secularization theory or abandon it.

A more important reason to rethink macro-level secularization theory afresh, and not simply to neglect or automatically discard it, is that something real at the level of macrosocial change, which secularization theory has tried to theorize, has actually happened in history, and we need to account for and understand that change. There are indeed some very important ways in which the influence of religion in the institutions and practices of public life at the macro level has in fact been diminished in the modern West. Most of sociology's founding thinkers—Comte, Durkheim, Weber, Toennies, Marx, Simmel—recognized this and wrote more than a little about it. It may be that the theory of secularization we have inherited is flawed. But that does not mean that the macrosocial transformations which that theory attempted to describe and explain were not real and important.[3] In some circles it is unfashionable to talk about secularization as religious decline; the focus instead is on the "relocation" or "restructuring" of religion. But this language too easily misses real historical changes in the cultural authority and control of resources that religion has enjoyed. We are not altogether wrong to consider macrosocial secularization as including real forms of decline. If so, we should not disregard the project of theorizing macrosocial secularization, but rather work to revise the theory itself to be adequate for making sense of the real social transformations that the theory has long sought to explain.

A third reason for rethinking macro-level secularization theory is somewhat more "practical": the question of what role, if any, religion should play in American public life has reasserted itself with new urgency and importance. The final two decades of the twentieth century witnessed a resurgence of publicly engaged religions in the United States and around the globe. Observers in mid-twentieth-century America might have assumed that the remains of religion in the modern world had been privatized, relegated to the sphere of personal preference and interest.[4] But religion seems to have since reawakened and reasserted itself with new vigor in American public life. This occurrence has produced an abundance of creative and significant philosophical, legal, and theological reflections on the question of religion's proper role in the public sphere.[5] Many accomplished philosophers, theologians, and legal scholars have advanced a variety of incisive arguments rethinking the normative issues, providing much-needed clarification and elaboration, enlivening and enriching the debate, and advancing the state of thinking on the matter. But this robust and growing body of normative literature has not been matched by an equally illuminating body of scholarship in sociology on the issues in question. Historical sociology could very well contribute to public deliberations about religion's role in American public life an enhanced understanding of where we have come from, where we have come to, and how and why we got from there to here.[6] This sociological-historical perspective could surely illuminate a debate often marked by more heat than light. But sociologists have been nearly silent on the matter—at best producing a variety of uneven contemporary analyses of the "Religious Right." One reason why sociologists have not stepped up to this challenge and opportunity, so relevant to a question pressing with increasing urgency, is that the dominant theoretical tradition which historically has framed the question of religion in public life for sociologists—secularization theory—is not adequate to the task. Its assumptions, causal logic, and substantive conclusions have little of interest to contribute to the discussion. If sociology is to advance anything valuable to contemporary debates about the proper role of religion in public life, it will first have to rethink its theory of macro-level secularization.

Secularization theory has for decades been the object of criticism (see, e.g., Martin 1969). But in recent years secularization theory has come under particular attack from a specific perspective, as it has become apparent that in the United States and elsewhere—at least by some measures—religion does not appear to be withering away. Finke and Stark (1992), for example, have shown that American history is one of ever-increasing church adherence. And Smith et al. (1998) have argued that American evangelicalism is thriving as a religious movement not despite the forces of secular modernity but in part precisely because of them. But these most recent critiques of secularization theory argue primarily at the micro level of individual belief and practice. Few of them address the organizational and macrosocial levels of secularization (see Dobbelaere 1981; Chaves 1994). On the one hand, the idea that religion has lost its significance and influence at the macro-institutional level of political, legal, educational, and economic life remains widely accepted. On the other hand, few contemporary scholars are happy with the theory that purports to explain this change. We need fundamentally to rethink macro-level secularization—as others have already reconsidered individual-level secularization—in order to develop a more satisfactory theoretical account of the historical evidence.

Problematizing the Secularization of American Public Life

Besides this rationale for rethinking secularization theory, a series of other considerations help to problematize the historical secularization of American public life in interesting ways. First, there is the curious contrast between the relative importance of religion in the lives of the vast majority of ordinary Americans versus the predominant irrelevance and absence (in some cases, exclusion) of religion in most institutions of public life. In 1993, according to the General Social Survey, for example, 77 percent of adult Americans said that faith in God was either "very important" or "one of the most important" things to them personally, yet relatively few traces of or responses to people's religious faith could be found, for example, in the public schools that educate their children. America is often observed as being at once the most religious and the most secular nation on earth. Whether or not this is precisely so, it is clear that the religious concerns of the majority of Americans are at best dimly reflected in the public spheres of education, business, law, government, mass media, and so on, which constitute the largely unavoidable institutional contexts in which much of their lives are lived. Americans disagree vehemently about whether this is a good or bad thing. But that does not change the fact: one need not be a Christian Right activist to recognize that religion is quite prevalent and strong among ordinary Americans, but largely absent in many of the institutions of American public life. This strength and absence may be correlated: given the positions and interests of the relevant actors involved, the strength of religion "on the ground" may itself have encouraged its removal by secular elites from the institutions of public life.

A second and related consideration that interestingly problematizes America's historical experience of macrosocial secularization is the comparative observation that the role of religion in public life in many other countries—including Western industrialized countries—is not like its role in the United States. A few examples will suffice: in the Netherlands— hardly a religiously overrun country—the government publicly funds on a nondiscriminatory basis Catholic, Protestant, Jewish, Hindu, Islamic, and private secular schools, which are formally free to be as religious or nonreligious as they wish. Likewise, in Australia the state finances Catholic, Anglican, Jewish, Lutheran, Adventist, Baptist, Pentecostal, Hare Krishna, as well as nonreligious private schools. Meanwhile, the German welfare state relies heavily on religious organizations in its delivery of health care and social services. In fact, when viewed in a comparative perspective, the United States is rather unique in its insistent removal of religion from state functions, especially educational ones (see Monsma and Soper 1997). This of course raises the point of historical non-inevitability: because things are different elsewhere, they perhaps might have turned out differently here. Indeed, in the future they still could become different, which is why Americans vehemently disagree about the matter: they have an interested stake in different outcomes that are real possibilities. For present purposes, this historical non-inevitability makes all the more interesting the question of exactly what social forces caused the American experience to turn out in the distinctive way that it did, and not in some other way.

A third factor to pique our interest in these matters is the retrospective observation that many of the justifications originally given for the historical secularization of American public life now appear to us so many years later to be hopelessly untenable. It might be the positivist Auguste Comte's simplistic, three-stage theory of social evolution, which easily abandons religions to the dustbin of primitive history. It might be University of Chicago President William Rainey Harper's 1905 optimism that the university's replacement of faith-grounded theological studies with "scientific" studies of religion would actually *strengthen* students' personal esteem for religion by associating religion with science instead of with women:

> If the university promotes the [scientific] study of religion, a larger respect
> and appreciation will be accorded these subjects by students as well as by
> people at large, because the problems are problems on which learned and sci-
> entific men are at work. An influence will be set at work to counteract the
> marked tendency . . . [to think] religious feeling is something peculiar to
> women and weak men. (quoted in Reuben 1996: 100)

Or it might be nearly any of the other myriad explanations and legitimations that were advanced by secularizers along the way—which one repeatedly encounters in studying this history—as to why traditional religion
should be moved out of the institutions of public life. In case after case, arguments that were once crucial in effecting secularization we would now regard as pathetically naive and often illegitimate. Realizing that our society's
course of action on an important matter has been guided by what turn out
to be naive beliefs and erroneous arguments, it is intellectually fascinating
to reconstruct more clearly why and how our forebears took that historical
course of action and perhaps reasonable to consider whether or not it is
sensible now to continue that course of action.

Fourth, and related to the previous point, the contemporary view of historians of science about the relationship between religious faith and science
also ought to prompt in us an interest in rethinking macrosocial secularization in America. A popular view of the science-religion issue pits the two in
an enduring "warfare" of fact against faith. Science and religion in this perspective are thought of as two antithetical means to knowledge, inherently
incompatible kinds of claims to truth that have been ever battling each
other for human allegiance. This common view, however, turns out to be
less a reflection of historical reality, and more an interest-driven ideological frame first promoted by certain late-Victorian academics—most notably
New York University chemist John William Draper, who in 1874 published
History of the Conflict between Religion and Science; and Cornell University's first
president, Andrew Dickson White, who in 1896 published *A History of the
Warfare of Science with Theology in Christendom* (also see Shipley 1927). University of California sociologist Stephen Shapin, in *The Scientific Revolution,*
a masterful synthesis of the historical literature, observes, "It has been a very
long time since these ["warfare"] attitudes have been held by historians of
science." Rather, Shapin says, in the historiography of science, "the intimate
connections between science and religion have been a leading concern"
(1996: 195). According to the seminal work of University of Wisconsin historians David Lindberg and Ronald Numbers, *God and Nature: Historical Essays on the Encounter between Christianity and Science,* recent decades have seen
"a developing consensus among scholars that Christianity and science had
not been at war" (1986: 6; see Turner 1978).[7]

Histories less biased by the "warfare" lens show instead, for example, that
the Catholic Church was in fact not a particular enemy of science (Shapin:

"There is no longer any sustainable and interesting sense in which it can be said that the Catholic Church was 'unscientific' or even unambiguously opposed to 'the new science'" [1996: 198]). They show, for instance, that most of the early leaders of the Scientific Revolution were theists, if not Christians, who viewed science and religious faith as mutually reinforcing (Shapin again: "In speaking about the purposes of changing natural knowledge in the seventeenth century, it is obligatory to treat its uses in *supporting* and *extending* broadly religious aims. There was *no such thing* as a necessary seventeenth-century conflict between science and religion" [1996: 136; italics in original]). And they show, for example, that nineteenth-century orthodox Christians engaged evolutionary geology and biology not with simple obscurantist antagonism but by articulating a broad range of complex positions, including quite supportive perspectives (Lindberg and Numbers: "Reconcilers experienced little difficulty accommodating the testimony of the rocks. When conflict occurred, it was not along a simple line separating scientists and clerics. . . . The issues raised by Darwin also provoked widespread controversy . . . but the conflicts surrounding Darwin were far more complex than the science-versus-religion formula suggests" [1986: 13–14]; also see Livingstone 1987; Moore 1979; Dupree 1986). Randall Collins says it succinctly: "Science is theologically neutral" (1998: 571).

Two points here are relevant. First, the received "warfare" view of religion and science is not a useful assumption that should frame our historical analysis. Rather we ought to view it as one of the ideological moves of late-nineteenth-century activist secularizers, itself historical data which we need to examine and understand as part of the secular revolution. To be clear: central to the vision of this book is the idea of a political struggle between various religious and secular activists.[8] But that was a struggle for social status and institutional control by identifiable contending social groups, *not* an inherent logical warfare between faith and science—a key distinction to bear in mind. Second, if science and religion are *not* in fact inherently incompatible and mutually hostile ways of knowing, then the secularization of America's public institutions becomes all the more curious. One of the key rationales for secularization was the categorical distinction constructed between science as objective and truthful versus religion as irrational and obscurantist. But if this distinction is problematic, we might, as suggested above, wish to rethink the significant political and institutional uses to which it was put.

A fifth consideration that helps problematize America's historical experience of macrosocial secularization is an important development in philosophy that parallels the preceding observations about the history of science and religion. For centuries, many philosophers have—typically assuming some version of classical foundationalism[9]—prevailed in arguing that religious faith and belief in God are irrational, that religion fails to satisfy the criteria of reliable knowledge or warranted commitment. That view is now changing. Classical foundationalism has in recent decades withered under a broad series of cogent attacks. And a group of leading philosophers in epistemology and the philosophy of religion—especially William Alston of Syracuse University, Alvin Plantinga of Notre Dame University, and Nicholas Wolterstorff of Yale University—have elaborated a school of thought known as "Reformed Epistemology." Their approach contends that religious faith and belief in God are *not* irrational, but rational, certainly no less rationally warranted than agnosticism or atheism.[10] Some skeptical philosophers still contest Reformed Epistemology—a normal process in working out the significance of any major shift in thinking. But Reformed Epistemology has decisively altered the terms of the debate. The burden is now on those who believe in religion's particular irrationality to defend that position. Meanwhile, many philosophers have been persuaded. Even atheist philosopher Richard Rorty has conceded Reformed Epistemology's accomplishment: "Plantinga's *God and Other Minds* is quite convincing on many points, and I admire Wolterstorff's *Reason Within the Bounds of Religion.* . . . I admire them both as remarkable philosophers . . . [who] show why we atheists should stop praising ourselves for being more 'rational' than theists. On this point they seem to me quite right."[11] If Reformed Epistemology is right, then a crucial historical, philosophical rationale for the secularization of American public life evaporates. If religious beliefs are in fact particularly irrational, unwarranted, and unreliable, it makes sense to bar them from informing public debate or shaping public institutions. Religion should be sequestered to people's private lives—for those who still insist on clinging to such superstitions—or better yet, discarded altogether. However, if religious beliefs are, as Reformed Epistemology claims, no less rational, warranted, or epistemically reliable than basic nonreligious commitments, then it is unclear why religious views should be automatically excluded from public debates and institutions—at least for the reason of religion's supposed irrationality. And it is therefore all the more intellectually enticing a puzzle to try to reconstruct more clearly, in this light, how and why secularization history unfolded the way it did.

This book lays out a theoretical framework for a "secular revolution" approach to macrosocial secularization, and examines a set of specific institutions to see how this analytical approach might work in particular cases. This work is a provisional start in a new direction of analysis, not a final or comprehensive alternative theoretical statement. It intends to alter the way we make sense of the historical secularization of the institutions of public life. But it is only among the first steps to that end. The next section clears theoretical ground for a secular movement analysis by critically examining problems in the old secularization theory. The final section of this introduction elaborates a broad analytical framework for an alternative secular movement approach. Chapter 2 and those that follow continue by presenting specific historical case studies that engage and evaluate the proposed secular movement framework with regard to specific fields and institutions, to see in what ways it might improve our understanding of the historical secularization of American public life.

WHAT'S WRONG WITH SECULARIZATION THEORY?

Reason is no abstract force pushing inexorably toward greater freedom at the end of history. Its forms and uses are determined by the narrower purposes of men and women; their interests and ideals shape even what counts as knowledge.
PAUL STARR, *The Social Transformation of American Medicine*

If we want to think more clearly about the secularization of American public life, we should begin by thinking critically about traditional secularization theory. By assessing what is wrong with the old theory, we may be better able to formulate a new approach that is more useful. This section critiques the once-dominant secularization theory, and then attempts to develop an alternative analytical framework for understanding the secularization of American public life.

On "Differentiation"

The two fundamental images of social change that are most frequently employed in social theory to explain secularization are "rationalization" and "differentiation." The main classical source of the rationalization approach is the work of Max Weber, and the primary spring of the differentiation perspective is that of Emile Durkheim. These two basic images often intermingle in secularization accounts and also sometimes combine with other images—the literature has often not been careful to specify which levels (micro/individual, meso/organizational, or macro/societal) and processes (implausibility, differentiation, accommodation, etc.) of secularization are under consideration. Broadly speaking, however, rationalization is often used to explain individual-level loss of religious belief, commitment, or orthodoxy. Differentiation is often employed to explain macrosocial-level decline in religious authority and jurisdiction, the result of which is said to be religious privatization.[12] Although individual-level theories of secularization have in recent years suffered increasingly damaging criticism (e.g., Finke and Stark 1992; Smith et al. 1998), it is this project's primary focus to rethink secularization at the macrosocial level, which requires us to reconsider the key image of differentiation.

That theorists usually conceptualized macrosocial secularization fundamentally as differentiation is clear. David Martin, for example, writes that "[t]he church becomes partially differentiated from other institutional spheres: such as justice, ideological legitimation, the state apparatus, social control, education, welfare; and . . . this is paralleled by a compartmental-ization of an individual's religious role which may encourage a range of vari-ation in personal religion which contributes to institutional disintegration" (1978: 3). Peter Berger puts the matter in simpler terms: "By secularization we mean the process by which sectors of society and culture are removed from the domination of religious institutions and symbols" (1967: 107). Karel Dobbelaere conceives of secularization "as a process of laicization, conceptualized as a process of differentiation, i.e. a process of growing in-dependence of institutional spheres (such as politics, education, economy, and science), each developing its own rationale, which implies the rejection of the over-arching claim of religion. . . . Secularization is basically a conse-quence of a differentiation process that results in a process of specialization of sub-structures" (1981: 14, 31). In the same work, Dobbelaere writes that "[l]aicization . . . is a process in which autonomous institutional 'ideologies' replace, within their own domain, an over-arching and transcendent uni-verse of norms. Church religion, an institutionally specialized social form of religion, is pushed to the periphery of modern industrial societies" (15). Bryan Wilson concurs, arguing that "[t]he presidency that the Church once exercised over social life has gone, as other agencies have assumed the func-tions that it once fulfilled" (1976: 16). And Thomas Luckmann advances the same perspective, suggesting that "[t]he relation between industrializa-tion and secularization is indirect. . . . Industrialization and urbanization were processes that reinforced the tendency of institutional specialization. Institutional specialization, in turn, tended to 'free' the norms of the vari-ous institutional areas from the influence of the originally superordinated 'religious' values" (1967: 39).

It is important for our purposes, however, to recall that the notion of dif-ferentiation in sociological theory came under a barrage of criticism in the 1960s and 1970s. As part of the collapse of structural-functionalism and modernization theory's postwar theoretical dominance, the concept of dif-ferentiation, which comprised macrosocial secularization's fundamental ex-planatory image, was attacked and undermined by sharp critics. By the mid-1970s, Jeffrey Alexander notes, "Differentiation theory was given up for dead" (1990: 10).[13] What killed it, says Alexander, was its "lack of phase-specific analysis, its failure to address institutional and structural levels, [and] its negation of process" (8). Attempts have been made to revive and revise differentiation theory (e.g., Rueschemeyer 1977; Rhoades 1990), al-most all of which contend for the need to pay closer attention to the role of power, agency, and elites in the differentiation process. These are precisely some of the factors that the next section attempts to bring back into secu-larization theory.[14] To be clear, the position here is that "differentiation" may well describe a general process at work in secularization, but that, taken by itself, the idea is badly incomplete; one of the tasks of this book is to elaborate in more concrete analytical terms the hows and whys of differentiation in secularization. Before moving to that discussion, however, we need first to conduct a more thorough and general critical accounting of the defects of the old secularization theory. We need to know more exactly what is wrong with secularization theory that makes it so uninteresting and unhelpful. Here I review seven specific defects.

Seven Defects

Traditional secularization theory suffers from (1) far too much abstraction; (2) a lack of human agency; (3) a sense of over-deterministic inevitability; (4) an orientation (primarily among historians) of idealist intellectual history; (5) an over-romanticization of the religious past; (6) an overemphasis on religious self-destruction; and (7) an under-specification of the causal mechanisms of secularization.

1. *Over-Abstraction*

First, secularization theory is often cast in abstract terms that mask important historical specificities. In a review article in which he claims that sociologists "underestimate the degree of coherence that obtains in the writings on secularization," Oliver Tschannen summarizes the main conceptual elements of the "secularization paradigm." These include "differentiation," "autonomization," "privatization," "generalization," "pluralization," "scientization," and "sociologization" (1991: 413, 401). Many of these terms border on the abstruse. Other theorists discuss "transcendentalization," "historization," "societalization," and other recondite conceptual abstractions in their works. Of course theories by definition entail abstractions. But the over-abstraction that often characterizes secularization theory obscures concrete social and political factors crucial to understanding the matter in question—including specific historical actors, interests, ideologies, cultural codes, institutions, resources, power relations, and so on. In this way, our view of how and why the role of religion in American public life has been transformed is clouded rather than enlightened.

2. *Lack of Human Agency*

Often as a result of its conceptual over-abstraction, secularization theory suffers from lack of human agency in historical process. Typically, it offers transformation without protagonists, action without actors, historical process without agents. Rarely do we hear of interest- and norm-driven parties proactively struggling together and at odds to accomplish goals, to reform institutions, to transform social structures. Seldom do secularization accounts involve historical agents who, for example, take strategic actions to edge religion out of public life. Instead, we hear of broad social processes and forces as causes and encounter passively phrased summaries ("the declining importance of religion," "the reduction of religion's authority") as effects. Occasionally, even secularization theorists recognize this flaw. Karel Dobbelaere, for example, writes,

> Too little attention has been paid to the question of just which people in just which social positions became the "sacralizers" or the "secularizers" in given situations. . . . Laicization is not a mechanical process to be imputed to impersonal and abstract forces. It is . . . carried out by people and groups who manifestly want to laicize society and its sub-structures. . . . Secularization as laicization is the result of opposing interest groups. (1981: 61, 67, 69)

But the tradition as a whole has not corrected itself on this point—even Dobbelaere most recently uses the passive "is being reduced" (1999: 232) to define secularization. In some cases, secularization theorists are actually at pains to deny human agency in the process. Warren Nord's lucid synopsis of secularization theory, for example, makes a point of saying that "*[t]he secularization of the modern world is not the work of secularists.* . . . It was not secularists that secularized the world—it was Protestantism and pluralism, science and technology, economic and political liberalism. Indeed, the secularization of modern civilization was largely unintended" (1995: 39). This absence of human agency, however, is theoretically inadequate. It submerges from view a host of important historical, intentional struggles, movements, social constructions, and accomplishments responsible for the formation of our contemporary situation regarding religion and public life.

3. Over-Deterministic Inevitability

Secularization theory suffers from a strong sense of over-deterministic inevitability, as if the historical outcome were destined by an inexorable fate. Shaped somewhat by functionalism's tautological predisposition to view everything social that exists as serving a necessary social function that itself explains its existence, much secularization theory typically conveys the impression that the "functional requisites" of a modern society necessitated the historical privatization of religion.[15] Religion's marginalization from public life is portrayed as a natural and inevitable process like cell mitosis or adolescent puberty (again, functionalism's heavy conceptual reliance on biological and corporatist metaphors is evident; positivist, linear social evolutionism in the tradition of Comte and Spencer are also discernable here). Typically, this sense of inevitability is implicit in secularization analyses, but sometimes it manifests itself explicitly. Durkheim foreshadowed the mentality when he wrote, "If there is one truth that history teaches us beyond doubt, it is that religion tends to embrace a smaller and smaller portion of social life" (1933: 169). More recently, Peter Berger has written that

> *[i]nevitably*, there develops an affinity, both in structure and in "spirit," between the economic and the political spheres. Secularization then passes from the economic to the political sphere in a *near-inexorable* process of "diffusion." . . . The decisive variable for secularization [is] . . . the process of rationalization that is the prerequisite for *any* industrial society of the modern type. (1967: 132, italics mine)

In discussing secularization as social differentiation and privatization, Richard Fenn writes, "The development of social structures *always* tends to separate institutions from personal [religious] goals and values" (1978: 65, italics mine). Bryan Wilson has concluded that "[r]eligions are always dying. In the modern world it is not clear that they have any prospect of rebirth" (1976: 116). Peter Glasner wrote that the anti-religious processes of disenchantment and rationalization are "an *inexorable* part of the development of a society rooted in the Judaeo-Christian tradition" (1993: 573). Robert Bellah once wrote that "[i]t was *entirely necessary* during the course of modern Western history for science in general and social science in particular to differentiate themselves from theology" (1970: 243). Ronald Inglehart has written, "One of the key trends associated with Modernization was secularization. . . . Secularization is *inherently* linked with Modernization" (1997: 45, 72).[16] And Anthony Wallace asserted bluntly that "[t]he evolutionary future of religion is extinction. Belief in supernatural beings and supernatural forces that affect nature without obeying nature's laws will erode and become only an interesting historical memory. . . . Belief in supernatural powers is doomed to die out, all over the world, as the result of the increasing adequacy and diffusion of scientific knowledge" (1966: 265). As a result of this analytical inexorability, history is stripped of any sense of contingency, of its possible-though-unrealized alternatives. Rather, we are stuck with a "what-became-had-to-be (and likely all for the better)" mentality. Consequently, the de facto contemporary situation of religion in public life becomes regarded as natural and unavoidable, undermining any real sense of available alternatives or responsible choice.[17]

4. *Idealist Intellectual History*

An obvious source for correcting some of these problems might be historical studies of the American religious experience, since historians generally respect specificity and contingency much more than do sociologists. Clearly there is much in the work of historians that can be synthesized within a historical sociology framework to understand better the socially transformed role of religion in American public life. Nonetheless, historians in the secularization tradition exhibit some assumptions and orientations that also limit their usefulness in illuminating the matter at hand. Perhaps most important, many relevant historical works construe the subject matter as one of *intellectual* history. The task is set up as if history is formed by great thinkers advancing compelling ideas that transform social relations, institutions, and structures. The focus of these analyses are big ideas and innovative intellectual systems that appear either to float into history from beyond the analytical horizon or to spring directly from the minds of "great men." James Turner (1985), for instance, has written a fascinating account of how religious unbelief spread in the United States during the second half of the nineteenth century. His book, he states, is "a study of the fate of one idea: the belief that God exists," and "how the *available ideas* in the culture changed so as to make unbelief viable" (xiv; italics in original). Owen Chadwick's study, *The Secularization of the European Mind* (1975; note the focus here on the *mind*), certainly accounts for such social forces as technological innovation and urbanization; yet Chadwick appears to place primary explanatory emphasis on the transformative force of the philosophy of political liberalism, evolutionary theory, Marxist ideology, and so on. And even George Marsden's excellent *Fundamentalism and American Culture* (1980: e.g., 21) portrays the engines of history ultimately as big philosophical and theoretical ideas (German Idealism, Darwinism, theological liberalism, etc.), giving only passing mention to forces of urbanization, immigration, industrialization, and urban social problems.

From a sociological perspective, however, for any robust explanatory account, the force of ideas and philosophies must be situated in relational and institutional contexts, which account for real interests, power, authority, resources, role relations, social conflict, and so on. Randall Collins writes,

> We arrive at individuals only by abstracting from the surrounding context. . . .
> It is possible to demonstrate that the individuals who bring forward such ideas are located in typical social patterns: intellectual groups, networks, and rivalries. . . . We need to see through the personalities, to dissolve them into the network of processes which have brought them to our attention as historical figures. (1998: 3–4)

Culture, philosophy, and intellectual systems certainly matter. But they cannot be abstracted from the real historical social, political, legal, and institutional dynamics through which they worked and were worked upon.

5. *Romanticized History*

A fifth problem that plagues secularization theory is the strong tendency to romanticize a religious past as a "golden era" from which modern religious and nonreligious actors have fallen. Many scholars are aware of this problem, yet it continues to shape much analysis. It simply appears extremely difficult for scholars to break away from a mentality that takes twelfth-century Catholic Europe as the template for pristine and robust religious life, against which all else then fails to measure up. Secularization theorist Bryan Wilson, for example, has written that "[r]eligious thinking, religious practice, and religious institutions were once at the very centre of the life of western society, as indeed of all societies" (1966: ix). Likewise, historian W. Warren Wagar claims categorically that before the nineteenth century, "nearly everyone in Christendom was a practicing and believing Christian, in a society where churches . . . had at their disposal immense economic, political, and educational power" (1982: 6). These views merely echo that of Peter Laslett:

> All our ancestors were literally Christian believers all of the time. . . . Not everyone was equally devout of course, and it would be simple-minded to suppose that none of these villagers ever had their doubts. Much of their devotion must have been formal, and some if it mere conformity. But their world was a Christian world and their religious activity was spontaneous, not forced on them from above. (1965: 71–72)

But positing this kind of mythic historical baseline against which to contrast more recent developments surely sets researchers up for all sorts of misguided and faulty understandings. David Martin, for example, has argued as follows:

> Secularist history tends to accept Catholic laments about the period when men were truly religious. In this instance the backward-looking utopia of medievalism becomes the basis for writing about secularization. . . . The more sophisticated versions of this fairy tale story select certain features of Catholicism which happen to be empirically coexistent from the eleventh to the thirteenth century and use these as a definition of religion. Broadly, the selective elements are the temporal power of the Church, extreme asceticism, realism in philosophy, and ecclesiastical dominance in the sphere of artistic patronage and learning. Clearly, if these are defined as religion, it is difficult to cope with any religious change in immediately succeeding centuries except in terms of secularization. (1969: 30–31, 36)

And anthropologist Mary Douglas has written even more forcefully:

> Secularization is often treated as a modern trend. . . . [But] the contrast of secular with religious has nothing whatsoever to do with the contrast of modern with traditional or primitive. The idea that primitive man is by nature deeply religious is nonsense. The truth is that all of the varieties of skepticism, materialism, and spiritual fervour are found in the range of tribal societies. They vary as much from one another on these lines as any chosen segment of London life. (1973: 36–37)

This suggests the need to depart from secularization theory by descending from broad generalizations about some quixotic religious past. We must instead force ourselves to operationalize more precisely what we mean by "religious social influence," "religious cultural hegemony," "religious authority in the public sphere," and so on. Having specified measures of those concepts, we will be able through historical investigation better to assess just how extensively and effectively religion did engage public life in the past and also to assess exactly the extent and kinds of changes that have occurred over time.

6. *Overemphasized Religious Self-Destruction*

A sixth problem with secularization theory is its unbalanced emphasis on the religious sources of religious decline. More than a little in secularization theory would lead one to surmise that secularization may be attributed essentially to religion's own self-destruction. The theme is present in both Weber and Durkheim. The latter, for example, wrote that "originally, [religion] pervades everything; everything social is religious; the two words are synonymous" (1933: 169; notice the romanticized history again). But then, Durkheim says, "God, who was at first present in all human relations, progressively withdraws from them; he abandons the world to men and their disputes" (1933: 169). God's abandonment is a mere figure of speech, of course. But this analytical theme of religion's own responsibility for secularization continued well beyond Durkheim and Weber.

Peter Berger, for example, in the historical segment of *The Sacred Canopy,* suggests that the Judeo-Christian tradition "carried the seeds of secularization within itself" (1967: 110–129). Ancient Israel's monotheism, he explains, originated a transcendentalization, historization, and rationalization of ethics, which initiated the secularization process. Roman Catholicism was a temporary restraint on the disenchantment of the world, but the Protestant Reformation set the secularization process back into full motion. In addition, the social formation of the Christian church as one institutional sphere among many also unintentionally promoted the decline of religion. Thus, Berger concludes that "historically speaking, Christianity has been its own gravedigger" (1967: 129). Dobbelaere (1981), Beckford (1989), and Wallis and Bruce (1992) reiterate Berger's argument directly, and other secularization theorists make analogous claims. Parsons (1967), for example, locates the sources of secularization in the Protestant Reformation. Richard Fenn theorizes that "the origins of secularization" lie in religion's separating off distinct institutions from the rest of society (1978: 34). Bryan Wilson states that Christianity's tendency toward division and denominationalism "has in itself promoted a process of secularization" (1966: 19–35). Randall Collins (1998) attributes secularization to the stalemates and exhaustions that derived from Europe's post-Reformation religious wars. And Berger (1967) and Wilson (1976) both claim that modern resurgences of religion (cults, fundamentalism, etc.) and religious attempts to adjust to secularization only reflect and advance the secularization process. Religion, it would seem, has nobody to blame but itself for its own demise.

We do know that religious actors played key roles in the marginalization of religion in American public life, liberal Protestants in particular. But religious actors are only *some* of the players we need to recognize on the field. What most versions of secularization theory overlook is the important role played by other, nonreligious and anti-religious actors in the process of secularization (two exceptions are Dobbelaere, Billiet, and Creyf 1978; and Martin 1978 [209–243]). At the very least, our analytical framework should include room to account for all of the players who may have been involved in any particular process of change. The irony of the idea of religion becoming its own gravedigger might have been too irresistible for secularization theorists not to accentuate. But this thematic overemphasis on the *religious* sources of secularization obscures other important actors also involved in the process.

7. Under-Specified Causal Mechanisms

A seventh problem with secularization theory is that scholars in this tradition often under-specify the causal mechanisms that are presumed to link the social factors that are claimed to have transformed the role of religion in public life with the secularization outcome. Bryan Wilson, for example, weaves into his writings a variety of factors that are said to have caused secularization: "sustained involvement in rational organizations . . . which impose rational behaviour"; "political movements, and the growth of organizational and manipulative techniques"; "the expansion of literacy and the development of the secular Press, as well as . . . the cinema and subsequently . . . the radio and television"; "the growth of a pragmatic *Weltanschauung*"; "the expansion of science" (1966: 37, 38, 41, 42); "a shift from society conceived as a moral order to society conceived primarily as a technical order" (1976: 19); and so on. Yet precisely how all of these changes caused secularization is left largely unexplained.

Sometimes with Wilson what at first appears to be an explanation (e.g., "Secularization occurs because . . . ") proves in fact to be a mere definition or description: "Secularization . . . occurs as our social organization becomes increasingly dominated by technical procedures and rational planning" (1976: 39). At other times, Wilson speaks in terms of simple correlations: "The more developed the economic techniques of a society, and more affluent its circumstances, the lower the proportion of its productive wealth will be devoted to the supernatural" (1976: 25). But the causal linkage still remains unspecified. At still other times Wilson simply asserts the incompatibility of modernity and traditional religion: "The moral intimations of Christianity do not belong to a world ordered by conveyor belts, time-and-motion studies, and bureaucratic organizations. The very thought processes which these devices demand of men, leave little place for the operation of the divine" (1976: 6–7).[18] But why should we automatically believe that God and conveyor belts are incompatible? We are not told. This is the kind of argument that is persuasive only to people who are already predisposed to believe it. At best, Wilson offers a causal explanation for secularization based on shifts in relative capacities for social control:

> Secularization is intimately related to the decline of community, to increased social mobility, and to the impersonality of role-relationships. . . . Christianity was an effective religious system as long as cultural constraints were solemnized in community life. It functioned to legitimate moral and social order. But once anonymity and impersonality became the dominant experience of man in western society, so Christianity, like any institutionalized religion, lost its grip on culture. (1976: 99, 103)[19]

But social control raises the issues of power, interests, resources, and struggles for legitimacy and authority—factors often ignored in secularization accounts.

Likewise, Peter Berger repeats that secularization is set in motion by industrialization. "The original 'carrier' of secularization is the modern economic process," he writes, "that is, the dynamic of industrial capitalism. . . . Today, it would seem, it is industrial society in itself that is secularizing, with its divergent ideological legitimations serving merely as modifications of the global secularizing process" (1967: 109). Elsewhere he writes, "The original 'locale' of secularization . . . was in the economic area, specifically, in those sectors of the economy being formed by the capitalistic and industrial processes. . . . Modern industrial society has produced a centrally 'located' sector that is something like a 'liberated territory' with respect to religion. Secularization has moved 'outwards' from this sector into other areas of society" (1967: 129). And he writes, "Their roots are in the process of rationalization released by modernization (that is, by the establishment of, first, a capitalist, then an industrial socio-economic order) in society at large and in the political institutions in particular. The . . . 'liberated territory' of secularized sectors of society is . . . centrally 'located,' in and around the capitalistic-industrial economy" (1967: 132). We are told here, then, that industrialization causes secularization, but we are not told why and how it does so. Berger later does offer one kind of causal explanation:

> A modern industrial society requires the presence of large cadres of scientific and technological personnel, whose training and ongoing social organization

presupposes a high degree of rationalization, not only on the level of infra-structure but also on that of consciousness. . . . On the level of structure, this means above all the establishment of highly rational bureaucracies; on the level of ideology, it means the maintenance of legitimations that are adequate for such bureaucracies. (1967: 132)

But if one does not accept Berger's strong linkage between "structure" and consciousness (also see Berger et al. 1973), this too proves to be a mere as-sertion about, not an explanation of secularization.

Even one of the most nuanced secularization theorists, David Martin, seems to lapse here as well. "Certain broad tendencies toward secularization in industrial society have already been fairly well established," he wrote. They are of the following kinds: "That religious institutions are adversely af-fected to the extent that an area is dominated by heavy industry; that they are more adversely affected if the area concerned is homogeneously prole-tarian; that religious practice declines proportionately with the size of an urban concentration" (1978: 2–3). Industrialization and urbanization are thus said to correlate with secularization. But the causal mechanisms of influence are not specified. Later on, Martin observes that industrialization took structures on a human scale and "replaced them [with] the structures of large scale bureaucratic rationality. . . . The consequences can be stated quite simply. The most generalized tendency is toward an apathy which re-tires from explicit institutional religion" (1978: 91–92). Traditional reli-gion, according to Martin, is thus replaced by astrological interests, hedo-nistic consumerism, fragmentation, and meaninglessness. But exactly why and how this happened is left unexplained.

Historians working within the secularization framework also often un-der-specify the causal links between key social forces and their allegedly sec-ularizing effects. Historical works often simply report a standard set of social factors that are said to have undermined religious relevance or au-thority, and then proceed to spend much ink detailing ways in which vari-ous actors responded. Robert Handy, for example, writes in *A Christian America*, "In the thirty years following the outbreak of the Civil War, some uncomfortable realities stood in the way of evangelical hopes for the early triumph of Christian civilization in America. . . . The facts of industrializa-tion, urbanization, immigration, and intellectual revolutions posed serious challenges to evangelical expectancies which had been nurtured in the pre-dominantly rural atmosphere of the early nineteenth century. Nevertheless, the Protestant forces rallied confidently" (1984: 57; also see Handy 1991: 3–4). Similarly, George Marsden writes,

Change was rapid and doubtless often disconcerting. The social changes were the most dramatic. America was changing rapidly from a culture dominated by small towns and the countryside to one shaped by cities and suburbs. Waves

of "uprooted" immigrants, together with rapid industrialization, created virtually insurmountable social problems. Industrialization, with the drive for
efficiency usually overcoming traditional moral restraints, created ethical, social, labor, and political problems beyond the capacities of traditional solutions. The characteristic response in America was neither panic nor rigid con-
servativism. (1980: 21–22)

But sociologists and historians give too little attention to explaining exactly
how and why these social changes had their supposed detrimental effects on
religion. Exactly why did urbanization or technological developments have
to undermine religious authority? Exactly how did industrialization and
immigration work to produce religious privatization? Why should we treat
these as some kind of "great gears of history" that inexorably grind their way
toward religious privatization? Rather than all nodding our scholarly heads
together in what could be premature analytical closure, we need to go back
and force ourselves to answer these questions again. Doing so might open
up new insights into the real social processes by which religion's role in the
public sphere was transformed. I suggest that moves in this direction will
again lead us back to more concrete organizational and institutional factors
involving human agents with interests, power, authority, ideologies, resources, social struggle, and so on.

Secularization Theory as Anti-Religious Ideology?

Picking up on these and other flaws, some able critics have suggested that
academic secularization theory itself functions as a pro-secular ideology
veiled in scientific garb. Peter Glasner, for example, suggests that secularization theory is a "scientific myth" that is "used to legitimate a broad range
of prior value orientations" (1977: 2). "Most 'theories' of the secularisation
process," Glasner claims, "are really generalisations from limited empirical
findings used by sociologists to bolster an implicit ideology of progress"
(1977: 64). Glasner suggests that secularization theory is not a balanced
analysis of the objective social process of the decline of religion; it is rather
an ideology actively sympathetic to "progress," which legitimates and therefore at least indirectly facilitates the decline of religion. Robert Bellah had
already said as much years earlier, when he suggested that secularization is
"a myth, because it functions to create an emotionally coherent picture
of reality. It is in this sense religious, not scientific at all. This theory or myth
is that of the Enlightenment, which views science as the bringer of light
relative to which religion and other dark things will vanish away" (1970:
237).

Jeffrey Hadden has elaborated this view, claiming that secularization is
really a "doctrine," not a theory, "sustained by a deep and abiding antago-

nism to religious belief and . . . organized religion" (1987: 588). "The founding generation of sociologists were hardly value-free armchair scholars," Hadden notes, but rather "believed passionately that science was ushering in a new era which would crush the superstitions and oppressive structures which the Church had promoted" (590). Hadden observes that "beneath the theoretical statement [that religion is vanishing] is a silent prescriptive assertion that this is good" (607). The secularization concept thus made intuitive sense to most sociologists, given their normative commitments. And until recently, Hadden suggests, secularization's "presuppositions . . . have gone unexamined because they represent a taken-for-granted *ideology* rather than a systematic set of interrelated propositions. . . . Its status was so obvious that it scarcely constituted a problematic issue requiring empirical investigation" (588). Evidence to support these claims is not scarce; it can be found historically and in more contemporary work. Occasional side remarks by some secularization theorists displaying a normatively hostile orientation to religion—for example, Bryan Wilson's characterization of faith in the supernatural as based on "arbitrary unexplained authority" (1976: 13), hardly a neutral or sympathetic reading—lend some credence to the secularization-as-ideology view.[20] So may the many old, self-assured prophetic statements about religion's demise, like Anthony Wallace's above, that "the evolutionary future of religion is extinction," or Peter Berger's of 1968 that "by the 21st century, religious believers are likely to be found only in small sects, huddled together to resist a worldwide secular culture" (quoted in Stark and Finke 2000).

Summary

If we want adequately to make sense of the significant historical changes at the macrosocial level that secularization theory has attempted to explain, and if we hope to understand the actual historical processes that generated the contemporary situation of religion and public life, traditional secularization theory will misguide more than help us. If we are to have any hope of reconstructing secularization theory as an interesting and helpful theoretical tool, we will have to face squarely these seven problems and construct an alternative perspective that corrects or transcends them. Any new version of secularization theory will need to (1) be far more analytically concrete; (2) include a stronger sense of human agency in historical process; (3) reflect an appreciation for historical contingency and foregone alternative outcomes; (4) balance individual and "ideal" factors with institutional, structural, and material factors; (5) pay close attention to the religious specifics of the historical "baselines" from which society will be said to have secularized; (6) account not only for religious factors, but also for nonreligious and anti-religious forces that might have contributed to secularization; and (7) carefully specify the causal links and mechanisms that it claims fostered secularization.

TOWARD THEORIZING THE SECULAR REVOLUTION

Be robbers and conquerors, as long as you cannot be rulers and owners, you lovers of knowledge! Soon the age will be past when you could be satisfied to live like shy deer, hidden in the woods! At long last the pursuit of knowledge will reach out for its due: it will want to rule and own; and you with it!

FRIEDRICH NIETZSCHE, *The Gay Science*

Getting Started

I address the theoretical task at hand by first trying to lay out the historical problem that needs explaining. Later chapters address aspects of this problem in much greater detail. To get started, I summarize the problem of the historical loss by Protestant establishment elites of the influence they once wielded in American public institutions by laying out a provisionally oversimplified story that runs as follows.

In 1870, American society was under the influence of a Protestant establishment that significantly ordered the dominant culture, governed key social institutions, and regulated many of the affairs of private life. America's Revolutionary era had been rather religiously derelict. But an entrepreneurial American Protestantism bounded into the nineteenth century with programs of mass revival and denominational expansion. These helped to establish a triumphalist Christian America—albeit one that had worked out significant compromises with key aspects of the Enlightenment—over which mainstream Protestantism presided.

Most important, the nineteenth-century Protestant establishment controlled socially legitimate knowledge through its Scottish Common Sense Realist epistemology and Baconian philosophy of science. What science discovered and what the Bible and Protestant theology taught constituted in that world a single, unified whole that invariably authenticated Christian truth. Christianity was believed to be the only basis for a virtuous and prosperous civilization, and a Christian moral order was institutionalized in most spheres of society. Most schools, for example, explicitly educated their students in the Christian world view and Protestant beliefs and morals; schools also worked to Protestantize the new immigrants who increasingly came to America's shores. Early American colleges, which were founded primarily to train Protestant clergy and magistrates, were joined by many hundreds of new denominational colleges springing up in small towns across the frontier. In this system of higher education, most college presidents were Protestant clergymen, the curriculum was classical and friendly to Protestant faith, and the mission was to graduate broadly learned men of Christian character.

The United States Constitution's First Amendment formally prohibited a federal-level religious establishment. But mainstream Protestantism in fact functioned openly as the quasi-official religion centering the nation's cultural and social life. American laws—on matters from the Sabbath to marriage to blasphemy—reflected and reinforced a broad Protestant moral order. Politicians frequently had to pass informal, and sometimes formal, religious membership tests even to get elected. As late as 1890, the constitutions of thirty-seven of the existing forty-two states acknowledged the authority of God in preambles or main articles. Indeed, in 1892, the U.S. Supreme Court wrote in a unanimous ruling that if one takes "a view of American life as expressed by its laws, its business, its customs and its society, we find everywhere a clear recognition of the same truth . . . that this is a Christian nation."[21] Protestant voluntary societies and moral reform movements were pervasive in their social and political activity. Publishing houses largely respected Protestant sensibilities in the works they produced. Magazines, newspapers, and even academic journals addressed issues and problems from explicitly Christian viewpoints. And most of the culture's important opinion makers were Protestant moralists, pastors, authors, and activists.

On the broadest scale, the Protestant establishment maintained that Christian virtue, free market capitalism, and civic republicanism were working together to beget a civilization higher than humans had ever known— begetting perhaps even the kingdom of God itself. Flush with the consolidation of Christian influence at home, the nineteenth-century Protestant establishment bolstered its global missionary crusade to spread the gospel and the progress of Christian America worldwide. A strong thread of secular Enlightenment culture had continued in American public life from the Revolutionary era through the nineteenth century, but Protestant culture nevertheless dominated. It was not that all or even most Americans were devout Christians; rather, a minority of Protestant leaders had significant control over many public institutions. Altogether, then, Christian America in 1870 abounded in optimism, confidence, and apparent strength.

But somewhere about 1870 was the beginning of the end. The following five decades saw the Protestant establishment routed from social power, its cultural authority greatly diminished, and its institutional influence significantly reduced. Succeeding decades then witnessed remnants of the deposed Protestant establishment's former influence in American public life progressively discarded. Early on, more than a few Protestant leaders were somewhat slow catching on to the momentous changes that were marginalizing them and their moral order. One senses that the changes were too traumatic to face. But very real and profound the changes were.

By the 1880s, Scottish Common Sense Realism and Baconian science had been decisively displaced by a "progressivist" vision of knowledge and science in which religious concerns had little significant role to play. Religious views came quickly to be defined as largely irrelevant to, not as unified with, true scientific knowledge. By the 1890s, Christian higher education was being definitively supplanted by an education revolution championing a fundamentally secular model of higher education and inquiry, and relegating religion to chapel services and baccalaureate prayers. These two transformations, effectively excluding religion from the core institutions of socially legitimate knowledge production and distribution, were the most crucial in the process of secularizing American public life. This late-nineteenth-century secularization of science and higher education paved the way for the movements of secularization that followed in the next decades.

This same era saw the legal field renovated by a "science of law" movement that replaced reliance on individual judges' sense of justice—which at that time would have been significantly influenced by Protestant ethics and morals—with a "scientific" method of deducing the law for any case from a small set of supposedly predetermined abstract principles. Then, by the 1910s, when a "legal realism" movement in jurisprudence again freed judges to take into account their own sense of justice and changing social circumstances in judicial decision making, far fewer judges believed that Protestant morality and ethics were directly relevant to their work. The 1910s also witnessed the emergence of publishing houses whose editorial policies were no longer primarily attuned to standards of Protestant establishment respectability. The decade also produced the rebellion of an elite of young, dissident literary intellectuals who openly flouted the Victorian-era Protestant establishment's cultural sensibilities and conventions, and promoted a modernist, liberated, secular worldview and lifestyle.

The decade of the 1920s was a crucial phase in secularization, when the effects of the secular transformation of core public institutions (science, universities, publishing) spread into American popular culture. Secularism's rising current crested, overflowed the banks, and began flooding the Main Streets of America. By the 1920s, the mass public education system had largely ceased functioning as a socializing agent for the Protestant establishment and had adopted a secular institutional logic that in the next five decades would root out most vestiges of Christian influence in the schools. In the 1920s, Protestant views of the divinely created human person, which focused on morality and character, were pushed aside by modern psychological constructions of the self centering on personality, instinct, and desire. In that same decade, both the Interchurch World Movement (which was prominent in Protestantism's worldwide missionary endeavor) and the Social Gospel movement (the Protestant establishment's last major effort of moral and social reform) faltered and collapsed. A new breed of anti-religious journalists—epitomized by H. L. Mencken—began in their newspaper columns to pour sarcastic contempt upon all manner of religious "meddlers" and "do-gooders." The old Protestant establishment moralizers and pastoral opinion makers were mostly swept aside in the 1920s by new cultural authorities in the social sciences, journalism, advertising, and Hollywood. By the 1920s, the old Victorian struggles with religious doubt had finally been replaced with a distinct cultural sense, among social elites and beyond, of religion's mere irrelevance.

By the time the Great Depression hit America, the Protestant establishment was in shambles. And as the American economy sank into deep depression, mainline American Protestantism followed with its own religious depression. Many of America's institutional elite were still mainline Protestants, but Protestantism's cultural hegemony was over. Christian faith would survive and often thrive in grassroots America. Mainline Protestant thinkers like Reinhold Niebuhr and Paul Tillich would later attempt to reestablish a Christian intellectual contribution to American public life. And efforts at token public respect for a bygone Christian America—such as the addition of "In God We Trust" to currency and "under God" to the Pledge of Allegiance in the 1950s—would occasionally appear. But in reality, disestablished Protestantism would remain largely at the margins of the action in American public life. The nation's scientific establishment, universities and colleges, public schools, judicial system, and mass media would remain under the cultural influence not of a mainline Protestant establishment or any other religious group.

This brief summary tells the story in stark and general terms. The reality, of course, was much more complex and slippery than this, as later chapters will show. Nevertheless, this brief story about the loss of the Protestant elite's institutional influence does point to a broad historical change that was real and requires explanation. The question thus remains: How can we explain this major transformation? Such a profound, observable displacement of a dominant social and cultural authority in such a relatively short span of time is so sociologically tantalizing that we want to try our best to explain it. But how can we?

Should we understand this case of secularization as the natural by-product of a global process of "modernization?" Can we explain it as the inevitable result of a force at work in the world called "differentiation?" Was American society simply "rationalizing" itself to keep up with the functional requisites of modernity? Was industrialization or bureaucratization somehow responsible for Protestantism's disestablishment?

Such traditional theoretical accounts of secularization fail adequately to explain Protestantism's disestablishment and the secularization of American public life. At best, they formulate generalized, abstract concepts that attempt to *describe* aspects of the secularization process. But they actually *explain* very little. "Differentiation," "modernization," "rationalization," "pluralization," and so on try to depict something that happened, but they do very little to tell us who made it happen, why they made it happen, and how they made it happen. What are fatally missing from the traditional theoretical accounts of secularization, in other words, are things like agency, interests, mobilization, alliances, resources, organizations, power, and strategy. Nobody serious would try to explain events like the Russian revolution, the rise of feminism, the collapse of the British Empire, or the spread of political liberalism by simply observing that these things did happen and are the result of "differentiation" or "modernization." Yet that is precisely what we have done for years to explain secularization. It is time to try something different.

I propose that we rethink macrosocial secularization from the analytical perspective of the field of study most attentive to the factors missing from traditional secularization theory: the sociology of revolutions and social movements. Students of revolutions and social movements are the ones who have most closely examined and theorized issues of agency, interests, mobilization, alliances, resources, organizations, power, and strategy in social transformation. To be sure, this is not an altogether novel approach—some historians of secularization in Britain (Turner 1978; Moore 1986a, 1986b) and at least one historian of secularization in America (Hollinger 1989) have made similar arguments. Thus, Hollinger has defined secularization as "the growth in size and in cultural authority of de-Christianized academic elites, and . . . the corresponding decline in the role played by churches in public life" (1989: 119). In 1994, Mark Chaves made an important contribution to thinking carefully about secularization by emphasizing the importance of shifts in religious authority—that is, socially legitimate power—in arguing for a theory that "situates religion and religious change in a concrete historical and institutional context" (1994: 752). Chaves continues,

> Secularization occurs, or not, as the result of social and political conflicts between those social actors who would enhance or maintain religion's social significance and those who would reduce it. Secularization . . . is carried by some social actors and resisted by others. The social significance of the religious sphere at a given time and place is the outcome of previous conflicts of this nature. Understanding and explaining secularization thus requires attending to these conflicts. (752)

More recently, Randall Collins has written likewise that "secularization is more structural than doctrinal. Secularization does not mean that no one is concerned with religion any longer. Religious movements may still flourish, but now they become private movements. Secularization means removing control of intellectual production from the authority of the church" (1998: 573; also see Dobbelaere 1981; Gorski 2000). By following the lead of these earlier theorists and more thoroughly developing the idea that macrosocial secularization is something like the outcome of an intentional struggle for cultural authority—"the probability that particular definitions of reality and judgments of meaning and value will prevail as valid and true" (Starr 1982: 13)—we may continue to move forward in our theoretical understanding of secularization.

In this section I first briefly lay out some of the major analytical issues and questions that scholars of revolutions and social movement use to understand and explain the events they study. What I review here is not a set of full-blown theories but simply an inventory of several important theoretical tools borrowed from different schools of thought in revolution and social movement studies. I do not use them to delineate a formal theory of secularization. This section's ambition is more modest. I seek merely to begin to describe in broad terms a particular analytical agenda for rethinking secularization, to consider some hypotheses that establish a framework of investigation, to suggest the outlines of a research program that addresses an old question in a new way.

Basic Theoretical Issues and Questions

If the secularization of American public life might be the political accomplishment of a secular revolution, then we must begin to focus on the type of issues and ask the kinds of questions about secularization that scholars of social and political revolutions and movements ask about the phenomena they study. Among the most important of these, very briefly, are the following ten issues and questions:

1. *Activists: Who were the actors who mobilized for activism, and how were they constituted as a group?* First one must identify the relevant actors in the struggle, the kind of people they were, their social and institutional locations, what they did and did not share in common, and how they were linked in networks and social groups.

2. *Motivation—Interests and Grievances: What were the material and symbolic interests at stake and benefits that the activists stood to gain through movement success? What were the sources and substance of the discontent, grievances, or moral outrage that helped to motivate the insurgent forces?* What specific interests of the various actors were implicated in the social movement struggle? Who stood to be winners and losers of which benefits, depending on the conflict's outcome? What grievances provoked activists to mobilize? What specifically did they oppose and seek to change? What cultural

norms, expectations, practices, or aspects of a moral economy may their opponents have violated?

3. *Culture and Ideology: What ideologies of moral order shaped the actors' cultural perspectives in ways that evoked and reinforced their commitment to activism? What cultural traditions and structures could activists draw upon to propel and strengthen their cause?* Existing packaged sets of narratives and discourses can help to define and communicate the structure of social relations and moral obligations in ways that move people under their influence to action. How did ideologies function to interpret the world for activists and adversaries in ways that fueled their activism and resistance?

4. *Political Opportunities: What changes in the sociopolitical environment altered the structure of power relations in ways that increased the opportunities for insurgents to act successfully upon their existing interests and grievances?* Political opportunity can take many forms: increased access to power within the given political system; internal divisions among establishment elites; instability of broad elite alignments that undergird the established regime; an increased presence of powerful allies for the movement; or a reduced capacity of the established regime to repress opposition. Were there instances of these kinds of opportunities that significantly enhanced the power of the insurgents?

5. *Material Resources: Were there shifts in the availability of material resources that facilitated activism and altered the likelihood of success?* Where did the movement's financial and institutional support come from? How were material resources mobilized, managed, and deployed to achieve the movement and its target's purposes?

6. *Issue Framing: How did actors actively frame the agendas, assumptions, issues, and evidence in ways that politically strengthened their cause?* How did the activists define and interpret the existence of a problem that demanded action and change to remedy? How did they diagnose the sources of that problem and define a prognosis that promised to solve it? How did actors in the struggle work to legitimate their framing of reality and to undermine their opponents' framings? How and why did certain frames win out over others?

7. *Strategy: What plans of action did the activists and their opponents implement?* Given the structure of the situation the relevant actors faced, how did each group undertake to pursue its purposes? And how did the particular combination of interacting strategies shape the outcome?

8. *Organizations: What organizational structures facilitated the revolution or movement's mobilization?* What preexisting or newly created organizations did the activists co-opt or form to coordinate their insurgent communications and actions? How were different organizations in the same field

of contention related to one another? How did organizational factors influence the outcome of the conflict?

9. *Publics: What broader public or publics were contending actors struggling to persuade?* Whose opinions matter in establishing an acknowledged claim for the legitimate control of a particular kind of knowledge and work? Among which groups of people can the relevant social and cultural authority be established? How do public opinion, legislatures, courts, other professions, and so on relate to the struggle?

10. *Identity and Solidarity: On what basis was any solidarity in a moral community or shared sense of collective identity established, and how did it motivate or facilitate the insurgents' activism?* In what kind of "identity work" did activists engage to sustain commitment and purpose in the movement? In what rituals, ceremonies, or other identity-building practices did the activists engage to sustain their movement relationally?

If these are some of the basic issues and questions to consider when studying revolutions and social movements, then what do we find when we begin to use them to rethink the secularization of American public life? The following chapters present case studies of specific fields and institutions that engage and evaluate this "secular movements" approach. The remainder of this chapter considers some of these analytical issues and questions in thinking about macrosocial secularization in America more broadly—so as to provide a larger framework within which to read the succeeding chapters. In the following pages, given the space limitations of this volume, I focus on only the first five of the issues and questions introduced above—the theoretically most crucial ones—to begin to outline a secular movements interpretation of the historical secularization of American public life. Again, what follows is not a definitive or comprehensive theory, nor does it account for the historical specifics, complexities, and variations we will see in succeeding chapters. What follows is merely a set of broad, inter-related observations—building on the insights of previous work (e.g., Chaves 1994; Dobbelaere 1981)—that sketch the outlines of an analytical framework for a secular movements research program.

The Activists

The secularization of the institutions of American public life did not happen by accident or happenstance. It did not merely befall society by fate or luck. Nor was it simply the effect of some abstract process or force that caught everyone unaware, like a natural disaster or serendipitous windfall. Religion's historical marginalization in science, the universities, mass education, reform politics, and the media was a historical accomplishment, an achievement of specific groups of people, many of whom intended to marginalize religion. The people at the core of these secularizing movements, at least, knew what they were doing, and they wanted to do it. They were activists, secularizing activists—actors who operated with the same kind and level of agency as people who go shopping, get married, and vote.[22] Of course many of the actors involved were, as with any revolution or social movement, swept along by the currents of change. But the currents themselves were also partially the result of active agents seeking change.

Furthermore, many of the groups in American history who worked in various ways to secularize public life had some important things in common. They often accomplished their purposes in different decades and in distinct spheres of life, and they did not all share the same motives in their secularizing activism. Nevertheless, compared to the larger populations from which they were drawn, we can identify certain similar features of the secularizing activists as a whole and of distinct subgroups of activists.

For one thing, almost all of these activists were intellectual elites—professional definers, producers, legitimators, and distributors of social knowledge. They belonged to the American knowledge class—the academic, scientific, and literary intelligentsia of their day. These belonged to the class of educated people that previous generations sometimes called "men of letters": writers, researchers, university presidents, college faculty, publishers, lawyers, public lecturers, reformers, and so on. I mean, for instance, people like Edward Youmans, Daniel Coit Gilman, Andrew D. White, Robert Ingersoll, William Graham Sumner, Bertrand Russell, John Dewey, John William Draper, Mabel Dodge, Walter Lippmann, Oliver Wendell Holmes, Clarence Darrow, H. L. Mencken, and Leo Pfeffer. Of course, behind these famous figures stood many thousands of unrenowned aspiring scientists, college professors, teachers, lawyers, journalists, administrators, and artists who shared their interests and causes. The fact that these were intellectuals is crucial in explaining secularization, as I explain below. For now it is sufficient to note that the movements to secularize American public life were mobilized primarily from among particular kinds of knowledge elites.

Edward Shils (1972: 18) has noted that Western intellectuals have generally moved within one of four major historical traditions: scientism, romanticism, apocalypticism, or populism.[23] Those intellectuals most responsible for the historical secularization of American public life came largely from the first two traditions—they were scientific intellectuals and romantic intellectuals. The former were mostly academics and scientists, situated within the scientism tradition, which, according to Shils,

> denies the validity of tradition as such; it insists on the testing of everything which is received and its rejection if it does not correspond with the "facts of experience." . . . It is critical of the arbitrary and irrational. In its emphasis on the indispensability of firsthand and direct experience, it sets itself in opposition to everything which comes between the mind of the knowing individual

and "reality." It is easy to see how social convention and the traditional authority associated with institutions would fall prey to the ravages of this powerfully persuasive and corrosive tradition. (1972: 18)

The romantic intellectuals, on the other hand, were mostly journalists, independent writers, and other artists. At first glance, scientists and romantic artists might seem very unlike, even quite opposed to each other—and in some ways they definitely are. But in relation to the nineteenth-century Protestant establishment, scientism and romanticism were united on some crucial commitments. They shared a dedication to the ultimacy of individual experience, and a deep antagonism toward external authority and traditional conventions. Shils explains,

> The romantic tradition appears at first sight to be in irreconcilable opposition to the tradition of scientism. . . . In many important respects, however, they share fundamental features. Romanticism starts with the appreciation of the spontaneous manifestations of the essence of concrete individuality. Hence, it values originality, i.e., the unique, that which is produced from the genius of the individual . . . in contrast with the stereotyped and traditional action of the philistine. . . . Institutions which have rules and which prescribe the conduct of the individual members by conventions and commands are likewise viewed as life-destroying. The bourgeois family, mercantile activity, the market, indeed civil society in general, with its curb on enthusiasm and its sober acceptance of obligation, are repugnant to the romantic tradition—all are the enemies of spontaneity and genuineness; they impose a role on the individual and do not permit him to be himself. . . . The affinities of the romantic tradition to the revolutionary criticism of the established order . . . are obvious. It too [along with scientism] is one of the most explosive antiauthoritarian . . . powers of modern intellectual life. (1972: 18–19)

I elaborate this point below. But already we catch a glimpse of how two quite different types of American intellectuals came to share common interests in disempowering Protestantism.

Second, stated somewhat differently, most of these activist secularizers were carriers of some version of the skeptical or revolutionary Enlightenment traditions received from eighteenth-century Europe (May 1976). The more skeptical imbibed Hume and Voltaire's irreverent, disbelieving, witty assault against traditional religion. One thinks here of Robert Ingersoll or H. L. Mencken. The more revolutionary reflected William Godwin and Thomas Paine's optimism about constructing a new, rational world by destroying the old, traditional world. One thinks here of Edward Youmans or Lester Ward. These two Enlightenment traditions can be as different as Friedrich Nietzsche and Auguste Comte. But American activist secularizers tended to be formed by and to promote versions of one or both of these traditions. This typically meant the rejection and suppression of received religion, or at least the uncoupling of moderate forms of Enlightenment from their historical religious frameworks. And this, ironically, often took the form of quasi-religious visions of building a new world order founded on science and reason emancipated from the myths and ignorance of traditional religions.[24]

Third, and related to the previous point, most of America's activist secularizers took their cues from earlier secular activists in Europe. I elaborate on this point below. For now, suffice it to say that few of America's secularizers were native thinkers, but rather looked to Germany, France, England, and Austria for authoritative ideologies and models. That these heirs of the skeptical and revolutionary Enlightenment were living and working as a progressive intelligentsia in a country that was at the time on the periphery of the world system of modern knowledge production—the United States—compelled them to look to Europe, the core of the system, for inspiration, leadership, teaching, and examples. For this reason, insofar as ideas and cultural codes matter, the ideology for the secularization of American public life came ultimately not from New World thinkers, but from the likes of Hume, Voltaire, Paine, Nietzsche, Swinburne, Carlyle, Owen, Holyoake, Darwin, Huxley, Wells, Spencer, Durkheim, Comte, Brewster, and Freud.

A distinct and important group of players in the secularization of American public life were the many liberal Protestant leaders who capitulated early to the basic assumptions and standards of the secularizers and so helped pave the way for their eventual success. American mainstream Protestantism produced more than a few pastors and theologians whose "survival" strategy was radical accommodation to secular modernism. Rather than formulate and advance creative intellectual counters to the early secular movements from an historically orthodox Protestant perspective, they opted instead to embrace their challengers' suppositions and agendas and to redefine Christian faith in secular modernity's own terms (e.g., Moore 1985). Some historians, like James Turner (1985), regard these religious liberals as a primary cause of secularization in America. I am among those scholars—such as Cashdollar (1989: 473) and Reuben (1996: 14)—who remain unpersuaded. Liberal Protestant clergy were important players in the secularization struggles, it is clear. But the liberal Protestant capitulation was a *response to something*. It was a (not very successful) survival strategy in relation to an external challenge. These Protestants did not simply talk themselves into liberalism, agnosticism, and atheism willy-nilly. Their secularized position developed through social and intellectual engagement with the advocates of skeptical and revolutionary Enlightenment. Rather than viewing liberal Protestantism as another case of religion secularizing itself, we might more accurately conceptualize liberal Protestantism as a strategic move partially to defect from an established religious regime—which served as a political opportunity for the secular movements. Liberal Protestants then occupied the intermediary position directly linking Protestantism and secular modernism. Thus, division within the establishment produced a new elite ally for the challengers. Conceived in this way, the liberal Protestants play their historical role in secularization, but not in a way that obscures the key protagonistic role of the secularizing activists.

Crucial to understanding the opportunity for and timing of the secularization of American public life is recognizing the rapid numerical growth of a new knowledge class during the last decades of the nineteenth century and first decades of the twentieth century. Between 1870 and 1930, the number of Americans gainfully employed in knowledge-class occupations that proved relevant to secularization grew more than nine times, an increase of more than twice the rate of growth of the total American labor force (see Hurlin and Givens 1933; Barabba 1975). The American economy, for example, grew from employing fewer than one thousand professional authors in 1900 to about twelve thousand in 1920. The number of professional editors and journalists grew ten times between 1870 and 1930, from five thousand to fifty-two thousand. Similar increases were enjoyed by college professors, lawyers, welfare workers, and various kinds of artists (Hurlin and Givens 1933; Barabba 1975). While the vast majority of Americans remained employed in agriculture, manufacturing, and trade during this era—84 percent in 1870 and 69 percent in 1930—the number of Americans employed in knowledge-class professions more than doubled as a percentage of the population (Hurlin and Givens 1933: 284). What mattered with secularization, however, was not so much absolute size, but *critical mass*. The secular movements were propelled by a new critical mass of secular intellectual elites drawn from the ranks of those who earned their livelihoods as knowledge producers within these professions. This new critical mass is key to answering the question of the historical timing of secularization.

An important part of this new knowledge-class growth that helped create critical-mass conditions favorable to secular movements was the rapid increase in the number of young Americans in higher education. In 1870, all American colleges enrolled a total of about 52,000 students; ten years later that number had risen to 116,000, and by 1890 to 157,000 (Barabba 1975: 383). Then, between 1900 and 1930, the number of students in American colleges and universities increased from 284,683 to 1,178,318—a growth rate nearly seven times that of the total population growth for this period (Judd 1933: 329). The number of American graduate students enrolled between 1900 and 1930 increased nearly eightfold, from 6,000 to 47,000. And the number of employed university professors grew in rates proportional to the growth of students—from 5,553 in 1870 to 23,868 in 1900 and to 82,386 by 1930 (Coben 1991: 49; Barabba 1975: 383). As a consequence, for the first time in American history, the number of Americans who were being exposed to Europe's secular Enlightenment ideology through higher education and going into knowledge-elite professions was reaching a critical mass and forming into self-conscious communities. It was from among a new critical mass of these elites that movements emerged seeking to marginalize the cultural authority of the Protestant establishment and secularize America's public institutions.

Motivation: Interests and Grievances

To sustain a social movements interpretation of the secularization of American public life, I must give a plausible account of what motivated the secularizing activists to challenge the ruling religious establishment. We can think about motivations in terms of interests and grievances. Social movement activism can be motivated both by group interests in gaining advantages and reducing liabilities, and by a felt sense of injustice and outrage. Often, interests and grievances mingle together in ways impossible to untangle. A good place to begin is to ask, Who benefited and who lost from the social changes that were being contested? And in what ways were activists' sense of justice and right violated that compelled them into activism?

The central argument of this book is that American public life was secularized by groups of rising scientific, academic, and literary intellectuals whose upward mobility—made possible by expanding industrial capitalism and an enlarging state—was obstructed by the Protestant establishment. Seeking to increase their own cultural authority and class autonomy—and to reinforce their own intellectual identities—these knowledge elites struggled to displace Protestantism's authority and to advance themselves as new, alternative cultural authorities. At issue was the cultural construction of jurisdiction over socially valued activities, struggles over who could make claims to knowledge and competence, and make those claims stick. What these secularizers were actually pursuing was not primarily a neutral public sphere, but a reconstructed moral order which would increase their own group status, autonomy, authority, and eventually income.

Assumptions

Behind this approach lie three assumptions, drawn largely from the work of Pierre Bourdieu and Alvin Gouldner on intellectuals. The first is that intellectuals are not any more "above" the pursuit of status, power, and wealth than others. Intellectuals pursue their own discernable group interests with the means available to them. Thus, things academic and literary are also political and acquisitive. As Bourdieu notes, "The theories, methods, and concepts that appear as simple contributions to the progress of science are *also* always 'political' maneuvers that attempt to establish, restore, reinforce, protect, or reverse a determined structure of relations of symbolic domination" (1971: 121). According to Gouldner (who uses the phrase "new class" for the kind of intellectuals I am discussing), "the new class . . . does not seek struggle for its own sake. No class does. It is concerned simply about securing its own material and ideal interests with minimum effort" (1979: 17). The intellectual products of the intelligentsia, therefore, can be viewed in part as reflecting the pursuit of group interests. Here is Bourdieu again: "Intellectual, artistic, or scientific stances are also always unconscious or semiconscious *strategies* in a game where the stakes are the conquest of cultural legitimation or in other terms for the monopoly of the legitimate production, reproduction, and manipulation of symbolic goods and the correlative legitimating power" (1971: 118).

My second assumption is that the primary resource of intellectuals in pursuing their interests is the power to construct reality through the production and control of knowledge. Intellectuals typically do not enjoy much capacity to issue authoritative commands that govern social relations, as do, for example, business managers, lawmakers, and school principals. But they do possess a special ability to manipulate symbols, to produce culture schemas, to define and regulate knowledge. Bourdieu argues, "Cultural producers hold a specific power, the properly symbolic power of showing things and making people believe in them, of revealing, in an explicit, objectified way the more or less confused, vague, unformulated, even unformulable experiences of the natural world and the social world, and of thereby bringing them into existence" (1990: 146). As Dick Flacks puts it, "Social theories are levers intellectuals use to influence power structures, to facilitate political outcomes, to enable groups interested in exercising control to improve their practice, to justify their ascendancy, to achieve their goals, or to advance their interests" (1991: 3). Peter Berger likewise suggests that "the ideology of the new class, at least as it impinges on public concerns, enhances the power and privilege of the new class. . . . The 'humanism' of the new class, especially in its intense moralism, may then be seen in essentially Marxian (or, even better, Nietzschean) terms—as a weapon in the struggle for power" (1979: 53).

Third, I assume that adequately understanding the status and authority work of intellectuals requires investigating their contentious interactions with other influential social groups on fields of cultural and political struggle. Intellectuals, like other actors, do not pursue their group interests in a vacuum, but always in relation to antagonists and allies with conflicting and aligning interests. And the fate of each player is profoundly affected by its relative "position" on the field. According to Bourdieu, "the ultimate cause of the conflicts, real or imagined, which divide the intellectual field along its lines of force and which constitute beyond any doubt the most decisive factor of cultural change, must be sought at least as much in the objective factors determining the position of those who engage in them as in the reasons they give, to others and to themselves, for engaging in them" (1971: 179–80).

But why should intellectuals pursuing status and authority struggle to secularize American public life? What do intellectuals' interests have to do with religious authority? To begin to answer these questions, I argue, first, that a number of features of Western intellectuals predispose many of them to be alienated from and adversarial toward the established traditions which their societies embrace. And the dominant cultural tradition and social establishment of nineteenth-century America was conspicuously Protestant. Second, certain characteristics of intellectuals also predispose many of them to be antagonistic to religion per se. Traditional religion, I suggest, often violates what most kinds of intellectuals hold dear. Finally, I argue that, in specific ways, the nineteenth-century Protestant establishment stood in the path of upwardly mobile academic and literary intellectuals, blocking their bids for increased group status, autonomy, authority, and income. Realizing their interests therefore required displacing the authority of the Protestant establishment. In what follows, I speak in broad generalizations about intellectuals—who, we should recall, come in different types[25] and often operate differently at national versus local levels—but I hope these generalizations will nonetheless contribute to a better understanding of actors and agency in secularization.

Adversarial Intellectuals

Most scholars who study intellectuals concur on one point: intellectuals have a strong tendency to become alienated from and adversarial toward their own societies. True, some intellectuals play the "clericy" role, defending the status quo,[26] but, more strongly and frequently, they seem drawn to the role of prophet, denouncing the failings of their societies. "Intellectuals," argue Lipset and Dobson, "are among the major critics of the way in which . . . society operates, sometimes calling into question the legitimacy of the social order and its political structure" (1972: 137). According to Shils, the "culture of intellectuals in the West, particularly in modern times, has included a marked distrust and even abhorrence of the nonintellectual elites in politics and the economy. Institutions, established traditions, incumbents in positions of authority, and intellectuals who have accepted these have come in for severe criticism and rejection" (1982: 226; also see Kristol 1979; Hollander 1987; Rubenstein 1987; Brown 1980; Ross 1990; Aron 1955; Nettl 1969). This adversarial tendency of intellectuals is rooted in their particular social role and social position.

To begin, modern intellectuals are heirs of a clear historical tradition of disaffection and protest. The term *intelligentsia* itself was created by a mid-nineteenth-century generation of critical Russian thinkers and writers—such as Boborykin, Turgenev, Belinski, and Chernyshevski—who derided traditional Russian society and sought to modernize it through "higher" education and "intelligence." They called themselves and were called the "intelligentsiya" (Bell 1980: 121–22).[27] Likewise, the term "intellectual" was popularized in 1896–98, by a protest movement of French writers and academics led by novelist Émile Zola, who published the "Manifesto of the Intellectuals" against the French army's controversial conviction of Jewish army captain Alfred Dreyfus on disputed charges of espionage. Through their intervention in this infamous "Dreyfus affair," the French knowledge elite asserted themselves as a leading critical body set on influencing public opinion (Eyerman 1994: 53–54). The first known use of the word *intellectual* in the United States—in an 1899 letter penned by William James—reflects a clear sense of elite autonomy from and criticism of established social institutions: "We 'intellectuals' in America must all work to keep our precious birthright of individualism, and freedom from those institutions (church, army, aristocracy, royalty). Every great institution is perforce a means of corruption—whatever good it may also do. Only in free personal relation is full ideality to be found" (quoted in Bell 1980: 121).

But this critical history merely expresses critical features that tend to be inherent in the intellectual role itself. One of these is a detached and skeptical frame of mind, which intellectuals by definition nearly all share. Hence, Max Weber observed, "The skeptical point of view has been common to the intellectual strata of every period" (1978: 568). Ralph Dahrendorf concurs: "All intellectuals have the duty to doubt everything that is obvious, to make relative all authority, to ask all questions that no one else dares to ask" (1969: 51). Edward Shils expands: "The rational-empirical outlook—the outlook of independent curiosity, openness to experience, disciplined inquiry and analysis, reasoned judgment, and the appreciation of originality—has been a major property of the intellectual in most countries in the nineteenth and twentieth centuries" (1972: 71).

Another feature of intellectuals that often predisposes them toward alienation and an adversarial stance toward society is their characteristic interest and investment in intellectual principles and ideals. While most people in a society are preoccupied with solving pragmatic problems generated by what *is,* intellectuals recurrently find themselves absorbed in ideas about what could and should be. "In modern times . . . in the West," observes Shils (1972: 9), "the major political vocation of the intellectuals has lain in the enunciation and pursuit of the ideal." This concern with ideals, Shils notes, has consequences: "The process of elaborating and developing further the potentialities inherent in a 'system' of cultural values

entails also the possibility of 'rejection' of the inherited set of values. . . . It
is practically given by the nature of the intellectuals' orientation that there
should be some tension between the intellectuals and the value orientations
embodied in the actual institutions of any society" (1972: 7).[28] According to
Hollander, "American intellectuals, even the most severe social critics
among them, harbor high expectations about their society, and it is the frustration of these expectations that often turns into bitterness and rejection"
(1987: 81).[29]

Often, this critical attention to social ideals encourages intellectuals to
think of themselves as uniquely responsible for and having the right to take
the lead in reforming society to fulfill those ideals. "Western intellectuals
have presented themselves as prophets," observes Eva Etzioni-Halevy. "Like
the prophets of antiquity . . . they have done so by admonishing society for
its shortcomings and by providing society with advice and guidance towards
the future" (1985: 1). Ron Eyerman observes that "[f]rom the beginning,
the intelligentsia connoted more than a modern cultural orientation:
bound up with the idea was a sense of mission, the desire and even obligation to carry enlightenment into the darkness of this vast continent. . . . A
practice central to the role of intellectual . . . was that of public educator, a
dispenser of culture" (1994: 21, 62). Similarly, in his study of nineteenth-
century French intellectuals, César Graña remarks, "Once the intellectuals
were compelled to trust ideas alone and to see themselves as creatures of
large and articulate intentions looking upon all of life, it became an article
of faith to them that, if only ideas were properly organized, distributed, and
listened to, an intellectual task force might actually transform society"
(1964: 54–55).[30]

This tendency of intellectuals to see themselves as an avant-garde,[31] particularly burdened by some truth that they must proclaim for society's ren-
ovation or emancipation, is based on their elite status and often superior
self-concept. Intellectuals not only know that they are not ordinary people;
they also often desire to be above common people. This spirit is clearly
expressed by William James, speaking in 1907 to the alumnae of Radcliffe
College:

> We alumni and alumnae of the colleges are the only permanent presence [in
> America] that corresponds to the aristocracy in older countries. We have con-
> tinuous traditions, as they have; our motto, too, is *noblesse oblige;* and, unlike
> them, we stand for ideal interests solely, for we have no corporate selfishness
> and wield no powers of corruption. We ought to have our own class-con-
> sciousness. *"Les Intellectuels!"* What a prouder clubname could there be than
> this one? (quoted in Ross 1990: 101)[32]

Interacting with and complicating these factors is what many scholars
consider to be intellectuals' uncomfortable social structural position, which

not infrequently generates status insecurity and resentment. First, because elites do not directly produce or control material wealth, they are typically dependent upon those who do—whether royal patrons or government grants. David Swartz writes,

> Intellectuals are in the contradictory position of being both dominant and dominated in terms of their class location. They are in the dominant class because they enjoy the power and privileges that come with the possession of considerable cultural capital. That power comes from their capacity to provide or withdraw legitimation of the social order. Yet, they are dominated in their relations with the holders of political and economic power. In the final analysis, the autonomy of cultural capital is only relative, not absolute. (1997: 223)

Yet this dependence does not sit well with intellectuals' sense of superiority or (we will see below) their quest for autonomy. Second, because the work and lifestyles of intellectuals are often—perhaps especially in the culturally activist and pragmatic United States—not understood or valued by ordinary people, intellectuals can often feel slighted and unappreciated. Those who perhaps most need what they have to offer often ignore and sometimes even disdain them. Thus, for example, Daniel Aaron writes that the sharp social criticism of American literary elites has "also reflected the hostility of the artist to a world that slights his needs and holds his values in contempt" (1992: 1). And Shils argues that "American intellectuals were pained by their membership in a society, the rulers of which seemed to have no need for them. . . . They disapproved of American society because intellectuals were not actually incorporated into its symbolic ornamentation" (1982: 232).[33]

Altogether, intellectuals tend to encounter an incongruous existence of detachment and idealism, skepticism yet committed prophetic judgment, and a superior self-concept in the face of class domination and lack of popular appreciation. This is an unstable compound that often begets alienation. In Weber's view, intellectuals' "very universal aspirations and socially irrelevant, deconstructive, or outright destructive musings render them untrustworthy: intellectuals are inherently a universally alien and alienated caste" (Sadri 1992: 73). Moynihan has written that, since "about 1840, the [American] cultural elite have pretty generally rejected the values and activities of the larger society" (quoted in Lipset 1979: 68–69). Such alienation often tends to breed a contempt for all things common and all orders established, a contempt recurrently expressed in the history of Western intellectuals (Carey 1992). Graña, for instance, writes that for nineteenth-century European intellectuals, "Genius was unleashed as an all-powerful, radical, and unequaled event, a gift of nature which must be allowed to take its course no matter how disruptive to common perceptions. It was now not only the right of intelligence to be respected, but also the duty of genius to tear up norms, to shatter the confines of rule and to permit a whole new world of reality, uniquely perceived, conceived, and expressed, to emerge" (1964: 52). Likewise, Coser observes that Western intellectuals in the romantic tradition

> express their estrangement from genteel society with laughing contempt. . . . Bohemia, the antithesis of respectable society, turns all convention upside down, and evolves its counterculture, its countersymbols, and its norms within a community of the uprooted. Flaubert called it "the fatherland of my breed." It certainly provided a congenial setting for some of the most creative men of the nineteenth and early twentieth centuries. It brought artists and writers together in their struggle with the bourgeois world (1997: 8).[34]

Thus intellectuals have tended toward a general alienation from and adversarial position toward mainstream society, a predisposition that continued into late-twentieth-century America and persists in the new millenium.[35]

Anti-Religious Intellectuals

Something about many modern intellectuals predisposes them not only to be alienated and adversarial toward conventional society generally, but also often to be suspicious of traditional religion specifically—or at least those religions dominant in their societies and directly associated with commercial and political life. Both the history and social identity of modern Western intellectuals are wrapped up in movements and concerns that often tend to be antagonistic to traditional religion per se.

For one thing, modern Western intellectuals are historically the emancipated offspring of the Christian church, and so owe their independent existence to the achievement of secularization. As Bell notes, "If to be an intellectual is to be involved in learning, then the historical source of the intellectual is the church, where literacy, learning, and preaching are bound together in a ministry" (1980: 122). So, as Mannheim observes, modern intellectuals are the direct product of a decline in church control: "From a sociological point of view, the decisive fact of modern times, in contrast with the situation during the Middle Ages, is that [the] monopoly of the ecclesiastical interpretation of the world which was held by the priestly caste is broken, and in the place of a closed and thoroughly organized stratum of intellectuals, a free intelligentsia has arisen" (1936: 11–12). Hollander agrees: "The evolution of intellectuals in the Western societies as a critical and moralizing elite is a by-product of secularization, of the decline of the virtual monopoly of the moralizing functions held by the clergy" (1987: 69). Like children who never want to return to a family and home they remember as suffocating, such a history naturally tends to make many

intellectuals suspicious of religious authority and friendly toward secularization. Shils elaborates:

> When intellectuals ceased to be solely bearers of religiosity, the very act of sep-
> aration . . . set up a tension between the intellectuals and the religious
> authorities. . . . Ecclesiastical . . . authority became an object of distrust of in-
> tellectuals. . . . In the West, where the separation of religious and other intel-
> lectual activities has become more pronounced, a more general feeling of dis-
> tance from authority has been engendered and has become one of the
> strongest of the traditions of the intellectuals. . . . The tradition of distrust of
> secular and ecclesiastical authority—and in fact of tradition as such—has be-
> come [a] chief . . . tradition of the intellectuals. As such, it is nurtured by many
> of the subsidiary traditions, such as scientism, revolutionism, progressivism,
> etc. (1972: 17)

This intellectual suspicion of religion has been widespread, but was expressed most sharply in the many European anticlerical movements (recall
Diderot's assertion, "Men will never be free until the last king is strangled in
the entrails of the last priest") and later in the Marxist tradition (Marx himself: "The first requisite for the happiness of the people is the abolition of
religion").

A second factor that disposes modern intellectuals to be suspicious of religion derives from the fact that intellectuals universally value autonomy as
one of their most prized possessions. Autonomy from external interests re-
inforces intellectuals' detached and skeptical self-identity, enables them to
focus on ideals which transcend the pragmatics of everyday life, creates
space for prophetic social criticism, and helps to alleviate their dependent
social status.[36] According to Gouldner, intellectuals typically cast their (supposed) autonomy in benevolent terms, saying it is "grounded in the specialized knowledge or cultural capital transmitted by the educational system, along with an emphasis on the obligation of educated persons to
attend to the welfare of the collectivity. In other words, the *ideology* of 'professionalism' emerges" (1979: 19). But autonomy is also for intellectuals a
self-interested pursuit of power:

> "Autonomy" . . . is not simply to be understood as a spiritual value important
> to intellectuals, or as desired because without it they are unable to work prop-
> erly. Autonomy is . . . also an expression of the social *interests* of the new class
> as a distinct group. . . . Autonomy is the ideology of a stratum that is still sub-
> ordinated to other groups whose limits it is striving to remove—partly con-
> sciously and in part unconsciously. This quest for autonomy expresses a *polit-
> ical* impulse. (1979: 34, italics original)

Intellectuals' love of autonomy easily disposes them against the historical
religious traditions of the West, for these traditions make it impossible to escape that which violates autonomy, namely dependence and authority with

regard to things beyond and above oneself—on God at least, if not also on Scriptures, bishops, church teachings, moral commands, and clergy (the term *religion* itself likely derives from the Latin word *religio*, which means "to bind"). Of course, all humans—including positivist scientists and bohemian rebels—inescapably live, move, and have their being within historical traditions entailing real dependence on authority, verbal testimony, and the binding power of collective narratives. But some traditions often attempt invisibility and delude their devotees into thinking they act autonomously. In these cases such devotees predictably react against other traditions more explicit about dependence and authority. Gouldner observes,

> The deepest structure in the culture and ideology of intellectuals is their pride in their own autonomy, which they understand as based on their own reflection, and their ability to decide their course in the light of this reflection. Thus any authority that demands obedience or any tradition that demands conformity without reflection and decision is experienced as a tyrannical violation of self. (1979: 33–34)

Among these authorities and traditions, religious ones are for intellectuals often foremost, and therefore most offensive. We have reason then to think that, under the right conditions, many intellectuals would perceive a direct relationship between a decline in traditional religion's authority and an increase in their own autonomy, and would believe both to be in their interest. As Gouldner notes, "Professionalism silently installs the new class as the paradigm of virtuous and legitimate authority, performing with technical skill and with dedicated concern for the society-at-large. Professionalism makes a focal claim for the legitimacy of the new class which tacitly deauthorizes the old class" (1979: 19). In the decades between 1870 and 1930 and beyond, the old class that ascending scientific, academic, and literary intellectuals struggled to de-authorize consisted primarily of the Protestant establishment authorities who dominated America's public institutions.[37]

A third reason why many modern intellectuals may be predisposed to hostility toward religion concerns the particular kind of discourse that forms their tradition. Intellectuals, Gouldner observes, are not identified simply through occupational status, but are constituted by a common discourse: "The new class of intellectuals and intelligentsia is distinguished by the fact it is also a *speech* community. They speak a special linguistic variant . . . the culture of careful and critical discourse" (1979: 27). According to Gouldner, participants in this culture of critical discourse believe that they should justify their assertions through persuasive efforts alone, and so think of themselves as rejecting any appeal to established authorities or status positions. Furthermore, everything can (allegedly) be questioned and discussed, all statements are potentially wrong and so must be critically scrutinized, and all talk must be universally accessible—not dependent on or only meaningful within the particularities of context, situation, belief, or commitment (Gouldner 1979: 28–29). According to Gouldner, this culture of critical discourse is radicalizing, because, at least from the intellectuals' perspective,

> it experiences itself as distant from (and superior to) ordinary languages and conventional cultures. A relatively situation-free discourse is conducive to a *cosmopolitanism* that distances persons from local cultures, so that they feel alienation from all particularistic, history-bound places and from ordinary, everyday life. The grammar of critical discourse claims the right to sit in judgment over the actions and claims of any social class and all power elites. . . . Truth is democratized and all truth claims are now equal *under* the scrutiny of the culture of critical discourse. . . . Traditional authority is stripped of its ability to define social reality and, with this, to authorize its own legitimacy. (1979: 59, italics original)

That this culture of critical discourse's "grammar is the deep structure of the common ideology shared by the new class" (Gouldner 1979: 28) helps to dispose many intellectuals to be suspicious of religion. For this tradition of discourse embraces and embodies the Enlightenment faith in unencumbered individuality, the autonomy of reason, the universality of standards of persuasion, and the renunciation of tradition and authority. Insofar as religion inescapably entails a sense of orthodoxy, authority, and historical narrative; distinctiveness in tradition and language; boundaries of inclusion; and particularity in beliefs, commitments, and practices, religion stands as alien to intellectuals' discursive practices. The culture of critical discourse therefore tends often to position itself to scrutinize, judge, and de-authorize religious claims and perspectives. To be clear: it is not that religious people cannot think critically; rather that the particular version of critical thinking that dominates modern Western intellectual discourse tends to stand in tension with much of religion. Thus, Lasch observes that "among elites [religion] is held in low esteem. . . . A skeptical, iconoclastic state of mind is one of the distinguishing characteristics of the knowledge classes. Their commitment to the culture of criticism is understood to rule out religious commitments" (1995: 215).[38]

To summarize, many modern Western intellectuals exhibit a propensity for hostility toward religion. This is because historically they are themselves the direct products of emancipation from church control, and because religion is often implicated in established social orders which frequently they more generally condemn. It is also because intellectuals aspire to an autonomy and engage in discursive practices that are both in many ways at odds with religious sensibilities and practices. These factors then create another dynamic whereby relatively secular intellectuals come automatically to associate religion itself with the uncultivated mass of ordinary people (philistines, babbitts, fundamentalists, bumpkins, etc.), against whom intellectuals cultivate distinctions which reinforce their own positions and identities as enlightened and superior (Carey 1992). In the end, through complex processes of class reproduction, becoming and remaining a good member of the intellectual community requires leaving religion behind and below—or at the very least, keeping it privately within. Thus, Berger notes that "the new class is indeed a highly secularized part of the American population . . . a highly secularized group" (1979: 50–51).[39]

Ambitious Intellectuals

But the fact that many modern intellectuals may tend to be adversarial generally and anti-religious specifically does not itself adequately explain why certain knowledge elites in late-nineteenth and early-twentieth-century America would have intentionally worked to marginalize religion from public life. If this is indeed what happened, what more precisely motivated them? And why did whatever they were pursuing require the marginalization of religion?

The answer, in short, is that broad social structural changes opened potential opportunities for certain groups of knowledge producers to enhance their group status and cultural authority. But these opportunities involved spheres of activity that were until then significantly controlled by the Protestant establishment—science, higher education, public schooling, literary production, and so on. It was clear that a continuing influence of the Protestant establishment in these fields would restrict the potential autonomy, status, and authority of these aspiring knowledge elites. Fully capitalizing on these new opportunities, therefore, would require de-legitimizing religion's relevance in these spheres of activity, and reconstructing them as fields over which knowledge elites would enjoy autonomous jurisdiction. Religion had to go, in part, because it was entrenched in a knowledge system and moral order that these upwardly mobile knowledge elites stood to gain by deposing. Certain Enlightenment ideologies (elaborated below) proved crucial in achieving this transformation—supplying insurgent elites a moral vision that constituted and ratified their interests, and an alternative public discourse with which to displace religious legitimacy. Finally, this secularizing insurgency was intensified by these aspiring elites' growing experience of the Protestant establishment's exclusivism, censorship, repression, and narrowness—all of which deeply offended their elite sensibilities and interests. It was this combination of group self-interest, ideological conviction, and grievances against the ruling regime—operating against the backdrop of intellectuals' recurrent adversarial and anti-religious posture—that worked to generate the movements to secularize American public life.[40]

I am not claiming—nor to sustain my thesis do I need to claim—that all of the activists who participated in secular movements that worked to secularize American public life were motivated primarily or exclusively by personal animosity toward religion per se. Some were, and they were important. But many were motivated by more complex mixes of motives, involving ideological commitments, material self-interest, personal experience, and constructions of social identity. Some activists clearly were personally friendly to religion, but were motivated nonetheless intentionally to displace religion's cultural authority. Nor do I argue—or need to argue—that these activists all worked with big-picture blueprints for a secular America. Some did, and they were important. But many were focused primarily on their own more narrow concerns and interests, such as the status of university research or professional journalism. Moreover, there was no single umbrella agency coordinating a unified secular strategy. Nor were there many actors who saw the secularization process through from "beginning to end." What I *am* claiming is that, for a variety of identifiable motives, the secularizing activists did have an array of real reasons—interests, ideologies, grievances—to work intentionally to marginalize religion from public life, and that they did precisely this.

Space limits of this theoretical chapter prevent a detailed examination of the interests of upwardly mobile knowledge elites in all relevant fields of public life. The following chapters elaborate, substantiate, and evaluate this approach with historical evidence that pays much greater attention to complexity and variation in specific fields and institutions. Before moving on into those empirical analyses, however, I need first to elaborate other dimensions of the larger theoretical framework.

Grievances

The motivations behind America's secularizing activists' efforts to marginalize religion in public life are more complex than sheer self-interest. Working behind and through the aspirations of these knowledge elites for increased status and authority was also a set of moral grievances against the Protestant establishment. These activist secularizers were not simply out on quests for status mobility, but also on moral crusades against offensive and seemingly obsolete religious beliefs and practices. There was, in fact, more than a little about the Protestant establishment that secularizing elites could rightly—or at least understandably—be disgruntled about.

Perhaps foremost among the rising intellectuals' grievances with the Protestant establishment was its censorship of ideas considered dirty or dangerous. Censorship is a cardinal sin for knowledge elites, whose identities and livings are built around the free and imaginative production and expression of creative ideas. Censorship inherently violates who and what intellectuals are at heart. For this reason, Coser observes, "censorship, perhaps more than any other single factor, has been responsible for the typical alliance of so many intellectuals with the forces of liberalism and radicalism" (1997: 7). Victorian Protestant sensibilities, for example, exercised a censorship role in the acquisition of books for public libraries around the country. In 1875, for instance, the policy of the Boston Public Library's Board of Examiners was that

> [t]here is a vast range of ephemeral literature, exciting and fascinating, apologetic of vice, confusing distinctions between plain right and wrong; fostering discontent with the peaceful, homely duties; . . . responsible for an immense amount of the mental disease and moral irregularities which are so troublesome an element in modern society—and this is the kind of reading to which multitudes naturally take, which it is not the business of a town library to supply. (Geller 1984: 20)

Championing this approach, Frederick Beecher Perkins, a Boston Public Library administrator (and relative of Protestant luminaries Lyman Beecher, Harriet Beecher Stowe, and Henry Ward Beecher) wrote of both popular "sensational" novels and older literary classics (e.g., Balzac and Rabelais) that "all such baneful literature should be as inexorably excluded from the public library as arsenic and . . . rum should be refused to children. This criterion . . . is demanded by all considerations of Christian civilization" (Geller 1984: 22). Among the more famous of the innumerable works restricted by Protestant establishment censors were Benjamin Franklin's *The Autobiography of Benjamin Franklin;* Nathaniel Hawthorne's *The Scarlet Letter;* Walt Whitman's *Leaves of Grass;* and Mark Twain's *The Adventures of Huckleberry Finn*—the last of which was banned in 1885 from the Concord Public Library of Massachusetts, among other places, as "trash suitable only for the slum" (Sova 1998a: 3; also see Sova 1998b; Haight and Grannis 1978; Lewis 1976; Bald 1998). This censorship in public libraries continued well into the early twentieth century, affecting works such as Ernest Hemingway's *The Sun Also Rises* (1926) and *A Farewell to Arms* (1929) and Sinclair Lewis's *Elmer Gantry* (1927; see Sova 1998a).

Multiple Protestant voluntary and moral reform societies—whose strategies, as the nineteenth century wore on, increasingly were based less on persuasion and more on coercion—devoted themselves to censorship with significant success (Parker 1997; Boyer 1968). In 1873, for example, the Society for the Suppression of Vice successfully lobbied the U.S. Congress to pass the "Comstock law," barring from delivery in the U.S. mail "every obscene, lewd, lascivious, or filthy book." And, according to Geller, this helped to create a self-censoring atmosphere in the publishing industry: "[T]o avert prosecution and . . . maintain their reputations, American publishers carefully censored the language, actions, and heroes and heroines of their publications" (1984: 22). For America's ascending academic and literary elites of the late nineteenth and early twentieth centuries, this Protestant censorship of the free expression of ideas in a modern society was outrageous, and they demanded the throwing off of Victorian Protestant hands from the control of public knowledge and discourse. According to Coser, "Censors gave [these] authors a collective cause, a banner around which to rally. It made for the strength of a collective consciousness. . . . The censor came to be the very symbol of the philistinism, hypocrisy, and meanness of bourgeois society. 'Comstockery' became the incarnation of the perverted morality of the dominant middle classes" (1997: 89, 95).

The censorship of ideas considered dangerous happened not only in public libraries and publishing houses, but also in institutions of higher education. Colleges and universities still under Protestant establishment influence often suppressed or dismissed their faculty who expressed alarming beliefs and views. According to Shils, "[W]hen American universities began to bestir themselves intellectually . . . academics . . . were sporadically harassed, threatened, and dismissed from their posts for criticism of existing . . . institutions and for those who exercised authority in them" (1982: 236). Instances of the institutional repression of threatening faculty are myriad, but two will suffice to make the point here. First, in 1878, the eminent Vanderbilt University geologist and theistic evolutionist Alexander Winchell published a tract, *Adamites and Preadamites,* that argued for the pre-Adamite origins of the human race (in part on the basis that Negroes were too racially inferior to have descended from the biblical Adam). Winchell believed that the laws of evolution operated according to the will of God, and his tract contained many references to the scientific truth of the Bible. But, attacked by religious journals and the dean of Vanderbilt's Bible Department for trying to undermine the Bible and the Gospel, Winchell was terminated that year by Vanderbilt's president, Methodist Bishop Holland McTyeire. Second, in 1879, Noah Porter, the president of Yale University, wrote to William Graham Sumner, a prominent sociologist on his faculty, demanding that Sumner desist from using Herbert Spencer's *Study of Sociology* as a course textbook. Porter believed that Spencer's philosophy of science undermined theistic religion. In response, Sumner circulated a forceful letter of protest among the university faculty and trustees, in which he threatened to resign. The university refused to accept Sumner's resignation, and in the end Sumner discontinued using the Spencer text (Hofstadter and Metzger 1955: 330–38). Histories of universities during these decades are replete with similar cases, all of which grated against the academic elites' desire for autonomy and made clear their need to supplant the Protestant establishment's institutional authority.

The idea that a paternalistic American Protestantism might smother all nonconformists was, during the Protestant establishment's zenith, not entirely far-fetched. In 1863, for example, a group of Protestants mobilized the National Reform Association (NRA), among whose goals it was to pass a federal Constitutional amendment declaring the United States an explicitly Christian nation (Green 1987). The second article of the NRA's Constitution read, "The object of this Society shall be to maintain existing Christian features in the American government . . . to secure such an amendment to the Constitution of the United States as will declare the nation's allegiance to Jesus Christ and its acceptance of the moral laws of the Christian religion, and so to indicate that this is a Christian nation, and place all the Christian laws, institutions, and usages of our government on an undeniable legal basis in the fundamental law of the land" (Handy 1991: 25–26). The NRA, which was supported by Reformed Presbyterians, Methodists, and Episcopalians, succeeded in bringing petitions to the U.S. Congress for votes in 1874 and 1896. Despite losing both votes, the NRA continued to publish its periodical, the *Christian Statesman,* well into the 1920s (McAllister 1927; Handy 1991: 26). In retrospect, we see that the NRA's chances of carrying their Constitutional amendment were slim. But for many of America's rising knowledge class, increasingly doubtful about the social value of religion, NRA activism would have appeared bizarre, if not positively menacing.

Yet another dimension of nineteenth-century Protestantism that surely aggravated rising knowledge elites at century's end was its tendency toward anti-intellectualism. The democratizing forces of America's Revolutionary era and the mass revivalism of the Second Great Awakening both fostered the rise of populist brands of Protestant faith (Hatch 1989). This created a religious environment that tended to emphasize emotions, personal experience, anti-institutionalism, and naive biblicism, while discounting the value of serious intellectual work for Christians (Noll 1994). This anti-intellectualism was often expressed loudly and clearly by popular mass evangelists. Dwight Moody, for instance, the renowned urban evangelist of the last quarter of the nineteenth century, was not shy in expressing his disdain for intellectualism. "My theology!" he quipped, "I didn't know I had any. I wish you would tell me what my theology is." As to the reading of books: "I have one rule about books: I do not read any book, unless it will help me to understand *the* book [the Bible]" (Bradford 1927: 61, 25–26). Likewise, the famous early-twentieth-century evangelist Billy Sunday made clear his views about education and scholarship: "Thousands of college graduates are going as fast as they can straight to hell," Sunday claimed. "If I had a million dollars I'd give $999,999 to the church and $1 to education." And as to potential conflicts between faith and science: "When the word of God says one thing and scholarship says another," Sunday declared, "scholarship can go to hell!" (McLoughlin 1955: 132, 138). It is not hard to imagine the kind of contempt these anti-intellectual versions of religious faith would have evoked among many American intellectuals of this era. These voices and the populist religion they represented certainly would have made it hard for intellectuals to see how religion could have had much of value to contribute to knowledge, public welfare, or national progress.

Finally, many American intellectuals were becoming increasingly alienated by what they considered the twisted moral repressiveness of Victorian-era Protestantism. For many reasons beyond the scope of this chapter to explain, Victorian culture broadly in this era was being supplanted by modernist culture, and so seemed increasingly old-fashioned and obsolete (Coben 1991; Singal 1991). Late-nineteenth-century American Protestantism was firmly rooted in and conventionally associated with the Victorian ethos and, insofar as it had difficulty transitioning out of Victorianism, came itself to be seen as embarrassingly out-of-date and irrelevant. The most conspicuous aspect of this perceived obsolescence was the texture of its morality. Victorian moral culture idealized men and women of "character" exemplifying virtues of intense self-mastery: self-improvement, sexual self-control, delayed gratification, order, thrift, diligence, conscientiousness, dependability, punctuality, patriotism, piety, and a self-denying devotion to home, family, community, and nation (Howe 1976; May 1980; Coben 1991; Turner 1990). This morality was grounded in strong dualistic notions separating human from animal, civilized from savage, public from private, and male from female (Singal 1991; McDannell 1986). Historians debate just how repressively destructive this moral system actually was (e.g., Gurstein 1996; Himmelfarb 1994). But for many American intellectuals living through this transition, at least, there was no question—they saw Victorian Protestantism as clearly repressive and destructive. As the avant-garde of modernist enlightenment and liberation, many intellectuals viewed established Protestantism as a pernicious social force, whose crabby, small-town moralizing had no legitimate place in their envisioned future world of progress, reason, and science. Thus, according to Steven Biel, early-twentieth-century literary intellectuals shared the "assumption that the Victorian moral code had neither enhanced the life of individuals nor served the collective welfare. Few terms appeared in their writings of the 1910s and 1920s with such urgency and frequency as 'self-fulfillment' and its synonyms 'self-realization,' 'self-expression,' and 'self-development'" (1992: 143). Biel continues,

> [This] generation of critics recognized personal satisfaction as the basic ingredient of the good life and denounced older morality that condemned individuals to miserable lives of self-denial and thwarted expression. "We have surrounded ourselves with so many moral hedges," [Randolph] Bourne observed in 1913, "having imposed on ourselves so many checks and balances, that life has been smothered." . . . Bourne and his contemporaries generalized . . . free expression . . . into a "new morality" based on "giving our good impulses full play" instead of clinging to "the rigid mastery which self-control im-

plies." Demanding and articulating a new morality became one of the central pursuits of this generation. (1992: 143–44)[41]

And the propagation of this new morality, it was clear, could only happen when the antiquated Protestantism that stood in its way was finally cast aside.

To summarize, it is clear that activist intellectual secularizers were not motivated only by instrumental self-interest. Inextricably enmeshed in their projects of enhancing their own cultural status and authority were sincerely felt moral grievances and discontents against the old Protestant establishment. Both are related, but neither is entirely reducible to the other. The secularizers sought to increase their own power in part because they genuinely saw themselves as bearing the vision and means for a better world. Likewise, their special propensity to see and feel the oppressions of the old moral order correlated with their particular social location as rising elites who stood to benefit considerably by the replacement of the old order with a new one over which they would preside.

Culture and Ideology

Examining the secularizing actors and their interests and grievances goes a long way toward explaining the secular revolution in American public life. But the analysis so far has not gone far enough. We must take culture and moral order more seriously if we are to understand the enormously powerful cultural movement that helped to both constitute and propel the secularizing activists. Activists are motivated by interests. But interests are not pre-existent, self-evident entities simply waiting to be pursued. Real historical interests are themselves cultural formations, defined and valuated by specific cultural traditions. Likewise, activists are animated by particular grievances. Yet grievances are not objectively given, but are rather generated vis-à-vis cultural worldviews and moral orders involving expectations of goodness, justice, and right. In fact, even historical actors are not self-composed, but are always constituted and directed by the narratives of the cultural traditions within which their lives are embedded and to which they are committed. Apart from the specific, historical cultural traditions that compose and move them, there simply could be no actors, no interests, no grievances.

The cultural tradition whose logic and power we need to appreciate in order to understand the secularization of American public life is that of the skeptical and revolutionary Enlightenment, deriving from eighteenth-century Western Europe (May 1976). "The Enlightenment" is a label for a movement with many complex and diverse expressions, and some observers prefer to refrain from even speaking in such broad terms. Nevertheless, for our purposes, we can describe a core body of convictions, sensibilities, and aspirations that comprise the Enlightenment. "Dare to think!" was Kant's summary of the movement in his essay, *Was ist Aufklärung?* (What is Enlightenment?). The Enlightenment promoted the belief that critical and autonomous human reason held the power to discover the truth about life and the world, and to progressively liberate humanity from the ignorance and injustices of the past. "The time will come," announced Condorcet, "when the sun will shine only on free men who have no master but their reason" (quoted in Outram 1995: 1). The Enlightenment declared that the then-emerging scientific method would progressively yield new discoveries giving true knowledge about natural and social life. And the Enlightenment advocated a skeptical attitude about all institutions and traditions of the past, reflecting, in Kant's words, "man's release from his self-incurred immaturity."[42]

Two Enlightenment figures who were particularly important for American secularizing activists were Auguste Comte and Herbert Spencer. The intellectual structure of much of nineteenth-century American science and higher education, and of religion's legitimate role in it, had been built on Scottish Common Sense Realism and Baconian science. But these intellectual systems came under attack in the latter half of the century, shifting the grounds upon which religion in science and higher education might try to stand. In particular, ideological activists—who very consciously wanted to discredit the authority of religious knowledge and set their own secular doctrines in its place—advanced Spencerian evolutionism and Comtean positivism deliberately and strategically against religious interests.

Auguste Comte (1798–1857) was a Frenchman who wrote his *Cours de Philosophie Positive* between 1830 and 1842. In it, he advanced a three-stage interpretation of history, in which the "positive" stage inevitably superceded earlier "theological" and "metaphysical" stages. Comte built on Hume and Kant to claim that the human mind can only know about the phenomenal, never the divine or supernatural. He argued that a new science of society, for which he coined the name "sociology," would crown all sciences and help to fundamentally reconstruct society. And he proposed a new, nontheistic "Religion of Humanity" emphasizing altruistic service to humankind—complete with priests, rituals, prayers, a calendar of saints, and other rather Romanish adornments. Comte's work was picked up, discussed, and often actively promoted by British and Scottish thinkers, particularly John Stuart Mill, Alexander Bain, David Brewster, George Henry Lewes, David Masson, Frederic Harrison, Robert Blakey, George Eliot, James Morison, and Harriet Martineau—the last of whom translated Comte into English in 1852. By mid-century, Comte had become a familiar name to most British readers. Thereafter, Comte's positivism spread to America through Martineau's translation and a variety of English-language journals.

Some Americans forcefully opposed Comte's positivism as threatening Christian orthodoxy; others were more intrigued with rethinking their own religious beliefs in light of Comte's views. John Stuart Mill's 1865 publication of *Auguste Comte and Positivism* catapulted Comte's philosophy to the status of "a sensational popular topic" (Cashdollar 1989: 141). From there, a variety of American popularizers and commentators, ranging from sympathetic critics to zealous apostles of positivism, devoted themselves to expounding and propagating positivism far and wide. These included John Fiske, David Croly, Henry Edger, John Metcalf, Octavius Brooks Frothingham, Francis Ellingwood Abbot, J. Stahl Patterson, Andrew Preston Peabody, and Joseph Henry Allen.

Herbert Spencer (1820–1903) was a British railway engineer turned magazine writer, who became popular with Britain's growing, middle-class reading audience by advocating a social evolutionism that combined Darwinian evolution and laissez-faire liberalism. Like Comte, Spencer contended that human knowledge is limited to the phenomenal realm and was himself an agnostic. Spencer likewise claimed that history developed in evolutionary stages, the better understanding of which was the task of science, especially sociology. Although the world was, for Spencer, growing progressively better, he argued that the state should generally not intervene in individual affairs or with social reform, since evolutionary selection should be free to run its course. Nevertheless, sociology should study the differentiations through which society as a social organism has evolved. This, for Spencer, clearly included the evolution out of archaic religious stages of social development, which were based, as he saw it, on fear, ignorance, and emotion. Like Comte, Spencer attracted a coterie of British and American devotees who promoted his work, including Edward Youmans, William Henry Appleton, William Graham Sumner, Andrew Carnegie,[43] John Fiske—who after meeting Spencer in 1873 wrote to a friend, "I first saw our God the 9th Oct." (Boller 1971: 53)—and many contributing authors of *Popular Science Monthly*.

Despite their differences, the intellectual programs of both Spencer and Comte sought to limit human knowledge to the phenomenal only, not the supernatural, and to provide purely naturalistic understandings of causation. Both offered new theories of historical development and classifications of science that many intellectual elites found appealing. And both represented direct attacks on the intellectual legitimacy of the knowledge claims of orthodox Christianity (Cashdollar 1989: 147). Despite generally reserved, critical receptions among American academics early on, with such deliberate and persistent ideological sponsors promoting their views, Spencerian evolutionism and Comtean positivism both ended up exerting significant effects on American and British science, higher education, and intellectual and political life (Harp 1995; Bryant 1985; Wright 1986; Lightman 1987; Hawkins 1938). By the 1880s, positivist activists had largely discredited Common Sense Realism and Baconianism among American intellectual elites, shifting the terms of "respectable" intellectual assumptions and redefining science in the positivist image.

Also very important in the secular revolution was the spread in America of German Enlightenment idealism, historicism, and rationalism through the graduate training of thousands of aspiring American scholars in German universities. For most of the nineteenth century, American colleges did not offer programs for graduate training and advanced degrees. Young American scholars who aspired to graduate-level education had to travel to Europe for their advanced academic work. Germany was the clear destination of choice. Between 1815 and 1914, nearly ten thousand aspiring American scholars pursued graduate studies in German universities—far more than studied in the less prestigious French and English universities (Diehl 1978; Hofstadter and Metzger 1955: 367; Herbst 1965). Most returned to the United States to become college professors, eager to adapt and put into practice at home what they had learned abroad. This circumstance created a structural tie that brought many foreign ideologies and practices to the United States that weakened religion's position in American higher education. When American students voyaged to study in places like the Universities of Berlin and Göttingen, they were confronted with a host of academic practices alien to the American system: the compartmentalization of theology as one professional program among many in service of the state;[44] the partitioning of academic departments into autonomous scholarly units; the narrow research specialization required for scholars to advance *Bildung;* the freedom of professors to pursue their work unconstrained by governing religious or ideological interests (*Lehrfreiheit*); and the independence of students to pursue their studies and conduct their social lives free from close university regulation (*Lernfreiheit*). German scholarship was also on the forefront of the Enlightenment erosion of orthodox Christian theology and biblical studies. And so these American wayfarers also confronted in Germany a variety of ideological influences at odds with American Common Sense Realism and Baconian science: German historicism, idealism, and romanticism; the German classical Greek revival; and mature German biblical higher criticism and theological liberalism.

It is difficult to overestimate the awe with which many American college leaders and aspiring scholars viewed "the German model." "German thought and methods have done much to elevate scholarship in every land," wrote Harvard University's Charles Gross in 1893, in the *Educational Review* (1893: 31). "Many of the best American professors have been inspired by German teachers, and are now communicating to others the spark enkindled by German learning." Similarly, in 1896, Alja Crook of Northwestern University wrote in the *Chautauquan* journal,

The German university is known as a scientific factory where facts collected from the universe are shaped and fitted and sent to the thought markets of the world. . . . [The German professor] can think and teach what he regards as the truth without regard to civil or ecclesiastical rulers. . . . We never hear of heresy trials in Germany. That matter of "protecting the truth" has not been employed for many decades. Thus it is that the German professor is aided by freedom in thought and in time, and by fine equipment; and these conditions will enable him to lead in the educational world and to attract students. We may expect Germany to retain the first rank in the educational world. (1896: 564)

With German universities serving for many decades as America's graduate schools, the best of America's formally trained college faculty were increasingly the products of the German system (Marsden 1994). Nearly all of those who became leaders in the American higher education revolution had made their academic pilgrimage to Germany. Thousands of these young academics brought back to the United States a vision for restructuring American higher education that required replacing the existing college system with research universities emphasizing graduate studies, disciplinary specialization, faculty research, elective courses, seminar instruction, student independence, and laboratory and clinical methods (Cowley and Williams 1991: 135–36). An 1880 editorial in *Harper's New Monthly Magazine* observed that "[t]he comparison universally made is between our colleges and the German universities. It is shown that the conditions of higher education in the United States are in a sad state . . . ; that in Germany, on the contrary, it is in a flourishing one; *ergo,* let us turn our colleges into German universities" (1880: 254). For our purposes, it is important to note that these academic pilgrims—especially in the last decades of the century—had also assimilated and brought back home a set of German philosophical and theological systems that effectively undermined the existing American view of the intellectual authority of religious knowledge: German historicism, idealism, theological liberalism, higher biblical criticism, and the ideal of academic freedom as autonomous rationality. By the 1880s, large numbers of better-educated Americans were increasingly trading in their Baconian and Common Sense Realist views for new German doctrines (Marsden 1994). With this crucial shift in basic assumptions and standard beliefs, those who sought to retain a significant religious influence in science and higher education were increasingly intellectually and politically vulnerable. Those who wanted to eliminate religion from science and higher education grew more secure and bold.

The Enlightenment comprised many complex and dissonant tendencies, and it would be foolish to claim that it directly "caused" anything historically. Yet the Enlightenment did set in historical motion a set of compelling cultural traditions and visions for moral order that have profoundly shaped the world since. For our purposes, four general points are important. First, nineteenth-century American Protestantism was composed mostly of religious groups that were significantly influenced by elements of the European Enlightenment—particularly the moderate, didactic Enlightenment (May 1976)—in one way or another. Second, insofar as American Christianity was nevertheless also grounded in a historical tradition antecedent to and distinct from the eighteenth-century European Enlightenment, it had been somewhat successful in sustaining a religious worldview significantly in tension with the Enlightenment. Third, much of American history and society generally, and the Protestant establishment specifically, represent versions of a somewhat tenuous compromise between evangelical Protestant Christianity and Enlightenment liberalism. And fourth, the secularizing movements we are investigating here represent a decisive breaking of the old Protestant establishment compromise, through a quest for the final dominance of Enlightenment moral order in the public sphere and the relegation of Christian and other religious concerns to private life.

In more immediate terms, grasping the influence of Enlightenment culture helps us to appreciate dimensions of activist motivation for which the previous discussion did not adequately account. America's secularizing activists were not only people seeking status mobility and enhanced cultural authority by any means possible. They also really *believed* in the particular causes they championed—Science, Progress, Reason, Liberation, the Nation, and so on. These activist secularizers not only instrumentally drew upon Enlightenment cultural tools to construct for themselves strategies of action; more fundamentally, they were *possessed* by the Enlightenment tradition, encompassed and carried forward by its vision of moral order. The activists were in fact themselves constituted in the Enlightenment's image as particular historical actors with agency, interests, dreams, animosities, ends, and means. Having drunk deep from the wells of the Enlightenment, these secularizing activists pressed out its moral order, as if on a mission, in their own careers and professions.

All of this helps us better understand the potency of the secular movements, seeing that in them were met the forces of self-interest and moral vision. The lure of increased status and authority merged with the noble call of reason and progress. The acquisitive came cloaked in the ideal, as the virtuous coincided with the rewarding. The right thing to do and the profitable thing to do converged for our aspiring knowledge elites into irresistible historical projects, an important element of which involved the displacement of religion from public life. Kristol observes that

> [t]he appeal of any such [secular political] movement to intellectuals is clear enough. As intellectuals, they are qualified candidates for membership in the elite that leads such movements, and they can thus give free expression to

their natural impulses for authority and power. They can do so, moreover, within an ideological context which reassures them that . . . they are disinterestedly serving the "true" interests of the people. (1979: 335)

Against such powerful motives and forces, the structurally vulnerable Protestant establishment regime found itself in a losing position.

The historical evidence is clear that our American secularizing activists drew most of their inspiration, ideas, and models from European carriers of Enlightenment culture. Secular movement ideology was almost entirely imported from Europe—particularly from England, France, Germany, and Austria—where Enlightenment battles against establishment churches had spawned hard-line anticlerical movements more radical than any ever seen in the United States. In the world system of knowledge-production during this era, Western Europe was the core and the United States was the periphery. As these dynamics typically work, the production of knowledge elites on the periphery was developed according to the concerns and interests of knowledge elites in the core. According to Shils,

> The long persistent . . . preoccupation of American intellectuals . . . with Europe was part of an attachment to a culture in which they thought intellectuals "counted." The preoccupation with Europe was dominated by the fact that Europe was, in literature, in science, in scholarship, and in art, the very center of creativity. . . . Europe was for American intellectuals a place where intellectuals were respected and taken seriously by those strata of society which exercised power. (1982: 227)

Aaron also observes that

> [p]reparation [for intellectual rebellion] is usually marked by the pursuit and discovery of a philosophical system . . . often of a foreign origin, to sanction the movement. American intellectuals . . . have always been great borrowers; Europe has traditionally provided the theory, America the application. . . . Coleridge, Carlyle Fourier, Taine, Spencer, Tolstoy, Nietzsche, Freud, Shaw, and Marx are only a few of the European prophets who have been domesticated and sometimes vulgarized to serve American intellectual purposes. (1992: 3)

In some cases, our American knowledge elites only read translations of European authors, which were often promoted by secular activists in publications specially designed to disseminate European Enlightenment ideas in America, such as Edward Youmans's *Popular Science Monthly* and H. L. Mencken's introduction to the first English translation of Nietzsche's work in America. In other cases, as we have seen, Americans were exposed to European Enlightenment culture through their formal graduate studies in Europe. Other American intellectuals made journeys to Europe to soak up European knowledge. Steven Biel, for example, observes of those who became the 1920s Greenwich Village "Young Intellectuals,"

> For Brooks, Lippmann, Bourne, Reed, Stearns, and others, the first mature
> exposure to Europe came in the form of a trip after college. Seeing Europe as
> cultured young men still awed by Ruskin, Morris, Shaw, Wells, Nietzsche, and
> Anatole France, they inevitably found themselves confirmed in their belief
> that the Old World valued its thinkers infinitely higher than the United States
> valued or even recognized its own. While still at Harvard, Brooks made the
> common observation that "all Americans are born Philistines, and whatever
> they may acquire that is anti-Philistine comes from contact with Europe."
> (1992: 98–99)

Still other American intellectuals—particularly literary intellectuals of the
1920s seeking to escape this American Philistine culture—actually exiled
themselves as expatriates living in Paris and London. Finally, between 1933
and 1945, waves of European intellectual exiles fled to the United States
from Nazi Europe—particularly Jewish intellectuals from Germany and
Austria—who continued the diffusion in America of intellectual perspectives not oriented to the concerns of the old Protestant establishment
(Coser 1984).

It was through such channels that many American knowledge elites encountered evolving European Enlightenment assumptions, beliefs, and
practices that called the moral order of the old American Protestant establishment into question: that it is possible and necessary to discard the customs, traditions, and authorities that have governed knowledge in past ages;
that autonomous human reason itself will provide truth and understanding;
that religious knowledge is mythical and unreliable, if not irrational and oppressive; that humanity can and must take the reigns of progress into its own
hands; that individual experience through the scientific method is the real
source of authentic knowledge; that naturalism ought to frame our understanding of the world and the universe; that the advance of civilization will
be led by intellectual and scientific experts. Since at least the Revolutionary
era, certain American intellectuals—romantics, transcendentalists, secularists, literary critics, and so on—had carried on a strong secular-Enlighten-
ment tradition in America. But in the postbellum period, American intellectuals became enthralled with Europe. They looked from the periphery
to the world system's core of knowledge-production with reverence and admiration. There they found cultural traditions with resonant programs for
moral order that happened also to promise to increase their own social status and cultural authority, even as they secularized public life. The fit of vision and interest was irresistible.

Political Opportunities

Revolutions and social movements do not emerge, nor are they sometimes
successful, simply because activists have some interests at stake, grievances

to redress, and moral orders they want to institutionalize. Many people have numerous interests, grievances, and ideologies that never mobilize revolutionary activism, or at least never successfully. Actors always operate in socially structured situations that profoundly shape their willingness to mobilize action and their chances of success. Randall Collins has suggested that "secularization began as a type of political revolution; as with all revolutions, its structural key was breakdown at the top, caused by internal struggles among elites, and brought to a crisis by costly escalation and exhaustion of resources" (1998: 537). This line of thinking leads us to focus on a crucial factor that social movement scholars call the structure of political opportunities. Insurgent movements enjoy greater political opportunities when institutional political systems become more open for participation; when broad elite alignments that undergird a polity become unstable; when some elite groups ally themselves with the insurgents; and when the established regime's capacity or propensity to repress opposition is reduced (McAdam 1996). Overall, the explanatory focus here rests not on the efforts of the challengers, but on weaknesses in the regimes they challenge. The secular movements that marginalized religion in American public life in fact enjoyed versions of all four of these forms of political opportunity.

As noted earlier, Protestantism's Christian America in 1870 abounded in optimism, confidence, and apparent strength. The last qualifier is crucial. For although the Protestant establishment's abundant optimism and confidence were real, in retrospect we see that its strength was indeed only apparent. In fact, the Protestant establishment at its height suffered a variety of organizational, political, and intellectual weaknesses that made it quite vulnerable to the insurgency of motivated challengers. Some of this vulnerability was rooted in the structural weakness of America's multi-denominational religious structure, which, in a context of formal religious disestablishment, necessitated coalition rule. Some of it stemmed from inattention to the kind of intellectual work in theology and philosophy that would have been needed to withstand the discursive challenges of secularizers. Some of it came from a failure to build ties with natural political allies. And some of it was caused by internal splits that developed as a result of early secularizing challenges.

Minority Status

To begin, we should remember that, for all of the Protestant establishment's cultural and institutional influence, its membership never came even close to a majority of Americans. At the time of Protestantism's greatest cultural hegemony, Protestant church membership was less than one in five Americans. Handy observes that "by 1880, the leading Protestant denominations—Baptist, Congregational, Disciples of Christ, Episcopal,

Lutheran, Methodist, Presbyterian, Quaker, and Reformed—has an estimated total of close to nine million members, or about 18 percent of the
population. . . . Although their still-growing formal membership never
came close to enrolling half the population in this period, they often spoke
as if they were prescribing the moral direction of the nation as a whole"
(1991: 8–9). This should not be astounding, since we know that social
dominance is seldom a direct function of numerical strength—consider,
for example, South Africa's old apartheid regime. Still, institutional Protestantism's minority status meant that its power was somewhat presumptuous
and precarious. Had Protestantism comprised a solid majority of committed members, it might have been much harder for challengers eventually to
marginalize it in public life. But we know that "nominal" elements of religious traditions are not only the least committed, but also the most susceptible to "conversion" to other faiths. Protestant establishment leaders presumed that most of the 80 percent of Americans who were not Protestant
church members (and not Catholic and Jewish) were nonetheless "theirs."
But in retrospect we see that numerous Americans of this era were neither
deeply committed to the integrity of the Christian tradition nor committed
to maintaining a position for it in the public sphere. When new knowledge
elites began to articulate alternative visions of knowledge, science, truth,
reason, progress, and authenticity, many Americans were readily persuaded. Protestant establishment leaders bewilderedly discovered themselves to be a defensive minority.

Unwarranted Self-Confidence

A second and related form of vulnerability of the Protestant establishment
arose from a presumptuous self-confidence that underestimated—if not
often totally ignored—the potential for loss of cultural control. Decades of
self-assured pronouncements by Protestant leaders make it clear that they
often naively took their dominance for granted, which led to some very unrealistic thinking. Speaking in 1870, for example, Methodist Bishop Edward
Thompson told audiences that he looked forward to a day in the not-too-
distant future when America would be "without an adulterer, or a swearer,
or a Sabbath-breaker, or an ingrate, or an apostate, or a backslider, or a
slanderer; hundreds of thousands of homes without a prodigal, a quarrel,
or heart-burn, or a bitter tear" (Kirby 1967: 302–3). In 1897, Sidney Gulick
of the American Board of Commissioners for Foreign Missions declared
that "Christianity is the religion of the dominant nations of the earth. Nor
is it rash to prophesy that in due time it will be the only religion in the
world" (1897: 307). As late as 1909, Northern Baptist leader Samuel Batten
wrote that, of the three "great facts" of modern society—Christianity, the

state, and democracy—Christianity was "the most potent force in our modern civilization" (1909: 10).

What is striking in these myriad sanguine pronouncements of Protestant leaders is the absence of any clear account of the legitimate basis of their social influence. It appears that, never having been seriously challenged, these Protestant leaders simply allowed themselves to rest upon rather flimsy justifications for their religious dominance. Since the First Amendment formally disestablished religion—an arrangement most Protestants enthusiastically supported—Protestant leaders largely relied instead on sheer enthusiasm, commitment, and voluntary activism to build their Christian America (Handy 1984). In the 1909 words of Samuel Batten, "the Christian order of society is inspirational rather than institutional" (1909: 425). This approach allowed Protestant leaders to suppose that their hegemony was not coercive, but voluntary, and it generally worked well in the absence of serious challengers. But it also enabled Protestants to get by without ever formulating a cogent rationale for their influence in public life. Consider the argument of Presbyterian minister Isaac Cornelison in his 1895 treatise on church-state relations:

> The government of these United States was necessarily, rightfully, and lawfully Christian. . . . Christianity in a proper sense is the established religion of this nation; established, not by statute law, it is true, but by a law equally valid, the law of the nature of things, the law of necessity, which law will remain in force so long as the great mass of the people are Christian. (1895: 341, 362)

Christianity, he says, is clearly the established religion of America—despite its constitutional disestablishment—because of the law "of the nature of things" and "of necessity," which draws its "force" from the Christian commitment of the "great mass" of Americans. This fuzzy argument might have persuaded those who already believed it.[45] But even as Cornelison wrote, new groups of intellectuals were already rising for whom Christian public influence was anything but "of necessity," and whose cultural activism proved able to win over many of the "great mass" of Americans. When serious secularizing forces arose, Protestantism's old reliance on enthusiasm to justify its authority proved an insecure defense.

What is also striking in all of this is Protestantism's inability to step back, take stock of the threat, and formulate a more defensible rationale for its influence in public life. In the spirit of "Let them eat cake," most Protestant leaders appear simply to have ignored the danger of loss and pushed ahead with naive confidence. In 1900, for example, William Dodge, a leader of the New York Ecumenical Missionary Conference, declared, "We are going into a century more full of hope, and promise, and opportunity than any period in the world's history" (1900: 11). In 1909, Christian social activist Washington Gladden proclaimed that "[a] considerable part of the life of civilized society is controlled by Christian principle. We have come to a day in which it does not seem quixotic to believe that the principles of Christianity are soon to prevail; that all social relations are to be Christianized" (1909: 7–8). Even when they did recognize the serious threats they faced, Protestant leaders often assuaged their concerns with unrealistic expectations of eventual success. For example, having thoughtfully considered the threats and challenges of the new urban society they confronted, the Northern Methodist Bishops concluded their 1900 Episcopal Address with these words:

> However disquieting some present aspects of morals and religion may be, we nevertheless close this address in joyful confidence. The Church is not fighting a losing battle. The Christian era enlarges; the Christian populations gain on the non-Christian; the Church itself was never more sound in its faith, more pure in life, more influential within Christendom, more aggressive and hopeful without. (*Methodist Journal* 1900: 63–64)[46]

According to Handy, "In arousing enthusiasm, Protestant leaders of many types sounded much alike. It was believed that good intentions and an abundance of zeal would with God's help be adequate to handle the difficult problems. The self-assurance and crusading spirit of the time could almost but not quite conceal deeper currents of unrest and anxiety" (1984: 124). Protestant leaders remained unaware that active forces of opposition would bring down their establishment within a matter of years.

Internal Division

A third factor in the vulnerability of the apparently strong Protestant establishment to outside attack was the internal fragmentation of the Protestant regime. During its many decades of cultural hegemony, Protestant leaders continually emphasized the "common faith" that transcended denominational particulars and united them into one broad Christian establishment. But not far beneath this united Protestant front lay a series of ideological, organizational, and geographical divisions that badly fragmented American Protestantism. For starters, the American system of denominationalism itself separated Protestants into many different organizational structures and cultures. Although this unregulated, fragmented religious economy may have stimulated entrepreneurial competition for church membership (Finke and Stark 1992), it did little to facilitate the kind of Protestant solidarity and cooperation at a national level that might have produced a more effective response to the eventual challenges of secularizing elites. Recognizing this unity problem, some nineteenth-century Protestants mobilized to create trans-denominational ecumenical structures that linked different kinds of Protestants in common cause—such as the Evangelical Alliance for the United States, begun in 1847 (Jondan 1982). But coalition politics of this type create particular troubles of their own, including least-common-denominator problems, which I discuss below.

American Protestantism in the latter half of the nineteenth century was also geographically sundered. In mid-century, the debate over slavery and the Civil War—which was sometimes complicated by earlier theological quarrels—had divided most Protestant denominations into antagonistic northern and southern wings. The Methodist Episcopal Church, for example, split over slavery in 1844 and remained split until 1939; the Southern Baptist Convention seceded in 1845 and has remained separate since; the Presbyterian Church divided in 1857; and so it went. These splits were acrimonious and deep, and tensions during the Reconstruction era only sharpened them. Not until long after the Protestant establishment's demise did these divisions begin to heal. In the meantime, they contributed to a structurally divided and weakened American Protestantism during the crucial years of secularization. "The failure to mend and heal in the 1860s and 1870s," observes Marty, "shaped the destiny of Protestantism for the ensuing century" (1970: 134).

American Protestantism was also divided racially and ethnically. While white northern Protestants generally condemned slavery, few were prepared to work together with their black brothers and sisters in the faith within congregations and denominations. As a rule, white and black Protestants maintained separate churches and separate denominations, between which there was little affection or communication (Emerson and Smith 2000). To further complicate the picture, certain sectors of American Protestantism were segregated by strong ethnic boundaries—as with Dutch Reformed Calvinists, German Lutherans, Swedish Baptists, Swiss and Russian Mennonites—across which members did not often communicate.

Moreover, American Protestantism was polarized by revivalist movements, given the emotionalism, anti-traditionalism, subjectivism, and sectarianism they fostered and the social class divides they sharpened. The First Great Awakening of the eighteenth century had sparked great theological controversy among the Presbyterians, Lutherans, Congregationalists, Unitarians, and Reformed churches, playing a role in the splintering off of more than a dozen hybrid denominations (Askew and Spellman 1984: 84). Yale President Ezra Stiles was typical of opponents in protesting that revivals depended on driving people "seriously, soberly, and solemnly out of their wits" (Ahlstrom 1975: 404). The Second Great Awakening of the nineteenth century was more contentious. For one thing, it represented a controversial shift away from traditional Calvinist theology, de-emphasizing God's sovereignty and placing increased emphasis on human calculation and technique to prompt conversion. Revivalist ministers began openly professing, "We are not personally acquainted with the writings of John Calvin, nor are we certain how nearly we agree with his view of divine truth; nor do we care" (Hatch 1989: 174). Revivalism also opened yawning education and social class gaps between the opposing sides. Congregational minister Lyman Beecher condemned the preaching of "ignorant and un-lettered men . . . utterly unacquainted with theology," arguing that such "illiterate men have never been the chosen instruments of God to build up his cause" (1814: 5–8). The Calvinist minister Asahel Nettleton—who labeled Charles Finney's followers "the *ignobile vulgus*"—charged that revivalism was doing the "cause of Christ great mischief" (Finke and Stark 1992: 97–98). Revivalists attacked such views as pretentious and unbiblical, pointing to their many thousands of converts as proof of their cause's justice. Revivalist defender Lorenzo Dow saw in Beecher's disdain "a Snake in the grass," saying, "I see no gospel law that authorizes any man . . . to forbid . . . any man from preaching the gospel" (Hatch 1989: 20). In recurrent battles running through most of the nineteenth century, advocates and enemies of revivalism disputed the propriety of preaching in the vernacular, of uneducated evangelists, of female leadership, of disregard for local clergy authority, of threats of anarchy, of the human manipulation of spiritual experiences, and of the general spectacle and emotionalism of revivalist "enthusiasm" (Long 1998; McLoughlin 1959). Lyman Beecher insisted that revivalism "threatens to become one of the greatest evils which is likely to befall the cause of Christ," setting the nation "back in civilization, science, and religion, at least a whole century" (Beecher and Nettleson 1828: 80, 99). These controversies exacted a toll on American Protestantism. "Revivalism," Frank observes, "spawned new denominations, fractured old ones . . . and fomented interminable theological controversies" (1986: 12). Revivalism did add more sheep to the Protestant fold. But its deeper structural effect was to diminish American Protestantism's solidarity and increase its organizational, ideological, and social class fragmentation.

　The Protestant establishment thus went into the crucial decades of secularization (1870–1930) already internally divided along denominational, regional, racial, ethnic, methodological, and social class lines. One further internal division in the Protestant house would prove decisive in sapping Protestant attention and energy, polarizing its leaders and institutions, supplying elite allies to secularizers, and delegitimating the evolving version of orthodox Protestantism. That was the modernist-fundamentalist split that emerged in the late nineteenth century and came to a climax in the mid-1920s. American Protestantism had long struggled with ideological disputes between different kinds of theological traditionalists, especially Calvinists, and theological innovators—Arminians, Transcendentalists, Unitarians, "New Lights," and so on. Even so, by 1870, mainstream Protestantism's theological center of gravity remained a moderate evangelical orthodoxy that sustained consensus on theological essentials and tolerated differences on secondary particulars. As the century neared its end, however, that consensus broke down, and Protestantism began to split into two vocally antagonistic parties (Szasz 1982). Thus, precisely when the Protestant establishment might have been focusing its energy on confronting the new challenges of activist secularizers, it was instead bashing itself in two in a bitter family fight.

The case is more complex than this, however, for this family fight was itself in large measure a product of the successful activism of earlier secularizers. What drove the wedge that split Protestantism was not some inexorable force of abstract ideas or a happenstance of history, but many decades, even centuries, of persistent waves of activist intellectuals seeking to undermine the authority of the traditional Christian knowledge system. Those Protestant leaders who eventually became liberals and modernists did not simply wake up one day and decide they wanted to try a radically new way of thinking. Rather they were caught in an ongoing intellectual debate and cultural struggle with forces that sought to subvert their tradition. And through an interactive process, they opted for a particular strategic response to those antagonistic forces: survival through accommodation. The faith-salvaging Kant was, of course, responding to the skeptic Hume, just as Schleiermacher was responding to religion's "Cultural Despisers." Likewise, liberal and modernist American Protestants were not in calm waters throwing traditional orthodoxy overboard for the fun of it. They were rather trying to lighten the boat's load to see if they could somehow keep it afloat amid the skeptical, positivist, and Darwinian gale blowing westward from Europe. The Henry Ward Beechers, Charles Eliot Nortons, and Horace Bushnells of the world were in fact up against the Comtes, Spencers, Feuerbachs, Darwins, Huxleys, and Buechners of the world, within a theological context set up by the Kants, Schleiermachers, Tindals, and Strausses of the world. It was their confrontation with these forces that decisively shaped their options and choices. And it was their intermediary social positions— maintaining social positions within Protestantism while simultaneously forming intellectual and social alliances with secular modernism—that made them crucial players in the process of secularization. Thus, the modernist-fundamentalist split that opened a major political opportunity for secular movements was one their secularizing progenitors were instrumental in creating.

Crucial for present purposes, however, is recognizing the political opportunity the modernist-fundamentalist split did open for activist secularizers. The controversy plunged many Protestant bodies into wracking battles not only over theological doctrine, but also over the control of congregations, presbyteries, seminaries, missions boards, conference centers, publishing houses, and entire denominations. These clashes involved caustic altercations in religious newspapers, journals, and books; partisan political machinations and skirmishes in denominational governing bodies; blatant administrative and faculty maneuvering for hires and fires at theological seminaries; high-profile resignations of protest against apostasy; schismatic movements of purity to found new seminaries and denominations; and the bitter, sarcastic, public belittling of rivals. Moderate voices were drowned out as ever more shrill ideological voices controlled the airwaves. Altogether, the battles of this very unhappy period of Protestant church history commanded great attention, consumed tremendous energy, alienated large sectors of denominations' members, and bred an enormous amount of animosity (Marsden 1980; Longfield 1991; Marty 1991). It was exactly the kind of event that any revolutionary would hope might distract and destabilize the established regime they intend to overthrow. It split establishment leaders, muted moderate voices, consumed institutional resources, supplied a growing body of modernist allies to secularizers, and created a fundamentalist movement whose defensive version of orthodoxy was easy for adversaries to lampoon. Precisely when the secular movements turned up their pressure on the old Protestant regime—and in part because of that pressure—the regime itself had become exceptionally weak and vulnerable internally.

Alienation of Allies

A fourth source of political vulnerability against secularizing activism was the Protestant establishment's deep-seated anti-Catholicism. While Protestants and Roman Catholics have been at odds historically over many issues, when it comes to contending with the challenge of secular modernism, Protestants and Catholics could logically be—and actually have been in some historical cases—natural political allies. Relative to secular modernists, Protestants and Catholics have many broad, common interests, and in other countries, they have capitalized on these shared interests to carve out for themselves significant legitimate spaces for religious communities and their concerns in public life. In the Netherlands, for example, for much of the nineteenth century, Calvinists and Catholics were distrustful and antagonistic toward each other. But the growing power of the secular Enlightenment liberal party, which then controlled the parliament, began to bring Protestants and Catholics together. When the liberals in 1878 passed a new education law providing generous financial subsidies to state public schools but not to religious schools, a firestorm erupted. The Calvinists and Catholics joined ranks, mobilized a massive protest, and formed cooperative political parties. Their alliance then became a major political force, which in 1888 won an absolute majority of the lower house of Parliament. The Calvinists and Catholics proceeded to legislate a pluralistic program of public education, in which the state supported both secular and religious schools. This was eventually enshrined in the Dutch Constitution of 1917 that is still in effect today (Monsma and Soper 1997: 55–62).

But the United States was a different story altogether. Until well into the twentieth century, most Protestants were typically virulently anti-Catholic (McGreevy 1997). Historically they were much more ready to make common cause with Enlightenment liberals, deists, and skeptics than with Catholics. Low church evangelicals and Enlightenment deists, for example, had united in the eighteenth century to win passage of religious antiestablishment statutes in the federal and state constitutions. And by the nineteenth century, most mainstream Protestants had hitched their wagons to the moderate Scottish "didactic" enlightenment as a strategy to maintain respectability and control of social knowledge (Noll 1995). Nineteenth-century Anglo Protestants often viewed Roman Catholics as dirty, ignorant, antidemocratic, ungodly outsiders, quite likely bound for hell. They were seen as enemies of liberty of conscience, free speech, freedom of the press, and free schools. Between 1800 and 1860, Protestant America published at least twenty-five newspapers, thirteen magazines, and more than two hundred books that were explicitly anti-Catholic (Billington 1932). Mid-nineteenth-century Protestant fears of Catholicism erupted into anti-Catholic riots in New York, Boston, Philadelphia, Louisville, Cincinnati, St. Louis, and other Eastern cities, as well as attacks on Catholic convents, seminaries, and churches. And numerous anti-Catholic societies and political parties thrived in this era (Maynard 1942; Billington 1963; Hunter 1991: 36–37). In 1885, Josiah Strong reckoned "Romanism" the second of many "perils which threaten the nation," asserting that

> [t]here is an irreconcilable difference between papal principles and the fundamental principles of our free institutions. . . . It is as inconsistent with our liberties for American citizens to yield allegiance to the Pope as to the Czar. . . . If alive, [Romanism] must necessarily be aggressive; and it is alive. . . . Those degraded people are clay in the hands of Jesuits. (1885: 53–54, 58)

Even nominal Catholics were a threat to America, Strong contended: "Apostate Catholics are swelling our most dangerous classes. Unaccustomed to think for themselves, and having thrown off authority, they become the easy victims of socialists or nihilists, or any other wild and dangerous propagandists" (1885: 55–56). It is not easy to imagine late-nineteenth-century American Protestants and Catholics negotiating a political alliance to defend their shared interests, given circumstances and history. But had American Protestantism somehow managed—as in the Netherlands—to make American Catholicism its strategic ally, instead of its demonized enemy, that could have created a different structure of political opportunities less favorable to the secular movements. Protestants would have been less politically isolated, and they might have learned a bit of theological language that would have less readily played into the hands of secular liberalism.

Coalition Politics

A fifth source of political vulnerability in the Protestant establishment derives from the coalitional nature of its identity. In concrete terms, the singular label "American Protestantism" is a fiction: what actually existed were Presbyterians, Methodists, Baptists, Congregationalists, Lutherans, Episcopalians, Brethren, Reformed Calvinists, and other denominational types. None of them alone could dominate nationally. To maintain cultural and institutional hegemony, they were forced to operate as a broad, informal coalition of moral and institutional authorities—for example, through trans-denominational voluntary societies. This situation had important consequences for secularization. It compelled the power-sharing denominations to emphasize a thin "common" religion to hold Americans together. It undercut claims regarding the importance of religious particularity, and helped create the emotionally charged cultural category "sectarian," which became a powerful means of exclusion eventually used against religion generally.

In a social context that censured religious establishments, it was potentially awkward for Protestant leaders to operate as a de facto establishment, so they devised various rationalizations to obscure and legitimate their control. They contended, for example, that their social influence was based not on coercion but on voluntary acceptance of it by the people. More relevant to my point, Protestant leaders also crafted and emphasized a distinction between "sectarian" religion and "general," or "common," religious faith. The former was pernicious and unacceptable, the latter beneficial and necessary. "Sectarian" often functioned as a negative code word for Roman Catholicism. But it also referred to cases of specific Protestant groups who especially promoted their group's particularities—predestination, the tactile succession of bishops, believers-only baptism, and so on. By not being "sectarian" in public life and emphasizing only a "common" religious faith, Protestant leaders in coalition constructed their establishment in a way that did not violate strictures against establishments. But there was a price for this defense of dominance: it worked to redefine religion in a way that ultimately weakened any rationale for its role in public life. What mattered about religion was no longer the particularities of real historical theological traditions and communities that deserved respect and space in public life, and which might contribute to public deliberation. What mattered was an increasingly thin, least-common-denominator version of Protestantism that was sufficiently standard that all good Americans could affirm it.

Two things then happened. Without a grounding in particularistic historical religious traditions, this "general religion"—in conjunction with the new belief, increasingly promoted by secularizers, that morality did not need a religious foundation—eventually shriveled into a secularized apparition of faith. Theological commitments and faith practices became "Christian principles and values," the coming kingdom of God, then "broad principles of revealed religion," then piety and morals, then humanity and manners, and eventually civilization, science, and reason. Second, activist secularizers—particularly in the fields of education and law—themselves took up the exclusionary "sectarian" label and began applying it to all religious views and practices. Religion per se was made "sectarian" by definition. Having once been a tool in the hands of dominant Protestants to exclude versions of faith that did not serve their purposes, the term *sectarian* was commandeered by rising secularizers to expurgate religion per se from the public sphere. Thus, the structural situation requiring coalition politics for Protestantism's establishment and its strategic choice of superficial commonality instead of pluralistic particularity effectively increased Protestantism's political vulnerability to secular activist challengers.

Intellectual Vulnerability

To these five sources of political vulnerability we can add a sixth and final source: that the mainstream of late-nineteenth-century American Protestantism had become intellectually weak. Much of Protestantism had ceased engaging in the kind of rigorous intellectual activity that would have been necessary to respond to the intellectual and cultural challenges advanced by activist secularizers. The reasons for this were multiple. One we have already seen: that the mass revivalism that added many new converts to churches also tended to discourage sustained and careful thought about faith and life. What mattered was personal spiritual experience, emotional conversion, and new life. Questions about faith and knowledge, reason, science, social pluralism, and so on were beside the point. According to Hofstadter, in revivalism,

> The work of the minister tended to be judged by his success in a single area—the saving of souls in measurable numbers. . . . The Puritan ideal of the minister as an intellectual and educational leader was steadily weakened in the face of the evangelical ideal of the minister as a popular crusader and exhorter. Theological education itself became more instrumental. Simple dogmatic formulations were considered sufficient. In considerable measure the churches withdrew from intellectual encounters with the secular world, gave up the idea that religion is a part of the whole life of intellectual experience, and often abandoned the field of rational studies on the assumption that they were the natural province of science alone. (1963: 86–87)

Another source of Protestantism's intellectual weakness came from the pietistic movements that spread through much of American Protestantism in the eighteenth and nineteenth centuries. Pietism reacted against cold formality, empty ritual, and rationalistic dogma in churches by emphasizing the need for intense, personal, inner spiritual experience and commitment. While pietism brought spiritual renewal to many churches, it also tended to discount the importance of intellectual belief and self-conscious thought about faith and the world. Pietists were eager to focus on personal devotion, inner holiness, the "feeling of absolute dependence," and spiritual perfection. They were less interested in working out a theological agenda that would have energetically engaged the emerging intellectual issues of the day (Noll 1994: 47–49; Burtchaell 1998: 838–46). According to Hofstadter, "By 1853 an outstanding clergyman complained that there was, 'an impression, somewhat general, that an intellectual clergyman is deficient in piety, and that an eminently pious minister is deficient in intellect'" (1963: 87).

Yet another source of nineteenth-century American Protestantism's intellectual weakness was its crusading activist spirit. Protestants of this era were ever eager to fight for temperance, the abolition of slavery, urban reform, uplifting the poor, overseas missions, the education of immigrants and Indians, the end of secret societies, orphanages, the censorship of smut, and a host of other causes. Often inspired by the postmillenialist belief that their activism was helping to hasten the coming of Christ's kingdom on earth, nineteenth-century Protestants relentlessly formed volunteer societies to attack a host of social and personal sins and ills (Smith 1980; Parker 1997). However significant their activist zeal and accomplishments might have been, however, one thing this Protestant proclivity to activism did not foster was a thoughtful culture that valued sustained intellectual reflection on larger matters of philosophical and scientific importance. What mattered to kingdom builders was not so much faithfulness and creativity in the life of the mind, but victorious Christian social change.

Nineteenth-century Protestantism's intellectual weakness also derived from the logical structure of the Baconian philosophy of science that it embraced, which facilitated a certain form of intellectual laziness. Baconianism involved a great confidence in the capacity of the objective, neutral scientist to observe and collect a host of individual facts about the world. The scientist's job was then carefully to organize these verified facts into classification systems and, through strict induction, to work from those classified facts to knowledge of the general laws of nature. The particular perspective or position of the observer was not especially relevant, as long as the observations were disinterested and unbiased. Furthermore, the facts and laws themselves, once carefully and objectively observed and induced, would not change, since the universe was stable and ordered by the very natural laws being discovered (Bozeman 1977; Marsden 1989). Science, thus conceived, consisted of an ongoing expansion upon—though not a significant alteration of—knowledge already attained. In one sense, this Baconian science encouraged incessant scientific work of a particular kind—of collecting and classifying more and more facts with which to discover through induction general natural laws. But in another sense, Baconianism assumed a rather static view of the world that lent itself to a kind of intellectual lethargy. Nature itself was fixed, and the considerable number of facts and laws so far discovered would not change. One could therefore acclaim science's achievements, elaborate them incrementally, and otherwise occupy oneself with passing on the extant body of enduring knowledge to the next generation. Missing from this approach was an appreciation of science as an uncertain, dynamic, and innovative enterprise. Baconians had little awareness that humans actively construct knowledge through and within changing perceptual and theoretical frameworks. They were inattentive to the governing influence of theoretical paradigms in framing human knowledge; to legitimate alternative interpretations of empirical evidence; to the importance of the observers' particular position and perspective in shaping their knowledge. All of these Baconians dismissed as useless "metaphysical speculation" (Noll 1994). This static view of knowledge produced among its followers a relatively static intellectual program that did not foster creativity, innovation, and agility. As late-nineteenth-century scientific activists increasingly contested the source and control of socially legitimate knowledge, Protestant intellects shaped by the Baconian paradigm found themselves ill equipped to respond. Thus Noll has observed,

> So much . . . depended on assumptions, and thus so little actual thought went into developing the philosophical, psychological, and ethical implications of these views. All was well as long as Christian energies guided the nation. But once those energies were frustrated by the new social conditions after the Civil War, once they were challenged by new ideas from Europe that also penetrated American life . . . there was very little intellectual strength to meet the new challenges. . . . When Christians turned to their intellectual resources for dealing with these matters, they found that the cupboard was nearly bare. (1994: 105–6)

MATERIAL RESOURCES

Revolutions and social movements are not simply the result of interested and aggrieved activists capitalizing on new political opportunities. To mobilize and prevail, activists also need access to material resources sufficient to sustain their cause. In some cases, the difference between successful and failed revolutions and movements can be traced largely to increasing and decreasing supplies of resources. The secular revolution succeeded in part because new sources of material resources outside of the control of Protestant authorities became available for secular activists to deploy in the cause of secularization. This story is long and complex, and varies in different spheres of public life. Given space limitations, I focus here on the core economic transformation that shaped activists' secularizing of American higher education and science: the boom and incorporation of industrial capitalism.

One of the most profound social changes taking place during the crucial decades of the secularization of higher education and science was the incorporation of industrial capitalism. The magnitude of this transformation, Barrow (1990) shows, was astounding. Spurred by the "epoch-making innovation" of the national railway system established between 1861 and 1907 and the national markets it opened up, the structure of America's productive capacity, ownership of wealth, and class system was profoundly altered. Before the Civil War, only about 7 percent of U.S. manufacturing took place in corporations; by 1900, that figure had grown to nearly 66 percent. Economic centralization merged industries into massive corporate trusts. Between 1897 and 1905, more than 5,300 industrial firms were merged into only 318 corporations. More than 1,200 mergers took place in the single year of 1899. By 1904, there were 26 different major trusts that controlled at least 80 percent of the production in their particular fields. In the process, the structure of the labor market was also revolutionized. At the start of the nineteenth century, the vast majority of American workers were self-employed entrepreneurs; but by century's end, two-thirds of workers had become wage and salaried employees. The ownership of wealth was centralized dramatically as well. During the 1840s, there were fewer than twenty millionaires in what was still a primarily agricultural United States. By 1893, a mere 9 percent of the most prosperous Americans had come to own 71 percent of the nation's wealth (Barrow 1990: 14–30). In sum, in a relatively short time of historically unprecedented growth and centralization of wealth, American capitalism had incorporated under the control of the Morgans, Rockefellers, Mellons, Carnegies, and Du Ponts of the country.

This economic transformation had important consequences for the place of religion in American higher education and science. The interests of corporate, industrial capitalism proved in certain ways unfriendly to religion's playing a significant role in science and higher education. It was not that capitalism and Protestantism were in a direct and logical way intellectually and socially irreconcilable—as with Wilson's suggestion that people simply can't believe in God in an age of conveyor belts (1976: 6–7). But corporate capitalism did significantly influence resources that facilitated activist secularizers who were working to undermine religion's authority in American higher education and science.

Perhaps the most obvious and crucial influence that expanding corporate capitalism exerted on American higher education was its financial patronage of secular research universities, which effectively marginalized religion. Most of America's Christian colleges depended financially on the support of local towns, affiliated denominations, and student tuition. The education they managed to produce with these limited funds was impressive, all in all. But corporate capitalism's centralization of the production and ownership of wealth at the end of the nineteenth century created vast new pools of financial assets, some of which many industrial philanthropists chose to devote to the cause of reforming higher education (Hollis 1938). As it turns out, the most important American research universities that self-consciously pioneered functionally secular education and scholarship were either created *ex nihilo* or were significantly endowed by affluent capitalist benefactors: Johns Hopkins University by Johns Hopkins, Cornell University by Ezra Cornell, the University of Chicago by John D. Rockefeller, Stanford University by Leland Stanford, Clark University by Jonas Gilman Clark, and so on. Andrew Carnegie, Andrew Mellon, Cornelius Vanderbilt, James Duke, and many other wealthy industrialists also had a hand in endowing what became major research universities. Industrial money also flowed into secular universities through Rockefeller's General Education Board, founded in 1902 with assets of $46 million; through the Carnegie Corporation with assets of $151 million in 1911; and through the Commonwealth Fund established by Mrs. Stephen V. Harkness in 1918 through a $43 million endowment. This massive supply of new financial resources for universities came with few mandates seeking to preserve substantial religious interests in higher education. Rather, the concern of these capitalist patrons was to rationalize American higher education through uniform national standards and to promote advanced scientific research modeled on the German university system. This they viewed as serving the interests of the nation and its economy. In effect, the hundreds of millions of dollars that capitalist moguls pumped into their new research universities created the financial basis for autonomy from religious bodies. They also decisively institutionalized a new model of specialized, secular scholarship and learning, which quickly became the national ideal standard for higher education and scholarship.

In some cases, big corporate money actually came with explicitly *anti*-religious mandates. In 1905, for example, Andrew Carnegie gave $10 million to establish a professor's pension fund. Carnegie put Henry Smith Pritchett in charge of the project, the secularized son of a Methodist preacher, of whom it was said that "[h]is 'faith' was science" (Lagemann 1983: 35). Pritchett's rules governing access to funds stated that all denominational colleges and universities were categorically excluded from the plan; only schools with no formal ties to religious denominations could participate. Pritchett argued that denominational influences on colleges made for unsound education, encouraged the existence of too many small schools, were institutionally inefficient, and compromised the public good (Marsden 1994: 281–83). In response, fifteen colleges immediately severed their ties with their religious denominations in order to get a share of the Carnegie money—including Wesleyan, Dickinson, Swarthmore, Brown, Bowdoin, Rutgers, Rochester, and Occidental (Bass 1989).

All of this reflected in part the fact that corporate capitalist interests required a different kind of graduate than those earlier Christian colleges had been educating. In the previous economic era, American colleges specialized in training and graduating gentlemen broadly educated in the classics and intellectually socialized into a coherent Protestant moral universe. They would go into the traditional professions to become leaders and sustainers of the prevailing social order. But corporate capitalism did not need classically educated gentlemen. It needed technically and professionally trained employees in management, finance, law, advertising, engineering, and other material sciences. Similarly, corporate capitalism needed scholars in higher education whose research agendas differed from those dominating earlier Christian colleges. Traditional faculty scholarship in Greek, Hebrew, and Latin languages, moral philosophy, theology, literature, science as inductive Baconian specimen-gathering, and the like contributed little to the industrial corporation's production of material wealth and accumulation of capital. Rather, corporate capitalist interests were better served by technical knowledge generated by basic and applied scientific research producing scholarship useful for boosting material production and economic growth. Not geology focused on harmonizing with the Genesis creation account, but geology intent on locating and excavating minerals and petroleum was what corporate capitalism, by systemic logic, was interested in—regardless of the particular religious beliefs of any individual capitalist magnate. Capitalism thus undercut the justification for the scholarly task of a college system that privileged religious knowledge in its education, bolstering instead a rationale for a kind of technical, instrumental scholarship that was at the very least indifferent to religious concerns and interests. The moral order of Christian higher education simply did not much aid the interests of an expanding corporate capitalist system, and the material rewards for academic achievement shifted to a different version of success in higher education.

To what extent, in and through all of this, corporate magnates—some of whom were personally devout—actually perceived a threat to their capitalist interests from the public authority of particularistic religious traditions is unclear. We know theoretically that historical religious faiths foster "substantive rationalities" with definite moral and social imperatives rooted in their specific traditions. Capitalist interests, on the other hand, are theoretically best served by systems of "procedural rationality" which foster universality, "neutrality," interchangeability, and a public/private partitioning of life. Together, these allow the "invisible hand" of the market to do its work, unencumbered by moral critiques, inefficient lifestyle particularities, or other potential obstructions grounded in substantively rational moral and religious traditions. Labor is then mobile as needed, consumers purchase what is promoted, workers perform as demanded, managers execute as expected—and profits flow. And what the Torah, or the Pope, or Jesus may say in opposition is not relevant, because those are *private* matters. Historically, in fact, we do know that more than a few religiously driven social activists struggled during this era against capitalist interests. Groups such as the Evangelical Ministers Union, for example, mobilized for decades to close down all businesses on Sundays in observance of the biblical Sabbath (Mirola 1999). The American labor movement after the Civil War also drew extensively on Christian languages of morality to justify their struggles over working conditions, pay, and shorter work hours (Mirola 1998). And many Social Gospel reformers agitated to restructure industrial capitalism to conform to the will of Jesus, as they saw it (White and Hopkins 1976). Had they been either theoretically reflective or intuitively perceptive, late-nineteenth-century capitalist industrialists would have recognized the economic advantages of privatizing religious authority. To what extent they actually did so, however, is beyond the scope of this chapter to ascertain.

What we do know, however, is that in many spheres of public life capitalism created the material conditions necessary to develop new systems for producing and distributing socially legitimate knowledge no longer under the supervision of dominant religious interests. In the case of higher education, capitalism supplied the resources to establish new secular universities whose intellectual labor was placed beyond the control of the Protestant establishment. Capitalism's growing interest in shaping higher education, in ways that proved detrimental to religious influences, is evident in the changing vocational makeup of the boards of trustees of colleges and universities during this era—the governing bodies that formally owned and guided the schools. In one sample of fifteen private institutions of higher education, the 39 percent of trustees that in 1860 were clergymen had by 1900 dropped to 23 percent, and by 1930 dropped again to only 7 percent. By contrast, the percentage of those schools' trustees who were businessmen, bankers, and lawyers grew from 48 percent in 1860 to 64 percent in 1900, and again to 74 percent in 1930. Since the proportion of trustees from the other represented vocations remained fairly stable over this period, the 26 percent gain for businessmen, lawyers, and bankers came directly out of the 32 percent decline in the clergy's representation. In the end, more than ten times more business than religious leaders served on these boards of trustees (McGrath 1936). A separate analysis of the boards of trustees of twelve other private colleges, universities, and technical insti-

tutes confirms these results. During the years 1861–80, clergymen constituted 41 percent of the trustees of these schools, but by 1881–1900 that
figure had dropped to 18 percent, and by the 1920s again to 9 percent.
Over that same time period, the percentage of businessmen and lawyers
grew from 32 to 66 percent (Barrow 1990: 36). A similar displacement of
religious by business leaders also occurred in a sample of private denominational and liberal arts colleges, whose trustees showed a 32-point decline
in clergy between 1861–80 and 1920–29, in contrast to a 39-point increase
in businessmen and lawyers over the same years (Barrow 1990: 47). Rightly,
then, did Thorstein Veblen observe in 1918 that

> [w]ithin the memory of men still living it was a nearly unbroken rule that the
> governing boards of . . . higher American schools were drawn largely from the
> clergy and were also guided mainly by ecclesiastical . . . notions of what was
> right and needful in matters of learning. . . . That phase of academic policy is
> past. . . . Academic authorities now proceed on grounds of businesslike expe-
> diency rather than on religious conviction. . . . For a generation past . . . there
> has gone on a wide-reaching substitution of laymen in the place of clergymen
> on the governing boards. The substitution is a substitution of businessmen
> and politicians; which amounts to saying that it is a substitution of business-
> men. So that the discretionary control in matters of university policy now rests
> finally in the hands of businessmen. (1918: 62–64)

With sufficient space, we might more thoroughly examine the influence
of other shifts in material resources—particularly through the expansion of
mass-consumer capitalism—that facilitated the secular revolution. We
might, for example, investigate how the emergence of a new mass market
for magazines and books generated new publishing houses managed by
non-Protestant entrepreneurs who were more interested in the profits that
could be earned by promoting *avant garde* literature than in sustaining
Protestant establishment cultural sensibilities and standards. We might explore the financial underwriting by wealthy sponsors of people and programs promoting a secular modernist worldview and culture (e.g., see
Wexler 1997). In these and other ways, shifts in the availability and alloca-
tion of material resources exerted significant direct and indirect influences
in the secularization of American public life.

CONCLUSION

This chapter has only begun to sketch an outline of a secular revolution approach to macrosocial secularization, merely to suggest some broad lines of
thought about a research program to address an old question in a fresh way.
Its terms are broad and general. Its analytical agenda has highlighted intentional actors, human agency, struggle and conflict, interests and griev-

ances, authority and power, knowledge and institutions, and culture and moral order. Much more could be said about strategy, material resources, organizations, issue framing, identity, solidarity, and other issues related to the secularization struggles. Much complexity, case-specific variation, national-versus-local differences, and cross-national comparisons need to be added as well. The following chapters undertake to put flesh on some of these bare bones, to specify in much greater detail how secularization worked in various fields of public life. Here I have suggested a general analytical framework in sweeping and sometimes imprecise terms. The chapters that follow engage the analytical agenda outlined in this chapter and explore its usefulness in different fields. The specifics of different cases vary, and different fields and institutions fit different aspects of the framework laid out in this chapter better than others. The first few chapters examine cases that tend to fit the thesis elaborated above more clearly, showing how secularizing activists worked intentionally to reduce the authority and relevance of religion in diverse spheres of public life, including science, higher education, primary and secondary education, moral reform politics, law, and in American Protestantism and culture itself. Latter chapters introduce some twists on the basic story. The chapter by Thomas, Peck, and De Haan, for example, compares national, regional, and local levels to show, among other things, how the secularizing effect of an activist elite "educational trust" was conditioned at local levels by the interposition of the superintendency. Flory's chapter on journalism reveals how a field of practice that never was strongly controlled by religious agents was nevertheless reshaped, through the adoption of secular models of authority and knowledge from other social fields, into a more thoroughly secular image. And the Evans chapter on science shows how a solidly secularized profession managed later in the twentieth century to prevent subsequent religious countermoves from succeeding. The larger purpose of this work is not necessarily to advance and defend a specific theoretical approach; rather, it aims to stimulate broad discussion and inquiry that will enhance our historical understanding of secularization in different fields of American public life.

NOTES

1. Most, however, suffered considerable "symbolic violence" (Bourdieu 1977: 190–97; Swartz 1997: 88–93).

2. Totals include those having "secularization" in their dissertation titles and dissertation abstracts, respectively.

3. I am much more skeptical, however, that secularization describes any real historical change at the micro level of individual belief, consciousness, and practice (see Smith et al. 1998; Stark and Finke 2000; but see Bruce 1992 for a different perspective).

4. Thus, Eisenstadt (1966: 21, 34) wrote, "The processes of cultural modernization, which include secularization, have weakened the certainty of the accepted,
long-established values and traditions and of their bearers and representatives. . . .
The major theme that developed in this [cultural] sphere throughout different
stages of modernization were those of traditionalism as against more autonomous
forces of cultural creativity. . . . The first specific form of cleavage . . . in this sphere
was that of religious freedom and of the possibility of an overall secularization of the
culture." Likewise, Brown (1976: 199) wrote, "Modern rationalism, with its endless
emphasis on inquiry and analysis, has undermined the religious faiths that sustained
modernization."

5. The literature is vast, but a few examples include Thiemann 1996; Perry 1997;
Audi and Wolterstorff 1997; Sandel 1996; Reichley 1985; Monsma and Soper 1997,
1998; Carter 1993; Wentz 1998; Monsma 1992; and Sullivan 1986.

6. Historical sociology has since the 1950s revitalized its roots in the classical sociological tradition and produced works of major importance in the 1970s–1990s
on the rise of modern capitalism and the global economic system; political revolutions and social movements; the evolution of empires and civilizations; the rise,
transformation, and decline of democracies; and social inequalities, gender relations, family systems, community change, and welfare states. But historical sociology
has contributed virtually nothing to our understanding of the transformed role of
religion in American public life—Thomas (1989) being the obvious exception—
despite the central focus on religion in the historical analyses of Max Weber, one of
historical sociology's key progenitors.

7. If anything, contemporary scholarship in the sociology of science has revealed
how very similar scientific practices often are to religious practices—for example,
science operates within paradigms that are resistant to empirical falsification in all
but the long run; science necessarily relies on testimony, authority, and trust in the
often unverifiable witness of others to sustain itself; and so on (e.g., Kuhn 1970; Latour 1987). On the latter point, for instance, Shapin (1994: xxv) notes "the ineradicable role of what others tell us": "No practice has accomplished the rejection of testimony and authority and . . . no cultural practice recognizable as such could do
so. . . . Knowledge is a collective good. In securing our knowledge we rely upon others, and we cannot dispense with that reliance. That means that the relations in
which we have and hold our knowledge have a moral character . . . [namely] trust."
Not all scientists, however, are sympathetic to this general approach (see, e.g., Gross
and Levitt 1994).

8. The secularizing activist T. H. Huxley professed, "Warfare has been my business and duty" (quoted in Huxley 1901: 227).

9. Classical foundationalism assumes that rational beliefs always have the particular structure of indubitable foundations and that beliefs derive either deductively
or probabilistically from those foundations.

10. See, for example, Alston 1991, 1992; Plantinga 1993a, 1993b, 2000; Plantinga and Wolterstorff 1983; Wolterstorff 1976, 1992; also see Kvanvig 1996; Runzo
and Ihara 1986; Clark 1993. Note that Reformed Epistemology advances a negative
or defensive apologetic (i.e., theism is *no less* rational or defensible than other perspectives), not a positive or offensive apologetic (i.e., that theism is *more* rational or
defensible than alternatives; see Meeker 1994). Its thrust is not to prove the validity

of theistic faith, but simply to establish that it is *not less* rational or warranted than other basic perspectives. In that it only sets religious belief on relatively *equal* ground with unbelief, it cannot finally resolve which alternative position deserves assent. Still, even this negative apologetic represents a major change in the epistemic status of religious belief.

11. Rorty is quoted in Louthan 1996: 179. Rorty remains opposed to religion, however, not on epistemological grounds, but on "practical" grounds: "I do not think that Christian theism is irrational. I entirely agree . . . that it is no more irrational than atheism. Irrationality is not the question but rather, desirability. The only reason I can think of for objecting to Christian theism is that a lot of Christians have been bigoted fanatics. But of course, so have a lot of atheists. . . . Atheism is more practical only if you wish to form a pluralistic, democratic society. In that situation, the persistence of the theist who claims to know that this or that is against God's will becomes a problem. So atheists find themselves wishing that these groups would wither away" (in Louthan 1996: 178, 183).

12. Both rationalization and differentiation are used to explain secularization at the meso/organizational level, although this level has received the least attention of the three in the literature.

13. Jeffrey Alexander—devoting nearly one half of his summary to religious marginalization—describes the "general outlines" of differentiation theory thus: "Institutions gradually become more specialized. Familial control over social organization decreases. Political processes become less directed by the obligations and rewards of patriarchy, and the division of labor is organized more according to economic criteria than by reference simply to age and sex. Community membership can reach beyond ethnicity to territorial and political criteria. Religion becomes more generalized and abstract, more institutionally separated from and in tension with other spheres. Eventually cultural generalization breaks the bonds of religion altogether. Natural laws are recognized in the moral and physical world and, in the process, religion surrenders not only its hierarchical control over cultural life but its institutional prominence as well" (1990: 1).

14. Our first clue in this regard is provided by the history of the word *secularization* itself: rather than suggesting an abstract modernization process, secularization originally referred to the forced disbanding of Catholic religious orders and the confiscation of their land and wealth by states, particularly after the Treaty of Westphalia.

15. The concepts of secularization as differentiation and rationalization, as I have said, derive from Durkheim and Weber, both of whom were mediated to American sociology through the work of the structural-functionalist Talcott Parsons. Since secularization theory came of age at the zenith of structural-functionalism's theoretical dominance of American sociology (the 1960s), secularization theory has reflected much of functionalism's character. And even though structural-functionalism virtually collapsed in the 1970s, under the weight of widespread criticism, secularization theory itself has in succeeding years retained much of the character of the structural-functionalist approach, including some of its heavily criticized features.

16. Inglehart continues as follows: "Modernization involves . . . the shift away from cultural traditions (usually based on religious norms) that emphasize ascribed

status and sharing, toward placing a positive value on achievement and accumulation. For Weber, the key to Modernization was the shift from a religiously-oriented worldview to a rational-legal worldview [then discusses secularization and bureaucratization]. . . . Modernization *does require* the dismantling of some core aspects of traditional religion—in particular, it abolishes traditional tendencies to equate the old with the good" (1997: 72–73, 80; italics mine).

17. In Berger's (1967) own terms, secularization theory circumvents intellectual and political anomie at the expense of alienation and intellectual bad faith; whereas what is needed is the humanizing effect of de-alienating historical process by re-introducing historical openness and contingency.

18. Likewise, Wilson asserts but does not explain that "[t]he emergence of industrial man, technological man . . . was a process of transforming human consciousness. . . . The consequence of this slow process of change in the thinking of men has been steadily to make religious belief and practice . . . difficult for modern man" (1976: 12).

19. Wilson also writes on social control: "Control has become a matter for mechanical and bureaucratic devices. It has become impersonal and amoral, a matter for routine techniques and unknown officials. Our world has become *de*-moralized" (1976: 20).

20. Modernization theorists Watson and Tarr's focus on cynical anti-religion jokes as (I think rather weak) empirical evidence of secularization raises similar questions: "Despite the large number of people who now claim religious affiliation there is a strong tendency toward secularism in American life. Secularization means that the bulk of one's life is determined by nontraditional, especially nonreligious, institutions. . . . At the same time that we recognize the place of religion in American life, we also discover a cynicism toward religion. . . . Cynicism can be recognized in the jokes about one-day-a week Christians and Eastertime Christians. We also find it in the behavior of parents who insist that their children attend Sunday school but who themselves never enter the church. The notion that church is good in its place but that business is business further exemplifies the cynical attitude toward religion held by Americans" (Watson and Tarr 1964: 258–60).

21. *Church of the Holy Trinity v. United States,* 143 U.S. 457 at 471.

22. Agency of course does not imply *complete* self-awareness, conscious calculation, and control of action, as even voting, shopping, and getting married involve the playing out of cultural scripts within social structures, actions that entail some degree of habit, conformity, and a rational process. But none of that negates the presence of human agency.

23. Shils (1972: 21) actually adds a fifth tradition, that of "anti-intellectual order," modern versions of which, however, in my view can be understood as a subtradition within scientism.

24. See Koch 1968; Royle 1974, 1976; Campbell 1972: 46–96; Haught 1996; Vitzthum 1995; Thrower 1971: 97–136; Lightman 1987; Baumer 1960; Lockerbie 1998; Trace 1983: 93–170; Robertson 1899; Lecky 1866; for historical background, see Manuel 1959, 1983; Bury 1952; Cairns 1881; Yolton 1983; Preus 1987; Haakonssen 1996; Redwood 1976; and Harrison 1990. By contrast, most elements of the old Protestant establishment embraced the views of the more moderate Scottish didactic Enlightenment, which was intellectually much friendlier to religion (Noll 1995).

And some later secularizing activists—such as mid-twentieth-century Jews fighting anti-Semitic discrimination—were often more concerned with less ideological matters of equity and autonomy than skeptical or revolutionary Enlightenment.

25. Bohemian intellectuals, for example, are of course quite different from mainstream progressive reformers; succeeding chapters seek to sort through the specifics of these kinds of differences in ways that this broad chapter cannot explore.

26. This is a point that Marxists and certain other progressives are most likely to emphasize (see, e.g., Chomsky 1997; Herman and Chomsky 1988).

27. Daniel Bell writes, "Intelligentsia was meant to apply to a generation . . . who were becoming critical of society—and received its definitive stamp in the novel of Turgenev, *Fathers and Sons,* the fathers being the critical thinkers and the sons the nihilists. The formulation . . . deals with . . . the primacy of the *ideological* as the focus of its concerns, and a sense of *alienation.* What is implicit in all this is . . . being involved in a war of ideas; of being concerned with new and novel ideas; and of detaching oneself from the society of which one is a part" (1980: 120–21).

28. Shils continues, "This applies . . . to the value orientations of those exercising authority in the society, since it is on them that the intellectuals' attention is most often focused, they being the custodians of the central institutional system. [Most interesting] is the rejection by intellectuals of the inherited and prevailing values of those intellectuals who are already incorporated in ongoing social institutions" (1972: 7).

29. Hollander continues, "The broad historical background against which such expectations are played out is that of secularization. . . . Political beliefs take on religious coloration when religion proper withers, at any rate among intellectuals" (1987: 81). In his study of leftist literary elites, for example, Daniel Aaron notes how their ideals generated their social criticism: "American literature . . . is the most searching and unabashed criticism of our national limitations that exists, the product of . . . years of quarreling between the writer and his society. The social criticism of writers . . . has usually sprung from an extreme sensitiveness to the disparity between ideals and practices" (1992: 1).

30. Thus Gouldner observes that "[t]he new class starts out by critiquing traditional normative systems . . . in the name of reason . . . [and] concludes by arrogating to themselves not only administrative decisional competence but, finally, even the role of judge and regulators of the normative structures of . . . society" (1979: 15).

31. Kristol writes, "The self-designation . . . 'avant-garde' is itself illuminating. The term is of military origin, and means . . . the foremost assault troops in a military attack. It was a term popularized by Saint-Simon to describe the role of his utopian-socialist sect vis-à-vis the bourgeois order, and was then taken over by modernist innovators in the arts. The avant-garde is, and always has been, fully self-conscious of its hostile intentions toward the bourgeois world" (1979: 338).

32. Often this desire is expressed with a much more elitist spirit, as with Graña's nineteenth-century French intellectuals, whose "view of the . . . proper society . . . was that of a hierarchical world resting on the discipline established by reverence to intelligence and to the spiritual poise and aesthetic and moral superiority of a new aristocracy—themselves" (1964: 69).

33. Kristol concurs, noting that nineteenth-century Victorian society deprived intellectuals of "the status that they naturally feel themselves entitled to. Artists and

writers and thinkers always have taken themselves to be Very Important People, and they are outraged by a society that merely tolerates them" (1979: 333). Noting that commercial society tends to reflect through the market the interests of common people, Kristol says that "artists and intellectuals see this as an inversion of the natural order of things, since it gives 'vulgarity' the power to dominate" (333).

34. Christopher Lasch notes about 1930s progressive elites that "[i]n the heyday of the socialist movement its attraction for intellectuals cannot be adequately explained without considering the way it overlapped with the bohemian critique of the bourgeoisie. Socialists and aesthetes shared a common enemy, the bourgeois philistine, and the unremitting onslaught against bourgeois culture was far more lasting in its effects . . . than the attack on capitalism" (1995: 233–34).

35. According to a study by Lipset and Dobson (1972), "intellectuality" per se was found to make a person more critical of policies of the existing regime. In the early 1970s, Kadushin found "the American intellectual elite to be to the left of any other sector of the American elite and even to the left of comparable American university professors. Thus there is no question but that the general climate of opinion of elite American intellectuals is one of opposition and generalized dissent. . . . They are not mid-America and even the more conservative among them when confronted with the simple choices of a public opinion poll find themselves on the opposite side of the fence from most Americans" (1974: 347–48). Data from the early 1980s show cultural elites to be highly alienated from the U.S. social system and most committed to [romanticist] expressive individualism (Lerner, Nagai, and Rothman 1996; also see Ladd 1979).

36. Eisenstadt observes that elites tend "to develop claims for an autonomous place in the construction of the cultural and social order. They [see] themselves as . . . potentially autonomous carriers of the models of a distinct cultural and social order. . . . Intellectuals . . . were able to transform their visions, in relatively autonomous ways, into the institutional premises of society. . . . In all the great revolutions that lay at the origins of modernity . . . intellectuals promoted the basic cultural and ideological visions that were promulgated in the crystalization of these revolutions and their impact on the crystalization of the basic premises of modern societies" (1987: 160, 164).

37. Note that intellectuals' recurrent alienation from established social orders often focuses specifically on religion per se when religion serves ideologically to legitimate that order, or when religion becomes associated with what intellectuals consider the crassness of commercial and political life. Graña, for example, shows how nineteenth-century European literary elites worked to "intrude into daily reality . . . their contempt for the established spiritual order." In one instance, French author Théophile Dondey published his "Profession of Faith," which Graña quotes: "Ah Eh he He! Hi! Hi! Oh Hu! Hu! Hu!" Dondey explained elsewhere that he wrote this because, "I despise society . . . and especially its excrescence, the social order" (Graña 1964: 71, 77–78).

38. Shils notes that "at the periphery of the Protestant churches, a certain kind of active, social-reforming, Christian intellectual was to be found, but, on the whole, literary and humanistic intellectuals had no affectionate connections with these circles. Theologians and ecclesiastical dignitaries . . . were regarded as alien to the valid intellectual tradition. [For American intellectuals] the church was hopeless: the Ro-

man Catholic hierarchy was the epitome of benightedness; and the Protestants, ranging from the despicable stuffiness and sycophancy of the Episcopalians and the Presbyterians . . . to the innumerable sects of ranters and Bible-pounders who had fallen out of the bottom of the Baptists and Methodists, were no better" (1982: 231, 235).

39. Berger elaborates: "There exists an international subculture composed of people with Western-type higher education, especially in the humanities and social sciences, which is indeed secularized by any measure. This subculture is the principal 'carrier' of progressive, Enlightenment beliefs and values. . . . They are very influential, as they control the institutions that provide the 'official' definitions of reality (notably the educational system, the media of mass communications, and the higher reaches of the legal system). . . . Why it is that people with this type of education should be so prone to secularization is not entirely clear, but there is, without question, a globalized *elite* culture" (1996: 8).

40. In Abbott's language on professions, groups seeking jurisdiction ask society to recognize their own particular cognitive structures through exclusive rights. "A jurisdictional claim before the public is generally a claim for the legitimate control of a particular kind of work. . . . Public jurisdiction, in short, is a claim of both social and cultural authority" (1988: 59–60). Moreover, rightly understanding issues of jurisdictional dispute requires a focus on interprofessional competition, as Abbott explains: "Control of knowledge and its application means dominating outsiders who attack that control. Control without competition is trivial. . . . The professions make up an interacting system, an ecology. Professions compete within this system, and a profession's success reflects as much the situations of its competitors and the system structure as it does the profession's own efforts. From time to time, tasks are created, abolished, or reshaped by external forces, with consequent jostling and readjustment within the system of professions" (2, 33).

41. According to Bell, "What united [the Young Intellectuals] was the protest against the genteel tradition, the domination of America by the small town and the crabbed respectability which the small town enforced. What enthralled them was the teeming vibrancy of urban ethnic life. What attracted them was an exuberance summed up in a series of catchwords. One of them was 'new.' . . . A second was 'sex,' a word which they used openly to proclaim a sexual revolution; and the word sex sent a *frisson* through the rest of society. And the third was the word *liberation.* Liberation, which the movement self-consciously ascribed to itself, was the wind blowing from Europe, the wind of Modernism come to the American shore. . . . And the favorite 'doctrine of the Rebellion' . . . was that happiness would follow completely instinctual self-expression" (1980: 125–26).

42. The Enlightenment, of course, also generated critical and reactive movements—including romanticism and skepticism—which, however, when disseminated among American knowledge elites, also typically worked to undermine Protestant establishment authority.

43. Spencer's ideology legitimated Carnegie's wealth. Troubled by religious doubts, Carnegie wrote that, upon reading Spencer, "light came in a flood and all was clear. . . . 'All is well since all grows better' became my motto, my true source of comfort." In his autobiography Carnegie confessed, "Few men have wished to know

another man more strongly than I to know Herbert Spencer" (quoted in Boller 1971: 54).

44. According to Moore, "The German clergy were not of the ruling class but functioned as an educational civil service, in most cases employed by the state. Neither the state nor the Protestant churches required them to subscribe a statement of belief, and thus in the theological faculties of the great universities there had been for many years a freedom of scholarship almost unknown in British and American institutions, where professors were bound by denominational creeds through most of the nineteenth century" (1986a: 332). Thus, the German periodical *Kreuzzeitung* observed of the late nineteenth century, "We have a double-entry system of spiritual bookkeeping. For the masses, [who] . . . attend elementary schools and . . . secondary schools as well, we have instruction in religion on the lines of positive Christianity in the name and by the authority of the state. In the universities, on the contrary, where young men are being educated who will in time succeed to the leadership of Church and state . . . something entirely different is often put forward in the name of science; doctrines are preached which stand in sharpest contradiction with those given to the people. . . . This is excused on the ground that religion is for the people, and for them it is good enough as it is; science, however, occupies another field and seeks a different patronage—the two do not come in contact" (quoted in Russell 1895: 391–92).

45. Likewise, the evidence cited by the U.S. Supreme Court in its 1892 ruling (quoted at the beginning of this chapter) to demonstrate that America was indeed a Christian nation consisted largely of social conventions: oaths appealing to the "Almighty," the opening of legislatures with prayer, the word "God" in the prefatory words of wills, Sabbath laws, and the widespread presence of Christian churches, charities, and missionary efforts (*Church of the Holy Trinity v. United States,* 143 U.S. 457 at 471).

46. Likewise, having confronted what he saw as the many forces threatening the future of Christian America—immigration, "Romanism," Mormonism, intemperance, socialism, mammon, and urban life—Josiah Strong, in his 1885 book, *Our Country: Its Possible Future and Its Present Crisis,* drew to a close optimistically:

> "When Napoleon drew up his troops . . . under the shadow of the Pyramids . . . he said to his soldiers: 'Remember that from yonder heights forty centuries look down upon you.' Men of this generation, from the pyramid top of opportunity on which God has set us, *we look down on forty centuries!* We stretch our hand into the future with power to mold the destinies of unborn millions. . . . Notwithstanding the great perils which threaten it, I cannot think our civilization will perish; but I believe it is fully in the hands of the Christians of the United States, during the next fifteen or twenty years, to hasten or retard the coming of Christ's kingdom in the world by hundreds, and perhaps thousands, of years. We of this generation and nation occupy the Gibraltar of the ages which commands the world's future." (1885: 179–80)

REFERENCES

Aaron, Daniel. 1992. *Writers on the Left.* New York: Columbia University Press.

Abbott, Andrew. 1988. *The System of Professions.* Chicago: University of Chicago Press.

Ahlstrom, Sydney. 1975. *A Religious History of the American People.* New Haven, CT: Yale University Press.

Alexander, Jeffrey. 1990. "Differentiation Theory: Problems and Prospects." In *Differentiation Theory and Social Change,* ed. Jeffrey Alexander and Paul Colomy. New York: Columbia University Press.

Alston, William. 1991. *Perceiving God.* Ithaca, NY: Cornell University Press.

———. 1992. *Faith, Reason, and Skepticism.* Philadelphia, PA: Temple University Press.

"American Colleges and German Universities." 1880. *Harper's New Monthly* 61: 253–60.

Aron, Raymond. 1955. *The Opium of the Intellectuals.* New York: W. W. Norton.

Askew, Thomas, and Peter Spellman. 1984. *The Churches and the American Experience.* Grand Rapids, MI: Baker Book House.

Audi, Robert, and Nicholas Wolterstorff. 1997. *Religion in the Public Square.* Lanham, MD: Rowman and Littlefield.

Bald, Margaret. 1998. *Banned Books.* New York: Facts on File.

Barabba, Vincent. 1975. *Historical Statistics of the United States.* Washington, DC: Bureau of Census.

Barrow, Clyde W. 1990. *Universities and the Capitalist State.* Madison: University of Wisconsin Press.

Bass, Dorothy. 1989. "Ministry on the Margin: Protestants and Education." In *Between the Times,* ed. William R. Hutchinson. New York: Cambridge University Press.

Batten, Samuel. 1909. *The Christian State.* Philadelphia, PA: Griffith and Rowland.

Baumer, Franklin. 1960. *Religion and the Rise of Scepticism.* New York: Harcourt Brace.

Beckford, James. 1989. *Religion in Advanced Industrial Society.* Boston: Unwin Hyman.

Beecher, Lyman. 1814. *A Reformation of Morals Practical and Indispensable.* Andover, MA: Flagg and Gould.

Beecher, Lyman, and Asahel Nettleson. 1828. *Letters of the Rev. Dr. Beecher and Rev. Mr. Nettleson on the "New Measures" in Conducting Revivals of Religion.* New York: G. & C. Carvill.

Bell, Daniel. 1980. *The Winding Passage.* New York: Basic Books.

Bellah, Robert. 1970. *Beyond Belief.* New York: Harper and Row.

Bendix, Reinhard. 1964. *Nation-Building and Citizenship.* New York: Wiley.

Berger, Peter. 1967. *The Sacred Canopy.* New York: Anchor Books.

———. 1979. "The Worldview of the New Class." In *The New Class?* ed. B. Bruce-Briggs. New York: McGraw-Hill.

———. 1996. "The Desecularization of the World." *National Interest* 46: 3–12.

Biel, Steven. 1992. *Independent Intellectuals in the United States, 1910–1945.* New York: New York University Press.

Billington, R. A. 1932. "Tentative Bibliography of Anti-Catholic Propaganda." *Catholic Historical Review* 18: 492–513.

———. 1963. *The Protestant Crusade.* Gloucester, MA: Peter Smith.

Boller, Paul. 1971. *American Thought in Transition.* Chicago: Rand McNally.

Bourdieu, Pierre. 1971. "Intellectual Field and Creative Project." In *Knowledge and Control,* ed. M. F. D. Young. London: Cullier-Macmillan.

————. 1977. *Outline of a Theory of Practice.* Cambridge: Cambridge University Press.

————. 1990. *In Other Words: Essays toward a Reflexive Sociology.* Stanford, CA: Stanford University Press.

Boyer, Paul. 1968. *Purity in Print.* New York: Scribner's.

Bozeman, Theodore. 1977. *Protestants in an Age of Science.* Chapel Hill: University of North Carolina Press.

Bradford, Gamaliel. 1927. *D. L. Moody.* New York: George Doran.

Brown, Bernard. 1980. *Intellectuals and Other Traitors.* New York: Ark House.

Brown, Richard. 1976. *Modernization.* New York: Hill and Wang.

Bruce, Steven, ed. 1992. *Religion and Modernization.* Oxford: Clarendon Press.

Bryant, Christopher. 1985. *Positivism in Social Theory and Research.* New York: St. Martin's Press.

Burtchaell, James T. 1998. *The Dying of the Light.* Grand Rapids, MI: Eerdmans.

Bury, J. B. 1952. *A History of Freedom of Thought.* London: Oxford University Press.

Cairns, John. 1881. *Unbelief in the Eighteenth Century.* New York: Harper and Brothers.

Campbell, Colin. 1972. *Toward a Sociology of Irreligion.* New York: Herder and Herder.

Carey, John. 1992. *The Intellectuals and the Masses.* New York: St. Martin's Press.

Carter, Stephen. 1993. *The Culture of Disbelief.* New York: Anchor/Doubleday.

Cashdollar, Charles. 1989. *The Transformation of Theology.* Princeton, NJ: Princeton University Press.

Chadwick, Owen. 1975. *The Secularization of the European Mind in the Nineteenth Century.* Cambridge: Cambridge University Press.

Chaves, Mark. 1994. "Secularization as Declining Religious Authority." *Social Forces* 72, no. 3: 749–75.

Chomsky, Noam. 1997. *Media Control.* New York: Seven Stories Press.

Clark, Kelly James. 1993. *Philosophers Who Believe.* Downers Grove, IL: InterVarsity Press.

Coben, Stanley. 1991. *Rebellion against Victorianism.* New York: Oxford.

Collins, Randall. 1998. *The Sociology of Philosophies.* Cambridge, MA: Harvard University Press.

Cornelison, Isaac. 1895. *The Relation of Religion to Civil Government in the United States of America.* New York: Da Capo Press.

Coser, Lewis. 1984. *Refugee Scholars in America.* New Haven, CT: Yale University Press.

————. 1997. *Men of Ideas.* New York: Free Press.

Cowley, William, and Don Williams. 1991. *International and Historical Roots of American Higher Education.* New York: Garland.

Crook, Alja. 1896. "German Universities." *Chautauquan* 23: 560–64.

Dahrendorf, Rolf. 1969. "The Intellectuals and Society." In *On Intellectuals,* ed. Philip Rieff. Garden City, NY: Doubleday.

Diehl, Carl. 1978. *American and German Scholarship, 1770–1870.* New Haven, CT: Yale University Press.

Dobbelaere, Karel. 1981. "Secularization." *Current Sociology* 29, no. 2 (summer): 3–213.

————. 1999. "Towards an Integrated Perspective of the Processes Related to the Descriptive Concept of Secularization." *Sociology of Religion* 60, no. 3: 229–47.

Dobbelaere, Karel; Jaak Billiet; and Roger Creyf. 1978. "Secularization and Pillarization: A Social Problem Approach." *Annual Review of the Social Sciences of Religion* 2: 97–124.

Dodge, William. 1900. *Ecumenical Missionary Conference, New York, 1900.* Vol. 1. New York: American Tract Society.

Douglas, Mary. 1973. *Natural Symbols.* London: Barrie and Jenkins.

Draper, John. 1874. *History of the Conflict between Religion and Science.* New York: Appleton.

Dupree, A. Hunter. 1986. "Christianity and the Scientific Community in the Age of Darwin." In *God and Nature,* ed. David Lindberg and Ronald Numbers. Berkeley: University of California Press.

Durkheim, Emile. 1933. *The Division of Labor in Society.* New York: Macmillan.

Eisenstadt, S. N. 1966. *Modernization.* Englewood Cliffs, NJ: Prentice-Hall.

———. 1987. "Intellectuals and Political Elites." In *Intellectuals in Liberal Democracies,* ed. Alain Gagnon. New York: Praeger.

Eisenstadt, S. N., and S. R. Graubard, eds. 1973. *Intellectuals and Tradition.* New York: Humanities Press.

Emerson, Michael, and Christian Smith. 2000. *Divided by Faith.* New York: Oxford University Press.

Etzioni-Halevy, Eva. 1985. *The Knowledge Elite and the Failure of Prophecy.* London: G. Allen and Unwin.

Eyerman, Ron. 1994. *Between Culture and Politics.* Cambridge: Polity Press.

Fenn, Richard. 1978. *Toward a Theory of Secularization.* Storrs, CT: Society for the Scientific Study of Religion Monograph Series, no. 1.

Finke, Roger, and Rodney Stark. 1992. *The Churching of America.* New Brunswick, NJ: Rutgers University Press.

Flacks, Dick. 1991. "Making History and Making Theory." In *Intellectuals and Politics,* ed. Charles Lemert. Newbury Park, CA: Sage.

Frank, Douglas. 1986. *Less Than Conquerors.* Grand Rapids, MI: Eerdmans.

Geller, Evelyn. 1984. *Forbidden Books in American Public Libraries.* Westport, CT: Greenwood.

Gladden, Washington. 1909. *The Nation and the Kingdom.* Boston: The Board.

Glasner, Peter. 1977. *The Sociology of Secularisation.* London: Routledge and Kegan Paul.

———. 1993. "Secularism." In *Blackwell Dictionary of Twentieth-Century Social Thought,* ed. William Outhwaite et al. Cambridge: Basil Blackwell.

Gorski, Philip. 2000. "Historicizing the Secularization Debate." *American Sociological Review* 65, no. 1: 138–68.

Gouldner, Alvin. 1979. *The Future of Intellectuals and the Rise of the New Class.* New York: Seabury Press.

Graña, César. 1964. *Bohemian versus Bourgeois.* New York: Basic Books.

Greeley, Andrew. 1995. *Religion as Poetry.* New Brunswick: Transaction.

Green, Steven. 1987. *The National Reform Association and the Religious Amendments to the Constitution.* Master's thesis, University of North Carolina, Chapel Hill.

Gross, Charles. 1893. "College and University in the United States." *Educational Review* 7: 26–32.

Gross, Paul, and Norman Levitt. 1994. *Higher Superstition.* Baltimore, MD: Johns Hopkins University Press.

Gulick, Sidney. 1897. *The Growth of the Kingdom of God.* Chicago: Student Missionary Campaign Library.

Gurstein, Rachelle. 1996. *The Repeals of Reticence.* New York: Hill and Wang.

Haakonssen, Knud. 1996. *Enlightenment and Religion.* Cambridge: Cambridge University Press.

Hadden, Jeffrey. 1987. "Toward Desacralizing Secularization Theory." *Social Forces* 65, no. 3: 587–611.

Haight, Anne, and Chandler Grannis. 1978. *Banned Books.* New York: R. R. Bowker.

Handy, Robert. 1984. *A Christian America.* New York: Oxford University Press.

———. 1991. *Undermined Establishment.* Princeton, NJ: Princeton University Press.

Harp, Gillis. 1995. *Positivist Republic.* University Park: Pennsylvania State University Press.

Harrison, Peter. 1990. *'Religion' and the Religions in the English Enlightenment.* Cambridge: Cambridge University Press.

Hatch, Nathan. 1989. *The Democratization of American Christianity.* New Haven, CT: Yale University Press.

Haught, James. 1996. *2000 Years of Disbelief.* New York: Prometheus Books.

Hawkins, Richmond. 1938. *Positivism in the United States.* Cambridge, MA: Harvard University Press.

Herbst, Jungen. 1965. *The German Historical School in American Scholarship.* Ithaca, NY: Cornell University Press.

Herman, Edward, and Noam Chomsky. 1988. *Manufacturing Consent.* New York: Pantheon Books.

Himmelfarb, Gertrude. 1994. *The De-moralization of Society.* New York: Vintage Books.

Hofstadter, Richard. 1963. *Anti-intellectualism in American Life.* New York: Alfred A. Knopf.

Hofstadter, Richard, and Walter P. Metzger. 1955. *The Development of Academic Freedom in the United States.* New York: Columbia University Press.

Hollander, Paul. 1987. "American Intellectuals: Producers and Consumers of Social Criticism." In *Intellectuals in Liberal Democracies,* ed. Alain Gagnon. New York: Praeger.

Hollinger, David. 1989. "Justification by Verification: The Scientific Challenge to the Moral Authority of Christianity in Modern America." In *Religion and Twentieth-Century American Intellectual Life,* ed. Michael Lacey. New York: Cambridge University Press.

———. 1996. *Science, Jews, and Secular Culture.* Princeton, NJ: Princeton University Press.

Hollis, Ernest. 1938. *Philanthropic Foundations and Higher Education.* New York: Columbia University Press.

Howe, Daniel, ed. 1976. *Victorian America.* Philadelphia: University of Pennsylvania Press.

Hunter, James. 1991. *Culture Wars.* New York: Basic Books.

Hurlin, Ralph, and Meredith Givens. 1933. "Shifting Occupational Patterns." In *Recent Social Trends in the United States.* President's Research Committee on Social Trends, Wesley C. Mitchell, Chair. New York: McGraw-Hill.

Huxley, Leonard, ed. 1901. *Life and Letters of Thomas Henry Huxley.* New York: Appleton.

Inglehart, Ronald. 1997. *Modernization and Postmodernization.* Princeton, NJ: Princeton University Press.

Jondan, Philip. 1982. *The Evangelical Alliance for the United States of America.* New York: Edwin Mellen Press.

Judd, Charles. 1933. "Education." In *Recent Social Trends in the United States.* President's Research Committee on Social Trends, Wesley C. Mitchell, Chair. New York: McGraw-Hill.

Kadushin, Charles. 1974. *The American Intellectual Elite.* Boston: Little, Brown.

Kirby, James. 1967. "Matthew Simpson and the Mission of America." *Church History* 36: 299–307.

Koch, G. Adolf. 1968. *Religion of the American Enlightenment.* New York: Thomas Y. Crowell.

Kristol, Irving. 1979. "The Adversary Culture of Intellectuals." In *The Third Century,* ed. Seymour Martin Lipset. Stanford, CA: Hoover Institution Press.

Kuhn, Thomas. 1970. *The Structure of Scientific Revolutions.* Chicago: University of Chicago Press.

Kvanvig, Jonathan, ed. 1996. *Warrant in Contemporary Epistemology.* Lanham, MD: Rowman and Littlefield.

Ladd, Everett, Jr. 1979. *Faculty Career Development.* Washington, DC: American Association for Higher Education.

Lagemonn, Ellen. 1983. *Private Power for the Public Good.* Middletown, CT: Wesleyan University Press.

Lasch, Christopher. 1995. *The Revolt of the Elites.* New York: W. W. Norton.

Laslett, Peter. 1965. *The World We Have Lost.* London: Methuen.

Latour, Bruno. 1987. *Science in Action.* Cambridge, MA: Harvard University Press.

Lecky, W. E. H. 1866. *History of the Rise and Influence of the Spirit of Rationalism in Europe.* New York: Appleton.

Lerner, Robert; Althea Nagai; and Stanley Rothman. 1996. *American Elites.* New Haven, CT: Yale University Press.

Lewis, Felice. 1976. *Literature, Obscenity, and Law.* Carbondale: Southern Illinois University Press.

Lightman, Bernard. 1987. *The Origins of Agnosticism.* Baltimore, MD: Johns Hopkins University Press.

Lindberg, David, and Ronald Numbers. 1986. *God and Nature.* Berkeley and Los Angeles: University of California Press.

Lipset, Seymour Martin. 1979. "The New Class and the Professoriate." In *The New Class?* ed. B. Bruce-Briggs. New York: McGraw-Hill.

Lipset, Seymour, and Richard Dobson. 1972. "The Intellectual as Critic and Rebel." *Daedelus* 101, no. 3: 137–98.

Livingstone, David. 1987. *Darwin's Forgotten Defenders.* Grand Rapids, MI: Eerdmans.

Lockerbie, D. Bruce. 1998. *Dismissing God.* Grand Rapids, MI: Baker Books.

Long, Kathryn. 1998. *The Revival of 1857–58.* New York: Oxford University Press.

Longfield, Bradley. 1991. *The Presbyterian Controversy.* New York: Oxford.

Louthan, Stephen. 1996. "On Religion—A Discussion with Richard Rorty, Alvin

Plantinga, and Nicholas Wolterstorff." *Christian Scholar's Review* 27, no. 2: 177–83.

Luckmann, Thomas. 1967. *The Invisible Religion.* New York: Macmillan.

Mannheim, Karl. 1936. *Ideology and Utopia.* New York: Harvest.

Manuel, Frank. 1959. *The Eighteenth Century Confronts the Gods.* New York: Atheneum.

———. 1983. *The Changing of the Gods.* Hanover, NH: University Press of New England.

Marsden, George. 1980. *Fundamentalism and American Culture.* New York: Oxford University Press.

———. 1989. "Evangelicals and the Scientific Culture: An Overview." In *Religion and the Twentieth-Century American Intellectual Life,* ed. Michael J. Lacey. Cambridge: Cambridge University Press.

———. 1994. *The Soul of the American University.* New York: Oxford University Press.

Martin, David. 1969. *The Religious and the Secular.* London: Routledge and Kegan Paul.

———. 1978. *A General Theory of Secularization.* New York: Harper and Row.

Marty, Martin. 1970. *Righteous Empire.* New York: Dial Press.

———. 1991. *The Noise of Conflict, 1919–1941.* Chicago: University of Chicago Press.

May, Elaine Tyler. 1980. *Great Expectations.* Chicago: University of Chicago Press.

May, Henry. 1976. *The Enlightenment in America.* New York: Oxford.

———. 1992. *The End of American Innocence.* New York: Columbia University Press.

Maynard, T. 1942. *The Story of American Catholicism.* New York: Macmillan.

McAdam, Doug. 1996. "Conceptual Origins, Current Problems, Future Directions." In *Comparative Perspectives on Social Movements,* ed. Doug McAdam, John D. McCarthy, and Mayer N. Zald. Cambridge: Cambridge University Press.

McAllister, David. 1927. *Christian Civil Government in America.* Pittsburgh, PA: National Reform Association.

McDannell, Colleen. 1986. *The Christian Home in Victorian America.* Bloomington: University of Indiana Press.

McGrath, Earl. 1936. "The Control of Higher Education in America." *Educational Record* 17: 259–72.

McGreevy, John. 1997. "Thinking on One's Own: Catholicism in the American Intellectual Imagination, 1928–1960." *Journal of American History* 84, no. 1: 97–131.

McLoughlin, William. 1955. *Billy Sunday Was His Real Name.* Chicago: University of Chicago Press.

———. 1959. *Modern Revivalism.* New York: Ronald Press.

Meeker, Kevin. 1994. "William Alston's Epistemology of Religious Experience." *International Journal for Philosophy of Religion* 35, no. 2: 89–110.

Methodist Journal. 1900. *Journal of the General Conference of the Methodist Episcopal Church, 1900.* Nashville, TN: Methodist Episcopal Church Press.

Mirola, William. 1998. "Asking for Bread, Receiving a Stone: The Rise and Fall of Religious Ideology in Chicago's Eight-Hour Movement." Unpublished ms.

———. 1999. "Shorter Hours and the Protestant Sabbath." *Social Science History* 23, no. 3: 395–433.

Monsma, Stephen. 1992. *Positive Neutrality.* Westport, CT: Greenwood Press.

Monsma, Stephen, and J. Christopher Soper. 1998. *Equal Treatment of Religion in a Pluralistic Society.* Grand Rapids, MI: Eerdmans.

———. 1997. *The Challenge of Pluralism.* Lanham, MD: Rowman and Littlefield.

Moore, James. 1979. *The Post-Darwinian Controversies.* Cambridge: Cambridge University Press.

———. 1985. "Herbert Spencer's Henchmen: The Evolution of Protestant Liberals in Late-Nineteenth-Century America." In *Darwinism and Divinity,* ed. John Ducant. New York: Blackwell.

———.1986a. "Geologists and Interpreters of Genesis in the Nineteenth Century." In *God and Nature,* ed. David Lindberg and Ronald Numbers. Berkeley and Los Angeles: University of California Press.

———. 1986b. "Crisis without Revolution." *Revue de Synthèse* 107: 53–78.

Nettl, J. P. 1969. "Ideas, Intellectuals, and Structures of Dissent." In *On Intellectuals,* ed. Philip Rieff. New York: Doubleday.

Nietzsche, Friedrich. 1974 [1882]. *The Gay Science.* New York: Vintage.

Noll, Mark. 1994. *The Scandal of the Evangelical Mind.* Grand Rapids, MI: Eerdmans.

———. 1995. "The Rise and Long Life of the Protestant Enlightenment in America." In *Knowledge and Belief in America,* ed. William M. Shea and Peter A. Huff. Cambridge: Cambridge University Press.

Nord, Warren. 1995. *Religion and American Education.* Chapel Hill: University of North Carolina Press.

Outram, Dorinda. 1995. *The Enlightenment.* Cambridge: Cambridge University Press.

Parker, Alison. 1997. *Purifying America.* Urbana: University of Illinois Press.

Parsons, Talcott. 1967. "Christianity and Modern Industrial Society." In *Secularization and the Protestant Prospect,* ed. James Childress and David Harned. Philadelphia, PA: Westminster.

Perry, Michael. 1997. *Religion in Politics.* New York: Oxford University Press.

Plantinga, Alvin. 1993a. *Warrant and Proper Function.* Oxford: Oxford University Press.

———. 1993b. *Warrant: The Current Debate.* Oxford: Oxford University Press.

———. 2000. *Warranted Christian Belief.* New York: Oxford University Press.

Plantinga, Alvin, and Nicholas Wolterstorff, eds. 1983. *Faith and Rationality.* Notre Dame, IN: University of Notre Dame Press.

Preus, J. Samuel. 1987. *Explaining Religion.* New Haven, CT: Yale University Press.

Redwood, John. 1976. *Reason, Ridicule, and Religion.* Cambridge, MA: Harvard University Press.

Reichley, A. James. 1985. *Religion in American Public Life.* Washington, DC: Brookings.

Reuben, Julie. 1996. *The Making of the Modern University.* Chicago: University of Chicago Press.

Rhoades, Gary. 1990. "Political Competition and Differentiation in Higher Education." In *Differentiation Theory and Social Change,* ed. Jeffrey Alexander and Paul Colomy. New York: Columbia University Press.

Robertson, John. 1899. *A Short History of Freethought.* New York: Macmillan.

Ross, Andrew. 1990. "Defenders of the Faith and the New Class." In *Intellectuals: Aesthetics, Politics, Academics,* ed. Bruce Robbins. Minneapolis: University of Minnesota.

Royle, Edward. 1974. *Victorian Infidels.* Manchester, U.K.: University of Manchester Press.

———. 1976. *The Infidel Tradition.* New York: Macmillan.

Rubenstein, William. 1987. "Jewish Intellectuals in Liberal Democracies." In *Intellectuals in Liberal Democracies,* ed. Alain Gagnon. New York: Praeger.

Rueschemeyer, Dietrich. 1977. "Structural Differentiation, Efficiency, and Power." *American Journal of Sociology* 83, no. 1: 1–25.

Runzo, Joseph, and Craig Ihara, eds. 1986. *Religious Experience and Religious Belief.* Lanham, MD: University Press of America.

Russell, James. 1895. "The University Crisis in Germany." *Educational Review* 9: 391–99.

Sadri, Ahmad. 1992. *Max Weber's Sociology of Intellectuals.* New York: Oxford.

Sandel, Michael. 1996. *Democracy's Discontent.* Cambridge, MA: Harvard University Press.

Schenkel, Albert. 1990. *The Rich Man and the Kingdom.* Ph.D. diss. Harvard University.

Senor, Thomas, ed. 1995. *Rationality of Belief and the Plurality of Faith.* Ithaca, NY: Cornell University Press.

Shapin, Stephen. 1994. *A Social History of Truth.* Chicago: University of Chicago Press.

———. 1996. *The Scientific Revolution.* Chicago: University of Chicago Press.

Shils, Edward. 1972. *The Intellectuals and the Powers.* Chicago: University of Chicago Press.

———. 1982. *The Constitution of Society.* Chicago: University of Chicago Press.

Shipley, Maynard. 1927. *The War on Modern Science.* New York: Alfred Knopf.

Singal, Daniel, ed. 1991. *Modernist Culture in America.* Belmont, CA: Wadsworth.

Skocpol, Theda. 1979. *States and Social Revolutions.* Cambridge: Cambridge University Press.

Smith, Christian; with Michael Emerson; Sally Gallagher; Paul Kennedy; and David Sikkink. 1998. *American Evangelicalism.* Chicago: University of Chicago Press.

Smith, Dennis. 1991. *The Rise of Historical Sociology.* Philadelphia, PA: Temple University Press.

Smith, Gary Scott. 1985. *The Seeds of Secularization.* Grand Rapids, MI: Eerdmans.

Smith, Timothy. 1980. *Revivalism and Social Reform.* Baltimore, MD: Johns Hopkins University Press.

Sova, Dawn. 1998a. *Banned Books: Literature Suppressed on Social Grounds.* New York: Facts on File.

———. 1998b. *Banned Books: Literature Suppressed on Sexual Grounds.* New York: Facts on File.

Stark, Rodney, and Roger Finke. 2000. *Acts of Faith.* Berkeley and Los Angeles: University of California Press.

Starr, Paul. 1982. *The Social Transformation of American Medicine.* New York: Basic Books.

Strong, Josiah. 1885. *Our Country.* New York: American Home Missionary Society.

Sullivan, William. 1986. *Reconstructing Public Philosophy.* Berkeley and Los Angeles: University of California Press.

Swartz, David. 1997. *Culture and Power.* Chicago: University of Chicago Press.

Synnott, Marcia. 1979. *The Half-Opened Door.* Westport, CT: Greenwood.

Szasz, Ferenc. 1982. *The Divided Mind of Protestant America.* University: University of Alabama Press.

Thiemann, Ronald. 1996. *Religion in Public Life.* Washington, DC: Georgetown University Press.

Thomas, George. 1989. *Revivalism and Cultural Change.* Chicago: University of Chicago Press.

Thrower, James. 1971. *A Short History of Western Atheism.* London: Pemberton.

Trace, Arther. 1983. *Christianity and the Intellectuals.* La Salle, IL: Sherwood Sugden.

Tschannen, Oliver. 1991. "The Secularization Paradigm: A Systematization." *Journal for the Scientific Study of Religion* 30, no. 4 (December): 395–415.

Turner, Frank. 1978. "The Victorian Conflict between Science and Religion." *Isis* 69, no. 248: 356–76.

———. 1990. "The Victorian Crisis of Faith and the Faith That was Lost." In *Victorian Faith in Crisis,* ed. Richard J. Helmstadter and Bernard Lightman. Stanford, CA: Stanford University Press.

Turner, James. 1985. *Without God, without Creed.* Baltimore, MD: Johns Hopkins University Press.

Veblen, Thorstein. 1918. *The Higher Learning in America.* Stanford, CA: Academic Reprints.

Vitzthum, Richard. 1995. *Materialism.* New York: Prometheus Books.

Wagar, W. Warren. 1982. "Introduction." In *The Secular Mind,* ed. W. Warren Wagar. New York: Holmes and Meier.

Wallace, Anthony. 1966. *Religion.* New York: Random House.

Wallis, Roy, and Steve Bruce. 1992. "Secularization: The Orthodox Model." In *Religion and Modernization,* ed. Steve Bruce. Oxford: Clarendon Press.

Watson, Bruce, and William Tarr. 1964. *The Social Sciences and American Civilization.* New York: John Wiley.

Weber, Max. 1978. *Economy and Society.* Berkeley and Los Angeles: University of California Press.

Wentz, Richard. 1998. *The Culture of Religious Pluralism.* Boulder, CO: Westview Press.

Wexler, Joyce. 1997. *Who Paid for Modernism?* Fayetteville: University of Arkansas Press.

White, Andrew. 1896. *A History of the Warfare of Science with Theology in Christendom.* New York: D. Appleton.

White, Ronald, and C. Howard Hopkins. 1976. *The Social Gospel.* Philadelphia, PA: Temple University Press.

Wilson, Bryan. 1966. *Religion in Secular Society.* London: C. A. Watts.

———. 1976. *Contemporary Transformations of Religion.* Oxford: Oxford University Press.

Wolterstorff, Nicholas. 1976. *Reason within the Bounds of Religion.* Grand Rapids, MI: Eerdmans.

———. 1992. "What Reformed Epistemology Is Not." *Perspectives* (November): 14–16.

Wright, T. R. 1986. *The Religion of Humanity.* Cambridge: Cambridge University Press.

Yolton, John. 1983. *Thinking Matter*. Minneapolis: University of Minnesota Press.

Young, Robert. 1973. "The Historiographic and Ideological Contexts of the Nineteenth-Century Debate on Man's Place in Nature." In *Changing Perspectives in the History of Science,* ed. Mikuláš Teich and Robert Young. Boston: D. Reidel.

———. 1985. *Darwin's Metaphor*. New York: Cambridge University Press.

2

Secularizing American Higher Education

The Case of Early American Sociology

Christian Smith

Higher education for most of its history in the West has been an enterprise pursued in a religious context and under religious influences. Most scholarship during the Middle Ages was carried on by monastics in cloisters and monasteries. With the founding of universities in Paris, Oxford, and elsewhere at the end of the twelfth century, Western higher education continued to be conducted for more than half a millennium under the purview of the Christian church. American colonizers carried on and intensified this religiously grounded educational tradition. The first American colleges—Harvard, Yale, William and Mary, New Jersey (Princeton)—were founded as religious institutions to produce a learned clergy and a lettered Christian people. Through most of their histories, until the end of the nineteenth century, the vast majority of America's hundreds of colleges were founded by religious denominations, governed by religious leaders, and guided by religious visions of knowledge and virtue.

This religious influence in American colleges was, however, decisively thrown off at the end of the nineteenth and beginning of the twentieth centuries by proponents of an education revolution in trend-setting universities that radically transformed the character and purposes of higher education. This education revolution redefined religious concerns and perspectives as irrelevant if not detrimental to the mission of higher education. Thereafter, in what were considered leading universities, religion often lingered on the margins of campus in voluntary chapel services and campus ministries. But religion had little or nothing to do with the real work of university scholarship and teaching. Within a handful of decades, religious influences, issues, and viewpoints had been decisively eliminated from the heart of American universities, making higher education an essentially secular concern.

This chapter seeks to explain this secularization of American higher education by employing the theoretical perspective of secular movements outlined in the previous chapter. A number of historical works have of course already addressed this question. The classic story has been told by Hofstadter and Metzger (1955), Rudolph (1962), and Brubacher and Rudy (1958). More recently, Marsden (1994) and Reuben (1996) have published excellent accounts of the marginalization of religion and morality in American higher education. But as insightful as these and other works are, I believe that a secular movements analysis can still contribute an important dimension to an understanding of the secularization of American higher education.

Hofstadter and Metzger's (1955) account is framed by an un-self-critical, normative, secular triumphalism that assumes the necessary and inevitable victory of scientific fact over religious faith, of academic freedom over denominational dominance. Their approach—itself an exemplary specimen of a secular-partisan rendition of history—indulges some of the same flaws that have plagued secularization theory generally. And their mid-twentieth-century, modern overconfidence in progress and intellectual autonomy helps to obscure some of the agency, contingency, and political struggle that were important in the historical secularization process. Both Marsden (1994) and Reuben (1996) take a more circumspect approach to the secularization of universities, and produce sophisticated and illuminating historical accounts, although both largely take for granted the secularizing activists who struggled to marginalize religion in higher education. Instead they focus primarily on the liberal Protestants and administrative reformers who *responded* in various ways to those activists and their movement. Their accounts are tremendously insightful, and both are more comprehensive than this chapter. But they also highlight actors and processes different from those I will emphasize here. This chapter aims to bring into the spotlight a set of players that other accounts have often left offstage or in the background. I intend here, in other words, to explore not so much how liberal Protestants and administrative reformers responded to the secular *zeitgeist,* but, more specifically, where that secular *zeitgeist* was coming from.

Rather than attempting a comprehensive interpretation of American higher education, I focus here on the discursive work of one set of secularizing activists—academic advocates of the nascent discipline of sociology—who operated as one element of a much larger secularizing process. I do not claim that early sociologists were representative of all academics of this era, nor that sociology was *the* crucial force at work in secularization. Sociology offers merely one case study, but one that is illuminating and suggestive about the larger process of higher education's secularization.

THE BROAD CONTEXT

American higher education was for most of its history an enterprise informed by religious concerns and perspectives. From the founding of Harvard College in 1636 until the rise of the secular universities at the end of the nineteenth century, religion played a significant role not only in the founding and funding, but also in the intellectual life of American higher education. Religiously interested actors and institutions not only sponsored higher education, but actually significantly influenced the academic goals, course curricula, faculty research, and student life of most American colleges and universities. The majority of American colleges maintained ties to Christian denominations. For example, during the years 1861 and 1880, Protestant clergymen constituted about 40 percent of the trustees of private U.S. colleges, universities, and technical institutes; and in 1861, about 60 percent of U.S. college presidents were drawn from the ranks of church ministers (Barrow 1990: 36, 81). The era's Baconian conception of science encouraged college faculty in the sciences and theology alike to make explicit connections between religious faith and the study of the natural world (Hovenkamp 1978; Bozeman 1977). Even in state-supported schools, most faculty not only were church members but were also free, if not encouraged, to express their Christian perspectives in class and in published scholarship (Marsden 1992). Students in these colleges were trained in a classical curriculum, which emphasized the unity, beauty, and moral coherence of life and the world (Reuben 1996). Though the system was by no means perfect, religious interests and viewpoints did enjoy an important place in the administrative, intellectual, and social life of higher education. How and why this changed dramatically within a few decades is the focusing question of this chapter.

The dominant history of American higher education has been constructed for us primarily by partisans of the secular research university model of higher education. Hofstadter and Metzger (1955) provide the most notorious example, but many other standard and derivative accounts employ similar perspectives. These stories indulge Whiggish and presentist interpretations of history, tracing the progress of higher education from "the great retrogression" and "sectarianism" of "the old college system," to the breakthrough of true science and academic freedom with the rise of the glorious, graduate-school research university. This standard account casts American higher education before the era of Johns Hopkins and Cornell as fragmented, elitist, socially irrelevant, intellectually repressive, poverty-stricken, pedagogically tedious, and institutionally precarious. In fact, much of the historical evidence of these accounts derives from the polemics of late-nineteenth-century higher education reformers—Francis Wayland,

George Ticknow, Henry Tappan, Andrew White, and F. A. P. Barnard—who themselves were struggling mightily to displace the old college system with their new university model (see Axtell 1971).

Thus, the history has been framed for us by storytellers with particular commitments, interests, and perspectives vis-à-vis the earlier religious college system, which scholars since have shown had a significantly distorting effect on their story. Much evidence countering the standard story has prompted many revisions of the old account (see, e.g., McLachlan 1978; Potts 1971, 1981; Finkelstein 1983; Axtell 1971; Naylor 1973; Herbst 1988; Stevenson 1986; Burke 1982; Noll 1989). For example, careful studies have shown that colleges were much more diverse and adaptive than the standard account allowed, sustaining extracurricular lives "of extraordinary intellectual, cultural, and social variety and vitality" (McLachlan 1978). Reanalysis of data reveals that the mortality rate of religious colleges was actually much lower than standard accounts estimated. Research on college faculty suggests that they did engage in progressive academic research that moved scientific knowledge forward. Contra to the standard account's images of the irrelevance, unpopularity, and decline of colleges, enrollment data reveal a steady increase in the popularity of colleges throughout the nineteenth century. Similarly, we see that rather than simply serving an aristocratic elite, colleges enrolled significant numbers of students from middling and poor economic backgrounds for whom education was a clear basis for social mobility. College faculty, it also turns out, were, despite their complaints, generally not impoverished, but were relatively well paid for their work. And, nineteenth-century colleges, especially earlier in the century, were for the most part not controlled by heavy-handed sectarian denominations, but were broadly Christian institutions that were well integrated into and supported by their local communities.

In sum, the nineteenth-century Christian college system was not nearly as moribund or repressive as the standard account has led us to believe. Clearly, these colleges did grapple with issues of financial constraint, faculty discontent, student behavioral problems, and resistance to institutional change—as do colleges and universities today. But on balance it is not clear that they were the institutional disasters of which the nation obviously needed to be rid—as later secular university partisan interpreters led us to believe. And yet, activist university reformers in the late nineteenth century *did* manage successfully to promote their alternative model of the academy to the dominant status of *the ideal standard* for higher education. Liberal arts colleges continued to educate students, of course. But a small group of new secular research universities established themselves as the real trendsetters, authoritatively defining the ideal model that other institutions of higher education would henceforth seek to mimic and by which they would judge themselves and others. In the process, the longstanding legitimacy of religious interests and viewpoints in the core work of higher education was eliminated. The former authority of religious knowledge was rendered irrelevant and illegitimate in the central labor of the new universities. The number of clergy who were presidents and board members fell precipitously—in Barrow's sample of twenty-six schools, for example, the 59 percent of U.S. college presidents who were clergy in 1861, declined to 15 percent by 1890, and to 0 percent by 1915 (Barrow 1990: 81). More important, university faculty began actively distancing themselves from religious issues and discourse. Higher education at its core had, in a handful of decades, been decisively secularized.

Theoretically, the old college system of American higher education could have evolved into more complex institutions of scientific and humanistic research where teaching would have served the nation's interests but still sustained a genuine overarching interest in—or at least an openness to—ways that religious knowledge and concerns might have related to emerging scientific knowledge. And, theoretically, as the nation became more religiously pluralistic—with the immigration of Roman Catholics, Jews, and others—American higher education could have evolved more pluralistic models of interaction between religion and science that might have left behind the offensive domination of Protestantism. But neither of these things happened. Instead, religion was simply eliminated from the central concerns, practices, and discourse of higher education.[1] Why was that?

Certain historical factors that both motivated the secularizing university reformers and helped them to win the contest over the character of American higher education begin to help to answer that question, and to put the case of nascent sociology, on which this chapter will primarily focus, into perspective. The literature on this transformation of American higher education is vast, complex, and—as I have argued—uneven in reliability. I do not review it all here. Suffice it to mention a few crucial factors about which much has already been written elsewhere. In chapter 1, for example, we saw the importance of Auguste Comte and Herbert Spencer, whose influence in American higher education and on American intellectuals was substantial. Both provided what proved to be key intellectual tools utilized by rising academic elites seeking to displace religious authority in order to make room for themselves as new, secular cultural authorities. The emerging social sciences employed two core positivist ideas in particular—that society developed through regular stages, and that it adapted to its changing environment—to advance a modern science of society that would provide the positive knowledge for a secular basis of a new and progressive social order. Likewise, the influence of nearly ten thousand aspiring American scholars who pursued graduate studies in Germany and brought back to America with them German idealism, historicism, and rationalism was crucial. Furthermore, we saw in chapter 1 that incorporating industrial capitalism created a base of material resources outside of the direct control of the church for new institutions of secular higher education.

Another factor in the secularization of American higher education worth mentioning was increasing denominational control over American colleges. Precisely when secular, European Enlightenment cultural ideals were diffusing widely among American elites, many American Protestant denominations were moving in a direction opposite these intellectual and institutional trends, by intensifying their organizational and ideological control over their affiliated colleges. The standard history of nineteenth-century American colleges (e.g., Boorstin 1965; Hofstadter and Smith 1961) is portrayed as one gradually running from early, strict sectarianism toward increasingly loose secularism. Historian David Potts, however, has argued persuasively that quite the contrary is true. The typical image of antebellum colleges as denomination-ruled strongholds of narrow-minded sectarian zeal, he observes, has been "written from an urban Northeast, European-inspired, . . . university-reformer point of view that seems severely limited— one might even say parochial—when compared with the facts" (1971: 366). The historical evidence—once extricated from the framing agenda of late-nineteenth-century university reformers—suggests instead that colleges evolved into increasing, not decreasing denominational control after the Civil War. Earlier in the century, American colleges were predominantly local enterprises with strong ties to their host towns, and only secondary connections to their affiliated denominations. They drew most of their support from local boosters who were not necessarily members of their denominations; in return, colleges provided their local communities valued economic and intellectual returns. The colleges' official denominations themselves provided mostly official sanction and verbal encouragement. After 1850, however, denominations began to strengthen their grips on colleges through increased financial investment and control, charter revisions and trustee reorganizations, the oversight of new denominational educational agencies, and greater attention to faculty hires and student campus life. Improvements in transportation and communication enhanced denominations' abilities to monitor colleges' local activities. The clear trend in colleges—contradicting broader intellectual and institutional trends—was that Baptist colleges were becoming more strictly Baptist, Methodist colleges more definitely Methodist, and so on. The goal was to ensure that colleges were more clearly serving their denomination's constituency and maintaining a distinctive denominational identity. According to Potts (1971: 371), this increased denominationalism in colleges peaked in the 1880s and 1890s—precisely the era of the positivist activists' discursive takeover of science, and the successful takeoff of the university reformers' revolution in higher education. For the thousands of faculty employed by these denominational colleges, these countervailing trends would have created an acute identity dissonance and intellectual contradiction. For more committed positivist science and university reform activists, this increasing denominational grip on American colleges would have been seen as a dangerous regression into sectarian ignorance and domination—exactly what they were mobilizing to battle and defeat.

Another factor which contributed to the historical secularization of American higher education was the crucial influence of leading educational reformers—such as Harvard's President Charles Eliot, Johns Hopkins's President Daniel Coit Gilman, and Cornell's President Andrew Dickson White—who, while often publicly extolling the value of a nebulous version of "religion" for human civilization, actually worked with capitalist tycoons to orchestrate the institutionalization of a new system of higher education that intentionally marginalized religion from its central work. President White, for example, authored *A History of the Warfare of Science with Theology* (1896)—the culmination of twenty years of activist writing against religion in science—which framed religion as the dark enemy of science, fighting an inevitably losing battle against the progress of true knowledge.

Still another influence in the academic secular revolution was the growth of university faculty as a self-conscious "class for itself," organizing collectively to defend its group interests in intellectual and academic autonomy (Hawkins 1992). Particularly important in this was the formation in 1915 of the American Association of University Professors (AAUP)—initiated by Johns Hopkins University faculty, and first led by John Dewey—which explicitly devalued all "parochial," "local," and "sectarian" standards and traditions; framed religion as belonging to the "intimate personal" sphere of life; and extolled as superior all things objective, expert, universal, scientific, rational, and autonomous. "In the early period of university development in America," the 1915 AAUP's founding report observed, "the chief menace to academic freedom was ecclesiastical." However, the report noted with relief that churches, which generally function as "an instrument of propaganda," are "rare, and are becoming even more rare" (AAUP 1915: 38). Thus, activism to protect their interests in autonomy and cultural authority led university faculty to work to privatize religion and subordinate it to the scientific knowledge they themselves produced and sought to control.

Finally, worth mentioning for its later influence on the secularization of American higher education was a wave of immigrant Jewish scholars and their children who fled the Nazi onslaught in 1930s Europe. These Jews, who altered the demographics of higher education, David Hollinger has argued, were "conspicuous in their devotion to science and to the building of a culture liberated from the Christian biases that barred Jews and other non-Christians from full participation in American life. . . . Jews who managed to find a place for themselves in the public intellectual life of the nation . . . reinforced the most de-Christianized of the perspectives already current among the Anglo-Protestants" (1996: x, 24; also see Coser 1984; Cooney 1986). Thus, many Jewish and other non-Protestant activists in the mid-twentieth century further dismantled many of the academic remains of the Protestant establishment that survived the revolution of higher education in the late nineteenth century.

These and other related factors broaden our understanding of forces contributing to religion's historical marginalization in American higher education. But many other scholars have explored most of these influences already. This chapter focuses instead on the specific case of the late-nineteenth-century emergence of sociology as an academic discipline and its leaders' active, discursive undermining of the authority of religious knowledge and secularizing of higher education. The previous discussion has helped to set a general framework for understanding this more specific analysis.

The remainder of this chapter elaborates a story about sociology and secularization by unpacking the following five points. First, early American "sociologists" were not a single group of actors, but at least two quite different groups—the "reformers" and the "academics"—with very distinct goals and discourses. Second, these two groups viewed each other differently: the early American reformer sociologists tended to view the academics as important strategic allies, while the academics viewed the reformers as amateurs and professional liabilities. Third, in contrast to the reformers, the vast majority of leading early American academic sociologists were personally non-religious and often anti-religious intellectuals whose generally negative views of religion significantly shaped their academic perspectives and agendas—which in turn shaped the movement they led. Fourth, the early academic sociologists believed that their scientific knowledge was crucial not only for helping to ameliorate certain social ills, but for building a new, secular social order—they therefore actively promoted their sociological knowledge as a new cultural authority deserving public honor and attention. And fifth, in the process of promoting themselves as new secular cultural authorities, early academic sociologists actively framed and constructed religion in their writings in ways that clearly delegitimated religious knowledge and privatized religious beliefs and practices. In sum, a certain group of largely irreligious early American sociologists who aspired to greater status and authority, viewed themselves as competing against religious rivals, and responded by working actively and intentionally to discredit the religious claims and concerns of their perceived competitors. In so doing, they were instrumental in making religion irrelevant in American higher education and privatizing religion in American culture.

By analyzing this illustrative case, this chapter aims to support the larger claim that the historical secularization of American higher education—and of American public life more generally—was not an abstract, natural, and inevitable by-product of some evolutionary modernization process. Rather, it was the achievement of intentional agents, influenced by particular ideologies and interests, seeking to enhance their own status and authority by actively displacing the competing status and authority of religious actors.

THE EMERGENCE OF AMERICAN SOCIOLOGY

American science in the mid-nineteenth century enjoyed little of the resources, disciplinary definition, social status, and institutional power that science later came to possess in the twentieth century. Science at that time was ill-formed and ill-funded, the scattered work primarily of independent amateurs collecting bits of information about the world. Whatever organization did exist was largely the creation of members of a gentry class who sought to maintain cultural authority in a fast-changing world that increasingly imperiled their social status. Threatened in mid-century by Jacksonian individualism and populism, and by emerging social problems that endangered the old social order and seemed to undermine American exceptionalism itself, members of the gentry founded groups like the National Academy of Science in 1863 and the American Social Science Association in 1865 as a means to elevate themselves above the popular authority of common sense and to reground their leadership in the nascent authority of science (Haskell 1977; Ross 1991; Bruce 1987). In this way, these American proto-scientists made claims to possess the means to acquiring the kind of expert knowledge that would properly reorder the nation and secure for it a progressive future—thereby guarding their own role in it as its natural leaders and authorities.[2] American social science of this era was elitist in its impulse, conservative in its intentions, individualistic in its explanations, and relatively amateurish in its practices.

The latter decades of the nineteenth century, however, witnessed the emergence of a new generation of scientific claims-makers who struggled to take over the incipient organizational structures and cultural authority established by earlier scientists and remake science in new ways. The impulses in the process were many and complex. There were drives to eliminate amateurs through professionalization. There were efforts to replace individualistic theories with more genuinely social, institutional, and structural explanations of society. There were moves to use science to establish the cultural authority not of the older gentry class or of female amateurs, but of upwardly aspiring sons of the middle class. And there were struggles to make science not a prop for an old social order but the catalyst for the building of a new order. The character and purpose of science was in this era considerably open and contested by diverse groups of scientific claims-makers (Furner 1975; Ross 1991; Haskell 1977).

Within this fluid, competitive context the self-designated discipline of sociology first emerged in America. The fundamental contention upon which most early sociologists staked their claim was that American society, undergoing such rapid social transformation and confronting so many new social problems, desperately needed a true science of society to discover the fundamental properties and laws of social life in order to provide the knowl-edge necessary for the management of social order and for the making of progressive social reform. Sociology, they promised, could do for society what the natural sciences had done with nature—provide knowledge that would increase human understanding, order, control, safety, health, and prosperity. "Society" was the new frontier for science to conquer, and soci-ologists were the right men for the job.

Just below the surface of these confident claims, however, lurked the fact that "sociologists" had little idea—not to mention consensus on—how so-ciology was to go about executing this task, what its outcome would actually look like, and who exactly was properly equipped to perform this science of society. "Sociology" was at this stage essentially a series of optimistic public promises offered by an assortment of self-promoting claimants hoping to acquire resources and authority for the proposed project. What remained to be sorted out were things like what a real sociologist actually was, what that person was supposed to do, and what results they would finally have to show. At best, American sociologists had Comte and Spencer to build on—but their sociologies also largely consisted of promises about a science of so-ciety, not the science itself. Thus, having declared American sociology into existence and promoted it to a level of importance, the assortment of people calling themselves sociologists faced the much more challenging task of actually defining and practicing "sociology."

This was a complicated and arduous process. For present purposes, we must note that among the various kinds of people who then called them-selves sociologists, two were particularly important for understanding the dynamics of the secularization of higher education: the religious reformer sociologists and the academic sociologists. The latter intentionally worked to exclude the former from the domain of legitimate sociology, motivated by group status aspirations and by personal anti-religious commitments. In so doing, I argue, they contributed significantly to the broader marginal-ization of religious interests, perspectives, and discourse from social science and from higher education.

American sociology is commonly spoken of as an outgrowth of the Social Gospel movement; early American sociologists were said to be largely Protestant ministers or sons of ministers who were motivated by religious faith to understand society better in order to reform it according to the moral imperatives of a liberal Christian gospel.[3] But this is a simplistic and misleading reading of history. It mistakenly views early American sociology as a single movement, and naively attributes genuine religious commitments and motives to sociologists based on superficial and sometimes selective readings of texts. William Swatos's (1983, 1984, 1989) careful historical investigation of this claim has demonstrated decisively that early American sociology was in fact advanced by two ideologically and organizationally distinct groups of proponents: religious reformers and irreligious academics. They developed two largely distinct social networks, formed different professional organizations, spoke in dissimilar rhetorics, and advanced disparate visions of the purpose of sociology. Swatos effectively uses personal correspondences, membership rolls, and some published articles to show the antipathy the academics held toward the reformers. Taking a cue from Swatos, the following pages explore more fully why and how the academics worked to eliminate all things religious from sociology.

Status Aspirations

The academic sociologists were motivated to win exclusive control of this new science of society in part by the status advantages such control promised. New research universities were offering members of middling classes unique opportunities for status mobility into newly created positions of scientific expertise. According to O'Boyle,

> Academic professionalization in the United States was . . . similar to the German experience in that it opened up new opportunities for a group not already integrated into a social or governing elite. . . . Perhaps most important, [faculty] won growing acceptance of the idea that only those with certain stipulated academic credentials had a legitimate right to judge in certain areas of knowledge. . . . The older patrician class, a largely professional group based in New England . . . were now . . . to a large degree displaced by the new experts, as Eliot of Harvard so often referred to them. Increasingly strong in the universities, their claims to leadership rested on certified, specialized training. In their own minds . . . the experts believed themselves to be the means of redeeming the democratic system, albeit by the undemocratic substitution of their own judgment for that of the mass of people.[4] (1983: 23–24)

Academics thus actively promoted their expertise as a new form of cultural authority (Kimball 1992: 198–300). "Confidence in experts," argued Harvard president Charles Eliot, for example, "and willingness to employ them and abide by their decisions, are among the best signs of intelligence in an educated individual or an educated community; and in any democracy which is to thrive, this respect and confidence must be felt strongly by the majority of the population" (1898: 412).

In order to establish themselves as new scientific experts, however, academic sociologists had to fight at least two battles—both of which set them in opposition to religious authority. The first was the battle to replace the religious classical education of the existing college system with a new education emphasizing original scientific research. The rising academic sociologists themselves were clear that the classical education of the traditional Christian college obstructed their disciplinary ambitions. John Burgess, for example, who began teaching at Amherst College in the 1870s, recalled unhappily of his senior colleagues,

> They regarded the college as a place for discipline, not as a place for research. To them the truth had already been found. It was contained in the Bible, and it was the business of the college to give the preliminary training for acquiring and disseminating it. Research implied doubt. It implied that there was a great deal of truth still to be found, and it implied that the truth thought to have been already found was approximate and in continual need of revision and readjustment. . . . They regarded research as more or less heretical. (1934: 147–48)

Likewise, Colby College sociologist Albion Small complained, "We are teaching a cut-and-dried Philology, by a method persistently unscientific, and allowing such instruction to take the place of study of the growth of the human mind" (Dibble 1975: 26). In response, the new academic sociologists fiercely attacked classical education's constraints on their careers. Columbia sociologist Franklin Giddings, for instance, characterized traditional classical education—which obstructed objective, scientific education—in terms which evoked (we will see below) his polemical association of contemporary faith with savage religion:

> It is vouched for by doctors of magic, heirs and assigns of the medicine men. It is a child of fear. It was born in the jungle and reared in the bush. It harks back to incantation and sorceries. Its curriculum, like that of the wolf-reared man-cub in Kipling's story of Mowgli, consists of "master words" of magical virtue. This education is arrogant and despotic. It crushes intellectual liberty when it can. It hates the scientific knowledge of nature with implacable hatred, for that knowledge exposes magic and discredits it. (1929: 1–2)

Yale sociologist William Graham Sumner was equally harsh. Classical education, he charged, promotes "dogmatism, pedantry, hatred of contradiction, conceit, and love of authority" (1911: 360). It is harmful for faculty and students alike:

> As a man goes on in life under this discipline, he becomes more self-satisfied and egotistical. He has little contact with active life; gets few knocks; is rarely forced into a fight or into a problem of diplomacy, gets to hate care or interruption, and loves routine. Men of this type, of course, are timid. . . . Such men

are ever fond of *a priori* reasoning and fall helpless the moment they have to face a practical undertaking. They have the whole philosophy of heaven and earth reduced, measured out, and done up in powders, to be prescribed at need. They know just what ought to be studied, in what amount and succession of doses. (Sumner 1911: 360–61)

Thus, Sumner complained, "It cost me years of discipline to overcome the limitations of the classical training and to emancipate my mind from the limited range of processes in which it had been trained" (quoted in Starr 1925: 337). Evoking a sense of masculine duty and courage, Sumner called on higher education to reform: "Certainly the notion that any body of men can now regulate the studies of youth by what was good for themselves twenty, forty, or sixty years ago is one which is calculated to ruin any institution which they control. It is always a hard test of the stuff men are made of when they are asked to admit that a subject of which they have had control would profit by being taken out of their control and entrusted to liberty" (1911: 360–61). Thus, Sumner asserted, classical education must give way to the new scientific authority: "The time when a college instructor fulfilled his duty if he looked on the book and said that the young men repeated from memory what was written in it, has gone by. . . . The instructors who are now demanded are men of thought, research, and genius, who can *make* books or even dispense with them, and teach directly, personally from an independent and original knowledge of the subject" (1870: 153). The new academic sociologists, of course, fully intended to be among those men of genius representing the liberty to which higher education should be entrusted. And counterposed to liberty, in this case, was the traditional religious influence in higher education.

The second battle that upwardly aspiring academic sociologists in search of cultural authority had to fight was against what they saw as a rival brand of amateur sociologists, the religious reformers noted above. Based primarily not in colleges and universities, but in churches, denominations, and religious voluntary associations, a network of Social Gospel activists were claiming the mantle of sociology for their liberal Christian reform movement (Greek 1992). They founded the Chautauqua Movement in 1874, the American Institute of Christian Sociology in 1893, and the Oberlin Institute of Christian Sociology in 1894. They published the periodical *Bibliotheca Sacra: A Religious and Sociological Quarterly,* and a host of articles and books with titles like *Applied Christianity* and *The Christian Society.* Among them were Josiah Strong, John Vincent, Richard T. Ely, George Herron, Walter Rauschenbusch, Francis Peabody, and Washington Gladden. "Sociology" to this group was not a neutral or irreligious science, but a crucial means by which the Christian church could redeem society. "Sociology can become a science," claimed Herron in 1894, "only by becoming a science of redemption. Only by grounding society in right social faiths and laying the axe of truth at the roots of social falsehoods, by regenerating society with right social visions" (1894: 18–19).

These religious reformers were aware that other sociologists were establishing a foothold in universities, but they did not view this as a necessary threat. As long as academic sociologists did not deny a spiritual reality or oppose the work of the Kingdom of God, the religious reformers viewed them as valuable strategic allies. Rauschenbusch, for example, argued that, "We need a combination of the Kingdom of God and the modern comprehension of the organic development of human society. . . . So directing religious energy by scientific knowledge that a comprehensive and continuous reconstruction of social life in the name of God is within the bounds of human possibility" (1907: 199, 209). Likewise, Strong contended that, "Science, by discovering the laws of nature, reveals the divine methods and enables us, by adopting them, to become efficient laborers together with God unto the kingdom" (1902: 104).

The academic sociologists, on the other hand, were clear that, were this formidable group of religious reformers to win jurisdictional control over the definition and practice of sociology, their budding science of society would become entirely subordinate to the interests and agendas of outside religious groups—and this definitely did not serve their interests. The academic sociologists thus saw their religious counterparts not as allies or complements but as competitors, professional liabilities. They did their best, therefore, in their speaking, writing, and organizing to cast the religious reformers as misguided amateurs, interlopers, and frauds. Even Albion Small, who was clearly sympathetic to religion, "was anxious to preempt the clerical amateurs and to separate sociology from the stigma attached to the radicals in the religious movement. He urged Ely to break with the radical social gospelers and probably decided to found his *American Journal of Sociology* in 1895 to head off their plans for a journal of Christian sociology" (Ross 1991: 127). Indeed, in 1894, Small and his collaborator George Vincent— son of Social Gospeler John Vincent—charged that "[t]he most dangerous social doctrinaires among us are not the theoretical anarchists who attack social order directly, but those zealous prophets of righteousness who teach that the only reason why the Kingdom of God cannot be established on earth tomorrow is that Christians will not put their knowledge of social principles into practice. . . . Sociology is just now passing through a stage of struggle for the application of scientific principles of investigation, in place of loose criticism and silly utopianism" (1894: 19, 32). Below I explore more thoroughly how the rising academics constructed sociology in ways that belittled and ostracized the religious reformers. Their interest in doing so becomes even more clear when we explore their own personal commitments regarding religion.

Personal Anti-Religious Commitments

Nearly all of the leading academic sociologists in America during the discipline's establishment were personally hostile to religion per se. Most had been raised in seriously religious families, but had subsequently rejected their own faith and become personally antagonistic toward things religious. For some, these anti-religious commitments were expressed in sustained, overt frontal assaults on religious faith and practice. Others were more politically discreet. They worked to undermine religion more subtly, feigning respect through the occasional use of religious language—in ways similar to the "colonization" discussed in chapter 4—all the while working intentionally to disabuse believers of their religious faith and divest religious organizations of public authority. These were not men who accidentally slighted religion. These were skeptical Enlightenment atheologians, personally devoted apostles of secularization.

The early American sociologist Lester Ward (1841–1913), for example—who wrote the groundbreaking *Dynamic Sociology* in 1883—was raised in a pietistic, evangelical, churchgoing family, the grandson of a church minister and son of a devout mother who encouraged Ward to enter the ministry himself. But after studying in Germany and reading Comte, Spencer, Darwin, Huxley, Tyndall, Paine, and Voltaire (of whose work he said, "I have never read a more instructive book"), Ward embraced atheism and naturalism, and completely rejected his family's faith. Ward then generalized the anti-Catholicism he had learned as a child into a damning critique of all faith, and became a zealous missionary of irreligion. He edited an "anticlerical and skeptical" periodical known as the *Iconoclast*, an "open attack on religious . . . superstition," which crusaded against the "errors of the churches and the dogmatism of theology." And he helped form the National Liberal Reform League in 1869 to fight religious dogmatism. Believing fervently that "religious ideas . . . consist entirely of error, their being no objective truth corresponding to spiritual beings," Ward constructed his sociology within the interpretive narrative of enlightened scientific progress battling against repressive religious control. Naturally, Ward opposed all attempts by religious reformers to associate with the social sciences. In response to a proposal at an American Economic Association meeting to construct the foundations of sociology on theology, one observer recorded that "Ward threw himself back in a chair with a gasp that was almost a groan, and a legible look of disgust and despair." In all of his interactions and personal and scholarly communications—some of which we examine below—it is clear that Ward was a zealous evangelist of secularization and secularism— of a new intellectual and social order over which he and other sociologists would preside as expert scientific authorities (O'Connor 1942; Scott 1974; Stern 1935; Hinkle and Hinkle 1954; Vidich and Lyman 1985: 20–35;

Swatos 1983: 41–42; Schwendinger and Schwendinger 1974: 238; Ross 1991).

Similarly, Yale sociologist William Graham Sumner (1840–1910) was raised in a devout Calvinist family. As an undergraduate, Sumner was outspokenly committed to orthodox Christian theological doctrines and aspired to ordained ministry. While studying at the University of Göttingen, Germany, however, Sumner became critical of traditional Christian faith and began a drift into agnosticism. After a stint as an Episcopal rector, Sumner took an academic position at Yale. There he became an ardent advocate of Herbert Spencer's secular, laissez-faire social evolutionism, which generated tremendous strife between himself and those at Yale he derided as "the Puritan theological crowd." Sumner also became an uncompromising foe of the "unscientific sentimentality" of the many religious reformers who claimed to be sociologists. At Yale, the last of Sumner's own religious faith disappeared. "I never consciously gave up a religious faith," he later recalled; "it was as if I had put my beliefs into a drawer, and when I opened it up there was nothing there at all." Sumner did, however, consciously and intentionally struggle at Yale to institutionalize a secular worldview and science that cared little for religious interests and perspectives. Science, Sumner thought, did and should replace religion: "In these last days, true science has become a religion . . . a revelation of truth to the mind of man." "If there is any salvation for the human race from woe and misery," Sumner claimed, "it is in knowledge and training to use knowledge" (Starr 1925; Keller 1933; Davie 1963; Swatos 1983: 36–37; Vidich and Lyman 1985: 36–49).

Albion Small (1854–1926), who established both the Chicago Department of Sociology and the *American Journal of Sociology,* is often regarded as a devout Christian who was amicable to religious influences in sociology. After all, he was a preacher's son and a Baptist minister of sorts himself, who wrote freely about "God," "the Gospels," "salvation," and "the brotherhood of man" in his academic work. However, the traditional view of this prominent early American sociologist is misinformed. In fact, like many secularizers of his day, Small actually held a completely functionalist view of religion devoid of the supernatural. Religion for Small was good not because it was theologically true, but because it could be *practically useful* for inspiring humane action and promoting social harmony. But Small was in fact a true adversary of any orthodox Christian. Like his more blatant secularist colleagues, Small had studied social science in Germany, had deeply imbibed Comte and Spencer, and viewed science as rightfully replacing traditional religion. Unlike others, however, Small was careful to segregate his audiences: he spoke candidly among certain trusted academic colleagues, reserving for more devout listeners—in whose financial resources evidence suggests he was interested—terms more congenial to religion. Small, in other words, was more rhetorically strategic than, say, Lester Ward. But Small also admired Ward tremendously and, at bottom, shared his essential views about science and religion. In fact, their personal letters reveal just how self-conscious and intentional these academics were about subverting religion. Referring to their purposeful efforts to marginalize the religious reformers from sociology, for example, Small wrote as follows to Ward in 1900: "At the same time as we are unloading some of the people who want a sort of sociological Christian science, but have no brains for sociology, the remnant [of true scientists] will make headway in elucidating the social situation in all its phases." And debating how explicit to be about their anti-religious naturalism, Small wrote that he regretted that Ward expressed his opinion "so freely upon religious subjects, for on that account, many are willing to throw aside your volume entirely, whereas, without injury to the course of thought, the omission of these references would have left such persons no occasion for suspicion of your methods." Ward replied bluntly that he "did not write for the feeble minded." Small answered, again imploring Ward to be more politic, "simply from the strategic or rhetorical point of view . . . for the sake of spreading discoveries of the truth. . . . There are thousands of men who hold to the substance of the traditional evangelical doctrines, who are yet theoretically willing to be convinced that any of them is untenable. . . . It is better in dealing with such . . . to adopt Beecher's advice, 'Don't let too many cats out of the bag at once.'" The exchange is revealing: Small is as interested as Ward in disabusing thousands of evangelical believers of their traditional doctrines by showing their incredibility— he simply advocates that they be more artful about their anti-religious purposes. Small was, as much as Ward and Sumner, an apostle of secularization; he was simply more tactically clever in that work (Stern 1933; Swatos 1983: 42; 1989: 367; O'Connor 1942; Christakes 1978; Dibble 1975; Ross 1991).

One could write similar stories about almost all of the other guiding lights of early American sociology. One could tell of Edward A. Ross (1866–1951), who founded sociology at Wisconsin in 1906—his strict Presbyterian upbringing; his faith-eroding studies of philosophy at the University of Berlin, Germany; his embrace of positivism, agnosticism, and social evolutionism after reading Darwin and Spencer; his coming to believe that religion is ultimately a "hollow sham" and "beyond the bounds of logic"; and his scientific vision for a "Christian society," which amounted to little more than building through science and education a secular, progressive social order over which sociology would preside in its expert knowledge (Bierstedt 1981; Pearman and Rutz 1981; Ross 1991: 231–32). One could write similarly about Franklin Giddings (1855–1931), the builder of sociology at Columbia University—about his evangelical Puritan family and strict Congregationalist pastor father against whom he rebelled; about his embrace of

Spencer, Huxley, and Darwin's positivist scientism, social evolutionism, and agnosticism in and after high school; about his reductionist view of religion and antagonism to the supernatural as "occultism"; about his editorial ridicule of the religious reformer sociologists; and about his vision for a managed society in which religion would be displaced by secular science and education, and sociology would help to engineer social morals and ethics (O'Connor 1942; Vidich and Lyman 1985: 105–125; Hinkle and Hinkle 1954: 3; Ross 1991: 127–28, 132). Variants of these stories exist for the lives of many other early American sociologists who significantly helped shape the discipline. All the biographical evidence points to the same conclusion: whether they sometimes strategically talked a vague language of religion or made outright attacks on all things religious, the academic sociologists who first defined and institutionalized sociology in American universities were mostly men who had personally rejected their own traditional religious faith, were antagonistic toward historical religion, viewed science as supplanting or subordinating religion, and intentionally sought to diminish the authority and influence of traditional religion in American social life. In all of this, these early American sociologists were personally committed apostles of secularization.

THE SOCIOLOGICAL CONSTRUCTION OF SCIENCE AND RELIGION

But how exactly were these irreligious and anti-religious interests and commitments expressed? How do we know that these interests and forces translated into actual discursive and institutional efforts to reduce the influence of religion in higher education? Is there some way that we might more systematically examine the secularizing work of early American academic sociologists?

One could demonstrate activist secularizing in many ways. For present purposes, I focus on the particular ways that the authors of important early American sociology textbooks constructed for their readers the nature, value, and purposes of science and religion. Sociology, as I have said, was at this time a new discipline needing definition and representation to the educated American public. At the same time, greatly expanding numbers of college and university students and faculty, government officials and administrators, and civic and religious leaders were increasingly looking to sociology—this new science of society—for trustworthy information, understanding, and guidance. General sociology textbooks therefore provide us with systematic disciplinary statements that both reflect their authors' interests and commitments, and frame the claimed importance and contribution of the emerging discipline of sociology in relation to other fields of social life, including religion.

These textbooks represent much more than "mere words," as somehow opposed to real action, for social life is itself necessarily and always constituted and enacted through language and discourse. And, particularly in their context of greatly contested and shifting grounds of knowledge and authority during their "unsettled times," these textbooks manifest these academic activists' political "frame alignment" work, which sought to construct persuasive, legitimate accounts for a particular ordering of knowledge and authority in opposition to competing orders (Snow et al. 1986). Thus, the discursive work of these sociological textbooks represents an important form of *social action,* of political action, intent on deconstructing one moral and epistemological order and institutionalizing another. They provide a revealing window onto the secularizing insurgency of early American academic sociologists.

In the forty-five years between the publication of Ward's *Dynamic Sociology* in 1883 and the end of the 1920s—by which time the Protestant establishment's domination of public life had been debilitated—sociologists published about 170 general sociology texts.[5] Many of these were unexceptional books that had little influence on sociology or beyond. But we know from historical records that a smaller group of these early sociology textbooks were very influential, widely read and cited, and consistently assigned as required reading in college and university social science classes. Specifically, national surveys of the state of sociology as a discipline by Frank Tolman (1902), L. L. Bernard (1909), and F. Stuart Chapin (1910), as well as historical analyses of sociology textbook usage by Morgan (1983) and McCarthy and Das (1985) provide a clear and consistent picture of the early American sociology textbooks that were in their day widely assigned, read, and cited. Combining the findings of these studies yields an inventory of the thirty-three most important early American sociology textbooks, grouped by the time periods during which they were most influential and ranked by importance within periods (see table 2.1).

The question is, How did these most influential early American sociology textbooks construct for their reading audiences what religion is and what its proper role in society should be? If sociology was the new science of society that would provide the factual knowledge essential for the reordering of modern social life, what did that science have to say about religion and its place in the new social order?

To answer these questions, I studied all of the textbooks listed in table 2.1, paying particular attention to their claims about religion, morality, ethics, knowledge, sociology, science, and related matters. I read to gain an overall sense of the textbooks' general perspective, but also to identify their specific arguments about religion. First, I found that the texts were remarkably similar on the question of religion in society. This was partly because these authors relied so heavily upon Comte and Spencer, as well as upon each other—particularly upon Ward (1883, 1893; they also tended to

TABLE 2.1 Important Early American Sociology Textbooks,
by Period of Greatest Influence

Up to 1900

Albion Small and George Vincent
    1894. *An Introduction to the Study of
       Society.*
Franklin Giddings
    1894. *The Theory of Sociology.*
    1896. *The Principles of Sociology.*
    1898. *The Elements of Sociology.*
Herbert Spencer
    1851. *Social Statics.*
    1874. *The Study of Sociology.*
    1876–97. *The Principles of Sociology.*

Lester Ward
    1883. *Dynamic Sociology.*
    1893. *The Psychic Factors of Civilization.*
    1898. *Outlines of Sociology.*
Carroll Wright
    1899. *Outline of Practical Sociology.*
Arthur Fairbanks
    1896. *Introduction to Sociology.*

1900–1910

Franklin Giddings
    The titles above, plus the
      following:
    1901. *Inductive Sociology.*
    1906. *Readings in Descriptive and
      Historical Sociology.*
Albion Small and George Vincent
    1894. *An Introduction to the Study of
      Society.*
Carroll Wright
    1899. *Outline of Practical Sociology.*
Edward Ross
    1901. *Social Control.*
    1905. *Foundations of Sociology.*
    1908. *Social Psychology.*
James Dealey
    1909. *Sociology.*

James Dealey and Lester Ward
    1905. *A Text-Book of Sociology.*
Lester Ward
    The titles above, plus the following:
    1903. *Pure Sociology.*
    1906. *Applied Sociology.*
Albion Small
    1905. *General Sociology.*
Arthur Fairbanks
    1896. *Introduction to Sociology.*
Charles Henderson
    1898. *Social Elements.*
Frank Blackmar
    1905. *The Elements of Sociology.*
Herbert Spencer
    1874. *The Study of Sociology.*
    1876–97. *The Principles of Sociology.*

1910–1930

This group includes many of the titles above, plus the following:

Robert Park and Ernest Burgess
    1921. *Introduction to the Study of
      Sociology.*
Edward Ross
    1925. *Principles of Sociology.*

Edward Hayes
    1915. *Introduction to the Study of
      Sociology.*
Frederick Bushee
    1923. *Principles of Sociology.*

cite Darwin, Huxley, Nietzsche, James, and writers in *Popular Science Monthly*). But, as I have suggested, this similarity is also partly due to their occupation of a similar social location whose status interests were well served by their shared views of religion. Second, I found that these authors tended to make claims about religion that often expressed internal tensions and sometimes inconsistencies. It appears that they thought they were adding nuances and qualifications to their otherwise bold claims about religion. But in the end it is not hard to discern which views of religion they themselves truly meant to promote. My thematic analysis below captures some of these tensions by contrasting the claims about religion to which I suggest these authors were truly committed with their weaker claims, set up apparently for purposes of "balance." Taken together, nearly everything that these important early sociology textbooks had to say about religion and its relationship to science and society can be summarized in the ten thematic claims discussed in the following sections.

1. *Science and religion are different ways of knowing, concerned with different orders of reality, but . . . they are actually absolutely incompatible and antagonistic sources of knowledge.*

At first glance, important early American sociologists appear to grant religion the dignity of possessing its own autonomous sphere of knowledge, distinct from that over which science presides. By this account, religion and science properly concern themselves with the aspects of reality that are their rightful domain, and each either supplements the other or simply leaves it alone. Thus Ward wrote, "The religious explanation is the supernatural, the scientific explanation is the natural" (1883: 273). And Bushee suggested, "Science and religion supplement each other. The one deals with the known and the other with the unknown; the instrument of one is knowledge and of the other faith" (1923: 535). Thus, if and when science does address religion, it must do so with proper deference: "To the sociologists as such, religion is one of the aspects of social life, and should be studied dispassionately and without prejudice" (Dealey 1909: 501). But certain concerns of religion are beyond the proper study of science—for instance, as Ward suggested, the afterlife, "the future state of existence—[is] a field of discussion which, of course, lies outside of the province of this work and of all scientific investigation" (1883: 286).

But this separate-spheres truce is immediately broken once the texts' authors begin to elaborate upon science's relation to religion, when two facts become immediately apparent. First, religion and science are actually considered ways of knowing that are inherently incompatible with and hostile to each other. Second, science is inevitably routing all religious dogmas, theologies, and "superstitions." The two knowledge systems are perpetually engaged in a war that religion is always losing.

Underlying these claims is the belief that science and religion are not actually distinguished by their two distinct domains of focus, but by their two opposite methods of understanding the world: fact-through-observation versus superstition-through-ignorance. Bushee explained, "Science as used here . . . refers to the spirit of investigating phenomena, of studying facts, as over against the spirit of mere speculation or of superstitious belief" (1923: 508). Likewise, Giddings contrasted the "speculations" of theology with the "actual knowledge" of science: "The oldest [tradition of conceptual thought] is the theological tradition, which was created by an elaborate process of reasoning and speculation upon the materials furnished by popular religious beliefs. . . . The scientific tradition is the sum of our actual knowledge of the world and of man, as distinguished from our conjectures about them" (1896: 144–45).[6]

Part of this difference between science and religion is that the latter, as Spencer pointed out, is governed by forces other than love of facts, which confound the truth: "Theological bias . . . producing conformity to moral principles from motives of obedience only, and not habitually insisting on such principles because of their intrinsic value, obscures sociological truths" (1874: 271). Science, by contrast, is nothing but the disinterested pursuit of truth: "The modification of the scientific tradition by fresh discoveries," said Giddings, for example, "has and needs no special name, for science makes no compromises with the old and the new. Whatever of the old is verified by later research is retained; whatever is disproved is discarded, and the net result is truth" (1896: 146). Religion and science thus generate different products, as Giddings explained: "Belief is so far separated from knowledge that not infrequently the most positive beliefs are affirmations of alleged truths which, upon investigation, prove to have absolutely no foundation in fact. . . . *Knowledge,* on the other hand, is truth that cannot be overthrown by any process of testing or criticizing" (1898: 142; italics in original). All of this meant, according to Ward, that there is no middle ground, that religious and scientific commitments absolutely cannot mix:

> No one is adjudged a true causationist who recognizes the possibility of teleological explanation anywhere. . . . The fundamental psychological character of the classification . . . is established on the line between the natural and the supernatural. The question whose answer determines to which class anyone belongs is not, 'To what extent do you admit the supernatural?' But, 'Do you admit the supernatural at all?' If so, you are a dogmatist. (1883: 32)

Because of religion's inherently weak epistemic position relative to science, its historical survival strategy has been resistant obscurantism. According to Bushee,

History gives us two well-marked periods of scientific advance, the Greek period . . . and the modern period. . . . In both cases emancipation from theological dogmas preceded scientific activity. . . . Previously, superstitious beliefs had hindered the progress of science. . . . But the new knowledge of the material world gradually relaxed the hold of these superstitions and prepared the way for . . . scientific observation. (1923: 514, 523–24)

But religion's obstruction of science is a strategy destined to fail. According to Ward, "Since the scientific era began there has been no such faith in the supernatural as exists among savages. Science was made possible by the diminution of this kind of faith and the concomitant increase in faith in natural causes. The history of science shows that those who still possess a large amount of the faith of primitive man oppose science and stubbornly resist its advance" (1906: 88).

Part of atheistic naturalism's power over religion is its ability to explain religion away. Ward, for instance, observed,

Eternal matter with its eternal activities suffices to account for all the phenomena of the universe, which are as infinite in causation as in duration or extent. All departments of science confirm this truth. Like many other once useful hypotheses, that of *theo-teleology* . . . has outlived its usefulness, and, where still called in, becomes a burden to the advancement of science. . . . And thus is science marching relentlessly forward, and reclaiming one field after another that has been so long given over to dogmatic conceptions, until there is now scarcely room to doubt that its conquest must ultimately become complete. (1883: 29)

In short, "All . . . phenomena are now satisfactorily explained on strictly natural principles. Among people acquainted with science, all . . . supernatural beings have been dispensed with, and the belief in them is declared to be wholly false and to have always been false" (Ward 1883: 268–69).

In view of these facts, science has a moral duty to do away with religious belief. For some, like Ward, society itself has the mission to do away with religion altogether:

In its efforts to bring about the general settlement of opinion, society should first specially aim to convert all pseudo-ideas into true ideas. There is no more insidious danger than that of mistaking settled belief of the illegitimate class for the attainment of truth itself. This has been the great fallacy of all ages. Dogmatic faith, firmly fixed in transcendental propositions, has always been to a greater or less extent confounded with positive truth, when in reality they stand at the very antipodes of consciousness. (1883: 413)

Therefore, "dislodging" the "errors thus forced into man's mind . . . [by] the sanction of religion" and "the illusions of nature and the errors of the primitive reason" was, for Ward, the "Herculean task . . . of science," the "chief

mission of science in its broadest sense." This would require that science un-
earth the scientific truths "that only reveal themselves to prolonged observation, experimentation, and reflection," that "can only be brought to light
by the most prolonged and patient research" (Dealey and Ward 1905: 279–
80; Ward 1898: 23). The outcome, however, was assured: "It has . . . been
the uniform mark of intellectual progress," Ward wrote, "that the supernatural should constantly give way to the natural method, and it has been on
this advancing line that the warfare of religion and science has been constantly waged. . . . The weapons of religion have been coercion and exhortation; those of science have been skill and strategy" (1883: 273).

For others, seemingly more benevolent toward religion, science would
not fully abolish but transform and enlighten religion. Thus, Bushee observed that "[b]etter knowledge of natural laws has offered new interpretations of the manifestations and methods of spirit forces. Increasing intelligence has constantly altered methods of approach to the unknown and
modified the cruelties and absurdities of early religious ceremonies" (1923:
546). More recently, claimed Henderson, science has corrected our understanding of the creation:

> Each science has made its contribution to religious thought and feeling. Ge-
> ology has taken the idea of God and enlarged it in time. . . . A few years ago
> the creation was a story of six thousand years, a mere speck in the infinity of
> time. Now the college lad is made familiar with aeons and cycles of time dur-
> ing which the solemn procession of creative events moves before the reverent
> mind. (1898: 267–68)

What is clear in all of this, however, is that science and modern human
interests are what dictate change, and religion is the thing that does the
changing. Ross, for another example, observed,

> Religious interests cannot but wax and wane with the relation of religion to
> men's necessities. The gods are remembered in danger, forgotten in security,
> valued when the state rests on authority, ignored when the government is
> founded on consent. . . . Every forward stride in man's mastery of Nature and
> control over men lessens his dependence on the Unseen. A sense of security
> . . . weakens the fears behind religion. As people come to look to the police-
> man for protection, to the physician for healing, to the inventor for victory,
> and to themselves for worldly success, their anxious zeal in worship abates. Re-
> ligion abides, purer and nobler to be sure, but less potent as a maker of his-
> tory. (1925: 55)

Thus, a potentially "purer and nobler" religion must first relinquish its
influence in history to the power of scientific mastery and the authority of
professional expertise. Dealey likewise made clear who in the science-religion relationship stays in place and who moves: "Ultimately religious teach-

ings must harmonize with well-established truths in science and philosophy; the two systems of teaching may occasionally seem to be in opposition, but a faith unreasonable in its basis is finally atrophied and sloughed off as credulity or superstition, or else is retained as a mere conventional belief. No religion founded on unreason and injustice, or in opposition to demonstrated scientific teachings can retain its hold on the minds of thoughtful men in an age when men are striving to come into harmony with the highest and best in the universe" (1909: 272). "Unquestionably," Dealey affirmed, "the influence of comparative science and philosophy will slowly modify [religion's] organization and teachings" (501).

This symbolic opposition of pure science and religion was no doubt in part constructed out of the cultural tools of the standard Victorian opposition of masculine versus feminine. The Protestant church of the era was undergoing a process of feminization, and women were very involved at the grassroots in the Social Gospel activism associated with the religious-reformer sociologists. This created a gendered social context in which the association of religion as private, emotional, and feeble-minded would have been for many of the era particularly plausible, since that version of cultural production was compatible with prevailing social conditions as interpreted through the dominant cultural categories. Thus, the structural homology of science/manly/strong versus religion/feminine/weak, combined with social Darwinism, was a key part of the identity construction and discursive work of sociological secularizers, and likely an important reason why many academics and other elites proved receptive to their claims.

Far from thinking about science and religion as different but compatible systems of knowledge, important early American sociologists constructed religion for their textbook-reading audiences as mere superstitions about the unknown, destined to be entirely remade in the image of scientific knowledge, if not fully eradicated by scientific truth.

2. *Sociology is an immature science,* but . . . *it will surely deliver the knowledge necessary for social salvation.*

Early American sociologists were quick to admit that sociology was a relatively immature science that had not yet produced the valuable social knowledge it pledged. They cautioned, for example, that social science itself was in transformation: "A process of reorganization and redistribution of subject-matter is in progress among the social sciences, and for that reason it is impossible to speak most accurately of these in a few words under their usual names" (Small and Vincent 1894: 54). And they warned that society was more complex than nature, and so would require extra hard work and patience to comprehend. Speaking of sociology's "immense possibilities . . . from a practical point of view," for instance, Ward suggested that "the laws of nature have always proved capable of being turned to man's advantage . . . and there is no reason to suppose that those of human nature and of society will form an exception. But it is admitted that they are more complex and difficult to understand, and therefore sociology requires more study than any other science" (1898: 199). Such claims seem designed to lower short-term expectations of sociology in order to buy more time to make good on its promises. But despite such admissions and cautions, these sociologists boldly claimed that sociology was destined to lay the foundation for true human happiness, ethical advance, the overcoming of evil, and the salvation of humanity and society. In fact, there seemed little of worth that sociology could not do.

To begin, early American sociologists—eager to hitch their wagon to the broader authority of natural science—insisted that sociology was a real, legitimate science. Giddings, for example, asserted that "[s]ociology has a province as definite as that of any science, and yet it is in perfect continuity with every science in the indivisible whole of knowledge. In the scientific division of labor, the sociologist has a distinct work" (1896: 51). Ward likewise spoke about the promise of "nothing less than the establishment . . . of a true science of sociology in all respects parallel and identical with the other less complex sciences of the hierarchy" (1893: 11). Like the natural sciences, sociology was assumed to be an objective science, free from the biases of human particularity. "Adoption of the sociological point of view," explained Hayes, "means that all prejudices and settled questions shall be subject to re-examination, in the light of adequate investigation and of the adopted conclusions of all previous sciences. We are to study . . . unprejudiced as if seated in a star and looking down upon earthly sects and parties" (1915: 8). Sociology was also a science based on a method capable of explaining all phenomena. "The effects observed must result of necessity from a definite cause actually existing in the nature of things," claimed Ward. "Whatever does so exist is capable of discovery . . . [and] every apparent anomaly in nature can be satisfactorily accounted for and scientifically explained. . . . It is here that the immense superiority of the necessitarian theory becomes evident, since it opens up to man a field of otherwise forbidden fruit" (1883: 43). This was the kind of science, believed Small and Vincent, that could produce trustworthy social facts: "The beginnings of Sociology . . . are in the development of the natural sciences . . . [in] a transition of thought from the fictitious to the real. . . . Until recently, opinion has dominated social doctrine. Sociology has entered the ranks of the sciences by turning from opinion to precise examination of social facts" (1894: 24–25).

For early American sociologists, it was obvious that such knowledge held great promise for human betterment. For one thing, it put the means to social welfare within human hands, as Small and Vincent suggested: "This manual has attempted to show that there is discoverable coherence throughout the whole range of social conditions and actions; that the factors of human welfare are intelligible; and that the forces by which the conditions of human welfare are to be secured and maintained are within human control" (1894: 374). These textbooks invariably proclaimed that sociology was the key to progressive social engineering. "Why," asked Ross, "is it not legitimate to sound social phenomena in hopes of discovering how they may be controlled to suit our wishes? . . . Indeed, attack upon the maladjustments among men is an inevitable consequence of the development of social science" (1925: 545). Dealey likewise promoted sociology, heralding that, "Sociologists now assert with increasing emphasis that the time is not far distant when some of the fundamental laws and principles underlying social activity will be so well understood that civilization can begin to exterminate the great handicaps to progress, such as crime, pauperism, intemperance, and sexual vice, and to build up with scientific precision a social order that will bring vigor and happiness to mankind" (1909: 65–66). Hayes similarly wrote about sociology developing "social arts which will make it possible to control social situations and mold them in the interest of human welfare" (Hayes 1915: 10–11).

This kind of pitch, however, made these academic sociologists sound uncomfortably like the religious reformer sociologists from whom they were working hard to distance themselves. The academics therefore also engaged in identity work to mark the slippery boundary between the two groups. Small and Vincent wrote derisively that, "Sociology is not a collection of interesting experiments and opinions concerned with methods of putting the world to right. Sociology is the philosophy of human welfare. . . . Sociology is not . . . a resort for social visionaries, so eager to reform social evils that they cannot stop to take advantage of available knowledge of social conditions" (1894: 32). Similarly, Ward asserted with tough-minded practicality that, in contrast to the "mantle of charity thrown over everything that exists," sociology provides the rational basis for social knowledge, making it possible to distinguish "those social conditions which are susceptible of modification" from those not. "In this way an enormous amount of energy otherwise wasted can be saved and concentrated upon the really feasible" (1906: 3–4).

By their own accounts, precious few social conditions would not be susceptible to sociological modification. For example, they said sociology would facilitate, through its hard work, the attainment of fulfilled human life: "The justification of Sociology will be its contributions to knowledge and its aid toward realizing the conditions of complete human life. The merit of such contributions must be earned by strenuous exertion" (Small and Vincent 1894: 373). Sociology would create the conditions for human happiness: "The problem of dynamic sociology is the organization of happiness. . . .

Most ... wrong conduct is due to defective ... correspondence between organism and environment. Something must, therefore, be done to complete the adaptation" (Ward 1883: 156). Sociology would also make ethics scientific: "Sociology aims at nothing less than the transfer of ethics from the domain of speculative philosophy to the domain of objective science" (Hayes 1915: 4). Furthermore, sociology would, through its knowledge about the liberation of "social energy," enable humans to conquer evil: "True morality not less than true progress consists in the emancipation of social energy and the free exercise of power. Evil is merely the friction which is to be overcome or at least minimized. This cannot be done by exhortation. It must be done by perfecting the social mechanisms" (Ward 1893: 114).[7] Sociology would foster a complete transformation of society: "The new truth being discovered leads to the further conquest of nature, which belongs to pure sociology. Applied sociology aims at the complete social transformation which will follow the assimilation of discovered truth" (Ward 1906: 85). Sociology would even earn society's very salvation and heavenly perfection. With sociology confronting human pain, scarcity, disease, and misery, Dealey said at the conclusion of his textbook, "there is a call to salvation":

> [Humanity] looks forward to the time when man will come into his kingdom; when misery, vice, and human discord shall have been outgrown, and peace, good will, and joyous emulation in achievement will prevail among men. In anticipation he feels himself to be part of this glorified humanity, since he also does his share in the world's work, and builds up, be it ever so little, the achievements and happiness of mankind. This joy in companionship with men, past, living, or future, is to him immortality, and when death comes, since he is also a true son of man, and like Moses has caught a glimpse of the promised land, he goes gladly. (1909: 503)

"When sociology lends itself so readily to a sort of religious interpretation of social movements," Dealey concluded, "it is not strange that many persons find in it a kind of inspiration for life. Back of statistics, the cold logic of science is a belief in the perfectability of mankind" (1909: 503–4).

These academic authors (following Comte) suggested that, as the scientific messiah destined to usher in through its advent humanity's secular millennial kingdom of perfection, sociology rightfully deserved to sit at the right hand of Knowledge on its throne as the supreme science of all sciences. Dealey declared, "Sociology may be considered as a science of sciences, since it incorporates into itself all information of human interest gathered by the other sciences" (1909: 54). And Ross proclaimed, with Pauline assurance in its second coming and glorification, that, although sociology was then only a minor science,

We know we can afford to bide our time. We do not need to plead or preach in order to win. In the long run the nature of things will prevail. Vested interests in learning will yield to the logic of facts. So far as social life is one, there will be one master science of social life. If not to-day, then to-morrow, if not by this generation, then by the next, the necessity for sociology will be fully recognized. There is a vacant chair among the great sciences, and sooner or later that chair will be filled. (1905: 15)

Such visions of disciplinary grandeur hint at the elitist tendencies present in these promises of scientifically improved human welfare. With apparent humility, Small and Vincent thus explained why only a small elite can ever aspire to sociological knowledge:

Easy sociology is probably false sociology. The right of free thought does not involve the competence of every man to think every order of thought. Sociology cannot be brought within the comprehension of everybody. Social relations are so wide and involved that the most capacious and penetrating minds will be most reserved about assuming that they have reached final conclusions about the economies of social action. . . . Sociology shall be exhibited as a realm of thought in which effective work can be performed only after critical use of the most diverse orders of facts, and the exertion of the maturest judgment. (1894: 373–74)

Similarly, Ross closed his massive text, *Social Control,* by asking—in language thick with biblical imagery—whether it is not unwise for sociology to demystify the foundations of social order, "to show faiths and moralities in all their nakedness as so many ways of luring a man from the pursuit of his individual welfare." Ross concludes condescendingly that it is prudent to reserve the use of the sociological good news for experts and elites alone:

The fact of control is . . . no gospel to be preached abroad with allegory and parable, with bold type and scare headlines. The secret order is not to be bawled from every housetop. The wise sociologist will show religion a consideration . . . [and] will venerate a moral system too much to uncover its nakedness. He will speak to men, not to youth. He will not tell . . . [the ordinary man] how he is managed. He will address himself to those who administer the moral capital of society—to teachers, clergymen, editors, law-makers, and judges, who wield the instruments of control; to poets, artists, thinkers, and educators, who guide the human caravan across the waste. In this way, he will make himself an accomplice of good men, for the undoing of bad men. (1901: 441)

The early American sociological project, then, was not simply about producing new social data and theories, or even about fostering progressive social amelioration. It was also about securing for sociologists a legitimate social role as expert social masterminds whose *gnosis* could both save and manage the new, secular social order. "The knowledge appropriate to Sociology," wrote Small and Vincent, "can be redeemed only by men skilled in the processes of real knowledge" (1894: 24). Though scorned by the world, Ward wrote, the sociological elite must persist in its mission: "The world is not ripe nor ready for the blessings of science that a few privileged men have given it, and therefore it receives only a small part of the advantages. . . . Society fails to avail itself of their services and allows them to be misapplied and wasted . . . and if applied sociology has any purpose it is to show how this can be prevented" (1906: 287, 292). Moreover, it is to these men skilled in knowledge, the "few privileged men," that society must defer. In a twist of equality and elitism, Giddings enumerated first among the kinds of "equality" essential for social harmony, "Equality of regard for certain fundamental social values, especially . . . respect for expert knowledge" (1898: 328). And thus, when Ross—explicitly contrasting it with religious manipulation—declared that "[o]f all the [social] controls, that of the State is the least sentimental because the state is an organization that puts the wise minority in the saddle" (1901: 74), we know from his writings that Ross clearly believed that sociologists belonged to that wise, ruling minority.

In sum, early American academic sociologists constructed sociology not simply as a valid scholarly enterprise, but in many ways as the functional equivalent of traditional Christianity.[8] In a world full of human ills and evils, sociology would provide knowledge and guidance for a salvation and regeneration that would bring human life to fullness and perfection. And it would do so with an authority and finality—notwithstanding present conditions seemingly to the contrary—that would be vindicated at a future time whose coming was most certain.

3. *Religion is concerned with the spiritual realm, which is beyond sociology's ability to examine, but . . . all religions are finally reducible to naturalistic, material, and social causes, and are clearly false in their claims.*

The writings of important early American academic sociologists commonly recognize that religion is focused on things spiritual or supernatural. But they also treat such things as definitely known to be unreal. The world, according to their constructions, should be viewed entirely in naturalistic and materialistic terms. Ward was the most forthright in promoting this belief: "There is no intelligent reason why anything should be as it is. That this little planet of ours happens to be peopled with life is merely an accident, or rather the convergence of a number of accidents" (1898: 30–31). But that essential belief permeated all of the textbooks. Consequently, religion itself was consistently represented as nothing but a psychological or social product, fully determined in character by its surrounding environment, to be understood always in historical evolutionary terms.

This approach came out most clearly in the textbook accounts of the social basis of religion, all of which were thoroughly and explicitly reductionistic. For Dealey, religion is grounded in primitive fear of the unknown: "Religion had its beginnings when primitive man felt a sort of dread of uncomprehending forces surrounding him and there arose a dull desire on his part to understand them. Fear, and the desire to comprehend the reason for his fears, so as to free himself from them, combined to give him beliefs respecting the world outside his own" (1909: 267). For Ross, religion derives from the need for social solidarity:

> As the social group grows farther and farther away from . . . natural society . . . it is necessary to enclose the members of the community in a network of half-metaphysical ties in order that feeling may play through it and unite them. . . . Where impulsive sympathy fails to answer the summons of a kinship theory, a special conscience must be formed. In other words, the feeling between man and man ceases to be wholly natural and begins to become *religious*. (Ross 1901: 202; italics in original)

Ward took a similar approach to defining the human soul: "We define the soul as the feelings taken collectively . . . the collective feelings of organic beings and their resultant efforts" (1893: 46). More than two decades later, Ross argued that religion comes from the desire to feel ecstasy: "A primary factor in the religious interest has been the desire to experience ecstasy. Primitive people know and highly value this enlargement of consciousness, and no one who has ever seen persons 'getting happy' at a camp meeting will doubt the reality or the seductiveness of such states"(1925: 54). Ward explained religion alternatively as an invented legitimation for rules guarding collective security: "It becomes difficult to distinguish morals from religion. The latter is little more than the addition of supernatural penalties for the violation of the laws of race safety. . . . At the beginning of all religion was race perception . . . and the creation of gods whose supposed will is thwarted by conduct dangerous to the race" (1903: 419). In another work, having discussed in detail "anthropomorphic" theories about the projections of "savages" as the basis for belief in spiritual beings, Ward concluded that "[t]he facts above enumerated constitute the basis of all religious ideas" (1906: 60).

Reductionistic explanations of religion's ultimate source were matched by reductionistic explanations of its historical development. Fairbanks, for example, suggested that ethnic interaction determined religious evolution: "All the great ethnic religions of the world . . . are the product of epochs and of countries where there was a vigorous interaction of different ethnic elements. The development of new and higher forms of thought and of life in Christianity itself may be traced to external stimulating influences of the same sort" (1896: 219). A more popular interpretation, however, focused on determining changes in family structure. Henderson, for instance, explained that

> [a]s the family expanded into the clan or tribe . . . the common ancestor became the common deity, and thus all the beliefs and sentiments of a larger group helped to cement them in a common life. It was in the tribe that the medicine man, weather prophet, sage acquaintance of the departed, laid the foundation for a special class in society, the priestly class. . . . From the long history of the family, religion has come to think out the meaning of its universal prayer, "Our Father which art in heaven." (1898: 265–67)

Hayes likewise observed that "[t]he patriarchate, through the development of reverence and worship for the spirits of departed ancestors, opens wide the way to belief in a father-god" (1915: 36). In all cases, through scores of pages detailing religion's historical evolution, these authors effectively draw their readers into a naturalistic, reductionistic worldview.

Within this framework, neither divine revelation nor religious ethical commands have legitimacy on their own terms. They are mere human, social products. "The religious man hears God's voice in the commands of duty as he hears it in the revelation of truth," observed Fairbanks, "but both the command or revelation and the power to apprehend them come through his shared social life. . . . Ideals are a social fact; the ideals which men create for themselves are proposed to them by the social group" (1896: 81, 119). Therefore, standards of religious morality have no legitimate binding status, as Small argued: "The actual standard is not absolute, but relative after all. For example, if the 'will of God' be taken as the absolute standard of conduct, each judgement about a specific act will be referred to some assumed expression of the will of God, . . . the divine will according to Moses, . . . Mahomet, . . . Paul, . . . Rome, or Constantinople, or Geneva, or Westminster, or Massachusetts Bay" (1905: 669). In fact, for some, religion amounted to simply another version of calculating human self-seeking. As early as 1883, Ward was laying the foundation for a reductionistic, rational, egoist interpretation of religion: "The religionist . . . is pre-eminently the true and practical exemplification of utilitarianism and even hedonism. . . . No voluntary action can be disinterested. . . . All ideas of advantage or disadvantage are grounded in the experience of pleasure and pain" (1883: 146–47). Years later, Ward reaffirmed that "[a]ll interest is essentially economic, and seen in their true light religious interests are as completely economic as the so-called material interests. All conduct enjoined by religion—not only the most primitive but also the most highly developed religions—aims at the satisfaction of desire" (1906: 46). And Ross argued similarly that "[t]he actual sweep of religion is, of course, due in large measure to self-seeking, propitiatory motives, and to its maintenance as a prop of social order" (Ross 1905: 16–17).

On occasion, three of these sociologists interjected the claim that none of their analyses implied judgments about the truth or falsity of religion per se. Near the end of a twenty-page discussion of the social origins and evolution of religion, Hayes notes, "The foregoing discussion has not raised the question whether the religious beliefs of the tribes of mankind correspond with any reality, but has only traced the method of the origins of these beliefs, considered as prevalent social phenomena. . . . It is no part of our task to raise the question what among all the teachings of religions concerning the hereafter is to be believed" (1915: 570, 633). Similarly, Henderson wrote that "[s]ocial theory does not consider whether creeds are true or false. That work belongs to metaphysicians, theologians, preachers. There must be division of mental labor, and sociology does not inquire into the grounds for the various beliefs of mankind, nor seek to criticize or reconcile the warring tenets of creeds" (1898: 261). And Dealey was sure to point out that his ethnological, historical, and comparative study of religion looked "merely . . . at the institutions and ethics of religion, leaving to philosophy and theology all discussion of fundamental beliefs" (1909: 267). But these claims of indifference to religion's ultimate truth status are belied by the massive weight of otherwise thoroughly naturalistic, materialistic, and reductionistic assertions about religion offered even by these few disclaiming authors. Dealey, for example, had already earlier explained away religion in this way: "Fear of the unusual, common to all animals, had become broadened . . . by crude attempts . . . to explain unusual phenomena. . . . Imagination and erroneous reasoning, handed on by tradition and enlarged by later generations, in time peopled the entire environment of man with supposed supernatural agencies" (108–9). Or, as Ward wrote even more frankly, "Religious ideas . . . consist entirely of error, there being no objective truth corresponding to spiritual beings" (1906: 65). Whether or not the likes of Hayes, Henderson, and Dealey had deluded themselves into believing that their analyses did not actually make final claims about the actual status of religion itself, it is naive to think that they had convinced their readers on this point. For the actual message of these textbooks was loud and clear: ultimately, religion is illusory, the reflection of something else more basic and real.

4. *Modern religion has advanced well beyond primitive religion, but . . . all religions are essentially identical in being based on the fear and ignorance of savages.*

Nineteenth-century Victorian culture was obsessed with establishing clear boundaries defining dichotomous opposites—such as male versus female, private versus public, and backwardness versus progress. Another cultural dichotomy that loomed large in the minds of Victorians was the distinction between savage and civilized. Early American academic sociologists, being post-Victorians, continually employed this savage/modern distinction in their analyses of religion. But part of the modernist project was to break down the boundaries between old Victorian opposites in order to create a unified and holistic world. And since early American academic sociologists were also very much budding modernists, their analytical claims about religion recurrently utilized the savage/modern dichotomy in order effectively to destroy that dichotomy. At one level, they nominally reaffirmed the widespread notion that modern people had evolved far beyond savages. But at another level, they suggested that modern religion was actually not fundamentally different from primitive religion, insofar as both were based on fear and ignorance. By implication, the only way for truly civilized people to escape complicity with barbaric and bloodthirsty savagery would be to renounce all religion per se entirely, in favor of modern secularity. This was a modernist discursive strategy that capitalized upon, while also undermining old Victorian sensibilities.

The first step was to establish the origins of all religion in savagery. Some, such as Ross, suggested that religion was the product of primitive fears: "The earliest non-religious force behind [religion] is fear. *Primos in orbe deos fecit timor.* After man has by propitiation of the unseen powers assured his personal safety, he seeks to utilize them" (Ross 1905: 176; also see Ross 1925: 54). Ward took the same approach: "Primitive man, living, as he must, in a pain economy, is and always has been a prey to innumerable fears. Fear of nature . . . wild animals . . . other men make him wild. . . . But all these sources of fear combined . . . are as nothing compared to another source, unknown to animals—the fear of spiritual beings. This great overshadowing awe he has created for himself" (Ward 1906: 62–63). Others, such as Giddings, emphasized the role of primitive ignorance in giving rise to belief in spirits: "The religious tradition is the sum of beliefs about the continued existence of the soul after the death of the body, and about invisible personal powers, from ghosts to gods, which are supposed to govern natural phenomena and to control human destinies. Savages think the world is peopled with spirits of the dead. They are regarded with fear, and beliefs about them are a confused web of superstition" (Giddings 1896: 144; also see Giddings 1898: 251; 1901: 122). Blackmar likewise observed, "Religion itself is a slowly evolving institution. . . . Perhaps the first religious notion [of savage or barbaric people] is found in the conception of a spiritual life or being. This comes not through reason but through instinct or feeling. . . . The savage mind rapidly passes from a state of unorganized superstition to that of organized superstition" (1905: 193–94). Ward also took up this theme: "All natural causes were explained after the analogy of human effort in the intentional production of effects, and the earth and air were peopled with invisible and often malignant spirits as the only recognizable agents.

And thus were built up great systems of magic, superstition, and mythology" (Ward 1898: 23).

Religion, then, was a primitive human invention. It helped fearful and ignorant savages to acclimate to their world, wrote Bushee: "Religion in all stages of development has expressed the effort of man to adjust himself, through acts and observances, to external forces. Religion then may be defined as the expression of the desire on the part of man to come into more perfect relations with the unknown powers of the universe" (1923: 535). It thus reflects, according to Burgess and Park, not divine existence, but human desire: "Faith, taken in the conventional religious sense of assurance of things hoped for, is a primitive form of will" (1920: 27). Naturally, as all civilized moderns knew, primitive religion was an illusion. Thus Ward declares, "All will no doubt admit that the conceptions of primitive man and those of existing savages . . . were and continue to be grossly false and erroneous" (1883: 265). Blackmar concurred: "We may consider much of [primitive] religion false, and in many instances, degrading" (1905: 200). In this spirit, Bushee reaffirmed how very far enlightened moderns had advanced over primitives: "When the savage offers sacrifices to the god of thunder in order to protect his life, he is performing a religious act; but when civilized man tries to protect himself by the use of lightning rods, he is not performing a religious act" (1923: 535).

But in fact, modern progress in this case does not consist of a more highly evolved religion, but of the scientific elimination of religion. Sacrifices give way to lightning rods. A more highly evolved religion would not solve the problem, because, for these academic sociologists, advanced religion is not essentially different from savage religion—both are based on fear and ignorance. Thus any religion surviving in the modern world represents an embarrassing holdover from the lowest stages of human evolution. Academic sociologists usually made this connection between primitive and civilized religion through expressions of shock and ridicule regarding modern religious believers who still carried on the beliefs and practices of savages. Although their favorite targets in this were the poor and "ignorant," such critiques had clear generalizable implications for readers, since, in all of these texts, anyone who maintained religious beliefs of any kind was by definition ignorant. Ward, for example, linked the savage and modern believer in this way:

> The unhappy condition of the lower classes of society is due as much to error as to ignorance. . . . Their minds are full of false ideas. They are nearly all superstitious and are slaves to a creed and to the priesthood whom they are supporting out of their hard earnings. . . . This is true for all religious sects. . . . From this source they are haunted and oppressed by nearly the same fears and terrors as the savage. Indeed, in some respects by worse ones, for the latter . . .

have invented at least one more terrible punishment than any savage priest-hood has ever devised, vis., that known as "eternal damnation." . . . This dia-bolical doctrine has been the cause of more suffering than all other religious errors combined, but it has been the main dependent in keeping the masses under complete spiritual subjection. (1906: 93–94)

Having expounded his "ghost" explanation for religion's origins, Giddings then expressed astonishment that "[i]n civilized lands, the ignorant still be-lieve in ghosts, and a majority of the people believe in the existence of per-sonal gods or of one omnipotent God" (Giddings 1896: 144). Likewise, in the context of his claim that "the [primitive] belief in immortality was un-doubtedly fostered in part because of its possibilities as an engine of social control," Hayes wondered that "[e]ven here and now many a Bible is put in the trunk with the same feeling that led the savages to take along his fetish" (1915: 633). Using identical form, Giddings noted that "[b]elieving in a spirit separable from the body, the primitive man could no longer think of death as the end of conscious life. . . . Many strange occurrences convinced the beholder . . . [of] spirits. . . . To this day the ignorant believe that an in-sane person is 'possessed'" (1896: 248–49). And Dealey observed that, even in his time, "[m]any aspects of biological and psychological phenom-ena are among the ignorant supposed to be caused by ghostly agencies beyond scientific comprehension" (1909: 56).

By collapsing the boundaries between savage and civilized in this way, these sociologists constructed a clear choice for their readers: either hold fast to religious faith and implicate yourself with savagery, or abandon reli-gious faith altogether and join the ranks of the most highly evolved and truly civilized persons. It is not hard to imagine which choice the textbook reader—the ambitious university student, the professionalizing college professor, or the well-read local civic leader—would feel compelled to make.

5. *Religion remains intrinsically important to the mass of humanity, but . . . reli-gion's only real potential value is in instrumentally promoting social harmony.*

Although our early American academic sociologists were personally antag-onistic to historical religion, they were also aware that traditional religion still held the loyalty of many of their contemporaries. They acknowledge that religious faith and practice were still important for many Americans. They largely disagreed with the reasons why religion should be valuable, but they did at least sometimes allow for one potential value that religion—despite its essential falsehood—might retain: its functional ability to foster social harmony. This was for these sociologists a normatively groundless power—if people really understood the true nature of religion, it would lose this effect. But promoting social harmony was a frequently observable effect of religious belief nonetheless. And for this socially instrumental capacity of religion, these sociologists were willing to grant some recognition.

Small and Vincent, for example, took note of "the almost inestimable service of religion in determining individual will to truly social conduct. . . . In the apparent conflict between self-interest and collective welfare, the religious motive exerts a most powerful influence in securing social or altruistic conduct" (1894: 363, 365). Likewise, Blackmar observed, "Religion has always been connected with social order. The control of families, tribes, groups, and even nations has been brought about through religious influences. It has also lent a powerful sanction to virtue and morality. . . . On account of service to an authority and to a superior, [man] trained himself in the arts of social life" (1905: 201–2).

But these sociologists did not merely recognize this social function of religion; some also affirmed and encouraged it. Thus, assuming that promoting social harmony is the one thing that the church is really good for, Henderson gives this normative charge to the church: "Social unification is a function of the church. . . . The church ought to seek the most perfect unity in order that it may more perfectly fulfill this function" (1898: 269). Henderson then quotes extensively from a magazine article penned by Edward Ross—who, he notes, is "a thoughtful, honest, and free-thinking teacher, who feels scorn at mere clericism"—which likewise makes normative recommendations to the church:

> To the sociologist, what keeps the church most alive is its power to fit human beings for harmonious social life. . . . People need to be trained or developed to the self-restraints, sacrifices, unselfishness, and helpfulness that must abound in the members of society if social life is to go on smoothly. . . . The church must always work, with energy and unremitting patience, at this hard task of fitting human beings for social cooperation and harmony. (quoted in Henderson 1898: 270–71)

Thus, having identified at least one feature of religion of some genuine value to modern society, these authors took it upon themselves to tell the church what it must—and by implication, also must not—be and do. Bushee, for example, took the liberty of using the instrumental value of social harmony as the litmus test for defining "true religion": "True religion is the instrument of those with a vision who seek complete harmony and the full realization of all their faculties" (1923: 538). At times, some of these scientists of society lapsed into quite rapturous language: "The social function of religious institutions is the unification of mankind on the most exalted levels; or rather the unification of mankind in an upward movement in which the divine attractions of the Perfect Life are at once the bond of affection, the object of faith, and the inspiration to unceasing creative energies of goodness" (Henderson 1898: 268).

Others, however, were less enthusiastic. Ross, for example, while applauding the social value of overseas missionaries, made sure to remind his readers that this in no way endorsed the truth claims of their religion:

> Whether or not their theology possesses objective truth, the twenty thousand educated Christian missionaries sent out from Europe and the United States are accomplishing a social work of vast importance. Generally . . . they propagate the best industrial, moral, and political ideas of their time, to say nothing of its philosophical and scientific conceptions. Thus, incidentally, their labors tend to level up the civilization of the belated peoples to that of the advanced peoples, so that the progress of the human race is more symmetrical. (1925: 493)

Likewise, Ross was at pains to make clear that the potentially instrumental social value of religion was an entirely different issue than the intellectual credibility of its beliefs, which were, of course, suspect: "In the long run, the domination of a system of belief in the supernatural depends less on its plausibility than on the perfection with which its control meets the needs of the social organism" (1901: 136). Still others, such as Ward, refused entirely to acknowledge any positive social function of religion.

This recognition of religion's potential merit in fostering social harmony was the closest these textbooks came to affirming any value in religion. It was the one honestly positive gesture many of them made toward religion. Still, we should notice the implied consequences for religion of this praise. First, the new social scientific expert, and not religious believers, is assumed to be the one who would determine religion's true significance. Second, religion's one possible remaining value to the world was defined in purely functional terms relative to the normative criterion established by the larger social order—that is, the desire for social harmony—and not by any historical religious tradition itself. Third, the status of the actual truth claims about reality that historical religions proclaim became irrelevant, since all that really mattered were instrumental consequences. And fourth, such praise domesticated religion by sanctioning only its propensities toward social harmony, while tacitly disapproving of religion's prophetic capacity and its prerogative to act as a disruptive force of social criticism or protest. In sum, the actual views and interests of religious traditions themselves no longer mattered. If religion was to have *any* place in the new social order, it would be on the terms of and in the interests of modern society and those scientific experts who governed it.

6.   *Religion is in the business of promoting morality,* but . . . *in actuality religion has been history's primary source of oppression, immorality, conflict, and error.*

Early American sociology textbooks often paid brief lip service to the idea that religion promotes good morals. Ideally, they suggested, religion helps people behave uprightly and teaches them how to get along together. Jesus, after all, they noted, taught "tolerance" of others. But these initial credits to religion invariably served as convenient setups for extensive, damning critiques of religion's actual propensity toward moral failure and misconduct. Bushee was atypically generous when he observed, "Religion, as a method of regulating social conduct, has had undesirable as well as desirable consequences" (1923: 539). Much more typically, these leading sociologists openly vilified religion for its immoral repressiveness, selfishness, and stupidity.

One source of religion's destructive energy is the teaching of inhumane theological doctrines, such as belief in sin, divine wrath, and an afterlife. "At its best . . . the church shows a truly statesmanlike intuition of the laws of collective life," observed Ross, "But behind the control of the devout lurks a very masterful and dangerous sentiment, namely, sympathy with the divinity's abhorrence of sin. . . . Hence the worshipper's sympathy with the mortification and wrath of the slighted divinity against the undevout drives him to excesses of Puritanical zeal" (1901: 73–74). For this reason, Ross warned, "We must beware of bringing back the hideousness, the immense *ennui* of life which the Puritan type created" (161). Likewise, in a chapter entitled "Social Pathology," Small and Vincent include a section subtitled "The function of the church exhibits certain pathological conditions," in which they discuss the distorting social effects of belief in an afterlife and of the learning of moral virtues through adversity on earth (1894: 296).

But the deeper problems underlying such misanthropic theological doctrines are epistemological and political: religious beliefs have no verifiable basis in fact, so religion must resort to ruthless, authoritarian coercion to maintain its power. As Bushee, in explaining historical resistance to the evolution of progressive morality, observed, "Moral codes are usually promulgated with authority, ordinarily that of religion, and they have about them an air of absoluteness and finality which forbids modification. . . . Continuous appeal to the unknown has caused religion to remain absolute in its dictates and arbitrary in its methods" (1923: 470, 539). Giddings, in summarizing many pages discussing religious tradition, emphasized the same problems: "The laws of the social force of tradition are: First, tradition is authoritative and coercive in proportion to its antiquity. Second, tradition is authoritative and coercive in proportion as its subject-matter consists of belief rather than of critically examined knowledge" (Giddings 1898: 154). Since religion has no relation to objectively known facts, its teachings are entirely arbitrary. "We have only to recall biblical interpretation," noted Ross, "by means of which the Scriptures are made to teach whatever the age thinks, and citation from the Fathers, by which the way may be paved for any new dogma the church wants to set up" (1901: 192–93). Thus, the source of religion's propensity toward conflict—in contrast to science's benevolent universalism—is epistemological weakness: "The reason why theological controversy so fatally descends into polemic is that *all discussions of things supernatural contain seeds of degeneration.* It is owing to this that we hear of an *odium theologicum,* but not of an *odium scientificum.* Theologians . . . after they have marshalled in vain their texts and their reasonings, they have nothing else to appeal to" (Ross 1908: 313).

This vulnerable position naturally leads religion toward the persecution of and war against outsiders. "The whole history of religious persecution," suggested Ross, "is the history of an organization trying to establish itself as a monopoly by ruthless destruction of the spokesmen of competing doctrines and movements" (1925: 209). Dealey concurred:

> A church . . . wars against its antagonists if it fears them and . . . if it maintains that its teachings only are inspired, and that it alone knows the truth. Such religions, animated by the proselytizing spirit, become fanatical when opposed, and develop a policy of "no quarter." Hence one of the saddest records in all history is that series of bloody wars and persecutions, waged by churches against their rivals and against those who seem to be advancing teachings at variance with what is claimed to be "the word of God" or the creed of the church. (1909: 273–74)

Similarly, Ross pointed out that, although Jesus taught toleration, "the Church came to cultivate hatred of heretic, while the belief in collective responsibility for individual error made each community or nation intolerant of heterodoxy. Thus Christianity became one of the most terrible dividers and embroilers of men and brought on the devastating 'wars of religion'" (1925: 225).

The "sectarian" denominationalism of American religion was particularly subject to antisocial impulses, according to Ross: "Sectaries are often clannish, slow to mingle socially with outsiders or to join with their neighbors in the furtherance of common interests as . . . the advancement of secular knowledge. In the American population there have been thousands of local groups sewed up in separatist dogmas and dead to most of the feelings which thrill the rest of society" (1925: 422). What does Ross suggest as an appropriate solution to this problem?

> A self-conscious society will therefore endeavor to limit sect-formation by providing for the widest possible diffusion of secular knowledge. . . . The general enlightenment resulting from a system of universal education narrows the power of the fanatic or the false prophet to gain a following. The public university, moreover, rears up a type of leader who will draw men together with unifying thoughts, instead of dividing them, as does the sect-founder, with his private imaginings and personal notions. (1925: 422)

Religion as so far portrayed, then, is arbitrary, coercive, ruthless, hateful, destructive, the source of "one of the saddest records in all history," and a "most terrible divider and embroiler of men." The "common interest" of Americans is, obviously, secular understanding. But nonprogressive religion kills any sentiments toward the interests of normal people. Therefore society must intentionally curtail religion through the propagation of secular knowledge.

But the sociological indictment grows more damning still. For one thing, religion—perhaps especially Christianity—tends to seek not only to defend itself, but to destroy rival claims to knowledge, according to Ward:

> Religion once installed in full power throughout Europe, Western Asia, and North Africa, its systematic warfare upon the progress of the past began. The schools of philosophy, art, and science were closed; the teachers of all branches were forbidden to impart their knowledge. . . . The last feeble flicker of ancient light was finally extinguished, and the complete supremacy of the religious over the scientific agencies of society was established. (1883: 303)

Christianity also leads to the degradation of superior (Anglo) races, according to Ross (echoing Nietzsche): "The Christian cult of charity as a means of grace has formed a shelter under which idiots and cretins have crept and bred. The state gathers the deaf mutes into its sheltering arm, and a race of deaf mutes is in the process of formation" (1901: 424). Indeed, religion in general is associated with mental inferiority. According to Ward, "For a century past there have been a few truly eminent men who have had no special attachment to any religion. . . . There are many thousands now who do not belong to any religion, and these always embrace the best minds. . . . A religion that is intolerant must be highly unfavorable to the production of genius" (1906: 161, 163). For this reason, theology and science can only "co-exist in . . . minds which have not deliberately and independently worked out a searching analysis, and made a candid and thoughtful comparison of their respective claims" (Ward 1883: 33).

Early American sociologists single out professional clergy as especially guilty of religion's iniquities. The clergy, for example, promote ignorance and passiveness: "The priest wants the *peons* ignorant in order that he may hold them submissive to his authority . . . and be relieved of the necessity of defending his doctrines" (Ross 1925: 131–32). People must beware of greedy clergy who manipulate passions for their own good: "The emotions associated with religion are so intense that the greedy priest may easily play upon them to his own profit" (Ross 1925: 145). The clergy are also vulnerable to an overconfidence that obstructs intellectual advance: "The nature of revelation has been such that others, with authority but without spiritual perception, have been able to supplement and reinterpret truths for selfish and even immoral purposes. And sometimes even genuine religious leaders, believing the religious truth in their possession to be all-inclusive and final, have crushed independence of thought and checked intellectual progress" (Bushee 1923: 539). Clergy are also likely to be out of touch with basic reality: "The teachers of religion, in too many instances, do not grasp realities, but, by conventional creeds and theological systems, spread conceptions of life which do not issue in the most social forms of conduct" (Small and Vincent 1894: 296). Clergy also hold an interest in tormenting people through professional and ideological domination: "The undue ascendancy of the religious profession gives rise to what may be termed 'clericism.' . . . Always . . . the clergy should be balanced by other intellectual groups lest they torment the people with those austerities which regularly develop in an unchecked clerical class" (Ross 1925: 680). Included in "the tendencies that lurk in clerical control" are encouraging "an unwholesome solicitude for one's soul, leading to a morbid introspection and devotionalism"; "cramping the economic development of the people"; and laying "a heavy tax on the people's time" (680–81). Ross concludes, "An ascendant spiritual class inevitably presents conduct in a false perspective. . . . In the end you get a people austere and devout, but not truthful, loyal, and kindly" (682).

Finally, according to these early American sociologists, religion is not a true or necessary basis of morals. This makes sense if religion in fact historically has tended to promote evil instead of morality. So, on this point these sociologists are clear: Modern people do not need religion at all in order to be moral. Morality is independent of and prior to religion, according to Ward:

> The moral sanction is in reality first, both in time and in authority, and it has therefore been lashed to religion as a means of carrying the latter through, and not the reverse. It is moral sanction which gives authority to religious dogma, and not religious sanction which gives authority to moral principle. It is morality which has saved religion, and not religion which has saved morality. Here . . . the apparent is the reverse of the real. (1883: 283)

Thus, progressive people in progressive societies can ground morality not in religion but in their own human existence, according to Dealey:

> In socially developed societies there are undoubtedly many persons to whom the prohibitions and regulations of society are unnecessary. These persons violate no criminal code, they need no stimulus of fear or punishment to inspire them to right action, and they voluntarily conform to the highest standards set by society. Such persons illustrate the possibilities of human progress, and indicate the path of social development. . . . Human nature developed and rightly trained can become a law unto itself. (1909: 280–81)

Hence, Ward assures readers worried about "individuals who disavow adherence to any creed or religion whatever"—using evidence drawn from a *Popular Science Monthly* article—that "[t]he greater part of them are found among the devotees of the exact sciences. Yet there is no more exemplary class of citizen in society than scientific men, whether believers or non-believers in any system of religion, and no distinction certainly can be drawn in point of morality between the religious and the non-religious scientific inquirer" (1883: 281–82). This explains why religious defectors remain moral people even when they cannot intellectually maintain their faith: "After independent reflection has been brought to bear . . . the initial state of belief can be supplanted by a later state of doubt or non-belief. Yet in no such case can it be urged that the transition has been attended with any signs of moral degeneracy" (Ward 1883: 282). Enlightened societies may dispense with religion, then, and continue to sustain personal and social morality indefinitely.

Given Ward's view that religion is such a wellspring of oppressive and destructive tendencies and is morally dispensable, it is no wonder that he concluded categorically, "There is no direction in which the belief in spiritual beings has advanced the temporal interests of mankind. . . . It is a fair speculation how much higher the human mind would have risen in its efforts to comprehend the natural universe, had no such explanation as a spiritual being or a personal god ever suggested itself" (1883: 286). And the next best thing to there never having been religion at all is making sure there will be no influence of religion in the future.

7. *Religion has always been an important force in social life, but . . . its influence and credibility in the modern world are for good reasons rapidly declining.*

Early American sociology textbooks often recognized that throughout history religion has served as a powerful force in social life. As Fairbanks observed, "When [man's religious need] is allowed to develop in normal religious life, the institutions to which it gives rise and their influence of every side of social life are a constant evidence of its social importance. . . . [It] so governs and controls the whole of life, that the history of religion may almost claim to be the history of society" (1896: 106–7). Some, such as Henderson, even suggested that religion remains a powerful force in contemporary life: "That religion is actually a mighty force in society no one doubts, and the marks and outward revelations of that force are everywhere manifest" (1898: 261). But, as with the themes discussed above, such positive statements were vastly overshadowed by more repetitive and insistent claims that modern people can no longer believe in or be influenced by religion.

"However serviceable it may have been in disciplining barbarians," Ross, for example, explained, "the wielding of supernatural sanctions seems to be today a decaying species of control. . . . In our time, that faith in the Unseen which calls forth dread and propitiatory effort is not being renewed as fast as it perishes" (1901: 139, 212). According to Henderson, "Religion may seem to be a smaller part of human life in our day because the outward institutions of the church are not, relatively, so much thought of by most men. Modern life has a greater variety of . . . legitimate interests than former ages. . . . There is neither need nor time for protracted sermons and repetitious prayers" (1898: 273). Dealey also explained that "[t]he old time religious basis of ethics is weakening. Many of the ethical teachings, of the Old Testament at least, are inferior to the practices of the present generation. . . . The church . . . is losing its control over education and, having no longer compulsory authority, it must teach morals and religion to the young attractively and without dogmatism" (1909: 412, 477). Thus, according to Giddings, "The pulpit has doubtlessly ceased to make itself felt in public affairs" (1896: 140).

Behind this apparent loss of religious influence, according to these sociologists, is the fact that modern people can no longer believe in supernatural miracles and religious dogmas. Ward, for instance, claimed about religious explanations of natural events, "All these phenomena are now satisfactorily explained on strictly natural principles. Among peoples acquainted with science, all such supernatural beings have been dispensed with, and the belief in them is declared to be wholly false, and to have always been false" (1883: 268–69). Thus, said Ross, "The triumph of science leads men to value knowledge rather than religion or power. Science grants the health vainly besought by the worshiper" (1905: 179). Consequently, old ideas must give way to new criteria of knowledge. "The standard of truth varies with the social group," noted Fairbanks. "Many ages and peoples have regarded the miracle as the best possible proof of things supernatural; today some classes find in miracles a stumbling-block to their faith" (1896: 79). Henderson, too, wrote about the need for "rejecting, of course, the doctrine of total depravity" (1898: 270).

Within this framework, if religion is to survive at all, it must overhaul itself in order to conform to modern secular standards of knowledge. For instance, in discussing his "process-conception" of life, toward which "the human race is visibly gravitating," Small asserts,

> The process-conception reaffirms the Ten Commandments, not as statutes, but as principles of social economy. . . . It challenges the authority of every dogmatic assertion of a moral principle, unless it can be justified by ascertained moral economies. . . . The ethical norms for [family, politics, finances, and international relations] are in a process of transition. As a single illustration of change in the philosophical postulates underlying ethical judgements, we may cite the shifting standpoint in a generation among certain theological thinkers. They used to say: "This or that is right because it is commanded in the Bible." They now say: "This or that is commanded in the Bible because it is right." (1905: 274–75)

To survive, religion will need to conform not only its beliefs but also its activities to modern standards. In a chapter section entitled "The Suppressors of Recreation Misconceive Human Nature," for example, Ross argues that, "Religion naturally dreads whatever unleashes the beast in man and hence has taken a critical attitude toward recreations. . . . Such a yoke may be assumed by the elect, but it cannot be imposed on the people as a whole. Even the religious groups have had to give up much of their old-time strictness" (1925: 614). Another variant of this accommodationist survival strategy, also suggested by Ross, is for religion to abandon claims to truth and knowledge, and retool itself to specialize in subjective aesthetic experiences: "A church which in its attitude towards science, morals, and social work is out of harmony with its time is not doomed to languish. It may win by specializing in religious aesthetics. With dusky and mysterious interiors, magnificent mosaics, wonderful Gregorian music, forests of lighted candles, and domes blue with incense smoke, it may attract those who are sensuous or mystic in temperament" (218). What will clearly not work, however, is for religion to try to defend its traditional truth claims and moral practices. For these—as the following passage from Henderson makes clear—will be overrun by the activist, progressive spirit of the modern age:

> Our age has not given itself enough time for meditation and devotion, and in this it has the defects . . . of an active and busy age. . . . But better far the useful, energetic life than one given over to droning forms and endless prayers to heaven for individual salvation. Better far to spend life for the good of fatherland and the poor, for education and patriotic service, than to dream dreams and avoid the burdens of social duty. Religion cannot ask any man to profess what he does not believe. It must not ask for blind faith. . . . It must not be thought of as repelling suggestions for improvement. (1898: 273–74)

To summarize, as readers looked to these academic sociologists to help them understand their social world, the message that these new cultural authorities proclaimed about religion was clear: Religion is not in fact an important force to reckon with. Religion is unbelievable. Religion is dying. In short, religion is nothing that any of these readers would want to be associated with. In socially constructing reality in this way, then, these early American sociologists not only described a secularizing world as they saw it, but also significantly helped to promote the secular world that they desired.

8. *Religion has historically been engrossed in politics and public culture, but . . . true religion in the modern world should confine its social role to the private life of individuals.*

In constructing for readers a secularizing view of religion, important early American sociologists did not restrict themselves to "objective" descriptions. They actually felt free authoritatively to *prescribe* normative roles, directive functions, and proper boundaries for religion. For example, on the one hand, these textbooks acknowledged that religion has a significant role in public and political life. As Blackmar wrote, "Priestcraft in Egypt, in Assyria, and, indeed, in Palestine, became the most potent force in social order. Even in modern civilization the power of priests and clergy has manifested itself in the control of the government of nations" (1905: 196). On the other hand, these sociologists insisted in their writings that religion is a private matter that must be limited to the private sphere of individual and family life.

For example, these sociologists did not simply describe and analyze the relations between religion, the state, and education—they argued explicitly for the separation of religion from the state and for public education freed of religious influence. Ross argued,

> We are in the era of educational monstrosities, born of the unnatural union of church and school. . . . We find religious instruction given as part of the regular curriculum; given during school hours . . . paid for with school funds. . . . A state educational machine with its semi-military organization of little children . . . is far from attractive. But its unloveliest features seem comely, compared with the harsh and forbidding traits of a state church. (1901: 175–76, 178)

The alternative to such "monstrosities," Ross counseled, is enlightenment, autonomy, and nonsectarian education: "Over against fraud and superstition has been elaborated a *technique of enlightenment.* Freedom of meeting, freedom of speech, . . . the autonomy of institutions of learning, the liberty of investigation, the freedom of teaching, the free public university, the free open library—not without good cause have these come to be prized by democratic peoples" (1901: 390–91). Fairbanks agreed, arguing that to mix political authority and religion both harms religion and violates the sacredness of individual freedom:

> Moral character is not to be created by force. . . . The moral and religious state of a Savonarola or a Calvin shows the utter futility of the effort to *make* men moral. The modern state has found it possible to remove some temptations to vice . . . [but] more than this can hardly be accomplished by the use of authority. . . . The use of authority in matters of religion helps to make religion formal and perfunctory, [and] . . . the religious liberty for which so many have died is not lightly to be thrown away. (1896: 172–73)

Likewise, expressing an allegedly sympathetic interest in seeing religion achieve its "complete development," Giddings argues for the total removal of religion from all matters involving the state: "The church as a voluntary organization may exist in a country like England that has an established religion, but it can attain its complete development only in a country where state and church are completely separated" (Giddings 1896: 190). Similarly, Ross proposes to maintain religious vitality by reducing its public influence, counterbalancing the social influence of clergy with that of other nonreligious elites: "Keep a balance between clergy and lawyers and between these and students of ethics and sociology so that religion may not become formal and dry" (1925: 508).

Allowing religion a significant public influence is senseless, according to Ross, because it produces "a blend of the gospel of enmity and the gospel of amity which is foolishness to the natural man" (1901: 75). It is also unnecessary, according to Ward, since morality is essentially an intellectual issue, not at all a religious concern: "The chief wrongs emanate from the head and not from the heart. . . . It follows . . . that what are called moral culture and moral education are matters of minor concern. The real moral education is intellectual education, the education of information" (1883: 360). Thus, for these sociologists, it is a very good thing that "in many modern societies religion [has changed] from being a social institution and has become a private matter" (Ross 1925: 583). Ross further notes that "[i]n the United States, the great universities, palatial high schools and splendid public library buildings that are rising are as characteristic of the age as the cathedrals that rose in Europe between the twelfth . . . and the sixteenth century. In fine, the School, once semi-private, has become a public institution, while the Church, once a public institution, has become semi-private" (596). Indeed, religion is out of place in public life, according to Fairbanks, but most comfortable in the private sphere of the family: "In this intimate union, the religious life finds its best inspiration; God comes nearest to his followers at the family altar, and the responsibilities and joys of the family open the heart to the divine life" (1896: 154–55). Therefore, Ross advised in a chapter section entitled "Let Religion Govern Individuals but Not Institutions,"

> Keep social institutions out of the grasp of religion. . . . The more that institutions are delivered to the rigid clasp of religion, the harder it is to adapt them to changing conditions. . . . Instead of being fixed for all time by the texts of an ancient book, ethical discriminations develop with changing conditions of social life and keep step with the progress of psychology and sociology. Rigid ecclesiastical dogmas . . . cannot survive the light of social science. Again, the dissociation of the state from religion gives it a freedom of development unknown to the theocratic state. (1925: 507–8)

Once again, it is the emerging social sciences that in a progressive society are said to rightly lead the way in authoritatively determining ethics and institutional purposes. "Dogmatic" religion must abandon all aspirations for public institutional or legal influence, and be content to speak to private individuals only: "Not that religion should not give a rule of life to the individual and should not affect society by influencing its members. But its authority should end with the individual conscience. It should not preside over nor determine laws and institutions" (Ross 1925: 507–8).

In prescribing the proper role of religion in these ways—far from assuming Hayes's objective "sociological point of view," "unprejudiced as if seated in a star and looking down upon earthly sects and parties" (1915: 8)—these sociologists revealed themselves to be activist, partisan advocates of privatized religion and a secular public square. Under the guise of objective scientific study, they thus pursued their mission as committed apostles of secularization.

9. *Sociology is indifferent to religious concerns per se,* but . . . *the modern church must renounce the making of truth claims and instead emphasize positive, subjective individual feeling and human idealism.*

According to these authors' professed views of science and religion, sociology is properly indifferent to the concerns of religion per se. It cannot evaluate religious truth claims, nor prescribe normative policy directions for religion. Sociology can only examine, describe, and analyze observable phenomena. This supposed empirical impartiality and objectivity of these professing positivists, however, did not prevent them from also freely engaging in theological criticism and advancing bold policy recommendations for the fundamental reconstruction of traditional religion into a secular religion of human idealism. Comte was not the only sociologist explicitly promoting a new religion of humanity—early American sociologists were also apostles of a new secular "religion" that would displace supernatural religions.

The rhetorical strategy these authors employed was to alternate between positive descriptive statements about how religion is changing under the pressures of the modern world, and self-confident and visionary prescriptive recommendations about how to recast what is useful in religion for the modern world. In some cases, they emphasized that religion itself is taking the lead in change. "It is advisable," counseled Dealey, for instance, "in an age of transition to call into question from time to time dubious standards of morality . . . so as to lead to the elimination of what may be obsolete. . . . Especially should prohibitory codes be carefully examined. . . . For instance, religious teachers no longer insist on lengthy series of prohibitions, as, for example, the tabu on certain amusements, or threats of punishment, . . . but they rather set up and emphasize spiritual and altruistic standards as ideals" (1909: 282–83). In other cases, they took the initiative as sociologists for prescribing change. For example, instead of being "absolute in [their] dogmas and therefore extremely resistant to change," Bushee advised, "ethical religions should free themselves entirely from the myths of nature religions and abandon the attempt to interpret natural phenomena. When religions confine themselves to ethical and spiritual phenomena, they will be unaffected by the changing hypotheses and interpretations of science in the material world" (1923: 537). In both cases, these sociologists were intentionally deconstructing traditional religion and promoting their own secularized alternative.

The first thing that had to go in the modern reconstruction of religion were the theological creeds inherited from church tradition. Church creeds represented all that was defective in religion. "Volumes have been written filled with criticism of the church, its creeds, its acts, its superstitions," noted Henderson with approval, "The criticism was necessary, for it is only by revelation of error that we advance to larger truth" (1898: 262). Ross also objected to any theological creeds that would claim authority over individual preferences:

> It is not good . . . that the sons should inherit creed . . . from their fathers; they should choose in freedom. . . . If, instead of inheriting their adherents, organizations had to win them, they would accommodate themselves to today. . . . When everyone chooses his religion instead of inheriting it, the people make the religion instead of the religion making the people. (1925: 220–21)

According to Dealey, "Prohibitive codes and minute regulations of all sorts are already rapidly becoming obsolete; a full freedom of conscience must be maintained, to be sure, but a wise social policy will see to it that individual minds are trained under such stimulating surroundings that they will easily and spontaneously turn toward the nobler standards of action" (1909: 295). For Bushee, since religion's "superstitions and dogmas have tended to disappear . . . the scope of beliefs has been narrowed down to those essential for social welfare" (1923: 555–56). And Hayes suggested that "[t]here is increasing prospect that Christianity will divest itself of its incubus of outgrown, man-made creed and observance, and stand forth in its essential simplicity and power" (1915: 686; also see 688, 690). Church creeds—"outgrown incubuses"—were thereby declared to be in error, hampering individual freedom, nonessential, and obsolete.

Naturally, rejecting church creeds required abandoning points of traditional theology that the creeds summarized. Thus, Dealey celebrated his observation that "[t]he doctrine of innate depravity of man has fortunately gone to join the hell from which it sprang, and in place of it religion teaches men to believe in the essential Godlikeness of humanity" (1909: 296). Likewise, Ward noted the belief that "the great purpose of life . . . [is] 'the glory of God'" and argued that "the holders of this doctrine would not admit that they do not believe God to be absolutely infinite in all respects. Deity must, therefore, be already infinite in 'glory.' It therefore involves an obvious absurdity to suppose that the acts of men can add to this attribute" (1883: 138). According to Ross,

> Nearly everyone takes for granted that a deity and a future life are the essentials for . . . a [religious] faith. But the most striking manifestations of the pure ethical-religious sentiment do not seem to warrant this view. . . . [Human progress and morality] will be found to spring not from belief in God or immortality, but from something deeper still, namely, the conviction of our fundamental identity in nature and destiny. (1901: 212)

Thus, the era of theological "dreaming" is over: "Dogmatic teachings and creeds are no longer to the front and there is a general lack of interest in the older teachings of heaven and immortality. . . . All is in flux and the church . . . is in need of wise leaders who see visions rather than dream dreams" (Dealey 1909: 276).

One implication of this is that the church should stop concerning itself with maintaining the theological orthodoxy of its ministers, but should, in Ross's words, "allow for the possibility of growth and change. The greater [a clergyman's] intellectual vigor and the more independent his mind, the more this . . . becomes a probability" (1925: 647). "Save in extreme cases," admonished Ross, "it will not pursue with a heresy trial the clergyman who has come into disagreement with its creeds. It will leave the question of his continuance in its pulpit to his conscience and sense of propriety" (647). Indeed, modern religious faith as a whole must be understood as an entirely relative "truth" freely adopted by autonomously choosing individuals: "Individuals differ in the demands their natures make upon religion. They will be happier if they may choose freely among several types. . . . A . . . liberation comes from looking upon truth as a personal relation, so that truth for you is not necessarily truth for me" (667–68).

But if traditional religion is outmoded, what is the "religious spirit" these sociologists were apparently so concerned to protect? Essentially, "true" religion is reducible to positive subjective individual feeling and human idealism. "Religion," wrote Henderson, "is an aspiration after ideal goodness, beauty, and truth. It is never complete attainment" (1898: 263). The purpose of the church, in Giddings' view, is "to foster spiritual development and to promote happiness" (1896: 175). At times, sociologists' visions of religion's mission were hazy to the point of being nonsensical. Hayes, for example, envisioned the church creating "a spiritually helpful environment . . . in which ideas and sentiments which ennoble life are communicated and heightened by social suggestion and sympathetic radiation so as to give stable character to the subconscious set" (1915: 686).

But these irreligious sociologists had more to say about the new, "pure," and "noble" religion they hoped would replace traditional, supernatural religions. The "social religion" they advocated was a religion of humanity and ethical idealism. Ross, for example, contrasted the dross-filled "legal religion" with a growing, pliant "social religion":

In Western society, the beliefs that create legal religion are perishing before our eyes. They stand in flat contradiction to our knowledge. . . . The idealism that creates social religion, however, is not suffering so much. These beliefs are more elastic. . . . Social religion, then, has a long and possibly a great career awaiting it. As it disengages itself from that which is transient and perishable, as the dross is purged away from its beliefs and the element of social compulsion entirely disappears from it, social religion will become purer and nobler. . . . It will take its unquestioned place with art, and science, and wisdom, as one of the free manifestations of the higher human spirit. (1901: 216–17)

Ross himself was perfectly clear that this "social religion" involved nothing supernatural, but was an entirely human affair: "The belief basis of social religion is not necessarily theological at all. It is simply idealistic. . . . Human, then—all-human is the affirmation that is the corner-stone of social religion. Not the doctrine about the gods, but the doctrine about men, is the pivotal point" (1901: 212–13). Dealey, too, was clear that religion is not about proclaiming God's will for humans, but about heralding humans' own "idealistic longings" for themselves:

The church of necessity must become either an anachronism, or else must work toward a higher stage of usefulness, cutting loose from routine and pettiness and endeavoring to serve again as a prophetic guide for man's idealistic longings. The present century is obviously transitional for the great religions. . . . Throughout Western civilization far less attention is given to the religion of fear and punishment, and greater stress is placed on religious fraternalism. (1909: 276)

"When dogmatic teachings and a rigid ecclesiastical system as a whole become susceptible of modification," Dealey noted, "the religious system as a whole much more readily adapts itself to a progressive civilization, and may thereby exercise a powerful influence over social life" (1909: 275). In other words, religion may maintain its social influence only by abandoning its traditional identity and aims and conforming itself entirely to the interests and directives of modernity. In sum, religion must reinvent itself to be not about God, but about Man. This was the modern gospel that these allegedly objective, positivist sociologists proclaimed about the purpose and future of religion in a progressive social order.

10. *Religion is a well-meaning agent of social reform,* but . . . *it is dangerous and irresponsible unless it submits itself to the knowledge and authority of the social sciences.*

Early American academic sociologists were often quick to recognize the good intentions of religious reformers. But just as quickly, they warned how reckless and thoughtless these religious reformers were, and how all of their work needed to be brought under the control of more expert academic sociologists. Small and Vincent, for example, warned against the "danger . . . that certain . . . preachers will be mistaken for sociologists" (1894: 19). Their critique continued as follows:

> Christian purpose and aspiration cannot furnish technical skill or information. Piety without knowledge of facts would work disaster in politics and economics just as in navigation or in pharmacy. . . . They imagine that it is practicable to achieve freedom by knowing only half the truth, and that . . . half remotest from immediate applicability. . . . It is vicious to encourage students to speculate about great questions of social reform, before they have learned to know intimately the facts of social structures and functions. . . . The faults of the Christian Socialists have been those of zeal without knowledge. They have been more eager to prescribe social remedies than to acquire precise understanding of social conditions. . . . They have been inclined to quarrel with economic facts rather than to discover the real meaning of the facts. (20, 35, 38)

Giddings likewise suggested this appraisal of well-intentioned reformers: "Private philanthropy vies with legislation in attempts to diminish poverty and crime and . . . to improve the general life-conditions of the masses. Much of this endeavor is sentimental, and not a little of it is mischievous" (1896: 351). A decade later, Small compared the religious "social agitator and the academic sociologist":

> The former is cocksure what things are going to the devil, and what things must be done this minute for social salvation. The latter realize that the most intricate problem which the human mind ever confronts is the problem of antecedent and consequent, of cause and effect, in human society. It is impossible for him to be as sure about anything as the irresponsible ranter is about everything. . . . In spite of the awful complexity of each problem, the sociologist must accept the responsibility at last of definite judgements about the conduct of life. (1905: 693)

Religious activists as a group are thus naive, uninformed, sentimental, mischievous, shallow, overconfident, and overzealous in ways that lead to "vicious" and "disastrous" results. By contrast, academic sociologists as a group are skilled, informed, judicious, and through their expertise alone capable of making "definitive judgements" about social life. Some, such as Dealey, did not entirely oppose religiously motivated social reform, but argued that all such efforts abandon their populist and emotional tendencies and come under the authority and tutelage of academic sociology:

> The churches need to adopt [a well-educated, scientific] viewpoint. Religious temperance agitation would better emphasize a scientific study of the question as a social problem, rather than make it a religious demand, involving a war against the saloon. Instead of arousing the combative and sympathetic

emotions of their audiences, the ministry would better appeal to the intellect by a careful presentation of the larger aspects of the question arising from social and scientific studies. (1909: 421)

In rather unusual treatments of the need to bring religious reform impulses under the influence of academic sociology, a few of these textbook authors actually suggested that religion and science might in the future unite in new movements of progress. Bushee, for example—having first noted that, because of the advance of science, religious claims about the natural world have "entirely disappeared, leaving spiritual phenomena only as the province of religion"—says, in almost mystical language,

> Religion and science . . . seem destined to reunite on a new basis. A religious phase which is practically new begins to emerge as man comes to a full realization of the unity of all force. The boundary line between science and religion then becomes vague and the two may merge whenever the human and the material elements are both involved, science furnishing the method and religion supplying the motive. (1923: 536)

Similarly, Dealey asserted,

> While sociology is not a religion . . . it finds much in common with the ethical aspirations of the church, so that the two will inevitably unite in ethical policy in coming years. The ethical generalizations of the great religions are broadened out into a common teaching, and their ethical applications in details are more and more compatible with scientific conclusions. The ethical aims of all religions and sociological teachings will increasingly harmonize, just as the theology of religion and the best teachings of science and philosophy tend to conform. (1909: 501–2)

However, once again, it is clear that any detente between religion and science is not based on a new openness of science to traditional religion. If the boundary line between the two were ever to become blurred, it could only be because religion had jettisoned all of its claims about the empirical world and entered a "new phase" based on "a full realization of the unity of all force," thus making religion "more compatible" with science. Historical religions must, in other words, discard the particularity of their traditions and reinvent themselves in order to conform to the views of science.[9] In short, the "reuniting" and "harmonizing" of religion and science consists of a unilateral move: "religion" changes itself entirely to accommodate the demands of science.[10]

CONCLUSION

To repeat, in their historical context, important early American sociology textbooks represent much more than "mere words," as opposed to real action, since social life is itself necessarily and always constituted and enacted through language and discourse. These textbooks embody the activist work of "frame alignment" (Snow et al. 1986)—seeking to mobilize political support by constructing for specific audiences persuasive, legitimate accounts of a particular ordering of knowledge and authority in opposition to competing orders. Thus the discursive work of these sociological textbooks represents an important form of political action reflecting a broader movement to deconstruct an existing moral order and institutionalize an alternative order. Accordingly, important early American sociology textbooks tell us a great deal about the commitments and intentions of their authors, about the moral order underlying the discipline those authors were mobilizing to institutionalize, and—particularly for our purposes—about the intended legitimacy and illegitimacy of religion within that discipline, its moral order, and its broader institutional context.

Further substantiation of this chapter's thesis would require evidence of other aspects of early academic sociologists' secularizing activism. One might, for example, examine institutional histories for the politics of academic institutional processes—such as faculty hirings and firings, intradepartmental and intraschool struggles over turf and boundaries, and departmental communications and conflicts with administrators. Accessing, for instance, the kind of faculty politicking that underlies a department's marginalizing of some of the "wrong" kind of faculty members might be more difficult than analyzing textbooks on library shelves. But even a survey of existing literature on early American sociology departments reveals evidence of the kind of institutional political work that a secular revolution thesis would suggest must have taken place. Yale University's William Graham Sumner, for example, led a group of maverick faculty in a "Young Yale" movement that battled mightily against an old-style religious administration and alumni, which Sumner scorned as a "little group of Congregational ministers" (Davie 1963; Keller 1933; Starr 1925). At the University of Chicago—ostensibly one of the most religion-friendly early sociology departments—Albion Small accepted some religious reformer sociologists (albeit liberals who largely shared his revisionist view of the faith) on his faculty for a time. But this was mostly at the insistence of President William Rainey Harper, who retained an interest in Social Gospel reformism. When President Harper died in 1906, however, five of the faculty he had hired left the department within years, some moving to the new, reformist social work School of Social Administration, established across campus. Small then moved to increase the visibility and influence of people like Ross, Ward, Giddings, and W. I. Thomas at Chicago, while refraining from hiring "obvious" religious-reformer potential candidates, such as Chicago Theological Seminary's Shailer Mathews (Diner 1997; Faught 1997). Numerous other early American academic sociologists also worked hard within their universities and associations to marginalize any remnant of "do-gooder," religious reformist sociologists through their own brand of (allegedly) neutral, rigorous, quantitative "objectivism." These included Giddings at Columbia, William Ogburn at Columbia and Chicago, F. Stuart Chapin at Minnesota, Luther Lee Barnard at Florida, Minnesota, and Washington University in St. Louis, among others (Bannister 1987; Furner 1975). Their attitude and agenda were expressed clearly, for instance, by a Giddings student and professor at Wisconsin, John Lewis Gillin, who contrasted sociology with religion in his 1926 presidential address to the American Sociological Society:

> In certain of our institutions, it has unfortunately been true that sociology has been advocated by men who had no adequate understanding of scholarship. In their hands it was a mess of undigested, unsystematized, unscrutinized generalities which made a popular appeal to sophomores and attendants at [religious reformist] Chautauquas. . . . While some of these, unfortunately, are still with us, the application of the scientific method and the increase in emphasis upon objective data have been acting as selective agents in consigning these enemies of sociology to a deserved innocuous desuetude. Doubtless we shall have to put up with them longer, inasmuch as there is no sociological orthodoxy and no sociological inquisition or holy office by which these fellows can be eliminated. Emphasis upon rigidly scientific methods will attend to them. (1926: 25)

To summarize, then, this chapter's analysis has suggested that the irreligious and secularizing tendencies we find in early American academic sociology—which contributed to and reflected a larger process of secularization of American higher education—are understandable in terms of a convergence of key group interests and social forces. First, early American academic sociologists personally tended to be strongly antagonistic to religion. Second, although they were likely to rise in social and cultural status as promising scientists-of-society—positioned uniquely to provide the social knowledge necessary to build and maintain a progressive social order— to secure this position, early American academic sociologists needed to remove two obstructions. First, they needed to undercut the traditional American Christian college's classical education system, which restricted their autonomy as innovative scientific researchers and publishers. Second, they needed to discredit the network of Social Gospel reformer activists who competed for jurisdictional control over the defining of this new thing called "sociology." In both cases, their efforts to remove these obstructions to their upward mobility set these early American academic sociologists against established religious interests and practices in education and in public life. Their personal commitments against religion greatly aided in attacking these obstructions. But so also did a set of larger social structural forces: the growing influence of the German university model; the positivist takeover of scientific discourse; increased attempts by Protestant denominations to expand their control over colleges; the religiously indifferent interests of booming corporate capitalism; the leadership of key research university reformers; and the growing power of the university professorate. These larger forces together meant that, in their activist secularizing work, the early American academic sociologists were swimming with, not against the tide.

It is important to be clear about this chapter's claims. To the extent that this case study supports the analytical interpretation of a "secular revolution," it is not because sociology itself was an established institution controlled by religious actors who were then displaced by secularist insurgents. Sociology was, as I have said, a new discipline in formation, and initial control of it was itself being contested. The established institution from which powerful religious authorities *were* displaced, which provides the general frame of this chapter, was American higher education. That was the site of the revolution. The struggles within and over sociology represent only one aspect of this much larger and more complex conflict within higher education, but an aspect that is revealing. I do not claim that early sociologists were representative of all academics of this era, nor that sociology was *the* crucial force at work in secularization. Again, sociology was merely one "piece in the puzzle" and so provides merely one illuminating and suggestive case study. But to the extent that early American sociology was not entirely atypical of larger processes at work in secularizing higher education, it does suggest evidence supporting the view that secularization did not just happen to American higher education as an automatic by-product of modernization. Rather, the view becomes more plausible that American higher education was intentionally secularized—by purposeful actors motivated by compelling interests and ideologies, acting with agency and intentionality to struggle against rivals in order to achieve their goals. These actors clearly operated within a larger social structural context that greatly facilitated their secularizing aims. But in the end it was not the structures, but the actors—with agency, interests, ideologies, and intentionality—who achieved this signal historical, even revolutionary change.

Of course, again, there was a complex of different groups of secularizing activists in the history of American higher education—faculty, administration, philanthropists, board members, and more. Important among them were early American sociologists, who were not disinterested observers of social life. They were upwardly aspiring profession builders, struggling to wrest jurisdiction over the emerging entity of "sociology" from religious competitors—even as they often struggled among themselves—and so to establish their own exclusive cultural authority as objective scientists of society. They were also—common scholarly misconceptions notwithstanding—overwhelmingly ideologically irreligious and anti-religious first-generation defectors from the Christian faith, personally committed as skeptical Enlightenment atheologians to undermining the public authority of religion and to persuading, if not ridiculing, others into also abandoning such "superstition." Their primary strategy was straightforward: to launch relentless partisan attacks on religion under the guise of scientific objectivity and impartiality, thus engaging an explicitly normative debate from the protected position of allegedly self-evident fact. Thus, for instance, in this passage from his 1883 introductory sociology textbook, Lester Ward accomplished many things:

> The weapons of religion have been coercion and exhortation; those of science have been skill and strategy. . . . [It was a] simple and necessary circumstance that, with the advancement of intelligence brought about through the operation of [science], the deeper and more obscure phenomena already claimed by religion were one after another recognized as coming within the domination of fixed laws and claimed so by science. Religion had nothing to gain and everything to lose; and it has, in fact, been constantly losing from the first, and must continue to lose to the last. It has thus been a true "warfare of science," science having all along been on the offensive. (1883: 273, 305–6)

Ward here constructed an absolute difference and hostility between religious and scientific knowledge, vilifying the first and ennobling the second. He also constructed a narrative of unilinear progress from religious ignorance to scientific intelligence, imbuing that narrative with an aura of inevitability and triumph. These constructions helped to achieve both Ward's professional aim of excluding religious reformers from sociology and his personal aim of subverting the credibility of religious faith. In retrospect, it is easy to see that the claims of Ward and his associates quoted above frequently rested on speculation—ironically the very things from which these sociologists had wanted to disassociate themselves. Nevertheless, in the end, the Lester Wards of American higher education won.

By focusing attention on the anti-religious discursive work of early sociologists as activist secularizers, this chapter has helped to suggest an alternative explanation for the historical secularization of American public life. Secularization was not a natural, inevitable, and abstract by-product of evolutionary modernization. Secularization was the outcome of a power struggle between contending groups with conflicting interests and ideologies that mobilized to win control over institutions governing the production of socially legitimate knowledge.

NOTES

1. Berkeley historian Henry May, for example, writes, "In the late thirties, when I was in graduate school, the progressive interpretation of American history had the allegiance of nearly everybody. Part of the progressive ideology was the assumption

that religion was and must be declining. Democracy and progress were closely associated with the liberation of mankind from superstition. Religion was dependent on a series of dogmas and legends that no serious intellectual could entertain. . . . For many these assumptions were deeply taken for granted, lodged in the unconscious, where assumptions are hardest to dislodge" (1991: 18).

2. Already, these actors were sowing the seeds of later, more full-blown secularization, according to Ross: "At the outset [the gentry intellectuals'] overriding concern was to show that the social sciences could reconfirm the traditional principles of American governance and economy and replace religion as a sure guide to American exceptionalism. . . . The gentry resolutely banished overt reliance on divine guidance, hitherto the fundamental support of an eternal natural and historical order in America. They were thrown into greater reliance than before on the order discernible within nature and history" (1991: 64).

3. See, for example, Hinkle and Hinkle 1954; Oberschall 1972; Morgan 1969; Carey 1975; Vidich and Lyman 1985; Greek 1992.

4. In Germany, " 'Knowledge for its own sake' . . . served to legitimize [the] creation of a new profession through which men from the lesser middle class could gain status and security in a country where opportunities for advancement were few, and . . . this process was permitted and even encouraged by an upper class who judged it a useful way to avoid social conflict. . . . The ideal helped those who professed it to move from a lowly class origin to a position of alliance with a governing class of aristocrats and patricians. . . . The learned formed a kind of aristocracy of intellect" (O'Boyle 1983: 4, 8, 9).

5. This is based on the number of general sociology texts catalogued in the U.S. Library of Congress, Washington, DC.

6. Similarly, William Graham Sumner wrote, "The practical utility of sociology consists in deriving the rules of right social living from the facts and laws which prevail by nature in the constitution and functions of society. It must without doubt come into collision with all other theories of right living which are founded on authority, tradition, arbitrary invention, or poetic imagination" (quoted in Greek 1992: 187–88).

7. Speaking more like the theologians and philosophers he ridiculed than an empirical scientist, Ward continued, "The tendencies that produce evil are not in themselves evil. There is no absolute evil. . . . All evil is relative" (1893: 114).

8. This helps to explain why many early American sociologists—having eviscerated traditional religion and declared themselves committed positivists and naturalists notwithstanding—employed explicitly religious language to express the importance of their academic sociological work. "Theological religions have always been ungenuine because they have made the mystical the key to the real," wrote Small, for example, in 1910, "The religion of social science will make the real the key to the mystical. In all seriousness then, and carefully weighing my words, I can register my belief that social science is the holiest sacrament open to men" (quoted in Swatos 1983: 43–44). Likewise, Giddings wrote in 1900 that "[o]nly in the spiritual brotherhood of that secular republic [of "democratic empire"], created by blood and iron not less than by thought and love, will the kingdom of heaven be established on earth" (quoted in Vidich and Lyman 1985: 119). Sociologist John Gillin wrote in 1919 that science offered "the Promised Land of wholesome social

life" (quoted in Ross 1991: 428). Such rhetoric among important sociologists continued in ensuing decades. William Ogburn, for instance, confessed in the 1930s that "[m]y worship of statistics has a somewhat religious nature. If I wanted to worship, to be loyal, to be devoted, then statistics was the answer for me, my God" (quoted in Ross 1991: 394). Similarly, George Lundberg wrote in his 1947 book, *Can Science Save Us?* "To those who are skeptical and unimpressed by the promise of social science, we may address this question: What alternatives do you propose that hold greater promise? If we do not place our faith in social science, to what shall we look for social salvation?" (1947: 104).

9. As the somewhat lesser-known sociologist Charles Ellwood wrote in 1923, "True religion must be a faith consistent with the established knowledge. . . . If there is truth in religious values it will be corroborated by the independent, dispassionate investigation of science" (1923: 4, 7). Ellwood made plain his belief that only sociology could save the church: "The religious revolution of the last two generations, which undermined theological Christianity . . . has left the Church all but prostrate and powerless before the immense social task which now confronts it. . . . [This sociology text will] help show how the breath of life may again be breathed into its nostrils, and how the Church can again become that 'spiritual power' which the world needs to energize and harmonize its life" (1922: ix); and "Religion must enlist the scientific spirit and employ scientifically tested knowledge of human life if it is successfully to accomplish its task" (1923: 9).

10. Sociologists were not the only academics of this era remaking religion in their own image. Economist Thomas Nixon Carver, for instance, wrote in his 1914 book, *The Religion Worth Having*, that "[t]he best religion is that which acts most powerfully as a spur to energy and directs that energy to the most productive economic means" (1914: 5).

REFERENCES

AAUP. 1915. "General Report of the Committee on Academic Freedom and Academic Tenure." *Bulletin of the American Association of University Professors* 1: 17–43. Reprinted in *The American Concept of Academic Freedom: A Collection of Essays and Reports,* ed. Walter P. Metzger. New York: Arno Press.

"American Colleges and German Universities." *Harper's New Monthly Magazine* 61: 253–60.

Axtell, James. 1971. "The Death of the Liberal Arts College." *History of Education Quarterly* 9: 339–52.

Bannister, Robert C. 1987. *Sociology and Scientism.* Chapel Hill: University of North Carolina Press.

Barrow, Clyde W. 1990. *Universities and the Capitalist State.* Madison: University of Wisconsin Press.

Bernard, Luther Lee. 1909. "The Teaching of Sociology in the United States." *American Journal of Sociology* 14: 164–213.

Bierstedt, Robert. 1981. *American Sociological Theory: A Critical History.* New York: Academic Press.

Blackmar, Frank. 1905. *The Elements of Sociology.* New York, London: Macmillan.

Boorstin, Daniel. 1965. *The Americans: The National Experience.* New York: Vintage.

Bozeman, Theodore. 1977. *Protestants in an Age of Science.* Chapel Hill: University of North Carolina Press.

Brubacher, John S., and Willis Rudy. 1958. *Higher Education in Transition.* New York: Harper and Row.

Bruce, Robert V. 1987. *The Launching of Modern American Science, 1846–1876.* Ithaca, NY: Cornell University Press.

Burgess, Ernest, and Robert Park. 1920. *Introduction to the Study of Sociology.* Chicago: University of Chicago Press.

Burgess, John. 1934. *Reminiscences of an American Scholar.* New York: Columbia University Press.

Burke, Colin. 1982. *American Collegiate Populations.* New York: New York University Press.

Bushee, Frederick. 1923. *Principles of Sociology.* New York: Holt.

Carey, James T. 1975. *Sociology and Public Affairs: The Chicago School.* Beverly Hills, CA: Sage.

Carver, Thomas Nixon. 1914. *The Religion Worth Having.* Los Angeles: Ward Ritchie.

Chapin, F. Stuart. 1910. "Report on Questionnaire of Committee on Teaching." *American Journal of Sociology* 15: 114–25.

Christakes, George. 1978. *Albion W. Small.* Boston: Twayne.

Cooney, Terry A. 1986. *The Rise of the New York Intellectuals.* Madison: University of Wisconsin Press.

Coser, Lewis. 1984. *Refugee Scholars in America.* New Haven, CT: Yale University Press.

Crook, Alja Robinson. 1896. "German Universities." *Chautauquan* 23: 560–64.

Davie, Maurice R. 1963. *William Graham Sumner.* New York: Thomas Y. Crowell.

Dealey, James. 1909. *Sociology.* New York: D. Appleton.

Dealey, James, and Lester Ward. 1905. *A Text-Book of Sociology.* New York: Macmillan.

Dibble, Vernon K. 1975. *The Legacy of Albion Small.* Chicago: University of Chicago Press.

Diner, Steven. 1997. "Department and Discipline." In *The Chicago School,* ed. Kenneth Plummer. New York: Routledge.

Eliot, Charles. 1898. *Educational Reforms: Essays and Addresses.* New York: Century.

Ellwood, Charles. 1922. *The Reconstruction of Religion.* New York: Macmillan.

———. 1923. *Christianity and Social Science.* New York: Macmillan.

Fairbanks, Arthur. 1896. *Introduction to Sociology.* New York: Charles Scribner's Sons.

Faught, Jim. 1997. "Presuppositions of the Chicago School in the Work of Everett C. Hughes." In *The Chicago School,* ed. Kenneth Plummer. New York: Routledge.

Finkelstein, Martin. 1983. "From Tutor to Specialized Scholar: Academic Professionalization in Eighteenth and Nineteenth Century America." *History of Higher Education Annual* 3: 123–44.

Furner, Mary O. 1975. *Advocacy and Objectivity.* Lexington: University Press of Kentucky.

Giddings, Franklin. 1894. *The Theory of Sociology.* New York: Macmillan.

———. 1896. *The Principles of Sociology.* New York: Macmillan.

———. 1898. *The Elements of Sociology.* New York: Macmillan.

———. 1901. *Inductive Sociology.* New York: Macmillan.

————. 1906. *Readings in Descriptive and Historical Sociology.* New York: Macmillan.

————. 1929. *The Mighty Medicine.* New York: Macmillan.

Gillin, John Lewis. 1926. "The Development of Sociology in the United States." *Papers and Proceedings of the Twenty-first Annual Meeting of the American Sociological Society.* Vol. 21, pp. 1–25. Chicago: University of Chicago Press.

Greek, Cecil. 1992. *The Religious Roots of American Sociology.* New York: Garland.

Gross, Charles. 1893. "College and University in the United States." *Educational Review* 7: 26–32.

Haskell, Thomas L. 1977. *The Emergence of Professional Social Science.* Urbana: University of Illinois Press.

Hawkins, Hugh. 1992. *Banding Together.* Baltimore, MD: Johns Hopkins University Press.

Hayes, Edward. 1915. *Introduction to the Study of Sociology.* New York: D. Appleton.

Henderson, Charles. 1898. *Social Elements.* New York: Charles Scribner's Sons.

Herbst, Jurgen. 1988. "American Higher Education in the Age of the College." *History of Universities* 7: 37–59.

Herron, George. 1894. *The Christian Society.* Chicago: Fleming Revell.

Hinkle, Roscoe C., and Gisela J. Hinkle. 1954. *The Development of Modern Sociology.* New York: Random House.

Hofstadter, Richard, and Walter P. Metzger. 1955. *The Development of Academic Freedom in the United States.* New York: Columbia University Press.

Hofstadter, Richard, and Wilson Smith, eds. 1961. *American Higher Education.* Chicago: University of Chicago Press.

Hollinger, David. 1996. *Science, Jews, and Secular Culture.* Princeton, NJ: Princeton University Press.

Hovenkamp, Herbert. 1978. *Science and Religion in America, 1800–1860.* Philadelphia: University of Pennsylvania Press.

Keller, Albert. 1933. *Reminiscences (Mainly Personal) of William Graham Sumner.* New Haven, CT: Yale University Press.

Kimball, Bruce. 1992. *The "True Professional Ideal" in America.* Cambridge: Blackwell.

Lundberg, George. 1947. *Can Science Save Us?* New York: David McKay.

Marsden, George. 1992. "The Soul of the American University: An Historical Overview." In *The Secularization of the Academy,* ed. George Marsden and Bradley Longfield. New York: Oxford University Press.

————. 1994. *The Soul of the American University.* New York: Oxford University Press.

May, Henry. 1991. *The Divided Heart.* New York: Oxford University Press.

McCarthy, E. Doyle, and Robin Das. 1985. "American Sociology's Idea of Itself: A Review of the Textbook Literature From the Turn of the Century to the Present." *History of Sociology* 5: 22–43.

McLachlan, James. 1978. "The American College in the Nineteenth Century: Toward a Reappraisal." *Teachers College Record* 80: 287–306.

Morgan, J. Graham. 1969. "The Development of Sociology and the Social Gospel in America." *Sociological Analysis* 30: 42–53.

————. 1983. "Courses and Texts in Sociology." *The Journal of the History of Sociology* 5: 42–65.

Naylor, Natalie A. 1973. "The Ante-Bellum College Movement." *History of Education Quarterly* 13: 261–74.

Noll, Mark. 1989. *Princeton and the Republic, 1768–1822.* Princeton, NJ: Princeton University Press.

Oberschall, Anthony. 1972. "The Institutionalization of American Sociology." In *The Establishment of Empirical Sociology,* ed. Anthony Oberschall. New York: Harper and Row.

O'Boyle, Lenore. 1983. "Learning for Its Own Sake: The German University as Nineteenth-Century Model." *Comparative Study of Society and History* 25, no. 1: 3–25.

O'Connor, William Thomas. 1942. "Naturalism and the Pioneers of American Sociology." Studies in Sociology, no.7. Washington, DC: Catholic University of American Press.

Pearman, William A., and Robert Rutz. 1981. *The Providence of Science: Selected Profiles.* Chicago: Nelson-Hall.

Potts, David B. 1971. "American Colleges in the Nineteenth Century: From Localism to Denominationalism." *History of Education Quarterly* 11: 363–80.

———. 1981. "Curriculum and Enrollments: Some Thoughts on Assessing the Popularity of Antebellum Colleges." *History of Higher Education Annual* 1: 88–109.

Rauschenbusch, Walter. 1907. *Christianity and the Social Crisis.* New York: Macmillan.

Reuben, Julie A. 1996. *The Making of the Modern University.* Chicago: University of Chicago Press.

Ross, Dorothy. 1991. *The Origins of American Social Science.* Cambridge: Cambridge University Press.

Ross, Edward. 1901. *Social Control.* New York: Johnson Reprint.

———. 1905. *Foundations of Sociology.* New York: Macmillan.

———. 1908. *Social Psychology.* New York: Macmillan.

———. 1925. *Principles of Sociology.* New York: Century.

Rudolph, Frederick. 1962. *The American College and University.* New York: Vintage.

Russell, James. "The University Crisis in Germany." *Educational Review* 9: 391–99.

Schwendinger, Herman, and Julia Schwendinger. 1974. *Sociologists of the Chair.* New York: Basic.

Scott, Clifford. 1974. *Lester Frank Ward.* Boston: Twayne.

Small, Albion. 1905. *General Sociology.* New York: Arno Press.

Small, Albion, and George Vincent. 1894. *An Introduction to the Study of Society.* New York: American Book.

Snow, David E.; Burke Rochford; Steven Worden; and Robert Benford. 1986. "Frame Alignment Processes, Micromobilization, and Movement Participation." *American Sociological Review* 51: 464–81.

Spencer, Herbert. 1851. *Social Statics.* New York: A. M. Kelley.

———. 1874. *The Study of Sociology.* New York: D. Appleton.

———. 1876–97. *The Principles of Sociology.* Vols. 1–2. New York: D. Appleton.

Starr, Harris E. 1925. *William Graham Sumner.* New York: Henry Holt.

Stern, B. J. 1933. "The Letters of Albion W. Small to Lester F. Ward." *Social Forces* 12: 163–73.

———. 1935. *Young Ward's Diary.* New York: G. P. Putnam's Sons.

Stevenson, Louise. 1986. *Scholarly Means to Evangelical Ends.* Baltimore, MD: Johns Hopkins University Press.

Strong, Josiah. 1902. *The Next Great Awakening.* New York: Baker and Taylor.

Sumner, William Graham. 1870. "The 'Ways and Means' for our Colleges." *Nation* 11, no. 271: 152–54.

———. 1911. *War and Other Essays.* New Haven, CT: Yale University Press.

Swatos, William H., Jr. 1983. "The Faith of the Fathers: On the Christianity of Early American Sociology." *Sociological Analysis* 44, no. 1: 33–52.

———. 1984. *Faith of Our Fathers: Science, Religion, and Reform in the Development of Early American Sociology.* Bristol, IN: Wyndham Hall Press.

———. 1989. "Religious Sociology and the Sociology of Religion in America at the Turn of the Twentieth Century." *Sociological Analysis* 50 (4): 363–75.

Tolman, Frank. 1902. "The Study of Sociology in Institutions of Learning in the United States." *American Journal of Sociology* 7: 797–838.

Vidich, Arthur J., and Stanford M. Lyman. 1985. *American Sociology.* New Haven, CT: Yale University Press.

Ward, Lester. 1883. *Dynamic Sociology.* New York: D. Appleton.

———. 1893. *The Psychic Factors of Civilization.* Boston: Ginn.

———. 1898. *Outlines of Sociology.* New York: Macmillan.

———. 1903. *Pure Sociology.* New York: Macmillan.

———. 1906. *Applied Sociology.* New York: Arno Press.

White, Andrew Dickson. 1896. *A History of the Warfare of Science with Theology in Christendom.* New York: George Braziller.

Wright, Carroll. 1899. *Outline of Practical Sociology.* New York: Longmans, Green.

3

Educational Elites and the Movement to Secularize Public Education

The Case of the National Education Association

Kraig Beyerlein

The National Education Association (NEA) is the largest, and arguably the most influential, organizational advocate for the cause of public education in the United States. It is also the oldest, with a history of more than 140 years.[1] During the mid-to-late nineteenth and early twentieth centuries, the NEA played an important role in American public education, providing a national forum to discuss public educational policy and to nurture educational leadership (Fenner 1945; Wesley 1957; Mattingly 1975). Although histories of the NEA either completely ignore or gloss over this fact, from its founding in 1857 until the early 1870s, leaders of the association fervently supported, through their discourse and formal organizational policy, the teaching of "common Christianity"—which included, among other things, devotional Bible reading—for all of America's public schools.[2] This began to change, however, in the middle of the 1870s and especially in the 1880s, when new NEA leaders, who were much less friendly to having religion in public education, contested the instruction of "common Christianity" for public schooling. By the 1890s and 1900s, the contest was settled. The NEA had come by then to support educational positions and policies forbidding public schools from engaging in formal religious teachings and expressions. This makes the NEA an exemplar of internal, or organizational, secularization, understood as the process by which NEA educators who advocated religious teaching for public education lost the ability they once had to maintain this policy within the association (Chaves 1997: 441–42). They lost this ability, I argue, as the result of struggles with other educators in the association who wanted public schools freed from religious instruction (Dobbelaere 1981; Chaves 1993, 1994, 1997). This chapter describes and seeks to explain this struggle and outcome.

To document and explicate the conflict over religion's role in public education among educators in the NEA, I analyzed the association's annual convention proceedings, covering the years 1857 through 1920. These annual conventions were crucial in NEA politics and identity, and helped shape the character of American education more broadly. As Wesley states, "The [NEA] itself became a lofty organization, a kind of super-holding company that coordinated the state associations by providing an annual convention where ideas, theories, and principles were discussed. . . . The annual conventions became marts for the interchange of educational ideas; the annual volume of *Proceedings* recorded and disseminated the best that was thought and said in American education; common standards emerged from diversity, and in this national forum state leaders became national leaders" (1957: 24). Through a systematic reading of the association's *Proceedings* from 1857 to 1920, I recorded all references to religion and items potentially relating to religion, such as the teaching of ethics or morals. I coded and analyzed arguments about religion and public education, and researched the biographies of many of the most important voices in these debates. I was thus able to identify changes in ways that different influential educators of the association viewed the proper role of religion in public schools over time. I focused especially on educators in formal positions of power (for example, president or vice president) in the NEA, who, not incidentally, frequently spoke at annual conventions. I gathered information about their religious and educational backgrounds by consulting biographies and biographical encyclopedias, various books on the history of American education, and NEA necrology committee reports and other obituary accounts. I did not attempt to document compositional changes regarding the religious and educational backgrounds of the association's rank-and-file, because during this time period rank-and-file NEA membership and attendance at convention meetings fluctuated greatly from year to year (Schmid 1963: 27). Furthermore, the rank-and-file of the association did not appear to have had a clear impact on organizational positions or policies.

In the next section, I describe the NEA's initial educational position calling for the teaching of "common Christianity" in public schools and the central themes of this position. I then show how and why new educational leaders joining the association contested this "common Christianity" in the decades that followed. In the final section, I explain how this "common Christianity" was decisively displaced in the NEA. Three caveats are warranted before proceeding. First, I do not claim to show the extent to which the NEA's policies and positions about religious instruction directly influenced the actual practices of this instruction in public school classrooms. Second, I cannot in one chapter elaborate all of the larger social structural and contextual forces that influenced the change in how the NEA viewed the relationship between religious teaching and public education (but see Tyack and Hansot 1982; Jorgenson 1987; and Thomas, Peck, and De Hann, chap. 8 in this volume). Instead, I focus more on factors internal to the association to help explain how and why opposing actors marginalized religious interests and perspectives regarding public education in the NEA. Third, I leave aside the normative question of whether the displacement of support for "common Christianity" in public schools within the association was positive or negative; the purpose of this paper is descriptive and explanatory, not evaluative.

THE ESSENTIAL ROLE OF RELIGION, 1857–1869

In 1857, the NEA began its life as the National Teachers' Association (NTA). Prior to the founding of the NTA, four separate attempts had been made to establish a national organization of teachers—by the American Institute of Instruction (Boston, 1830), the Western College of Professional Teachers (Cincinnati, 1831), the American Lyceum Association (New York, 1831), and the American Association for the Advancement of Education (Philadelphia, under the direction of Horace Mann, 1849). Not until 1857 did such an attempt succeed. In Philadelphia on August 26 of that year, forty-three educators assembled to create the NTA. The mission of the association, as stated in its Preamble, was "To elevate the character and advance the interests of the profession of teaching, and to promote the cause of popular education in the United States."

The NTA's board of directors—the president, twelve vice presidents, a secretary, treasurer, and one counselor from each state, district, or territory represented in the association, all of whom were elected by majority ballot vote—constituted the leadership of the association, although the president had greater leadership duties and privileges than other members of the board. The board of directors had the power to create committees and appoint which members of the association served on these committees. Any person regularly engaged in the profession of education, broadly defined, was eligible for NTA membership.[3] Upon submitting an application to the board of directors and the recommendation of this application by the board, individuals confirmed their membership in the association by paying two dollars and signing the constitution. To maintain membership in the association, members were to pay an annual fee of one dollar. The NTA's open membership policy and structure made it a voluntary, unitary organization (Wesley 1957: 55). The NTA was to hold annual meetings, and members not physically able to attend these meetings could have their papers read by other attending members. For the first thirteen years, NTA membership remained relatively small, never exceeding 190 individuals (Fenner 1945: 155; Wesley 1957: 397).

For NTA leaders, "to promote the cause of popular education" was *de facto* to promote the cause of a religiously based public education.[4] NTA leaders, however, did not originate this position regarding public education; they had received it from the previous generation of educational leaders, the common school reformers. The common school reformers of the 1830s, 1840s, and 1850s—especially the reformers in the Northeast, most notably Horace Mann in Massachusetts—zealously pressed for religious instruction in all of the nation's public schools (Tyack and Hansot 1982; Jorgenson 1987; Glenn 1988). It was not unusual that NTA educators espoused the common school reformers' thinking about public education. The majority of NTA leaders, like their common school reformer forebears, were liberal Protestants—Unitarians, Episcopalians, Congregationalists, liberal Presbyterians or Baptists—who had spent their educational careers serving public school systems in the Northeast. Hence, it was natural for these educators to advocate that public schooling should be religious.

NTA leaders regularly advocated the primacy of religious instruction in public schools during their annual meetings. In 1863, the year that he was president of the NTA, John Dudley Philbrick—then superintendent of public schools in Boston, Massachusetts, a position he occupied for more than twenty years (1856–1874; 1875–1878); 1864 NTA vice president; and Unitarian—asserted that, in regard to measures to be encouraged and advocated by the association for the advancement of public education, "moral and religious training ought to be much more prominent than it is" (NTA *Proceedings* 1863: 323).[5] Elbridge Smith—a devout Congregationalist; principal of the Free Academy, Norwich, Connecticut; NTA 1859–1860 vice president—was more explicit about the paramount role of religion in public education. In his 1859 address, entitled "The Place Christianity Should Occupy in Education," he said,

> The place of Christianity in education is the same that it is any where else—it is first and foremost. . . . Christianity alone can give the perfect health and soundness to the human soul—alone can give that state of soul which is most desirable in both pupil and teacher. . . . Education has something more to do with Christianity than to tolerate and patronize it—it must walk in its light and become strong in its strength. But how shall this be done? Shall Christian science be taught as a distinct branch in our public schools? Not so. [Christianity] should pervade and preside over our system of instruction rather than enter into it on the same level with other studies. (NTA *Proceedings* 1859: 176–77)

Many other NTA leaders routinely made similar statements about the important place of religion in public schooling.

Connected to their declarations that religion was to have principal status in public education was the belief of these NTA leaders that public school teachers had the great responsibility of preparing their pupils not only academically, but religiously. As James Pyle Wickersham—at that time, newly appointed state superintendent of public schools in Pennsylvania, a title he held until 1881; original member of the NTA; president in 1866; vice president in 1867 and 1869; and a Quaker—said, "Educators of American children, it is your highest duty to open this eye of faith that it may discern the mysteries which God, in the plenitude of his mercy, writes upon the soul of man, reveals in the Bible, and exemplifies in the life of his Son, Jesus of Nazareth" (NTA *Proceedings* 1866: 608). Similarly, Dr. John Nelson McJilton—an ordained and active Episcopalian minister; superintendent of public schools in Baltimore, Maryland; and vice president of the NTA from 1858 to 1863—stated that to the teacher's duty of molding the mind and character of this great nation "must be added the higher obligation of preparing the subject for the intelligent worship of God. The duty is one of highest moment, and the teacher ought to know it; and he ought to appreciate and feel it" (NTA *Proceedings* 1860: 288). And Zalmon Richards— committed Northern Baptist, original NTA member, first NTA president in 1858, NTA secretary in 1860, and NTA vice president in 1863—asserted, "Teachers of the public schools should be selected . . . [who] pay attention to the morals of the scholars, and bring [children] up in the love of Christianity" (NTA *Proceedings* 1858: 36). This discourse reveals that NTA educators believed that public school teachers, above all else, were to ensure that students were cultivated religiously.

Another theme NTA leaders frequently articulated at their annual conventions was the belief that morality and religion were inseparable and, consequently, the view that moral training devoid of religion would not effectively instill morality in children of the public schools. For instance, the year that Samuel Stillman Greene was president of the NTA—a devout Northern Baptist, serving as a deacon, instructing Sunday school; president of the Rhode Island Baptist Sunday-school Convention; professor for more than thirty consecutive years at Brown University beginning in 1851; and NTA vice president in 1866 and 1869—he criticized those who suggested teaching children morality not grounded in religion:

> Teach the children morality, we are told, but never resort to the Scriptures or to revealed religion to support your teachings, just as though God would admit the restriction, and my prejudices, or my attachment to some ecclesiastical party, would exonerate me or you from a duty which lies deeper than all party! A Christian education with Christianity left out! The whole idea is absurd. These very persons who exclaim against the teaching of piety and religious truth, are foremost in pressing the importance of moral teaching—but it must be moral training destitute of its vital power—the mere outward form without the inward spirit. (NTA *Proceedings* 1865: 492)

Though Greene acknowledged that others held different positions about how to teach morality, to him, and other NTA educators, these positions were "absurd." According to NTA educators, Christianity had to undergird morality if public school children were to find moral instruction persuasive.

Just as NTA educators insisted that religion was requisite for moral training to be effective in public schools, they also argued that public education needed religious instruction to preserve the features of the nation—such as civilization, liberty, or patriotism—that all citizens, they believed, held dear. Thus James Pyle Wickersham argued, "*Schools in this country should train the young to be religious.* All men in all countries should be religious; but religion as an element is more necessary in a republic than under any other form of government; for without it self-government is impossible" (NTA *Proceedings* 1866: 606; italics in original). Later in that same address, Wickersham added, "humanity, patriotism, [and] religion all demand" public school educators to inculcate an intense religious sense in their students (608). In 1859, when he was NTA president, Andrew Jackson Rickoff— influential educator from Ohio, serving as superintendent of public schools in both Cincinnati and Cleveland; and later NTA vice president in 1860, 1864, 1865, and 1866—asserted, "The only safeguard for the country . . . is education founded upon the principles of pure Christianity and true religion. Without religion there can be no prosperity, no liberty, no advancement in real knowledge" (NTA *Proceedings* 1859: 149). That same year, Elbridge Smith proclaimed similarly,

> If then Christianity is thus related to the human mind, and has performed so important a part in the civilization of the modern world, it is obvious that it must enter largely into our system of American education. . . . As American teachers, if we would contribute our share to the civilization which is to exist on this continent, we can do it most effectually, not by making mathematicians and linguists, engineers nor rhetoricians merely, not by teaching them to lay Atlantic telegraphs nor build Pacific railroads, not by teaching them to delve in California, El Dorado, nor to thunder in yonder capitol: but to raise them to a far higher elevation—till they all come in the unity of the faith and of the knowledge of the Son of God unto perfect men, even unto the measure of the stature of the fullness of Christ. (NTA *Proceedings* 1859: 177–78)

To Smith, Rickoff, and other NTA leaders, it was "obvious" that Christianity was needed to preserve the Republic. It followed then that religion must be an essential element in public education. Reflecting this belief, the association adopted the following resolution in 1859: "The inculcation of the Christian religion is necessary to the happiness of the people and the perpetuity of our intuitions, and we should be pleased to see every teacher in our broad land imbued with its spirit; yet we would not shut the doors of our school-houses upon well qualified and apt teachers because they do not hold membership in any religious denomination" (NTA *Proceedings* 1859: 139). The caveat at the end of this resolution—stipulating that competent teachers lacking particular denominational memberships would not be banned from teaching in public schools—is a clue to one of the most significant and recurrent topics discussed by NTA leaders during their annual convention meetings: the type of religion desired for public education.

The educators of the NTA continually made it a point to explicate what kind of religion was to be taught in public schools. According to NTA educators, the religion of the public schools was to be, above everything else, "nonsectarian," which, at least to these educators, meant a common, generalized Protestant Christianity. As Elbridge Smith stated at the 1859 NTA convention meeting, "By Christianity, I do not mean any form of ecclesiasticism, nor do I mean any form of sectarianism. I mean not the creed of Rome, of Oxford, or of Geneva, but of Nazareth. . . . I mean by Christianity, the teachings of the New Testament, as the inspired word of God, and more especially the life and teachings of Christ himself" (NTA *Proceedings* 1859: 176). Samuel Stillman Greene similarly argued,

> The principal argument against religious instruction, is the danger of some sectarian bias—the fear of a secret or open proselytism. This is not the teaching in question. God gave us Christianity and bade us [to] promulgate it—not to scramble for religious sects. . . . It is not the dogmas of any sect that we need. It is Christianity itself, pure and unsullied as it came gushing from the lips and life of the Master. It is its vital power that we want. It is not so much the teaching of Christian doctrine, as it is Christian teaching—teaching which in its very essence shall be fragrant with the sprit that animated our Lord and Master. The very presence of a teacher who is thoroughly imbued with its power, is Christianity in a living form. (NTA *Proceedings* 1866: 492–93)

James Pyle Wickersham also made such a pronouncement in 1866: "[We have] to plant a purer religion in the hearts of men than any the world has yet realized . . . our schools must most diligently inculcate, not sectarian doctrines, but a spirit of devotion and faith in the most important truths of our holy religion" (NTA *Proceedings* 1866: 607). By "our holy religion," Wickersham meant a common Protestantism. The version of religion that NTA educators wanted taught in public schools, then, was clearly a common Protestant Christianity.

NTA leaders were mostly liberal Protestants. For them, as for the common school reformers, common Christianity denoted a purified form of faith, superior to the particular doctrinal concerns of the more "sectarian" American Christian traditions they wanted to transcend (Michaelsen 1970; Glenn 1988). This common Christianity also reflected the political need of Protestant educational elites to find a common ground among the dominant American Protestant camps upon which they could unite in their cause for public schooling. Nevertheless, not all of American Protestantism accepted this version of religion for public education. Early in the common school movement, certain more orthodox Protestant traditions rejected "common Christianity" as the appropriate version of religion to be taught in public schools (Boylan 1988; Glenn 1988). These orthodox Protestant traditions wanted their distinctive theological tenets taught, and in some cases, they were willing to abandon the whole public school enterprise in favor of securing such teaching in their own denominational schools. By the time the NTA was founded in 1857, however, the vast majority of these dissenting Protestant traditions, largely in response to growing Roman Catholic demands for public funding to support parochial schools teaching specific Catholic doctrines, had joined their liberal Protestant brethren in advocating the teaching of common Protestant Christianity for public schools (Jorgenson 1987; Nord 1995; McClellan 1999). NTA educators' espousal of "common Christianity" clearly signified their disdain for Roman Catholics' educational position and, accordingly, their desire to exclude them from the NTA. As stated above, NTA leaders, like the common school reformers, stigmatized Roman Catholics primarily through discursive associations with terms like "sectarian," "dogma," "creed," and other maledictions during many of their addresses and discussions at annual conventions (Jorgenson 1987). The absence of Roman Catholic participants in the NTA is thus hardly surprising.

At the 1869 NTA annual convention in Trenton, New Jersey, the association's anti-Catholic spirit and the other themes mentioned clearly revealed themselves during a discussion of Joseph White's paper, "Christianity in the Public Schools." In his paper, White—secretary of the Massachusetts State Board of Education and committed Unitarian—concluded "that the state has the right and it is consequently her duty to recognize and teach Christianity in the schools—not the dogmas of sects, but the great duty of love to God and man, as set forth in the Bible, the word of God" (NTA *Proceedings* 1869: 717). In response to White's paper, Judge Richard Stockton Field—an active Episcopalian—suggested an apparent challenge: "You can not give religious instruction . . . in the public schools, and this might as well be acknowledged today as ever" (717). But by religious instruction, Judge Field meant particularistic doctrinal religious teaching, as his ensuing discussion clarified. After Judge Field had finished his remarks, Emerson Elbridge White from Ohio—devout Presbyterian; prominent educational author, lecturer, and institute leader; and later president of Purdue University (1876–1883), who regularly argued, as a prominent member of the Ohio Teachers' Association, that public education should include Bible reading—asked, "Is Judge Field opposed to the reading of the Bible in the common schools?" (718). Judge Field quickly reaffirmed his commitment to inculcating a "common Christianity" in public schools, responding that, "No, I would have it read there, and studied to the fullest extent, without trenching on the consciences of the children. No living being reverences the Bible more than I do. I would look on its expulsion from the schools as one of the greatest calamities" (718). Emerson Elbridge White then continued to discuss the matter, addressing two "extreme" positions regarding religious instruction in public schools:

> In the first place, there are those who believe that no instruction is in any just sense religious that does not teach religious doctrines, dogmas, catechisms, forms of worship, etc.; that does not teach *technical* religion. It is held that it is impossible to separate doctrines, creeds, rituals, etc., from Christian instruction. This is the Roman Catholic view, and consequently they denounce all schools as irreligious and godless in which the church does not come in to teach her doctrines and rites. Believing that every school should be fundamentally and doctrinally religious, they demand a division of the school fund and the establishment of sectarian schools where the church may come in and teach her creeds. Over against this extreme, is the demand that *all* religion be excluded from the common schools; that they be completely secularized. Those who make this demand urge that there can be no reading of the Bible in the schools and no act of religious worship, without trenching on the rights of conscience. . . . The whole mission of the public school is held to be secular education in its strictest sense, all religious exercises and instruction being handed over to the family, the Sabbath school and the church. (720; italics in original)

White then argued that neither the Roman Catholic position nor the secular position was acceptable for public schools. He dismissed the former because it emphasized particularistic religious teaching. White asserted, "We cannot give *technical* religious instruction in our schools. This is what the Catholics demand. We have no right to teach rituals, catechisms, or confessions of faith in the public school" (720; italics in original). White also rejected the secular position because morality, he thought, could not be effectively taught that was not grounded in religion. He asked, "What is moral instruction worth, which excludes the motives drawn from God's word? Which fails to attach human duty to the very throne of God? Shut all idea of God out of our schools, and you have largely destroyed the power of moral precepts" (720–21).

White declared that the solution for teaching religion in public schools was contained in his friend Joseph White's address, the familiar position regularly promoted at previous NTA meetings. White argued,

> There can be religious influence and instruction in our schools without invading the rights of conscience. It is done all the while. Exclude all different doctrines which separate Christian sects and you have left a common ground on which the teacher can stand and not violate the scruples of any one; and this common line points the soul to God. This "common Christianity" can not be shut out of schools, without making them infidel in character and spirit. . . . We shall therefore shut neither God nor His word out of our

schools. . . .This common Christianity, of which we have heard, is . . . [the common school's] life and its hope for the future. (NTA *Proceedings* 1869: 721)

This widely articulated position emphasizing religious teaching in public education was unanimously adopted that year as an official association policy. The resolution stated, "The Bible should not only be studied, venerated, and honored as a classic for all ages, peoples, and languages in educational institutions, but devotedly read, and its precepts inculcated in all the common schools of our land" (725). A second resolution was also adopted that year: "The teaching of partisan or sectarian principles in our public schools, or the appropriation of public funds for the support of sectarian schools is a violation of the fundamental principles of our American system of education" (725). For NTA educators, these two positions were not contradictory. NTA leaders saw devotional Bible reading and instilling biblical principles in public schools as completely "nonsectarian" religious practices (Michaelsen 1970; Tyack and Hansot 1982; Jorgenson 1987).

The NTA in the first thirteen years of its history had established that a "common Christianity" was to pervade public school classrooms. NTA leaders had no difficulty instituting this position within the association, as there was consensus about this role for religion in public schooling. Although they acknowledged that there were opposing positions regarding religious instruction in public schools—the "sectarian" and the "secular"—they failed to give them any credence. Like the common school reformers, NTA leaders were convinced of the truth of their position on religion in public schooling and confident that their view would triumph (Jorgenson 1987). NTA educators had good reason to be sanguine, since dissenting positions in the association were merely hypothetical. These positions were therefore easily written off, as NTA leaders were never directly challenged in their continual, mutual validation of their positions. But in the middle of the 1870s, and especially in the 1880s, support for secularized public education would actually be voiced in the association. Educators advocating this position took advantage of changes in the NEA's organizational structure, acquired leadership positions in the association, and began to attack the teaching of "common Christianity" in public schools.

REORGANIZING THE NTA

The 1870s and 1880s were years of organizational expansion. The NTA was increasingly being recognized as the organizational leader among educational associations, and it increased in size and importance "by the simple process of adoption" (Wesley 1957: 44). In 1870, the NTA absorbed three smaller educational associations—the American Normal Association (organized in 1858), the National Association of School Superintendents (organized in 1865), and the Central College Association (organized in 1868).[6] Its name was then changed to the National Educational Association (NEA), to reflect its broader scope. As Daniel B. Hagar, 1870 association president, stated, "Blending the three associations into one, we can preserve the advantages of each, and at the same time establish on a broad foundation an organization grand in its proportions, comprehensive in its objects, and powerful in its operations" (NTA *Proceedings* 1870: 738). To "preserve the advantages of each," the three adopted education associations were organized as departments within the NEA (the departments of normal schools, of school superintendence, and of higher education). Additionally, in 1870, the NEA created one new department devoted to elementary education. For the first time in its history, the association was not a unitary organization, but rather a federated one, divided into separate departments. Its constitution was amended so other new departments could be formed. By the end of the 1880s, the NEA had created and sustained ten different departments representing a wide range of educational areas.[7]

In the process of this organizational restructuring, NEA membership changed dramatically. Quantitatively, the association enjoyed a substantial surge in membership during the 1870s and especially the 1880s. NEA membership jumped from around 150 in the 1860s to about 250–300 in the 1870s, and to about 1,000 in the 1880s (Fenner 1945: 155; Wesley 1957: 397). But, for at least two reasons, the increase in rank-and-file NEA membership was itself not a significant factor in what would soon become the association's growing hostility toward religious instruction in public schools. First, it is not apparent that the NEA rank-and-file objected to NTA's position of "common Christianity" for public education. Second, even if the rank-and-file had objected to this position, it is extremely unlikely that they would have been able to change it. During the 1870s and 1880s, the NEA afforded little opportunity for rank-and-file members to attain leadership positions within the organization. What did matter considerably for changing the association's position on "common Christianity" for public schools was the numeric increase in educational elites who joined during this era. As a result of its growing national reputation, the NEA attracted many of the day's most prominent educators. Many were superintendents of various ranks (city, county, or state), while others were faculty and/or administrators at major universities. The vast majority of these educational elites were qualitatively different from NTA leaders of the 1850s and 1860s in an important respect: they promoted religion's removal from public education. These educational secularizers gained numerous leadership positions within the NEA. The association's newly adopted organizational policy calling for departmental divisions facilitated their acquisition of powerful NEA positions.

Almost all of the NTA leaders believed that modifying the organizational structure of their association, in the form of departmental divisions, would be beneficial. For instance, in 1870, Daniel B. Hagar—one of the leading founders of the NTA, committed Episcopalian, and NEA president that year—stated, "The needs of our own [association], and the experience of some other associations, give me confidence to recommend for your consideration the organization of this Association into sections or departments, each of which have special charge of those subjects which are its chief concern" (NTA *Proceedings* 1870: 737). Zalmon Richards was one of the few NTA educators who had reservations about dividing the association into different departments. At the 1870 NEA meeting, Richards stated,

> But it seems to me this division into sections will prove to be an elephant on our hands. The meetings of certain sections at the same time; it will occur that certain sections will draw most of those in attendance and as a matter of course other sections will be very slimly attended. . . . I must confess—though I do not want to be too forward in recommending what should be done—I would much prefer that we have all our exercises with one general meeting. I think the interest of the Association will be kept up better in that way. (NTA *Proceedings* 1870: 749)

But Emerson Elbridge White assuaged his friend's concern about unequal departmental attendance; offered solutions to other potential difficulties that might arise from dividing the association into departments; and, believing that he had provided adequate remedies for such problems, strongly encouraged the association to implement this structural change. Most other NEA members agreed with White, and, consequently, the association was divided into separate departments. Although White could have not known it at the time, altering the NEA structure in this way was to have important consequences for the position his association would adopt concerning the proper place of religion in public schooling. Dividing the NEA into departments and largely granting them the right to define their own membership policies—the only stipulation imposed was that of general associational membership—allowed for the creation of subunits in which particular members could meet, organize, and act separately from others of the association. These subunits had the potential to be "mobilizing structures" for those seeking to influence associational positions and policies (Kurzman 1998; McAdam, McCarthy, and Zald 1996: 3–4; McCarthy 1996).

The National Council of Education (NCE) was a crucial mobilizing structure. Established in 1880, the NCE was the "prestigious inner sanctum" of the NEA (Tyack 1974: 42). Prominent, nationally recognized educators of the era formed the NCE's core constituency. The council desired exclusivity and achieved this through "self-perpetuating" membership policies (Schmid 1963: 48). The original NCE consisted of 51 members. The NEA's five departments in 1880 elected 3 members each, and the NEA board of directors elected 12. Then that group of 27 elected the remaining 24 members of the NCE. In 1885, the council increased its membership to 60 and generally specified a six-year membership tenure, with 10 members' terms expiring annually. The NEA departments were not asked to provide selections for these additional members of the NCE; their election resided solely with the NEA board of directors and the council itself. That same year the NCE amended its constitution to assure this elite control over the annual election of 10 new members, all of whom were to serve six-year terms—the NEA board of directors and the council alone were to select 5 members each.

Although as a department the NCE was well organized, this was not true of the association as a whole, which had a rather "loose" organizational structure (Wesley 1957; Schmid 1963; Seely 1963; Tyack and Hansot 1982). During the NTA years, this loose structure was insignificant for the association's position regarding the role of religion in public schooling, as all leaders of the organization consented to religion's primacy in this schooling. But since the NCE had become a significant mobilizing structure in the association, and those who favored eradicating religious influences from public schools were NCE members, the loose structural nature of the association became extremely important in shaping its future position regarding religion and public education. Given its loose structure, "political control [of the NEA] was not a difficult task for a group of men who could cooperate and who were able to attend regularly the semi-annual meetings of the association" (Seely 1963: 170). The council clearly met these criteria. First, organizing and maintaining an exclusive department required a substantial amount of cooperation among NCE members. Such cooperation was evident, for example, in the council's continual reelection of NCE members to new terms. Second, the NCE formally established lengthy membership terms, requiring members to be physically present at meetings. It is therefore hardly surprising that during this era NCE members "dominated the councils, committees, and offices of the parent association [NEA]" (Schmid 1963: 48; see also Wesley 1957; Seely 1963; Tyack and Hansot 1982; Murphy 1990). This dominance was important, because the NEA educators who desired to remove religion from public schools were all NCE members—in some cases, very influential ones.

In sum, the association's change in 1870 from a unitary organization to a federated one and its decision to allow departments to control their own membership rosters created the opportunity for departments to become separate and influential subunits in the association that could operate as important mobilizing structures. Educational elites of the association took advantage of this opportunity, and the NCE became a vital mobilizing structure in their efforts to control the association. Coupled with the loose organizational structure of the NEA, this mobilizing structure enabled them to dominate the association politically for several decades to come. This was significant for the association's position on "common Christianity" in public schooling, since a great many of these controlling elites promoted the secularization of public education. In addition, the cause of religious instruction for public education in the association was further weakened in the 1870s and 1880s as prominent NTA educators—such as Samuel Stillman Greene, John Dudley Philbrick, and Dr. John Nelson McJilton—died.

THE STRUGGLE OVER RELIGIOUS INSTRUCTION, 1875–1890

During the early years of the 1870s, the NEA largely continued to support the teaching of religion in public schools, as many NTA educators maintained leadership positions within the association. For example, Emerson Elbridge White, who was NEA president in 1872, invited the Unitarian minister Amory Dwight Mayo to give a lecture before that year's General Sessions of the association on what he considered to be a central educational question, moral training in public schools. Only a few years before, Mayo, as member of the Cincinnati Board of Education, zealously defended a nonsectarian, generalized Protestantism for public schools against attacks in the so-called "Cincinnati Bible War" of 1869 and 1870 (Jorgenson 1987; Michaelsen 1970). Although this war was over, Mayo continued on his crusade to have "common Christianity" taught in public schools. Mayo's commitment to this crusade was apparent in his NEA address, as he frequently remarked about the importance of religion for instilling morality in public school children. Among his many remarks in the "Methods of Moral Instruction in Common Schools" was the following:

> A moral precept from the Proverbs or the Sermon on the Mount, written on the blackboard; a snatch of a Psalm, hung up as an illuminated motto; a reference to some stirring passage in a case of discipline; a talk with the school on the Golden Rule, the Ten Commandants, the Lord's Prayer; a promise of heavenly consolation brought out for some despondent or bereaved child; the wise and vital use of that divine treasury of wisdom and love will be such a help as only they who have long known its value can well understand. No American citizen has the moral right to insist that the Bible shall not be placed in the school-room as the textbook of morality and wisely used, on every occasion when a judicious teacher can apply it, in the formation of character. (NEA *Proceedings* 1872: 21)[8]

Following Mayo's address, President White added, "The presentation of this topic so convincingly and so impressively must, I think, have satisfied you all that this is one of the vital educational questions which now confront the American people" (24). NTA educator Joseph White also commented on Mayo's lecture:

I thank God that I am permitted to live . . . and to listen to-night to the doctrines of the address presented by our eloquent friend from Cincinnati, whose
words, as given to us to-night and as he has published them before, will live as
long as the English language is taught to our children. I believe that if such
ideas, with such a spirit, control the American teacher, the republic is safe;
without them, notwithstanding all our glorious history, we shall die the death
of the people who have gone before us. My creed is a brief one, and it is not
mine, but that of a leading mind now gone to this rest (Hon. Josiah Quincy
[influential Unitarian, former mayor of Boston and president of Harvard Uni-
versity]): "There can be no freedom without morality; there can be no morality without religion; there can be no religion without the Bible." (26)

However, many newly joining educational elites of the NEA would reject Joseph White's syllogism, along with other NTA educators' assumptions regarding the purpose of religion in public schooling. Since these elites would
acquire prominent NEA positions in the middle of the 1870s and in the
1880s, the association's position of religious instruction for public education would not be secure for long.

Although many in the NEA would begin to challenge this established position on religion, it was William Torrey Harris who initiated the first substantial attack. As NEA incumbent president in 1875, Harris—then superintendent of schools in St. Louis, Missouri—problematized the view that
religious teaching had a legitimate place in public education. He authoritatively announced before the beginning of the 1875 NEA convention that,
among other items, "the proper status of moral and religious instruction in
our common schools" needed to be reconsidered by the association (NEA
Proceedings 1875: 5–6). He thus opened for question what had been fixed
in previous years: the essential role of religion in public schools. Harris first
joined the association in 1870 and delivered the first of what would become
145 NEA convention addresses, the most given by any member of the association during this period (Wesley 1957: 48, 284). With respect to NEA annual convention speeches, Wesley notes that "while frequency of speaking
is not necessarily an index of ability and effectiveness, it is an indication of
prominence and status" (1957: 48). Reflecting this prominence and status,
Harris held many leadership positions in the association. He was an original member of the NCE, serving the council for twenty-nine consecutive
years until his death in 1909; he was NCE vice president in 1889, and NEA
vice president in 1881 and 1882. Harris was widely regarded as one of the
most politically powerful members of the association (e.g., see Seely 1963).
In addition to his high-ranking positions within the NEA, Harris served as
U.S. Commissioner of Education from 1889 to 1906 and played a major
role in the formation of public education in the latter decades of the nineteenth century (McCluskey 1958; Michaelsen 1970; Tyack 1974). Most important, as a young adult, Harris revolted against his orthodox Congrega-

tionalist upbringing and, in its place, reinterpreted Christianity through a Hegelian framework, which profoundly shaped how he viewed religion's role in public education. According to Harris, public schools were to be entirely free from religious teaching (McCluskey 1958; Curti 1959; Michaelsen 1970; Jorgenson 1987). He vehemently advocated secular public education throughout his tenure in the NEA.

Echoing the growing number of secularizing activists in science and higher education in this era, Harris argued that religion was about humanity, not inculcation into a "common Christianity." As Harris stated in 1884 before the NCE, "The ideal of education is the ideal of humanity, which is the true religious ideal" (NEA *Proceedings* 1884: 57). John Dewey and other educational progressives would articulate similar statements in the years to come (Dewey 1934; Michaelsen 1970; Thomas, Peck, and De Hann, chap. 8 in this volume).[9] Harris also appealed to legal reasons for banning religious instruction in public schools. In his paper, "The Function of the American Public School," he stated,

> Our government is careful to avoid legislation in regard to religious educa-
> tion. While there will be a very general agreement among intelligent people
> that religious education is more important than all others, yet the written con-
> stitutions of our State do not permit religious education to become a matter
> of positive prescription by the State. Hence the nation, as a whole, and the
> States individually will not undertake anything in this most essential species of
> education. (NEA *Proceedings* 1887: 268–69)

Harris argued later in his paper that religious teachings, while not allowed in public schools, ought to be taught outside of these schools on a voluntary basis: "It is evident that education must not be limited to what can be given in the public schools of a nation that is founded on a compromise in religion. There must be other education besides Public Education. In this country, therefore, it is presupposed that people can and will undertake to provide religious instruction voluntarily" (NEA *Proceedings* 1887: 269).

Although Harris was not antagonistic to religious instruction per se (McCluskey 1958; Curti 1959; Michaelsen 1970), he nonetheless actively pushed for religion's expulsion from public education. His position is clearly opposed to that of NTA educators regarding the role of religion in public schooling. At this time, promoting secularized public education for elementary and secondary levels was not commonplace in the field of American education (e.g., see Jorgenson 1987). Harris's strong advocacy of secular public education was revolutionary in the NEA and in American education more broadly.

Other newly enlisting NEA educational elites joined Harris in his call to secularize public education. Two particularly important elites that supported Harris in promoting a secularized view of public education during this period were John William Stearns and William Watts Folwell, both of whom were connected to American research universities. Recall that these were the decades when positivism was replacing Baconianism in science, and secular research universities were supplanting denominational colleges as the dominant forms of higher education (e.g., see Marsden 1994; Reuben 1996). These influences affected the NEA thorough members linked with these institutions. John William Stearns—professor of science and education, and later philosophy and pedagogy, at the University of Wisconsin at Madison, who left no record of a religious affiliation—made his first NEA appearance in 1884, when Harris appointed him to serve on a committee in the association. He was subsequently a member of the NCE from 1885 to 1890 and NEA vice president in 1886. Stearns argued before the General Sessions of the association in his paper entitled "The Public Schools and Morality" that, while "from a pedagogical stand-point we say that no teaching of children is good which has not an ethical purpose in it all," nevertheless, the foundation of this ethical teaching was not primarily to be found in religion (NEA *Proceedings* 1885: 81). Stearns was clear:

> It is important . . . to remark that this morality is secular. The inference that it is therefore opposed to any forms of religion is entirely unwarranted; on the contrary, it is supported and strengthened by religious motives wherever these can be called in to its aid. But it rests firmly and unassailably in *human experience,* which has demonstrated its wisdom and necessity. It is taught because it is the foundation of social order, and approves itself to all right-minded men. Its cogency is increased rather than weakened by a distinct recognition of its secular character; for none but a fool will avowedly set at naught experience, and array himself against the order of the universe. Indeed, by recognizing its secular sanctions, we are ushered, as it were, immediately into the presence of "that power not ourselves which makes for righteousness;" and so we become truly religious. The great formative influence of our schools becomes apparent when we thus direct attention to the moral aspect of their whole work, instead of limiting our thought, as many do, to the direct and formal teaching in them of ethical precept. (82–83; my italics)

Thus, secularized morality stands on its own, and religion provides, at best, secondary support. Only by embracing this secular morality could one become religious. This was a major shift away from the view of NTA leaders of the late 1850s and 1860s on the connection between morality and religion.

William Watts Folwell also wanted to separate morality from religion. Folwell was president of the University of Minnesota and professor of political science. Prior to his presidency, his commitment to the Episcopalian tradition had waned, and some charged that Folwell turned the University of Minnesota into a "godless concern" (Buck 1933: 193). He first arrived on the NEA scene in 1875. Like Harris, Folwell was an original member of the NCE, serving the council for six consecutive years (1880–1886), and he was

NEA vice president in 1883. In his paper entitled "Secularization of Education," Folwell asserted, "[P]ublic schools are best calculated to develop good morals and good character. It is no longer sound orthodox theology to found morality on religion, but to build religion on the bed rock of morality. The Bible presumes virtue. The public school, assuming the essential goodness of human nature, can and must inculcate sound morality founded on man's nature and developed by experience" (NEA *Proceedings* 1882: 44–45). Thus, schools teaching morality do not need religion. Religion is secondary to and derivative of a more fundamental morality based in natural human goodness. The year he was NEA vice president, Folwell complained before the General Sessions that the "apparatus of [denominational] evangelization" controlled higher education (NEA *Proceedings* 1883: 127). Later in his address he contended that Americans were "the most common-schooled, and least-cultured people in the civilized world" (128).

Professor Stearns advanced another argument against religion in public education. In response to Emerson Elbridge White's 1886 paper "Moral Training in the Public School," Professor Stearns cited a common Enlightenment liberal rationale for the exclusion of religion from public schooling (e.g., see Monsma and Soper 1997: 8):

> But, my friend, we have before us a system of public schools built for a great and diversified public, in which all stages of belief and disbelief exist, side by side. . . . Now there can be no one who does not recognize the fact that a large portion of our community does not favor anything approaching a religious teaching in the school; and of the portion which does, a part will insist that the religious teaching shall take such and such a definite form, and another part will insist that it shall take other forms. In short, if our public school is to exist for the whole people, it must be made of such a character, in this respect, that it will not divide us into factions but unite us all about it. The moment we start out with the affirmation that our moral teaching in schools must rest upon religion—and I say this realizing to the full extent how vague that word "religion" is . . . and we may explain that word as carefully as we will, it will be practicably impossible to stand upon this platform, without very soon dividing ourselves into factions and warring with one another. The war will spring out of that which is deepest and strongest in us; and prudence warns us that we must keep off that ground. (NEA *Proceedings* 1886: 140)

Similar to NTA educators, Professor Stearns underscored the two "extreme" positions regarding religion and public education: the "secular" and the "sectarian." But unlike NTA leaders of years past, he did not argue for the middle position of a "common Christianity." Instead, Stearns contended that because the public schools were for all people, anything that divides them—perhaps especially religion, which is "deepest and strongest in us"— must simply be excluded (Nord 1995: 74). "Common Christianity" apparently was no longer common enough. The earlier hypothetical voices outside of the NEA arguing for a secularized public education had now in fact joined the debate within the association. Because religion is divisive, they claimed, it must be kept out of public schools. In addition, secular morality was affirmed to be superior to and more basic than religion. Therefore, secular education was actually more beneficial for instilling morality in students than education based in religion.

Certain NTA educators who had promoted a nonsectarian, common Protestantism for public schools in the late 1850s and 1860s, and who still held leadership positions within the association, now came to support the new secular NEA advocates in their plea to end religious instruction in public schools. For instance, James Pyle Wickersham—1876 NEA vice president, original NCE member, and 1882 NCE vice president—agreed with the educational secularizers that since public schools were for all children, religion must be removed. In 1881, Wickersham stated that "because the public schools are 'common schools,' open to all . . . it has been found expedient either to confine religious instruction to the brief and simple exercises to which no one objects, or to dispense with them altogether" (NEA *Proceedings* 1881: 98). Although Wickersham entertained the idea that a religion agreeable to all might work in the public schools, later in his address he declared that he had become persuaded that a plurality of religious convictions meant the secular position was the proper one for public schooling: "[Public schools] have changed because the times have forced changes upon them—changed to suit the complex demands of modern society, with its multiplied sects and varied religious opinions. In circumstances like the present, public education must either be in good degree secular, or it must be abandoned. Schools organized as our fathers organized them could not last a day" (98). This was quite a change from Wickersham's earlier position in the NTA, as noted above, when he stressed the utmost importance of teachers and schools inculcating the "holy religion" of common Protestantism "revealed in the Bible and exemplified in Jesus of Nazareth" (NTA *Proceedings* 1866: 607–8).

Of all former NTA members, Emerson Elbridge White was best positioned to resist the NEA's growing call to separate religious teaching from public education. White was an original and regular member of the NCE, serving the council for twenty-one consecutive years. He was also NCE secretary in 1882, NCE vice president in 1883, NCE president in 1884 and 1885, and NEA vice president in 1882. Moreover, White was second only to Harris in the number of career NEA convention lectures delivered, giving ninety-two in total (Wesley 1957: 48, 284). But much like Wickersham, White abandoned his earlier advocacy of a "common Christianity" for public schools in the NTA. In 1886, White—Cincinnati's newly elected superintendent of public schools—again referred, as he had at the 1869 NTA convention, to the two "extreme" positions regarding religion and public schools in his address, "Moral Training in the Public School." But his solution to this problem seventeen years later was to "thin out" religion, moving closer and closer to secular education:

> The truths which we have considered clearly indicate that there is a *practical mean* between these two extreme views. They show that what is needed to give efficiency to moral training in school is not formal religious instruction so much as the quickening of the conscience and the influencing of the will by the wise use of religious motives and sanctions. . . . I share Mr. Huxley's serious perplexity in seeing how the needed measure of religious influence in our schools can be secured without the presence of a Bible; and yet, to this end, its formal and stated reading may not be essential, since there are other ways in which its vitalizing truths may be brought home to the conscience and the life. . . . At least three avenues are open for the introduction of religious ideas and sanctions into all our schools. These are sacred song, the literature of Christendom, and, best of all, faithful and fearless Christian teachers, the living epistles of the Truth. (NEA *Proceedings* 1886: 137–38; italics in original)

And in response to the arguments of Professor Stearns regarding his paper "Moral Training in the Public School," White attenuated religion even more: "[My address] did not even assume that the teaching of religion should have a place in the schools at all. . . . [We] do want recognition of God and humble obedience to his will. . . . [But] I do not set up any definitions of God. The whole paper is away from it . . ." (148). White had nearly entirely flattened religion. Little substance was left that might belong in public schools. This was the same Emerson Elbridge White who challenged Judge Richard Stockton Field in 1869 when he heard him advocate the exclusion of Bible reading in public schools; the same White who fervently called for "common Christianity" rooted in God's Word for the public schools (see NTA *Proceedings* 1869: 718, 720–21). White seemed to be following the trend of moral instruction divorced from explicit religious contexts (e.g., see Jorgenson 1987).

RESISTANCE TO SECULARIZED PUBLIC SCHOOLING

The movement to secularize public education within the NEA did not advance without resistance. The Unitarian minister Amory Dwight Mayo spearheaded the charge against the new secularizing activists of the association. Mayo, much like his Unitarian educational predecessor Horace Mann, whom he deeply revered, and other NTA educators of years past, ardently battled back to have "common Christianity" taught in public schools. As he did in his 1872 NEA address, Mayo argued in 1880 that moral teaching for public schools was to be religiously based: "For all public and private purposes the moral training and discipline required in common schools is an instruction in and application of the simple Christian morality . . . [a]

code of Christian morals, the soul of the Sermon on the Mount, the Ten Commandments, the Lord's prayer, the law of love, and the golden rule . . . the morality of Christendom, of the gospel of Christ" (NEA *Proceedings* 1880: 9–10). As with NTA educators of the late 1850s and 1860s, it was inconceivable to Mayo that such a noble common expression of religion could be removed from public schools. He equated the "banishment of religion and morals and the Bible from the school-room" with "exhausting the oxygen from the atmosphere" (NEA *Proceedings* 1876: 65). And much like the NTA leaders, Mayo was confident that his view would prevail:

> If "Secularism in schools" means that a little squad of people who believe in nothing that anybody else calls religion shall have the power to forbid the United States of America teaching school and enforcing Christian morality and to brush the Holy Bible, of all books on earth, from the teacher's desk, it will not be accepted. Surely, . . . this National Association of teachers with no uncertain voice, should demand that the national school shall forever be kept the training school of the loftiest type of American character for American youth. (NEA *Proceedings* 1876: 27)

According to Mayo, there were good reasons why secularism would "not be accepted." For one, he thought that arguments against religious instruction in public schools were fallacious. Mayo asserted, for example, in response to the claim that religion inevitably gives rise to divisiveness, "Religious and moral instruction have always been a source of distraction in national schools; let the American people cut the knot by putting out all that anybody chooses to call religious instruction. The theory was specious, as are all wholesale ways of disposing of a public inconvenience" (NEA *Proceedings* 1880: 7). But other prominent members of the association, such as Stearns and Wickersham, did not find this theory specious. As previously mentioned, both argued that religious instruction ought to be "put out" of public schooling precisely for the reason that it generates discordance. Mayo also believed that secularism would "not be accepted" because it lacked political strength. He stated,

> The city of Cincinnati was selected as the place most thoroughly exasperated against the Papal program and, therefore, the fit theatre for the inauguration of the new secularism. After a long and bitter struggle, the theory was placed in school regulations of that city. But, there, the movement came to halt, and, with the exception of a few cities exasperated by the operations of the priesthood, the new secularism has found tardy favor. (NEA *Proceedings* 1880: 7)

Mayo was referring to the "Cincinnati Bible War," in which he was directly involved. Regarding the NEA, however, Mayo was again missing the mark, on at least two counts. First, this "new secularism" was indeed spreading in the association. Second, its spread was not, as Mayo suggests, due to Roman

Catholic influence. Rather, powerful NEA elites desiring an end to religious instruction in public schools were behind secularism's diffusion in the association. But Mayo could do little beyond asserting himself vocally to challenge the NEA secularizers, as he never occupied leadership positions in the association. Mayo was never elected to the NCE, nor as president, vice president, or secretary of the NEA.

An influential member of the association who joined Mayo in protesting the growing call to secularize public education was the committed Northern Baptist Zalmon Richards. Richards had been a prominent NTA member, and he continued to occupy leadership positions in the NEA, holding membership in the NCE for twelve consecutive years (1885–1897) and serving as NEA vice president in 1886. Richards was also a frequent lecturer in the association, giving more than twenty-five in his career (Wesley 1957: 48). He voiced hostility to the increasing secular nature of public education in his 1888 address, "The Relation of Industrial to Intellectual and Moral Training in Our Public Schools":

> [By] slow degrees, the religious and moral element of . . . [our fathers'] system, so wisely devised at first, because they were loyal to both church and state, has been disappearing from our public schools to such an extent that by many very little importance seems to be attached to the moral and religious character of our teachers, or of the instruction given in our schools. . . . Such a state of things reflects no honor on us, and bodes no good to our boasted Christian country—and it should exist no longer. In the name of all that is good we must *protest* against the growing neglect and almost total disregard of religious or moral instruction and qualifications on the part of our teachers. . . . The moral condition of child-nature should receive the highest consideration and attention. No system of education which ignores the religious nature of the child is worthy of recognition for a moment. (NEA *Proceedings* 1888: 564–65; my italics)

Richards continued to voice opposition to the banishment of religion from public schools in a response to an 1890 paper on the subject of state school systems:

> The hue-and-cry of our Catholic friends about what they have seen fit—unwisely, I think—to stigmatize as "our Godless schools"; their determination to organize parochial schools and force their children into them, because, as they say, the moral and religious characters of the children in our public schools are neglected, demands the immediate attention of all true educators. While I do not sympathize with their wholesale aspersion of our public schools, I am forced to acknowledge, after much careful observation and study, that there is too much truth in these complaints; that the thousands of defalcations, swindlings, breaches of trust, forgeries, and stealings, to say nothing about burglaries, show most unmistakably that there is, somewhere, a terrible deficiency in the moral training of our youth. Need we wonder at

this state of things, and at these complaints, when we look at these facts: that in some of our most highly lauded schools the subjects of "instruction in manners and morals" and "the reading of the Bible" have been stricken from their course of instruction? . . . [We] must meet and overcome it, or it will meet and overcome us! (NEA *Proceedings* 1890: 446)

But, as we have seen, many of Richards's former NTA colleagues then holding positions of power in the NEA—such as James Pyle Wickersham and Emerson Elbridge White—did not join him in the attempt to "overcome" the mounting secularization of public education in the association. As a result, secularization was, as Richards warned, on its way to "overcoming" the NEA's position regarding religious instruction in public schools.

THE CHANCE FOR A LIBERAL PROTESTANT/LIBERAL CATHOLIC ALLIANCE

In the Netherlands during this same era, orthodox Protestant Reformed groups and Roman Catholics put their historical animus aside, and formed a political alliance that enabled them to thwart liberal secularist attempts to drive out religious schooling (Monsma and Soper 1997: 55–62). In the United States at this time, the forming of such an alliance was unlikely, since liberal and orthodox Protestants had joined forces to counter Roman Catholic attacks on public education and efforts to obtain public monies for their parochial schools (Jorgenson 1987; Glenn 1988; Nord 1995; McClellan 1999). Although many Protestants assumed Catholics were monolithically against public education, this was not true, at least among the American Catholic hierarchy.[10] Conservative Catholic elites did strongly disdain public schools, but liberal Catholics of the hierarchy were much less hostile, even friendly in a sense to these schools (Cross 1958; Vinyard 1998; Fraser 1999). Consequently, the possibility seemed to exist for liberal Catholic elites and some of their liberal Protestant counterparts to join forces to combat the educational secularizers. For a time, this possibility took form in the NEA, as a number of prominent liberal Catholic leaders actively participated in the association.

At the 1889 NEA annual convention, for example, Cardinal James Gibbons of Baltimore, Maryland, delivered a paper, "Should Americans Educate Their Children in Denominational Schools?" on his view of the schooling situation in America. Cardinal Gibbons expressed concerns similar to those of Mayo, Richards, and other past NTA educators. As he asserted in this paper,

[It] is not enough for children to have a secular education; they must receive a religious training. . . . Our youth cherish the hope of one day becoming citizens of heaven, as well as of this land; and as they cannot be good citizens of this country without studying and observing its laws, neither can they become

citizens of heaven unless they know and practice the laws of God. . . . The religious and the secular education of our children cannot be divorced from
each other without inflicting a fatal wound upon the soul. . . . The only
efficient way to preserve the blessings of civil freedom within legitimate
bounds, is to inculcate on the mind of youth whilst at school the virtues of
truth, justice, honesty, temperance, self-denial, and those other fundamental
duties comprised in Christian code of morals. (NEA *Proceedings* 1889: 111–13)

Nevertheless, Cardinal Gibbons's proposed solution differed from the ideas
of Mayo, Richards, and other previous educators of the NTA. Gibbons
stated, "The combination of religious and secular education is easily accomplished in denominational schools" (NEA *Proceedings* 1889: 113). But,
unlike the NEA secular advocates pushing for religion's removal from public schools, Gibbons was ambivalent about the place of religious teaching in
public schools: "To what extent religion may be taught in the public schools
without infringing the rights and wounding the conscience of some of the
pupils is a grave problem beset with difficulties, and very hard to be solved,
inasmuch as those schools are usually attended by children belonging to the
various Christian denominations, by Jews also, and even by those who profess no religion whatever" (113). Cardinal Gibbons acknowledged that the
plurality of religious positions posed a problem for teaching religion in
public schools, but he did not conclude, like the secularizers, that the solution was to expunge religious teaching from schools. Rather, he advocated
effort to keep religion in public schools and public support for denominational schools: "[Children] should as far as possible breathe every day a
healthy religious atmosphere in [public] schools in which not only is their
mind enlightened, but the seeds of faith, piety and sound morality are
nourished and invigorated. This would be effected if the denominational
system, such as obtains in Canada, were applied in our public schools"
(113). Taken at face value, such statements suggested that Mayo, Richards,
and other NEA Protestant educators desiring religious instruction to remain in public education had a potential supporter in Cardinal Gibbons.

During the 1890 NEA convention meeting, Archbishop John Ireland of
Minnesota—according to conservative Catholic elites, the most infamous
of the liberal Catholic leaders—made even stronger statements supporting
the public school system than his good friend Cardinal Gibbons. In "State
Schools and Parish Schools—Is Union Between Them Impossible?" Archbishop Ireland asserted before the General Session of the association that
he was "a friend and the advocate of the state school" (NEA *Proceedings*
1890: 179). But, he continued,

In the circumstances of the present time I uphold the parish school. I do sincerely wish that the need of it did not exist. I would have all schools for the
children of the people state schools. . . . I repeat my regret that there is the

necessity for . . . [the parish school's] existence. In behalf of the state school I call upon my fellow Americans to aid in the removal of this necessity. (NEA *Proceedings* 1890: 179–80)

Still, Ireland was presently opposed to the public schools because of their growing secular character. Similar to Richards and Cardinal Gibbons, he explained,

> There is dissatisfaction with the state school, as at present organized. The state school, it is said, tends to the elimination of religion from the minds and hearts of the youth of the country. This is my grievance against the state school of to-day. . . . Do not say that the state school teaches morals. Christians demand religion. Morals, without the positive principles of religion giving them root and sap, do not exist. (NEA *Proceedings* 1890: 181–82)

Archbishop Ireland made an explicit appeal for Protestants to join him in challenging the secularization of education:

> Believe me, my Protestant fellow-citizens, that I am absolutely sincere, when I now declare that I am speaking for the weal of Protestantism as well as for that of Catholicism. I am a Catholic, of course, to the tiniest fiber in my heart, unflinching and uncompromising in my faith. But God forbid that I desire to see in America, the ground which Protestantism occupies exposed to the chilling and devastating blast of unbelief. Let me be your ally in stemming the swelling tide of irreligion, the death-knell of Christian life and of Christian civilization, the fatal foe of souls and of country. . . . Let us be on guard. In our jealousies lest Protestants gain some advantage over Catholics, or Catholics over Protestants, we play into the hands of unbelievers and secularists. We have given over to them the school, the nursery of thought. Are we not securing to them the mastery of the future? (NEA *Proceedings* 1890: 181)

Nonetheless, Archbishop Ireland disagreed with Mayo, Richards, and certain other liberal Protestants that the best solution for this instruction was a nonsectarian, "common Christianity." Instead he said, "The state school is non-religious. It ignores religion. There is and there can be no positive religious teaching where the principle of non-sectarianism rules" (NEA *Proceedings* 1890: 181). He continued,

> Well-meaning and well-deserving men have proposed as a remedy in this instance, that there be taught in connection with the schools a common Christianity. This will not do. Catholics in fidelity to their principles cannot accept a common Christianity. What comes to them not bearing on its face the stamp of Catholicity, is Protestant in form and in implication, even if it be Catholic in substance. This being the settled fact, American Catholics will not, of course, inflict Catholicism upon non-Catholic or Protestant children, and with similar fair-mindedness American Protestants will not inflict Protestantism upon Catholic children. Some compromise becomes necessary. Is it

not ten thousand times better that we make the compromise rather than allow secularism to triumph and own the country? (183)

As the preceding statements by Mayo and Richards reveal, they were unwilling to make compromises in their position of "common Christianity" for public education. It never occurred to them, as it did to Archbishop Ireland, that compromising with Catholics might thwart the secularization of pubic education. Mayo and Richards could not, in good faith, compromise with Catholics, if this meant providing governmental funds to support Catholic doctrinal instruction, regardless of whether this instruction took place only before and after regular school hours.[11] They believed that such instruction was sectarian and, therefore, pernicious. Moreover, Mayo deeply resented Catholics, as he believed that they were greatly responsible for secularizing America's public schools (Jorgenson 1987). Although much less so than Mayo, Richards expressed dislike for Catholics as well, since, according to him, they had overstepped themselves in stigmatizing the public schools as "Godless" (see NEA *Proceedings* 1890: 446). Mayo and Richards were not the only members of the association, past or present, to resent Catholics. Anti-Catholicism had pervaded the NEA from its founding (Tyack and Hansot 1982; Jorgenson 1987). In 1889, Cardinal Gibbons and John J. Keane, liberal rector of Catholic University, experienced the association's anti-Catholicism firsthand. After they had presented their papers at the NEA annual convention, John Jay, a committed Episcopalian and stout defender of the public schools, blamed Catholics for destroying the religious character—by which he meant common Protestantism—of public schools. Among Jay's many comments was the following:

> [Roman Catholic policy has denounced] the common school as a Godless and heathenish institution that must be destroyed. . . . A preliminary and significant step in the war against our common-school system was taken a few years since, when it was complained of by some Roman Catholic ecclesiastics connected with the mission to America as being sectarian in its character, for the reason that there was allowed the reading of passages from the Holy Scriptures in a version deemed by their church as erroneous and heretical. (NEA *Proceedings* 1889: 152–53)

Mayo, Richards, Jay, and other Protestant allies of "common Christianity" for public schooling, it appeared, were sooner prepared to lose the struggle with educational secularists in the NEA than compromise with Catholics, despite the latter's openness to public education—which is exactly what happened. NEA Protestant educational leaders desiring religious instruction in public schools never attempted to cooperate with liberal Catholic elites, who continued to participate in the association for some time. Perhaps, a liberal Protestant/liberal Catholic elite alliance would have prevented the educational secularizers from advancing in the association. Perhaps not. At this moment in NEA history, political momentum was certainly moving against the liberal Protestant educational defenders of religious teaching in public schools. They had become outnumbered in an increasingly complex organization they could no longer dominate. In a short time, their old position and policy would be swept away by the educational secularizers.

THE NEW ORTHODOXY

In the 1890s, the NCE continued to have considerable political power within the NEA. Also during this time, the Department of Superintendence (DOS)—one of the association's original four departments—became an important political force (Schmid 1963; Seely 1963; Murphy 1990). Ever since 1870, the DOS had generally met during the annual meetings of the NEA, which took place in the summer. The DOS held another set of annual meetings apart from the association in the winter. Previously, the DOS had always made leadership decisions and policies during its summer meeting in the NEA. But all this changed in 1889, when the DOS decided to cease meeting altogether at the NEA's annual meetings, and meet only in the winter. These DOS meetings quickly gained prominence within the NEA and before long, became known as the winter meetings of the association. Membership in the DOS, like that of the NCE, was highly selective, consisting mainly of influential superintendents and other prestigious educational leaders. DOS members did not challenge NCE members for political control of the association, as they were largely one and the same. As it had in the past, membership in the DOS and the NCE continued to overlap substantially (Wesley 1957; Schmid 1963; Seely 1963). Given that the elites of the association were NCE and DOS members, they now had two mobilizing structures to help them secure political control of the NEA. For example, they frequently used NCE and DOS meetings to decide important NEA policies and positions (Schmid 1963: 53).

Among the NEA's leaders at this time, Nicholas Murray Butler—eminent professor of philosophy and education at Columbia University, who, though reared as a Presbyterian, now basically rejected all of Christianity's premises—was particularly influential (Schmid 1963; Seely 1963; Marrin 1976; Murphy 1990). Butler was a member of the NCE from 1891 to 1909, active participant in the DOS, vice president of the NEA in 1896, and president of the NEA in 1895. William Torrey Harris, who continued to be part of the association's ruling elite, recruited Butler to participate in the NEA. The two had been loyal and close friends since Butler's graduate school days in the early 1880s. Harris was a mentor of sorts to Butler, who eagerly pursued Hegelianism. Butler and Harris shared a strong mutual admiration, and they were political allies in the NEA. Harris greatly facilitated Butler's attainment of power in the NEA, serving as a "useful bridge" between the younger Butler, then in his thirties, and the association's older leaders (Seely 1963: 177). Like Harris, Butler held the view that religious teaching was not to be part of public schooling. In the NEA, Butler had a reputation for advocating that the family and church were the sole institutions responsible for religious instruction (see, for example, NEA *Proceedings* 1901: 80). As we shall see, Butler strongly promoted the association's policy in 1902 calling for the Bible to be studied like any other piece of human literature.

As he had done for the previous fifteen years in the NEA, Harris, now United States Commissioner of Education, continued vehemently to promote the banishment of religious teaching from public schools. In 1894, for example, Harris asserted, "My notion . . . [has] been that the trend of modern religious movements was towards the separation of the Church from State, and of all religious education from the people's schools. . . . To me, it seems necessary that the separation should be complete" (NEA *Proceedings* 1894: 482). In his address, "The Five Co-Ordinate Groups of Studies," Harris explained, "[Religion] is so different, in fact, that it furnishes a ground for removing the study of religion from the school in which the other branches are studied. The method of religion is essentially the method of authority" (NEA *Proceedings* 1896: 295). Similar examples of Harris's attack on religion in public schools could be multiplied, if space permitted.

Although Harris and prominent NEA member Charles DeGarmo disagreed about the educational merits of a movement called Herbartianism, very important in those days, they did agree that religion should not to be taught in public schools. Along with Charles and Frank McMurry, DeGarmo headed the Herbartian movement in the United States. This movement— founded on Johann Friedrich Herbart's (1776–1841) educational theory, which emphasized the development of moral character—achieved wide recognition in the field of American education from 1890 until 1910.[12] Herbartianism made a strong impression on DeGarmo during his graduate days at the University of Halle in Germany, where he earned a Ph.D. in 1886. At the 1892 NEA meeting in Saratoga Springs, New York, DeGarmo played a major role in organizing the Herbart Club. And in 1895, he was instrumental in expanding this club into the National Herbart Society for the Scientific Study of Teaching (name changed in 1902 to the National Society for the Scientific Study of Education). Although this society was never officially made a department of the NEA, it became closely identified with the association. A Herbartian sympathizer, Nicholas Murray Butler was among the society's first executive council members. Butler and DeGarmo previously had established a connection in the NEA, through their NCE membership, both having become council members in 1891. DeGarmo remained a member of the NCE for nine consecutive years and held many leadership positions in the council, serving as NCE secretary in 1894, NCE vice president in 1897, and NCE president in 1898. DeGarmo was also an active member of the DOS during this time, frequently giving lectures at their annual meetings.

As a Herbartian, DeGarmo greatly desired that public schools provide moral training. But this training, he argued, like other educational secularizers of the association, should not be based on religious doctrines or teachings (DeGarmo 1895). DeGarmo believed that since religious instruction was currently being expunged from public schools, this was even more reason for educators to employ a Herbartian approach to moral training, given that it did not depend on religious instruction (DeGarmo 1895: 54–56). This he made clear in many of his lectures before the NEA. For instance, in 1890, DeGarmo—then professor of psychology at the University of Illinois—argued in his paper "Relation of Instruction to Will-Training," presented to the General Sessions,

> This inquiry [into will-training] has assumed a new importance through the rise and development of the public school, for the old-time direct religious instruction has been, or in the nature of the case soon must be, banished from the school; while but few teachers have much faith in the bare dictation of moral maxims. American school-men must show that secular instruction can and will develop moral character, or the Catholic position with regard to religious instruction in school under the leadership of the church will become the only tenable one to the conscientious Protestant. Again, the conditions of modern life demand that we take a broader view of will-training than that accounted sufficient by our mediaeval ancestors. (NEA *Proceedings* 1890: 119)

DeGarmo was pushing for religion to be expelled from schools, arguing that secularism must itself be able to develop moral character. At the NEA's annual meeting the following year, in his address, "A Basis for Ethical Training in Elementary Schools," DeGarmo acknowledged that "the authoritative basis of moral instruction found in the Bible has been taken from the public schools, and nothing tangible has been devised to take its place" (NEA *Proceedings* 1891: 170). But unlike Mayo, Richards, and other past NTA educators who sought the authority of the Bible as a foundation for moral instruction, DeGarmo promoted a purely secular foundation for moral instruction. In the concluding section of that same address, he asserted, "The basis for ethical training in elementary education advocated in this paper is to be found, therefore, primarily in a graduated course in classical literature, beginning with fairy tales, myths, legends, and folklore, and culminating with the higher dramatic literature; and secondarily, in the concrete biographical and narrative elements of history" (177). This was a dramatic change from the explicit biblical principles that NTA educators had argued must be applied when teaching morals and ethics in public schools. In 1894, DeGarmo, then president of Swarthmore College, continued to assert the necessity of moral training devoid of religion in his NEA address before the General Sessions, "Moral Training Through the Common Branches":

> It takes a weary time for the world to acknowledge the validity of a new idea or to view old problems from new standpoints. The notion that specific religious doctrines and observances are the indispensable basis of any moral development worthy the name has been so long prevalent in the world, that it is difficult to get serious attention to other means, which, if not so good in some respects, have the advantage of being at free disposal. Teach morals through the inculcation of religious systems we cannot, but not a hand will be raised to stay us when we propose to utilize to their highest extent the value of the common studies as instruments of moral training. (NEA *Proceedings* 1894: 165–66)

In earlier years of the association, DeGarmo's secular view of moral instruction would have been severely challenged. But by the 1890s, this view of moral instruction had become the norm in the NEA. Although old NTA defenders of religious instruction in public schooling continued, as they had in the 1870s and 1880s, to hold some leadership positions in the association, they either persisted in "flattening out" religion or simply capitulated to the secular promoters of public education. During this era, for instance, Emerson Elbridge White remained a member of the association's controlling elite. Beyond White's continued service to the NCE, he was a long-standing and influential member of the DOS, and NEA vice president in 1892. Butler considered him one of the preeminent educators of the day. But just as he had done during NEA meetings in the 1880s, White failed to defend his earlier NTA promotion of "common Christianity" for public education. He stated in his 1893 address, "Religion in the School,"

> The important fact to be kept in mind is that religion is not the end of the school, but only a means to an end; that end, *effective moral training.* . . . It follows that neither the state nor the school is an agency for the advancement of religion as an end, but each may use religion for its own ends. . . . The public school cannot make religion its end, or religious instruction and worship its necessary function. It must leave to other agencies that religious instruction and training that looks to the salvation of the soul. . . . What is needed, that religion may serve the ends of the school, is not the formal teaching of the Bible, or the catechism, or other technical religious instruction; not formal religious services or worship, but the wise and reverent use of those common religious sanctions and motives which quicken the conscience and enforce moral obligation. (NEA *Proceedings* 1893: 296–97, 299; italics in original)

According to White, religion was appropriate in public schooling when it instrumentally supported morality. Again, this was a very different defense of religion in public schools from that argued in earlier decades of the association, when NTA educators claimed that religion was a valued *end.*

Other important members of the NEA, who previously advocated religious instruction for public schooling, entirely capitulated to the claims of the association's secular advocates during the 1890s. Although less prominent in the association than White, Zalmon Richards was still an influential member of the NEA, holding membership in both the NCE and DOS until the late 1890s. Contrary to his resistance to the association's educational secularizers in the 1880s, Richards now acquiesced. In his 1892 lecture, "Moral Training in Elementary Schools," Richards stated,

> In the first place, all sound educators agree that a certain amount of what may be called "secular education" ought to be acquired by every child. We may assume, also, that much the largest portion of all respectable people desire to have their children carefully trained in all the moral virtues, as a necessary preparation for good citizenship. And we may assume that they would prefer to have this moral training given during the school period, while receiving their secular training; for the most effectual moral and intellectual training is always given in the days of childhood and youth. This is the period also for giving the most effectual religious training. But on account of the numerous conflicting and antagonistic views of religion entertained, both by religious and non-religious people, no one system of *religious instruction* can be required in a free public school supported by common taxation. . . . As the prejudices and inconsistencies of people cannot be easily overcome, we must meet them by providing a public school system for all our youth, in which the secular branches, combined with a good training in moral virtues, shall be faithfully taught and exemplified. This is the kind of public school education which we must have. (NEA *Proceedings* 1892: 318; italics in original)

However, Richards was not entirely happy about this. In that same address, he lamented,

> It is a latter day notion that pure morality—or, if you please, sound religious instruction—is to be ruled out of our free elementary schools. Within the memory of some of us, in some parts of the country, the first step in the examination of a common school teacher was the presentation of a well-vouched certificate of a good moral character. . . . But in these days of boasted improvement and enlightenment, we have become so refined and reformed, that in some places the Bible, prayer, and even "instruction in morals" have been expurgated from the school curriculum. What is stranger and more alarming than all, the moral and religious qualifications of teachers are so far ignored that no preliminary test of moral and of religious fitness for teaching is required. (NEA *Proceedings* 1892: 320–21)

Even the Unitarian minister Amory Dwight Mayo, who once had strongly advocated a "common Christianity" for public education in the association as if demanded by God, joined the capitulation, stating in 1898,

> Finally, the American people, in the development of the American common school, have solved what has been called the religious question. . . . The edu-

cational public of our country has solved this distracting question by showing that the new education in its American form—thru its fundamental idea of human nature, as revealed in the child; its expansive ideal of the possibilities of human culture; its spirit of benevolent discipline; its natural method of instruction; its invitation of woman to every opportunity as student, teacher, and administrator in the common school; and in its broad and profound conception of the manhood and womanhood essential to good American citizenship—is, in fact, the last and highest incarnation and organization of the absolute religion taught and lived by the world's great Teacher, as far as it relates to the entire realm of American public affairs. And this idea, never so completely apprehended and applied as in our own country, will be one of our most important contributions to the long-delayed, but inevitable and final, Christianization of Christendom. (NEA *Proceedings* 1898: 227–28)

Unlike Mayo's past commentary in the NEA, he no longer believed that promoting a "common Christianity" for public schooling was the "Christianization of Christendom." For Mayo in 1898, the new "Christianization" of public education was culture, progress, and citizenship (Herberg 1961). This was Mayo's last speech in the association; he died in 1907, and Zalmon Richards had died in 1899. Even had these educators lived, it appeared that they would only have added to the call in the NEA to secularize public education, as they had given up their defense of an explicit religious influence in public schooling. Emerson Elbridge White, one of the controlling members of the NEA and former NTA member, had died as well in 1902. But again, his continued involvement in the association would have posed little threat to the educational secularizers. White had long before given in to the ruling elite secularizers of the NEA, diluting, almost entirely, the religious context of public schooling.

At the turn of the century, the educational secularizers' position regarding the proper place of religion in public schooling was made official organizational policy. Without dissent, the association approved the following in its "Declaration of Principles":

It is apparent that familiarity with the English Bible as a masterpiece of literature is rapidly decreasing among the pupils in our schools. This is a direct result of a conception which regards the Bible as a theological book merely, and thereby leads to its exclusion from the schools of some states as a subject of reading and study. We hope for such a change of public sentiment in this regard as will permit and encourage the reading and study of the English Bible, as a literary work of the highest and purest type, side by side with the poetry and prose which it has inspired and in large part formed. (NEA *Proceedings* 1902: 27)

This is a striking difference from the NTA's 1869 policy regarding the place of the Bible in public schooling. The devotional reading of the Bible was gone. The Bible was to be read and studied merely as a piece of literature, like any other. It no longer had primacy, a belief the controlling leaders of the association were quick to clarify and defend in 1902. Before the General Sessions, Nicholas Murray Butler, now president of Columbia University, stated in his address, "Some Pressing Problems,"

> In what I am going to say about the English Bible I want to make myself clearly understood. I want to make this fundamental distinction clear: I am not now talking about instruction in religion, important as many conceive that to be. I am not talking now about instruction in theology, important as some feel that to be. I am merely laying down this thesis: the neglect of the English Bible incapacitates the rising generation to read and appreciate the masterpieces of English literature, from Chaucer to Browning, and it strikes out of their consciousness one element, and for centuries the controlling element, in the production of your civilization and mine. I hold this to be true, even if there were not one person living in the United States who subscribed to a single article of any Christian creed. I am speaking now about literature and life, not about religion and theology. . . . I want once more to make it perfectly clear that I am not talking about religious teaching in school; that I am not talking about theological influence in education; but that I am protesting against sacrificing the knowledge of our civilization to theological differences. I beg that I may be understood distinctly on this point. (NEA *Proceedings* 1902: 72, 79)

If there was any ambiguity about what the ruling elite of the association desired regarding religion and public education, they continued to make it clear. Harris stated, "The principle of religious instruction is authority; that of secular instruction is demonstration and verification. It is obvious that these two principles should not be brought into the same school, but separated as widely as possible" (NEA *Proceedings* 1903: 353). James Mickleborough Greenwood—superintendent of public schools for forty years (1874–1914) in Kansas City, Missouri; long-standing and prominent DOS member; NCE member for twenty-six consecutive years (1885–1911); NEA treasurer from 1891 to 1894; NEA president in 1898; and NEA vice president in 1899—backed Harris in a discussion of Harris's paper:

> I believe that the position of entire separation of church and state is the correct one, because if we admit that the state and church in this country should be united, with our freedom of speech and liberality of opinions, it would be only a short time until great complications would arise. There are so many great religions in the world, it would be only a short time until we should have to get a council to decide what particular religion should be selected for our people to practice. . . . In my opinion it is sound statesmanship to maintain with firmness and decision the plan of our forefathers outlined in all matters of religion. Let the parents look well to the religious instruction of their children in Bible history, and teach them those lessons which they ought to know. Bible literature is of a higher spiritual order than the literature of Greece and Rome, and more of it should be put in our reading books. With the proper teaching at home, in the church, and in the Sunday School, supplemented by

the great truths of morality inculcated in our public schools by our teachers, the religious training of the young will not suffer. (NEA *Proceedings* 1903: 362)

Like Harris and Butler, Greenwood argued that public schools were not to engage in religious instruction, which was the responsibility of the family and the church. Not all NEA members were satisfied, however. John W. Carr—then superintendent of public schools in Anderson, Indiana, and a fairly influential NEA member, belonging to both the NCE and DOS—responded to Harris's address with this remark:

I had hoped, Mr. President, that Dr. Harris would have given the weight of his great name to help on what I believe is destined to be the greatest movement in education of the last half-century—the introduction of a workable form of religious instruction in the public schools. But if I understand his paper right—and I hope I do not—he would completely divorce the public schools from all religious instruction. (NEA *Proceedings* 1903: 361)

But Carr *had* understood Harris's paper correctly. Tellingly, Carr himself eventually joined his fellow NEA ruling elite in marginalizing religion's role in public schooling (see NEA *Proceedings* 1908: 449–52, 1911: 351–77). Some other less prominent members of the association continued to desire that religious teaching be part of public schools, but they were never to see their dreams realized. Harris, Butler, Greenwood, and the other leaders of the NEA had decided that only secular education was the proper answer to the question of religious instruction in public schools. By the turn of the century, the educational secularizers in the association had won. Only vestiges of the old religious system remained. In 1903, for instance, the Hon. Patrick A. Collins, mayor of Boston, remarked at the NEA convention held in his city, "I have noticed tonight, and I think it must have passed under the observation of everybody on the platform, that Dr. [Rev. Edward Everett] Hale tested whether you, engaged in secular employment and in imparting secular education, have still a grip upon the spiritual. But that was settled when you joined in repeating Our Lord's prayer" (NEA *Proceedings* 1903: 42). The NEA still engaged in such token expressions of religion. But the important fact was that the NEA, as Collins observed, truly was "engaged in secular employment and in imparting secular education."

CONCLUSION

In the decades to come, the NEA would undergo numerous transformations in organizational leadership and structure (Selle 1932; Wesley 1957; Schmid 1963; Murphy 1990). Nonetheless, the association's new position and policy regarding religion and public education remained: normative religion was not to be taught in public schools. Gone were the days when leaders of the association strongly promoted the teaching of "common

Christianity"—including devotional Bible reading—for public schooling. The leading organization in American public education had become a leading advocate for secularizing public education.

NOTES

For excellent research assistance on various aspects of this project, I thank Amy Bailes, Karen Benjamin Guzzo, Brandon Canady, Brandy Farrar, Heather Kane-O'Donovan, Venecia Rock, and Michael Straight. I thank David Baker, Pamela Barnhouse Walters, John Bukowczyk, John Evans, Paul Kemeny, Kelly Moore, David Sikkink, Christian Smith, George Thomas, and Michael Young for helpful comments on earlier drafts of this chapter.

1. The National Education Association (NEA) was not adopted as the official title of this organization until 1906. Before then, it was known as the National Teachers' Association (1857–1869) and the National Educational Association (1870–1905). Throughout the remainder of this section, I refer to both of these organizations as the NEA.

2. Fenner 1945, Schmid 1963, and Butler 1987 omit any mention of religion in their historical accounts of the NEA, while Wesley 1957 treats religion as only tangential to the association's history.

3. Female educators did not become eligible for full membership in the NTA until 1866. Before that time, women were granted honorary membership in the NTA and could have their essays read at the association's annual meetings by any male member.

4. I use the terms *popular education, public education, public schools,* and *common schools* interchangeably.

5. For brevity, I use NTA *Proceedings* to refer to *Proceedings of the National Teachers' Association.*

6. Both the American Normal Association and the National Association of School Superintendents met in conjunction with the NTA in 1866, 1868, and 1869. Prior to their merger, there was substantial overlap in membership between these two organizations and the NTA. Topics discussed in both the National Association of School Superintendents and the American Normal Association reveal nothing conspicuously negative or positive regarding the relationship between religion and public education. It does not appear, then, that members of these organizations, who were not already NTA members, had a substantial impact on the NEA's view on religious teaching in public schools in the years to come. The Central College Association did not meet in connection with the NTA in 1868. Although information on the Central College Association is harder to identify, it seems that many of this organization's members remained when it was reorganized as the NEA's Department of Higher Education in 1870.

7. In addition to the departments mentioned above, the NEA created the following departments in the 1870s and 1880s: Industrial Education (1875), National Council of Education (1880), Art Education (1883), Kindergarten Instruction (1884), Music Education (1884), and Secondary Education (1886).

8. For brevity, I use NEA *Proceedings* to refer to the *Journal of Proceedings and Addresses of the National Education Association.*

9. Dewey considered Harris a good friend and significant intellectual influence (e.g., see McCluskey 1958).

10. Evidence from certain locales indicates that a fair number of rank-and-file Catholic parents sent their children to public schools during this time period (for references, see Cross 1958: 266–67, nn. 43–46).

11. As a possible solution to Protestant and Catholic differences regarding the issue of schooling, Ireland referred to the Poughkeepsie Plan during his NEA address (for details of this plan, see Jorgenson 1987: 115).

12. For more information on Johann Friedrich Herbart, Herbartianism, and the Herbartian movement in America, see DeGarmo 1895, McMurry 1946, and Dunkel 1970.

REFERENCES

Boylan, Anne E. 1988. *Sunday School.* New Haven, CT: Yale University Press.

Buck, Solon, ed. 1933. *William Watts Folwell.* Minneapolis: University of Minnesota Press.

Butler, Susan. 1987. *The National Education Association.* Washington, DC: National Education Association.

Chaves, Mark. 1993. "Intraorganizational Power and Internal Secularization in Protestant Denominations." *American Journal of Sociology* 99: 1–48.

———. 1994. "Secularization as Declining Religious Authority." *Social Forces* 72: 749–74.

———. 1997. "Secularization: A Luhmannian Reflection." *Soziale Systeme* 3: 437–48.

Cross, Robert. 1958. *The Emergence of Liberal Catholicism in America.* Cambridge, MA: Harvard University Press.

Curti, Merle. 1959. *The Social Ideals of American Educators.* Paterson, NJ: Pageant.

DeGarmo, Charles. 1895. *Herbart and the Herbartians.* New York: Charles Scribner's Sons.

Dewey, John. 1934. *A Common Faith.* New Haven, CT: Yale University Press.

Dobbelaere, Karel. 1981. "Secularization: A Multi-Dimensional Concept." *Current Sociology* 29: 1–216.

Dunkel, Harold B. 1970. *Herbart and Herbartianism.* Chicago: University of Chicago Press.

Fenner, Mildred. 1945. *NEA History.* Washington, DC: National Education Association.

Fraser, James W. 1999. *Between Church and State.* New York: St. Martin's Press.

Glenn, Charles L. 1988. *The Myth of the Common School.* Amherst, MA: University of Massachusetts Press.

Herberg, Will. 1961. "Religion and Education in America." In *Religious Perspectives in American Culture,* ed. James Ward Smith and A. Leland Jamison. Princeton, NJ: Princeton University Press.

Jorgenson, Lloyd. 1987. *The State and the Non-Public School.* Columbia, MO: University of Missouri Press.

Kurzman, Charles. 1998. "Organizational Opportunity and Social Movement Mobilization: A Comparative Analysis of Four Religious Movements." *Mobilization* 3: 23–49.

Marrin, Albert. 1976. *Nicholas Murray Butler*. Boston, MA: Twayne Pub.

Marsden, George. 1994. *The Soul of the American University*. New York: Oxford University Press.

Mattingly, Paul. 1975. *The Classless Profession*. New York: New York University Press.

McAdam, Doug; John D. McCarthy; and Mayer N. Zald. 1996. "Introduction: Opportunities, Mobilizing Structures, and Framing Processes: Toward a Synthetic, Comparative Perspective on Social Movements." In *Comparative Perspectives on Social Movements*, ed. D. McAdam, J. D. McCarthy, and M. N. Zald. New York: Cambridge.

McCarthy, John D. 1996. "Constraints and Opportunities in Adopting, Adapting, and Inventing." In *Comparative Perspectives on Social Movements*, ed. D. McAdam, J. D. McCarthy, and M. N. Zald. New York: Cambridge.

McClellan, B. Edward. 1999. *Moral Education in America*. New York: Teachers College Press, Columbia University.

McCluskey, Neil. 1958. *Public Schools and Moral Education*. New York: Columbia University Press.

McMurry, Dorothy. 1946. *Herbartian Contributions to History Instruction in American Elementary Schools*. New York: Teachers College Press, Columbia University.

Michaelsen, Robert. 1970. *Piety in the Public School*. New York: Macmillan.

Monsma, Stephen, and J. Christopher Soper. 1997. *The Challenge of Pluralism*. Lanham, MD: Rowman and Littlefield.

Murphy, Marjorie. 1990. *Blackboard Unions*. Ithaca, NY: Cornell University Press.

National Educational Association. 1871–1920. *Journal of Proceedings and Addresses of the National Educational Association*. Washington, DC: National Education Association.

National Teachers' Association. 1857–1870. *Proceedings of the National Teachers' Association*. Syracuse, NY: C. W. Bardeen Publisher.

Nord, Warren. 1995. *Religion and American Education*. Chapel Hill: University of North Carolina Press.

Reuben, Julie. 1996. *The Making of the Modern University*. Chicago: University of Chicago Press.

Schmid, Ralph Dickerson. 1963. "A Study of the Organizational Structure of the National Education Association, 1884–1921." Dissertation Thesis, Education, Washington University, St. Louis, MO.

Seely, Gordon Medard. 1963. "Investigatory Committees of the National Education Association: A History of the Years 1892–1918." Dissertation Thesis, Education, Stanford University, Stanford, CA.

Selle, Erwin. 1932. *The Organization and Activities of the National Education Association*. New York: Teachers College Press, Columbia University.

Tyack, David. 1974. *The One Best System*. Cambridge, MA: Harvard University Press.

Tyack, David, and Elisabeth Hansot. 1982. *Managers of Virtue*. New York: Basic Books.

Vinyard, JoEllen McNergney. 1998. *For Faith and Fortune*. Urbana: University of Illinois Press.

Wesley, Edgar. 1957. *NEA*. New York: Harper.

4

The Positivist Attack on Baconian Science and Religious Knowledge in the 1870s

Eva Marie Garroutte

How did American science become secularized? This chapter examines how a group of late-nineteenth-century science activists advanced a religiously hostile positivist discourse intentionally to supplant the dominant, more religiously open, Baconian scientific practice. The analysis here focuses on the discursive struggles recorded in the scientific journals most responsible for the advance of positivism, *Popular Science Monthly* and *Scientific American,* both of which were widely read and influential among college professors, scientists, and other intellectuals of the day. What follows shows that the secularization of science was a strategic achievement of interested activists, not an automatic, natural process of differentiation or rationalization.

Before we begin, it is useful to note that nineteenth-century commentators on American intellectual life frequently referred to a pitched battle of "science" with "religion," or sometimes, "theology." The idea was immortalized in the title of an enormously influential book by Cornell University's Andrew Dickson White, *History of the Warfare of Science with Theology in Christendom,* a two-volume work which appeared in multiple languages and endless editions (the most recent in 1997). Nevertheless, contemporary scholars agree that it is misleading to describe historic debates in terms of such a tidy division. Late into the nineteenth century, many of the leading men of science were men of deep faith, while clergymen and theologians also pursued scientific research. The intellectual conflicts of the day can be described in broad terms as struggles between two competing visions of inquiry into the natural world. One, which we might call Baconianism, imagined a fundamentally *sacred science,* sustained by contributions from diverse practitioners. The other, which I will call positivism, assumed a strictly *secular science,* nurtured and presided over by a bounded set of professionals. I first examine the assumptions underpinning the Baconian model of science, and then consider the discursive assaults upon it by positivist activists, which eventually led to its collapse.

For the first half of the nineteenth century, Baconian philosophy undergirded much of scientific inquiry, and it continued to find expression in the public discourse of scientists, churchmen, and ordinary people for decades after. Its tenets—articulated by British philosophers such as John Herschel, William Whewell, and John Stuart Mill, and spread about America by such powerful scientific intellects as Yale's Benjamin Silliman and Harvard's Louis Agassiz—were simple to grasp and use. The primary goal of Baconian science was to accumulate facts through refined observation. In this, it asked would-be scientists to employ a methodology different from everyday action only in being somewhat more self-conscious and disciplined. They should observe closely and honestly, taking care not to speculate about what was not actually observable, and to avoid preconceived notions about what they would find. Such speculations and preconceptions Baconians condemned roundly with their worst pejorative: "hypotheses." This concept of science fit perfectly with the deeply democratic presuppositions of nineteenth-century American culture, since it implied that any rational, intelligent person could contribute to scientific inquiry.

After careful observation, this religion-friendly approach proposed, scientists could compare the facts and develop classification schemes. As one's taxonomical system grew more refined over time, it would reveal the laws relating the facts so ordered. Thus one could achieve the accumulation of universal truths from particular facts in a process labeled "induction." The laws discovered by induction were understood teleologically as descriptions of the mediate intervention of the divine in the world. Laws, for these thinkers, were the means by which God carried out His will for humanity. Scientists, by revealing these laws, participated in a holy calling.

This Baconian view troubled itself little with the possibility that the products of its method of inquiry might be inaccurate—that observations might be false or distorted. This complacency derived from its roots in the philosophy of Scottish Common Sense Realism. From here Baconians had derived the argument that God willed them to know the truths of nature because, in so doing, they would be inspired to reverence for its creator. Perceptual error could only derive from careless observation, and the single necessary precaution against this was greater meticulousness. Furthermore, this approach's truthful God did not merely guarantee the accuracy of their perceptions in principle, but also in practice. God provided that correct human perceptions should be accompanied by "compelling intuitions"— overwhelming impulses to believe in them, which reasonable people could not resist (Marsden 1982). For instance, as one Baconian contributor to *Popular Science Monthly* claimed, "The fundamental truths of morality and religion are self-evident, as well as those of geometry, and . . . the belief in a God and in a future state is as primitive, universal, and necessary, as the belief in the uniformity of Nature or the indestructibility of force" (Bixby 1876: 702).

But for all of its concern with sensory perceptions, the broad Baconian approach did not depend entirely upon sight, smell, touch, taste, and hearing for the facts it loved to assemble. Facts could also be received from God through revelation. These thinkers argued straightforwardly that nature constituted one set of facts and that the biblical scriptures constituted another, and that scientists and theologians could apply the very same scientific method to the study of both (Hovenkamp 1978: 11; Daniels 1968: 182). Charles Hodge, that consummate Baconian divine, stated the nature of the scriptures with utmost clarity: "The Bible is to the theologian what nature is to the man of science. It is his storehouse of facts" (1871: 10). The physical sciences were primarily responsible to the factual "revelation of God in the world" (that is, nature), whereas the "theological sciences" were responsible to the equally factual "revelation of God in the Word" (that is, the biblical text). According to the straightforward biblical literalism of the Baconians, the Bible spread out before its readers a chronicle of facts entirely comparable to those supplied in nature. For them, the two kinds of facts—natural and revealed—were complementary and absolutely noncontradictory. As the chancellor of New York University, a Presbyterian clergyman, put it, "Science and religion are at one. They both come from God and lead to God" (Crosby 1872: 182). A truly complete scientific theory would account for *all* the facts, assembled from *all* sources, natural and textual.

The dominance of the Baconian philosophy of science for so much of the nineteenth century carried important social consequences for different speakers. In particular, it set up an expectation that science should pass certain religious tests—that it should be held responsible for spiritual faithfulness. This science, far from producing morally neutral knowledge, was explicitly expected to "point from the law to the Law-Giver; from the effect to a cause; from the force to the living well" (Bixby 1876: 702). Scientists as individuals thus encountered certain expectations in relation to religious faith: good scientists had to be good Christians.

The infusion of religious elements into discourse about nature implied a relative disadvantage to many scientific speakers. "The claim that science was the 'handmaiden of theology' . . . was compromising to [their] professional aims. . . . The role forced scientists either to impose severe limitations upon themselves or to contrive special justifications when they approached controversial areas" (Daniels 1967: 163–64). By contrast, for clergymen, theologians, and others without particular training in scientific research, this philosophy opened up broad vistas of authoritative speech, offering them the occasion to comment extensively on scientific issues. This opportunity they accepted with alacrity, regularly addressing such topics as evolution and geologic history in sermons, scholarly articles, lectures, and public debates with scientists. This religion-friendly view also provided theologians and clergymen access to scientific discourse by providing a vehicle that enabled them to move freely between evidence and conclusions relevant to both physical and spiritual worlds. This not only meant that believers drew upon scientific findings for apologetic purposes; it also meant that they could challenge scientific claims on the grounds of spiritual deficiency. In such efforts, the charge of "speculativeness" proved a convenient weapon with which to deflate unorthodox scientists. Theories displeasing to religious interests could always be accused of an excess of hypothesis (Bozeman 1977: 156).

In short, what I am calling the Baconian philosophy set up an extremely permeable boundary between discourses. "Science" was an activity of worship, and "religion" the product of reasoning, empirical observation, and verification. Users of religious symbols enjoyed legitimate access to discussions about nature, while scientific speakers were prevented from securing exclusive authority in those discussions.

THE POSITIVIST ATTACK

Important changes were afoot by the 1870s, and there occurred a noticeable shift in scientists' public discourse. Baconianism had certainly encountered doubts before the 1870s. A number of the men who would become known as the century's great scientific minds had begun quietly shrugging off its assumptions at least two decades earlier. But at the time, their intellectual defections were generally matters of private conclusion that they were not eager to air publicly. It was not until the 1870s, with its greater political opportunities for dissenting intellectuals, that anti-religious scientific thinkers directly confronted Baconianism (Daniels 1967). In that decade, a set of ambitious, secularist scientists and science popularizers undertook a broad positivist attack on this model of science.

One of the most important men at the center of this movement was Edward L. Youmans, a friend and American apostle of Herbert Spencer. He persuaded William Henry Appleton, of D. Appleton and Company Publishers, to underwrite the publication of *Popular Science Monthly* and to publish a series of books by Spencer, Darwin, Huxley, and other evolutionists and positivists. Youmans then used this publishing enterprise to promote the most earnest advocates of naturalism, positivism, and evolution, both American and European. These included John Tyndall, a British physicist devoted to "spreading the gospel of naturalism" at home and in America through writing and speaking tours; Thomas Huxley, famous agnostic and anti-religious evolutionist; Andrew D. White, president of Cornell University; and many others (Boller 1969; Roberts 1988; Leverette 1965). *Popular*

Science Monthly's remarkably large circulation of eleven thousand copies per month in 1874 (Mott 1938: 499) helped make it "one of the major sources of popular scientific influence in the late nineteenth century" (Walker 1956: ii).

Another publication that shaped ideas about science in important ways was *Scientific American*. Founded in New York City in 1845 by New England inventor Rufus Porter, this weekly newspaper strongly reflected its creator's interest in new technologies. Nevertheless, within a few years, *Scientific American* also began to report on developments in the sciences, and shared an interest with *Popular Science Monthly* in treating issues regarding the nature of scientific inquiry. *Scientific American* was well-known to men such as Thomas Edison and Samuel Morse, to whom it provided advice on patent law, enhancing its reputation in the process. By the Civil War era, it enjoyed a weekly circulation of forty thousand copies (Post 1979: 79–80). While *Scientific American* was less intellectually ambitious than *Popular Science Monthly*, both publications were "intended for audiences attentive to science" rather than for a mass audience (LaFollette 1990: 24; Whalen and Tobin 1980: 199). It was vital that the positivist activists influence this group of scientifically literate individuals, since it included many of those who exercised control over universities and the scientific thinking and research that occurred there, along with opportunities for funding and publication.

The motivation for the anti-religious attack of the 1870s is apparent. One of the central requirements of professionalization is that a group of actors must succeed in drawing clear boundaries between those who have the authority to speak on a certain subject and those who do not (Abbott 1988). This creation of boundaries by scientists was precisely the circumstance for which Baconianism did not allow. It simply distributed the authority to speak about science too broadly to allow for full professionalization. In order to establish an autonomous space in which they could speak about any subject and draw any conclusion, without challenges based on religious values and assumptions, professionalizing scientists needed openly to abrogate all treaties with the religion-friendly view. The antagonistic frame of mind with which activist positivists approached this purpose is evident, for example, in this quotation from Andrew White's series of articles in *Popular Science Monthly*. Here, he declares war against all religious "intrusions" into science:

> In all modern history, interference with science in the supposed interest of religion, no matter how conscientious such interference may have been, has resulted in the direst evils both to religion and science, and invariably. And, on the other hand, all untrammeled scientific investigation, no matter how dangerous to religion some of its stages may have seemed, for the time, to be, has invariably resulted in the highest good of religion and of science. I say "invariably." I mean exactly that. It is a rule to which history shows not one exception. (1876: 385)

A staff writer for *Scientific American* likewise proclaimed the secularizing scientists' clear intention to subjugate speakers who grounded their claims in religious authority: "Science, by experience made conscious of her superiority, has lifted up her head, and in place of being the handmaid of theology, and being judged by theologians, has placed herself in position to judge the teachings of theology, and to decide which are true and which are erroneous" (Staff 1872: 151). The grounds under the two models of science were not gradually shifting. An evolutionary process of differentiation was not underway. Rather, interest-driven positivist activists were mobilizing to overthrow a model of inquiry that stood in the way of their achieving full professional autonomy and authority.

Elsewhere (Garroutte 1993), I have elaborated the idea that positivists defeated the Baconians primarily by a process of discursive *colonization*—that is, a process by which one discourse compromises the symbols and assumptions of another discourse, explaining them in foreign terms. Colonization does not require a straightforward confrontation between specific, demonstrable claims generated by different claimants. It operates, instead, by shifting the grounds of argumentation, by attacking the deep structures of discourse. This makes colonization an extremely subtle process, and also an extremely powerful one. It is so subtle that speakers may not even realize that it is occurring, and so powerful that a targeted discourse simply appears suddenly to collapse, to be replaced with another that is "obviously" superior in its capacity to "make sense of" the world.

In this earlier work, I examined in detail the complex, discursive interactions that led to the colonization of Baconian discourse. Anti-religious scientists slowly created a new vocabulary for discussing natural events and objects, and challenged implicit (yet vital) religion-friendly assumptions about the relationships that could occur in the natural world. They also replaced Baconian *generative structures*—my name for the underlying textual formulas, or "plot templates," that allow for the creation of a large number of specific claims.

I have shown that the new terminology, assumptions, and generative structures, once inserted into discussions about the nature of scientific inquiry, implied very different criteria for the evaluation of claims than Baconians had assumed. They also reassigned intellectual property rights, radically expanding the domain in which positivist scientists could legitimately speak, and relentlessly contracting the domain in which others could legitimately speak. In the end, such discursive strategies allowed positivist activists to proffer themselves not only as the only relevant scientific "experts," but also as the only capable judges of what qualified as "true religion." (This turned out, in their hands, to be a "progressive" religion that made peace with secular science by completely subordinating itself to it.) Such colonization strategies even allowed positivists to argue that science had advanced so far as to be capable itself of fulfilling the vestiges of spiritual functions that remained after religion's demolition. They suggested, for example, that science could foster proper ethical and moral concerns and rightly order human relationships, an activity previously considered a religious task.

In short, my previous, more detailed treatment of the positivist colonization of Baconian discourse shows it to have been a complex and consequential process. It occurred on many fronts, but in this brief chapter I explore only one strategy of the anti-religious scientists' broad and intense attack. This was to dispute assumptions about the nature of *texts* and the nature of *knowledge*. Like the other strategies for the colonization of religion-friendly scientific discourse in the 1870s, the positivist re-envisioning of these key concepts helped to destroy the credibility of their Baconian opponents in the eyes of much of the attentive public.

The First Positivist Attack on Language

The positivist attack strategy upon which I focus here involved, first, a radical re-envisioning of assumptions about the nature of language. In particular, it opened a rift between language and the realities it described. Baconians had frequently referred to practitioners of "theological science" as primarily responsible to "the revelation of God in the Word" and to natural scientists as primarily responsible to the "revelation of God in the world." They rested upon the sacred language recorded in the scriptural text as the source of their authority to speak on scientific matters. These words constituted a set of facts exactly comparable to those available through the observation of nature, and just as reliable. As Baconian theologian J. S. Lamar writes in *Popular Science Monthly,* the scriptures can "speak . . . in a voice as certain and unmistakable as the language of nature heard in the experiments and observations of science." Language is "regulated by laws as fixed as any in nature." The dependability of scriptural texts is especially well developed, Lamar adds, given that the Bible was "made by the unerring hand of God," who had "written [it] for the purpose of *making known* those things which are necessary to our enjoyment here and our salvation hereafter" (Lamar 1860: 176, 87, 193, 90).

By the 1870s, however, positivist activists writing in *Popular Science Monthly* and *Scientific American* began explicitly to separate language from the facts it conveyed. These popular periodicals were not the original source of the new ideas about language. Congregational clergyman Horace Bushnell, for instance, had much earlier expressed the idea that language—more particularly language about religious truths—was always inadequate to the task of representation, and in 1850 he had very nearly been tried for heresy for his views. But by the 1870s, the scientific periodicals analyzed here played a key role in broadcasting the once clearly heterodox conception of language and giving it increased currency among the general public.

An article by a staff writer for *Scientific American* illustrates the derision newly directed at language and at texts. In it, he condemns "the so-called theologian who, neglecting the study of God's own handiwork, confines himself to the discussion of the old obscure literary traditions" (Staff 1872: 151). A piece by Frederick A. P. Barnard, president of Columbia College, develops a similar theme at greater length. Complaining that the problem with the modern education system is that the typical student is "bidden to mind his book and not to look out of the window," he discloses the superiority of natural observation to book learning:

> Is it not evident that Nature herself . . . is a better guide to the study of her own phenomena than all the training of our schools? . . . Is it not because the ample page which she spreads out before the learner is written all over, not with words, but with substantial realities? . . . [O]ur earliest teachings must be things and not words. . . . [T]he knowledge of visible things should be made to precede the study of the artificial structure of language. (1873: 697, 696)

Words here are something clearly different and separate from the "visible things" and "substantial realities" that the scientist observes. Language *itself* is not a fact, as it was for Baconians. Instead, language can only *convey* facts. There can be no guarantee, moreover, that it accomplishes this task reliably.

Consequences of the First Positivist Attack

Once the religiously hostile scientists had opened a chasm between the word and the world, Baconian speakers lost the prerogative of literalism when drawing upon the biblical text. Literalism presupposes a perfect communion of facts and perceivers—an immediate relationship undistorted by potentially intrusive influences. But now language had been re-envisioned as just such an influence. The language of the scriptural text only more or less adequately *carried* truths; it did not *embody* them. The literal facts might still lurk behind the narratives that contained them, but determining what they were could be no straightforward process. Religious persons might still sift for occult profundities through the haystacks of their texts, but the process now seemed hugely prone to error.

Various authors in *Popular Science Monthly* and *Scientific American* underscored the nonsensicality of biblical literalism with sneering commentary. British physicist John Tyndall, in commenting upon a colleague's insistence upon a literal interpretation of the miraculous nature of Christ's birth, death, and resurrection, goes so far as to declare it "blasphemous" (Tyndall 1875b: 132). And in an article penned only under his initials, one-time Anglican clergyman and Cambridge intellectual historian Leslie Stephen jeers that, although Darwin's theorizing might cause some of "the old literal interpretations of the Scriptures" to be abandoned, "after all they were in far too precarious a position already to be worth much lamentation." He acknowledges that, in the past, assertions contradictory to literalism have "flutter[ed] the dove-cotes of the church." He admits that they might still cause some anxiety "in remote country towns and small clerical coteries." Yet "most men have grown beyond [literalism and related beliefs] . . . and have found some broader basis for their hopes and aspirations" (1872: 188, 190, 191).

Even suggestions such as these left room for the possibility that important facts might be buried *somewhere* in Scripture, and that these might be available for excavation. But professionalizing secularizers did not rest content to leave the religion-friendly scientists even this shaky basis for authoritative speech. They argued that biblical texts were so far from factual documents that they were more adequately likened to an art form—particularly poetry. This argument appears in various statements. One example describes the Genesis account of creation as "merely a poetic rendering of the doctrine of [the earth's] . . . slow evolution" (Knight, quoted in Tyndall 1879: 267). Another asserts, "Religion is no more likely to leave the world because we have new views as to the mode in which the world began, than poetry to vanish as soon as we have ceased to believe in the historical accuracy of the account of the siege of Troy" (Stephens 1872: 191).

Such Bible-poetry parallels are significant, since poetry represents an art form definitionally impossible apart from language; it is constructed entirely out of language. The comparison, then, makes available the possibility that the meaning of religious texts is *exhausted* by language—that they are *nothing but* linguistic accomplishments. It suggests the secularized proposition that the Scriptural texts that served as the foundation for Baconian claims might have *no* necessary connection to any reality outside the text—that there may be no higher truth beyond the potentially misleading medium of language for even the diligent exegete to uncover. Biblical texts might imply no *necessary* factual referent at all.

Besides dealing a death-blow to Scriptural literalism, the positivist prizing apart of language and facts also deprived Baconians of one of their most useful tools—the one they had used to justify the right of ordinary people, with or without scientific training, to pass judgment on scientific claims: the "compelling intuition." Baconians had proposed that one recognized correct observations or ideas by their ability to *force* themselves upon perceivers. Because powerful ideas forced themselves on everyone equally, the wide distribution of ideas was evidence of their truth. As one Baconian letter to the editor of *Popular Science Monthly* (written by journalist and literary figure Parke Godwin) declared,

> There are certain broad, deep, ineradicable instincts of the human mind, which . . . are now become the inexpungible basis of all human credence and all human action. The convictions of the reality of Nature, of the independence of Mind, and of the being and authorship of God, in spite of every effort of Philosophy to get rid of them . . . always return as the final no less than the initial postulates of thought.

Such "ineradicable instincts," or compelling intuitions, were grounds for Baconian speakers to discredit scientific claims that they found offensive. As the same correspondent concluded, "Any scheme of the universe, therefore, which leaves any of them [the foregoing ideas] out, declares itself impotent. . . . Innumerable such schemes have gone before, and floated as bubbles for a while, but the first touch of these Realities broke them into thin air" (Godwin 1873: 109–110).

This reasoning had seemed convincing earlier in the century. But with the splitting apart of language and the world beyond it, secularizing scientists could advance a very different way of thinking about the source of beliefs that seemed to "compel" the consent of most people. For example, one positivist author takes on the issue of widely accepted religious claims in the following way. If such claims appear absolutely compelling to many people, he argues, it is *not* because they are true. Their pervasiveness, and the pervasiveness of religion in general, shows only that "[m]an possesses certain spiritual organs, whose function it is to produce religion." Here, the prevalence of belief does not reflect some characteristic of the "external" world of facts, to which language is no longer tightly joined. Rather, it reflects some shared characteristic of believers' *internal* worlds: "The inference . . . from the universality of any creed is not that it is true . . . but that it satisfies more or less completely the spiritual needs of its believers" (Stephens 1872: 191, 202).

Compelling intuitions were, in fact, so far discredited with the divorce of language from facts that *Popular Science Monthly* editor E. L. Youmans was able to turn the widespread acceptance of religious ideas into an argument *against* their truth. Referring particularly to the theory of a six-day creation, he writes, "How deep and tenacious was the old error is shown by the fact that . . . the traditional view is that which generally prevails among the multitude" (1874: 23).

Here, general agreement actually *diminishes* the credibility of a theory of cosmic origins: the consent of "the multitude" only reveals the belief to be an especially entrenched error. Scientific speakers could scarcely have moved farther from the Baconian assumption of the compelling intuition than this statement.

The Second Positivist Attack on Language

Another element of the anti-religious scientists' assault upon language, and therefore on the authority of claims based on texts, involved their explicit attention to hermeneutic issues. The older, religion-friendly view had typically adopted a blasé attitude toward questions of textual interpretation. The Scottish theologian Thomas Chalmers, for instance, had written that whereas new mathematical truths "can only be arrived at by the footsteps of a lengthened demonstration," the conviction of the truth of a statement received through revelation "may arise on the first moment of its utterance, as if in the light of an immediate manifestation." No interpretative processes, no thought-work at all, were required to appreciate the facts of scripture: they "are no sooner read than they are recognised of all men" (1849: 386). Similarly, J. S. Lamar had argued that the properly inductive study of biblical texts "leaves . . . [scriptural facts] free to speak their own clear and unbiased language" (1860: 37). For Baconians, the Scriptures presented an objective fact, and readers received it in much the same way that an apple drops into a shopping bag.

By contrast activist, secularizing writers in the 1870s urged recognition of the distinctly subjective processes impinging upon both the reception and production of religious texts. One expression of this pattern focused on the hermeneutic processes in which readers become entangled. Accordingly, an author offers an extended, practical example of the torturous difficulties of proper Scriptural interpretation. He points out that, in the past, people have read the Bible as a straightforward document, including passages such as "Suffer not a witch to live." The results were fearful, leading to the paradox that, "it has been the pious, the sincere, the believers in duty, those wishing to render a loving obedience to God's word, or what they thought was his word, who have in every age been the persecutors." Anticipating a protest, the author continues, "But you say that they were acting under a delusion. They mistook what was the word of God." Then, snapping shut the trap he had laid, he demands, "But how are they to know what is his word, if direct commands like the foregoing are not his?" (Boyd 1876: 230). The author leaves no room for a possible response to his query.

The demand for recognition of hermeneutic activity at the level of textual reception revealed that language was entangled with the necessary subjectivity of its human readers. But other secularizers argued that yet another level of subjectivity complicated the enterprise of interpreting the supposed facts of the scriptural text. Baconianism had entailed an assumption that God adapted the structure of *nature* to articulate with the structures of the human mind (so to guarantee that human intellect would easily be able to assimilate natural truths). Positivists now suggested, by contrast, that it was *revelation* that was necessarily so adapted to the mind. One contributor to

Popular Science Monthly revived a sentiment expressed by no less a scientific personage than Galileo to support his argument:

> "The Bible constantly requires interpretation to explain how very different the true sense of the words is from their apparent signification. . . . In truth, Holy Scripture . . . [is] the dictation of the Holy Ghost; . . . [nevertheless] it was fitting that, in the Scriptures, the language should be adapted to the people's understanding in many things where the appearance differs widely from the reality. . . . I therefore think it would be wise to forbid persons from using texts of Holy Scripture, and from forcing them, as it were, to support as true certain propositions in natural science, whereof the contrary may tomorrow be demonstrated by the senses or by the mathematical reasoning."
> (Galileo, quoted in Mezieres 1877: 389)

This is a remarkable passage in its affront to Baconian convictions about language. Scripture is confirmed as actual "dictation": words from God's mouth to human ears. Yet those words are slippery, elusive. They must not be understood to support particular conclusions about events in the real world. They only do so when "forced, as it were." They are unreliable because they are contaminated by subjectivity—but not, this time, with the subjectivity of their human interpreters. Instead, revealed texts here are contaminated by the subjectivity of *God,* who has not said exactly what He meant, but rather that which humans can grasp. In this construction of scriptural language, God sacrifices the letter of meaning to the spirit of communication, in accordance with personal goals. Like the examples above, this argument portrays language as a medium shot through with subjectivity—but this special case of religious language introduces the additional influence of a divine subjectivity, rather than a merely human one.

Consequences of the Second Positivist Attack

We may only adequately understand the import of the pronounced association of language with subjectivity by placing it within events occurring in American society in the nineteenth century. The mainstream of theology written before the Civil War is commonly described as rationalistic. Yet Baconianism also gave a positive evaluation of emotion, intuition, and subjectivity, which, like Scripture and nature, were considered sources of facts. The cultural climate changed markedly, however, as Americans passed through an unspeakably bloody war that deprived them of much of their earlier romantic idealism. "As American intellectuals sought to comprehend the suffering caused by the war, they began to interpret the carnage as a resounding negation of the early nineteenth century's 'feeble sentimentalities.' The 'charming sentiments' of the philanthropists died with the soldiers who fell at Shiloh, Antietam, and Gettysburg. . . . A vocabulary of toughness, realism, masculinity, and efficiency began to take hold" (Holifield 1983: 136). In an earlier era, when intuitions and emotions were valued as sources of facts, any linkage of language with these subjective processes might not have threatened its perceived dependability as a vehicle of objective fact. In the postwar context, however, when the Romantic movement had largely played itself out and when people had grown suspicious of subjectivity, this association linked language with an intellectual commodity whose stock was clearly falling.

The association of language with hermeneutic process also meant that language acquired a dangerous fecundity. It literally swelled with meanings. Biblical texts, asserted the secularizers, "are susceptible of a thousand different interpretations" and "are not so strictly limited in their significance as the phenomena of Nature." Thus, "natural effects brought under our eyes by the experience of our senses, or deduced from absolute demonstrations . . . can in no wise be called into question on the strength of scriptural texts" (Mezieres 1877: 389). How could one ever isolate a text's single and necessary signification, as the religion-friendly scientists had placidly supposed?

Some anti-religious contributors to our scientific periodicals went so far as to argue that language, far from being a dependable, docile instrument, actively *threatened* its readers with its uncontrollable ability to spawn meanings. Philosopher and chemist Charles Peirce, for example, suggests that language has an inherent tendency to *obscure* rather than elucidate facts. It can even impair the ability to think clearly. Remarking upon nations whose language is scanty, he observes, "far happier they than such as wallow helplessly in a rich mud of conceptions"—the inevitable outcome of an overly elaborated language. Such unfortunates will require the passage of generations to "overcome the disadvantage of an excessive wealth of language and its natural concomitant, a vast, unfathomable deep of ideas" (1878: 288).

Physicist John Tyndall also accuses words, in and of themselves, of interfering with clear thought. In a disparaging review of a book by the Rev. Mr. James Martineau, Tyndall observes that its linguistic "excesses . . . reach far beyond the reader, to their primal seat and source in Mr. Martineau's own mind; mixing together *there* things that ought to be kept apart; producing vagueness where precision is the one thing needful; poetic fervor where we require judicial calm; and practical unfairness where the strictest justice ought to be . . . observed." For this positivist author, language injures the ability to think lucidly. It conduces to infelicitous mixings and blurrings, to inequities, to improper mental process. Martineau, reproaches Tyndall, leaves his listeners "lost in an iridescent cloud of words" (Tyndall 1875b: 135, 137), or in what he elsewhere calls "the interior haze and soft penumbral borders, which the theologians love" (Tyndall 1875a: 140).

Finally, a staff writer for *Scientific American* points out that it was a fascination with the literary that led to Don Quixote's storied difficulties: "The Don lived in his [library], and forgot for a time the world outside; he became a believer in written authorities, whose statements he had no means of verifying; he passed his existence amidst a waste of words, and lost the use of his own perceptions; and thus . . . he is wisely represented by the satirist as an egregious madman" (Staff 1871: 216). Given the demand for interpretation, the many possible meanings that swell within language can scarcely be pinned down or limited. A quoted admission from the dean of Canterbury concedes the problem, painfully acknowledging a sentiment that became increasingly common toward the end of the nineteenth century: "Possibly . . . in our exegesis of Scripture, we have arrived only at partial truth; and do not distinguish with sufficient accuracy between what is certainly revealed and what is nothing more than a possible explanation of the divine word" (Staff 1874: 503). Scriptural revelation invites confusions of meaning because language may lead to a multitude of possible interpretations, some of them flawed. Language, it seems, chronically underdetermines meaning. Although texts undoubtedly mean *something,* the secularizing scientists argued, it is no longer possible, given the hermeneutical problem, to say with certainty *what* they mean. The knowledge that positivist science produces, by contrast, is obvious, certain, and universal.

THE DISPOSSESSION OF RELIGION-FRIENDLY SCIENCE

The final outcomes of the secularizing attacks were far-reaching. Perhaps most important, Baconians lost access to the facts they had once so un-self-consciously claimed. Theologian Charles Hodge had once portrayed his fellow Baconians as almost literally enslaved to facts: "No sound minded man disputes any scientific fact. Religious men believe with Agassiz that facts are sacred. They are revelations from God. Christians sacrifice to them, when duly authenticated, their most cherished convictions" (1871: 131–32). By contrast, *Popular Science Monthly* and *Scientific American* urge such claimants to abandon the delusion that they possess facts. Their arguments, one positivist asserts, "are, in the estimation of science, absolutely futile. . . . There is nothing in natural religion [i.e., Baconian claims] to answer the demands of modern thought for actual proof" (Fowle 1872: 28, 34). Indeed, to cling to the notion that Scripture consists of factually accurate truths, one author accuses, is to be "unable to distinguish between the essence and the remotest accidental accompaniment of the faith." Such claims are unimportant to religion, anyway, he continues: "What interest can the highest part of our nature really take in a dispute as to whether certain facts did or did not occur many ages ago?" (Stephen 1872: 191). Religion should not even care, argue the secularizers, whether or not the claims its texts allege are objectively, literally true. To do so, they assert, is to misunderstand genuine piety.

Theology, deprived of its Baconian "facts" could no longer claim for itself the name of science. Positivists instead gave it the title of "pretended science" (Boyd 1876: 230), asserting that "theological science, so called, is a misnomer and a mockery" (Youmans 1877: 497). Theologians and other religious speakers, for their part, no longer had a spot on which to stand, from which they might deliver critiques of scientific findings. Accordingly, upon contemplating the question, "Are ministers fitted to discuss the bearing of modern science upon religion?" Harvard physicist John Trowbridge answers negatively. He concludes, instead, that "the most successful sermons seem . . . to be those in which argument and logic are laid aside, and simple faith and enthusiasm take their place" (1875: 739).

Lastly, proponents of religion-friendly science were stripped of their ability to direct scientific inquiry into certain channels, or toward specific conclusions. They had once taught that science had the "proper, moral end of enabling beneficent works" (Taylor 1989: 12). One sought truth because truth led to salvation, moral uplift, and the glory of God. But once the secularizers had accomplished their insurgent discursive work, strategically re-envisioning the nature of language, scientific truth no longer needed to justify itself in these ways. Any desirable perceived moral outcomes of scientific study were now accidental accompaniments. Even when such moral outcomes were absent, science could still be pursued by the autonomous experts who controlled it.

At the same time as positivists deprived Baconian speakers of their access to facts by a process of discursive colonization that problematized deep, underlying assumptions about the nature of language, they established their own claim on facts even more securely than before. They promised that their new, secular science would deliver direct, indubitable, universal knowledge. The process by which they legitimated this claim was as sophisticated and subtle as their attack on language, and its discussion is beyond the scope of this chapter (see Garroutte 1993). Nevertheless, the following example provides a sense of the arguments by which anti-religious scientists elevated the facts of nature over the Baconians' non-facts of language. Here, philosopher and chemist Charles Peirce makes an assertion that he argues is applicable to "all scientific work":

> Different minds may set out with the most antagonistic views, but the progress of investigation carries them by a force outside themselves to one and the same conclusion. This activity of thought by which we are carried, not where we wish, but to a foreordained goal, is like the operation of destiny. No modification of the point of view taken, no selection of other facts for study, no natural bent of mind even, can enable a man to escape the predestinate opinion. (1878: 300)

Such statements showed the facts of "the world" to be all that the Baconians' "Word" was not. The positivists' natural facts operate directly upon the observer, even in disregard of his desires. They act with the power of a co-ercive "external force." Unlike language, the stubborn facts of nature do not require interpretation, and therefore do not allow us to err in our con-struction of them. They can mean only one thing, and they will literally force observers into agreement about that meaning. As Peirce continues, "All the followers of science are fully persuaded that the processes of inves-tigation, if only pushed far enough, will give one certain solution to every question to which they can be applied" (299).

In and through all of their arguments, the anti-religious activists explic-itly called for the entire separation of the domains of "religion" and "sci-ence." Against all of the anxious Baconian "reconciliations" of these spheres of inquiry, positivists simply asserted that the two *could not* contradict. This was not because, as for earlier thinkers, science and religion composed a single, self-consistent whole, but because they were completely disjunct; they simply had nothing to say to each other. The obvious conclusion of this new vision of a positivist science was that scientists and their disciplines were not answerable to evaluative criteria of religious origin. To the contrary, in Tyndall's words, "all religious theories, schemes, and systems which em-brace notions of cosmogony or which otherwise reach into its domain must . . . submit to the control of science and relinquish all thought of control-ling it" (1874: 684).

CONCLUSION

Late-nineteenth-century scientific periodicals lay out before us fascinating discursive movements, revealing a confrontation between two models for the conduct of science. A group of science activists argued their vision, ad-vancing revolutionary ideas about the nature of language, among many other claims, to secure the considerable professional advantages associated with the positivist model. This philosophy intentionally restructured the re-sponsibilities of science and scientists by redistributing the authority to make claims. The redistribution excluded many people who had formerly justified their right to comment upon scientific activity by reference to the Christian scriptures.

By mobilizing wide agreement with the suggestion that possessors of revealed evidence alone either should not or could not seek to make de-pendable claims, the anti-religious activists undermined the ability of reli-gion-friendly scientists to formulate meaningful claims about nature— indeed, about anything that had to do with reality. The secularizers ensured that Christian institutions could not be the source of the authoritative rhetorical formulations guiding the culture. Religious speakers categori-cally, they successfully contended, should not concern themselves with facts, because they did not have access to them. Therefore the responsibility to speak the truth of this world did not devolve upon them. Baconian claims were deconstructed by secularizers as having no necessary truth value that could challenge those of positivist scientists.

Through such activist discursive moves to redefine the nature of facts, secularizing scientists colonized the discourse of their rivals by strategically attacking its supporting (and frequently subtle and implicit) assumptions. These scientists then made themselves the sole inheritors of the right to control the intellectual territory from which they had successfully displaced religious interests. In subsequent decades, their accomplishment in science reverberated through most other institutional fields in American society. It provided a model of allegedly objective and universal scientific knowledge, in which religion was irrelevant at best. The model served as a key authority in the secularization of American public life more broadly.

REFERENCES

Abbott, Andrew. 1988. *The System of Professions*. Chicago: University of Chicago Press.

Barnard, F. A. P. 1873. "Science and Our Educational System." *Popular Science Monthly* 2 (April): 695–98.

Bixby, J. T. 1876. "Science and Religion as Allies." *Popular Science Monthly* 9 (October): 690–702.

Boller, Paul. 1969. *American Thought in Transition*. Chicago: Rand McNally.

Boyd, D. 1876. "Science and the Logicians." Review of C. F. Deems, *Science and Religion*. *Popular Science Monthly* 9 (June): 224–31.

Bozeman, T. D. 1977. *Protestants in an Age of Science: The Baconian Ideal and Antebellum American Religious Thought*. Chapel Hill: University of North Carolina Press.

Chalmers, Thomas. 1849. *Institutes of Theology*. Vol. 1. Edinburgh: Sutherland and Knox.

Clifford, W. K. 1877. "The Ethics of Religion." *Popular Science Monthly Supplement* 1–6: 335–45.

Crosby, H. 1872. "Introduction to *The Great Problem*." Review of *The Great Problem: The Higher Ministry Of Nature Viewed in the Light of Modern Science; and as an Aid to Advanced Christian Philosophy*. *Popular Science Monthly* 2 (December): 182–83.

Daniels, G. 1967. "Process of Professionalization in American Science: The Emergent Period, 1820–1860." *Isis* 58: 151–66.

———. 1968. *American Science in the Age of Jackson*. New York: Columbia University Press.

Fowle, T. W. 1872. "Science and Immortality." *Popular Science Monthly* 1 (May): 26–40.

Garroutte, Eva Marie. 1993. "Language and Cultural Authority: Nineteenth-Century Science and the Colonization of Religious Discourse." Ph.D. diss. Department of Sociology. Princeton University.

Godwin, P. 1873. "Correspondence: The Sphere and Limits of Science." Letter to the editor. *Popular Science Monthly* 3 (May): 105–11.

Hodge, Charles. 1871. *Systematic Theology.* Vol. 1. New York: Charles Scribner's Sons.

Holifield, Brooks. 1983. *A History of Pastoral Care in America: From Salvation to Self-Realization.* Nashville, TN: Abingdon Press.

Hovenkamp, H. 1978. *Science and Religion in America, 1800–1860.* Philadelphia: University of Pennsylvania Press.

LaFollette, M. C. 1990. *Making Science Our Own: Public Images of Science, 1910–1955.* Chicago: University of Chicago Press.

Lamar, J. S. 1860. *The Organon of Scripture, or, the Inductive Method of Biblical Interpretation.* Philadelphia, PA: J. B. Lippincott.

Leverette, William. 1965. "E. L. Youmans's Crusade for Scientific Autonomy and Respectability." *American Quarterly* 17: 12–33.

Marsden, G. M. 1982. "Everyone One's Own Interpreter? The Bible, Science, and Authority in Mid-Nineteenth-Century America." In *The Bible in America,* ed. N. O. Hatch and M. A. Noll, 79–100. New York: Oxford University Press.

Mezieres, A. 1877. "The Trial of Galileo." *Popular Science Monthly* 10 (February): 385–402.

Mott, F. L. 1938. *A History of American Magazines, 1865–1885.* Vol. 3. Cambridge, MA: Harvard University Press.

Peirce, Charles. 1878. "Illustrations of the Logic of Science." *Popular Science Monthly* 12: 286–302.

Post, R. 1979. "Science, Public Policy, and Popular Precepts: Alexander Dallas Bache and Alfred Beach as Symbolic Adversaries." In *The Sciences in the American Context: New Perspectives,* ed. N. Reingold. Washington, DC: Smithsonian Institution Press.

Roberts, Jon. 1988. *Darwinism and the Divine in America.* Madison: University of Wisconsin Press.

Staff. 1871. "Scientific Education and Religion." *Scientific American* 24, no. 14: 216.

———. 1872. "Science and Theology." *Scientific American* 27, no. 10: 151.

———. 1874. "Literary Notices." Review of J. Le Conte, *Religion and Science. Popular Science Monthly* 4: 502–3.

Stephen, Leslie. 1872. "Darwinism and Divinity." *Popular Science Monthly* 1 (June): 188–202.

Taylor, C. (1989). *Sources of the Self: The Making of the Modern Identity.* Cambridge, MA: Harvard University Press.

Trowbridge, J. 1875. "Science from the Pulpit." *Popular Science Monthly* 6 (April): 734–39.

Tyndall, John. 1874. "Inaugural Address before the British Association." *Popular Science Monthly* 5: 652–86.

———. 1875a. "Reply to the Critics of the Belfast Address." *Popular Science Monthly* 6: 422–40.

———. 1875b. "Martineau and Materialism." *Popular Science Monthly* 8: 129–48.

———. 1879. "Virchow and Evolution." *Popular Science Monthly* 14: 266–90.

Walker, D. D. 1956. *The "Popular Science Monthly," 1872–1878: A Study in the Dissemination of Scientific Ideas in America.* Ph.D. diss. University of Minnesota.

Whalen, Matthew, and Mary Tobin. 1980. "Periodicals and the Popularization of Science in America, 1860–1910." *Journal of American Culture* 3, no. 1: 195–203.

White, Andrew Dickson. 1876. "The Warfare of Science." *Popular Science Monthly* 8: 385–409.

Youmans, E. L. 1874. "Herbert Spencer and the Doctrine of Evolution." *Popular Science Monthly* 6 (November): 20–48.

———. 1877. "The Latest Cases of Heresy." *Popular Science Monthly* 11 (August): 494–97.

5

Power, Ridicule, and the Destruction of Religious Moral Reform Politics in the 1920s

P. C. Kemeny

"In the great war now ended," explained W. H. P. Faunce, president of Brown University, "the most important results have been unintended." Faunce, speaking before the annual meeting of the New England Watch and Ward Society, held at the historic First Baptist Church of Boston in May of 1919, discerned two such unintended results. "We have learned," he said, "the great truth that effectiveness in war and in peace depends on physical fitness, and that physical fitness depends absolutely on character." In short, "private morality is a public concern." Americans had also realized that "the defense of character is as truly the concern of the Government . . . as the defense of property." Among the "great enemies" facing America's social order, Faunce believed, were "men who are willing to become rich on the license of others." In his estimation, New England was fortunate to have the Watch and Ward Society to combat such people. The Watch and Ward Society, as Frederick B. Allen, president of the society, expressed in his 1919 annual report, "does not fight the victims of temptation, but its promoters. Our enemy is commercialized vice" (New England Watch and Ward Society 1918–19: 26–27, 29, 18).[1]

Raymond Calkins, pastor of the prestigious First (Congregationalist) Church in Cambridge, promised in 1919 that the Watch and Ward Society would continue its effort to combat vice as long as "the public conscience of our New England communities" remained strong. Judging by the list of prominent citizens who supported the work of the society, the social conscience of the region appeared to be rather healthy. In fact, the leadership of the society was the Protestant establishment writ large. The fourteen-member board of directors, which supervised the daily operation of the organization, included such esteemed Bostonians as the physician William Norton Bullard, grandson of Harvard Divinity School Dean Andrews Norton and nephew of Harvard English professor Charles Eliot Norton, and Edward Cummings, Unitarian pastor of the prestigious South (Congregational) Church (and father of the poet e. e. cummings). The honorary positions of vice president were held by a nine-member board, a number of whom were Brahmins. Among those willing to lend the prestige of their name in support of the society's work were Charles W. Eliot, retired president of Harvard University; George A. Gordon, the prominent liberal Protestant theologian and pastor of the Old South Church; and William Lawrence, Protestant Episcopal Bishop of Massachusetts. The multimillionaire manufacturer Godfrey Lowell Cabot, a member of Boston's unofficial first family, served as both a director and the treasurer of the society. Financial support came from more than eight hundred contributors as well as from a $130,000 endowment fund. When President Faunce closed his speech with the solemn pledge that "the best citizens" of Connecticut would join those of Massachusetts "to face the powers of evil and say, 'They shall not pass,'" the Watch and Ward Society entered the 1920s with a heady optimism that it had the public's support in its efforts to make America a more moral nation (*AR* 1918–19: 21, 33).[2]

Writing in the *Harvard Graduates Magazine* in 1930, the novelist and editor Bernard De Voto opined that the very name of the Watch and Ward Society "is irresistibly funny" and its aims "are most of all comic." The only course of action for the "educated public of Boston" to take was "to laugh" at this "preposterous" organization (1930: 30–31). To Horace Kallen, the "New England conscience" was not the source of social responsibility but "repressions, intolerances and witch-burning" (1929: 290). The *Boston Herald* told the society to stop making the city look "ridiculous" in the eyes of the nation.[3] Instead of praising the organization, Ivy League educators, like Harvard history professor Samuel Eliot Morison, assailed it for engaging in "a crusade against intelligence."[4] Joseph Wood Krutch may have best expressed the modern temper when he wrote that people who engaged in moral reform "may be drawn from many classes—from the stupid, the humorless, the fanatical, and the prurient—but the one class from which they cannot be drawn is the class of decent and intelligent men" (1927: 163).

What had made Boston, as Kallen put it, "the laughing stock of the civilized world" was the fact that the "precious Watch and Ward Society," maintained "an *Index Expurgatorius*" that prevented the legal sale of works by such modern authors as Theodore Dreiser and D. H. Lawrence (1929: 290–91). Although Massachusetts had laws banning obscene literature that dated back to the early eighteenth century, the current law had its origins in an 1881 statute that the Watch and Ward Society helped write. The law forbade the importation, publishing, or distribution of books, pamphlets, ballads, pictures, figures, images, or any other printed material "containing obscene, indecent or impure language or manifestly tending to corrupt the morals of youths" (New England Society for the Suppression of Vice 1881). Massachusetts was just one of several states that passed antiobscenity laws following the 1873 federal Comstock Act that made it illegal to sell or distribute "obscene" images in literature and art, and also information regarding birth control or abortion through the mail. The Massachusetts state obscenity law was a critical institutional structure that helped empower the Watch and Ward Society as it exercised jurisdiction over literature in Boston. According to the law, a book could be found obscene based upon a single passage. Moreover, the law's definitions of the key terms *obscene* and *impure* were vague, and interpretation was thus left to the discretion of the Watch and Ward Society. A landmark 1909 State Supreme Court decision upheld the obscenity conviction, which was based on a 1908 Watch and Ward Society complaint, of Joseph E. Buckley for selling Elinor Glyn's *Three Weeks* (1907). The court defined obscenity as "offensive to morality or chastity, to be indecent and nasty," and "impure" as "language is offensive, impure and indecent when it manifestly tends to incite in the minds of people susceptible to such influences obscene thoughts, impure thoughts, and indecent thoughts" (*AR* 1908–9: 20). These two factors, which gave the society wide latitude in its efforts to suppress books it deemed obscene, became the focus of debate in the late 1920s and aroused the wrath of such cultural modernists as De Voto and Kallen.

The Watch and Ward Society also served as the region's unofficial censors, determining what was and was not acceptable reading material for bookstores to sell. After the prosecution of several booksellers for obscenity in 1915, Richard Fuller, owner of the Old Corner Bookstore in Boston, and a colleague met with the Watch and Ward Society to discuss how to protect booksellers from legal action. The formation of the Boston Booksellers Committee resulted from these discussions. It consisted of three members from the city's Bookseller Association, reportedly representing 90 percent of all Boston bookstores, and three from the society. If someone found a book offensive and issued a complaint to either the booksellers or the society, the committee reviewed the work. If the committee unanimously decided that the work violated the state's obscenity law, an "informal notice" would be sent out to all Massachusetts booksellers who would "quietly" withdraw the book or risk prosecution.[5] Since Boston's booksellers had, in Frederick Allen's estimation, a "tender conscience," not to mention a fear of economic reprisal, many works were pulled from the shelf (*AR* 1915–16: 32). To be sure, the Watch and Ward Society was not the only religious organization interested in suppressing "impure" literature. The fundamentalist Lord's Day Alliance, though most concerned with enforcing Blue Laws, supported the censorship of salacious material (Chase 1921). Likewise, William Cardinal O'Connell established vigilance committees in 1913 to safeguard Catholic youths from "indecent picture shows, vile books, papers, and gangs" and regularly warned parishioners against "unclean" books in the pages of the archdiocese periodical, the *Pilot* (O'Leary 1980: 233). However, it was not Boston fundamentalists or Catholics but a liberal Protestant moral reform organization, the Watch and Ward Society, that had the cultural authority to dictate (through the Booksellers Committee) what type of literature was available for public consumption. It also had a similar arrangement with the New England Magazine Sellers Association. While the society vowed never to "supplant" the police but "always to supplement" their work, the arrangement with the book and magazine sellers gave the organization the power to decide on behalf of all Boston citizens what type of literature was morally acceptable to read (*AR* 1923–24: 6). But by 1930, the Watch and Ward Society had lost this power.

The demise of the Watch and Ward Society's censorship of literature did not occur simply and voluntarily according to some self-evident, consensual political logic; it was the result of a secular revolution spilling over into popular culture. Significant changes in American culture throughout the 1920s provided new political opportunities for the emergence and mobilization of an anticensorship coalition of activists. An ideological antagonism toward Christianity, economic self-interests, and a commitment to civil liberties fueled in varying degrees this coalition of cultural modernists, avant-garde publishers, and civil libertarians. The coalition mobilized public sentiment against censorship politically by ridiculing the society and its members and legally through judicial action. As a result of these attacks, members of the society defected, further weakening the organization's cultural authority. Secular activists achieved a decisive victory when they successfully revised the state's obscenity laws in 1930.

Secularization, Mark Chaves (1994) argues, is best understood not as the decline of religion per se but as the declining scope of religious authority. Likewise, Karel Dobbelaere contends that at the societal level secularization refers to the process of differentiation whereby politics, education, science, and other institutions gain autonomy from the religious institutions of a society (Dobbelaere 1981: 49–87). The coalition of anticensorship activists took from the Watch and Ward Society the cultural authority to determine what literature was morally acceptable for people to read. While the intention to secularize varied within this coalition, the result of the its activism was the decline of a religious institution's cultural authority—secularization, in short. By situating religion and religious change in its concrete and institutional context, as Chaves argues, one can more fully account for the decline (or rise) in religion's social significance (1994: 750, 752). An analysis of the secularizing activists' effort to curtail the religiously inspired moral reformers of the Watch and Ward Society from this one particular dimension of civic life offers a window into a critical juncture in the history of secularization of American culture.

THE RATIONALE FOR CENSORSHIP OF "PERNICIOUS BOOKS"

Echoing the infamous words of Chief Justice Oliver Wendell Holmes's Supreme Court decision upholding the 1919 Espionage Act, Bliss Perry asserted in 1923 that "the public is now facing a 'clear and present danger' through unclean books." Perry's warning grew even more dire. "Many booklovers, neither prudish nor prurient in their tastes have been shocked and bewildered by certain English and American novels in the last two years." "In fact, no one whose professional work brings him into contact" with the contemporary publishing industry can be "ignorant" of this critical fact (1923: 4–5). Perry, who served as the editor of the *Atlantic Weekly* before he became an English professor at Harvard, was one of the leading "men of letters" of early twentieth-century America. Like other men of letters, such as Henry Van Dyke and William Dean Howells, he was an apostle of Victorian culture. For more than a generation these Victorians exercised authority over the leading periodicals, enjoyed connections with the major book publishers, and held prestigious chairs at major universities, though such appointments were secondary to their professional identities. By 1923, new developments in the literary world were well underway that were threatening their professional status as the custodians of American literature. Because of its favorable copyright laws and better means of transportation, New York had already supplanted Boston as the nation's leading city of letters. Prior to this, however, the emergence of the left-wing literary radicals, such as Van Wycks Brooks, and the right-wing New Humanists, such as Irving Babbitt, began to challenge the men of letters for authority over the world of high culture literature in the 1910s. Within the university, philologists and literary historians with Ph.D.s dominated the academic study of literature. Since literature was a source of cultural and symbolic capital, the men of letters had a vested interest in preserving their position of cultural authority (May 1959: 3–106; Shumway 1994: 25–60; Graff 1987: 55–97). So when the New England Watch and Ward Society invited Perry to address their annual meeting, held at the historic Old South Church on Copley Square, it gave him an excellent opportunity to assert his authority. Perry's lecture, entitled "Pernicious Books," provides a useful touchstone for unraveling the thicket of motives that bound together the Protestant establishment's rationale for censorship.

Perry discerned four different types of pernicious books. One "deals with sex-perversion" and another "deals with sex-obsession." A third type "turns to pathology, to Freudian psychology, [or] to pseudo-science" for inspiration. The final class identified "human behavior with animal behavior." Perhaps, Perry added, "the most truly pernicious of all books, the book, namely, that harps with cynical insistence upon the meaninglessness, the emptiness, the futility of life." Although every pernicious book "breeds its own specific varieties of mental and moral disorder," not every work, most notably those in the final category, was liable to legal action for violating obscenity laws (Perry 1923: 8–10).

While not every book might be legally "actionable," every artist, Perry believed, has to answer to a higher law. That higher law, "as invisible as gravitation and as inexorable," is "the eternal trinity of Truth, Goodness, and Beauty." The value of traditional literary culture, the belief in the certainty and universality of moral values, and the inevitability of progress, Henry May observes, comprised the credo of Victorian culture. This Neoplatonic trinity of truth, goodness, and beauty served as a standard by which literature could be judged. William Dean Howells's best-known book, *The Rise of Silas Lapham* (1885), for example, is a work of sober realism. Lapham is a modest Boston manufacturer whose prosperity parallels the postbellum industrial boom. Through circumstance and his own poor choices, he slips into corruption. However, his personal scruples intervene. Although his business and social standing collapse, his personal morality triumphs and he makes a valuable contribution to society's ethical economy (Perry 1923:11; May 1959: 30–51; Bradbury 1983: 1–19). Judged by this trinity, pernicious books were simply not good literature.

Pernicious books posed more than just a threat to the aesthetic sensitivities of Victorians. Certain books were noxious because they were thought to imperil the character of the reader. Brown University President Faunce, for instance, viewed threats to people's character as a matter of national security. Victorians viewed character as a set of eternal and fixed virtues, such as perseverance, honesty, respectability, conscientiousness, and self-control, that could be mastered and incorporated into the self (Coben 1991: 3–35). *Character* served as a code word that indicated the moral rectitude of a person or even a novel. While upper-class Victorians could pass on economic capital to their children, the middle class concerned itself with the cultural capital that character possessed. In America's nineteenth-century economy of scarcity, virtues like hard work, self-restraint, and faithfulness were considered valuable assets that could help individuals prosper. By the 1920s, however, the modern mass-consumer economy had supplanted the economy of scarcity, and the Victorian cult of character had been eclipsed by the ideal of "personality." The personality ideal was neither bound to an external authority nor limited to a list of external virtues to be acquired. Instead, the personality ideal became its own higher law and was considered to be an ongoing, dynamic process (Hunt 1999: 4, 121; Beisel 1997: 4–7, 162–63; Rodgers 1980: 7, 95, 100–107, 121, 125–26). One of the cardinal features of the new consumer culture, William Leach observes, was that individuals achieved self-fulfillment through the acquisition and consumption of consumer goods and self-pleasure (1993: 3–4).

Beneath these fears concerning the risk that pernicious literature posed to a reader's character lay certain convictions about the nature of culture and the consumption of cultural forms through reading. "Obscenity is clearly an infectious disease," William T. Sedgwick, a professor at Massachusetts Institute of Technology, insisted in an address to the Watch and Ward Society in 1916. "It can spread like wildfire under the right conditions and in combustible material, as in a boys' or girls' school, where it has spread more than once" (AR 1915–16: 37). To justify censorship, the Watch and Ward Society mobilized the quasi-scientific discourse of the social hygiene movement. For instance, in 1905, Edward Cummings said, "You do not hesitate to support the organizations which are trying to prevent the spread of the physical diseases which threaten the health of the community. This organization is trying to prevent the spread of diseases that prey, not simply upon the body, but upon the soul" (AR 1904–5: 36). Moreover, the medical establishment's knowledge of germ theory and disease provided the society with well-respected terms that could be employed to analyze the impact of literature on a person's character. Obscene literature was likened to an "infectious disease" (AR 1915–16: 37). Not surprisingly, the society called for a "moral quarantine" (AR 1905–6: 35). If the "character" of literature was either pure or pernicious, then the consumption of that cultural form, they believed, would have either a morally constructive or detrimental effect upon the reader. "Literary critics," Perry observed, "have a defective social sense if they dismiss as negligible the pathological consequences of books which they know to be morally unwholesome" for the reader (1923: 7).

The Watch and Ward Society's rationale for censorship also resonated with the ideas of influential criminologists, psychologists, and sociologists of the day. Perry might have disliked Freud's influence on contemporary literature, but the society showed little hesitation to invoke his work to substantiate their fears about the impact of reading upon a person. "If the New Psychology is true," the society reported in 1924, "that which affects the imagination deeply impresses the subconscious self and brings a 'trauma' to the spirit that it is not easy to heal. It gives rise to wishes that must be suppressed unless the home life is to be endangered. These suppressed wishes return and haunt life with an impure atmosphere" (AR 1923–24: 9). In the development of modern social thought, Ruth Leys contends that the "imitation-suggestion theory" of William James and of Gabriel Tarde "introduced a new approach to crime and delinquency by proposing that these were the product not of biological degeneration but of the appropriation or incorporation of deviant forms of behavior" (1993: 280; Parker 1997: 21–22). The social sciences gave warrant to the society's fears about the impact of pernicious literature upon the behavior of readers. For example, G. Stanley Hall, who was president of the organization in 1909–1910, cited a German study of forty thousand youth in a 1909 lecture that reportedly demonstrated that "license and vice" has a detrimental effect on the health of individuals (*AR* 1908–9: 22). This theory not only informed the landmark 1909 *Massachusetts Commonwealth v. Buckley* decision but continued to guide prosecutions of pernicious literature well into the 1920s. Therefore, the discoveries of the social sciences affirmed scientifically much of what the Watch and Ward Society had already believed, namely, that pernicious literature was dangerous because a reader might imitate it.

The final piece in the Watch and Ward Society's rationale for censorship consisted of several important theological convictions. To fully appreciate the significance of these theological beliefs, we must understand the Watch and Ward Society in its larger theological context. While its members often described their mission in militaristic terms, the Watch and Ward Society was not a fundamentalist organization. The society consisted largely of first- and second-generation liberal Protestants. Boston's liberal Congregationalists, Episcopalians, Methodists, and Unitarians looked down upon the fundamentalist battles taking place in the 1920s in the northern Baptist and Presbyterian churches as a rearguard action (Gordon 1925: 230–31). Boston liberals had had their controversies with conservatives a generation earlier. For example, when Trinity Church's celebrity preacher and a founder of the Watch and Ward Society Phillips Brooks won election as bishop of Massachusetts in 1891 over the objections of conservatives, it signaled the triumph of the Broad Church theology in the Episcopal Church (Hutchison 1976: 76–144). While liberal Protestants clearly stood on the sunnier side of the street when it came to views of human nature, they did not deny the reality of human sin. One of their leading theologians, George A. Gordon, the "pulpit prince" of Old South Church and a founder of the Watch and Ward Society, carefully balanced his liberal optimism about society's progress with moral realism. His view on human sin and social evil offers an insight into the Watch and Ward Society's theological rationale for censorship. In his *New Epoch for Faith* (1902), Gordon expressed great enthusiasm for society's progress. The slow but "universal movement from darkness to light," he contended, assures believers "that injustice and inhumanity are not here to stay. The moral evil of society is among things temporal." One key source obstructing the "speedy realization" of the Kingdom of God was personal evil. Gordon discerned three sources of personal evil: atavism, a "weakness of human reason," and the "perversity" of the human will. "The believer in human progress," Gordon concluded, "must reckon with the fact of wickedness" (1902: 17, 361, 36–41). Pernicious literature threatened to unleash an animalism and foster a perversity that would undermine character and ultimately delay the coming Kingdom of God.

As much as the Watch and Ward Society worried over pernicious literature's impact on individual character, the focus of the organization's mission was the institutional, not individual, expression of evil. This institutional focus was a direct result of their theological conviction about the nature of sin. According to Gordon, all three sources of human wickedness—brutality, ignorance, and perversity—had "invaded the institutional life of mankind" and gained "immense influence" through expression in custom, law, government, trade, society, politics, and even religion (Gordon 1902: 43). To be sure, the society hoped to regulate the conduct of individuals by overseeing the type of literature available. The object of the society, however, was to thwart the invasion of the evils of animalism, irrationalism, and perversity on an institutional level. There was a growing market for allegedly pernicious literature in America's consumer economy in the early twentieth century. In 1926, Oswald Garrison Villard reported that one "sex magazine" publisher made more than 8.8 million dollars in 1924 (1926: 395). Like a talismanic refrain, the leadership of the Watch and Ward Society repeatedly insisted that "[w]e attack the promoters of vice, not the victims of vice; corrupting agencies, not corrupted individuals. We concern ourselves with fighting vice as a business, not vice as a diversion; public immorality, not private immorality." To combat the "systemized evil," the Watch and Ward Society reasoned that "an equal organization of the forces of good" was necessary (AR 1914–15: 5, 21).

The Watch and Ward Society recognized that some critics viewed the organization as a group of self-appointed censors who threatened individual freedom. Perry responded to these charges in his 1923 address. Censorship, he contended, was justified because it guaranteed "the rights of others." An individual may hold whatever "private opinions he pleases," but the law will hold this person responsible. So just as seditious literature might incite overt acts against the government and therefore deserved suppression, Perry reasoned, "obscene words constitute a 'present injury' upon listeners and readers" and likewise deserved suppression. The accusation that the society functioned as an unofficial censor was a red herring to Perry. What these "writers and publishers of indecent books are really afraid of, is not inquisitors," Perry insisted, "but the law." No book "can possibly be suppressed in this country by any secret body of inquisitors. It is either suppressed in the open courtroom, by one's fellow citizens, or it is not suppressed at all." "That sound old doctrine is exactly what the Watch and Ward Society is following today. It believes in no censorship except that which one of its agents has called the *democratic* censorship of *law*." The law, he acknowledged, provided no "accurate test of what constitutes obscenity" and judiciously forbade expert testimony on the matter. The decision, he argued, was wisely "left to *ordinary citizens*" who made it "in the light of *common sense,* and by giving to the words of the book their ordinary meaning." No doubt Perry expected the prevailing views of "good literature," and its impact on character development, to inform conventional thinking on the matter (1923: 3, 12, my italics, 13).

Although Perry asserted that pernicious literature received a fair hearing in a court of law, not all banned books actually made it into an open courtroom. The society repeatedly insisted that its most effective work was done outside of public notice. "The effort is always to suppress these books quietly," explained the secretary in 1925, "so that they may not receive the notice and advertising which a public prosecution would bring with it" (*AR* 1924–25: 8). The very name of the organization—Watch and Ward—indicates the importance of this tactic. However, if booksellers continued to sell a banned work, they might receive a warning from an agent of the society. These agents, in tracking down pernicious literature and, more commonly, in following up leads about illegal gambling and illicit drugs, worked incognito. Given the nature of illicit business, they reasoned, "no uniformed officer" could secure the evidence necessary for a warrant or conviction. So it was necessary to employ "agents who may pass for average members of the public" (*AR* 1907–8: 6). Occasionally, the police even looked to the society for help. In 1924, for example, the Springfield police called upon the society to assist them in investigating illegal gambling (*AR* 1923–24: 13). When prosecution proved necessary as a "last resort," the organization enjoyed remarkable success. Of the 2,167 cases that went to trial between 1916 and 1925, more than 99 percent ended with convictions (*AR* 1915–16: 25; *AR* 1924–25: 9).

The society's commitment to censorship as a means of social reform was an expression of the mainline Protestant sense of its custodianship over American society. To Protestants like Faunce and Perry, private and public morality were inseparable. In fact, they believed that they were combating the partitioning of private religion and social ethics. Perry was certain that "the great public is with us" (1923: 15). Mainline Protestants presumed that most citizens shared their values and appreciated the work of the myriad of organizations and institutions that comprised the Protestant establishment. Nationally, the seven major denominations that made up the mainline Protestant establishment enjoyed cultural hegemony far disproportionate to their numbers (Hutchison 1989b: 4). In Boston, with its growing Catholic population and sizeable fundamentalist community, this cultural authority was likely even more disproportionate.

"To me the interesting part of our preventive work," explained society president Calkins in 1925, "has been the way in which the big business interests have come forward and accepted our leadership in this matter of suppressing obscenity" (*AR* 1924–25: 12). Besides their vested economic interest, some evidence suggests that the older established publishers and booksellers shared the society's opposition to certain types of modern literature. According to Perry, the "Boston booksellers, as high-minded a group of business men as any in this city, have shown their willingness to co-operate with any movement for decency" (1923: 15). Some of the more staid publishing firms refused to publish works that they considered pernicious.

The Watch and Ward Society conceived of pernicious literature as a "social problem" and therefore identified itself as one of many late-nineteenth-century voluntary societies that attempted to reform different troubling aspects of American culture. The society was founded in 1878 by a broad range of Boston ministers, educational leaders, and other prominent citizens. Besides several leading liberal Protestants, including Brooks, the Unitarian minister Edward Everett Hale, and Boston University president William F. Warren, the original call for the organizational meeting included the signatures of the pastor of the conservative Clarendon Street Baptist Church, A. J. Gordon, and the president of Boston College, the Jesuit Robert Fulton. Although the presence of Gordon and Fulton suggests an ecumenism remarkable for late-nineteenth-century Boston, the organization was dominated by liberal Protestants. There is no evidence that Fulton was ever involved in the society. Outside of Gordon's service as an honorary vice-president from 1878 until his death in 1895, conservatives do not appear to have been active in the society. Although the original impetus for the organization was the growing prevalence of pernicious books, periodicals, and picture postcards, over the years the organization's interest expanded to include gambling, illicit drugs, and "white slavery" (AR 1924–25: 6–8). Similar organizations existed in New York, Philadelphia, Baltimore, Cincinnati, Chicago, and San Francisco. These organizations were part of a larger, late-nineteenth-century movement of extralegal law enforcement agencies that attempted to reform municipal governments and to curb police malfeasance. The Society for the Prevention of Cruelty to Children, founded in 1872, is just one example (Gilfoyle 1994: 185–91). Other voluntary and professional organizations, such as the Women's Christian Temperance Union (WCTU), which established its own Department for the Suppression of Impure Literature in 1883, all supported censorship (Parker 1997: 5–6, 35–36). Protestant denominations also supported censorship. The Methodist Board of Temperance, Prohibition, and Moral Reform, for example, launched a national censorship campaign in 1925.[6] In Washington, DC, the International Reform Federation served as a lobbying organization for censorship and other moral reform causes (Crafts 1911). Thus the Watch and Ward Society was hardly alone in its censorship activities; it was part of a broad array of Protestant and Catholic church and parachurch organizations that advocated censorship.

The Watch and Ward Society's advocacy of censorship as a popular reform helps to situate the society within the larger context of the Social

Gospel movement. Although its concern with "pernicious literature" certainly makes it appear to be like late-nineteenth-century religious conservatives, the Watch and Ward Society was not concerned with evangelizing and reforming individuals but with combating the commercialization of vice on an institutional level. As the Episcopalian Clifford Gray Twombly put it in a 1924 address, "[T]he old way of simply trying to convert souls out of the corruption of the world is not enough to save America! *We must convert the conditions also which are ruining so many souls faster than we can save them*" (*AR* 1923–24: 26). While not all early-twentieth-century liberal Protestants espoused social Christianity and not all leaders of the Watch and Ward Society were advocates of the Social Gospel, the society's leadership did include a number of Social Gospelers and champions of other progressive causes. For example, Reverend Raymond Calkins, a Harvard graduate, was involved in numerous progressive causes, such as the Fellowship of Reconciliation. He also used his pen and pulpit at First Church, conveniently located near Harvard Square, to advocate a Social Gospel. In a sermon before the National Council of Congregational Churches in 1919, for instance, he urged the church to go beyond an "individualistic religion" and embrace Jesus' "social creed" of "Justice, democracy and brotherhood." The church, he argued, had to expand its "moral aims" beyond "dilettante" charities and address "the burning questions of sexual immorality, undoubted economic injustices, corporate dishonesty." The goal of the Watch and Ward Society, like the hundreds of other Protestant reform organizations, as Calkins put it, was to help the church "reach the source and springs of social currents and movements of our day and control and direct them toward the ultimate attainment of the Kingdom of God among men" (Calkins 1919: 4, 7, 13).

THE INTELLIGENTSIA AND
THE COLLAPSING WALL OF VICTORIAN CULTURE

Writers like Emerson, Hawthorne, Lowell, and Longfellow once made Boston "the undisputed literary capital of the United States." "But where is Boston now?" asked the writer and recent Harvard graduate, Charles Angoff, in 1925. "In literature," he believed, "it is as dead as the Hittite Empire." Angoff laid part of the blame on the "illiterate" population but most of it went to "the unceasing activity of that famous organization of smut hounds, the New England Watch and Ward Society." With boosters among Boston's editors and educators, "including no less a personage than Professor Bliss Perry," these "smellers see to it that Boston is kept in the gutter." Angoff found the absence of "a civilized minority" even more depressing. Boston had "a small Russian-Jewish intelligentzia [*sic*]," "a handful of advanced Rotarians," and a massive "horde" of "Irish-Catholic anthropoids" who "have no more interest in ideas than a guinea-pig has in Kant's *Critique of Pure Reason.*" Not surprisingly, Angoff concluded, Boston "lunges down-ward toward the cultural level of Port au Prince and Knoxville, Tenn" (An-goff 1925: 439–44).

As Angoff's diatribe against the Watch and Ward Society suggests, not everyone shared the Victorians' aspirations for "pure" literature. Angoff's vicious and racist attack was but one expression of a growing rebellion against Victorianism. Although many had been cheerfully laying dynamite in the hidden cracks of nineteenth-century culture long before 1914, as Henry F. May has observed, it took a world war in Europe to detonate the explosives that collapsed the walls of Victorian American culture (May 1959: ix). The war marked a crucial turning point, and the signs of rebellion were everywhere. "Both in literature and outside of it," wrote Helen McAfree in 1923, the war "created a precocious Younger Generation—too early ma-tured by the shock and prolonged tragedy, . . . [whose] work has met with severe criticism. 'It is morbid.'" And she adds, "To this, the Younger Gener-ation retorted: 'We have a right to be morbid. Life as we have seen it is macabre. Civilization isn't getting anywhere'" (McAfree 1923: 233–34).

"A phenomenon new to America," observed the critic Salwyn Schapiro in 1920, "is the growing sympathy among men and women of education with ideals and methods of the revolutionary proletariat." "What is taking place in America now—something with which Europe has long been familiar— is the formation of an intellectual *class,* revolutionary in tendency and bound together by a common antipathy for the present order of things." Ac-cording to Schapiro, they were rebelling against the "triumphant middle classes" who "imposed upon society their morals and ideas, as well as their political and economic systems" (Schapiro 1920: 820–21, 824; Coben 1991: 48–68). The very fact that they styled themselves an intelligentsia suggests that they set themselves against conventional beliefs and the ma-jority of American culture. While some fled for France in disgust, frustration produced activism in others. Harold Stearns's 1922 symposium, *Civilization in America,* for example, brought together thirty authors to "diagnose . . . our national disease," as one reviewer described it. In a sweeping review of all aspects of American culture, ranging from science to sex, these cultural modernists unleashed a brutal attack on the genteel tradition that had left "intellectual life" "sour and déraciné" (Stearns 1922: 148). Beyond their jaded cynicism lay the hopes of regenerating American culture as well as a quest to increase their own cultural authority. This intelligentsia comprised a loosely knit community of independent intellectuals who struggled to maintain a position of critical disinterestedness and, as Steven Biel argues, also hoped to influence and transform society (Biel 1992: 54–84).

In order to cultivate a new civilization, the intelligentsia had to overcome "the shrewd janitors of orthodoxy," as Ben Hecht called them. "Our ene-mies the censors," he observed, "commissioned, elected, [and] delegated by the proletaire [*sic*] are not worthy [of] our steel." The malady which gave rise to these "psychopathic repressions," Hecht believed, was the Frankenstein spirit of Puritanism. In the 1920s, "Puritanism" became a term of contempt and derision (Hecht 1922: 23, 30, 17, 20). Because the intelligentsia, according to Schapiro's analysis, was "primarily interested in the social problem as a form of self-expression," they were the leading protagonists for "freedom of speech and freedom of the press." In their rebellion against Victorian culture, the modernists loathed the Protestant establishment that dominated literary culture. In order to elevate their own social status, the rebels had to restrict the Protestant establishment's cultural authority. In Boston this meant toppling the Watch and Ward Society.

To be sure, some individuals and groups well before 1920 opposed censorship. Colonel Bob Ingersoll's National Liberal League, established in 1876, attempted to combat the Comstock Act's censorship by the postal authorities (Goodheart 1991). But unlike previous efforts to curb censorship, the revolution to overthrow Protestant suppression in the 1920s had new political opportunities and also several new resources and organizations to subvert Protestant hegemony. Besides having reached a critical mass of uncompromising anti-Victorian intellectuals who were located in strategic knowledge-producing and knowledge-disseminating institutions, cultural modernists also had the financial resources and support of avant-garde publishers and civil libertarians at their disposal.

Modernists were not alone in their quest to overthrow the Protestant establishment. Beginning in the 1910s, the Young Intellectuals found a host of entrepreneurial publishers eager to promulgate their ideas. The nineteenth-century denizens of the industry—such as Doubleday, Page, and Company, Harper and Brothers, Charles Scribner's Sons, Houghton, Mifflin, and Company, and Little, Brown, and Company—remained in the hands of the founders' families in the very early twentieth century. While New York had become the locus of publishing by the turn of the century, the prevailing influence in the established publishing houses remained in the hands of the New England Brahmins and their editors. When the novels of Booth Tarkington nearly guaranteed Doubleday a million dollars every other year, the works of the rebels, as Dreiser's experience suggests, found little interest among the old guard. A whole array of upstart publishers—B. W. Huebsch, Horace Liveright, Charles Boni, Random House, Covici-Friede, Simon and Schuster, the Viking Press, and, most important, Alfred A. Knopf—emerged to fill a growing niche in the market. Some, however, first worked for the established firms, like Knopf at Doubleday, before striking out on their own. Another reason that some young publishers started their own presses was that they were Jewish, and anti-Semitism limited possible career advancement within the old publishing houses. Cerf recalled that American publishing was "a closed corporation" for young

Jewish editors. As outsiders, they did not have contacts with established writers upon which to build a publishing firm. So they recruited heavily among the intelligentsia, who were also alienated from the establishment. Arthur Schlesinger Sr. recalled that Knopf hosted "Lucullan feasts" in Boston to attract authors (Schlesinger 1963: 123). They also recognized that European authors were not being published by the old guard firms. In 1917, for example, fifty-three of Knopf's titles were written by foreigners. In the new publishing companies, the rebels against Victorianism found kindred spirits and willing allies to get their ideas into the marketplace. To be sure, the established houses published some of the new authors. Doubleday, for instance, published novels by Frank Norris, and Harper put out Dreiser's *Jennie Gerhardt*. But many others were shut out. While the genteel publishers could unofficially exclude the avant-garde from the publishers' club, they could not ignore their success (Gilmer 1970: 5–6, 9, 1–2; Cerf 1977: 41). In addition to a common economic interest, the intelligentsia and avant-garde publishers shared an ideological commitment to the free exchange of ideas. "A censorship over literature and the other arts," Liveright wrote in 1923, "is stupid, ignorant, and impudent, and is against the fundamental social principles of all intelligent Americans" (Liveright 1923: 192–93).

The modernists and their avant-garde publishers found ready allies in the fledgling civil libertarian movement and its similar quest to disestablish the Victorians as the nation's arbiters over literary culture. The nationwide and institutionalized suppression of free speech that followed from the U.S. entrance into the European conflict helped to generate an organized opposition. The American Union against Militarism, an organization of pacifists established in 1914, led to the independent creation of the National Civil Liberties Bureau in 1917 to defend free speech. When the National Bureau was reorganized as the American Civil Liberties Union (ACLU) in 1920, civil libertarians had a national organization to continue their defense of free speech in the face of a majoritarian view of democracy. Initially, however, the ACLU was most concerned with labor and political causes (Walker 1990: 11–47; Murphy 1979).

Some of the nation's most prominent cultural modernists and civil libertarians were brought together in Dayton, Tennessee, in the summer of 1925 at the Scopes trial. While the Scopes trial did not halt the rising tide of fundamentalist antievolution agitation, it did successfully arouse in civil libertarians and cultural modernists anxieties about the danger that religiously motivated political activists, such as the Watch and Ward Society, could pose to intellectual freedom. The ACLU's confrontational strategy centered around publicizing the threats to free speech. "Hays was cynical about the legal process and saw court proceedings as a platform for broad and philosophical statements, an opportunity to educate both the judge and the public," explains ACLU historian Samuel Walker (1990: 53). Cultural modernists and civil libertarians framed the conflict over teaching evolution in terms that could be easily mobilized to discredit the intellectual credibility of other religiously inspired reform movements, such as the Watch and Ward Society. According to Arthur Garfield Hays, the lead ACLU attorney, Dayton was "a battle between two types of minds—the rigid, orthodox, accepting, unyielding, arrow, conventional mind and the broad, critical, cynical, skeptical and tolerant mind" (Hays 1928: 27–28). Framed in this way, the civil libertarians clearly stood on the high ground intellectually. In his analysis of the media coverage of the Scopes trial, Edward Caudill concludes that because the media shared the civil libertarians' empiricist view of knowledge, they were "biased in favor of Darrow" (1989: 32, 21). H. L. Mencken, dispatched to cover the "monkey trial" by the editors of the *Baltimore Sun,* created a caricature of Bryan and the fundamentalists that quickly became a commonplace stereotype. Mencken presented the trial as a contest between "rustic ignoramuses" and the enlightened guardians of American civil liberties. To Mencken, Bryan "was, in fact, a charlatan, a mountebank, a zany without shame or dignity" deluded by "an almost pathological hatred of all learning" (1926: 68). After Bryan's sudden death five days after the trial, Mencken privately gloated, "We killed the son-of-a-bitch" (Larson 1997: 200). A brief sampling of the *Nation*'s coverage suggests that the intelligentsia did not view Dayton as a debacle for fundamentalism but as a possible harbinger of even greater menaces to civil liberties. Joseph Wood Krutch, for example, warned that the trial "has shown conclusively that the danger, often referred to by liberals, of the laws that will reduce the United States to a bondage more complete than that of the darkest Puritan village of colonial New England, is no fanatic danger but one real and present" (1925: 137).

Liberal Protestants, like those who dominated the Watch and Ward Society, viewed the events in Dayton with chagrin. For instance, the liberal weekly *Congregationalist* insisted that "true religion" was getting a "raw deal" from all the bad publicity flowing out of Dayton. There could be no conflict between science and "true religion," they believed, because the divine was immanent in nature, and science and religion constituted two entirely different modes of discerning truth ("Raw Deal for Religion" 1925). Liberal Protestant protests notwithstanding, critics of Christianity had depicted religion as science's stubborn foe for more than a generation. To many cultural modernists, the disparity between fundamentalists and liberal Protestants was a distinction without a difference. Mencken asserted that liberal Protestants, by "depriving revelation of all force and authority, [robbed] their so-called religion of every dignity. It becomes, in their hands, a mere romantic imposture, unsatisfying to the pious and unconvincing to the judicious" (1931: 412). The journalist and political philosopher Walter

Lippmann also excoriated liberal Protestantism in his *A Preface to Morals* (1929) for its half-hearted compromise with science. He too looked to science to provide a solid foundation for the religion of the future. But Lippmann's religious aspirations were not for a strict scientism, but rather a humanism that was guided by a disinterestedness similar to the scientific search for truth.

The secular intelligentsia's critique stunned liberal Protestantism. For instance, the Watch and Ward Society's vice president, George A. Gordon, complained that Lippmann had unfairly judged liberal Protestantism to be a theological compromise with modernity. This interpretation, Gordon believed, stemmed in part from Lippmann's misguided assumption that Christians in previous generations had no spiritual doubts but utter epistemological certainty as a basis for their faith (Gordon 1929: 636–39). Gordon's response, penned the day before he died, suggests that at least intellectually the aging liberal Protestant establishment was now as vulnerable as fundamentalists were to modernist criticisms.

THE "ANTI-CHRIST" OF BALTIMORE COMES TO BOSTON IN 1926: H. L. MENCKEN AND THE MOBILIZATION OF SECULARIZING ACTIVISM

The rebels against Victorianism had reached a critical mass. In the aftermath of the Scopes trial, Mencken, the "heathen missionary zealously endeavoring to convert barbarian Christians away from the false gods of Humility and Restraint," as Krutch described him, saw a new political opportunity to challenge the cultural authority of the New England Watch and Ward Society (Krutch 1921: 733). Mencken, as he explained in an unpublished manuscript, intentionally set out in the fall of 1925 to subvert the "organized terrorism" that the Watch and Ward Society exerted over the market for literature in Boston. The plan, Mencken recounted, was not to "denounce the wowsers in a pontifical manner" but "to proceed against them satirically" in the *American Mercury* until "they writhed under the attack." He was especially eager to unmask the Protestant elites, like Charles W. Eliot and the other honorary vice presidents, who lent their "great" names to the society's "nefarious operations." Mencken was certain that if these "false faces" "could be brought to book," "the wowsers would lose their support." He especially despised J. Frank Chase, secretary of the society, who he thought was "the most potent and impudent" of all American censors (Mencken 1937: 45, 141). In September 1925, A. L. S. Wood penned a commentary on this Methodist minister's life and work in which he described Chase as "an unctuous meddler" (1925: 74–78). Chase, to Mencken's delight, was reportedly "furious and full of threats of revenge." Charles Angoff's "Boston Twilight," the brutal harangue summarized above, followed Wood's character assassination in the December issue. The

April 1926 issue of the *Mercury* contained two more articles taunting Chase. The first, written by Angoff under a pseudonym, was an iconoclastic piece on the Methodist church that included more disparaging comments about Chase (Bernard [Angoff] 1926). But it was the second article, an excerpt of Herbert Asbury's forthcoming book *Up from Methodism,* that pushed Chase over the edge. The author, a direct descendant of the founder of the Methodist church in America, Francis Asbury, described the sad life of a prostitute named Hatrack from his hometown in Missouri. Far from salacious, the article focused upon the hypocrisy of churchgoers who refused Hatrack church membership but welcomed her paid fellowship after Sunday evening services (Asbury 1926). Chase found the story obscene and advised the magazine committee to inform stores to withdraw the *Mercury*. Mencken and the *Mercury*'s publisher, Knopf, immediately consulted ACLU attorney Arthur Garfield Hays. "These dogs in Boston have banned the *American Mercury,*" Mencken announced. Finally, as Hays put it, "Chase swallowed the bait" (Mencken quoted in Hays 1928: 160–61, 167).

Mencken opposed censorship for several reasons. Most obviously, the ban posed a threat to the economic well-being of the periodical. In April 1926, the *Mercury* had an impressive circulation of 80,500. If Chase persuaded the postal authorities that the periodical was obscene, it could lose its second-class mailing privileges, which could spell economic ruin. Mencken himself had been censored in the past. During the war, the *Baltimore Sun* suspended Mencken's regular column because of his militantly pro-German position. Mencken had also fought moral reformers in the past and lost. In the summer of 1916, the New York Society for the Suppression of Vice banned Theodore Dreiser's novel *The "Genius"* (Hobson 1994: 138). Even though he thought that some of Dreiser's writings were "cheap" and "pornography," Mencken leaped to his friend's defense (Bode 1977: 83). He appealed to the Authors League of America for support and drew up a protest for writers to sign. Many of the Young Intellectuals, such as Willa Cather, James Branch Cabell, Edgar Lee Masters, and Sinclair Lewis, signed, but some of the older literary figures, including William Dean Howells, whom Mencken described as a "notorious coward," refused. Mencken's efforts failed. "When *The 'Genius'* was attacked by the Comstocks," Mencken wrote in 1920, "it fell to my lot to seek assistance for Dreiser among the intelligentsia. . . . It was, it appeared, dangerous for a member of the intelligentsia, and particularly for a member of the academic intelligentsia, to array himself against the mob inflamed—against the moral indignation of the sort of folk who devour vice reports and are converted by the Rev. Billy Sunday!" (Mencken 1920: 90–91). Mencken was even willing to capitulate to the censors. In 1922, he sat down with the secretary of the New York Society for the Suppression of Vice, John S. Sumner, to excise the pernicious sections of *The "Genius"* in order to make it acceptable for publication (Mencken 1993: 165, 355, 390–91). But Dreiser refused to compromise with the censors and soon backed out of the agreement. Mencken's publisher also had experience in surrendering to the censors.

"My whole life, once I get free from my present engagements," Mencken wrote Dreiser in 1916, "will be devoted to combating Puritanism" (Hobson 1994: 190). The Puritan, Mencken's classic definition explained, suffered from "the haunting fear that someone, somewhere, may be happy" (1949: 624). Beneath his witticism, however, lay a set of intellectual and professional grievances that fueled his opposition to the Watch and Ward Society. Mencken did not use the term "Puritan" in a historical sense. Rather it functioned rhetorically in his social philosophy to embody all of his antipathies. He favored the works of Joseph Conrad, James Branch Cabell, and especially Dreiser because of their skepticism and unyielding naturalism. By contrast, he alleged that the "Puritan" reduces everything to a morality play. This is why Mencken hated Victorians, such as Van Dyke, and the New Humanists, like More. Not only had Puritanism's "moral obsession" discolored American literature, but it also endangered the social status of avant-garde writers. The enlightened minority, Mencken explained in his influential 1917 essay, "Puritanism as a Literary Force," labored "under harsh Puritan restraints." Puritanism, moreover, posed a danger to Mencken's civil liberties. He accused the Puritans of having "put an almost unbearable burden upon the exchange of ideas in the United States." His contempt for Puritanism made him one of the leaders in the literary revolt against Victorianism. To Mencken, Puritans were "Philistines" (1917: 198–99, 202, 210).

Intellectually, Mencken's antipathy toward Puritanism arose from his commitments to social Darwinism and agnosticism. His father and grandfather were confirmed skeptics. Mencken was sent to a local Lutheran church on Sunday mornings, not for theological training, but so that his father could read the paper in a quiet house (Mencken 1943: 32). Nietzsche, Darwin, Shaw, and Huxley were the central influences that shaped Mencken's social philosophy. Mencken served, according to Krutch, as a "liaison officer between American intelligentsia and European ideas" (1921: 733). To Mencken, Charles Darwin's *Origin of Species* provided scientific evidence that refuted traditional Christian belief. In Nietzsche, he found an uncompromising social Darwinist and scientific naturalist, and in 1908, he wrote *The Philosophy of Friedrich Nietzsche,* the first English introduction to his thought written for a general audience. Nietzsche's teaching, Mencken wrote, "leads to a rejection of Christianity and democracy" (1908: 28). Nietzsche's critique of "slave morality" convinced him that except for a "civilized aristocracy" the vast majority of Americans "constitute the most timorous, sniveling, poltroonish, ignominious mob of serfs and goose-steppers ever gathered under one flag in Christendom since the end of the Middle Ages"

(1922: 10). George Bernard Shaw's plays provided Mencken with a role model of a sham-smasher in action. In 1905, he wrote the first study of Shaw published in America. Thomas H. Huxley, Mencken wrote, "gave order and coherence to my own doubts and converted me into a violent agnostic" (Hobson 1994: 52). In 1922, Lippmann called Mencken a "new Machiavelli" who dreamed of seeing "himself as the companion of a small masterful minority who rule the world and who, because it is so simple to rule the world, have ample leisure for talk. In that circle Mencken is the gayest spirit of the lot, the literary pope, of course, but with a strong flavor of Rabelais and Voltaire about him" (Lippmann 1922: 14). Before Mencken could realize his dream, however, the ruling literary establishment had to be displaced.

The ban on the *American Mercury* turned Mencken from a typewriting iconoclast into a secularizing activist. Mencken was the one who began to break the Watch and Ward Society's stranglehold on reading consumption in New England. In addition to supportive allies among the Young Intellectuals and civil libertarians, Mencken had a strategic advantage in 1926 that he lacked before—he was the editor of the most popular literary magazine in America in the 1920s. With Knopf's financial backing, Mencken and George Jean Nathan had created the *American Mercury* in 1924. It was soon called "the bible of the sophisticates" (Dulles 1945: 284). The *Mercury* followed in the tradition of the "little magazines" of the late nineteenth century and early twentieth century, such as *Lark* and *M'lle New York*. The chief aim of the *Mercury,* the editors explained in the first issue, was "to attempt a realistic presentation of the whole gaudy, gorgeous American scene" without the "messianic passion" that clouded other periodicals. The audience Mencken and Nathan hoped to reach was "the normal, educated, well-disposed, unfrenzied, enlightened citizen of the middle minority" (Nathan and Mencken 1924: 30, 27–28). When Mencken told Dreiser about plans for the new endeavor, he invited him to "attack the Methodists by name, and call the Baptists the Sewer Rats of God if you please" (Riggio 1986, 2: 498).

In this first major attack on the Watch and Ward Society's cultural authority, Mencken employed a two-pronged strategy: ridicule the censors and challenge them in court. Mencken, Knopf, and Hays determined that Mencken should travel to Boston and violate the ban. This act, Mencken explained, would not only "force an open court fight" but would also "arouse those Bostonians who were ashamed" of the society and "eager to find a stick to flog it with." They convinced Chase to meet Mencken at the famed "Brimstone Corner," where the conservative Park Street Congregational Church was located, on the Boston Common on April fifth. Chase would make the purchase of the banned journal and order Mencken's arrest.[7] The corner of Park and Tremont Streets was a symbolically significant location for this confrontation over whose morality would dominate the public square. According to one popular explanation, "Brimstone Corner" had gained its colorful name when seventeenth-century Puritans allegedly spread hot ashes over the area to illustrate the texture of Hell to unbelievers. Now Chase, a descendant of the original Puritans and a defender of twentieth-century Protestant values, was poised to preserve Boston from the onslaught of secular values. A crowd of nearly five thousand, including a large contingent of Harvard students, had gathered to witness the confrontation. One *Boston Evening Transcript* reporter likened the crowd to a group of people waiting for a circus parade to pass through the city.[8] It was an apt description because Mencken was about to make a clown out of Chase. Mencken had a long history of using ridicule to debunk everyone and everything he hated. It was an effective tactic. Mencken was a delightfully funny writer who created demeaning stereotypes that were nearly impossible to refute. By laughing at Mencken's humor, moreover, readers, even if they disagreed with the author's agenda, temporarily consented to the truthfulness of the parody. Short, burley, with wire-rimmed glasses and a fastidious moustache, the middle-aged Chase even looked like the "blue nose," "vice-chasing," "Pecksniff" caricature that Mencken had created. Chase, who typically worked clandestinely, had stepped onto a vaudeville stage to play the straight man to Mencken's slapstick humor. The crowd cheered as Chase stepped forward and bought the banned issue. When Mencken bit the silver half-dollar to ensure it was real, the crowd roared again. Mencken was hauled off to jail with a "joyous crowd" of supporters trailing, but it was the Protestant establishment that was soon to be swept away by a coalition of cultural modernists, civil libertarians, and progressive publishers (Mencken 1937: 51–60; Greenslet 1943: 178).

When Mencken's lawyers learned that he was to come before an Irish Catholic judge "who was notoriously friendly to the Watch and Ward Society," they made "the specious plea" that the judge's docket was too crowded and got his trial moved before Judge James P. Parmenter, "who was neither a Methodist, nor a Catholic, but a Unitarian." Hays, as he wrote two years later, "made the familiar argument that the Bible or Shakespeare would not stand the test of Chase's temperature. Reference was made to the illiberal spirit throughout the country pursuant to which small groups of people gathered together to compel others to accept their ideas" (1928: 168–69). When he took the stand, Mencken argued that "Chase's customary method of proceeding was grossly unfair and disingenuous." Judge Parmenter suspended proceedings to read the magazine for himself.[9] That evening Mencken dined at the St. Botoph Club—"one of the most holy places of the Boston Brahmins"—as the guest of Ferris Greenslet, head of Houghton Mifflin. Parmenter dismissed the charge the next day with a simple, extemporaneous decision "that no offense has been committed." "It seemed a good chance to spread some terror among the enemy," Mencken believed, "so I hinted . . . at damage suits against Chase and his associates." That afternoon Mencken lunched as the guest of honor at the Harvard Union. After complimentary speeches by noted civil libertarian lawyers Felix Frankfurter and Zechariah Chafee, students hailed Mencken as a conquering hero with the Harvard cheer, "three times *fortissimo*" (Mencken 1937: 63–65, 69–72).[10]

The Hatrack controversy put the Watch and Ward Society on the defensive. "It must be understood that opinion is bound to differ as to whether a given article or story is indecent or obscene or not," explained Chase in his annual report for 1925–1926. "There seemed no reason for not taking this action, because the article appeared in a brilliantly edited magazine like the *Mercury*" (*AR* 1925–26: 8–9). When the U.S. Post Office barred the *Mercury* from the mail and a judge fined a Harvard Square magazine stand owner for selling the April issue, Chase concluded that society had been "vindicated." However, Mencken's strategy of trying to get the society into court in order to contest the obscenity law proved to be effective. Although the society saw itself justified by the postal ban on the *Mercury,* that consolation was short-lived. Hays got an injunction against the ban from a New York federal court in November 1926, and the following May a federal judge denied the postal authority's appeal (Hays 1928: 169–82). While this decision, like the Boston injunction, did not stop the society's censorship activities, it did demonstrate that the organization could be fought successfully in open court. Mencken boasted to reporters that he had won a "decisive victory."[11] However, despite his bravado, he was still leery of getting into another row with them. He consequently pulled Bernard De Voto's piece on "Sex and the College Girl" from the May 1926 issue (Mencken 1937: 79, 90–165).

At least in the eyes of fellow modernists, Chase gave credence to Mencken's sarcastic caricatures of vice-hunters. Mencken had done to the Watch and Ward Society in Boston what he had done to the fundamentalists at Dayton. As an editorial in the *Nation,* "A Libertarian Laughs," put it, "We have seldom enough called censorship the thing it evidently is, a comedy; here is one who acts out as such" (1926: 440). Several months after the Hatrack controversy, Lippmann judged Mencken as "the most powerful personal influence on this whole generation of educated people" (1926: 413). Although the society's action annoyed a few supporters—the *Congregationalist* first deemed the ban "ill-advised" and later called it a "decided failure" that brought about "a certain loss of prestige" for the organization—the media in Boston and elsewhere took issue with Mencken ("Without Aid of Police," 1926; "What Is the Sense of Censorship?" 1927). Even

Mencken himself complained that the "newspaper comments were predominantly against us—indeed, they were overwhelmingly so" (Mencken 1937: 100).

Although Mencken's efforts to make a spectacle out of the society and its elite Protestant supporters did not mobilize the organized opposition that he envisioned, it did temporarily bring together cultural modernists, like Mencken; civil libertarians, such as Chafee and Frankfurter; and progressive publishers, such as Greenslet, who had taken over as head of the once conservative Houghton Mifflin. Such constructive interactions among the intelligentsia boded well for future cooperation. Perhaps the most important consequence of the Hatrack controversy was that it may have helped put Chase in an early grave in November 1926. Mencken's threats of suing Chase personally for damages made front page news, and his attorneys even met with Chase about the matter. Fear over possibly losing his savings and house to Mencken reportedly caused Chase so much anxiety that he had something of a nervous breakdown that made it difficult for him to recover from an illness.[12] The society remembered Chase as a "vigilant, resourceful foe of every form of evil which threatens the welfare and moral health of the community" (*AR* 1926–27: 2). Mencken thought differently. "Now he was dead at least in defeat and dismay, and we were rid of him" (Mencken 1937: 151).

BOSTON "BOOK WAR": NEW POLITICAL OPPORTUNITIES
AND THE CLARIFICATION OF THE SECULAR ACTIVISTS' GRIEVANCE

"Boston 'Book War' Opens" screamed front-page headlines in April 1927.[13] A battle had been brewing for more than a month. Disgusted by recent titles, individuals, such as a woman from the Back Bay who read Ernest Pascal's *The Marriage Bed*, began making complaints directly to the police. In March, the police superintendent Michael Crowley banned nine books, including Boni and Liveright's recent title, *The Plastic Age* by Percy Marks (Smith 1928: 215).[14] Unsure of which titles were obscene, the frustrated Booksellers Association sent Middlesex County District Attorney William Foley a package of forty-nine books that were reportedly under "surveillance," including Theodore Dreiser's long awaited *American Tragedy* and Sinclair Lewis's *Elmer Gantry*. Which of these books, they asked, were obscene? Foley returned the package unopened. While he expressed little affection for "certain morbid moderns who would like to be considered as fit companions of Shakespere [sic]," his office would only prosecute obscenity charges, not review books like the Watch and Ward Society.[15] For the secularizing activists, the "Book War" marked a propitious, if temporary, breakdown in the Watch and Ward Society's cooperative arrangement with booksellers because it provided them with a new opportunity to challenge censorship in court.

The "Book War" caught the Watch and Ward Society flatfooted and left booksellers and publishers at one another's throats. Chase's death had left the cooperative arrangement between the society and the booksellers "temporarily inoperative." Ironically, of the fifty-seven titles reportedly banned, only one had actually been deemed obscene by the society (*AR* 1926–27: 10). The society, nevertheless, was blamed for starting the war.[16] While some of the blacklisted titles were thoroughly forgettable, such as *Mr. Gilhooley,* by Liam O'Flaherty, other works were very popular. *Publishers' Weekly* estimated that the ban cost Boston bookstores the sale of an estimated 3,000–5,000 copies of *Elmer Gantry.* New York bookstores immediately began advertising the censored works in their store windows as "Banned in Boston."[17] This soon gave rise to the phrase as a contemptuous epithet. Yet Boston bookstores did not fear that they were losing sales to New York. Since the ban was only in Suffolk County, customers simply had to cross the Charles River to find *Elmer Gantry* in a bookstore in Cambridge, which was located in Middlesex County. At the same time, Boston booksellers felt economic pressure from another source. The creation of the Book-of-the-Month Club in 1926 threatened to put many out of business. In fact, Richard Fuller, the president of the Boston Booksellers Association, was involved in a lawsuit against the Book-of-the-Month Club. Publishers, on the one hand, typically benefited when the Book-of-the-Month Club selected one of their titles for distribution (Lee 1958: 44–59). On the other hand, Boston booksellers faced a dilemma: they could pull the banned books off their shelves and lose business or risk six months in jail. Hoping to find a way out of their troubles, booksellers issued an open invitation for publishers to challenge the recent ban with a test case. Booksellers tried to position themselves as a neutral party in the debate.[18] While area publishers declined the offer, a group, which included Ellery Sedgwick of *Atlantic Monthly* and M. A. DeWolfe Howe of Little, Brown, and Company, did write an open letter protesting "the high-handed, erratic, and ill-advised" action of the police.[19] Still publishers, as Greenslet explained, had an "awkward" time explaining to "desirable" authors like John Dos Passos why his popular book *Manhattan Transfer* was not for sale in Boston (Greenslet 1943: 178). Despite booksellers' and publishers' common grievance with censorship, the antagonism between them prevented any coordinated action. Publishers, the *Nation* cynically concluded, "have meekly submitted to the Watch-and-Warders and their kin. It is expensive to be a martyr, it interferes with business, it results in advertising of uncertain value. The publishers, like so many other persons, do not believe in censorship, but—" (Editorial Note 1927a: 305).

While the Boston ban may have cost many authors, publishers, and book-stores money, certain ones were actually helped by censorship. In fact, some authors, such as Sinclair Lewis, may have had a vested interest in generating controversy. He intentionally declined the Pulitzer Prize for *Arrowsmith* (1925) in 1926 in order to provoke some publicity for his forthcoming novel, *Elmer Gantry*. While Lewis was in Kansas City doing research on the novel, a pastor invited him to address his congregation. Lewis leaped at the opportunity to mock Protestantism and to arouse some publicity for his next work. From the pulpit of the Linwood Boulevard Christian Church on April 18, 1926, Lewis gave God ten minutes to strike him dead as an infidel in order to prove His existence. His antics made headline news across the nation. For more than a year, Harcourt, Lewis's publisher, leaked controversial tidbits about *Elmer Gantry*. Upon its release, the book was immediately banned in several cities. Harcourt fed reporters regular updates on the controversy. "The making, the advertising, the marketing of Sinclair Lewis novels," observed one journalist, has "become one of the great industries almost to be compared with Ford cars, Camel cigarettes, the movies, radio or Aimee McPherson crusades" (Williams 1927: 577). Despite the boom that the ban had provided to sales, the publisher still saw the censorship of free speech as an issue possibly worth pursuing as a matter of principle. Harcourt threatened to sue Richard Fuller for payment on the more than one hundred copies of *Elmer Gantry* that Fuller had returned to the publisher. Harcourt soon withdrew from the lawsuit, as he explained to Lewis, because the attorneys were "extremely doubtful [that] we could win the case under the present statute" (Smith 1952: 243).

Unlike Lewis and Harcourt, Theodore Dreiser, his publisher, Horace Liveright, and their attorney, Arthur Garfield Hays, were three mavericks willing to go to the wall to combat the practice of censorship. *An American Tragedy* earned the author more than $47,000 in royalties in 1926. By April of 1927 sales had begun to sag. Outraged by the ban of the novel, Liveright sent Donald Friede, the firm's chief agent, and Hays to Boston to test the ban in the usual manner; by repeating Mencken's exploits. Such a "grand stunt," as Friede described it, would also boost lagging sales and show up other publishers as well (Gilmer 1970: 165). While the Watch and Ward Society believed that unofficial censorship, as they put it, "safeguarded" the public's interest and did "no injustice" to authors or publishers, critics argued that the practice was an extralegal proceeding in which an author, publisher, or bookstore is found guilty without a fair and legal trial (*AR* 1926–27: 10; Grant and Angoff 1930: 43). Having the opportunity to actually contest the practice of censorship in court was crucial to subverting the Watch and Ward Society's cultural authority. Because the police refused to get lured into another vaudevillian act on the Boston Common, Friede had to make the sale in the quiet office of Superintendent Crowley.[20]

The April 1927 trial over the sale of Dreiser's *An American Tragedy* and the subsequent 1929 appeal represented the most direct challenge to the Watch and Ward Society's cultural authority to date. Although they were not directly involved, the society had helped write the obscenity law and, moreover, stood to lose its ability to censor books if Dreiser's work was not found obscene. The 1927 trial and 1929 appeal also brought the specific legal factors preserving the Watch and Ward Society's cultural authority into bold relief. If the society was to be overthrown, then the state's obscenity statutes would have to be rewritten. Moreover, it exposes why the cultural modernists and their avant-garde publishers found censorship so offensive. If literature constituted cultural capital, book banning imperiled more than the economic well-being of the modernist writer and publisher. Censorship threatened their social status and, moreover, one of their most deeply held virtues, intellectual freedom. Thus, the "Book War" helped to mobilize an anticensorship coalition.

Dreiser's standing as the leader of the literary revolt against the genteel tradition in letters made his challenge to the cultural authority of the Watch and Ward Society especially significant. In his 1930 Nobel Prize speech, Sinclair Lewis said that Dreiser, "more than any other man, marching alone, usually unappreciated, often hated, has cleared the trail from Victorian and Howellsian timidity and gentility in American fiction to honesty and boldness and passion of life" (Lewis 1953: 7). Like many other cultural modernists, Dreiser was an outspoken atheist. After his freshman year at the University of Indiana, he later recalled, "I was thoroughly satisfied that there was nothing in the Catholic or any other sectarian pretense to divine authority and very little substance to the Christ legend either" (Dreiser 1931: 30, 503). Like Mencken, he found intellectual confirmation for his unbelief by reading Herbert Spencer's *Data of Ethics* and *First Principles*. "They nearly killed me, took every shred of belief away from me; showed me that I was a chemical atom in a whirl of unknown forces; the realization clouded my mind" (Harris 1919: 91). Dreiser was militantly anti-Christian. In 1930 he told a reporter for the *El Paso Evening Post* that "[r]eligion in America is just a total loss. . . . Boot out your El Paso ministers along with all other religionists and your city and America will be much better off. At least you will have cleared this country of just so much pure dogmatic bunk. That is all this religion is—just fool dogmatic bunk" (Swanberg 1965: 361).

The trial over the sale of *An American Tragedy* is also significant because Dreiser advocated a moral vision that represented the repudiation of all traditional Protestant values. Dreiser's stark naturalism inverted conventional morality, and his work boldly defied the Victorian literary notions of truth, goodness, and beauty. Whereas Howells's *Silas Lapham* lost everything but kept his virtue and thus the novel serves as a moral lesson about good character, in his groundbreaking work, *Sister Carrie*, Dreiser's protagonist, Caroline Meeber, is a wanton sexual libertine who uses several men in her climb to fame and fortune. In *An American Tragedy,* Dreiser traces the social rise of Clyde Griffiths from poverty to the cusp of prosperity. The protagonist, however, ends up in the electric chair for murdering a young woman whom he had gotten pregnant. As he had done in *Sister Carrie,* Dreiser only intimated that the couple had sexual relations. The central theme of the novel is that Griffiths did not have a free will but was driven to murder by circumstances and forces beyond his control. Since Griffiths and Meeber are rather grotesque characters, Dreiser's works are a social protest against the American dream (Bradbury 1983: 25–26; Cowley 1955; Farrell 1955). To critics, Dreiser's naturalism reduced the human will to that of an animal. The New Humanist Stuart Sherman found neither "moral value" nor "memorable beauty" in Dreiser's fiction because his characters simply act upon their "jungle motive." Sherman called Dreiser's works a "sermon" illustrating "a crude and naively simple naturalistic philosophy, such as we find in the mouths of exponents of the new *Real-Politik*" (Sherman 1915: 648–50). Spurning Victorian notions about character formation and human freedom, modernists deemed unbridled liberty the gateway to the full development of one's own personality. They found the restraint of individual freedom offensive and immoral. Victorian critics of modern fiction recognized that writers like Dreiser were advancing a radically different moral order. The Watch and Ward Society also realized that the naturalist works, like those by Dreiser, constituted a new genre of literature that made defining "what is and what is not lascivious and obscene . . . increasingly difficult." In the spring of 1927, the society attempted to clarify the principle by which it would determine if a book should be censored, saying, "It has not been our policy to express an opinion concerning the illegality of novels which may contain a few passages which could in a strict sense be called obscene or indecent—but only those the whole purport and tenure of which could reasonably be called subversive of these standards of morals upon which the common welfare of the community may be said to depend" (*AR* 1926–27: 11).

While the modernist impulse in American fiction may have symbolically been put on trial, at the 1927 trial and 1929 appeal Arthur Garfield Hays unmasked the specific legal issues that had empowered the Watch and Ward Society. The vague definition of obscenity, critics complained, "is capable of broad interpretation, and therein lies its danger" (Editorial Note 1927b: 465). Hays attacked three other factors crucial to preserving the Watch and Ward Society's cultural authority. At both trials, the district attorney read selected passages to illustrate the work's pernicious character. At the 1929 trial, Hays put Dreiser on the stand and asked him which sections would demonstrate to the jury that those passages read by the prosecution "were not salacious." Dreiser answered, "The whole book."[21] The district attorney objected, and only long passages were permitted to be read aloud. Lifting a passage out of its larger literary context clearly contradicted the most basic rules of scholarship; this had the potential of arousing widespread outrage among thoughtful people of every political and religious persuasion, not just enlightened intelligentsia. Critics complained that failure to consider an allegedly obscene passage within its context was an "injustice" (Smith 1928: 214).[22]

Not only was the defense unable to place allegedly obscene passages in their broader literary context, but legal precedent precluded Hays from introducing expert testimony from leading professors, writers, and other intellectuals. Perhaps the most damaging testimony came from the police officer who had arrested Friede. Hays asked him at the 1927 trial if his morals had been corrupted by reading the objectionable passages. He answered that they were not but added that he was not assigned to "the book-censor department."[23] When the audience chuckled, Hays had successfully contested the "imitation-suggestion theory," or philosophy of reading, that informed the Watch and Ward Society's rationale for censorship. However, the jury at the 1927 trial still convicted Friede for selling obscenity.[24]

The intelligentsia seemed especially uncomfortable that working-class people were standing in judgment over an important novelist like Dreiser. An editorial in *Publishers' Weekly* condescendingly noted that the jury was "composed of an auto washer, a painter, a janitor, a hatter, two machinists, two clerks, three salesmen and one treasurer."[25] This comment suggests that the intelligentsia viewed the fight over censorship as a contest between the socially superior and their inferiors. The free expression of ideas was central to Dreiser's identity as a member of the intelligentsia and as a writer. However unpalatable Victorians found his fiction, Dreiser insisted that he had a freedom, if not a duty, to express his ideas. Moreover, the coercion of morality through the state's obscenity law threatened his class interests. In the courtroom, however, the defense's inability to place objectionable passages in their larger literary context as well as the exclusion of expert testimony from other members of the intelligentsia underscored the subservient position of the modernist writers and publishers to the cultural authority of the moral reformers. Censorship is the cardinal sin of knowledge elites because it violates what intellectuals are at heart. Banning books undermined the intelligentsia's efforts to propagate their views, although more than anything else, these independent intellectuals believed that the free exchange of ideas was essential for society's improvement. These factors cut to the heart of the modernist authors' grievance with censorship. They were writers by profession, and their fiction expressed the deepest hopes and aspirations for the renewal of American society. Yet the law was written in such a way as to keep the intelligentsia in a marginal position to the Watch and Ward Society's cultural authority.

Given the peril that censorship posed to modernist writers' income, identity, and social status, cultural modernist writers viewed censorship as a violation of their most basic civil liberties. The current obscenity statutes left Hays little legal ground other than to defend Dreiser's work. Throughout the trial and appeal, Hays and his allies turned to the freedom of the press and freedom of speech for inspiration and, more important, as a grounds for defense. While waiting for the appeal of Friede's conviction to reach the higher court, Hays wrote a classic defense of civil liberties in *Let Freedom Ring*. He insisted in the preface that "I should not deny to any of these people the right to express their views; or to persuade others. I don't want to control them. But I don't want them to control me" (1928: xvi). In a remarkable reversal of moral judgment, civil libertarians viewed censorship as "pernicious" and "indecent" (Krutch 1927: 162–63). Despite the appeal to basic civil liberties, the moral reformers' view prevailed and Friede was fined three hundred dollars in 1929.

FAILED ATTEMPTS TO TOPPLE THE WATCH AND WARD SOCIETY AND COALITION POLITICS, 1928–1929

After the "Book War" died down, the society hired Charles Bodwell, a person whom it believed had the "education, culture, training, [and] experience," to succeed Chase. A Unitarian minister, Bodwell had undergraduate and divinity degrees from Yale University and experience working with the Division of Immigration and Americanization in the State Department of Education as well as the Lawrence, Massachusetts, Federation of Churches (*AR* 1926–27: 5).[26] By November of 1927, the society's cooperative arrangement with the booksellers and the police was back in full swing. That month, Bodwell reported, book censorship occupied "a large place" in his new work (Secretary's Report 1927). While the society attempted to resume its place as the moral custodian of literature, a local anticensorship coalition began to form. Twice, this loosely knit coalition launched challenges to the state's obscenity laws, only to be rebuffed by the Watch and Ward Society. Not until the ACLU got involved in the action in the fall of 1929, however, did the society's cultural authority appear to be genuinely threatened. While the initial attempts to restrict the society's jurisdiction over literature failed, they helped to strengthen an emerging coalition of anticensorship activists. Moreover, other events in Boston and the nation at large in the late 1920s strengthened the resolve of the anticensorship coalition and consequently made the Watch and Ward Society more vulnerable to subversion. While cultural modernists, avant-garde publishers, and civil libertarians joined the effort to overthrow the Watch and Ward Society's cultural authority, the society was unable to match this growing opposition by expanding its own base of support into Boston's fundamentalist and Catholic communities.

Between the spring of 1927 and the fall of 1929, calls to end censorship increased. More moderate voices began to insist upon bringing an end to the Ward Society's practice of "preventive charity." *Publishers' Weekly*, the leading trade journal of the industry, called the society's work "illegal" and suggested that a change in the law would be the only "way out of the ridiculous situation in which Boston has got itself."[27] An informal survey of letters published in the city's newspapers ran decidedly against censorship. One critic said it made Boston "the hickest hick town in the United States."[28] Whereas the Watch and Ward Society once depended upon Boston's newspapers for support, the local media had largely turned against censorship. A *Boston Herald* editorial succinctly summarized most newspapers' position with a question: "[Is] it a square deal to pounce upon a reputable bookseller as though he were peddling narcotic drugs in a dim alley, or caught in the act of burglary?"[29] After World War I the American Library Association reversed its position on censorship. Eager to assert their own professional expertise in an effort to increase their own cultural authority, its members also piped up in the discussion. One librarian from Salem, for instance, called censorship "an act of tyranny quite out of keeping with the rights and privileges of American civilization."[30] Although mainline Protestants remained firmly behind the practice of censorship during this period, some fissures began to appear in the establishment's commitment. For instance, in a lecture to a group of Wellesley business leaders, Daniel Evans, a professor at the liberal Andover Theological Seminary, adopted the secularists' anticensorship rationale *tout court*. Ecclesiastical and political censorship, he argued, threatened "the freedom of faith and the progressive ideas of moral and social life." Evans also wanted censorship stopped in order "to save Boston from being the laughing stock of the country."[31] In an open letter to the city's business leaders published in the *Boston Evening Transcript* two days after Christmas 1927, A. Lincoln Filene, the department store magnate, was certain that censorship was hurting the region's efforts to sell goods across the nation. "Have the censors weighed against their moral triumphs the economic losses which they entail?" People in other parts of the country, he wrote, "think we take" censorship "seriously and diagnose our general mental outlook accordingly."[32] This fear that Boston looked foolish in the eyes of the nation indicates that the modernist strategy of using ridicule to diminish the social prestige of the advocates of censorship was beginning to take hold. Censorship, the argument went, threatened the cultural status of Bostonians and therefore jeopardized their economic well-being.

By January 1928, a loosely organized opposition emerged to challenge the Watch and Ward Society. Three bills were offered in the Massachusetts State House that month to revise the existing obscenity law. One legislator proposed creating a commission to investigate the matter and make recommendations. The Booksellers Association, working in cooperation with the Watch and Ward Society, recommended some minor alterations in the enforcement of the existing law. The third alternative, called the Sedgwick Bill after its principal author, Ellery Sedgwick, editor of the *Atlantic Monthly*, called for a more specific, clearer definition of obscenity and a consideration of the entire book in obscenity trials (Minutes 1928).[33] Since the success of a revolution depends partly upon turning opinion into effective political action, Sedgwick and the bill's sponsor, Henry Shattuck, a Republican from Cambridge, worked hard to gather support for this measure. They also created an *ad hoc* committee of publishers, librarians, and others. Despite these efforts, however, the measure died in committee.[34] In the fall of 1928, the Massachusetts Library Club made another push to revise the law. Their proposal, which came before the legislature in January 1929, had the support of newspapers, librarians, and publishers. The Legal Affairs Committee sent the measure to the full Senate with its unanimous support. "This bill, it is confidently predicted, will pass," reported *Publishers' Weekly* in late March. By a vote of 20–17, however, the senate killed the bill for another year.[35]

The Watch and Ward Society twice thwarted the coalition of booksellers, publishers, and librarians by effectively persuading "twenty clear-headed, straight-thinking men," as one society director put it in 1929, not to be "stampeded" by "the energetic propaganda" of the pro-revision coalition.[36] To stop the revisionist movement, the Watch and Ward Society applied direct political pressure to key legislators, a strategy like that which the Anti-Saloon League had employed to obtain and then maintain the Eighteenth Amendment (Kerr 1985). The society issued a press release to counter a Library Club pamphlet and mailed a position paper as well as a copy of Bliss Perry's *Pernicious Books* lecture to each legislator. Moreover, it contacted ministers in critical districts and encouraged them to speak directly with representatives or have influential congregants attempt to persuade senators to vote against the proposed revision (Minutes 1928; "Protect Our Youth," n.d.). While the pro-revision coalition had marshaled several prominent and well-respected supporters and had the blessings of the local media, it was not enough to overcome the status quo. In a *Publishers' Weekly* article entitled "Mobilizing the Author and the Publisher," published just before the Watch and Ward Society successfully scuttled the proposed revision, noted civil libertarian lawyers Morris Ernst and William Seagle offered a suggestion to those trying to overcome existing censorship laws. Having successfully defended several works against the New York Society for the Suppression of Vice, Ernst and Seagle, like Mencken, suggested that when all else fails, "ridicule is the best weapon against censorship."[37]

Twice foiled by the Watch and Ward Society, the secularizing activists were extremely frustrated in the spring of 1929. Unable to limit Watch and Ward Society's cultural authority by revising the state's obscenity law, the secularizing coalition turned to ridiculing the censors. On the night before the jury was to render its decision at the April 1929 appeal of Friede's conviction for his illegal sale of Dreiser's *American Tragedy*, the intelligentsia gathered at the twenty-first anniversary celebration of the Ford Hall Forum to burlesque censorship. Placards were hung around the balcony with titles of banned books and signs reading "Verboten" and "taboo."[38] Arthur M. Schlesinger Sr., professor of history at Harvard University and civil rights activist, served as toastmaster (Schlesinger 1963: 128). Seated on stage, the *Boston Globe* reported, were a host of "undesirables," including the attorneys Darrow and Ernst, the *Nation* editor Oswald Garrison Villard, and the author Percy Marks. The frolic included various gags and speeches mocking censorship.[39] The jury in the Dreiser case probably did not enjoy being mocked by the intelligentsia. At least that is what Friede's lawyers argued the following day when they asked the judge to set aside the guilty verdict. Newspaper accounts of the frolic, they feared, might have prejudiced the jury.[40]

In the aftermath of Friede's 1929 conviction, the Massachusetts Civil Liberties Union (MCLU) joined the effort to overthrow the Watch and Ward Society's jurisdiction over literature in Boston. "A well-organized program to fight censorship in all its phases was launched last night," announced a front page *Boston Globe* story. The October 1929 meeting, sponsored by the MCLU, drew more than a thousand people. This was no publicity stunt intended to boost lagging sales for another banned novel. The roster of speakers included some of Boston's most respected citizens. Harvard Law School professor Zechariah Chafee, Tufts College professor Clarence Skinner, Tufts Medical School professor Abraham Myerson, and *Atlantic Monthly* editor Edward Weeks each denounced censorship. These civil libertarians vowed to restrict the Ward and Ward Society's censorship activities by changing the state's obscenity law.[41] This was not like the *ad hoc* committee that had failed to revise the obscenity statutes the two previous years. The secularizing activists now had the institutional support of an independent organization to contest the cultural authority of the Watch and Ward Society. Moreover, the social standing of many in this organization, such as Chafee and Weeks, equaled that of the Brahmin supporters of the society. They also had greater financial resources to try to match the Watch and Ward Society's endowment and donor list. Chafee announced the establishment of a "War Chest" to finance their effort to curb censorship.[42] The following month they held another meeting at the Old South Forum, where Roger Baldwin, head of the ACLU, encouraged the troops to make a frontal assault on censorship.[43]

In order to generate greater public participation in the campaign against censorship, the MCLU published a pamphlet, *The Censorship in Boston,* by Chafee. This essay is important because it reveals that an influential wing of the anticensorship coalition was motivated by more than self-interests. Chafee's pamphlet demonstrates that the opponents of the Watch and Ward Society were in part also motivated by ideas. To the anticensorship coalition, the First Amendment guaranteed the right to free speech and the free exchange of ideas. Lacking the histrionics of the Ford Hall Frolic, Chafee's essay offered a dispassionate review of book censorship as well as other perceived violations of civil liberties in Boston's recent past. In each instance, he pointed out that censorship transgressed the constitutionally guaranteed right to free speech. But Chafee's argument went beyond a technical discussion of the law. The essence of his argument was that he found it highly hypocritical that in the birthplace of democracy unpopular ideas could not be expressed freely. This violated the most basic American values of justice and equity. Chafee made a clarion call for action: "Only a determined opposition by an aroused public opinion can break down this entrenched—and for the most part lawless—assumption of the power of advance censorship." The "remedies" for this unjust situation, he reasoned, lie "in organized effort to bring actions in the courts and to pass bills in the legislation" (Chafee 1929: 4–5).

Several developments in the nation at large and in Boston in particular helped to spur the civil libertarians to take action against censorship. By the mid-1920s, the ACLU's interest in free speech rights extended beyond the defense of unpopular political views. Even more important, Prohibition had convinced many civil libertarians and other citizens that religiously in-spired social reform had trampled upon the Bill of Rights. Civil libertarians, such as Senator James Reed of Missouri, believed that the "modern moral reformer insists upon substituting statutory commands for ethical precepts and official surveillance for the restraints of morality" (Reed 1925: 1). In critics' eyes, enforcement of the Eighteenth Amendment subverted other constitutionally guaranteed civil liberties. In order to mobilize support to repeal the Eighteenth Amendment, the Association Against the Prohibition Amendment (AAPA) and other critics publicized shocking stories of agents shooting unarmed bootleggers or committing other outrageous acts in the name of enforcing the "noble experiment" (AAPA 1929; Merz 1931: 130–96, 282–304). The repeal movement found plenty of evidence in Boston to support its case. In January 1930, for instance, the Coast Guard killed three crew members of a rum runner caught off of Cape Cod.[44] Many found the use of spies and *agent provocateurs* reminiscent of the repressive activities of the government during the Great War and afterward in the Palmer raids. To many critics, as the *Wickersham Report* later confirmed, the unscrupulous be-havior of enforcement agencies provided the ammunition that the repeal movement needed to undermine public support for prohibition (Clark 1976: 111, 159–63, 166–67, 193–97; Kerr 1985: 221–31, 268–73).

The trial and execution of Nicola Sacco and Bartolomeo Vanzetti, two Italian immigrants and known anarchists, for the murder of a paymaster and guard at a South Braintree shoe factory in 1920 heightened many Bostonians' commitment to free speech rights. As Bostonians became more familiar with the story, especially from newspaper columns by the *Boston Globe*'s Gardner Jackson, many became convinced that Vanzetti was innocent and maybe even Sacco (Kempton 1955: 41–51). As the August 1927 execution date approached, a small defense committee, which included Felix Frankfurter, raised credible doubts about the prosecution's deceitful use of evidence and the presiding judge's lack of objectivity (Frankfurter 1927). Boston was also the site of several other bruising fights over free speech in the 1920s. For example, three times Catholic Democratic Mayor James Curley refused to allow Margaret Sanger to hold birth control meetings in the city. "You might just as well seek to convince me," the mayor wrote John Codman of the MCLU, that Boston's churches "should open their doors and give their pulpits to the missionaries of Sodom and Gomorrah" (Chafee 1929: 12–13). While both the Watch and Ward Society and the Boston archdiocese led by Cardinal O'Connell advocated the suppression of salacious literature, they differed over the censorship of birth control information. Since the Watch and Ward Society did not oppose the distribution of birth control literature, it never pursued prosecution of Sanger or any of her allies. This fact not only indicates one critical difference between the Watch and Ward Society and Boston Catholics but also suggests that early-twentieth-century cultural conservatives were hardly a monolithic movement, as many historians have assumed, but rather held a variety of different and sometimes opposing positions on the controversial issue of birth control.

The Episcopalian Chafee's belligerence with avowed agnostics and the Protestant Watch and Ward Society's silence over birth control raise questions about intentionality and social movement politics. To be sure, some opponents of the Watch and Ward Society, such as Mencken, Darrow, Hays, Lewis, Sinclair, and Liveright, were ideologically anti-Christian. Frankfurter and Chafee, however, were not aggressively antagonistic. Frankfurter described himself as "a reverent agnostic." Chafee, by contrast, was a lifelong Episcopalian. In reference to censorship, neither expressed the animus toward Christianity others in the coalition did. Their commitment to the principle of free speech alone drove their opposition to censorship. They shared only this common grievance with the cultural modernists and avant-garde publishers. Their commitment to free speech, moreover, was born out of personal experience with attempts to repress the civil liberties. Frankfurter had experienced anti-Semitism as the first Jew appointed to the Harvard Law School faculty. He had also authored controversial reports while serving on President Wilson's Mediation Commission during the war that branded him a radical sympathizer (Frankfurter and Phillips 1960: 291). The Espionage Act aroused in Chafee an academic interest in free speech (Smith 1986: 118–19). Chafee's 1920 book, *Freedom of Speech*, so outraged conservative Harvard alumni that he nearly lost his faculty position (Auerbach 1969: 531).

If the coalition of secularizing activists consisted of different groups, why was the Watch and Ward Society unable to arouse widespread support from the fundamentalist and Catholic communities of Boston? Mainline Protestants, fundamentalists, and Catholics certainly shared a common grievance: they all despised pernicious literature. For instance, Boston's fundamentalist Baptist newspaper, the *Watchman-Examiner*, viewed modernist writers' attempt to "exalt reality" the "most specious and most dangerous pretext in all this insidious effort to undermine Christian ideals of society and to destroy family life" ("The Tendency to Indecency," 1927: 1318). Through articles and editorials in the *Pilot*, Cardinal O'Connell warned Catholics about the peril that pernicious literature posed to their moral well-being. When *Elmer Gantry* hit Boston's book market, albeit briefly, the *Pilot* called it "commercialized bunk" and "an anti-religious tract" ("Commercialized Bunk," 1927: 4). Like the Watch and Ward Society, O'Connell embraced censorship as a reasonable tactic for reforming society. Not surprisingly, anticensorship activists frequently identified Boston's Catholic community with the Protestant establishment when it came to censorship. According to Elmer Davis, the "Puritans forged the sword and the Irish are wielding it" (Davis 1928: 43). While the Watch and Ward Society worked with Catholic police chiefs and district attorneys to enforce obscenity laws, there was no organized cooperation between the organization and the Boston archdiocese.

Key reasons for the Watch and Ward Society's failure to build a broad-based coalition for political action were the long-standing divisions and antagonisms within the Protestant community of Boston. Boston's Protestants, as noted above, had been divided into conservative and liberal factions for more than a generation. Several sources fueled the breach between Boston's mainline Protestant and Catholic churches. The most obvious tension concerned theology. Many late-nineteenth-century liberal Catholic theologians sought to revise traditional neo-scholastic theology in light of modern science and biblical criticisms. After Pope Leo XIII censored the theological movement of Americanism in 1899 and Pope Pius X condemned theological modernism as error in 1907, American Catholicism officially went in a direction opposite to that of mainline Protestantism. O'Connell was American Catholicism's leading ultramontanist in the early twentieth century. Moreover, in Boston in the 1920s, theological antagonisms were intertwined with Protestant nativism and Catholic responses. Nowhere did the tensions between the Protestant Brahmins and Irish Catholic community become more visible than in the 1928 presidential election. Charles M. Marshall expressed Protestant misgivings in an open letter to New York Governor Alfred E. Smith in the *Atlantic Monthly* in 1927. The essence of the criticism centered around whether the Catholic doctrine of the union of church and state contradicted the American principle of the separation of church and state and if Catholics tolerate non-Catholics by favor and not right (Marshall 1927: 540–49). "I recognize no power in the institutions of my Church," Smith replied in the following issue, "to interfere with the operations of the Constitution of the United States or the enforcement of the law of the land" (Smith 1927: 721–28). While historians would later argue that religion did not play a determinative role in the election, this would have been utterly lost upon Boston liberal Protestants and Catholics in 1927 and 1928, who traded accusations of religious intolerance. One final, crucial factor that helps explain the lack of cooperation between the Watch and Ward Society and pro-censorship Boston Catholics was O'Connell's conviction that associating with the Protestant establishment was not worth the effort. "The Puritan has passed into history," O'Connell announced with satisfaction at the centennial celebration of the See of Boston in 1908. "His children's children live, proud, as they well may be, of the great civic accomplishment of their fathers. But his creed has passed from the land. . . . The child of the immigrant is called to fill the place which the Puritan has left" (O'Connell 1911: 132).

THE DUNSTER HOUSE BOOK SHOP CONTROVERSY
AND VICTORY BY THE SECULARIZING ACTIVISTS, 1929–1930

Just days after the MCLU held its "War Chest" meeting and a few weeks before the Catholic church inaugurated its "Clean Book" campaign, a quiet conversation in a Cambridge bookstore set off an explosive chain of events that would quickly subvert the Watch and Ward Society's cultural authority over literature in Boston. On October 15, John Tait Slaymaker, a fifty-seven-year-old agent for the Watch and Ward Society, visited the Dunster House Book Shop near Harvard Square to see if a report that the store was selling D. H. Lawrence's *Lady Chatterley's Lover* was accurate (New England Watch and Ward Society 1930: 6). The store did not have the book, but he returned the next day and placed an order with James DeLacey, the store owner. Two weeks later, a clerk, James Sullivan, delivered a copy to Slaymaker. The November trial barely received the media's attention. Bodwell's monthly report also described it *pro forma*. Arthur Stone, who presided over the November trial, had even expressed appreciation for the society's work. "This is the worst book I have seen in my twenty-five years experience as a judge. . . . As for the methods employed in buying the book," he added, "they were the only methods that could be successfully employed in a case like this. I say that in this instance the New England Watch and Ward Society has rendered a service to the community."[45] By Thanksgiving, DeLacey and Sullivan had been convicted of selling obscene literature, fined, and sentenced to the House of Corrections.

If a Massachusetts court had found Dreiser's *An American Tragedy* obscene, it was unlikely that *Lady Chatterley's Lover* would fair any better. At the December appeal before the State Superior Court, the booksellers' new attorney, Herbert Parker, turned the tables on the society and accused them of entrapping his clients by using an *agent provocateur*. The media reported the allegation as a statement of fact. Not only was the coalition of secularizing activists outraged by the Watch and Ward Society's reported activity, but the organization drew harsh criticism from totally unexpected quarters. The controversy energized the renewed effort to revise the state's obscenity law. In fact, the secularizing activists, led by the MCLU, had just organized the Massachusetts Citizens Committee for Revision of the Book Law and were holding public meetings to cultivate wider support for overturning the key institutional structure that empowered the society's jurisdiction over literature in Boston. The controversy provided activists with a new political opportunity to challenge the Watch and Ward Society. Not since the Sacco-Vanzetti trial, the *Boston Evening Transcript* observed, had a conviction generated such a storm of public controversy.[46]

At the December appeal of DeLacey's and Sullivan's convictions, Parker waived his clients' right to a jury trial and opted instead to allow Judge Frederick Fosdick to determine their fate. Parker was no brazen ACLU agitator brought in from New York, but the retired Attorney General for the state of Massachusetts. Because of his stature, Parker's scathing attack on the society's tactics gained immediate credibility. He framed his questions in a way that made the society's investigation look like a clear-cut case of an *agent provocateur* entrapping an honest bookseller. Upon cross-examination, for instance, Slaymaker acknowledged that he had deceived DeLacey by giving his name as John Tait. Such dissembling was common among antivice organizations. Under Parker's badgering questions, Slaymaker also conceded that when he had first visited the store the novel was not available. "You kept after it until you got it?" Parker asked. "I got it," vindictively admitted Slaymaker. The society had always defended its agents and their tactics as honest. When Parker bullied Bodwell into acknowledging that the society had used these methods for decades, the media reports made it sound remarkably scandalous. Prohibition agents often disguised themselves to capture bootleggers. One infamous pair of federal agents, Izzy Einstein and Moe Smith, for instance, disguised themselves as grave diggers, vegetable vendors, fishermen, and even churchgoers to trap bootleggers. Parker, drawing on the widespread contempt for prohibition agents and their deceptive methods, had little trouble getting Slaymaker to admit that he went into the bookstore by posing as a salesman for the Automotive Legal Association. The Boston media helped Parker exploit the society's tactic by running front-page stories with sensational titles, such as "Gave False Name, Agent Confesses" (Merz 1931: 135–37).[47] The society had always professed that its guiding motive was to keep pernicious literature out of the hands of children. But when Parker pointed out Slaymaker's age, his accusation that the society was really out to get DeLacey seemed all the more credible. DeLacey, moreover, was not some street peddler hawking nude pictures to school boys but a Yale graduate with many respectable friends in the Harvard community. Stewart Mitchell, editor of the *New England Quarterly*, and Robert T. Hillyer, a Harvard English professor, testified to his good character. In his summation, Parker admitted that *Lady Chatterley's Lover* was "abominable," but said the tactics of the society constituted the real obscenity. He called them "miserable false pretenders posing as guardians of public morals."[48] The Watch and Ward Society might have survived Parker's harangue; after all, he was a paid defense attorney trying to save his clients from jail. They never expected what was to come next.

The society had always found willing allies in the judicial system. Now, however, both the judge and district attorney turned against it. Fosdick agreed with Parker: the Watch and Ward Society had "induced" DeLacey to sell the book. This entrapment "robs the offense of a great deal of its wickedness." Since Slaymaker might have been a "low panderer" who would in turn sell the book to a youth, DeLacey's "indifference" about who was buying the book troubled Fosdick. The judge said that while he held "no cordiality" for the methods of the society, he believed that only legislative action could "obviate such evils." He sentenced DeLacey to a $500 fine and one month in prison but set aside Sullivan's conviction because he was only a clerk carrying out his job.[49] Parker immediately appealed the decision to the State Supreme Court.[50]

Fosdick's criticisms proved to be gentle compared to the vociferous attack of the district attorney, Robert Bushnell. He called *Lady Chatterley's Lover* the work of a "filthy degenerate" but said it was the obligation of his office to uphold the state's obscenity law. Yet he adamantly opposed censorship by "self-appointed persons" and described the actions of the Watch and Ward Society as "the best illustration of the futility of the existence of private, snooping societies." Bushnell had apparently changed his position on censorship. Two years earlier at the height of the "Book War," he had proposed the creation of a citizen review board to censor books and plays. Other factors than the Watch and Ward Society's questionable activity may have come into play in his reversal. Bushnell had political ambitions to serve in a higher office. Soon after the trial concluded, he announced that he was going to run for Lieutenant Governor on the Republic ticket.[51] This is not to suggest that Bushnell railed against the society solely to demonstrate to civil libertarians in Cambridge that he shared their commitments. His attack, however, would certainly not hurt him politically.[52] In his closing argument, Bushnell warned that if the society even went "into a bookstore in this district, and procure[d] the commission of a crime which would not othrewise [sic] be committed, I'll proceed against them for criminal conspiracy." The courtroom, the *Globe* reported, sat in stunned silence.[53]

Outraged critics of the society soon joined Bushnell in protest. To be sure, not everyone opposed the society. A. Z. Conrad, the fundamentalist pastor of Park Street Church, "rapped" Bushnell from the pulpit for not doing more to protect society from "character-destroying books."[54] However, vocal opponents far outnumbered Watch and Ward Society supporters. Critics were upset that the existing law permitted the Watch and Ward Society's activity. Civil libertarians, cultural modernists, publishers, educators, newspapers, and even some religious leaders joined in the chorus denouncing the society's tactics and pointing to the DeLacey case as demonstrating the pressing need to revise the state's obscenity law.

The proposed revision came up for consideration in the state legislature just as criticisms were cascading down upon the society. January 1930 was a terrible month for the organization. It got pummeled by critics from all sides. For example, Gardner Jackson sarcastically mused in the *Nation* that it "must be frightfully uncomfortable to be 'an expert' in obscenity" (Jackson 1930: 64–65). Likewise, William Allen Neilson, president of Smith College, wrote in the *Atlantic Monthly*, that "[t]he saving of a man's soul, which one must presume is the object of the censorship," he concluded, "is after all a man's own affair, and is not to be achieved by external compulsion or guardianship" (Neilson 1930: 16). Some of the more progressive voices in Boston's Protestant establishment also joined the activist coalition. For instance, Dieffenbach, the pugnacious editor of the Unitarian *Christian Register*, sided with the secularists. "The idea that morals come ready made from Heaven is false," he asserted. "Every generation makes its own morals. The saccharine days of our Sunday School are past."[55] Society leaders felt besieged. Critics pursued the organization throughout the spring. In a lengthy April article in the *North American Review*, aptly titled "Banned in Boston," Bushnell detailed the DeLacey case. Despite the fact that "the few remaining Cotton Mathers and other quack doctors of public morals" still opposed liberalizing the obscenity statute, Bushnell contended, the vast majority of people believed it was time to bring the law "into accord with common sense" (Bushnell 1930: 518–25). In the past, advocates of censorship, such as Perry, employed "common sense" in their arguments advocating the censorship of what they considered to be socially destructive forms of literature.

Now critics had captured "common sense" and mobilized the phrase in arguments to restrict the activities of Boston's moral reformers.

As critics berated the organization, the Watch and Ward Society was rocked by the public defections of three prominent members. The first was the director, Julian L. Coolidge, a mathematics professor at Harvard. While he claimed that he was overwhelmed by academic duties, the *Boston Globe* reported in a front-page story that Coolidge's association with the society had cost him dearly at Harvard. He had recently been appointed master of the new Lowell House, but students were reluctant to sign up for rooms for the next academic year because they feared his *in loco parentis* oversight.[56] On New Year's Eve, the Boston press reported that the retired Episcopal bishop of Massachusetts and society vice president, William Lawrence, had abandoned the organization. Then word leaked out that David D. Scannell, a prominent surgeon, and another director had left the organization in protest. "I'm out, I'm free and I'm glad to be out," was the only comment that Scannell would make to reporters after his resignation.[57] These resignations fueled a feeding frenzy among Boston's newspapers. When the society's directors gathered to discuss the controversy at the Boston City Club in early January, the media laid siege in the hallway outside the meeting room ([Hiltz] 1930a; [Hiltz] 1930b).[58] Whereas the society's secretary, president, and directors ran the organization's daily operations, the honorary position of vice president proved to be a major organizational weakness in the structure of the society. When the press approached William Anderson, the bishop of the Methodist Episcopal Church of Massachusetts, for his position on the controversy, he said that he had read recent newspaper articles listing him as a vice president with "a good deal of surprise." He had never been notified of his "election." Anderson speculated that the honorary title was a "legacy" which he inherited from his predecessor.[59] The names of some of Boston's most prominent citizens provided the society with cultural capital and lent social credibility to its work, but amid the controversy swirling around the society, some found their association to be a major liability. Mencken's plan to unmask the "false-faces" of the honorary vice presidents had finally been realized.

Though staggered by the barrage of condemnation, the society attempted to reply to its critics. In December, immediately after the second trial, the directors met in emergency session and issued a press release. "This organization was founded by such men as Edward Everett Hale and Phillips Brooks. Some of Boston's best citizens have been in its service. . . . It is entitled to be treated with some respect."[60] In the face of media criticism, the directors grew indignant and sounded very much like the caricature of the self-righteous Puritan that Mencken had created. By reminding people that Hale and Brooks had founded the organization, they were attempting to cash in on their founders' virtuous character. Throughout 1930, Calkins, Bodwell, and other leaders repeatedly invoked the respectable names of their founders as a defense against questions about their own integrity. This was a weak response to genuine questions about the conduct of the organization, and it may have worked against them. The defection of three of Boston's most prominent citizens suggested that they may have found the media's negative attention undesirable and perhaps also the society's conduct dishonorable. Critics pointed out the apparent contradiction. Moreover, many of the society's critics, such as Chafee, Neilson, and Weeks, were hardly scoundrels.

In addition to the appeal to its founders' respectable reputations, the society vehemently denied the accusation that it had entrapped DeLacey. In fact, the charge seemed to have surprised the leadership. The society, they reasoned, had to use "detective methods" because it was the only way to secure evidence that could stand up in court. They flatly denied, however, that the society employed an *agent provocateur*. Because the case was pending before the State Supreme Court, the society refused to go into specific details (Calkins and Bodwell 1929). This reluctance, however, gave the impression that it was obfuscating.

In the past, the society had relied upon the judicial system to help them ensure that the only books legally sold were those that they deemed morally acceptable. But Fosdick and Bushnell had taken away that asset. The organization was desperate to regain its credibility. In January, it hired Thomas Proctor, a past president of both the Boston and Massachusetts Bar Associations, to review the society's role in the DeLacey case. Not surprisingly, Proctor's report exonerated the organization. Proctor determined that DeLacey had not only "voluntarily" sold the book to Slaymaker but did so at a profit of 200 percent. DeLacey had also sold five other copies of *Lady Chatterley's Lover*. "In conclusion," he wrote, "I have seen nothing in the activities of the agents . . . that was not in the public interest." Because of the pending Supreme Court decision, however, the society waited until July to publish his report (New England Watch and Ward Society 1930: 10).

Despite efforts to rebuff the tirade of criticisms, many longtime Watch and Ward Society members abandoned the organization. Some wrote and demanded that their names be removed from the society's rolls, as one person put it, for playing an "unprincipled trick" upon the Cambridge book dealer (Pierce 1930). Bodwell tried to reassure members that the society was innocent. "I would be among the first to resign," he told one member, "if I had to countenance any unethical methods" (Bodwell 1930). In a form letter sent to all members in January, Calkins complained that the "storm of newspaper criticisms" was "such as almost to deceive the very elect." Unfortunately, he told supporters, "our lips were partially sealed by law," and it

THE DESTRUCTION OF MORAL REFORM POLITICS

would be weeks before the society could fully explain its actions ([Calkins] 1930a). Not everyone disapproved of the society's actions. One person increased his annual contribution, albeit by only three dollars, to demonstrate his "hearty approval of the recent action" (Brigham 1930). Overall, however, the society had lost credibility among its members. If support for the society's role in the Dunster House Book Shop affair is judged by the annual financial contributions of members, then they overwhelmingly disapproved of the action. According to the treasurer's monthly report in July 1930, year-to-date contributions had dropped by almost 54 percent compared to the previous year ("Treasurer's Report" 1930). The Great Depression undoubtedly had a negative impact on giving. Numerous members apologetically returned the annual subscription form without a pledge, citing, as one put it, "[W]e've got our hands more than full" (Platt 1931). Because it severely weakened the society's financial resources, the Depression came at an opportune moment for the secularizing activists. A review of the society's financial records also reveals that many longtime members were passing away in the early 1930s. The society was desperately seeking funds. It sent out several fund-raising letters and reminders of overdue memberships. Even Harvard President Lowell stopped giving ("List of Subscribers" 1930). If not for the large endowment, the organization might have gone under. The 1931–1932 annual report claimed that the society's financial affairs were in "excellent condition" (*AR* 1931–32: 6), but they were putting a brave face on a desperate situation.

While the Watch and Ward Society was trying to save its reputation, the Massachusetts Citizens Committee was gaining support in its effort to rewrite the obscenity statute. In mid-December, the committee announced that it was going to push for specific wording that only considered a book "as a whole" to be obscene. The committee had gathered the signatures of a broad coalition of religious leaders, including Dieffenbach; George Spencer, secretary of the Massachusetts Bible Society; Charles Slattery, Episcopal bishop of Massachusetts; educators, including Morison, Neilson, Vida Scudder, English professor at Wellesley College, and Mary E. Wooley, president of Mount Holyoke College; publishers, including Greenslet and Howe; politicians, including former mayor Andrew Peters; and civil libertarians, such as Chafee. One name to appear on the list must have surely stunned the Watch and Ward Society: Bliss Perry joined the forces actively campaigning for revision.[61] But his defection may not be entirely mysterious. In his address on pernicious literature, he differentiated between books that violated obscenity laws and those that only transgressed the higher law of truth, goodness, and beauty. Although he might have found works like Dreiser's *An American Tragedy* offensive to his literary sensibilities, it is quite possible that he did not deem it obscene in a legal sense. He may have found the proposed revision a useful way to help clarify this distinction in a court of law. Given the list of elites in favor of revision, it was also in his best interest professionally to join the coalition.

At the meeting of the Legislative Affairs Committee in late January, the secularizing activists offered a compelling case for revision. Edward Weeks articulated the activists' position with a history of censorship in Boston and a straightforward explanation of their grievances against the current law. More than two dozen people, including former attorney general Parker, retired mayor Peters, George A. Gordon's successor at Old South Church, Russell Stafford, and the editor of the Methodist *Zion's Herald,* Lewis Hartman, offered more temperate testimony on behalf of revision. The opponents of revision were clearly outnumbered. Bernard Rothwell, a director of the Watch and Ward Society, was the lone representative at the hearings. He did not doubt the sincerity of the proponents of revision, but he questioned their familiarity with the difficulty of combating pernicious literature. Why, he begged the committee, expose the state's youth to "the moral sewerage of a depraved or decadent humanity"? Despite Rothwell's efforts, the committee sent the bill to the legislature for passage. Both the House and the Senate passed the measure with just one revision. The final version struck out the hotly contested phrase, "as a whole," as a compromise with opponents. Yet the exact wording of the new statute clearly accomplished the secularizing activists' goal. In the past, any book "*containing* obscene, indecent or impure language or manifestly tending to corrupt the morals of youths" could be deemed obscene and therefore illegal, but now only a book "which is obscene" would be barred from sale. In other words, the entire book, not merely a sentence or paragraph, had to be deemed obscene.[62]

The successful revision of the state's obscenity law severely curtailed the Watch and Ward Society's jurisdiction over literature in Massachusetts. Not only had the organization been thoroughly discredited, but the new obscenity law meant that allegedly obscene passages had to be read within their entire literary context. When the State Supreme Court upheld DeLacey's conviction in May, the society greeted the news as vindication. But it was a hollow victory at best. Upon Bushnell's recommendation, Fosdick remitted DeLacey's prison sentence. The coalition took up a collection to pay the five hundred dollar fine on his behalf. The list of contributions was a veritable who's who of the secular activists. Chafee, Codman, Frankfurter, Hillyer, Knopf, Mencken, Morison, Sedgwick, and Weeks were among more than two hundred opponents of censorship grateful for DeLacey's unintended service.[63]

Although wounded, the society attempted regain some of its former strength in the years that followed. In addition to the ongoing efforts to raise money, in June 1930 the organization attempted to replace Coolidge, Scannell, and Lawrence with equally prominent citizens. William Phelps, an

English professor at Yale with a reputation for criticizing modernist literature, for example, declined their invitation, but Henry Sherrill, the newly
appointed Episcopal bishop of Massachusetts, accepted (Calkins 1930b;
Sherrill 1930). The society also attempted to broaden its community of support beyond the Protestant establishment, even asking Cardinal O'Connell
to serve as an honorary vice president. Not surprisingly, he declined the offer (Calkins 1930c). The organization's Protestant heritage, the vestiges of
nativism, and the damage done to the society by the Dunster House Book
Shop affair prevented the organization from expanding its base of support
well beyond the aging mainline Protestant establishment.

The clearest evidence that the secularizing activists had successfully restricted the Watch and Ward Society's cultural authority over literature in
Massachusetts is that the organization curtailed its efforts to censor books it
found to be pernicious. In the society's annual report for 1930–1931, the
organization conceded defeat. Since revision, the society acknowledged
that it "does no more advance book censoring and cannot justly be criticized in the future on this score" (AR 1930–31: 15–17). This position, however, did not preclude the possibility of making official complaints to the
police about works it found obscene. The fact that the society had lodged
no such complaints about books during the past year, however, indicates
that it had restricted its activities to other areas, namely burlesque theaters,
gambling, prostitution, and "Unquestionable Obscenities," such as nude
pictures and sex magazines (Rothwell 1930). With the growing expansion
of the state and federal governments, many people in Massachusetts, as in
the nation at large, questioned the necessity and even the right of private,
voluntary, antivice organizations to exist. In January of 1932, some legislators on the Joint Committee on Rules proposed that the state investigate the
operation of the Watch and Ward Society and even threatened to eliminate
the organization by legislation. The society viewed the threats as little more
than a punitive attack on the part of secularizing activists. They successfully
argued that they were a voluntary organization, just like the Massachusetts
Society for the Prevention of Cruelty to Children. As such, they had a right
to insist that state's antivice laws were enforced and to complement the
state's efforts to enforce those laws (AR 1931–32: 8–13; [Dowling?] 1933).

Religiously inspired moral reform had not come to an end in the 1930s,
as the Catholic Legion of Decency's influence over Hollywood's Production
Code Administration indicates. Nonetheless, the censorship of modern
literature, a form of cultural consumption more established and not as popular as the new media of Hollywood movies, had certainly become less popular (Walsh 1996). On the national level, efforts to revise federal antiobscenity laws followed a course similar to the events in Massachusetts. Some
of the same activists involved in the effort to curb the Watch and Ward Society's jurisdiction over literature, such as Chafee, were also involved in the

struggle to lift the restriction on imported literature that postal and custom authorities deemed pernicious. This movement began with some colorful debates in the U.S. Senate between New Mexico Senator Bronson M. Cutting, a Harvard graduate and admirer of modern literature, and Reed Smoot, a conservative Mormon and senator from Utah, over revising importation prohibitions in the 1929 Tariff Act. The Senate eventually passed a bill that precluded the legal importation of obscene literature but left it to the courts to determine whether particular books violated the statutes (Walker 1990: 82–86).[64] In 1931, the ACLU launched a national "crusade," as Morris Ernst described it, to revise federal obscenity laws (Ernst 1932: 122–24). Protestant moral reform efforts fell on hard times in the 1930s. According to one longtime Watch and Ward Society member, the "same underlying spirit" animated the opposition to both his organization and the work of the Anti-Saloon League. The ACLU's efforts to revise obscenity laws paralleled the efforts of the Association Against the Prohibition Amendment to overturn the Eighteenth Amendment. In the very same week of December 1933 that Congress repealed the Eighteenth Amendment, Ernst won a landmark decision in federal court that allowed the legal importation of James Joyce's *Ulysses*.[65]

The demise of the Watch and Ward Society's cultural authority over literature was the result of a secular revolution. The cultural crisis surrounding the First World War proved to be critical. Among the Young Intellectuals, the war produced a violent backlash against Victorian culture. These militantly aggressive cultural modernists rejected the Victorian worldview, morality, and view of literature that had dominated American culture for more than a generation. Nowhere was this rebellion against Victorians more eloquently expressed than in literary realism. This new genre of literature and the avant-garde publishers who produced it flourished in America's mass consumer economy. The war not only helped to produce a generation of anti-Victorian intellectuals but also gave rise to the civil libertarian movement. Because of the growing repression of unpopular political ideas, the possible execution of two political dissidents, the widespread violation of basic rights by government agencies responsible for enforcing prohibition laws, and the apparent suppression of intellectual freedom as symbolized in the Scopes Trial, the value of safeguarding constitutionally guaranteed civil liberties gained popularity, as did the ACLU and various state civil libertarian organizations. The cultural modernists' use of ridicule to discredit the social credibility of the Watch and Ward Society and the judicial challenge to the state's obscenity laws proved to be successful tactics in subverting the Watch and Ward Society's cultural authority. The controversies surrounding Mencken and the *American Mercury* in 1926, Theodore Dreiser and *An American Tragedy* from 1927 through 1929, and the Dunster House Book Shop controversy in 1929, proved to be crucial political opportunities to restrict the Watch and Ward Society's cultural authority. Moreover, these controversies not only helped to mobilize a coalition of anticensorship activities but also cost the Watch and Ward Society invaluable support. The media, the judiciary, socially prominent vice presidents, and directors abandoned their support for the organization and its moral reform activities. The defection of rank-and-file members proved to be equally devastating. Not only were regular supporters passing away, but the Great Depression cost the Watch and Ward Society desperately needed resources. In its support for the censorship of obscene literature, like that for Prohibition, the Protestant establishment proved to be much more vulnerable and more easily toppled than anyone might have suspected in the heady days following the Great War.

NOTES

I would like to express my gratitude to Margaret Bendroth, Kraig Beyerlein, John Evans, Gillis Harp, Alan Hunt, Allison Parker, Jon Roberts, and Chris Smith for their helpful criticisms, as well as to Bryn Dunham, Lucy Pearce, and Dave Premawardhana for their help as research assistants.

1. Annual reports of the New England Watch and Ward Society are hereafter cited in text as *AR*, with the year.

2. The phrase "Protestant establishment" and its synonyms are used in a descriptive, not normative, sense. A "Protestant establishment" can be defined both as a group of denominations, namely the Congregationalists, Episcopalians, Presbyterians, Disciples of Christ, the United Lutherans, and the white branches of the Baptist and Methodist churches, and as an informal network of leaders who dominated various inter-denominational institutions, such as the Federal and later National Council of Churches (Hutchison, 1989a: x–xi; Hutchison, 1989b, 3–5).

3. *Boston Herald,* April 14, 1927: 10.

4. *Boston Globe,* March 17, 1930: 7.

5. *Publishers' Weekly,* May 28, 1927: 2120.

6. *Publishers' Weekly,* June 13, 1925: 1937.

7. *Boston Post,* April 30, 1926: 9.

8. *Boston Evening Transcript,* May 4, 1926: 4.

9. *Boston Evening Transcript,* April 6, 1926: 1, 9; and April 7, 1926: 1–2.

10. See also the *Boston Post,* April 8, 1926: 2.

11. *Publishers' Weekly,* April 10, 1926: 1277.

12. *Boston Post,* April 6, 1926: 1, 14.

13. *Boston Herald,* April 14, 1927: 1, 14.

14. *Boston Herald,* April 14, 1927: 1, 14.

15. *Boston Evening Transcript,* April 14, 1927: 6; *Boston Globe,* April 15, 1927: 15.

16. *Publishers' Weekly,* March 12, 1927: 1058.

17. *Publishers' Weekly,* March 19, 1927: 1254–55; *Publishers' Weekly,* April 16, 1927: 1570; *Boston Globe,* April 13, 1927: 4.

18. *Boston Herald,* March 15, 1927: 3.

19. *Publishers' Weekly*, April 23, 1927: 1651.
20. Ibid.
21. *Boston Globe*, April 17, 1929: 11.
22. See also *Publishers' Weekly*, April 23, 1927: 1943.
23. *Publishers' Weekly*, April 30, 1927: 1712.
24. *Publishers' Weekly*, December 7, 1929: 2676.
25. *Publishers' Weekly*, April 27, 1929: 2022.
26. *Boston Herald*, June 22, 1927: 18.
27. *Publishers' Weekly*, July 16, 1927: 206.
28. *Boston Herald*, October 23, 1927: E-3.
29. *Boston Herald*, June 2, 1927: 20.
30. *Boston Herald*, June 9, 1927: 18.
31. *Publishers' Weekly*, December 10, 1927: 2112.
32. *Boston Evening Transcript*, December 27, 1927: sec. 1, 18.
33. *Boston Evening Transcript*, January 25, 1928: sec. 1, 10; *Publishers' Weekly*, January 28, 1928: 349–50.
34. *Publishers' Weekly*, February 4, 1928: 444–47; *Publishers' Weekly*, May 12, 1928: 1963–64.
35. *Boston Evening Transcript*, April 2, 1929: 1, 7.
36. *Boston Evening Transcript*, April 4, 1929: 16.
37. *Publishers' Weekly*, March 2, 1929: 963.
38. *Boston Globe*, April 17, 1929: 17.
39. *Boston Evening Transcript*, April 17, 1929: 3.
40. *Boston Globe*, April 17, 1929: 17.
41. *Boston Globe*, October 10, 1929: 1–2.
42. *Boston Evening Transcript*, October 10, 1929: 3.
43. *Boston Evening Transcript*, November 2, 1929: sec. 2, 8.
44. *Boston Evening Transcript*, January 2, 1930: 1.
45. *Boston Evening Transcript*, November 25, 1929: 5.
46. *Boston Evening Transcript*, January 11, 1930: 1.
47. *Boston Globe*, December 21, 1929: 1.
48. *Boston Globe*, December 21, 1929: 1, 28.
49. *Boston Globe*, December 21, 1929: 1–2; *Boston Evening Transcript*, December 20, 1929: 1, 8.
50. *Boston Evening Transcript*, December 21, 1929: 10.
51. *Boston Evening Transcript*, January 17, 1930: 1.
52. *Boston Evening Transcript*, April 15, 1927: sec. 1, 3.
53. *Boston Globe*, December 21, 1929: 1, 2; *Boston Evening Transcript*, December 20, 1929: 1, 8.
54. *Boston Globe*, December 30, 1929: 19.
55. *Boston Globe*, January 4, 1930: 5.
56. *Boston Globe*, December 14, 1929: 1, 19.
57. *Boston Globe*, December 31, 1929: 27.
58. *Boston Globe*, January 13, 1930: 1, 11.
59. *Boston Globe*, January 7, 1930: 32.
60. *Boston Globe*, December 25, 1929: 21.

61. *Boston Evening Transcript,* December 13, 1929: 1, 12.

62. *Boston Globe,* March 19, 1930: 1; *Boston Evening Transcript,* March 20, 1930: 7; *Publishers' Weekly,* May 12, 1963 (my italics); and *Boston Evening Transcript,* March 25, 1930: 1.

63. *Boston Globe,* June 7, 1930: 1, 5.

64. *Publishers' Weekly,* October 5, 1929: 1735.

65. Since 1930, the Watch and Ward Society has changed its name and merged with several other organizations. In 1957 the organization was renamed the New England Citizens' Crime Commission, in 1967 it became the Massachusetts Council on Crime and Correction, in 1975 the Crime and Justice Foundation, and in 1999 the Community Resources for Justice. The organization still exists today, albeit in a new form with a new mission. It operates several halfway houses for disabled adults and also for adult offenders released from prison, and it conducts advocacy programs for prison reform.

REFERENCES

AAPA. 1929. *Scandals of Prohibition Enforcement.* Washington: Association Against the Prohibition Amendment.

Angoff, Charles. 1925. "Boston Twilight." *American Mercury* 6: 439–44.

Asbury, Herbert. 1926. "Hatrack." *American Mercury* 7: 479–83.

Auerbach, Jerold. 1969. "The Patrician as Libertarian: Zechariah Chafee, Jr., and Freedom of Speech." *New England Quarterly* 42: 511–31.

Beisel, Nicola. 1997. *Imperiled Innocents: Anthony Comstock and Family Reproduction in Victorian America.* Princeton, NJ: Princeton University Press.

Bernard, James D. [Charles Angoff]. 1926. "The Methodists." *American Mercury* 7: 421–32.

Biel, Steven. 1992. *Independent Intellectuals in the United States, 1910–1945.* New York: New York University Press.

Bode, Carl, ed. 1977. *The New Mencken Letters.* New York: Dial.

Bodwell, Charles. 1930. Letter to Clifton Johnson, 31 Jan. New England Watch and Ward Society Records. Harvard Law School Library. Box 6, Folder 1.

Bradbury, Malcolm. 1983. *The Modern American Novel.* New York: Oxford University Press.

Brigham, William. 1930. Letter to Charles Bodwell, 3 Jan. New England Watch and Ward Society Records. Harvard Law School Library. Box 12, Folder 1.

Bushnell, Robert. 1930. "Banned in Boston." *North American Review* 229: 518–25.

Calkins, Raymond. 1919. *The Church and the Social Conscience.* New York: National Council of Congregational Churches.

[Calkins, Raymond]. 1930a. Letter to "Friends," 1 Jan. New England Watch and Ward Society Records. Harvard Law School Library. Box 12, Folder 1.

———. 1930b. Letter to William Phelps, 2 June. New England Watch and Ward Society Records. Harvard Law School Library. Box 10, Folder 8.

———. 1930c. Letter to Cardinal O'Connell, 2 June. New England Watch and Ward Society Records. Harvard Law School Library. Box 9, Folder 4.

Calkins, Raymond, and Charles Bodwell. 1929. Letter to "Members of the New

England Watch and Ward Society," 24 Dec. New England Watch and Ward Society Records. Harvard Law School Library. Box 9, Folder 5.

Caudill, Edward. 1989. "The Roots of Bias: An Empiricist Press and Coverage of the Scopes Trial." *Journalism Monographs* 114: 3–37.

Cerf, Bennett. 1977. *At Random: The Reminiscences of Bennett Cerf.* New York: Random House.

Chafee, Zechariah. 1929. *The Censorship in Boston.* Boston: Civil Liberties Committee of Massachusetts.

Chase, William S. 1921. *The Case for the Federal Supervision of Motion Pictures.* Brooklyn, NY: n.p.

Chaves, Mark. 1994. "Secularization as Declining Religious Authority." *Social Forces* 72: 749–74.

Clark, Norman. 1976. *Deliver Us from Evil: An Interpretation of American Prohibition.* New York: W. W. Norton.

Coben, Stanley. 1991. *Rebellion against Victorianism: The Impetus for Cultural Change in 1920s America.* New York: Oxford University Press.

"Commercialized Bunk." 1927. *Pilot* 90: 4.

Cowley, Malcolm. 1955. "Sister Carrie: Her Fall and Rise." In *The Stature of Theodore Dreiser,* ed. Alfred Kazin and Charles Shapiro. Bloomington: Indiana University Press.

Crafts, Wilbur. 1911. *Patriotic Studies of a Quarter Century of Moral Legislation in Congress.* Washington, DC: International Reform Bureau.

Davis, Elmer. 1928. "Boston: Notes on a Barbarian Invasion." *Scribner's Magazine* 77: 140–52.

De Voto, Bernard. 1930. "Literary Censorship in Cambridge." *Harvard Graduates Magazine* 39: 30–42.

Dobbelaere, Karel. 1981. "Secularization: A Multi-Dimensional Concept." *Current Sociology* 29: 1–213.

[Dowling, John?]. 1933. Letter to John Mackay, 22 May. New England Watch and Ward Society Records. Harvard Law School Library. Box 7, Folder 4.

Dreiser, Theodore. 1931. *Dawn.* London: Constable.

Duffus, R. L. 1927. "Our Changing Cities: Unruffled Boston." *New York Times Magazine* 10: 6–7.

Dulles, Foster Rhea. 1945. *Twentieth-Century America.* Boston: Houghton Mifflin.

Editorial Note. 1927a. *Nation* 124: 305.

Editorial Note. 1927b. *Nation* 124: 465.

Ernst, Morris L. 1932. "Sex Wins in America." *Nation* 135: 122–24.

Farrell, James. 1955. "Dreiser's *Sister Carrie.*" In *The Stature of Theodore Dreiser,* ed. Alfred Kazin and Charles Shapiro. Bloomington: Indiana University Press.

Frankfurter, Felix. 1927. *The Case of Sacco and Vanzetti: A Critical Analysis for Lawyers and Laymen.* Boston: Little, Brown.

Frankfurter, Felix, and Harlan Phillips. 1960. *Felix Frankfurter Reminisces.* London: Secker and Warburg.

Gilfoyle, Timothy J. 1994. *City of Eros: New York City, Prostitution, and the Commercialization of Sex, 1790–1920.* New York: W. W. Norton.

Gilmer, Walker. 1970. *Horace Liveright: Publisher of the Twenties.* New York: Lewis.

Goodheart, Lawrence. 1991. "The Ambiguity of Individualism: The National Liberal League's Challenge to the Comstock Law." In *American Chameleon: Individualism in a Trans-National Context,* ed. Richard Curry and Lawrence Goodheart. Kent, OH: Kent State University Press.

Gordon, George A. 1902. *The New Epoch for Faith.* Boston: Houghton Mifflin.

———. 1925. *My Education and Religion: An Autobiography.* Boston: Houghton Mifflin.

———. 1929. "A Review of Mr. Lippmann's *A Preface to Morals.*" *Congregationalist* 114: 636–38.

Graff, Gerald. 1987. *Professing Literature: An Institutional History.* Chicago: University of Chicago Press.

Grant, Sidney S., and S. E. Angoff. 1930. "Massachusetts and Censorship." *Boston University Law Review* 10: 36–60, 147–94.

Greenslet, Ferris. 1943. *Under the Bridge: An Autobiography.* Boston: Houghton Mifflin.

Harris, Frank. 1919. *Contemporary Portraits,* 2d ser. New York: Published by the author.

Hays, Arthur Garfield. 1928. *Let Freedom Ring.* New York: Boni and Liveright.

Hecht, Ben. 1922. "Literature and the Bastinado." In *Nonsenseorship: Sundry Observations Concerning Prohibitions, Inhibitions, and Illegalities.* New York: G. P. Putnam's Sons.

[Hiltz, Orrie?]. 1930a. Letter to Raymond Calkins, 30 Apr. New England Watch and Ward Society Records. Harvard Law School Library. Box 4, Folder 6.

[Hiltz, Orrie?]. 1930b. Letter to Charles Bodwell, 9 Aug. New England Watch and Ward Society Records. Harvard Law School Library. Box 4, Folder 6.

Hobson, Fred. 1994. *Mencken: A Life.* Baltimore, MD: Johns Hopkins University Press.

Hunt, Alan. 1999. *Governing Morals: A Social History of Moral Regulation.* Cambridge: Cambridge University Press.

Hutchison, William R. 1976. *The Modernist Impulse in American Protestantism.* Reprint, New York: Oxford University Press, 1982.

———. 1989a. "Preface: From Protestant to Pluralist America." In *Between the Times: The Travail of the Protestant Establishment in America, 1900–1960,* ed. William R. Hutchison. Cambridge: Cambridge University Press.

———. 1989b. "Protestantism as Establishment." In *Between the Times: The Travail of the Protestant Establishment in America, 1900–1960,* ed. William R. Hutchison. Cambridge: Cambridge University Press.

Jackson, Gardner. 1930. "My Brother's Peeper." *Nation* 130: 64–65.

Kallen, Horace. 1929. "Fear, Freedom, and Massachusetts." *American Mercury* 18: 281–92.

Kempton, Murray. 1955. *Part of Our Time: Some Monuments and Ruins of the Thirties.* New York: Simon and Schuster.

Kerr, K. Austin. 1985. *Organized for Prohibition: A New History of the Anti-Saloon League.* New Haven, CT: Yale University Press.

Krutch, Joseph Wood. 1921. "Antichrist and the Five Apostles." *Nation* 113: 733–34.

———. 1925. "Darrow vs. Bryan." *Nation* 121: 136–37.

————. 1927. "The Indecency of Censorship." *Nation* 124: 162–63.

Larson, Edward. 1997. *Summer for the Gods: The Scopes Trial and America's Continuing Debate over Science and Religion.* New York: Basic Books.

Laws, Curtis Lee. 1923. "A Little Journey to Boston." *Watchman-Examiner,* 11: 267–69.

Leach, William. 1993. *Land of Desire: Merchants, Power, and the Rise of a New American Culture.* New York: Vintage Books.

Lee, Charles. 1958. *The Hidden Public: The Story of the Book-of-the-Month Club.* Garden City, NY: Doubleday.

Lewis, Sinclair. 1953. "The American Fear of Literature." In *The Man from Main Street: Selected Essays and Other Writings, 1904–1950,* ed. Harry Maule and Melville Cane. New York: Random House.

Leys, Ruth. 1993. "Mead's Voice: Imitation as Foundation, or, the Struggle against Mimesis." *Critical Inquiry* 19: 277–307.

"A Libertarian Laughs." 1926. *Nation* 122: 440.

Lippmann, Walter. 1922. "The New Machiavelli." *New Republic* 12–14.

————. 1926. "H. L. Mencken." *Saturday Review* 111: 413–14.

————. 1929. *A Preface to Morals.* New York: Macmillan.

"List of Subscribers." 1930. New England Watch and Ward Society Records. Harvard Law School Library. Box 12, Folder 1.

Liveright, Horace. 1923. "The Absurdity of Censorship." *Independent* 110: 192–93.

Marsh, Daniel. 1930. Letter to Raymond Calkins, 25 June. New England Watch and Ward Society Records. Harvard Law School Library. Box 8, Folder 1.

Marshall, Charles. 1927. "An Open Letter to the Honorable Alfred E. Smith." *Atlantic Monthly* 139: 540–49.

May, Henry F. 1959. *The End of American Innocence: A Study of the First Years of our Own Time, 1912–1917.* Reprint, New York: Quadrangle Books, 1964.

McAfree, Helen. 1923. "The Literature of Disillusion." *Atlantic Monthly* 132: 225–34.

McDaniels, George. 1926. "Intolerance Elsewhere, Idolatry Here." *Watchman-Examiner* 14: 1035.

Mencken, H. L. 1908. *The Philosophy of Friedrich Nietzsche.* Boston: John W. Luce.

————. 1917. "Puritanism as a Literary Force." In *A Book of Prefaces,* 197–283. New York: Knopf.

————. 1920. "The National Letters." In *Prejudices: Second Series,* 9–101. New York: Knopf.

————. 1922. "On Being an American." In *Prejudices: Third Series.* New York: Knopf.

————. 1924. "Editorial." *American Mercury* 3: 420–22.

————. 1926. "In Memoriam: W. J. B." In *Prejudices: Fifth Series,* 64–74. New York: Knopf.

————. 1927. Review of "Elmer Gantry," by Sinclair Lewis. *American Mercury* 10: 506–8.

————. 1931. "Editorials." *American Mercury* 24: 409–12.

————. 1937. "Hatrack." In *The Editor, the Bluenose, and the Prostitute,* ed. Carl Bode. Boulder, CO: Robert Rinehart, 1988.

————. 1943. *Heathen Days, 1890–1936.* New York: Knopf.

————. 1949. *A Mencken Chrestomathy.* New York: Knopf.

———. 1993. *My Life as Author and Editor.* Edited and with an introduction by Jonathan Yardley. New York: Knopf.

Merz, Charles. 1931. *The Dry Decade.* New York: Doubleday, Doran.

Minutes of the Directors' Meetings. 1928. New England Watch and Ward Society Records. Harvard Law School Library. Box 14.

Murphy, Paul L. 1979. *World War I and the Origins of Civil Liberties in the United States.* New York: W. W. Norton.

Nathan, George Jean, and H. L. Mencken. 1924. "Editorial." *American Mercury* 1: 27–30.

Neilson, William Allen. 1930. "The Theory of Censorship." *Atlantic Monthly* 145: 13–16.

New England Society for the Suppression of Vice. 1881. *Massachusetts Laws Concerning Offences against Chastity, Morality, and Decency.* Boston: Beacon Press.

New England Watch and Ward Society. 1904–1932. *Annual Report of the New England Watch and Ward Society.*

———. 1930. *The Dunster House Book Shop Case: A Statement.* Boston: New England Watch and Ward Society.

O'Connell, William Cardinal. 1911. *Sermons and Addresses of His Eminence William Cardinal O'Connell, Archbishop of Boston.* Cambridge, MA: Riverside Press.

O'Leary, Robert A. 1980. "William Henry Cardinal O'Connell: A Social and Intellectual Biography." Ph.D. diss. Tufts University.

Parker, Alison M. 1997. *Purifying America: Women, Cultural Reform, and Pro-Censorship Activism, 1873–1933.* Urbana: University of Illinois Press.

Perry, Bliss. 1923. *Pernicious Books: Address by Professor Bliss Perry of Harvard University. Delivered at the Annual Meeting of the New England Watch and Ward Society at the Old South Church, Copley Square, Boston, Mass., April 22, 1923.* Boston: Printed for Watch and Ward Society.

Pierce, Marty. 1930. Letter to Watch and Ward Society, 3 July. New England Watch and Ward Society Records. Harvard Law School Library. Box 10, Folder 6.

Platt, Mrs. T. Beade. 1931. Letter to Watch and Ward Society, 3 Jan. New England Watch and Ward Society Records. Harvard Law School Library. Box 12, Folder 2.

"Protect Our Youth: Reply to 'A Responsible Statement.'" N.d. New England Watch and Ward Society Records. Harvard Law School Library. Box 6, Folder 12.

"Protection of Souls," 1929. *Pilot* 92: 4.

"The Raw Deal for Religion." 1925. *Congregationalist* 110: 134.

Reed, James. 1925. "The Pestilence of Fanaticism." *American Mercury* 5: 1–7.

Riggio, Thomas, ed. 1986. *Dreiser-Mencken Letters: The Correspondence of Theodore Dreiser and H. L. Mencken, 1907–1945.* 2 vols. Philadelphia: University of Pennsylvania Press.

Rodgers, Daniel. 1980. *Work Ethic in Industrial America, 1850–1920.* Chicago: University of Chicago Press.

Rothwell, Bernard. 1930. Letter to Raymond Calkins, 13 Aug. New England Watch and Ward Society Records. Harvard Law School Library. Box 11, Folder 1.

Russell, Bertrand. 1924. "New Morals for Old: Styles in Ethics." *Nation* 118: 497–99.

Sapir, Edward. 1929. "The Discipline of Sex." *American Mercury* 16: 413–20.

Schapiro, Salwyn. 1920. "The Revolutionary Intellectual." *Atlantic Monthly* 125: 820–30.

Schlesinger, Arthur M., Sr. 1963. *In Retrospect: The History of a Historian.* New York: Harcourt, Brace, and World.

Secretary's Report. 1927. New England Watch and Ward Society Records. Harvard Law School Library. Box 16.

Sherman, Stuart. 1915. "The Naturalism of Mr. Dreiser." *Nation* 101: 648–50.

Sherrill, Henry. 1930. Letter to Raymond Calkins, 3 June. New England Watch and Ward Society Records. Harvard Law School Library. Box 11, Folder 11.

Shumway, David. 1994. *Creating American Civilization: A Genealogy of American Literature as an Academic Discipline.* Minneapolis: University of Minnesota Press.

Smith, Alfred E. 1927. "Catholic and Patriot: Governor Smith Replies." *Atlantic Monthly* 139: 721–28.

Smith, Donald. 1986. *Zechariah Chafee, Jr.: Defender of Liberty and Law.* Cambridge, MA: Harvard University Press.

Smith, Harrison, ed. 1952. *From Main Street to Stockholm: Letters of Sinclair Lewis, 1919–1930.* New York: Harcourt, Brace.

Smith, Helena Huntington. 1928. "Boston's Bogy-Man." *Outlook* 140: 214–16, 233.

Stearns, Herald. 1922. "The Intellectual Life." In *Civilization in the United States,* ed. Herald Stearns. New York: Harcourt, Brace.

Swanberg, W. A. 1965. *Dreiser.* New York: Charles Scribner's Sons.

"The Tendency to Indecency." 1927. *Watchman-Examiner* 15: 1318.

"Treasurer's Report." 1930. New England Watch and Ward Society Records. Harvard Law School Library. Box 15.

Villard, Oswald Garrison. 1926. "Sex, Art, Truth, and Magazines." *Atlantic Monthly* 137: 388–98.

Walker, Samuel. 1990. *In Defense of American Liberties: A History of the A.C.L.U.* New York: Oxford University Press.

Walsh, Frank. 1996. *Sin and Censorship: The Catholic Church and the Motion Picture Industry.* New Haven, CT: Yale University Press.

"What Is the Sense of Censorship?" 1927. *Congregationalist* 112: 485.

Williams, Michael. 1927. "The Sinclair Lewis Industry." *Commonweal* 4: 577–79.

"Without Aid of Police." 1926. *Congregationalist* 111: 420.

Wood, A. L. S. 1925. "Keeping the Puritans Pure." *American Mercury* 6: 74–78.

6

"My Own Salvation"

The Christian Century *and Psychology's Secularizing of American Protestantism*

Keith G. Meador

I had baptized the whole Christian tradition in the waters of psychological empiri-
cism, and was vaguely awaking to the fact that, after this procedure, what I had left
was hardly more than a moralistic ghost of the distinctive Christian reality. It was
as if the baptismal waters of the empirical stream had been mixed with some acid
which ate away the historical significance, the objectivity and the particularity of the
Christian revelation, and left me in complete subjectivity to work out my own salva-
tion in terms of social service and an "integrated personality."

CHARLES CLAYTON MORRISON, *"How My Mind Has Changed,"* 1939

It is no longer uncommon to interpret Christianity as a vague set of therapeutic practices dedicated to personal health and well-being. During the
course of the twentieth century, many of America's pastors and preachers began envisioning themselves as agents of psychological and self-help
interventions (Witten 1993). Yet in 1939, Charles Clayton Morrison responded with regret at the secular therapeutic culture forming within
American Protestantism. Morrison recognized that "psychological empiricism" had eaten away at what he elsewhere called his "Christian inheritance," an American public life thoroughly shaped and informed by Protestantism. In this moment Morrison acknowledged his own culpability as a
leader in the secularization of American public life and named psychology
as a secularizing force acting within and through American Protestantism.
Morrison was well situated to make this claim, because for fifty years he
wrote for and edited what became the most influential American Protestant
journal of his era, the *Christian Century*. During his long tenure, Morrison
and his staff introduced and popularized psychology with a language of instinct and personality, which displaced the Christian theological language
of morality and grace. I trace this displacement by analyzing the first four
decades of the *Christian Century* as a reflection of trends in American Protestantism, through which we can examine the central and active role of

psychology in the secularization of American public life. I systematically reviewed each issue of the *Christian Century* published during the period 1900–1940 for psychological language and articles about psychology by reading through each advertisement, book review, column, and essay. The use of psychological language was noted by context and frequency, and then compiled and reviewed. I prepared an annotated bibliography of pertinent articles on psychology and related topics that served as representative primary sources from the *Christian Century*.

It seems paradoxical to speak of American culture as secularized, for Americans profess their personal religious beliefs in study after study. Yet the governing institutions in which Americans live out their lives—business, education, entertainment, law, and medicine alike—bear little evidence of this faith. As Dorrien observes, "Most Americans believe in God, but this affirmation does not lead them to make serious commitments to any community of faith or distinctively Christian ethic" (Dorrien 1995: 216). Americans bracket off their individual beliefs from their public lives.

Sociologists, historians, and other cultural observers traditionally explain the disjunction between the beliefs Americans profess and the institutions in which they live as a normative experience of modernity, a natural outcome of modernizing societies. By naming secularization as an expected process, these observers turn an interpretive lens into a predictive tool: as cultures develop, they will secularize. By employing standard secularization theory, observers narrate secularization as a process intrinsic to modernity, which elides the agency of cultural participants and institutions. In truth, secularization did not occur on its own, but was achieved by the active work of individuals and institutions with variable levels of agency and intentionality. For example, William James, the paradigmatic "tolerant scientist," claimed that "no scientist will ever try actively to interfere with our religious faith, provided we enjoy it quietly with our friends and do not make a public nuisance of it in the market-place" (James 1897: xi). When James praised people for keeping religion in the parlor and out of public life, he echoed his own account of religion as an essentially individual state or experience, and he privileged a decidedly American and Protestant version of religion that embodies its own secularization. Standard secularization theories rightly recognize a dramatic transformation in American public life, as religious faith now resembles what James believed to be its essence, an atomized, individual experience with only a peculiar place in public life—but the mechanism and implications of this process merit ongoing consideration.

H. Richard Niebuhr, a prominent Yale theologian, recognized the significance of the transformation in American public life ushered in by psychologists when he described psychology's marriage with theology as a "sterile union" resulting from the "revolution introduced by William James and his followers" (Niebuhr 1927: 47).[1] Niebuhr was right to name this "revolution" as culturally significant, for it was the work of psychologists like James and others that actively imbued Protestantism with psychology. Many have emphasized the degree to which American Protestantism, broadly construed, was predisposed to embrace the psychology of James, Freud, and their followers (Rubin 1994). I want to propose a model for American secularization that does not assume some prior inevitable trajectory toward secularization, but appreciates the predispositions and affinities of American Protestantism toward the secularizing agent of psychology. As an example of these inclinations, Rieff observes, "[T]here was something about Protestantism itself that made it ready . . . for psychoanalysis. . . . When Freud analyzed actions symptomatically, he appealed chiefly to persons, trained and yet troubled, in just those cultures that had once been Calvinist, or otherwise rigorously ascetic. The therapeutic of the psychological age is successor to the ascetic of the religious age" (Rieff 1990: 12).

Historically, Protestant theology has viewed the Christian life through two distinct yet complementary lenses: one focused on the life and history of the institutional church, and the other on the individual's personal experience. Both lenses were shaped within the American context. American Protestants have long emphasized the latter view much more than their European counterparts and fostered a form of Protestant individualism that pervades American culture (Weber 1930). But even the institutional church was seen from a distinct and complex perspective by the Puritan settlers. They founded America as an ideal Christian community, a "city that is set on a hill." The American Puritans sought to be a people set apart from worldly vice and entrapments, and envisioned a church coterminous with the state in its intentions and eschatological vision. This system was not a theocracy; nor was it a system in which church and state coexisted as two separate branches of authority, as in England. Rather, American Puritanism was a system designed to assure that government would always reflect the life and spirit of the church (Noll 1992). But by the end of the first century of American Puritanism, this vision of a city on a hill was already obscured by increasing numbers of diverse settlers, who foreshadowed the denominational multiplication characteristic of American Protestantism by appropriating their own religious experiences in the formation of new churches.

The fiery preacher and forceful Puritan theologian Jonathan Edwards planted the first seeds of what blossoms into the "*ganz Americanish* psychology" (Rieber 1998: 192). Best remembered for his role in the First Great Awakening, Edwards brought his training in British empiricism into his devout Puritanism. Rieber shows that Edwards sought in his theology "a 'natural' method for the pursuit of salvation and self-knowledge." Edwards therefore "emphasized the teaching of proper moral action and the 'cure of the soul'" that would eventually grow into "the twentieth century concept of mental hygiene and psychotherapy" (Rieber 1998: 192). Though he himself maintained the Puritan tradition, he instigated the first theological deviations that prepared American Protestantism to embrace psychology. His empiricism led him to see personal experience as the foundation of faith and, according to Taylor, "[T]he result was America's first articulation of a science of religious consciousness" (Taylor 1999: 28). The conflicted Christianity that results from the marriage of his Calvinism and his proclivity to locate religious authority within personal experience runs throughout American Protestant history.

Throughout the nineteenth century, Protestantism increasingly emphasized the centrality of personal experience. The practice of revivals in the Second Great Awakening strove to elicit emotional, individual responses, and their success signaled a mass migration of Americans into newer denominations (e.g., Methodists and Baptists) that approached salvation more individualistically (Noll 1992). The central experience of American Protestantism remained the personal surrender of a believer to God, but this surrender's aim changed during the nineteenth century from salvation in a future kingdom to a cathartic shedding of emotional burdens in service of the kingdom within.

Whether this change was inherent to the Protestant project in general or a feature endemic to American Protestantism in particular is beyond the scope of this essay. For now, it can simply be acknowledged that several factors within American Protestant culture, ecclesiology, and theology predisposed American public life to secularization through psychology. However, American Protestants did not bracket off their faith from their public lives because of theological or ecclesiological innovations; they were taught do to so, in part, by the early American psychologists. So the question remains: How did agents of psychology secularize American public life by acting within and through American Protestantism?

Social movement theory's appeal to shifts in socially legitimate power provides an apt lens for observing this secularization process. Viewed through this lens, American Protestantism and psychology are cultural authorities that played significant and often complementary roles in the process of macro-secularization in America as American Protestantism increasingly located "religious experience" between individual believers and their God, and psychology was called upon to interpret that experience. The early American psychologists were formed in the individualism of American Protestantism, but felt incapable of confessing the Christian faith of their ancestors in an age of Darwinian scientific progress. Instead, they embraced psychology as an appropriate replacement for the Protestant faith of their childhood, as a way to make Christianity "scientific." The students of the early American psychologists became leaders within American Protestantism and proselytized for this new American faith, a fully psychological religion, from pulpits, classrooms, and newspapers alike. Psychology actively secularized American public life through a social movement that targeted both broad social structures and individual lives, a movement within American Protestantism. I am chiefly concerned with the agents and cultural structures that actively advocated macro-secularization through psychology in American Protestantism and the ideologies these agents and structures disseminated. During the first four decades of the twentieth century, Charles Clayton Morrison and the staff of the *Christian Century* embodied this process; the *Christian Century* was both a voice of mainline American Protestantism and a purveyor of a psychological interpretation of Protestantism.

THE *CHRISTIAN CENTURY* SINGS THE THERAPEUTIC GOSPEL

Charles Clayton Morrison purchased the *Christian Century* at a 1908 sheriff's sale for $1,500. At the time, the bankrupt publication served a readership of three hundred Disciples of Christ subscribers from its Chicago headquarters, publishing news from local churches, traveling missions, book reviews, and brief theological articles. For years, the *Century* had sought in vain to increase its readership through subscription drives that appealed to the rural background of its readers, offering family Bibles, denominational hymnbooks, groceries, and even hunting rifles in exchange for subscriptions. All to no avail: the *Century* would have certainly folded into the recesses of local history if not for its transformation by Morrison, a young pastor and occasional contributor to the magazine. Morrison had moved to Chicago after graduating from Iowa's Drake College in 1898, and spent the intervening decade pastoring a local church and pursuing graduate studies in philosophy at the University of Chicago under Edward Scribner Ames, James Rowland Angell, John Dewey, and George Herbert Mead. Upon taking the *Century's* reins, Morrison imbued the paper with the functional psychology for which these Chicago professors were famous, and expanded the reach and the aims of the paper from a regional and parochial publication into a national "undenominational journal of religion" that brought the leading Protestant voices of its time into churches, homes, libraries, and schools across the nation. The *Century's* fervent plea, the song sung by this gathered congregation of Protestants, is aptly summarized by Morrison in a 1916 advertisement for a hymnbook that he coedited. Morrison acclaims the hymnbook's three chief features as "Hymns of Christian Unity. Hymns of Social Service. Hymns of the Inner Life." Morrison sang these songs of an ecumenical Protestantism that nourishes the individual self, what he later ruefully recalled as "my own salvation in terms of social service and an 'integrated personality,'" from the pages of the *Century*.

Morrison began his career as a minister of the Disciples of Christ, a denomination that developed out of Presbyterianism on the American frontier, far from established churches and denominations, into a loose confederation of thousands of churches, mostly located in the American Midwest and South (McAllister and Tucker 1975). These churches shared no creed or proscribed liturgy; indeed they saw their pluralism as their strength, as an embodiment of their call to "Christian unity" without creeds. Their rallying cry became, "In essentials, unity; in nonessentials, liberty; in all things, charity" (Disciples of Christ [Christian Churches] 1909: 11). Yet at the end of the nineteenth century, the Disciples were far from unified in their publishing efforts: without a centralized publishing house, a score of their publications vied for readers, notably the conservative *Christian Standard* in Cincinnati and the liberal *Christian-Evangelist* in St. Louis.[2] In 1884, Des Moines Disciples entered their own journal into this crowded market, the *Christian Oracle,* to serve liberal Disciples of Christ pastors and parishioners (McAllister and Tucker 1975). Pastors filled the back pages with reports from across the Midwest, announcing recent converts in Omaha and successful missions in Sioux City. The editors printed portraits of exemplary Disciples preachers on the covers, featured upcoming Disciples conventions, and sang the praises of Disciples colleges like Drake and Bethany. At the time, Americans were swelling the booming midwestern cities in a mass migration from the rural countryside. In 1891, the *Oracle's* editor, D. R. Lucas, followed his readers from Iowa to Chicago. The move would prove beneficial, for Chicago was home to a thriving Disciples community whose leaders included two pastors who were also professors at the University of Chicago: Edward Scribner Ames in philosophy, and Herbert L. Willett in Old Testament.

Ames and Willett were intellectual leaders for Disciples nationwide, working diligently to bring Disciples theology out from the revival tents and frontier churches. Willett in particular saw the Disciples publications as the ideal vehicles for bringing his sophisticated biblical criticism to Disciples in their homes, and he became an informal advisor to the *Oracle's* editors. Indeed, Willett and other prominent Chicago Disciples supported the *Oracle* throughout its tenure, but we can infer its small influence from the fact that Willett published a regular column in St. Louis's *Christian-Evangelist* rather than Chicago's *Oracle.*

In a flush of centennial fever, the editors rechristened the *Christian Oracle* as the *Christian Century* on January 4, 1900. They moved from an oracle, a disembodied image of God's wisdom, to the century, a messianic vision of the inbreaking of the kingdom of God through social witness. The editors called the new name "an inspiration, a programme and a platform. It is almost a creed. It expresses the faith and hope of its present corps of editors. We can wish nothing better for the twentieth century than that it may be Christian in a larger and better sense than any other since Christ was here."[3]

The editors hoped for a century unrivaled in its Christian character, and explicitly figured this character as a "progressive" and "constructive" vision, an "optimistic and hopeful, tolerant and liberal" Christianity (January 4, 1900).

The *Century's* editors embraced psychology as a progressive science of the mind, and psychology texts and innovations appeared often in the *Century* between 1900 and 1903, but the topic faded from prominence from 1904 to 1908. The *Century* did not discuss the German psychology tradition, but limited itself to the William James–John Dewey school of functionalism, focusing chiefly on the application of the "new" psychology to religion and education. During these years, James, George Coe, and Edwin Starbuck published the first book-length psychological accounts of religion. The works of Coe and Starbuck, especially on conversion, were recommended to readers and cited as "scientific" evidence that "emotionalism" needs to be downplayed in conversion experiences. For example, Carlos C. Rowlinson cited psychology as a caution against infant baptism:

> Pioneering work is being done in the study of the psychology of religious experience. One fact is clearly evident from these studies, namely, that there is a time when a man is religiously a minor, and there is a time when he reaches his majority. If he is led to perform the outward functions of a man while he is still a child, the results are usually disastrous both for himself and for the kingdom of heaven. Premature conversions are very common and very unfortunate. (Jan. 9, 1902)

James was praised as first among his peers, and the publication of *The Varieties of Religious Experience* in 1902 occasioned a series of appreciations from the *Century's* writers as well as from its readers. Ames himself hailed it as the first "scientific" examination of religion. "No field can plead exemption from the modern seekers after knowledge, and the last two years have marked the invasion of this inmost realm of human interest—personal religious experience. The beginnings made by Professors Starbuck and Coe have now been confirmed and greatly extended by Professor James of Harvard, who is perhaps the greatest living psychologist" (Jan. 1, 1903). However, articles about the psychology of religion appeared only when significant texts were published, and so diminished in number after this initial flurry. Psychology was introduced more regularly through articles on education, especially religious education. The *Century* praised psychology for remaking education on the basis of the different developmental stages of childhood and the educational needs particular to each stage. Its contributors approvingly cited G. Stanley Hall as the nation's foremost educational expert, as the psychologist who best combined science and education. Although the articles on psychology were enthusiastic, they were also infrequent and vague, providing only fleeting glimpses of psychological theories. Instead of being explored, psychology was more often praised for being scientific, for being new.

The *Century* commended the scientific in all matters, especially evolution, for science heralded the dawn of a new era of Christian unity. It extolled the virtues of a "scientific" biblical criticism for helping people see anew the person of Jesus, "to know him more intimately" and to gain "personal contact with the living Christ . . . as we study His superhuman personality" (Jan. 4, 1900). The editors broached the subject of evolution more cautiously, since evolution was still deeply unpopular in many Disciples colleges and most churches. Yet the majority of the writers believed Darwin's evolutionary theory as a scientific description of the means by which God created the universe. Evolution also resonated with the *Century* as the best metaphor for understanding human life: Humans develop progressively toward God through science and social service. Jesse B. Haslon wrote that "the most emphatic practical tendency in our modern Christianity is a social direction, dealing with our faith as a social force . . . to create a social consciousness, a sense of personal responsibility for public conditions and evils." Notably, Haslon attributed the vigor of this movement in part to an evolutionary spirit, writing that "the evolutionary and vital trend is translated . . . into a conviction of the tremendous power and importance of education" (March 13, 1902). Evolution also operated as a kind of liberating knowledge that in and of itself encouraged human development. In the view of writers like Carey E. Morgan,

> The printing press is our machine gun, and it bombards the citadels of ignorance and superstition with magazines and newspapers and books and school houses. . . . Knowledge goes to the attack by rail and steamship. . . . The railroad is the enemy of heathenism. . . . All these inventions that abridge the distance bring civilization face to face with heathenism. There can be but one result. The fittest will survive. (Jan. 17, 1901)

The *Century* barely survived the decade. Between 1900 and 1908, the *Century* went bankrupt three times and was edited by a series of prominent Chicago Disciples, including Willett, George A. Campbell, J. J. Haley, Frank G. Tyrrell, and Charles A. Young, each unable to turn a profit. The paper proved incapable of transforming a small local readership into a national readership. Even the acquisition of the Washington, DC–based Disciples paper the *Christian Tribune* on June 7, 1900, after which the *Century* declared itself "a national paper," failed to broaden the subscriber base. Subscribers praised the *Century's* staff for their equanimity and liberalism in published letters to the editor—but there were few subscribers. In the end, the issues became thinner, and the editors even took to putting Dr. P. Chester Madison, a wealthy Chicago ophthalmologist, on the masthead, writing breathless articles about the benefits of eye exams in exchange for cash to shore up the paper's sagging financial assets. The editors of the *Century* began the decade buoyed by their prophetic hope in American Protestantism and modern, scientific religion. They looked to end their first decade with little more than that hope until Charles Clayton Morrison became editor in 1908.

Morrison's life spanned a period of dramatic change in American Protestantism, from December 4, 1874, to March 2, 1966. Morrison was the second of four children born to Anna MacDonald Morrison and Hugh Tucker Morrison, a carpenter and itinerant preacher. In the early 1870s, Hugh converted to the Disciples of Christ and spent the next four decades pastoring Disciples churches and organizing frontier revivals from Nova Scotia to Oregon, but chiefly in the Midwest. Hugh steeped his son Charles in Disciples theology and groomed him for the pulpit. Charles embraced his calling at an early age, becoming a full-time pastor at a Disciples church in Woodbine, Iowa, after graduating from high school in 1892. A year later, Morrison matriculated at Drake, a Disciples college in Des Moines, Iowa. Morrison initially floundered there, and even dropped out for a time to conduct revivals in rural Iowa, but eventually returned and graduated from Drake in 1898. His education came as much from Disciples churches as from the college, for Morrison paid for his education by pastoring a Disciples church in nearby Perry, Iowa. At the Perry church, Morrison met H. O. Breeden, a Disciples pastor committed to evolution and biblical criticism. Breeden's talks fired Morrison's nascent intellectual life and led him to question the unadorned frontier faith of his family. When Prof. Willett visited the church from Chicago and spoke on biblical criticism, Morrison was won over and decided to enroll in graduate studies at the University of Chicago. Accordingly, Morrison moved to Chicago in October 1898 and began pastoring a local Disciples church and saving money for tuition (Morrison 1966).

In the fall of 1900, Morrison entered the Disciples Divinity House and enrolled as a graduate student in philosophy and psychology, rather than in divinity, explaining in his unpublished autobiography that "I had a theory that the problems of theology originated in philosophy" (Morrison 1966). Elsewhere, he describes his experience at the university in passionate terms:

> Besides Dewey, . . . my teachers were mainly G. H. Mead, J. H. Tufts, J. R. Angell and E. S. Ames. When I left, I was thoroughly immunized against every form of rationalism, apriorism, or speculation of any kind based on dogmatic or authoritarian ideas. Ideas, I saw, arise in experience, they are conditioned by experience, they refer to experience—whether to concrete experience out of which they have arisen or to a possible experience toward which they point. In a word, ideas are functional for experience. (Morrison 1939: 1370)

Morrison was also "immunized" against his own revivalist faith, which he abandoned in favor of a modern theology that accepted evolution and biblical criticism. But Morrison did not abandon the church. He always imagined himself a preacher, and left his doctorate unfinished, believing it an unnecessary degree for a preacher. Instead, after three years of graduate studies, he devoted himself full-time to the pastorate of the Monroe Street Church on Chicago's West Side in 1906. However, the Monroe Street Church offered little to interest the restless pastor, who now had purchase in the university as well as the revival tent, and after two years his mind began to wander, so he began editing the ailing *Century* during the summer of 1908. On October 10, 1908, he quit the Monroe Street Church and became the *Century's* editor and publisher, positions he held until 1947 (Morrison 1966).

Morrison later explained the transition by saying that "I had resigned from the pastorate to become an editor, but I never lost my sense of being a Christian minister. My desk became my pulpit, and the subscribers were my congregation" (Oct. 11, 1928). Morrison understood the *Century* as the ideal combination of the university and the frontier congregation, a union of "scientific" theology with the enthusiasm of revivalism. For at least the first decade, Morrison sustained the *Century* on his own passion, writing and editing the bulk of the paper, for a miniscule "congregation" of subscribers that left the *Century* ever scrambling for money. During the early years, the rest of the *Century's* material was produced by an older generation of Chicago Disciples, including most of the writers previously associated with it. Morrison depended especially upon Ames and Willett, the prominent University of Chicago Disciples. Ames wrote often for the *Century* on psychology, mysticism, and the "inner life." Willett introduced biblical criticism to the *Century's* readers as the author of a regular column and served as Morrison's coeditor for the first five years. Whatever Willett offered certainly did not temper Morrison's embrace of liberal theology. Morrison was not chastened by the failure of his liberal predecessors to win an audience, nor even by the paper's tenuous financial position, for he not only retained but accelerated the *Century's* commitment to what he called a "progressive and constructive" Christianity.

Morrison's commitment to liberal theology was strengthened by two early doctrinal disputes—on literal interpretations of the Bible and baptism by immersion—between the *Century* and the more conservative Disciples paper, the *Christian Standard*. Since the late 1890s, the Cincinnati-based *Standard* had attacked Ames, Willett, and the Chicago Disciples associated with the Disciples Divinity House for breaking with tradition. When Morrison became editor, he hoped to avoid the controversies that had roiled Disciples publications, but was quickly drawn into the disputes. The first dispute came when Morrison defended Willett's commitment to liberal biblical criticism; the second when Morrison argued in favor of accepting Christians not baptized by immersion (the standard practice of the Disciples) on "functional" grounds (Garrison 1948). These contentious debates embold-ened Morrison to cast the *Century* as a strident voice for theological liberal-ism within the Disciples, as a "Progressive Religious Weekly for Christian Homes."

Morrison and his writers believed a "progressive" bent was necessary be-cause science required Christianity to renew, revive, and even rewrite itself to be intelligible to contemporary Christians. In an unsigned editorial, they asserted, "The religious discussions of the last century are meaningless to-day. . . . Church rites, rituals, ordinances and orders are given a truer value as incidentals, not essentials of the religious life. . . . What is the duty of the church in a changing world? Manifestly to accept the law of change as fun-damental and inevitable; to adapt itself to the changes" (Sept. 28, 1911). Morrison and his writers believed the spirit of their age to be unrelenting change, or as Earle Marion Todd wrote,

> Progress is growth, development. What has been can never be again, and what is to be . . . has never been before. Change, unceasing change, is the eternal law. . . . Not only are things changing; they are growing. The world, the uni-verse, is becoming more beautiful, more wonderful, more complex. . . . [T]he church, like every other institution that is to continue to live and discharge a vital function, must adapt herself to the changed conditions. (Jan. 20, 1910)

And it is the church, not science, that must conform to the new culture shaped by science. In an unsigned editorial on Charles Darwin, the editors claimed that

> [i]n olden times religion was a thing apart. It had special days for itself and special places. . . . The religion that is typical of modern times is getting on friendly terms with other human interests. It is abdicating its absolutism and bending down to the life men really live. It accepts the challenges of a practi-cal age to justify itself by its fruits. It sees that its power and worth reside in its vital relations with the rest of life, not its holy exclusiveness. (Feb. 20, 1909)

The editors notably hailed the formation of a "modern" church with the metaphors of development and evolution. Morrison and his writers under-stood evolution not only as the scientific principle by which God operates, but also as the chief rule of contemporary life: Adapt or become extinct. The church is not exempt, but must, like all organisms, "grow or perish" (March 15, 1917).

Accordingly, Morrison hailed Darwin as the most important figure of the nineteenth century and regularly proclaimed him an "emancipator" just like President Lincoln, since both men freed humanity from ignorance.[4] Morrison also defends Darwin from religious conservatives, believing that evolution does not contradict but affirms the Christian account of creation. Evolution became the foundation of modern theology for contributors to the *Century*, as in this article from Orvis F. Jordan:

> If there is any word which is especially dear to all modern liberals it is the word evolution. We have never seen a liberal who is not an evolutionist. . . . He insists that a theology which does not square with the assured results of modern science is one which is built on sand and one which can never make headway among intellectual people. . . . It is the humanity of Christ that makes his life in any sense an example for us. It is only his humanity that can afford a bond of sympathy with the human race. (April 28, 1910)

In an editorial a year later, the *Century* explicitly connected Darwin to an individual account of religion. Morrison began by recalling Darwin's journeys on the H.M.S. *Beagle* and the many religious traditions he encountered, eventually concluding that all people need a "personal religion."

> They know that they must believe in God, a God who is real and personal. . . . The answer must be personal and individual. No man can answer for his brother. But it is a satisfaction to believe that the trend of modern thought, in the light of all the new knowledge, and in the face of all the new criticism, is toward the constructive and world-embracing view which the Christian church in its nobler thinkers and confessors is today reaching (Oct. 5, 1911).

Morrison saw science as bringing about a new era,

> a day when there is more knowledge about more things in possession of more people than at any other time in the history of man. The things known locally have become universalized. The provincial is passing. . . . Not only the unknown, but much that was considered unknowable, has become well known. . . . Inquiring thought has been turned in three most promising and perilous directions, toward God, toward human relationships and towards the inner self of the inquirer. We call these fields of theology, sociology and psychology. . . . Our knowledge of the inner-self life and of the outer social is growing every day. Experts are leading in the study. (April 27, 1911)

And the experts of the "inner-self life" are psychologists, not preachers.

Morrison embraced psychology as the science of religion, as the way to make religion scientific, to make it fit the new Darwinian era. The *Century* embraced the tradition of James and Dewey, and so hailed the role of the will and the formation of good habits, and continued to focus on the application of psychology to education and religion. Accordingly, the works of George Albert Coe and G. Stanley Hall were praised for their insight into child education, especially for characterizing the different stages of childhood development. H. D. Maclachlan wrote a weekly "Teacher Training Course" introducing psychology to Sunday School teachers, which the *Century* advertised as "An Ideal Primer in the Fascinating Science of Psychology" (April 22, 1909). Indeed, Willett at one point said that "the new psychology is really the effort to determine by actual experiment the methods by which the child acquires knowledge" (Aug. 18, 1910). The *Century* sold

Sunday School books whose "ruling principle" was "modern psychology" (Aug. 25, 1910). The *Century* acclaimed psychological studies of religion, especially the work of Ames and Coe. In 1910, Ames published *The Psychology of Religious Experience,* and the *Century* responded with almost a dozen appreciative articles, features, and reviews. Throughout this period, the book reviews brimmed with psychology books, and the *Century* sold many of these books directly to its readers. Morrison also published another dozen articles extolling the therapeutic practices of the Emmanuel Movement as a truly scientific religion.[5] Morrison dramatically increased the number and frequency of the *Century's* psychology stories.

More significant was Morrison's prescription of psychology as religion's salvation; psychology becomes the only way to make religion a science. For example, in an unsigned editorial called "From Laboratory to Pulpit," the editors declared,

> It has long been our conviction that the most important testimony to the truth of religion and the reality of a spiritual world is yet to come, not from theologians but from psychologists. The day of dogma is past. The scientific method of study and proof sweeps the field. . . . A new type of proof is forthcoming— the professors call it a new apologetic—which grounds itself in the bed-rock of experience and follows the most rigid method known to any science and comes out, fairly and without stumbling, on the side of faith. The psychologists are the apostles of this new gospel. (Oct. 6, 1910)

And the gospel they preach was summarized by Frank E. Boren as "Salvation is self-realization. We are saved when we escape the lower possibilities of our natures and achieve the higher possibilities" (April 22, 1915). Psychology also offered empirical proof that religious practices need to be reformed. Morrison wrote that "[t]he study of the psychology of religious experience has revealed the various possibilities of Christian development, stamping some as desirable and some as undesirable. Probably no one discipline has so shaken the practice of evangelism in the church or so much strengthened the educational method in religious work, as has this" (March 15, 1917).

However, it would be misleading to suggest that Morrison and the *Century* were exclusively focused inwardly, for they often agitated for the Social Gospel.[6] Indeed, Morrison believed the Social Gospel to be organically related to his interest in psychology, as he explained in a fascinating series of eleven articles entitled "Why I Am a Disciple:"

> As a teacher of religion, my liberalism extends in other directions also,—in the direction where modern psychology is working to give us newer and clearer understanding of the inner life, and in the direction of where modern social theories are breaking up the crust of established custom and introduc-

ing principles of reconstruction which, it seems to me, are bound to give us a plan of living together far happier and more just than the social scheme to which long ages have grown accustomed. My interest in these activities of scholarship and my sympathy with their results tends to liberalize my thinking on the matters of religion. (March 17, 1917)

For Morrison, the Social Gospel and psychology were important because they were contiguous planks in the liberal platform, not because they were the practices of the church. Indeed, it was his scholarship that "liberalized" his faith: the shift in cultural authority from religion to psychology was continuing. Before examining the implications of this progressive shift in cultural authority for both the *Christian Century* and twentieth-century Protestantism, we must first examine more closely the primary actors who represent psychology's secularizing influence within American Protestantism.

RELIGION BECOMES PSYCHOLOGY

Psychology renarrated Protestantism through the efforts of individuals and groups acting as agents of secularization through a "revolution" in American Protestantism (Niebuhr 1927). We should not imagine psychology and religion as distinct, for they often intersect and overlap in American culture. Indeed, it is only in the nineteenth century's last decades that psychology began to understand itself as a science; before that historical moment, what we now call psychology could be located in literature, medicine, physiology, philosophy, and theology. Psychology's disparate roots developed throughout late-nineteenth- and early-twentieth-century American life, both in a host of popular "mind cure" movements, including Christian Science, mesmerism, and New Thought, and in the academic work of American psychologists (Cushman 1995). William James surely stands as the chief American psychological pioneer, for he was the first to craft a distinctly American psychology and the first to provide a compelling psychological account of religion. Yet James did not till this field alone, but was joined by an increasingly large number of laborers, including several of his own students and the mind-cure healers whom he sought out to soothe his own troubled mind. In their varying ways, all these pioneers renarrated religion through psychology. In so doing, they shifted cultural authority away from religion and toward psychology and, perhaps even more startlingly, made psychology's standards the measure of religious truth. This shift in cultural authority was often literal for the early American psychologists; most of them were the sons of Protestant pastors or began their academic careers training for the ministry. Of course, many of their churchgoing peers remained in the church, but committed themselves just as fervently to psychology. The *Christian Century's* writers and editors can be classed in this category: they looked to psychologists for advice, heartily recommended psychology texts and methods to pastors and laypeople alike, and believed the future of Christianity belonged to psychologists with their "scientific" understanding rather than to theologians.

To understand why the *Century's* staff were so receptive to academic psychology, one must consider the history of American psychology and its significant agents, groups, and ideologies. Moreover, one must consider how these agents influenced American religious life, as well as how American religion received psychological interpretations and authority as its own. This story begins with a recognition of American psychology's debt to nineteenth-century science, especially the German "physiological psychological" tradition and the work of Darwin. From this foundation, American psychology developed this science and transformed it along therapeutic lines, most notably in the work of William James and his students and colleagues at Harvard. Finally, it embraced "functionalism," the psychological school associated chiefly with the University of Chicago in the early twentieth century. As a response to increasing embarrassment with overt confessions of faith in public arenas, many American Protestants appropriated and were deeply comforted by the potential of this psychological tradition (especially its functionalist form) to transpose religion into the interior sensations of the psychological self. Indeed, American Protestantism's predisposition toward individualism and obsession with the sensations of the self blossomed under the influence of the functionalists. The extent of this influence is evident throughout the first forty years of the *Christian Century*, as the journal actively engaged and promulgated a "functionalist" psychology of religion as a way to recast Protestantism for a psychological era.

What was meant by *psychology* is contested throughout the nineteenth century, but by the century's end, American psychology characterized itself as an empirical science of the mind, or, as William James began his epochal text *The Principles of Psychology*, "Psychology is the science of mental life" (James 1890). By claiming that American psychology derived its authority from its empirical practices, its ability to observe, test, and measure, James rendered obsolete a metaphysical definition of psychology. As late as 1853, Noah Webster defined psychology as "a discourse or treatise on the human soul; or the doctrine of man's spiritual nature" (quoted in Benjamin 1986: 941). James and his colleagues shifted the subject of psychology from the soul to the self, a move certainly indicative of shifts in American theology, but also a legacy of scientific psychology's roots in the secularized German academy, where many early American psychologists received their formal training.

Scores of Americans studied with Wilhelm Wundt, the German psychologist whose work embodied this shift from a metaphysical to a scientific psychology. Wundt created an institutional space for psychology as a discipline distinct from both physiology and philosophy in the German university.

According to Wundt, "immediate experience" can be reduced to its constituent "sensations" and "feelings" and measured in experiments and trials. Wundt defined psychology as "the science of immediate experience . . . the empirical discipline whose results are most immediately useful in the investigation of the general problems of the theory of knowledge and ethics, the two foundations of philosophy" (Wundt 1896: 16). Wundt positioned his new scientific psychology above all other natural and humanistic sciences, claiming that psychology addressed "immediate" experience while other sciences addressed only "mediate" experience, experience mediated through abstractions. In naming psychology the chief and fundamental science, Wundt established psychology as a discipline whose authority is *scientific* rather than philosophical or religious (Hamner 1997). Thus he elevated psychology above theology; by declaring immediate experience the only certain reality, he crafted psychology as a field radically inhospitable to any distinctly Christian claims.

Americans embraced Wundt and his "physiological psychology" as an exemplar of scientific psychology. Wundt's American disciples, especially E. B. Titchener and his "structuralist" school of psychology, self-consciously understood themselves as a separate class of "new" psychologists because of their devotion to empirical methods—they proclaimed their findings not mere speculations but verifiable mechanisms of the human mind. Wundt himself never seriously considered a psychology of religion, because he did not have to—at least in the secularized universities of late-nineteenth-century Germany. However, American psychologists conducted their work from within Protestant (or newly secular) universities and so tried to fit their old religion with their new psychology. The work of James and his followers suggests that German psychologists taught them to see psychology as new, and the work of Charles Darwin, which scientifically explained creation as the natural selection of favorable individual differences generated by chance, taught them to see religion as old.

While other evolutionary theories, most notably Spencer's, had their adherents during this period, it is Darwin's theory of evolution that undergirds almost every psychological theory since the nineteenth century (Gruber 1998). Many American psychologists understood Darwin and his work as a liberation from (or at least as a "scientific" modification of) the Christian narrative of creation. Hall wrote in his own autobiography with rapturous joy of discovering evolution as a student and realizing that "all worlds and all in them had developed very gradually and by an inner and unremitting impulsion from cosmic mist and nebulae . . . while all religions, gods, heavens, immortalities, were made by mansoul" (Hall 1924: 359–60). For the founders of American psychology like Hall, the work of Darwin provided the final empirical challenge to the Christian faith of their parents and culture, and rendered that faith untenable as previously articulated.

James fashioned the first distinctly American psychology by weaving together British evolution and German psychology in the *Principles*. The publisher Henry Holt commissioned James to write the *Principles* in 1878 for Holt's American Science Series, but it took James twelve arduous years to complete the fourteen-hundred-page text. The two volumes of the *Principles* were immediately hailed as seminal works, published in nine editions, widely translated, abridged, and used as the American psychology textbooks for decades of university students. The work was also used as the library for American psychological research because James both presented his own psychological theories and ably summarized those of his American and European counterparts.[7] Indeed, James described such a variety of psychological methods that any American psychological school, from mathematical psychology to parapsychology, can trace its genealogy back to the *Principles* (King 1992). Accordingly, scholars usually attribute the success of the *Principles* to its pluralism, James's vision of psychology as a science, or his eloquence as a writer.

While these explanations are credible, they are not complete, for they neglect the cultural context in which James wrote and published the *Principles*. Indeed, the success of these texts might finally be better attributed to James's ability to elucidate a compelling account of the individual self in the midst of a tumultuous American political and economic culture than to the breadth of his scholarship. James wrote the *Principles* as corporate capitalism developed out of the post–Civil War explosion and diversification of the consumer goods industries and markets. Like many of his contemporaries, James thought he was witnessing a transformation of capitalism and the development of a consumer culture. James strove in the *Principles* to describe the individual self in a manner strong enough to stand against the bureaucracies that were reshaping American public life and politically identified himself as a progressive, even a socialist (Livingston 1994). However, James did so by elevating the individual self above all institutions; without a shared authority by which to understand individual lives (let alone communal lives), James embraced them all through his tolerant pluralism. Pluralism led James to define the individual self so broadly that he actually legitimated a consumer culture. James called a man's self, "the sum total of all that we CAN call his, not only his body and psychic powers, but his clothes and his house, his wife and children, his ancestors and friends, his reputations and works, his lands and horses, and yacht and bank-account" (James 1890: 291). In this, James recognized that the self is constituted by its social and cultural contexts, but the only contexts he can name are contractual contexts, relationships mediated by commerce and law. In his desire to free people from the invasive reach of bureaucracies, James fashioned a high view of human nature that finally elevated the self to a kind of lonely materialism. Likewise, James extolled "habits" as the practices of a consumer nation. "The great thing, then, in all education, is to *make our nervous system our ally instead of our enemy*. It is to fund and capitalize our acquisitions, and live at ease upon the interest of the fund" (James 1890: 123). Rieber calls this "the first statement of psychology's role as a capitalistic business enterprise" (Rieber 1998: 210), but it also marks a transformation of the Protestant language of covenant and moral living into a psychological language tending to the self. James freed himself from the constraints of Protestantism as a lived faith, but continued to speak with a denuded Christian language. Instead of preaching the gospel, James offered pithy aphorisms steeped in a modest hope familiar from today's self-help books, declaring, for instance, that "Self-esteem = success/pretensions," and uncannily foreshadowed self-help gurus when he gushed, "How pleasant is the day when we give up striving to be young,— or slender! Thank God! we say, *those* illusions are gone" (James 1890: 310, 311). James formulated American psychology as a secular answer to and peculiar legitimization of the developing consumer culture.

The *Principles* influenced generations of American psychologists, but James established psychology as a distinct discipline within the American academy through his teaching at Harvard as well as through his writing; the most famous of James's students is G. Stanley Hall, who earned the first American doctorate in psychology. Born into a storied New England family of Congregationalists, Hall attended Williams College and Union Theological Seminary with intentions of entering the ministry. While enrolled at Union, he studied in Germany with the financial help of the eminent Brooklyn pastor Henry Ward Beecher. Hall traveled to Germany in 1868, and discovered in German psychology and philosophy a more apt faith, a faith for which he relentlessly proselytized as one of America's leading psychologists.

If James can be thought of as American psychology's Paul, its most eloquent expositor, then Hall is its Peter, the founder of the chief institutions of American psychology. He established the first American department of psychology as well as the American Psychological Association and four psychology journals. He published widely in several fields, but typically focused on developmental psychology (his work is deeply indebted to Darwin and Darwin's cousin, the eugenicist Francis Galton), and his major works concerned adolescence, aging, childhood, and sexuality. Hall earned renown chiefly as a proponent of "applied psychology," of bringing the empirically determined conclusions of scientific psychology to bear upon practical problems. In particular, he led the nationwide child study movement, which trained teachers in psychologically derived pedagogical methods, and advocated the reorganization of education around the developmental patterns of children. Yet Hall identified himself first and foremost as a scientific psychologist (Ross 1972).

Hall trained as a scientific psychologist with both James and Wundt. After returning from Germany, he eventually graduated from Union Theological Seminary and then spent the next decade teaching philosophy in American high schools and colleges, and studying psychology at Harvard under James. In 1878, Harvard awarded Hall his doctorate, and he then returned to Germany to work with Wundt and his colleagues for two years, a period he considered the formative years of his professional life. In Germany, Hall immersed himself in the laboratory and abandoned metaphysics for a scientific psychology. In Germany, he encountered a continental life blissfully free from the strict restrictions of his upbringing. He wrote that in Germany the "hated Puritan Sunday which all my life before had been a dreaded day of gloom and depression now became one of joy and holiday recreation," as people danced, drank, and attended concerts rather than church services (Hall 1924: 219). Hall championed German culture and its university system throughout his life, chiefly in *Aspects of German Culture* (1881), for its secularized and scientific bent. He disparaged his American peers as unable to engage philosophy without reference to theology, and excoriated American psychologists as insufficiently empirical. By the end of the nineteenth century, however, it became apparent that Hall's criticisms were better directed at himself. This son of Congregational New England never fully embraced a secularized or even a scientific psychology, never absorbed what he himself proclaimed as the lessons of his German education (Ross 1972). Although Hall noisily proclaimed his freedom from the strictures and institutions of his Christian upbringing, his biographer noted that he spoke and wrote with strong "moral and religious overtones," and that he turned "the language of science into 'mythopoeic' terms" (Ross 1972: 268–69). Hall littered his writing with psychological terms, but a denuded religious language so pervades all of his work that even James complained of his "religious cant" (quoted in Ross 1972: 269). Examining Hall's work today reveals that he engaged in startlingly few experiments for a professed empirical scientist. Instead, his psychology reads as a recasting of the faith of his childhood for a new scientific era.

Even more than James, Hall transformed his Protestant heritage into a pious psychology, especially in his two-volume account of the life of Jesus, *Jesus, The Christ, in the Light of Psychology*. By the turn of the century, Hall had channeled his reaction to his Christian upbringing into a psychological refurbishment of Christianity and its practices—religion became, like education before it, the subject of Hall's "applied" psychology. For example, Hall urged the reform of Sunday school in his study of children, calling for children to be raised with a less doctrinal and a more emotional sense of faith. Hall's religious enthusiasm culminated with the publication of *Jesus* in 1917, a revised collection of essays on the historical Jesus that he had been preparing since 1895 but hesitated to publish because of its theologically unorthodox content. In many respects, *Jesus* is a fairly typical liberal Protestant account of the historical Jesus and owes a great debt to Ernest Renan's *The Life of Jesus*, so that Jesus is not the one *in whom* Christians believe, but the one *with whom* Christians believe. What makes Hall's account so notable is its embodiment of the continued shift of cultural authority from religion to psychology. This cultural authority was mediated through the influence of the psychologist, who is assumed to possess special insight into the machinations of the mind. Read through the lens of this authority, Jesus belongs to all people rather than to a church or a gathered community of believers. Hall reinterpreted Jesus to Christianity. Psychology rather than theology tells the story of Jesus in a new scientific era, and this reinterpretation is necessary because "Christianity is less and less a solution, and more and more a problem. . . . It should take the psychology that deals with the deeper things of humanity to its very heart of hearts, instead of maintaining an attitude of suspicion and exclusion, and help to show forth the new sense in which our scriptures are being revealed as the world's chief text-book in psychology" (Hall 1917: xv–xvi). Central to this reinterpretation of Christianity was Hall's account of Jesus' mental state during his public ministry and the charismatic effect of the "master psychologist" upon his ancient and contemporary disciples. His characterization of Jesus included the speculative conclusions that Jesus must have been tall, strong, beautiful, and endowed with a magnetic personality. He called Jesus a mythic creation of humans, but also the "paradigm" for human experience, whose cycle of death and resurrection each individual must reenact through a personal conversion.

In writing *Jesus*, Hall proudly announced that he drew upon the latest research of Sigmund Freud, whom he literally introduced to American psychology. Hall's interest in German psychology in general, and in developmental psychology in particular, led him to begin incorporating Freud into his work near the end of the nineteenth century (Ross 1972). He hailed Freud's work as the dawning of a new era in psychology because it shifted the subject of psychology from consciousness to the unconscious, but he criticized Freudian analysis for its emphasis on sex (Hall 1924).[8] More important, Hall brought Freud (and his then disciple Carl Jung) to America, for his first and only visit, in September 1909 for a psychology conference at Clark University. Hall was then in the midst of his thirty-one-year tenure as Clark's president and organized the conference as a celebration of the fledgling university's twentieth anniversary.

Freud delivered his famous *Five Lectures on Psycho-Analysis* to an audience of America's foremost psychologists, including James and Titchener, and a small but influential gathering of psychoanalysts, including A. A. Brill, Sandor Ferenczi, and Ernest Jones. Freud succinctly summarized (and brightened) the major points of his psychoanalytic theory in the lectures he prepared each morning as he walked the grounds of the university (Evans and Koelsch 1985). In return, Clark awarded Freud an honorary doctorate and gave both him and his psychoanalytic theory a congenial welcome. The conference stands as a critical moment in American psychology, a gathering of the men who collectively introduced and popularized Freudian methods. With his remarks, Freud inaugurated a new era in American psychology, as it became more and more a therapeutic practice (Hale 1971).[9] At the same conference, Wundt's protégé, E. B. Titchener, delivered a series of lectures exhorting psychologists to remain in their laboratories, to further develop psychology as an experimental science. Titchener scorned applied psychology, particularly its therapeutic application to the "cure of souls" (Hale 1971: 4). In his comments, Titchener perhaps intimated the future of American psychology after Freud, as experimental psychology became the poor relation of the vastly more popular therapeutic psychology. Freud appeared to understand the stakes as well, for he greeted Titchener with the remark, "O, Sie sind der Gegner," "Oh, you are the opponent" (Evans and Koelsch 1985: 944).

Any account of psychology as a secularizing force in American public life must consider the impact of Freud. In the words of Peter Gay, Freud "advertised his unbelief every time he could find, or make, an opportunity" (1987: 3). Freud first characterized religion as humanity's shared neurosis in his 1907 paper on "Obsessive Actions and Religious Practices," but he did not speak of religion when he visited Clark in 1909. Freud shrewdly focused on psychoanalysis as a therapeutic practice rather than as a cultural critique. I do not speak at length here of Freud's role as an agent of secularization for three reasons. First, my interest is in the formative years of American psychology, the years most pertinent to the *Christian Century's* beginning. Freud's impact on America is gradual, and does not truly start ascending until after the First World War (Hale 1971). Second, Freud's role in the secularization of American public life has been well discussed (Rieff 1966).[10] Although such accounts do not fully characterize Freud as an agent of secularization, it is the challenge of this argument to traverse less well-trod scholarly territory and develop a framework within which to interpret Freud's secularizing influence. Finally, Freud constructed psychology in opposition to religion and was therefore more cautiously received by American Protestants in general.[11] However, James, Hall, and their contemporaries crafted a psychological religion widely embraced in their own time and are therefore more instrumental in the accommodation that literally facilitated secularization within and through the broader culture of American Protestantism during the period upon which we are focusing this discussion.[12]

Even if one only considers Hall's students at Clark, it becomes apparent how engaging the prospect of a psychological religion appeared at the beginning of the twentieth century. From the beginning of Hall's presidency, work in religious psychology was popular at Clark. In 1904, Hall capitalized on this interest and began publication of the *American Journal of Religious*

Psychology and Education with the assistance of several colleagues and students, most notably James H. Leuba and Edwin D. Starbuck. The Clark University Library records that 122 papers in the field of religious psychology were presented at the university between 1893 and 1912, most of which were published in the journal (Wilson 1911: 3). To these religious observers, psychology seemed to open a whole new set of questions and methods, from how to apply psychology to mission work to analyses of conversion experiences and revival sermons for their psychological effects.

In 1897, Starbuck published a paper on conversion that earned wide renown and led him to write the first of many books with the now ubiquitous title, *The Psychology of Religion,* in 1899.[13] Starbuck, like his mentor Hall, strove to understand the religious experience, especially of children, to foster "greater wisdom in religious education" (Starbuck 1899: 8). He pioneered the use of the questionnaire in psychology, tabulating his results in charts and graphs showing the age, height, and weight at which and the reasons why people convert. Starbuck focused throughout on the individual experience, especially conversion and religious development. He described conversion as a natural experience of human development, and typified conversion as either a response to sin or a sudden awakening after a period of struggle. Despite his professed interest in reviving Christianity with psychology, Starbuck announced in the book's opening line, "Science has conquered one field after another, until now it is entering the most complex, the most inaccessible, and, of all, the most sacred domain—that of religion" (Starbuck 1899: 1). For Starbuck, like so many of the psychologists of religion, this shift in cultural authority is figured with a panoply of metaphors, from the conquest of religion, to religion as a subsidiary art. "Psychology is to religion what the science of medicine is to health, or what the study of botany is to the appreciation of plants. The relation is the same as that of any science to its corresponding art" (Starbuck 1899: 8). Whatever the metaphor, the outcome is the same: Psychology judged the fitness of religion.

Leuba, another of Hall's influential protégés, also focused on the conversion experience of individuals, but figured the relationship between the "science" of psychology and the "art" of religion in an even less irenic manner than Starbuck. Leuba said that religion needed "the kind of purification and guidance that science provides. It needs in particular the insight into the dynamics of conscious life which can be contributed, not by studies in comparative religion nor by criticism of sacred texts, but only by psychology" (Leuba 1912: viii). Leuba claimed that "religious experience ('inner experience') belongs entirely to psychology—'entirely' being used in the same sense as when it is claimed that the non-religious portions of conscious life belong entirely to science" (212). Leuba praised the "psychotherapeutic cults" of Christian Science and New Thought for beginning to remake Christianity into "a new religious faith acceptable to the modern world" (296). Throughout his work, Leuba explicitly advocated religious practices on the basis of their "psychological" merit.

It was this burgeoning psychological religion, especially as set forth in the works of Starbuck and Leuba, that James expanded upon and articulated so compellingly in his 1902 Gifford Lectures, *The Varieties of Religious Experience*.[14] In the decade between the *Principles* and the *Varieties*, James steered his philosophy away from psychology and positivism, and became more interested in metaphysical and religious questions. That James nurtured these interests anywhere but within "organized" religion reflects his thoroughgoing pluralism and anti-authoritarian individualism, for, as his biographer reported, James "grew up in a circle in which heresies were more gladly tolerated than orthodoxies" (Perry 1947: 204). Indeed, James lived his adult life in a similar circle, for late-nineteenth-century Boston teemed with mental healers, mediums, and aura readers (Taylor 1999). James engaged these various practitioners both as a client and as a scientist, but always as a pluralist. He hypnotized students, received mind-cure treatment, wrote at length about the famed Boston medium Leonora Piper, and even attended daily prayer at Harvard (but apparently because the sparsely attended services had become the underdog of Boston's religious activities), without ever distinguishing between their different accounts of the world (Perry 1947). Far from disparaging religion as Freud did, James encouraged religious practice indiscriminately and individually. To a friend, James declared, "I am intensely an individualist, and believe that as a practical problem for the individual, the religion he stands by must be the one which he finds best for *him*, even though there were better individuals, and there religion better for them" (quoted in Perry 1947: 262–63). It is precisely this religious form of consumerism (for what finally is James's pluralism but consumerism?) that James articulated so well in the *Varieties*, an expansive piety centered on what best appeases the individual seeker.

In the *Varieties*, James presented religion as an individual and pluralist version of Christianity. James subtitled his lectures "A Study in Human Nature" and named his method scientific and psychological. Yet James had broken from laboratory psychology as surely as he had broken from orthodox Christianity and marshaled the evidence for his study from the lives of recognized saints and holy fools alike, "individuals for whom religion exists not as a dull habit, but as an acute fever" (James 1902: 6). James sheared these lives from their cultural and political contexts and found in their stories that all religious experiences are an individual's experiences of a further reality. In this respect, James extended the "great man" view of history he articulated in his 1880 essay "Great Men and their Environment" to the religious sphere, again finding in the midst of the disorder of the post-Darwinian universe hope in the inspiring lives of geniuses (Hauerwas 2000).

Accordingly, he defined religion as "the feelings, acts, and experiences of individual men in their solitude, so far as they apprehend themselves to stand in relation to whatever they may consider the divine" (James 1902: 31). Just as Wundt distinguishes between immediate and mediate experience, James distinguished between the individual's immediate experience of the divine and the mediate experience of churches, which "live at second hand upon tradition" (30). James's pluralism shaped his understanding of both the individual and the divine, which he alternately figured as the "higher universe" or "higher power" or the "Eternal" and imagined competing theologies as attitudes. "The divine can mean no single quality, it must mean a group of qualities, by being champions of which in alteration, different men may all find worthy missions. Each attitude brings a syllable in human nature's total message, it takes the whole of us to spell the meaning out completely" (487).

Although the traditions in which James found these images of the divine are numerous and rich, his own account is finally a threadbare version of pious Christianity, for James was, as he aptly characterized himself to a friend, "a Methodist minus a Saviour" (quoted in Perry 1947: 259). Whereas Hall is best understood as a religious liberal steeped in Schleiermacher and the other bulwarks of liberal Christian theology, James's intense but diffuse piety eluded the usual distinctions between liberal and conservative. James's biographer Ralph Barton Perry rightly noted that James's own religion "was closer to the simple piety of the evangelical sects than to that of modern religious liberalism. To James, as to Methodism, religion was a clearly recognizable and memorable event in the history of the individual" (Perry 1947: 259). This description presages the subsequent psychologizing of evangelical American Protestantism, but further development of this process is beyond the scope of this chapter. In the *Varieties,* James turned his own religion into a systematic form of evangelical humanism, an inspired and distinctly American religion that embraced religious vigor in all its nonpublic forms. What James did not embrace was the Christian sense of sins as evil practices from which Christians must turn away and for which they can or should be forgiven. Instead, he replaced sin with illness, and described healthy and unhealthy states of the self. The result was that James found Luther, Wesley, and the mind-cure movement speaking the same consoling thought: "*God is well, and so are you*" (James 1902: 108).

In synthesizing these irreconcilable sources, James created a psychological religion that was, in many respects, the culmination of American Protestantism's development. Indeed, the *Varieties* captivated Americans like no theology text of its day and uncannily foreshadowed today's consumerist, personal, frequently privatized religion. Within the academy, James's *Varieties* fostered a whole new discipline, the psychology of religion, and the *Va-*

rieties is still frequently taught in American universities.[15] Yet James never wrote for the academy alone, and would surely be gratified to observe the wide audience the *Varieties* has found throughout American culture. Taylor and others cite the *Varieties* and its typography of healthy, sick, and divided souls as a signal event in the relationship between religion and therapeutic practices (Taylor 1999). Indeed, in many respects James narrated religion as many scholars now believe it is practiced in America, as a dynamic, individual, syncretic, and pious Christianity for the good of our "self."[16] James notably employed the new language of consumerism when he circumscribed his study to personal rather than communal religion, saying that "the individual transacts the business by himself alone, and the ecclesiastical organization, with its priests and sacraments and other go-betweens, sinks to an altogether secondary place. The relation goes direct from heart to heart, from soul to soul, between man and his maker" (James 1902: 29). Like a good American, James urged on each of us the ethos of tolerance, saying that "for each man to stay in his own experience, whate'er it may be, and for others to tolerate him there, is surely best" (James 1902: 488). The claims of Christianity are no longer claims about ultimate things, but about how best to live our individual lives; or, as the theologian Stanley Hauerwas concludes, James considered religion as "another name for the hope necessary to sustain a modest humanism" (Hauerwas 2001: 63).

Perhaps the man most influenced by James's account of the will was John Dewey, the leader of the functionalist school of psychology. Raised as a devout Congregationalist in Vermont, Dewey first studied psychology as a doctoral student from 1882 to 1884 at Johns Hopkins, during G. Stanley Hall's five-year stint as a professor there. In 1887, Dewey published *Psychology*, a popular textbook which both Hall and James disparaged as too metaphysical (Ross 1972). After publishing the book, Dewey reanalyzed his idealist psychology with a concern for biological function, an ideological shift from Hegelian idealism to Darwinian naturalism that was crystallized by his reading James's *Principles*.[17] Like James, Dewey rejected Wundt's division between the mind and body, and Dewey explicitly countered Wundt and his American students with his 1896 essay "The Reflex Arc Concept in Psychology." Dewey declared the structuralist distinction between stimulus and response to be a mere partial view of a complete reflex circuit. Dewey thus rejected structuralism as a fragmented view of individual elements in favor of a functionalist view of constituent elements as parts of a whole that operated together for a common cause (Buxton 1984). In time, Dewey, building upon James's account of the will, articulated the therapeutic concept of adjustment "in its active sense of *control* of means for achieving ends." We can transform our surroundings as well as our selves through education, which is "the acquisition of those habits that effect an adjustment of an individual and his environment" (Dewey 1916: 46). Dewey, like James before him, shifted the Christian meaning of habits as particular ways of living that form us in the Christian story, to a sense of the development of habits as a process of personal and social growth toward an ever-better, ill-defined, integrated personality.

Dewey and his functional psychology proved extraordinarily influential in both the academy and American public life. After Dewey abandoned the religious faith of his early years, finding Christianity untenable after Darwin and only recovering a purely moralistic account of religion in his later years (Dewey 1934), he continued to write with a religious fervor for the great secular institutions of American life, especially the schoolhouse. Dewey revolutionized American education by applying the new psychology to education, encouraging teachers to tailor their instructions to individual students. His influence extended to the pastoral care movement, where Holifield called him the "man who did the most to define the meaning of adjustment for the pastoral care writers" and hailed Dewey's 1916 bestseller, *Democracy and Education,* as a "hidden classic of the pastoral care movement" (Holifield 1983: 223).

Within the academy, Dewey formed the functional school of psychology with a group of like-minded young scholars, first briefly at the University of Michigan, and from 1894 on, at the University of Chicago, where his colleagues included Edward Scribner Ames, James Rowland Angell, and George Herbert Mead. Each of these professors shared with Dewey a devout Protestant upbringing from which they broke away, and a devotion to James and his psychology. Indeed, when Dewey collected papers in philosophy and psychology to commemorate the university's tenth anniversary in 1903, he dedicated the volume to James and admitted "the pre-eminent obligation on the part of all of us to William James, of Harvard University, who, we hope, will accept this acknowledgment and this book as unworthy tokens of a regard and an admiration that are coequal" (Dewey 1903: xi). In return, James publicly celebrated Dewey and his Chicago compatriots for formulating "real thought and a real school" that "deserves the title of a new system of philosophy" (James 1904: 2).

Functionalists like Dewey, Angell, and Mead are more interested in the mind's adaptations than its elements. Ames, a philosophy professor and a Disciples of Christ minister who pastored a church in Hyde Park and educated ministerial students at Chicago's divinity school, made clear the implications of this interest for a psychological account of religious faith. In his 1906 landmark essay, "Theology and Functional Psychology," Ames described the mind as the "chief instrument" used by the organism in adapting to its environment.[18] Since functional psychology addressed the roots of consciousness, Ames concluded that there was no distinction between religion and psychology in functional psychology. To understand theology "requires a psychological study of the religious consciousness" (Ames 1906: 221). Likewise, the most rigorous psychology of religion (he named the *Varieties* as the only worthy text) was the best theology. Accordingly, religious questions are rewritten as psychological questions. No longer should theologians ask whether God exists, asking instead,

> Is the idea of God of value in actual experience? Does it serve to organize the highest interests of life, and to vitalize them with dynamic power in eliciting and controlling efficient reactions of the will? If the idea of God has these values and performs these functions, it is true. Without these, it is irrelevant and untrue. By the same criterion, that conception of God is truest which aids most in guiding, ennobling, comforting, and strengthening man in his devotion to moral ends. The idea of God in this view becomes the great 'working hypothesis' of religion. It corresponds precisely to the hypothesis of natural science. It guides activity and is progressively modified by these results. (Ames 1906: 229)

This is what the peculiar blend of German psychology, Darwinian evolution, and an American psychological religion produced: religious communities, doctrines, and histories became "working hypotheses" valuable only to the extent that they helped people adapt to their environment. Ames, a theologian, became a major proponent of Darwin's conviction that religious faith must prove its evolutionary or adaptive advantage. When an avowedly religious man, let alone a pastor and seminary professor like Ames, made such a statement, then, in the words of Holifield, "theology finally becomes therapy" (Holifield 1983: 201). Ames disseminated this therapeutic (and, inherently, increasingly secularized) theology through his preaching, his teaching of influential pastors and students like Charles Clayton Morrison, and in the pages of the *Christian Century*.

BAPTIZING PROTESTANTISM AND THE *CHRISTIAN CENTURY* IN PSYCHOLOGICAL EMPIRICISM

In the 1920s, mainline Protestant seminaries began teaching the concept of "self-realization," which conceived of the self as an entity whose fulfillment and full potentiation were paramount within the spiritual life. As a result, helping people "adjust" and "adapt" in service of the self became the goal of pastoral care and counseling. Through continual adjustment and adaptation, people would grow in their perceptions and come closer to the ultimate goal of self-realization (Holifield 1983). George Albert Coe, a professor of religious education at Union Theological Seminary, pioneered this movement by incorporating psychology into pastoral care and counseling, seminary training, and Sunday school classes. Coe applied Dewey's educational philosophy to religious education. Holifield concluded that "Coe's research into the psychology of religion convinced him that the functionalists were right when they turned their attention from such well-worn topics as 'perception' and 'attention' and looked instead at persons' interests, preferences, and yearnings for self-realization" (Holifield 1983: 225). Coe's 1916 book, *The Psychology of Religion,* drew more consciously upon the Chicago tradition. It is precisely through religious education programs like Coe's that psychology permeated the churches, for they introduced Dewey's psychology and educational reforms into Protestant Sunday schools and seminary education alike. Coe wrote that religious education promoted "The Growth of the young toward and into mature and efficient devotion to the democracy of God, and happy self-realization therein" (Coe 1917: 55). Likewise, "We believe in God primarily because we need God" (Coe 1904: 203). Coe eventually concluded that God "is immanent in all choices of ours that make us personal and still more personal; that this immanence, having the form of a choice within our choices, is that of a personal being; and that this being, in that he realizes himself by promoting our self-realization in a society of persons, is ethical in the profoundest sense" (Coe 1929: 94). Coe described his approach to education as coming from historical Christianity but also as a "dynamic" departure from the traditional ecclesiology that the church simultaneously served individuals and their community. "The whole situation, ecclesiastical and extra-ecclesiastical, is here confronted with a principle, already within historical Christianity, that could re-create Christian education, and by doing so make an indispensable contribution to the healing of our sick society. This principle is neither dogmatic nor ecclesial, but dynamic. It is most intimately personal, and therefore most intensely social" (v). By this point, parts of American Protestantism were becoming difficult to distinguish from the secular alternative of psychology, and many American Protestants began to forego traditional religious practices entirely in favor of a more direct alleviation of suffering from the psychologists, whom even churches hailed as the true "physicians of the soul."

The result is what Charles Clayton Morrison eloquently lamented in the quotation that began this essay—we are left with a church as a loose conglomeration of subjective selves. Later in the same article, Morrison remarked that

> [t]here was a genuine satisfaction in the procedure of translating Christianity into terms of psychological experience. It generated an unction of its own. I was relieving people of a burden—the burden of having to believe the historical particularities of Christianity. I was engaged in "simplifying" religion, and surely this was a worthy service. That I was really oversimplifying it by leveling down its objective particularities to a psychological common denomina-

tor, did not for some time occur to me. But the cumulative effect of this procedure gradually began to register in my consciousness. I found that, having
baptized the Christian verity in the waters of psychological experience, something seemed to have been washed away from it—something that belonged to
it as a part of my Christian inheritance. It no longer could be described in
terms of an "inheritance." The tang of *history* had gone out of it. Its particularity had gone. Its objectivity as something *given* to me from beyond myself,
had been reduced to my own subjective processes. (Morrison 1939: 1371)

Morrison may have regretted it in 1939, but in the first decades of his
tenure at the *Century,* he committed himself fully to the Social Gospel and
psychology's renewed understanding of the "inner life" as the perfect tools
for building Christian unity. Morrison identified the chief obstacle to Christian unity as "denominationalism," especially the Catholic variety, and
praised ecumenical efforts among Protestants. The *Century* described the
religion that they sought to build, following James's formulation, as an individual and solitary affair, as "the expression of the soul's desire for the
infinite life. It rests upon the capacity of man to know God and to achieve
character. . . . It is the result of a developing life, aspiring after fuller realization of friendship with God and with man. All religion has the same essential elements" (Oct. 20, 1910). Morrison and his writers discussed the
church infrequently; instead, they focused their efforts on articulating the
individual's relationship with God. When they did speak of the church, it
was usually from a functional perspective, as when Ames described the
church as a communal "mind" created through "our interaction and common endeavor to get some result we seek." Ames noted the scientific belief
that few people use their entire brain capacity, and rhetorically asked why
the church did not use all of its own "mind" capacity (Aug. 16, 1917). So
even though the *Century* remained a Disciples publication, it was never truly
committed to a specific, embodied church. Indeed, a specific commitment
was actively discouraged. To foster a national, nondenominational Christian identity, the *Century* began publishing a regular column called "The
Christian World: A Department of Interdenominational Acquaintance" in
1911 and supported the Federal Council of Churches and other liberal ecumenical movements. Morrison's plea for unity manifested itself as vitriol
when he considered Judaism and Catholicism, faiths that required the most
specific commitments.[19] Roman Catholics were mocked for standing in "an
unchanging and eternal church," rather than a liberal Protestant church
which "admits change and argues in behalf of it as the one principle which
guarantees the continued life of religion" (Jan. 25 1917). What irked Morrison about Catholicism was the church's authority in the lives of its members. "There is as complete a non-communion between Protestantism and
Catholicism as between Protestantism and Mohammedanism. They stand

over against each other as religious antitheses. . . . If it were possible Catholicism would establish a complete segregation of her own people from all other classes" (April 22, 1915). Indeed, Morrison believed Catholicism to be near its end, for it was

> simply inconceivable that there should be progress in every sphere of human thought and interest, save that of religion. . . . A religion of mere ceremony is rapidly becoming a thing of the past; a religion based upon outward authority is fast crumbling away, and in its place coming a religion based upon the inward authority of the spirit. . . . The present day movement of development is also a movement from the limited to the universal. (June 18, 1914)

For Morrison, the paramount plea for Christian unity required a transformation in church practices and structures, a move akin to an evolution "from the limited to the universal."

Morrison helped create exactly such a universal institution when he adopted a new motto for the *Century* on December 6, 1917 as "An Undenominational Journal of Religion." In so doing, Morrison declared the *Century* a journal for all Protestant Christians rather than a paper specifically intended for Disciples. The *Century* retained its commitment to Christian unity, the Social Gospel, and the psychological inner life, but reimagined its audience. Morrison later remarked that the change was a happy accident: going through the subscription list, he recognized the names of several prominent Protestants who were not Disciples (Morrison 1928). Since the *Century* was still in a precarious financial position after another decade as a Disciples paper, Morrison saw the change both as a natural expansion of the Disciples' call to Christian unity and as a marketing decision meant to increase circulation.[20] In the loose ecclesiology of the Disciples, the *Century* was not affiliated in any formal way with a church body or publishing house, and was indeed a subsidiary of its own corporation, the Christian Century Press, of which Morrison was the editor and publisher, so he was free to make the change. Two months later, Morrison published an advertisement announcing a drive to double circulation. The advertisement's tagline declared, "Our Hope: Every Reader a Cooperator." Morrison and the *Century* were not just catering to an audience, they knowingly created a nondenominational, "spiritual" audience of liberal Protestants, bound more closely by the *Century* and thus less by concrete ecclesial ties. In a time when denominational papers were declining, Morrison overhauled the *Century* into a paper for American Protestantism, shifting its resources from local coverage to national and international coverage. He eliminated several columns devoted specifically to Disciples and Midwestern audiences and featured nationally prominent Protestants, including Jane Addams, Harry Emerson Fosdick, Joseph Fort Newton, and Reinhold Niebuhr. Morrison realized that the *Century* could become a national journal for mainline Protestantism, the Christian equivalent of the *Atlantic Monthly* and the *Nation,* two of the secular magazines that began advertising in the *Century* at this time. The newly oriented *Century* quickly met with success, reflected both in a swelling of the subscription rolls and increased cultural prominence.[21]

As the *Century* gained national attention, it became known as the chief proponent of the Social Gospel, a movement renewed at the conclusion of the "Great War." The outbreak of war in Europe provoked a long series of reflections by the *Century* on possible American involvement in Europe. Morrison was reluctant to commit American troops to a European war, but fully supported the Americans after they entered. Afterwards, he focused the *Century's* attention on the changes the war wreaked upon religion. In an unsigned editorial, the *Century* wrote that "the war is bringing to pass radical changes on the economic and temporal side of the social order. The spiritual and eternal aspect of things human can in no way escape" (Dec. 6, 1917). In this and later articles, the *Century* insisted that the failure of religious communities to prevent the war showed two things: that earlier forms of Christianity were not liberal and scientific enough and that in the war's wake Americans had another opportunity to begin the Christian century, to bring Christian peace and unity to the world. This mood was well captured in an editorial entitled "The New Mysticism":

> The world tragedy has made us mystics, if we were not so before, and the demand is for a religion that is real, inward, and endlessly rich in inspiration for new adventures in service. Disillusioned of a materialistic civilization, distrustful of a barren intellectualism, and dissatisfied with a religion which has none but claims of external authority to put forth, men are seeking God and finding him, where he is surely found, in the human soul; in what Boutroux called "the Beyond that is Within." (March 17, 1921)

As these comments intimate, Morrison and his writers believed that the war showed materialism and mere intellectualism to be dangerous endeavors. In response, they called their readers to return to Christianity, though not to a specific church, through social service and a renewed attention to their inner lives. The *Century's* rallying cry in those years was the Social Gospel, which translated into support for unions, suffrage, and prohibition. Yet the quieter, insistent plea beneath this was the call to an inner life, an inner life best understood and nurtured by the psychologists. Longtime *Century* contributor Alva W. Taylor sounded this sentiment in an article entitled "The Inner Life and Social Reform," where he declared that "the pressing problems of social readjustment in our time find fundamental solution in Jesus' principles of the inner life" (June 28, 1923).

Morrison generally published two classes of articles about the "inner life," articles about mysticism and articles about psychology. Even though Christian mysticism has most often been associated with the Roman Catholic and Orthodox traditions the *Century* reviled, Morrison and his writers acclaimed the mystic life as exemplary for contemporary Christians. Mysticism was in vogue throughout the early years of the twentieth century, especially as described in James's *Varieties*, Rudolf Otto's *The Idea of the Holy*, and Evelyn Underhill's *Practical Mysticism*, each of which the *Century* reviewed enthusiastically. These writers privileged the individual's experience in religion at the expense of the communal church and saw this union between the individual and the divine as the heart of all religions. Morrison and his writers were moved by mysticism because it seemed to pare religion to its essential core, a relationship between the believer and God. Morrison published scores of articles and book reviews on mysticism, many of which connected mysticism to the Social Gospel. In "The Social and the Mystical," Laura H. Wild wrote that "the next step in Christian progress is to be the coupling of these very real, very modern, and seemingly paradoxical expressions of our religious life, the rational and the mystical, practical service and inner realization" (Jan. 19, 1922).

But who was to lead the searching Christian on this inward turn? By their own admission, Morrison and the *Century* saw psychologists, rather than Christian mystics, as the guides to the inner life. As American psychology began to absorb the implications of the Freudian "unconscious" and observe the therapeutic applications of psychology, the *Century* increased its coverage of psychology, which became an accepted feature of American life during this period. In 1918, the *Century* praised psychologists for giving American military recruits psychological exams to accompany their physicals, thus increasing military efficiency. Later in the same year, the *Century* cheered Morrison's alma mater, the Disciples college Drake University, for naming a new president whose qualifications included a doctorate in psychology. The *Century* even employed psychology to explain social ills: H. O. Pritchard named four factors that create racism, the last of which was the "psychological basis of race prejudice." In conclusion, Pritchard suggested that healing the psychological basis of racism might ultimately eliminate the other three problems (Aug. 11, 1921). The *Century* also located the difference between fundamentalists and modernists in psychology, saying "our essential differences are in our more or less unconscious foundations, not in our conscious superstructures. These foundations of theology are for the most part hidden; they are not logical, but psychological, not metaphysical but naïve, not expressed but implied" (March 20, 1924).

Morrison continued to review a raft of psychology books and to sell psychology books directly to subscribers. In a full-page ad for Richard LaRue Swain's *What and Where Is God? A Human Answer to the Deep Religious Cry of the Modern Soul*, Morrison suggested that he and his readers were saturated with psychology books, saying, "The author is one of those psychologists—and alas! all too few is their number—who have gone into the technique of psy-

chology and thought their way through into real life again" (Feb. 17, 1921).
The subject remained popular, and all the publishers advertising in this period offered multiple volumes on psychology. Indeed, in a later advertisement, they hailed Swain's book as "by far the most popular book ever sold
by The Christian Century Press," surpassing the theology titles and Bibles
they sold (June 1, 1922). Apparently buoyed by this success, Morrison advertised *A Dictionary of Religion and Ethics,* edited by longtime *Century* contributor and University of Chicago Divinity School professor Shailer Mathews. To give readers a sense of the work, the *Century* dedicated one page to
a sample entry from the book, selecting a passage on the psychology of religion. The ad promised that "especial regard has been paid to the psychology and history of religion" (June 8, 1922). The *Century* reviewed and advertised books in every issue, but often published special spring and fall
book issues, many of which were given over to books on psychology.

Just as psychology became a part of everyday American life in the 1920s,
Morrison and the *Century* integrated their psychology coverage throughout
the paper during this era as psychology became not only *a* language of the
self, but *the* language of the self. For the first time, Morrison published articles that introduced psychological principles without mentioning religion.
However, the bulk of the articles still applied psychology to religion. For example, Douglas Horton explained the relationship between the Freudian
theory and preaching, finding in Freudian psychology "the basis of a scientific apologetic for the practice of that art [preaching] which more powerfully than any other agency is competent to make real the life of God in
the hearts of men" (Jan. 13, 1921). Other attempts to reconcile Freud and
Christian practices included an unsigned editorial, "The New Psychology:
Why Do We Sin?" which defined sin as

> living under the influence of subconscious instincts, desires and habits when
> the time has come to pass under the higher rule of reason and conscience....
> Jesus was a supreme psychologist, in that he sought to liberate and sublimate
> the native powers of man and use their energy for higher ends—forging pas-
> sion into power, and the cunning of greed into the strategy of righteousness.
> If the old exhortations no longer appeal, it is because the time has come for
> understanding, for a wiser approach, for a more Christ-like insight and skill.
> (August 24, 1922)

Not all of the *Century's* coverage of Freudian psychoanalysis was so enthusiastic, for several writers found Freud's theories prurient and obtuse. Still,
the overarching trend was to accommodate Christian theology to the
newest psychological theory. John Buckham described the effect as "revolutionary":

> Modern psychology has partly uncovered a wide realm of experience hitherto
> unexplored.... The mere coining of the term subconscious and its applica-

tion to our inner life has worked something almost like a revolution in our thought of that wonderful world within ourselves. . . . There is room in this realm . . . for interaction with a supreme Self. . . . Prayer in the light of psychology, may thus be conceived, not as the mechanical granting of petitions by a deistic Ruler of the Universe, but as cooperant spiritual activity in a realm of immeasurable personal and even physical potencies. (June 17, 1920)

Morrison continued to preach church unity with fervor, and simultaneously stepped up the criticisms of Catholicism.[22] In a typical editorial, Morrison wrote that "The Roman pontiff feels no need of compromising with modern civilization; he defies it. . . . A multitude of people still seek the comfort of sacramentalism, finding in it a cheap and easy way to commend themselves to Deity." The editors went on to imply that Catholics will eventually be conquered not through political repression but through the Americanizing (secularizing) institutions of the school and press: "One has only to wait for free schools, a free press and a free public forum to accomplish its work" (April 12, 1923). Finally, what troubled Morrison was that "Catholicism is not essentially a form of worship or of faith. It is essentially a form of government. It is a corporate control over the minds, consciences and conduct of its adherents—of all the world, so far as circumstances permit—by a very small self-perpetuating group" (May 22, 1924). Elsewhere, Morrison declared that the conflict between Catholicism and Protestantism "is really a conflict between democratic and aristocratic Christianity. In one case, a privileged class stand between the soul and God, and hold special powers in the government of the church. In the other case the simple democracy of Jesus is professed as a theory and largely recognized in practice" (Feb. 12, 1920).

Morrison eventually recognized the implications of this secularizing process as he guided the *Century* to ever greater cultural prominence. The paper became less and less distinctly Christian and indistinguishable from its secular peers. By 1938, the *Century* was the recognized voice of mainstream American Protestantism and so successful that Morrison ran several subsidiary publications, yet he commemorated his twentieth anniversary as editor by reevaluating the magazine's role during the last thirty years, what he called "the most crucial" period since the Reformation. Morrison described the magazine's rise to fame as a daily effort to resist the temptation of secularization.

I recall with many an inward chuckle, one morning some ten or a dozen years ago when the business manager came into my office to tell of a dream he had had that night. It seems that I was drowning in Lake Michigan. He and my editorial colleagues were standing on the shore, having exhausted all their efforts to rescue me. I was just going down for the third and last time, but before the water covered my mouth I thrust up my hand and cried, "Keep it religious! Keep it religious!"

They knew that "it" meant *The Christian Century,* and that my exhortation was in keeping with the determination, shared by us all, against the temptation to break away from religious journalism and make the paper an organ of secular idealism. I speak of it as a "temptation," for that it truly was. (Morrison 1938: 1186)

A year later, Morrison published the remarkable article "How My Mind Has Changed," with which this essay began, where he named "empirical psychology" as a secularizing "acid" of American Protestantism. Morrison returned again and again to the passage quoted, reworking each phrase many times in the autobiography he left unpublished at his death in 1966.

In *Can Protestantism Win America?* published in 1948, the year after he finally retired as the *Century's* editor, Charles Clayton Morrison saw three competitors for the future of America: Protestantism, Catholicism, and secularization, which he believed to be mutually exclusive. He again excoriated Catholicism, but now took Protestantism to task for embracing the modern culture that wound up secularizing American public life. According to Morrison, Protestantism

> must also rid itself of the illusion that it has an ally in modern culture. The assumption that modern culture has been moving toward a Christian goal has been the undoing of Protestantism. It has weakened its will and confused its faith. . . . Liberalism did not propose a radical criticism of this culture in the light of Christian faith. Instead, it proposed a radical criticism of the Christian faith in the light of modern culture. The question it propounded was: What must Christianity now do to adjust itself to science and to the type of mentality produced by contemporary education? Its major assumption was that the cultural scene represents "progress," while the Christian faith is cluttered with tradition. To make an adjustment, it took over into Christianity the idea of progress as it was secularly conceived, and undertook to insert the Christian ethic of the Kingdom of God into the social process by identifying it with the secular goal. (Morrison 1948: 87–89)

Morrison identified Dewey's language of "adjustment," the Darwin-inspired language of "progress," and the whole American Protestant project as an accommodation to psychology whose final result was the secularization of American public life.

NOTES

1. Niebuhr made this statement in the *Christian Century,* but his criticism does not diminish the overall activity of the journal as a harbinger of psychologizing secularization.

2. David Harrell, a Disciples historian, notes that in the absence of a central church authority, Disciples periodicals were the highest authority in discerning answers to difficult questions: "The simplest, and probably the best, way to trace the

course of Disciples history is to study the editors and periodicals of the church" (Harrell 1973: 16). In his unpublished autobiography, Morrison concurred, noting that "the Disciples had no ecclesiastical structure above the local church by which this or any other issue could be settled by authority. They represented on a national scale the concept of a town-meeting democracy. In such a body, the denominational newspapers exercised a far greater influence than in other denominations. They provided a kind of parliament for the discussion of questions of interest to the denomination" (Morrison 1966). Thanks to the Morris Library of Southern Illinois University for permission to quote from Morrison's autobiography.

3. All quotations from the *Christian Century* are cited in the text by author's name, when known, and date of publication. Individual articles are not included in the bibliography.

4. Although he does not mention it, Morrison may have known of Darwin's opposition to slavery, and this association presumably resonated with at least some of the *Century's* readers. That Morrison frequently celebrated Lincoln during these years is notable, because, as Delbanco writes, it is Lincoln's thinking that crystallized "the process by which Christian symbolism, even as it was weakening, was transformed into the symbol of a redeemer nation, and, thereby, into a new symbol of hope" (Delbanco 1999: 77).

5. The Emmanuel Movement was the first American mental health practice operated as a church ministry. In 1906, Elwood Worcester and Samuel McComb, the pastors of Boston's Emmanuel Episcopal Church, along with two local psychiatrists, opened a "psychotherapy" clinic in the church, offering individual counseling and twice-weekly group therapy sessions. Worcester and McComb were steeped in academic psychology as well as Christian theology (Gifford 1997). They understood their work both as a reclamation of the church's ancient healing ministry and as a new—scientific—endeavor. Worcester exulted that, armed with psychology, "the Church of to-day has weapons at her disposal which were denied to the Church of the early centuries" (Worcester, McComb, and Coriat 1908: 301).

6. Dorrien provides the fullest account of the Social Gospel movement in American Protestantism and the role of Morrison and the *Century* in popularizing social gospelers like Jane Addams, Shailer Mathews, Reinhold Niebuhr, and Walter Rauschenbusch (Dorrien 1995).

7. For example, Ames used the *Principles* as the central text of his first university courses. He later recalled that "[i]t was not difficult to get up vigorous class discussions over the 'stream of consciousness,' the nature of the 'self.'. . . The most worn and abstruse topics, like conception and reasoning, came to life under the magic touch of James's lively style and homely illustrations" (Ames 1959: 45–46).

8. This is mostly a defensive posture, for contemporary critics complained that Hall's own work, particularly *Adolescence,* his book most influenced by Freud's view of sex, was prurient (Ross 1972).

9. Americans also appropriated the therapeutic psychology of Pierre Dubois and French physician Pierre Janet, "who twice toured American medical school faculties to explain his theories about the psychological sources of hysteria and other disorders," but Freud proved to be the catalyst (Holifield 1983: 193).

10. Freud's formative influence on early clinical pastoral counseling within American Protestantism is well described, and constitutes a parallel and comple-

mentary perspective to this essay (Holifield 1983; Stokes 1985).

11. In time, Freud was certainly well received by American Protestants; for example, as early as 1925, Freudian psychology dominated the *Century's* psychology coverage. Stokes convincingly describes the history of the Freudian strain of liberal Protestantism as the "Religion and Health" movement, and sees it as a parallel of the Social Gospel tradition. She charts its influence on widely influential Protestants like Norman Vincent Peale and Paul Tillich (1985).

12. Taylor compellingly argues that the fateful visitor at Clark was Jung rather than Freud (1999: 212), as does Rieff: "Better a forthright enemy than an unworthy friend. Jung's psychological religiosity is too strictly for therapeutics, those for whom a god is the need of needs. Freud declared that God did not exist—and identified Him as the universal figure of authority. I am not sure whether one should prefer Freud's strong nonexistent God to Jung's weak existent one" (Rieff 1966: 91).

13. Starbuck began his training at Harvard under James, but eventually moved out to Clark and earned his doctorate under Hall. However, Starbuck asked James, rather than Hall, to write the preface for *The Psychology of Religion*. James returned the favor in 1902 by using Starbuck's research as the empirical basis for the lectures on conversion in *The Varieties of Religious Experience*.

14. James wrote to Leuba in 1904, "I have no living sense of commerce with a God. I envy those who have, for I know that the addition of such a sense would help me greatly. The divine, for my active life, is limited to impersonal and abstract concepts which, as ideals, interest and determine me, but do so faintly in comparison with what a feeling of God might effect, if I had one" (quoted in Perry 1947: 266).

15. For example, the entry entitled "The Psychology of Religious Experience" in the *Encyclopedia of the American Religious Experience* locates the field's origin with the *Varieties* and narrates the discipline in James's terms (Capps 1988).

16. Taylor's own *Shadow Culture* embodies this connection. Taylor, a longtime scholar of James, understands the *Varieties* as the model for his own work, and his book's dust jacket declares, "Writing a modern *Varieties of Religious Experience*, Eugene Taylor traces the lineage of the American visionary tradition through three centuries." Taylor self-consciously understands his project to be a history of American spirituality and mental healing, what he calls a "shadow culture," which is now becoming the mainstream of American religious life. In some respects, this essay can be understood as an alternate account of the same history.

17. Dewey wrote in his autobiography that James's *Principles* was the "one specifiable philosophic factor which entered into my thinking so as to give it a new direction and quality" (quoted in Buxton 1984: 452).

18. In his autobiography, Ames described James's *Principles* as that "great revolutionary work," which "opened new doors to the understanding of the human mind. [James] himself spoke of it as 'psychology without a soul,' thereby indicating in startling phrase the fact that he had discarded the old, speculative, metaphysical conceptions and had turned to the living stream of everyday experience. He viewed the mind as functioning within an elaborate physical organism and presented in detail the results of new studies in experimental laboratory research. His book had profound significance for all further inquiries in philosophy and theology" (Ames 1959: 37). It is surely no accident that Ames entitled his autobiography *Beyond Theology*.

19. Morrison's anti-Judaism grew acute in the 1940s (Williamson and Blaisdell 1991: 133–34).

20. Morrison was careful not to offend his Disciples audience (and his Disciples financial backers), and certainly hedged his bet in this disclaimer below the motto:

> The Christian Century is a free interpreter of the essential ideals of Christianity as held historically by the Disciples of Christ. It conceives the Disciples' religious movement as ideally an unsectarian and unecclesiastical fraternity, whose common tie and original impulse are fundamentally the desire to practice Christian unity in the fellowship of all Christians. Desiring to be a worthy organ of the Disciples movement, The Christian Century has no wish at all to be regarded as an organ of the Disciples' denomination. Published by Disciples, it is not published for Disciples alone, but for the Christian world. It strives to interpret the wider fellowship in religious faith and service which it believes every church of Disciples was intended to illustrate. It desires definitely to occupy a catholic point of view and it seeks readers in all communions. (Dec. 6, 1917)

21. Exact subscription and circulation figures for the Century are not available. However, we can surmise that roughly ten thousand copies were printed each year from 1908 through 1913. By 1926, the Century had doubled its circulation; by 1928, it printed thirty-five thousand copies a year (Ayer & Son 1907–1939).

22. The Century, especially through the work of the famed modernist preacher Harry Emerson Fosdick, also criticizes the fundamentalist movement that became prominent during this era.

REFERENCES

Ames, Edward Scribner. 1906. "Theology from the Standpoint of Functional Psychology." *American Journal of Theology* 10 (April): 219–32.

———. 1910. *The Psychology of Religious Experience*. Boston: Houghton Mifflin.

———. 1959. *Beyond Theology: The Autobiography of Edward Scribner Ames*. Ed. Van Meter Ames. Chicago: Chicago University Press.

Ayer & Son. 1907–39. *N. W. Ayer & Son's American Newspaper Annual and Directory*. Philadelphia, PA: N.W. Ayer & Son.

Bakan, David. 1998. "American Culture and Psychology." In *Psychology: Theoretical-Historical Perspectives*, ed. Robert W. Rieber and Kurt D. Salzinger, 217–25. 2d ed. Washington, DC: American Psychological Association.

Benjamin, Ludy T. 1986. "Why Don't They Understand Us? A History of Psychology's Public Image." *American Psychologist* 41, no. 9 (Sept.): 941–46.

Buxton, Michael. 1984. "The Influence of William James on John Dewey's Early Work." *Journal of the History of Ideas* 45, no. 3 (July): 451–63.

Capps, Donald. 1988. "The Psychology of Religious Experience." In *Encyclopedia of the American Religious Experience: Studies of Traditions and Movements*, ed. Charles H. Lippy, 51–70. New York: Scribner.

Coe, George A. 1904. *Education in Religion and Morals*. Chicago: Revell.

———. 1917. *A Social Theory of Religious Education*. New York: Charles Scribner's Sons.

———. 1929. *What Is Christian Education?* New York: Charles Scribner's Sons.

Cushman, Philip. 1995. *Constructing the Self, Constructing America: A Cultural History of Psychotherapy*. Boston: Addison-Wesley.

Darwin, Charles. 1989. *The Autobiography of Charles Darwin.* Vol. 29 of *The Works of Charles Darwin.* Ed. Paul H. Barrett. London: William Pickering.

Delbanco, Andrew. 1999. *The Real American Dream.* Cambridge, MA: Harvard University Press.

Dewey, John. 1896. "The Reflex Arc Concept in Psychology." *Psychological Review* 3: 357–70.

———. 1910. *The Influence of Darwinism on Philosophy.* New York: Henry Holt.

———. 1916. *Democracy and Education: An Introduction to the Philosophy of Education.* New York: Macmillan.

———. 1934. *A Common Faith.* New Haven, CT: Yale University Press.

———, ed. 1903. *Studies in Logical Theory.* The University of Chicago Decennial Publications, 2d series, vol. 11. Chicago: Chicago University Press.

Disciples of Christ (Christian Churches). 1909. *Program of the International Centennial Celebration and Conventions of the Disciples of Christ (Christian Churches).* Cincinnati, OH: American Christian Missionary Society.

Dorrien, Gary J. 1995. *Soul in Society: The Making and Renewal of Social Christianity.* Minneapolis, MN: Fortress Press.

Evans, Rand B., and William A. Koelsch. 1985. "Psychoanalysis Arrives in America: The 1909 Psychology Conference at Clark University." *American Psychologist* 40, no. 8 (Aug.): 942–48.

Freud, Sigmund. 1961 [1928]. *The Future of an Illusion.* Trans. James Strachey. New York: W. W. Norton.

Garrison, Winfred Ernest, and Alfred T. DeGroot. 1948. *The Disciples of Christ: A History.* St. Louis, MO: Christian Board of Publication.

Gay, Peter. 1987. *A Godless Jew: Freud, Atheism, and the Making of Psychoanalysis.* New Haven, CT: Yale University Press.

Gifford, Sanford. 1997. *The Emmanuel Movement (Boston, 1904–1929): The Origins of Group Treatment and the Assault on Lay Psychotherapy.* Boston: Francis Countway Library of Medicine.

Gruber, Howard E. 1998. "Diverse Relations between Psychology and Evolutionary Thought." In *Psychology: Theoretical-Historical Perspectives,* ed. Robert W. Rieber and Kurt D. Salzinger, 226–52. 2d ed. Washington, DC: American Psychological Association.

Hale, Nathan G., Jr. 1971. *Freud and the Americans: The Beginning of Psychoanalysis in the United States, 1876–1917.* New York: Oxford University Press.

Hall, G. Stanley. 1917. *Jesus, the Christ, in the Light of Psychology.* Garden City, NY: Doubleday.

———. 1924. *Life and Confessions of a Psychologist.* New York: D. Appleton.

Hamner, Martha Gail. 1997. *Habits of a Christian Nation: An Alternative Genealogy of American Pragmatism.* Ph.D. diss. Duke University.

Harrell, David Edwin. 1973. *The Social Sources of Division in the Disciples of Christ: A Social History of the Disciples of Christ, 1865–1900.* Vol. 2. Nashville, TN: Disciples of Christ Historical Society.

Hauerwas, Stanley. 2001. *With the Grain of the Universe: The Church's Witness and Natural Theology.* Grand Rapids, MI: Brazos Press.

Haynes, Nathaniel Smith. 1915. *History of the Disciples of Christ in Illinois, 1819–1914.* Cincinnati, OH: Standard Publishing.

Holifield, E. Brooks. 1983. *A History of Pastoral Care in America: From Salvation to Self-Realization.* Nashville: Abingdon Press.

James, William. 1890. *The Principles of Psychology.* New York: Henry Holt.

———. 1897. *The Will to Believe.* New York: Longmans, Green.

———. 1899. *Talks to Teachers on Psychology and to Students on Some of Life's Ideals.* New York: Henry Holt.

———. 1902. *The Varieties of Religious Experience: A Study in Human Nature.* New York: Longmans, Green.

———. 1904. "The Chicago School." *Psychological Bulletin* 1: 1–5.

King, D. Brett. 1992. "Evolution and Revision of the *Principles.*" In *Reinterpreting the Legacy of William James,* ed. Margaret E. Donelly, 67–76. Washington, DC: American Psychological Association.

Lesser, M. X. 1998. *Jonathan Edwards.* Boston: Twayne.

Leuba, James Henry. 1912. *A Psychological Study of Religion, Its Origin, Function, and Future.* New York: Macmillan.

Livingston, James. 1994. *Pragmatism and the Political Economy of Cultural Revolution, 1850–1940.* Chapel Hill, NC: North Carolina University Press.

McAllister, Lester G., and William E. Tucker. 1975. *Journey in Faith: A History of the Christian Church (Disciples of Christ).* Saint Louis, MO: Bethany Press.

Morgan, Edmund S. 1967. *Roger Williams: The Church and the State.* New York: Harcourt, Brace and World.

Morrison, Charles Clayton. 1914. *The Meaning of Baptism.* Chicago: Disciples Publication Society.

———. 1928. "The First Twenty Years." *Christian Century,* Oct. 11, 1220–22.

———. 1938. "Looking Ahead After Thirty Years." *Christian Century,* Oct. 5, 1185–88.

———. 1939. "How My Mind Has Changed." *Christian Century,* Nov. 8, 1370–74.

———. 1948. *Can Protestantism Win America?* New York: Harper.

———. 1966. *Memories, Thoughts of Faith: The Autobiography of Charles Clayton Morrison.* Unpublished book. Carbondale, IL: Morris Library, University of Southern Illinois.

Niebuhr, H. Richard. 1927. "Theology and Psychology: A Sterile Union." *Christian Century,* Jan. 13, 47–48.

Noll, Mark. 1992. *A History of Christianity in the United States and Canada.* Grand Rapids, MI: W. B. Eerdmans.

Perdue, Leo G. 1991. "The Disciples and Higher Criticism: The Formation of an Intellectual Tradition." In *A Case Study of Mainstream Protestantism: The Disciples' Relation to American Culture, 1880–1989,* ed. Newell Williams, 71–106. Grand Rapids, MI: W. B. Eerdmans.

Perry, Ralph Barton. 1996 [1947]. *The Thought and Character of William James.* Nashville, TN: Vanderbilt University Press.

Reed, Edward S. 1997. *From Soul to Mind: The Emergence of Psychology from Erasmus Darwin to William James.* New Haven, CT: Yale University Press.

Rieber, Robert W. 1998. "Americanization of Psychology before William James." In *Psychology: Theoretical-Historical Perspectives,* ed. Robert W. Rieber and Kurt D. Salzinger, 191–216. 2d ed. Washington, DC: American Psychological Association.

Rieff, Philip. 1966. *The Triumph of the Therapeutic: Uses of Faith after Freud.* New York: Harper & Row.

———. 1990. *The Feeling Intellect: Selected Writings.* Ed. Jonathan B. Imber. Chicago: University of Chicago Press.

Ross, Dorothy. 1972. *G. Stanley Hall: The Psychologist as Prophet.* Chicago: University of Chicago Press.

Rubin, Julius H. 1994. *Religious Melancholy and Protestant Experience in America.* New York: Oxford University Press.

Schull, Jonathan. 1992. "Selection—James's Principal Principle." In *Reinterpreting the Legacy of William James,* ed. Margaret E. Donelly, 139–52. Washington, DC: American Psychological Association.

Starbuck, Edwin Diller. 1899. *The Psychology of Religion: An Empirical Study of the Growth of Religious Consciousness.* New York: Charles Scribner's Sons.

Stokes, Allison. 1985. *Ministry after Freud.* New York: Pilgrim Press.

Taylor, Eugene. 1999. *Shadow Culture: Psychology and Spirituality in America.* Washington, DC: Counterpoint.

Weber, Max. 1930. *The Protestant Ethic and the Spirit of Capitalism.* Trans. Talcott Parsons. New York: Scribner.

Williamson, Clark M., and Charles N. Blaisdell. "Disciples and Mainstream Protestant Theology." In *A Case Study of Mainstream Protestantism: The Disciples' Relation to American Culture, 1880–1989,* ed. Newell Williams, 107–38. Grand Rapids, MI: W. B. Eerdmans.

Wilson, Louis N. 1911. "List of Papers in the Field of Religious Psychology Prepared at Clark University." *Publications of the Clark University Library* 2, no. 8 (July): 2–9.

Witten, Marsha Grace. 1993. *All Is Forgiven: The Secular Message in American Protestantism.* Princeton, NJ: Princeton University Press.

Worcester, Elwood, Samuel McComb, and Isador H. Coriat. 1908. *Religion and Medicine: The Moral Control of Nervous Disorders.* New York: Moffat, Yard.

Wundt, Wilhelm. 1897. *Outlines of Psychology.* Trans. Charles Hubbard Judd. 1896; reprint, New York: Gustav E. Stechert.

7

From Christian Civilization to Individual Civil Liberties

Framing Religion in the Legal Field, 1880–1949

David Sikkink

In 1943 the U.S. Supreme Court overturned an earlier decision that Jehovah's Witnesses could be disciplined for not saying the Pledge of Allegiance in public schools. Earlier the Court saw the Pledge requirement as contributing to social order in the classroom and as a legitimate expression of the national moral order. But in a dramatic overruling of that decision, the Court framed the Pledge issue as one of individual freedom of religious expression. The about-face was symbolic of the transformation of religion in the legal field, which resulted from two political struggles over the dominant legal culture.

The first shifted the legal field toward a "science of law." Through most of the nineteenth century, many judges creatively used common law to insert community and religious notions of justice and fairness into legal decisions. But in the late nineteenth century the actions of the emerging legal elite within the universities expanded the influence of a "science of law," which narrowed the role of religion in legal decision making while defending the expression of religion in public life as a universal moral order. Led by the likes of Christopher Langdell, James Barr Ames, Jeremiah Smith, and Samuel Williston at Harvard, this movement sought to establish the position of the law professor and claim a legitimate role for the law school within the university. Within this "classical" movement, law professors and Supreme Court judges defended "general religion" as a legal concept compatible with establishing general and universal principles of law, and limited the role of religion in legal decision making through this systemization of the common law.

In the second watershed political struggle within the legal field, which occupied the first half of the twentieth century, the dominant legal framework for religion in public life shifted from a general religion that enhanced the social order to one in which religion figured as one expression of the legal doctrine of individual civil liberties. This shift in jurisprudence was the result of political struggles among legal elites—especially between elite corporate lawyers of the bar and elite academic lawyers—that dismantled the nineteenth-century form of jurisprudence, legal formalism, which had attempted to apply abstract and ahistorical legal principles to judicial cases. Civil liberties activists, who emerged in response to state suppression of dissent during World War I, provided a cultural framework that filled the vacuum left by legal formalism. The events of World War I fostered both the insurgent consciousness and the cultural milieu in which the civil liberties activist groups were successful in framing religion cases as issues of individual freedom of expression. Cultural elites' understanding of Hitler's Germany as the expression of a coerced uniformity, the subordination of the individual to the collectivity, only furthered this movement. Through the symbolic contrast of democracy and fascism, legal elites reinforced their view that the defense of individual religious expression rather than cultural consensus was the foundation of social order.

That opened the way for the Supreme Court, led in the 1940s by justices well connected to the civil liberties movement and the movement against legal formalism, to defend a jurisprudence that attempted to deal with the issue of the Pledge in schools and other issues of religion and public life by first accounting for religious pluralism rather than national moral consensus. Through the convergence of movements within the legal field and responses to the events of World Wars I and II, the major legal tradition—the frame—that legal elites used to understand religion's role in the public sphere was that of individual civil liberties. Rather than the individual bending to the general religion, the common moral order, the dominant schema for cases of religion in public life pitted the individual over against community. Religion came to be viewed with suspicion, as something people and society often needed by law to be protected from.

A JURISPRUDENCE OF THE HEAD

The transformation of the role of religion in law cannot be understood apart from the efforts of university law professors after the Civil War to limit the work of judges to systematic application of general legal principles to particular cases. Earlier in the nineteenth century, judges were free to draw on biblical traditions to decide cases in favor of the less powerful and in the name of notions of justice—a jurisprudence of the heart (Karsten 1997; see also Grossberg 1985). And in an era when many judges, especially outside of the Northeast, were deeply religious and strongly influenced by the evangelical moral reform movements of the day, it was much more likely that common law would be creatively appropriated to ensure that biblical

notions of concern for personal and practical justice, including the defense
of community, of children, and of the weak against growing corporate interests, would trump a formal decision that blindly followed an established
legal precedent. Moreover, judges seemed justified in doing so, since the
dominant legal culture assumed that Christianity was and should be an integral part of the common law (Banner 1998).

But elite university law professors, led by Christopher Langdell and
James Barr Ames of Harvard, championed a jurisprudence of the head,
which classed the jurisprudence of the heart as old-fashioned and unscientific. The ways in which religion could legitimately enter the judicial process were narrowed as the movement of legal formalism—or the classical
style—swept through the legal field, attempting to systematize the common
law as a set of general principles that would govern particular cases.

The Essential Classical Style

The science-of-law movement was rooted in changes in legal training pioneered by Langdell in the 1870s (Horwitz 1977; Wiecek 1998). Langdell
took advantage of the increasing publication and distribution of case reporters, which catalogued legal cases from across the country. In Langdell's
view, the burgeoning of case law confronted the lawyer and judge with a ca-
cophony of legal arguments and precedents for any particular case. Under
earlier notions of common law (as well as recent legal theories of law; see
Burton 1991; Farber 1992; Perry 1988; Van Zandt 1991), many legal commentators would see this myriad of decisions as the natural result of attempting fairly to apply legal concepts and rules to the particularities of individual cases. Langdell saw something quite different: the expansion of
case reporters was evidence that law was overly subjective and lacked a scientific classification scheme. He thought he could see an almost Platonic
order behind this legal messiness, and believed that it was time to use the
methods of modern science to reveal this order. Thus, Langdell saw the case
reporters as providing useful data from which university professors could
build jurisprudence for the new era.

Langdell grew up on a farm in New Hampshire, and through incredible
doggedness and the support of his sister, who had moved to Massachusetts
to work in the clothing factories, entered Harvard, where he became
friends with Charles W. Elliot, who would later transform Harvard toward a
more secular university model. Because Elliot and Langdell shared a common intellectual commitment to emerging positivist perspectives in science, Elliot called on Langdell to be the first dean of the Harvard Law
School in 1870. Remembering his early days with Langdell, Elliot lauded his
scientific approach to law: "He told me that law was a science: I was quite

prepared to believe it. He told me that the way to study a science was to go to the original sources. I knew that was true, for I had been brought up in the science of chemistry myself; and one of the first rules of a conscientious student of science is never to take a fact or a principle out of secondhand treatises, but to go to the original memoir of this discoverer of that fact or principle" (Sutherland 1967: 159). The tight connection between Elliot and Langdell placed the science-of-law movement in the context of the secularization of the universities, where religious claims were either ignored or thwarted (Smith, chap. 2 in this volume).

Langdell took it on faith that law was a self-contained system. He argued that

> [l]aw, considered as a science, consists of certain principles or doctrines. . . .
> To have such a mastery of these as to be able to apply them with constant fa-
> cility and certainty to the ever-tangled skein of human affairs, is what consti-
> tutes a true lawyer. . . . If these doctrines could be so classified and arranged
> that each should be found in its proper place, and nowhere else, they would
> cease to be formidable from their number. It seemed to me, therefore, to be
> possible to take such a branch of law as Contracts, for example, and, without
> exceeding comparatively moderate limits, to select, classify, and arrange all
> the cases which had contributed in any important degree to the growth,
> development, or establishment of any of its essential doctrines; and that
> such a work could not fail to be of material service to all who desire to
> study that branch of law systematically and in its original sources. (Sutherland
> 1967: 174)

The task of the academic lawyer, then, was to discover the general principles within the common law, and create a rational system of universal legal principles. In case decisions, the judge must determine the general principle that applies to the facts, and write the decision by deducing the legal argument from the applicable general principle to the particular case. Since there was little concern for social and historical context of "the facts"—and even less reflexivity about the general principles—legal discourse had a mechanical flavor to it, as if particularities could be swept aside in favor of a logical, scientific system of law (Gilmore 1977; Wiecek 1998).

Within the legal academy, the movement to institutionalize legal formalism came largely through law school efforts to mimic the Langdellian case method, which trained law students almost exclusively through reading selected cases that illustrated the general and universal principles governing a particular area of law. Through networks of elite university professors, this innovation spread rapidly to law schools throughout the country (Friedman 1998). In the process, the science-of-law supporters had not only mobilized to dominate the teaching of law, but also created cultural tools to dominate the legal field.

Aims of the Early Legal Reformers

The science-of-law movement had several objectives. The first was to refurbish lawyers as professionals, which would stem the declining status of lawyers in the Jacksonian era (Johnson 1981; Stevens 1983). But another important motive of these reformers was their desire to win a place within the legal field for the position of the law professor. The scientific movement in law went hand in hand with the establishment of "jurisdiction" (Abbott 1988) for an academic lawyer over the analysis of case law and the establishment of general legal principles (Bledstein 1976), which granted legitimacy to the previously marginal role of the academic law professor (Friedman 1998).

Thus the movement emerged out of the university professor's identity as (and interest in being) an arbiter of legitimate knowledge within the legal field. Rather than simply training lawyers as apprentices, the movement to make law systematic—in which the legal elite sits above the fray of the courtroom—placed academic lawyers in a stronger role vis-à-vis other elites—in particular, elites in the fields of politics and religion, but also judges.

How the movement would create this space within the legal field depended on a related interest among these academic legal professionals: their desire to secure a legitimate place for law schools within the emerging secular university (Kronman 1993; Smith 1999), built on German models (Marsden 1994; Reuben 1996; Smith, chap. 2 in this volume). As Langdell argued, "If law be not a science, a university will best consult its own dignity in declining to teach it" (Sutherland 1967: 175). For this task, it was clear to the reformers that the taint of religion within jurisprudence would offer no help. Instead, the classical reformers pursued a science of law that was meant to parallel botany or other physical sciences. The library played the role of the natural world, and academic lawyers classified cases and in the process built a neat system of legal concepts and principles. Langdell summed up his views in an 1886 Harvard anniversary celebration:

> It was indispensable to establish at least two things; first that law is a science; secondly, that all the available materials of that science are contained in printed books. If it be not a science, it is a species of handicrafts, and may best be learned by serving an apprenticeship to one who practices it. If it be a science, it will scarcely be disputed that it is one of the greatest and most difficult of sciences, and that it needs all the light that the most enlightened seat of learning can throw upon it. Again, law can be learned and taught in a university by means of printed books. . . . We have also constantly inculcated the idea that the library is the proper workshop of professors and students alike; that it is to us all that the laboratories of the university are to the chemists and physicists, all that the museum of natural history is to the zoologists, all that the botanical Garden is to the botanists. (Sutherland 1967: 175)

Langdell and the classical reformers were emotionally and intellectually committed to have law take its place—and a prominent place indeed—among the high-status natural sciences in the emerging secular university.

By establishing dominant models of legitimate legal education and pushing for laws that required formal university training to practice law, these reformers created "legal science" as a legitimate subject in the university. They accomplished this partly by distinguishing the university from other competitors that provided legal training, such as apprenticeship programs and independent law schools scattered throughout the country (Stevens 1983). Langdell argued that "if printed books are the ultimate sources of all legal knowledge, if every student who would obtain any mastery of law as a science must resort to these ultimate sources, and if the only assistance which it is possible for the learner to receive is such as can be afforded by teachers who have traveled the same road before him, then a university, and a university alone, can furnish every possible facility for teaching and learning law" (Sutherland 1967: 175). The many and varied legal training institutions were gradually left behind as the university law school model dominated the field. As part of this effort, Langdell changed the admission policy at Harvard from admitting anyone with "good moral character" to requiring some measure of "intelligence." He barred "weaker" students from degree candidacy and instituted stringent qualifying examinations. He extended the program from eighteen months to three years, and instituted qualifying exams that students had to pass in order to move on to the next year of study (Sutherland 1967). More generally, efforts to professionalize the bar and to standardize the educational and testing requirements for practicing law solidified the base of legal formalism by granting further legitimacy to the position of law professor and to the university law school's monopoly on legal training (Johnson 1978).[1] Ironically, these two structural conditions created political opportunities for later challenges to the classical style, which came under attack in the twentieth century.

Outcomes for Religion in Law and Public Life

The Langdellian science-of-law movement joined forces with proponents of academic professionalization throughout the university to downplay the role of religion in public institutions. In this context, what served the interests of law professors was a jurisprudence that built on the distinction between a jurisprudence of the head and jurisprudence of the heart, which allowed them to claim a corresponding position of objectivity and neutrality within the secular university.

To accomplish this, legal elites sought to establish a system of law that created distinction within the dominant religious culture in America. Specifically, they sharpened the boundary between legal discourse and the "religion of the heart"—the enthusiastic religions of the Baptists and Methodists, and of evangelists such as Charles Finney and Dwight Moody—that was making solid gains with the growth of upstart sects. For legal reformers, religion in law became problematic within a cultural context that placed head in opposition to heart and increasingly identified religion as a matter of emotion, irrationality, and heart (Miller 1965). Because the jurisprudence of the heart was more strongly supported by evangelicals clamoring for "public morality" and less favored by the liturgical, mainline faiths (Karsten 1997: 317)—which were increasingly the only respectable religious association for the legal elite, especially those in the universities—the traditional jurisprudence became guilty by association in the eyes of the reformers. For law professors, this cultural context and their structural position pointed in one direction: attacking the jurisprudence of the heart, with its diversity and tendency to appeal to religious principle, in favor of the supposed pure gaze of the scientific law professor. In sum, academic lawyers developed a jurisprudence that furthered their interests as professors within a secular university by creating distinction from the emotional, "sectarian" religion.

This movement succeeded in further delegitimating the religious basis for legal decision making. The jurisprudence of the heart, which drew on biblical traditions, lost standing (Karsten 1997). Clearly, the reformers could not look to "sectarian" religion as a basis for establishing general legal principles. But, unlike figures like Justice Holmes (discussed below), they were not yet ready to abandon a commitment to law as an independent, almost transcendent object (Gilmore 1977; Smith 1999). Instead, legal formalists seemed to claim a "direct line to God's mind through their knowledge of the principles of legal science" (Gordon 1997). The opposition of established and "enthusiastic" religion was transposed into the legal field by the reformers not as a push for a positivist conception of law that eliminated religion altogether—after all, a metaphysical assumption lay behind their view that law had to be "discovered" through careful scholarship of existing case law (Banner 1998)—but as a "religion of the head" within law. The implication of legal formalism for transforming religion in the legal field was the narrowing of the legal conceptions of religion to that of "general religion." What made most sense in this legal science scheme was a general religion that was analogous to the universal claims of the legal principles themselves.

THE SUPREME COURT, THE CLASSICAL STYLE, AND THE FRAMEWORK OF GENERAL RELIGION

The defenders of the classical style found one form of religion that they were willing to defend within a science of law: the concept of a general religion that was presumed to provide the foundation of civilization. The interest in a rationalization of law led legal elites to adopt a rational and universal understanding of legitimate religion in public life. As we have seen, the dominant frame of jurisprudence among the reformers set a small number of general principles over a clearly defined set of particular cases; by analogy, religion was classified in terms of the opposition of the universal and particular. Judges in the classical style transposed a frame of principle versus emotion to make a similarly strong distinction between general religion and the particular religions of the "sects," which included, in their view, the Catholic Church. The beauty of the "general religion" concept for the reformers was that it simultaneously fit the cultural style of legal formalism and created further distance between "enthusiastic" sectarian religion and public life. In Sewell's terms (1992), the schemata of the general and the particular were transposed by the legal elite to classify religion as either contributing to a common moral order or lapsing into mere sectarianism. Legal decisions in the classical style flowed mechanically from a framework that granted legitimacy to religion as a common moral order.

One example of the classical style as applied to religion is the *Watson v. Jones* case in 1871. In the midst of struggle for control of a church in Kentucky (with slavery issues central to the struggle), the Supreme Court wrote,

> Conscious as we may be of the excited feeling engendered by this controversy, and of the extent to which it has agitated the intelligent and pious body of Christians in whose bosom it originated, we enter upon its consideration with the satisfaction of knowing that the principles on which we are to decide so much of it as is proper for our decision, are those applicable alike to all of its class, and that our duty is the simple one of applying those principles to the facts before us. (*Watson v. Jones*, 80 U.S. 679 [1871])

The condescending tone and feigned praise for "intelligent and pious" religion had meaning within an institutional framework in which the legal elite sought distinction and autonomy from a religious culture. The Court made a strong distinction—common to the Victorian era—between "excited feelings" and the objective process of knowing and applying legal principles. Piety in religion is contrasted with the rational and systematic form of law within legal formalism.

A legal schema of general religion was evident in other Supreme Court decisions in the late nineteenth century. In these decisions, the legitimate religious expression in the public square was explicitly connected to "general Christianity." In reviewing the founding documents and letters of the founders, the Court concluded that

> [t]here is no dissonance in these declarations. There is a universal language pervading them all, having one meaning; they affirm and reaffirm that this is a religious nation. These are not individual sayings, declarations of private

persons: they are organic utterances; they speak the voice of the entire people. While because of a general recognition of this truth the question has seldom been presented to the courts, yet we find that in *Updegraph v. The Commonwealth,* 11 S. & R. 394, 400, it was decided that, "Christianity, general Christianity, is, and always has been, a part of the common law of Pennsylvania; . . . not Christianity with an established church, and tithes, and spiritual courts; but Christianity with liberty of conscience to all men." (*Church of the Holy Trinity v. United States,* 143 U.S. 457 [1892])

Interestingly, the decision juxtaposed "universal languages" with "religious nation," and "general Christianity" with "organic" and "public" utterances that speak the voice of the people. The legal concept of general religion, then, meant that public religion had to have a collective dimension that embodied the entire society. Religion with legal standing in public life was a civil religion, which was thought to provide moral glue and a national identity. And this legal framework for religion had no room for the collective representation in public life of, say, the Catholic Church or the "upstart sects."

In a case in which a church hired a foreign pastor, the Court was explicit about the defense of general religion in the public square and interpreted the diversity of collective representations of religion as merely proving the public legitimacy of general religion, the religion of a "Christian nation":

If we pass beyond these matters to a view of American life as expressed by its laws, its business, its customs and its society, we find everywhere a clear recognition of the same truth. Among other matters note the following: The form of oath universally prevailing, concluding with an appeal to the Almighty; the custom of opening sessions of all deliberative bodies and most conventions with prayer; the prefatory words of all wills, "In the name of God, amen;" the laws respecting the observance of the Sabbath, with the general cessation of all secular business, and the closing of courts, legislatures, and other similar public assemblies on that day; the churches and church organizations which abound in every city, town and hamlet; the multitude of charitable organizations existing every where under Christian auspices; the gigantic missionary associations, with general support, and aiming to establish Christian missions in every quarter of the globe. *These, and many other matters which might be noticed, add a volume of unofficial declarations to the mass of organic utterances that this is a Christian nation.* In the face of all these, shall it be believed that a Congress of the United States intended to make it a misdemeanor for a church of this country to contract for the services of a Christian minister residing in another nation? (*Church of Holy Trinity v. United States,* 143 U.S. 457 [1892])[2]

Note that this case for religion in the public square was narrowly construed to "universal" religion. The public prayers were "to the Almighty." The Christian missionary movement was notable for its "general support." The argument for Sabbath laws seems the most explicit case that particular religion can inform law, but, as I show below, the Court defended these laws strictly on the basis of their contribution to the general social welfare.

An important piece of the Court's defense of religion in the public square was not only that religion provided a kind of collective conscience, but also that legitimate religion in the public square provided a basis for civilization and good order. This conception of religion owed much to Victorian moralism, which saw the need for restraints (through religion) on the animal and base instincts of man (Benedict 1985). And this understanding of general religion in the legal field was essentially utilitarian; general religion was justified in public life because it built individual character and maintained public morals. In an 1890 case, *Latter-Day Saints v. United States,* the Court affirmed that "[t]he principles of the law of charities are not confined to a particular people or nation, but prevail in all civilized countries pervaded by the spirit of Christianity" (*Latter-Day Saints v. United States,* 136 U.S. 1 [1890]). In one sentence, the justices brought together all the elements of their concept of religion: general principles of law were associated with a general and universal religious impulse that pervaded the culture of entire nations and therefore upheld civilization itself.

That the Court defended religion in public life in terms of its contribution to social welfare and its role in the civilizing process was clear in decisions regarding Sabbath laws. Judges defended these "blue laws" in terms of their secular benefit to workers; the laws were essential to social well-being. One case concerning whether trains could run on Sunday explicitly adopted a utilitarian view of religion as the foundation of social order by appealing to the decisions of Justice Field:

> [R]elating to the Sabbath day, [J. Field] said: "Its requirement is a cessation from labor. In its enactment, the legislature has given the sanction of law to a rule of conduct, which the entire civilized world recognizes as essential to the physical and moral well-being of society. Upon no subject is there such a concurrence of opinion, among philosophers, moralists and statesmen of all nations, as on the necessity of periodical cessation from labor. One day in seven is the rule, founded in experience and sustained by science. . . . The prohibition of secular business on Sunday is advocated on the ground that by it the general welfare is advanced, labor protected, and the moral and physical well-being of society promoted." (*Hennington v. Georgia,* 163 U.S. 299 [1896])

The concern with labor is ironic, since legal elites would later attack the classical style for not accounting for changing social conditions as the organization of work concentrated power in the hands of management and owners. The Court established, however, a principle for dealing with religion in public life that connected religion with a good social order, with something akin to natural law, and with civilization as a whole. The decision went on to claim that

[l]eisure is no less essential than labor to the well being of man. Short intervals of leisure at stated periods reduce wear and tear, promote health, favor cleanliness, encourage social intercourse, afford opportunity for introspection and retrospection, and tend in a high degree to expand the thoughts and sympathies of people, enlarge their information, and elevate their morals. They learn how to be, and come to realize that being is quite as important as doing. Without frequent leisure, the process of forming character could only be begun; it could never advance or be completed; people would be mere machines of labor or business—nothing more. *If a law which, in essential respects, betters for all the people the conditions, sanitary, social and individual, under which their daily life is carried on, and which contributes to insure for each, even against his own will, his minimum allowance of leisure, cannot be rightfully classed as a police regulation, it would be difficult to imagine any law that could.* (*Hennington v. Georgia,* 163 U.S. 299 [1896])

The Court transformed the religious basis of Sabbath laws to a socially instrumental one—classed as a police function, Sabbath laws could be considered public.

The decision also claimed that civil duties are different from religious duties, but the two may overlap:

Courts are not concerned with the mere beliefs and sentiments of legislators, or with the motives which influence them in enacting laws which are within legislative competency. That which is properly made a civil duty by statute is none the less so because it is also a real or supposed religious obligation; nor is the statute vitiated, or in anywise weakened, by the chance, or even the certainty, that in passing it the legislative mind was swayed by the religious rather than by the civil aspect of the measure. Doubtless it is a religious duty to pay debts, but no one supposes that this is any obstacle to its being exacted as a civil duty. With few exceptions, the same may be said of the whole catalogue of duties specified in the Ten Commandments. Those of them which are purely and exclusively religious in their nature cannot be, or be made civil duties, but all the rest of them may be, *in so far as they involve conduct as distinguished from mere operations of mind or states of the affections.* (*Hennington v. Georgia,* 163 U.S. 299 [1896])

In their legal conception of religion, the judges maintained support for public religion, defined to include only those aspects of religion that were consistent with some definition of the health of society.

In effect, this line of argument separates religion from public life. General religion leads to morality, which in turn leads to public benefits. Legitimate claims for religion in the public square were connected to a general religion that forms character and conforms to general morality. There is no defense of a diversity of religious groups active in public functions within the public square.

The Mormon Polygamy Cases

The legal discourse regarding the Mormons, framed in the legal tradition of general religion in the public square, contrasted sharply with how other minority religions would fare in the mid–twentieth century. Within the framework of general religion, monogamy in these cases is presented as civilized and Christian. In the 1890 case of *Davis v. Beason,* Justice Field states that

> [b]igamy and polygamy are crimes by the laws of all civilized and Christian countries. They are crimes by the laws of the United States, and they are crimes by the laws of Idaho. They tend to destroy the purity of the marriage relation, to disturb the peace of families, to degrade woman and to debase man. Few crimes are more pernicious to the best interests of society and receive more general or more deserved punishment. To extend exemption from punishment for such crimes would be to shock the moral judgment of the community. To call their advocacy a tenet of religion is to offend the common sense of mankind. (*Davis v. Beason,* 133 U.S. 333 [1890])

It is clear in this passage that a general religion that guided legal understandings was one of "common sense," of civilization, and thus not a "sectarian" religion. For the Court, legitimate religion in public life was that which upheld the moral judgment of the community as a whole. In this way, the Court reduced religion to the presumed moral order of Western civilization.

The particularity of the Mormon religion had no legal standing since, according to the Court, the Mormons were sectarian and advanced social policies that were opposed to civilization. Justice Bradley argued that one of the distinguishing features of the Mormon church was

> the practice of polygamy—a crime against the laws, and abhorrent to the sentiments and feelings of the civilized world. Notwithstanding the stringent laws which have been passed by Congress—notwithstanding all the efforts made to suppress this barbarous practice—the sect or community composing the Church of Jesus Christ of Latter-Day Saints perseveres, in defiance of law, in preaching, upholding, promoting and defending it. It is a matter of public notoriety that its emissaries are engaged in many countries in propagating this nefarious doctrine, and urging its converts to join the community in Utah. The existence of such propaganda is a blot on our civilization. The organization of a community for the spread and practice of polygamy is, in a measure, a return to barbarism. It is contrary to the spirit of Christianity and of the civilization which Christianity has produced in the Western world.
>
> The State has a perfect right to prohibit polygamy, and all other open offences against the enlightened sentiment of mankind, notwithstanding the pretence of religious conviction by which they may be advocated and practiced. (*Latter-Day Saints v. United States* 136 U.S. 1 [1890])

This passage again marked a strong boundary between general Christianity and organized communities of believers, which were classified as sectarian religions. The Victorian worldview came through as well in Justice Field's 1890 decision:

> There have been sects which denied as a part of their religious tenets that there should be any marriage tie, and advocated promiscuous intercourse of the sexes as prompted by the passions of its members. And history discloses the fact that the necessity of human sacrifices, on special occasions, has been a tenet of many sects. Should a sect of either of these kinds ever find its way into this country, swift punishment would follow the carrying into effect of its doctrines, and no heed would be given to the pretence that, as religious beliefs, their supporters could be protected in their exercise by the Constitution of the United States. (*Davis v. Beason,* 133 U.S. 333 [1890])

The Court linked sectarianism with the antinomian passions and contrasted these to the civilizing effect of general religion. Of course, not all "sects" would have elicited such condemnation from the Court, but it is important to see that the schema of general religion versus sectarian religion was linked to the Victorian opposition of civilization and savagery, of rational social order and slavery to passions.[3]

Whatever one thinks of whether the Mormons should have been prohibited from practicing polygamy, these cases show the formation of a legal consensus around general religion that embodied the moral order of a "civilized" nation. It also showed the strength of the legal schema that defined general religion and sectarian religion against each other. General religion that provided the basis of civilization was defensible in Court. Its opposite was sectarianism, which had its place in private life, but was limited in public expression by its tendencies toward barbarism. The Mormon cases could not be handled in any other way, given the constraints of a conception of religion as general and universal—if somewhat abstract and separate from particular religious expressions. Under this schema of religion and public life, there was no room for accommodating minority, religiously motivated views of marriage.

While this classical approach perhaps made the task of the judge more certain, it was ushered out in the early twentieth century by the second reform movement among the academic legal elite. And with it went the legitimacy of the dominant conception of religion in law in the classical era, the general religion frame.

FROM GENERAL RELIGION TO CIVIL LIBERTIES

Origin of Challenges to the Classical Style

In the late nineteenth and early twentieth centuries, law professors such as Oliver Wendell Holmes, John Chipman Gray, Ernst Freund, Roscoe Pound, and Felix Frankfurter made up the activist core of a broad attack on legal formalism. In a nutshell, the conflict within the legal field was between those who argued that judges "find" law and those who thought judges should "make" law—or at least have a larger and independent role. This was not an effort to bring back the role of religious tradition in the jurisprudence of the heart, but to govern legal decision making according to a pragmatic instrumentalism (Summers 1982), which would incorporate policy concerns and findings from the emerging social sciences. In this struggle, law professors were in a unique position to bring about change in the legal field: they were now solidly based in a law school within the university, and by that position they maintained an image within the legal field of autonomy from the particulars of the legal process and thus were supposed to have a pure gaze on legal issues.

The movement depended heavily on the influence and writings of Holmes—a complicated figure who contributed to the construction of law as a science yet at the same time could not stomach Langdell's codification efforts. Oliver Wendell Holmes Jr. was born into "the center of Boston legal and literary cultures" (Gordon 1992: 1). He grew up in the company of literary notables, including Emerson and Nathaniel Hawthorne. The younger Holmes would acknowledge later that the doubting side of Emerson had provided the spark for his intellectual career. His grandfather was a well-known Calvinist minister, but his congregation turned Unitarian and eventually asked him to leave. Holmes's father was a famous physician and writer. He was the dean of the Harvard Medical School and one of the original founders of the *Atlantic Monthly,* which was central to the New England intellectual and cultural "awakening" in the first half of the century.

Doctor Holmes lauded the

> remarkable change [that] has taken place in the attitude of men towards each other in all that relates to spiritual matters, especially in this respect: Protestantism is more respectful in its treatment of Romanism, Orthodoxy in its treatment of Heterodoxy, supernaturalism in its treatment of naturalism, Christianity in its handling of humanity, . . . the virtue of humility found to include many things which have often been considered outside of its province—among others the conviction of the infallibility of our own special convictions in matters of belief, which appeal differently to different minds. (Morse 1896)

Following the Unitarians, Justice Holmes's father had a strong distaste for Calvinist theology, especially the doctrines of predestination and original sin. He could not see humans as "little fallen wretches, exposed to the wrath of God by the fact of that existence which they could not help." Attending Harvard while his Calvinist father was fighting against Unitarianism only reaffirmed Doctor Holmes's distaste for orthodox religion. Science became his religion. In his medical career, he learned "not to take authority when I can have facts" (Baker 1991: 36). Justice Holmes would take this mindset into law.

Oliver Wendell Holmes Jr., the future justice, was part of a skeptical generation that valued above all the willingness to question. Skepticism was "in the air," he said. He often heard his father challenging traditional theological principles. Of his father's Deism, Holmes said that he admired his father's "scientific way of looking at the world," but disparaged "a certain softness of attitude toward the interstitial miracle—the phenomenon without personal antecedents" (Baker 1991: 76). The elder Holmes had no use for Calvinism, and the younger had no room for a belief in God. While Justice Holmes maintained a nominal connection to the Unitarian Church, the influence of a nineteenth-century faith in science and reason left him in the end an agnostic. Seeing the worst of several battles during his service in the Civil War and barely surviving two serious wounds contributed to his life-long skepticism, especially of human institutions, which he often referred to in Social Darwinian terms as expressions of the will of the powerful. His perspective was undoubtedly affected by the growing conflict within the universities between the formalism of classical training and the positivist scientific method, which may have laid the groundwork for his later struggles against legal formalism.

Even under Unitarian rule, Harvard religious instruction while Holmes attended there remained explicitly Christian in many ways, particularly in public morality and views of religion and public life. As a protest against the vestiges of the Protestant Establishment, Holmes joined the Christian Union, a liberal student organization organized to oppose the Christian Brethren, whose members held to salvation by faith and other Calvinist doctrines. Holmes joined not because he "considered [his] life justified in belonging to [it]," but because "he wished to bear testimony in favor of a Religious society founded on liberal principles in distinction to the more 'orthodox' and sectarian platform of the 'Xtian Brethren.'" Holmes was disturbed by the claim that a Christian "has been let in on the ground floor by God—that he is privy to his ultimate judgments and a sharer in absolute truth" (Baker 1991: 76). Holmes found theological absolutes repugnant, and was skeptical of all rigid orthodoxies. While not able to reach eternal truths, he believed that there was recurrence of certain national phenomena. Truth was relative, and "largely personal"—only what "I can't help thinking."

Darwin's theories arrived at Harvard during Holmes's undergraduate days, and Holmes's theories of society and law owed much to Darwin. Frances Bowen, the professor who taught Holmes's "Natural Theology" course and with whom Holmes had a running battle, called Darwin's thought a fad and tried to subsume it within his orthodox Christian perspective. Asa Gray, Holmes's botany teacher, supported Darwin. There was no doubt where

Holmes stood on these questions; he trusted in the scientific method. It was axiomatic for Holmes that "all questions may be asked and that many venerable beliefs are not true." He thought he was the first to be "brought up in an atmosphere of investigation, instead of having every doubt answered" (Baker 1991: 87).

Holmes was connected to philosophical pragmatism, and specifically to Charles Peirce and his close friend, William James. A small, elite group of pragmatists formed the informal "Metaphysical Club," in which they "twisted the tail of the cosmos" (Baker 1991: 214). But Holmes later found he could not share James's interest in making room for spiritual faith. In many ways, Holmes brought pragmatism into legal thought. For Holmes, "the law and rights were only the systems imposed by force by whatever social groups emerged as dominant in the struggle for existence" (Gordon 1992: 1). As we will see, this view conflicted directly with the claim that religion was the foundation of common law, and that universal and objective legal principles could float above the fray of political and economic power struggles. If his connections to pragmatism weren't enough to ensure his opposition to the role of religion in law, Holmes's admiration for the positivism of Comte and Mill, including the supposed progression of history through theological, metaphysical, and positivist stages (Kelley 1990), led him to see law and legal theory as similarly evolving, "each generation taking the inevitable next step, mind, like matter, simply obeying a law of spontaneous growth" away from religious superstitions (Holmes 1897).

After serving in the Civil War, Holmes returned to Harvard Law School. He entered private practice in Boston but took time off to write for the *American Law Review*. This led to his landmark book in 1881, *The Common Law*, in which he attempted to uncover the historical development of common law doctrine in order to discover its missteps. He hoped that his historical approach would supplant dominant conceptions of common law, which gave it an independent moral standing, as if it were natural law. Holmes thought that "[t]he rational study of law is still to a large extent the study of history. . . . History must be part of the study, because without it we cannot know the precise scope of the rules which it is our business to know. . . . It is a part of the rational study, because it is the first step toward an enlightened skepticism, that is, toward a deliberate reconsideration of the worth of those rules" (Holmes 1897). In essence, Holmes profaned the absolute claims of Blackstone by showing how common law principles that Blackstone seemed to worship looked quite human when set in the context of ordinary history and social and political forces. His book was lauded in the *American Law Review* and in several law journals, as well as in the *Nation*.

The book landed him an appointment as a professor in the Harvard Law School. Elliot invited Holmes to teach constitutional law at Harvard to contribute to his efforts to modernize the university. But Holmes's argument for a "law of experience" brought him into direct conflict with Dean Langdell's legal formalism. Holmes's visceral, negative reaction to Langdell was un-equivocal: he called Langdell's casebook on contracts a "misspent piece of marvelous ingenuity" representing the "powers of Darkness," and said Langdell was "wanting in horse sense." For Holmes and his intellectual children, including Cardozo and Frankfurter, Langdell's sin was to consider law in a vacuum, divorced from political and social reality (Baker 1991: 208). Rather than study Langdell's selected cases from the past, Holmes thought law schools should be devoted to policy science (Holmes 1897). Holmes was suspicious of the early codification movement because, first of all, he did not think it was possible to construct a viable code without killing the "living law," and he thought the complexities and flexibility of the common law allowed it to evolve and adapt faster than the codifiers could respond to the changing society. The conflict contributed to Holmes's early exit from Harvard for a vacancy on the Massachusetts Supreme Court, which to Holmes was a move to participate in "the practical struggle of life" (Baker 1991: 270).

Legal Formalism and Cultural Wars

Movement activists like Holmes drew heavily on (and contributed to) broader cultural struggles to overthrow Victorianism and formalism (Himmelfarb 1995; White 1957), which included an opposition to the role of religion, especially established Protestantism, in public life. The broader cultural movement commandeered a position in the universities and had a direct parallel in the struggle over legal formalism. This massive revolt against conventional legal discourse included a rejection of its metaphysical commitments in favor of a practical and rational legal discourse (Smith 1999). A key part of this revolt was the academic legal elite's attack on the clearest expression of formalism within the legal field, the classical style.

To the reformers, the classical movement represented the expression within law of absolute principles, which appeared to be based on moral claims and were associated with Victorian culture and the God of the Protestant Establishment. Not only the absolute claims for legal concepts within legal formalism but judicial writings had a religious air to them, as if they were revealed from on high (Johnson 1981). Legal reformers threw down the cultural gauntlet. Holmes's famous words of derision for the classical style were telling: "The common law is not a brooding omnipresence in the sky" (*Southern Pacific v. Jensen*, 244 U.S. 205, 222 [1917]). The sacred nature of general principles, in the view of the reformers, paralleled the Protestant Establishment's conception of God: rational, omnipresent, omnipotent, and disembodied from human experience (i.e., ahistorical). The fact that Christianity was intimately tied to the Western legal tradition of law as a unified whole that develops according to an internal logic rather than simply in response to the social environment or instrumental pursuit of social goals (Berman 1983)—a view of law that remained intact within legal formalism—would create further animus toward the classical style among radical reformers. The classical style had to come under attack from Holmes, who was born and bred to believe that "truth was only what he couldn't help thinking on the basis of observation and experience, and his only absolute was an absolute abhorrence of absolutes" (Baker 1991: 11). In an 1897 article in the *Harvard Law Review* that marked a watershed that continues to define the legal field (George 2001), Holmes opposed "some text writers telling you that [the law] is something different from what is decided by the courts of Massachusetts or England, that it is a system of reason, that it is a deduction from principles of ethics or admitted axioms or whatnot, which may or may not coincide with the decisions" (Holmes 1897). Interestingly, Holmes here attacked legal formalism and a tight connection between law and morality as if they were one. Arguing against legal formalism, he argued for a strict separation of law and morality (Alschuler 2000); he "often doubt[ed] whether it would not be a gain if every word of moral significance could be banished from the law altogether, and other words adopted which should convey legal ideas uncolored by anything outside the law" (Holmes 1897).

Thus, Holmes led the attack on what he saw as the absolute and universal—quasi-religious—pretensions of the classical style. Holmes summed up his purpose in writing *Common Law,* which he wanted to supplant Blackstone's and Kent's commentaries. "What sounded so arbitrary in Blackstone, for instance, should give some reasonable meaning—that the law should be provided, if it could be, to be worthy of the interest of an intelligent man." To the reformers, the construction of classical versus modern approaches to the common law was the equivalent within law to the assumed opposition of faith and intelligence.[4] In *Common Law,* Holmes disparaged looking to logic, tradition, and God for jurisprudence, since law was not static but evolved in response to the social and economic environment. He attacked the view of legal formalism that "the only force at work in the development of the law is logic" (Holmes 1897). Holmes wrote, "The life of law has not been logic: it has been experience. . . . The law embodies the story of a nation's development through many centuries, and it cannot be dealt with as if it contained only the axioms and corollaries of a book of mathematics." And Holmes saw in legal formalism the religious impulse "toward the superlative." He argued that "the logical method and form flatter that longing for certainty and for repose, which is in every human mind." But this religious source for legal formalism could not stand in a scientific age in which "certainty is an illusion, and repose is not the destiny of man" (Holmes 1897).

Legal formalism, then, seemed to the reformers to embody claims about absolute and universal principles that had a sacred quality to them; the reformers saw the manner and orientation of the classical style as symbolic of the God of the Protestant Establishment. Holmes tellingly referred to Langdell as a "legal theologian" (Holmes 1880) and took positions that transposed current disputes between science and religion into legal discourse. Even the terms from these broader cultural wars were evident when Holmes chastised the Langdellians (and, by implication, a jurisprudence of the heart) for assuming "a transcendental body of law," which he dismissed as a "fallacy and illusion . . . there is no such body of law."[5] The reformers saw legal formalism as passé for the same reason that theological concepts from a Protestant Victorian culture were outmoded. To oppose the classical style was to oppose a Protestant culture, at least as that culture was expressed in public life.

The opposition of a key leader in the movement against legal formalism, Benjamin Cardozo, was reinforced through an analogous schema that pitted his orthodox Jewish upbringing against a "modern" religion. He believed that religious creeds were snares and hypocrisy if they were not adapted to the needs of life. He could not understand or approve of a morality that regarded formal membership in religion as more important than leading a good life. As shown in more detail below, the similarity of this view to Cardozo's critique of legal formalism was striking. As formal religion was worthless without a dynamic relationship to lived experience, so he condemned formalism in law because it was not dynamic, not adapted to "experience" and social needs.

In the reformers' view, then, the classical style was another Hegelian sacred that had to be dethroned in favor of experience and scientific empiricism. Looking back at a dissent in a case that struck down a minimum wage law, Holmes commented that his intent was to "dethrone Liberty of Contract from its ascendancy in the Liberty business" (Baker 1991: 579). Moreover, the animus of the new reformers toward the classical style was generated in part by the connection between that style and the defense of general religion. Holmes criticized the classical style by arguing that "the time has gone by when law is only an unconscious embodiment of the common will. The ground of decision really comes down to a proposition of policy" (quoted in Wiecek 1998: 180). From the perspective of the reformers, the reciprocal relationship between general religion and legal formalism made them both all the more suspect in an age of scientific positivism, Progressivism, and secular universities.

Sociological Jurisprudence as a Political Struggle with the Legal Field

The movement against the classical style coalesced in the legal field around "sociological jurisprudence" in the early twentieth century. Influenced by their increasingly secular and empiricist colleagues in the university, anti-legal formalists attacked the classical style for failing to make legal decisions that seemed just in changing social and economic circumstances. The attack of Charles Beard on an American historiography that failed to account for economic power and class interests had its parallel—as well as direct influence—in the legal reformers' sociological jurisprudence, which called for legal decision making that accounted for social change, especially industrialism and "big business." These reformers sought not a return to a jurisprudence of the heart but a policy-oriented law grounded in the social sciences (Smith 1999). The "new" disciplines, especially sociology, gave cultural tools for the challenge to the classical style (Wiecek 1998). Edward Ross, a pioneer sociologist, added his voice to the clamor against "unhistorical jurisprudence," as he put it (Weinberg 1972: 57), by which he meant that the specific social and economic context must have an independent role in the decision-making process. According to sociological jurisprudence activists, the judicial task was to account for the particularities of the case rather than attempting to apply abstract legal principles suited for another age. In step with the rest of the university, legal reformers wanted Hegel on his head.

The clash of sociological jurisprudence and classical formalism was not simply an academic debate within elite law schools. In fact, the political origins of the reform movement—specifically, the opposition of individualism and laissez-faire capitalism, and Progressivism—created a committed and activist cadre of reformers within the legal field.

The relationship between outside political struggles and struggles within the legal field depended on late-nineteenth-century movements. Conservative lawyers and judges used the federal judiciary as the key line of defense in their efforts to protect private property and interstate corporate enterprise. In the last decade of the nineteenth century, elite corporate lawyers, responding to social unrest and fear of immigrants as well as to a challenge from the newly formed National Bar Association, transformed the American Bar Association into a potent force for economic conservatism and opposition to the populist and labor movements (Haber 1991; Paul 1969; Smith 1986). These economic conservatives regarded state and federal legislatures, and to some extent state courts, as suspect. When the Supreme Court expanded its oversight of government regulatory actions in the name of the right of individual "freedom of contract," the stage was set for the opposition of legal conservatives (who at the time actually favored expanded federal judiciary power) and Progressives within and outside of the legal field, who believed that social reform was only possible if the Supreme Court power was limited and legislative power expanded (Purcell 2000).

The conflict within the legal field of elites in the bar and academic legal elites surfaced when Holmes was being considered for the U.S. Supreme Court. This conflict was structured in part by the fact that the practice of the law depended (and still depends) on assumptions about a metaphysical conception of law, which law professors following Holmes were combating within legal theory (Smith 1999). Holmes's status as a lightening rod in the growing struggle between the positions of legal theorists and lawyers emerged in a legal case in which Holmes claimed that "the law knows nothing of moral rights unless they are also legal rights." One justice strongly dissented, arguing that the decision must account for "natural justice," which he "had learned in a law office, not in a school" (quoted in Karsten 1997: 230). Thus, for political and ideological reasons, corporate lawyers described Holmes's views on labor as dangerous. Echoing the views of corporate lawyers, Senator Hoar claimed that "his accomplishments are literary and social, and as an investigator of the history of jurisprudence, and not judicial. He lacks strength." Regarding his appointment to the Massachusetts Supreme Court, the Boston legal establishment generally agreed with Senator Hoar's opinion that "all the strong men thought his appointment a distinct lowering of the standards of our Supreme Court. In his opinions he runs to subtleties and refinements and no decision of his makes a great landmark in jurisprudence or serves as a guide for the courts in after cases." The public would like Holmes, Senator Hoar argued, but he was "too much of a scholar" (Baker 1991: 350).

The conflict spilled over into issues of free speech at the university. Reformers Frankfurter, Pound, and Harold Laski were suspect in the eyes of the Boston corporate elite. Among conservatives, Pound's sociological jurisprudence was easily equated with socialism. Holmes wrote Harvard President Lowell, then being pressured by corporate lawyers and influential alumni, that Frankfurter and Pound "have and impart a ferment which is more valuable than an endowment and makes of a Law School a focus of life." The cultural opposition of legal and academic elites was clear.

For their part, the challengers to the conservatives, including Frankfurter, Pound, Louis Brandeis, and Zechariah Chafee, were spurred into action by the use of the classical style, especially under the guise of defending laborers' individual "freedom of contract," to stifle the labor movement in the early twentieth century and strike down state regulation of questionable business practices. One of the most important advocates of this view and a prominent leader of the sociological jurisprudence movement was Louis Brandeis, who, because of both Jewish origins and earlier radical stances in favor of the labor movement, was alienated from elite corporate lawyers and took up sociological jurisprudence to challenge the classical style that enforced their power (Glendon 1994; Johnson 1981). Brandeis and Holmes were close friends, and Brandeis's famous defense before the Supreme Court of an Oregon statute that restricted women's work hours was the first attempt to take seriously Holmes's contention that "the life of the law has not been logic; it has been experience." For Brandeis, that meant taking seriously the changing social and economic conditions brought on by industrialization. And the case marked the beginning of his long-standing involvement in legal fights over reforms advocated by Florence Kelley's National Consumer League. His commitment and activism in Progressive causes did not endear him to conservative elite lawyers; he was "thoroughly hated by most of the leaders of the bar" (Baker 1984).

Born in 1858, Brandeis grew up in Louisville, Kentucky. His family maintained only a casual relationship to the Reform Jewish synagogue. His mother saw religion as a matter of virtue, truth, and nobility. "This is my justification for bringing up my children without any definite religious belief," she said, "I wanted to give them something that could not be argued away or would have to be given up as untenable, namely, a pure spirit and the highest ideals as to morals and love" (Baker 1984: 22). Brandeis entered Harvard Law School in 1875, and struck up a friendship with James Bradley Thayer, who invited Brandeis to a lecture by Emerson at his home. Brandeis graduated from Harvard and established a law practice in Boston, but later returned to academic life with a paper for the *Harvard Law Review* entitled "The Right to Privacy," which treated the invasion of privacy by the news media. The argument here for "full protection in person and property" became the hallmark of Brandeis's legal career (Baker 1984). In making this argument, Brandeis was explicitly taking up a political battle within the legal field that was in part determined by political and class struggle outside of law.

The battle to overturn legal formalism depended as well on a precipitating event, the Lochner case on bakers' work hours (*Lochner v. New York*, 198 U.S. 45 [1905]). Holmes's landmark dissent in the case has become famous. The Court majority rigidly applied the general principle of the sacredness of autonomous individual contracts in employment, which seemed hopelessly anachronistic in a case where bakers were attempting to negotiate for reduced work hours vis-à-vis management and owners, who seemed to have disproportionate power in the new industrial context. For the activists, the Lochner case became a symbol of the mechanical application of general principles to the exclusion of establishing justice through attention to the context of the case, including the growing power of capitalist managers and owners (Wiecek 1998). And through his dissent, Holmes became the visible leader of the movement to overthrow legal formalism.[6]

In a way different from Brandeis but nearly as important, Holmes was tightly connected to the Progressive movement. His *Lochner* dissent and defense of free speech—at least in the eyes of the reformers—made him a hero with the Progressives. Opposing the abstract principle of "freedom of contract," Holmes believed that the courts must defer to legislatures, which had imposed regulations on business. Believing that legal elites opposed to legislative action were driven by political interest, Holmes argued that the majority in the Lochner case made their decision based on an economic theory that most of the country did not entertain. Despite the high regard he felt for Spencer, he argued that the Constitution was not meant to "enact Herbert Spencer's social statistics." Building on Holmes's work, legal reformers highlighted the relationship between political struggle and legal decisions. Translating political interests into the legal field, sociological jurisprudence reformers brought social and economic conditions—power relations—into consideration within law.

Sociological Jurisprudence and Religion Cases

Constructing what became an important reformer strategy, Brandeis profaned legal formalism by building legal defenses on "mountains of data," which led some to label his form of law "nascent" social science (Johnson 1981). Bringing the methods of the increasingly respected social sciences in the university to bear on the legal field, Brandeis was able to claim scientific objectivity and authority at the same time that he challenged the formalism and the objective and deductive claims of the classical style.

Justice Benjamin Cardozo, through landmark lectures and writings, called into question the autonomy, the pure gaze, of the classical judge, who supposedly was able to provide an objective and neutral application of general principles to carefully classified cases. Instead, he argued that "what judges actually do" is enmeshed in mundane, everyday life, including personal prejudices and morality, as well as class interests. While he was a complex and sometimes eclectic legal thinker, Cardozo pushed forward in the courts the effort to "modernize" law by accounting for social and economic conditions. And Cardozo was one of the most important players in the movement because he provided a reliable link between legal elites in the academy and key elites within the courts. Cardozo openly appreciated the work of academics and was one of the first judges to cite their work regularly in his opinions. The admiration was mutual (Kaufman 1998: 568–69).

Cardozo was born into an upper-class, conservative, Jewish family in New York, the son of a prominent lawyer and judge, who later was tainted by scandal. As a child, he was deeply involved in synagogue. He was trained for his bar mitzvah by Rabbi Mendes, who maintained an austere moral code, summarized by the "three R's" of Judaism: reverence, righteousness, and responsibility. Following the path of many intellectuals of his day, he lost interest in the faith after his bar mitzvah, and showed his streak of independence by refusing to attend synagogue, despite the prominent role his family had there. Although he was not religiously observant—he claimed to be a "heathen" who "didn't have religion"—he maintained ties to the synagogue, always valued his Jewish identity, and was a lifelong member of Shearith Israel. Good conduct, according to Cardozo, was the essence of religion. He said that "the submergence of the self in the pursuit of an ideal, the readiness to spend one's self without measure, . . . for something intuitively apprehended as great and noble, spend one's self one knows not why—some of us like to believe this is what religion means." He had a keen interest in the philosophy of Matthew Arnold: "Perfection, that is, the full and free development of man's being . . . is the supreme good." Not surprisingly, he shared the view of most intellectuals that associated the fundamentalism exhibited at the Scopes trial with "obscurantism" (Kaufman 1998). Undoubtedly, this shaped his support of freedom of speech, which he saw as an "indispensable condition of intellectual experimentation."

Cardozo was tutored by Horatio Alger, who was briefly a Unitarian minister before being accused of sexual abuse. At the age of fifteen, Cardozo entered Columbia. Though Columbia at the time was dominated by classical education, Cardozo was favorably introduced to Hume and problems of causality by Nicholas Butler, and to Social Darwinism by John Burgess. Cardozo would later use concerns about causality to call into question the classical view of legal decision making.

Cardozo entered Columbia Law School in 1885, as the battles over Langdell's case method were brewing. During his last year at Columbia, William Keener from Harvard brought the case method to Columbia. Cardozo was not impressed with the new science of law, partly because he did not appreciate the combative teaching style of Keener. After graduating, Cardozo gained a reputation as an effective lawyer; he was appointed to the New York Supreme Court and eventually rose to chief justice. In the 1930s, he was appointed to the U.S. Supreme Court.

Cardozo was closely connected to secular trends within the elite universities. He read widely, including philosophy and the emerging field of sociology. He was explicit about the value he placed on keeping up to date on "modern" ideas, including those of Alfred North Whitehead. He kept up with developments within physics, and, echoing Holmes, concluded that there was "no reason to believe that this is a rational universe. Perhaps the order of world is only in perceptions" (Kaufman 1998: 160).

Cardozo greatly admired Holmes, and considered Roscoe Pound a rare combination of learning and wisdom. While on the New York bench, his involvement in the American Legal Institute brought him into closer contact with elite lawyers and professors. Even before his appointment to the U.S. Supreme Court, he maintained personal ties to Felix Frankfurter and Learned Hand, both of whom were very active in the Progressive movement. In the 1920s, Cardozo served briefly on a subcommittee of the American Jewish Committee, one of the prime movers behind the emerging civil liberties doctrine. Cardozo was a strong proponent of civil liberties, especially freedom of speech, since he saw this as fundamental to human freedom in a democracy.

Cardozo opened up the debate about what judges do in his famous lectures at Columbia in 1910. One of his primary contributions was that decisions must account for social and economic factors, rather than retreat behind the supposed rationality of general and universal principles. As he put it, concern for precedent should not be deluded by the "demon of formalism [that] tempts the intellect with the lure of scientific order" (Kaufman 1998: 209). The religious symbolism reveals Cardozo's view that the classical style, with its certainties rooted in Scottish Common Sense Realism, represented Protestant religious culture. In contrast, Cardozo pitted the methods of sociology against the logic, coherence, and consistency of the classical style. As we will see below, the roles of Brandeis and Cardozo on the Supreme Court, combined at times with that of Justice Felix Frankfurter, linked Supreme Court decisions to the legal movement to overthrow the classical style.

Deconstructing Legal Formalism

While the movement of sociological jurisprudence placed shackles on the old school, the emergence of what was known as "legal realism" in the 1920s and 1930s sounded its death knell. Legal realists such as Karl Llewellyn, Felix Cohen, and Jerome Frank attacked the classical style not only by calling attention to social and economic conditions in which mechanical application of abstract principles would not lead to just outcomes, but by deconstructing the scientific process that supposedly governed legal reasoning under the classical style (Horwitz 1977; Schlegel 1995). Following Holmes's lead, many of the legal realists opposed legal formalism with "behavioral" accounts of law, which defined law as what in fact judges or state officials do (Smith 1999).

Legal realists claimed that the classical style was not what it pretended to be. Whatever judges do, the legal realists asserted, it is not a logical, formal, and inevitable process of discovering ultimate principles and straightforwardly and logically applying them to different types of cases. The legal realists believed it was impossible to define a set of principles from which individual case decisions could be deduced. Moreover, they pointed out that contradictory principles coexist in the supposedly rational, formal world of the classical style. Rather than rely on the absolute principle of general religion in the public sphere, and pigeonhole cases into the schema of general versus particular religion, legal realists challenged judges to balance individual free expression and community cohesiveness and order.

The combination of the movements of sociological jurisprudence and legal realism put the classical style to rest, discrediting in the process the legal concepts connected to the legal formalism of the nineteenth century, including the principle of general religion. This created the cultural space for a new approach to handling religion cases. Social movements of the 1920s were bringing the doctrine of civil liberties into focus. One of the most important factors in the rise of the civil liberties movement was state action to suppress dissent during World War I.

World War I and the Making of Individual Civil Liberties

President Woodrow Wilson along with other Progressives in government and community leaders outside of government went to great lengths to ensure support for the war effort and stifle even the slightest dissent to the war. Press restrictions and the failure to curtail vigilante pro-war community groups raised the question of whether the efforts to maintain national unity during World War I went too far (Murphy 1979). The backlash from cultural elites included activist groups in the legal field, such as pacifist groups, one of which was a precursor to the American Civil Liberties Union, that made the civil liberties frame more salient in legal discourse, and eventually structured legal cases concerning religion and public schools around the civil liberties frame (Paulson 1997).

The Progressive movement had granted legitimacy among the cultural elite to expanding the government's role in dealing with social ills. The common good was served through the collective action of government, according to Progressives such as Wilson. Wilson's natural inclination, then, was to greatly expand the role of the state in maintaining agreement on support for the war. He enlisted the state to address the "social problem" of consensus on the war effort. Public opinion was not left to informal social control, but became a matter of the state. Free speech was curtailed; the press was restricted. The Post Office, for example, was instructed to use its powers to thwart the mailing of antiwar material, including some magazines that were not fully supportive of the war. Wilson's particular concern was that nothing be said that would hinder the conscription effort. Thus the Justice Department along with most state governments did not deal firmly with the excesses of the patriotic voluntary groups that arose during this period and harassed open dissenters (Murphy 1979).

These decisions by Wilson contributed to an insurgent consciousness (Smith 1991) among cultural elites and religious minority groups. And these groups, which would play a key role in bringing cases before the Court framed in terms of individual civil liberties, constructed a particular version of Wilson's sin: Wilson had pursued organic unity, a collective consensus, over justice for individuals. He used appeals to a general, civil religion to drown out individual dissent. Moreover, the dissenters argued, he punished groups without regard for individual differences. The government and community groups, for example, put Germans as a social category under suspicion, without regard for individual differences among them.

The impact of censorship during World War I on the framing of religion in the legal field, then, is partly due to the fact that strong government action grew out of and was defended in the name of the collective or general moral order. This stance was upheld in legal decisions that appealed to the classical discourse about the common moral order. When the legal elite and others in the budding civil liberties movement began to question state censorship, they attacked not only the censorship but also the case for a unified, organic moral order. If the concept of general religion wasn't tainted enough through its association with the classical style, it lost further credibility because the cultural elite of the 1920s saw in it the logic behind the censorship during World War I.

The World War I experience went farther than simply discrediting the legal discourse that defended a common moral order; it would also shape the direction of the civil liberties movement. The use of government to create individual conformity had implications for cultural assumptions about the meaning of citizenship. The decision to put government in the business of monitoring and policing the expression of individual dissent solidified and enhanced a cultural frame in which autonomous individual selves were constructed by their relation of complementary opposition to the state (Thomas 1987, 1989). A paternalistic government, in the context of the rise and power of the government bureaucracy, reshaped the relation of the individual and the state, which created the cultural opportunity structure in which the defense of autonomous individual expression against collective constraints made sense. The cultural tinder was in place, and interest groups provided the spark.

Playing on the cultural opposition of state versus autonomous individuals, activists created interest groups to defend individual civil liberties against the bureaucratic social control that marked the war period. If the collective power of the state faced autonomous individuals, activist groups could match this power by collective representation of individuals. One of the important bridges between the legal elite's challenge to legal formalism and the emergence of the civil liberties movement was Zechariah Chafee of Harvard Law School, who was greatly influenced by Roscoe Pound (Murphy 1979). Born in Providence, Rhode Island, in 1885, Chafee was the son of an industrialist. He was influenced by the tradition of Roger Williams, who was one of his ancestors. He admired the Dorr Rebellion, which in 1833 fought for a People's Constitution and expansion of suffrage in Rhode Island. Chafee grew up in a devout Episcopalian home and was required to attend church. His father was active in the denomination, and helped to found St. Andrews School in Barrington. Chafee attended Brown University in 1903, which was developing into a modern university under the direction of E. Benjamin Andrews. The sociologist Lester F. Ward was on the faculty at the time, though Chafee did not have a course with him. Instead, Chafee was influenced by Ward through his mentor at Harvard, Roscoe Pound, whose philosophy of law owed much to Ward and to Edward Ross.

Chafee is perhaps best known for *Freedom of Speech,* which was one of the first statements that constructed Wilson's expansion of the state in terms of individual civil liberties. Though the first edition of the book was praised by H. L. Mencken and other Progressives, it did not attract widespread public attention. Still, within the small but growing civil liberties movement, Chafee was established as a leading legal innovator. In one of the key cases in overturning the influence of legal concepts of general religion, the Jehovah's Witnesses Pledge of Allegiance case, Chafee wrote an influential brief as a member of the ABA's Bill of Rights Committee. In this brief, Chafee drew heavily on his concern for "balancing interests," which would allow the jurists to account for the power of the majority culture in suppressing minority religious expression. He argued that reciting the Pledge of Allegiance should be considered a religious ceremony in relation to the Jehovah's Witnesses (rather than a public expression of community and nationhood) and that this impairment of religious liberty would not promote the public interest (Smith 1986). Chafee quoted a favorite biblical passage in his argument that formal structures could not in themselves contribute to a common moral order: "The law does not require national unity and it could not. National unity is a creation of the spirit, and the wind of the spirit 'bloweth where it listeth, and thou hearest the sound thereof, but canst not tell whence it cometh, and whither it goeth: so is everyone born of the Spirit. . . .' The nation which survived Valley Forge and the dark days of the Civil War without compulsory flag salutes will not go to rack and ruin because a few children fail to participate in this novel ceremony on account of their religious beliefs" (Smith 1986: 211). Clearly, Chafee had little time for blanket, formal legal principles such as the defense of a general religion. His work set the stage for new civil liberties organizations that would pursue individual civil liberties cases through sponsorship and coordination of test cases within the courts.

Among the major players who emerged in this context was Roger Baldwin, who founded the National Civil Liberties Bureau, which later became the American Civil Liberties Union. Baldwin was from the class of "Boston Brahmins" of the day, the son of a Unitarian minister.[7] Baldwin regularly attended a Unitarian church while in Boston, and Thoreau and Emerson were household names. Besides his father, his grandfather could only have reinforced the Unitarian dissenting tradition when he organized the Young Men's Christian Union to counter what he saw as the religious sectarianism of the early YMCA. Baldwin was also strongly influenced by his aunt, Ruth Bowles, who was the daughter of Samuel Bowles, editor of a Progressive newspaper in Boston. With this heritage, it is not surprising that Baldwin was unconventional and nonconformist even at a young age. As he put it years later, "My tendency is to look at the minority viewpoint. I am not at home with the majority" (Lamson 1976: 16).

In his view of religion, Baldwin seemed ready to follow Emerson, who, Baldwin said, "had left the Congregational Church with its acceptance of the divinity of Jesus Christ and all that sort of thing." The intellectual zeitgeist against traditional religion was deeply ingrained: when asked late in life whether he believed in Jesus Christ as the Son of God sent to redeem him, he was dismissive: "Oh, no, of course not." He noted with approval that a friend of his had "given up the ministry to become a Christian." His religion was self-described as consisting primarily of the "Christian underdog doctrine": to make democracy work, he had to protect the rights of the humblest citizens.

Keeping with his family position, Baldwin never had to think about whether and where he would attend college. While nonconformist Unitarianism was reinforced during his years at Harvard from 1901–1905, he veered from the ministry into social work. After some soul searching—and encouragement from his father's lawyer, Louis Brandeis—he ended up in St. Louis after college, directing a center organized by the Ethical Culture Society and providing the first course in sociology at Washington University. He had returned to Harvard for a summer to study sociology in preparation for the class. He said he liked the freedom and individualism in the Midwest, compared to the caste system of Boston, though he also admitted that he was able to connect with the "intellectual and cosmopolitan elite" in St. Louis. Most important, he became a well-known player in Progressive causes, including cleaning up government, reforming probate courts, and improving the lot of the poor. He later directed the Civic League, a reform organization solidly within the Progressive movement. He was instrumental in bringing the ballot referendum to city government, but was disillusioned when it was used to pass an ordinance to maintain residential segregation by race. From that experience, he was convinced that "in the case of minority rights, you can't trust the majority" (Lamson 1976: 51). But when the Supreme Court overturned the ordinance, he claimed to have put his progressive hopes and faith in the Court and judicial supremacy.

Baldwin's credentials in the loosely defined Progressive movement included his association with Jane Addams and the Hull House in Chicago, as well as with Clarence Darrow. He also led a protest of the city's refusal to allow Margaret Sanger to hold a meeting and speak in St. Louis. In addition, he strengthened his ties to the Industrial Workers of the World (IWW) while in St. Louis. One of the more important influences on Baldwin was his relationship with Emma Goldman, whom he greatly admired. Goldman reinforced his concern about "freedom from coercion," which for Baldwin meant individual freedom from the state. His job was to "protect the individual from the abuse of government." Baldwin took that general orientation into his very public marriage, which was reported in local newspapers as a "50/50" marriage (i.e., nonpatriarchal).

The original National Civil Liberties Bureau (NCLB) was tightly networked with the pacifist movement, which was connected to the literary and cultural elites who were beginning to crack the dominance of Victorian culture (Paulson 1997). Baldwin, with strong ties to the labor movement and Eugene Debs, had larger goals for the movement; he wrote, "Civil liberties, like democracy, are useful only as tools for social change" (Auerbach 1976). In the 1920s, the ACLU strategy for social change was primarily to publicize free speech concerns in cases involving the labor movement, and to get involved with publicity-generating test cases (which they expected to lose; Murphy 1972, 1979). But it was also active in interpreting cases, such as the Scopes case, which involved the legal concept of general religion, in terms of the dangers of collective conformity to individual freedom and democracy.

Another key player in cases involving religion and public life arose in this context, the American Jewish Congress (AJC), which was later dominated by Leo Pfeffer. Founded in 1918, the AJC was the first Jewish interest group to move from a strategy of "social reform," which attempted to ameliorate anti-Semitism allied with the Protestant Establishment through public education and public relations, interfaith contacts, and compromise with public authorities over what religious instruction could be aided by the state, to the "legal reform" model, in which the AJC focused on achieving church-state separation and systematically attempted to reduce institutionalized anti-Semitism through changes in law and litigation. Later joined in this legal reform effort by the American Jewish Committee and the Anti-Defamation League, the AJC sponsored test-case litigation, submitted *amicus curiae* briefs, intervened as a third party, and attempted informally to shape constitutional doctrine to remove Protestant majoritarianism (Ivers 1995).

The immediate grievance for these activists was discrimination against Jews in public life, but the means of achieving this goal was pursued through a frame of individual civil liberties. These two groups and one that emerged later, Protestants and Other Americans United for the Separation of Church and State, not only coordinated their legal actions, but also were by far the most influential interest groups on religion cases. They constituted a movement that framed test cases as matters of individual civil liberties and successfully carried them to the Supreme Court (Sorauf 1976). The fact that cases involving the free exercise of religion have been almost entirely about individual conduct, rather than the defense of religious group rights against state action (Gedicks 1989) owes much to the activists' successful promotion of the individual civil liberties frame in law (and in American culture) and to their sponsorship and framing of test cases.

The innovation of these groups was to construct civil liberties as universal and abstract rights attached to individuals. Consistent with ontological individualism, the protection of individual civil liberties was viewed as not just for the "deserving." The cultural milieu was dominated by the opposition between bureaucratic social control, symbolized by large corporations and a growing state, and the autonomous individual; civil liberties groups did not challenge this structure, but used it to frame their challenge. The decisions of Wilson and other governmental leaders during the war fostered a new structural relation: that between the growing state organization and the abstract, autonomous individual. The question, then, was, How can the individual be protected from the impositions of the growing power of state bureaucracies? Translated to cases of religion and public life, this framing of the problem motivated the ACLU and the American Jewish Congress to frame cases of religion in public life as the defense of individual freedom of expression versus the cultural hegemony of the Protestant establishment.

The hard-line stance of Wilson and the emergence of activists in the antiwar movement would eventually change the relation of religion and public life within jurisprudence. No doubt the actions of Wilson's administration and the antiwar activists had other targets, but one was clearly the connection between religion and nation that was inherent in the "general religion" of the classical style. Wilson's expansion of the state created a political and cultural backlash that swung hard to the pole of individual autonomy and freedom of expression, and this led to changes in how religion in public life was handled in law.

World War II: Constructing the Lessons for Democracy of National Socialism

If the defense of a general religion as part of a societal moral order had fallen on hard times, the reaction to Hitler and the defense of democracy against fascism created new pressures to abandon it altogether in legal decisions. Whatever National Socialism was, it was to the American legal elite the embodiment of the principle of general religion from the classical era. The legal elite interpreted general religion as similar in kind to the "organic unity," civil religion, propaganda, nationalism, and coerced uniformity of National Socialism (Auerbach 1976). Hitler's Germany—along with Soviet Communism after the war—resurrected images of an overzealous American state during World War I and the general religion principle of the classical style. This strengthened the hand of civil liberties activists who framed American democracy as the defense of individual freedoms against the pressure toward conformity from the collective moral order. Civil liberties frames gained greater currency.

With this frame in hand, legal elites not only saw democracy as standing against artificial organic unity, but also argued that trying to achieve this kind of national, religious unity leads to division and civil strife. A common religious moral order actually disrupted the social order—a view that the Supreme Court adopted for cases regarding religion in the schools.

This framing of National Socialism and its lessons for religion in a democracy was evident in Justice Jackson's decision in the 1943 case that overturned an earlier ruling allowing compulsory recitation of the Pledge of Allegiance in public schools:

> Struggles to coerce uniformity of sentiment in support of some end thought essential to their time and country have been waged by many good as well as by evil men. Nationalism is a relatively recent phenomenon but at other times and places the ends have been racial or territorial security, support of a dynasty or regime, and particular plans for saving souls. As first and moderate methods to attain unity have failed, those bent on its accomplishment must resort to an ever-increasing severity. As governmental pressure toward unity becomes greater, so strife becomes more bitter as to whose unity it shall be. Probably no deeper division of our people could proceed from any provocation than from finding it necessary to choose what doctrine and whose program public educational officials shall compel youth to unite in embracing. *Ultimate futility of such attempts to compel coherence is the lesson of every such effort from the Roman drive to stamp out Christianity as a disturber of its pagan unity, the Inquisition, as a means to religious and dynastic unity, the Siberian exiles as a means to Russian unity, down to the fast failing efforts of our present totalitarian enemies. Those who begin coercive elimination of dissent soon find themselves exterminating dissenters. Compulsory unification of opinion achieves only the unanimity of the graveyard.* (*West Virginia State Board of Education v. Barnette*, 319 U.S. 624 [1943])

This passage drew on earlier legal traditions of the divisive potential of sectarian religion but went further. The lesson of National Socialism was that the moral unity of the nation (and, by implication, the legal principle of general religion) created the social conflict it was intended to dispel. The Court was now prepared to equate Hitler's national "unity" with the attempts to enforce a general religion in the legal field.

In the pivotal Everson case of 1946, which ruled on parochial school transportation, the Court took up this same framing of religion as divisive sectarianism:

> The centuries immediately before and contemporaneous with the colonization of America had been filled with turmoil, civil strife, and persecutions, generated in large part by established sects determined to maintain their absolute political and religious supremacy. With the power of government supporting them, at various times and places, Catholics had persecuted Protestants, Protestants had persecuted Catholics, Protestant sects had persecuted other Protestant sects, Catholics of one shade of belief had persecuted Catholics of another shade of belief, and all of these had from time to time persecuted Jews. In efforts to force loyalty to whatever religious group hap-

pened to be on top and in league with the government of a particular time and place, men and women had been fined, cast in jail, cruelly tortured, and killed. (*Everson v. Board of Education*, 330 U.S. 1 [1947])

Religion no longer could provide a common moral order, but was detrimental to societal cohesion in Justice Black's view. In 1943, the lessons of National Socialism were summarized in the Court's contrast between democracy as freedom of individual expression and an artificial cultural consensus that ultimately led to social disorder. The Court argued, "To enforce those [individual free expression] rights today is not to choose weak government over strong government. It is only to adhere as a means of strength to individual freedom of mind in preference to officially disciplined uniformity for which history indicates a disappointing and disastrous end" (*West Virginia State Board of Education v. Barnette*, 319 U.S. 624 [1943]).

Through the events of World War I and National Socialism, civil liberties activist groups were increasingly successful in using their frame of individual versus community to dominate legal culture. As a result, the Court was much less likely to frame religion cases in the public schools and other public institutions as legitimate expressions of a general religion in the public square and was much more likely to frame them in terms of the defense of individual expression in the context of an oppressive collective moral order (Berman 1986). The Protestant Establishment was losing its grip on legal discourse (Handy 1991).

THE SUPREME COURT, CIVIL LIBERTIES, AND RELIGION

Bringing Society Back In

The reformers' struggle to overturn the classical style in judicial decision making did not have a widespread impact until the 1930s and 1940s. By then, Cardozo and Brandeis represented these views as justices on the Court, and the ACLU framed cases to highlight the importance of socioeconomic conditions and power relations for legal decisions. Moreover, corporate lawyers and conservative (but, ironically, activist) judges lost strength after President Franklin Roosevelt threatened to "pack" the Court if it continued to hide behind legal formalism to strike down New Deal legislation. In the context of the Great Depression, it was more difficult to argue that social and economic conditions should not be accounted for in legal decisions. As a result of academic reformers and activist organizations, Supreme Court decisions became marked with the imprint of Holmes and sociological jurisprudence. An "instrumental pragmatism" (Summers 1982), evidenced in concerns for the policy implications of Establishment religion and in the heightened concern with societal pluralism, dominated judicial decisions regarding religion in public life.

In 1943 the efforts of the reformers bore fruit in one of the key cases that would change the relationship of religion and public schools. This case reversed an earlier ruling that Jehovah's Witnesses could be required to say the Pledge of Allegiance in public schools. Rejecting the classical style, the Court held that abstract principles could not be fairly applied in changing social and economic circumstances:

> These [civil liberty] principles grew in soil which also produced a philosophy that the individual was the center of society, that his liberty was attainable through mere absence of governmental restraints, and that government should be entrusted with few controls and only the mildest supervision over men's affairs. We must *transplant these rights* to a soil in which the laissez-faire concept or principle of non-interference has withered at least as to economic affairs, and social advancements are increasingly sought through closer integration of society and through expanded and strengthened governmental controls. These *changed conditions often deprive precedents of reliability* and cast us more than we would choose upon our own judgment. But we act in these matters not by authority of our competence but by force of our commissions. We cannot, because of modest estimates of our competence in such specialties as public education, withhold the judgment that history authenticates as the function of this Court when liberty is infringed. (*West Virginia State Board of Education v. Barnette,* 319 U.S. 624 [1943])

Within the new legal discourse, judicial decisions required an analysis of the social environment, especially the impact of a dominant religious majority on individual religious freedom.

The key social change that reformers seized on was pluralism. In the early twentieth century, religious pluralism was increasing—or at least the salience of the religious pluralism increased in the legal field.[8] The reformers' push to account for pluralism is evident in the decision to protect Jehovah's Witnesses' freedom of public speech in 1947:

> The essential characteristic of these [civil] liberties is, that under their shield many types of life, character, opinion and belief can develop unmolested and unobstructed. Nowhere is this shield more necessary than in our own country for *a people composed of many races and of many creeds.* There are limits to the exercise of these liberties. The danger in these times from the coercive activities of those who in the delusion of racial or religious conceit would incite violence and breaches of the peace in order to deprive others of their equal right to the exercise of their liberties, is emphasized by events familiar to all. These and other transgressions of those limits the States appropriately may punish. (*Cantwell v. Connecticut,* 310 U.S. 296 [1940])

With sociological jurisprudence paving the way, religious freedom and religious establishment cases would now have to show how legal doctrine could be applied fairly in a context of social, cultural, and religious pluralism. In particular, the reformers required judges to account for the power of dominant religious groups over minority religious groups. In the 1943 case of religious freedom and the Pledge of Allegiance, the Court stated,

> If official power exists to coerce acceptance of any patriotic creed, what it shall contain cannot be decided by courts, but must be largely discretionary with the ordaining authority, whose power to prescribe would no doubt include power to amend. Hence validity of the asserted power to force an American citizen publicly to profess any statement of belief or to engage in any ceremony of assent to one, *presents questions of power* that must be considered independently of any idea we may have as to the utility of the ceremony in question. (*West Virginia State Board of Education v. Barnette,* 319 U.S. 624 [1943])

The reformers had succeeded in creating a legal framework in which minority religious faiths, in their expression through individual acts, took on new stature. If pluralism and power relations within the religious field must be accounted for in legal decision making, then the reformers had weakened one pillar of the schema of general religion versus sectarian religion. The potentially detrimental effect of support for general religion on a pluralistic society and culture had become a legitimate legal question.

The Demise of General Religion

The reformers went beyond throwing out the classical style by accounting for religious pluralism, and mounted a direct assault on the institutional vestiges of a general religion, or common moral order, in public life.

The Court did this largely by defending the religious expression of individuals of minority religions against any type of dominant religion in public spaces. Justice Black wrote in *Everson* that the "[First] Amendment requires the state to be a neutral in its relations with groups of religious believers and non-believers" (*Everson v. Board of Education,* 330 U.S. 1 [1947]). And in *Jones v. Opileka* the Court saw a conflict of dominant versus minority religions:

> The mind rebels at the thought that a minister of any of the old established churches could be made to pay fees to the community before entering the pulpit. These taxes on petitioners' efforts to preach the "news of the Kingdom" should be struck down because they burden petitioners' right to worship the Deity in their own fashion and to spread the gospel as they understand it. There is here no contention that their manner of worship gives rise to conduct which calls for regulation, and these ordinances are not aimed at any such practices. (*Jones v. Opileka,* 316 U.S. 584 [1942])

Completely reversing the logic of general religion, the reformers defended minority religious expression as necessary for social order. Social order in a pluralistic society, they argued, was predicated on voicing religious and other forms of diversity. In 1943, the Court argued that it was through freedom of expression that "those who follow false prophets are exposed. Repression has no place in this country. It is our proud achievement to have demonstrated that unity and strength are best accomplished, not by enforced orthodoxy of views, but by diversity of opinion through the fullest possible measure of freedom of conscience and thought" (*Martin v. Struthers*, 319 U.S. 141 [1943]). The views of Holmes, Cardozo, and Chafee were vindicated. The maintenance of societal peace depended not on consensus but on expressing differences and encouraging diversity. As the Court argued in 1943,

> Nevertheless, we apply the limitations of the Constitution with no fear that freedom to be intellectually and spiritually diverse or even contrary will disintegrate the social organization. To believe that patriotism will not flourish if patriotic ceremonies are voluntary and spontaneous instead of a compulsory routine is to make an unflattering estimate of the appeal of our institutions to free minds. We can have intellectual individualism and the rich cultural diversities that we owe to exceptional minds only at the price of occasional eccentricity and abnormal attitudes. When they are so harmless to others or to the State as those we deal with here, the price is not too great. But freedom to differ is not limited to things that do not matter much. That would be a mere shadow of freedom. The test of its substance is the right to differ as to things that touch the heart of the existing order. (*West Virginia State Board of Education v. Barnette*, 319 U.S. 624 [1943])

The reformers were skeptical of the unity of the Protestant Establishment—this order was artificial—and instead focused on the strength or seriousness of individual assent to the collective moral order. In the Pledge of Allegiance case in 1943, the Court argued,

> Any spark of love for country which may be generated in a child or his associates by forcing him to make what is to him an empty gesture and recite words wrung from him contrary to his religious beliefs is overshadowed by the desirability of preserving freedom of conscience to the full. It is in that freedom and the example of persuasion, not in force and compulsion, that the real unity of America lies. (*West Virginia State Board of Education v. Barnette*, 319 U.S. 624 [1943])

Defending the collective moral order made democracy possible in the nineteenth century; in the twentieth century, the defense of individual expression became the essence of democracy. As the Court argued in 1939,

> In every case, therefore, where legislative abridgment of the rights is asserted, the courts should be astute to examine the effect of the challenged legislation. Mere legislative preferences or beliefs respecting matters of public convenience may well support regulation directed at other personal activities, but be insufficient to justify such as diminishes *the exercise of rights so vital to the*

maintenance of democratic institutions. And so, as cases arise, the delicate and difficult task falls upon the courts to weigh the circumstances and to appraise the substantiality of the reasons advanced in support of the regulation of the free enjoyment of the rights. (*Schneider v. State,* 308 U.S. 147 [1939])

And in *Cantwell v. Connecticut* in 1940, the Court defined what they now saw as essential to democracy:

In the realm of religious faith, and in that of political belief, sharp differences arise. In both fields the tenets of one man may seem the rankest error to his neighbor. To persuade others to his own point of view, the pleader, as we know, at times, resorts to exaggeration, to vilification of men who have been, or are, prominent in church or state, and even to false statement. But the people of this nation have ordained in the light of history, that, in spite of the probability of excesses and abuses, these liberties are, in the long view, essential to enlightened opinion and right conduct on the part of the citizens of a democracy. (*Cantwell v. Connecticut,* 310 U.S. 296 [1940])

The transformation in the legal field, then, was from general religion — the supposed wellspring of civilization and social order — to a defense of pluralistic religious faith. The defense of a common moral order inspired by general religion could not be further from the Court's declaration in 1943 that "[i]f there is any fixed star in our constitutional constellation, it is that no official, high or petty, can prescribe what shall be orthodox in politics, nationalism, religion, or other matters of opinion or force citizens to confess by word or act their faith therein. If there are any circumstances which permit an exception, they do not now occur to us" (*West Virginia State Board of Education v. Barnette,* 319 U.S. 624 [1943]). The exceptions vividly occurred to the justices of the nineteenth century, but the classical style and the defense of general religion had been pushed aside in the legal field by the movement of sociological jurisprudence and legal realism.

Religion Cases Framed by Civil Liberties Doctrine

Responding to the influence of the civil liberties movement, especially the framing of cases by organizations like the ACLU, the Court swept religion cases into the civil liberties rubric. In 1942, the Supreme Court argued as follows: "Believing, as this Nation has from the first, that the freedoms of worship and expression are closely akin to the illimitable privileges of thought itself, any legislation affecting those freedoms is scrutinized to see that the interferences allowed are only those appropriate to the maintenance of a civilized society" (*Jones v. Opileka,* 316 U.S. 584 [1942]). While this passage affirmed the place of religion in the public square, it limited religion to a matter of individual free speech. By doing so, it subsumed religion within the legal concept of individual civil liberties (Boyle 1993). Similarly, in a 1940 case, Justice Stone writes as follows in his dissent:

> The guaranties of civil liberty are but guaranties of freedom of the human mind and spirit and of reasonable freedom and opportunity to express them. They presuppose the right of the individual to hold such opinions as he will and to give them reasonably free expression, and his freedom, and that of the state as well, to teach and persuade others by the communication of ideas. *The very essence of the liberty which they guaranty is the freedom of the individual from compulsion as to what he shall think and what he shall say, at least where the compulsion is to bear false witness to his religion.* Tested by this standard, I am not prepared to say that the right of this small and helpless minority, including children having a strong religious conviction, whether they understand its nature or not, to refrain from an expression obnoxious to their religion, is to be overborne by the interest of the state in maintaining discipline in the schools. (*Minersville v. Gobitis,* 310 U.S. 586 [1940])

By the 1940s, then, the civil liberties tradition shaped the form of religion that came before the Court and how it was framed in proceedings and decisions. The Court's connection of religion and civil liberties was perhaps best summed up in *Jones v. Opileka,* a case involving a tax on the distribution of Jehovah's Witnesses' literature:

> That burden should not be allowed to stand, especially if the accepted clergymen of the town can take to their pulpits and distribute their literature without the impact of taxation. Liberty of conscience is too full of meaning for the individuals in this Nation to permit taxation to prohibit or substantially impair the spread of religious ideas, even though they are controversial and run counter to the established notions of a community. If this Court is to err in evaluating claims that freedom of speech, freedom of the press, and freedom of religion have been invaded, far better that it err in being overprotective of these precious rights. (*Jones v. Opileka,* 316 U.S. 584 [1942])

In the Court's view, religion was a matter of individual expression, and, moreover, was constructed as a private, individual affair protected much as free speech, rather than as freedom of religion (Sandel 1996).

Whether or not religion was becoming a private affair for religious believers at the time, the legal understanding of religion was privatized (Myers 1991). In 1943, Justice Jackson declared that he was "unable to agree that the benefits that may accrue to society from the compulsory flag salute are sufficiently definite and tangible to justify the invasion of freedom and privacy that is entailed or to compensate for a restraint on the freedom of the individual to be vocal or silent according to his conscience or personal inclination" (*West Virginia State Board of Education v. Barnette,* 319 U.S. 624 [1943]). The schema of collective benefits versus individual free expression in this case defined religion as a matter of conscience—a personal and private affair. Similarly in *Everson* in 1947, Justice Black wrote, "But we cannot have it both ways. Religious teaching cannot be a private affair when the state seeks to impose regulations which infringe on it indirectly, and a public affair when it comes to taxing citizens of one faith to aid another, or those of no faith to aid all" (*Everson v. Board of Education,* 330 U.S. 1 [1947]). The conclusion in *Everson,* the foundation for many subsequent decisions on religion and schools (Sorauf 1976), defined religion in the legal sphere as a private affair. Justice Frankfurter in 1948 argued for strict separation of private religious faith and public institutions: "The preservation of community from divisive conflicts, of Government from irreconcilable pressures by religious groups, and of religion from censorship and coercion however subtly exercised, requires strict confinement of the State to instruction other than religious, leaving to the individual's church and home, indoctrination in the faith of his choice. . . . Separation means separation, not something less" (*McCollum v. Board of Education,* 333 U.S. 203 [1948]). Justice Frankfurter's separationist views have been influential in nearly every religion case since (Guliuzza 2000).

Within this legal context, it was not surprising that Justice Black, in one of the more celebrated and criticized lines, stated that the "First Amendment has erected a wall between church and state. That wall must be kept high and impregnable. We could not approve the slightest breach." Ironically, Justice Black was writing a decision that allowed public funding of parochial school bussing. But both his own framing of the issue and the dissenters on the bench made it very clear that religion in public life would have to be framed as an issue of private, individual religious expression. The dissenters wrote,

> That is a difference which the Constitution sets up between religion and almost every other subject matter of legislation, a difference which goes to the very root of religious freedom and which the Court is overlooking today. This freedom was first in the Bill of Rights because it was first in the forefathers' minds; it was set forth in absolute terms, and its strength is its rigidity. *It was intended not only to keep the states' hands out of religion, but to keep religion's hands off the state, and, above all, to keep bitter religious controversy out of public life by denying to every denomination any advantage from getting control of public policy or the public purse.* Those great ends I cannot but think are immeasurably compromised by today's decision. It was to create a complete and permanent separation of the spheres of religious activity and civil authority by comprehensively forbidding every form of public aid or support for religion. In proof the Amendment's wording and history unite with this Court's consistent utterances whenever attention has been fixed directly upon the question. (*Everson v. Board of Education,* 330 U.S. 1 [1947])

In the reformers' world, organized religion was divisive in the public square. General religion of the classical style had no place in the legal field. As in the classical era, however, the framework for handling religion in law did not have room to defend public action of diverse, organized religious groups (Carter 1993; Gedicks 1989).

CONCLUSION

Two social movements transformed what the legal elite considered the legitimate role that religion could play in law and in public life. The science-of-law movement led by Langdell and spread through university law schools reduced the role of religion in case decisions by replacing "judge-made law" with a formalized version of law that was beholden to emerging academic legal elites. These academic elites sought a respected position for law within the increasingly secular universities and therefore sought to marginalize the "jurisprudence of the heart," which was a primary means by which religion shaped legal decision making. The second movement, anchored by legal Progressives, attacked legal formalism and the defense of a common moral order within law, and thus further narrowed the ways in which the old Protestant Establishment could be institutionalized in public life. The Progressives were motivated in part by the remaining vestiges of religious influence in the legal theory of the formalists, who maintained the metaphysical element in law in their struggle to "discover" general principles of law within selected cases. This second movement eventually moved legal decision making toward pragmatic policy concerns, in part through an alliance with the emerging civil liberties interest groups. As the legal reformers in the academy increasingly influenced (or became) Supreme Court justices, and as civil liberties interest groups framed cases in terms of the opposition of the individual and collectivity, individual freedom of expression became the dominant frame for defining legitimate expressions of religion in public life.

Why this transformation? Activists within the legal field, using power bases in elite university law schools, attacked legal formalism and discarded the principles that the Court had defended in the classical era, including general religion. The development of a new frame for religion cases depended on events and social movements outside of the legal field. The decisions of Woodrow Wilson and the Progressives to thwart dissent during World War I energized an elite opposition with both the insurgent consciousness and structural conditions to promote a new version of civil liberties doctrine. The actions of interest groups, such as the ACLU and the AJC, redefined religion within the legal field as a matter of individual expression and ensured that the legal field would treat religion as it did other civil liberties. These groups framed cases concerning religion and public life in the legal discourse of civil liberties, especially as a conflict between social conformity and the "free" thoughts and expressions of individuals.

By the 1940s, the dominant frames in the legal field constructed religion in terms of individual freedom of expression and the divisiveness of organized religious group activities in the public square, which was considered a threat to the social order. In addition, the older frame of general religion, the defense of a common moral order as a foundation for civilization, became symbolic of exactly what legal decisions should try to avoid. These frames governed the Court decisions in the 1950s and 1960s regarding the Bible and prayer in public schools, as well as public aid to religious schools. These legal frames—whether in the nineteenth or twentieth century—did not and could not defend the involvement of religious groups in public life in a way that maintained their religious identity and particularity.

Conceptions of religion within law play an important role not only in the legal decisions that bear on the relationship of religion and public life, but also in constructing the dominant view of religion in the culture at large (Sullivan 1994). As we have seen, the classical movement placed limits on the expression of a jurisprudence of the heart, which limited the role of religious traditions within the common law. And a frame for religion as a common morality offered little room for defending the legitimate public role of Catholic religious schools (Jorgenson 1987). Nor does the dominant frame of religion as concerning individual civil liberties do justice to the reality of collective religious expressions within public life (Sandel 1996). For example, the Courts have failed to clarify support for free exercise rights of religious organizations.[9] Just as the Supreme Court has failed to provide an adequate conception of the place of political parties in representation (Ryden 1996), it has not yet developed a concept of collective religious representation within public life. In this sense, the science-of-law movement and its countermovement, which established religion as a matter of individual civil liberties, have been movements that *achieved* secularization of the public sphere.

NOTES

1. Moreover, the classical movement is both a cause and a consequence of competition between law schools for status within the legal field and vis-à-vis each other. The science-of-law movement created innovative methods for training lawyers that solidified Harvard's dominance in the legal field (Chase 1982).

2. All italics in Supreme Court quotations are mine.

3. The revivals of Charles Finney and the success of the "upstart sects" would only solidify among the legal elite the opposition between rational, general, public religion and emotional, particular, private religion.

4. Steven Smith summarizes the influence of growing secularism in the university on academic lawyers: "The intellectual climate of the time ensured that any sort of 'faith' of the kind seemingly implicit in the law could only be considered backward and disreputable, and that an enterprise built on such commitments was des-

tined to whither. . . . In particular, Holmes and his descendants could no more suppose that a respectable enterprise like law could be based on commitments of the kind that seemed evident on the face of conventional legal discourse than they could contemplate a department of astrology or witchcraft in the modern university. So they had no choice, in their new academic offices, but to set about putting law on a more respectable footing" (1999: 1097).

5. See Holmes's dissent in *Black & White Taxicab Co. v. Brown & Yellow Taxicab Co.*, 276 U.S. 518, 532–34 (1928).

6. One could argue that the contextless decision making of classical legalism was inevitably headed for contradictions, since even the most scientific, rational, and deductive framework for legal decision making would eventually founder on the near impossibility of dealing with the complexity and particularity of individual cases. But the overturning of the classical style depended on a new social construction of legal reality, which the legal elites based in law schools accomplished partly through constructing *Lochner* as a symbol of the irrelevance of the classical style.

7. The nonconformist Brahmins considered Unitarianism an avenue of respectable dissent.

8. The salience of religious difference in the legal field was increasing, partly because of social integration through expanding government, larger corporations, and consolidated schools.

9. See "Developments in the Law: Government Regulation of Religious Organizations," in the *Harvard Law Review* 100: 1016.

REFERENCES

Abbott, Andrew Delano. 1988. *The System of Professions: An Essay on the Division of Expert Labor.* Chicago: University of Chicago Press.

Alschuler, Albert W. 2000. *Law without Values: The Life, Work, and Legacy of Justice Holmes.* Chicago: University of Chicago Press.

Auerbach, Jerold S. 1976. *Unequal Justice: Lawyers and Social Change in Modern America.* New York: Oxford University Press.

Baker, Leonard. 1984. *Brandeis and Frankfurter: A Dual Biography.* New York: Harper & Row.

Baker, Liva. 1991. *The Justice from Beacon Hill: The Life and Times of Oliver Wendell Holmes.* New York: HarperCollins.

Banner, Stuart. 1998. "When Christianity Was Part of the Common Law." *Law and History Review* 27: 58–59.

Benedict, Michael. 1985. "Laissez-faire and Liberty: A Re-Evaluation of the Meaning and Origins of Laissez-faire Constitutionalism." *Law and History Review* 3, no. 2: 293–331.

Berman, Harold Joseph. 1983. *Law and Revolution: The Formation of the Western Legal Tradition.* Cambridge, MA: Harvard University Press.

———. 1986. "Religion and Law: The First Amendment in Historical Perspective." *Emory Law Journal* 35: 777–93.

Bledstein, Burton J. 1976. *The Culture of Professionalism: The Middle Class and the Development of Higher Education in America.* New York: W. W. Norton.

Boyle, Ashby. 1993. "Fear and Trembling at the Court: Dimensions of Understanding in the Supreme Court's Religion Jurisprudence." *Constitutional Law Journal* 3: 55–101.

Burton, Steven. 1991. "Law as Practical Reason." *Southern California Law Review* 62: 747.

Carter, Stephen L. 1993. *The Culture of Disbelief: How American Law and Politics Trivialize Religious Devotion.* New York: Basic Books.

Chase, William C. 1982. *The American Law School and the Rise of Administrative Government.* Madison: University of Wisconsin Press.

Farber, Daniel. 1992. "The Inevitability of Practical Reason: Statutes, Formalism, and the Rule of Law." *Vanderbilt Law Review* 45: 533.

Friedman, Lawrence Meir. 1998. *American Law: An Introduction.* New York: W. W. Norton.

Gedicks, Frederick Mark. 1989. "Toward a Constitutional Jurisprudence of Religious Group Rights." *Wisconsin Law Review* 99.

George, Robert P. 2001. "What Is Law? A Century of Arguments." *First Things* 112: 23–29.

Gilmore, Grant. 1977. *Ages of American Law.* New Haven, CT: Yale University Press.

Glendon, Mary Ann. 1994. *A Nation under Lawyers: How the Crisis in the Legal Profession Is Transforming American Society.* New York: Farrar, Straus, and Giroux.

Gordon, Robert W. 1992. *The Legacy of Oliver Wendell Holmes, Jr.* Stanford, CA: Stanford University Press.

———. 1997. "The Path of a Lawyer." *Harvard Law Review* 110: 1013.

Grossberg, Michael. 1985. *Governing the Hearth: Law and the Family in Nineteenth-Century America.* Chapel Hill: University of North Carolina Press.

Guliuzza, Frank. 2000. *Over the Wall: Protecting Religious Expression in the Public Square.* Albany: State University of New York.

Haber, Samuel. 1991. *The Quest for Authority and Honor in the American Professions, 1750–1900.* Chicago: University of Chicago Press.

Handy, Robert T. 1991. *Undermined Establishment: Church-State Relations in America, 1880–1920.* Princeton, NJ: Princeton University Press.

Himmelfarb, Gertrude. 1995. *The De-Moralization of Society: From Victorian Virtues to Modern Values.* New York: Alfred A. Knopf.

Holmes, Oliver Wendell. 1880. "Review of C. C. Langdell, *Selection of Cases on the Law of Contracts.*" *American Law Review* 14 (March): 234.

———. 1897. "The Path of Law." *Harvard Law Review* 10 (March): 457–78.

Horwitz, Morton J. 1977. *The Transformation of American Law, 1780–1860.* Cambridge, MA: Harvard University Press.

Ivers, Gregg. 1995. *To Build a Wall: American Jews and the Separation of Church and State.* Charlottesville: University Press of Virginia.

Johnson, John W. 1981. *American Legal Culture, 1908–1940.* Westport, CT: Greenwood Press.

Johnson, William R. 1978. *Schooled Lawyers: A Study in the Clash of Professional Cultures.* New York: New York University Press.

Jorgenson, Lloyd P. 1987. *The State and the Non-Public School, 1825–1925.* Columbia: University of Missouri Press.

Karsten, Peter. 1997. *Heart versus Head: The Judge-Made Law in Nineteenth-Century America.* Chapel Hill: University of North Carolina Press.

Kaufman, Andrew L. 1998. *Cardozo.* Cambridge, MA: Harvard University Press.

Kelley, Patrick. 1990. "Was Holmes a Pragmatist? Reflections on a New Twist to an Old Argument." *Southern Illinois University Law Journal* 14: 427.

Kronman, Anthony T. 1993. *The Lost Lawyer: Failing Ideals of the Legal Profession.* Cambridge, MA: Belknap Press of Harvard University Press.

Lamson, Peggy. 1976. *Roger Baldwin, Founder of the American Civil Liberties Union: A Portrait.* Boston: Houghton Mifflin.

Marsden, George M. 1994. *The Soul of the American University: From Protestant Establishment to Established Nonbelief.* New York: Oxford University Press.

Miller, Perry. 1965. *The Life of the Mind in America, from the Revolution to the Civil War.* 1st ed. New York: Harcourt, Brace & World.

Morse, John. 1896. *The Life and Letters of Oliver Wendell Holmes.* New York: Houghton Mifflin.

Murphy, Paul L. 1972. *The Meaning of Freedom of Speech.* Westport, CT: Greenwood.

———. 1979. *World War I and the Origin of Civil Liberties in the United States.* New York: W. W. Norton.

Myers, Richard. 1991. "The Supreme Court and the Privatization of Religion." *Catholic University Law Review* 41: 19.

Paul, Arnold M. 1969. *Conservative Crisis and the Rule of Law: Attitudes of Bar and Bench, 1887–1895.* New York: Harper & Row.

Paulson, Ross Evans. 1997. *Liberty, Equality, and Justice: Civil Rights, Women's Rights, and the Regulation of Business, 1865–1932.* Durham, NC: Duke University Press.

Perry, Michael J. 1988. *Morality, Politics, and Law: A Bicentennial Essay.* New York: Oxford University Press.

Posner, Richard A. 1995. *Overcoming Law.* Cambridge, MA: Harvard University Press.

Purcell, Edward A. 2000. *Brandeis and the Progressive Constitution: Erie, the Judicial Power, and the Politics of the Federal Courts in Twentieth-Century America.* New Haven, CT: Yale University Press.

Reuben, Julie A. 1996. *The Making of the Modern University: Intellectual Transformation and the Marginalization of Morality.* Chicago: University of Chicago Press.

Ryden, David K. 1996. *Representation in Crisis: The Constitution, Interest Groups, and Political Parties.* Albany: State University of New York Press.

Sandel, Michael J. 1996. *Democracy's Discontent: America in Search of a Public Philosophy.* Cambridge, MA: Belknap Press of Harvard University Press.

Schlegel, John Henry. 1995. *American Legal Realism and Empirical Social Science.* Chapel Hill: University of North Carolina Press.

Sewell, William H., Jr. 1992. "A Theory of Structure: Duality, Agency, and Transformation." *American Journal of Sociology* 98, no. 1: 1–29.

Smith, Christian. 1991. *The Emergence of Liberation Theology: Radical Religion and Social Movement Theory.* Chicago: University of Chicago Press.

Smith, Donald L. 1986. *Zechariah Chafee, Jr., Defender of Liberty and Law.* Cambridge, MA: Harvard University Press.

Smith, Stephen. 1999. "Believing Like a Lawyer." *Boston College Law Review* 40: 1041–1137.

Sorauf, Frank J. 1976. *The Wall of Separation: The Constitutional Politics of Church and State.* Princeton, NJ: Princeton University Press.

Stevens, Robert Bocking. 1983. *Law School: Legal Education in America from the 1850s to the 1980s.* Chapel Hill: University of North Carolina Press.

Sullivan, Winnifred Fallers. 1994. *Paying the Words Extra: Religious Discourse in the Supreme Court of the United States.* Cambridge, MA: Harvard University Center for the Study of World Religions.

Summers, Robert S. 1982. *Instrumentalism and American Legal Theory.* Ithaca, NY: Cornell University Press.

Sutherland, Arthur E. 1967. *The Law at Harvard: A History of Ideas and Men, 1817–1967.* Cambridge, MA: Belknap Press of Harvard University Press.

Thomas, George M. 1987. *Institutional Structure: Constituting State, Society, and the Individual.* Newbury Park, CA: Sage Publications.

———. 1989. *Revivalism and Cultural Change: Christianity, Nation Building, and the Market in the Nineteenth-Century United States.* Chicago: University of Chicago Press.

Van Zandt, David. 1991. "An Alternative Theory of Practical Reason in Judicial Decisions." *Tulane Law Review* 65: 775.

Weinberg, Julius. 1972. *Edward Alsworth Ross and the Sociology of Progressivism.* Madison: University of Wisconsin Press.

White, Morton Gabriel. 1957. *Social Thought in America: The Revolt against Formalism.* 2nd ed. Boston: Beacon Press.

Wiecek, William M. 1998. *The Lost World of Classical Legal Thought: Law and Ideology in America, 1886–1937.* New York: Oxford University Press.

8

Reforming Education, Transforming Religion, 1876–1931

George M. Thomas, Lisa R. Peck, and Channin G. De Haan

SCHOOL REFORM AND RELIGION

Current debates about the place of religion in public schools in the United States comprise the most recent in a series of episodic conflicts. Important periods include the Protestant and Enlightenment sources of mass education through the early years of the republic, the common school movement in the middle of the nineteenth century, the Progressive movements at the turn of the twentieth century, and the legal disputes and curricula reforms of the 1950s and 1960s. Each episode has a beginning, middle, and end. They are created by movements and countermovements entering into political and discursive conflict and end with some negotiated resolution. Each episode results in new understandings of the nature and interrelations of religion, mass education, and public schools. They thereby set the agenda for policy and reform and form the conditions for subsequent conflict.

In this work we study the Progressive reform period, 1876 through 1931. This is a critical period because Progressives revolutionized educational ideology and thereby framed all subsequent debate. When these movements first emerged, there was a diffuse Protestant civil religion institutionalized in the common school. Progressive intellectuals marginalized and transformed religious discourse in public education. Their influence was mediated by institutional structures and felt throughout mass education. When the episode ended, there was a secularized educational ideology and bureaucratized public school system, formally secular but with local religious practices.

We focus on the interplay between people organizing movements to reform mass education and the institutional contexts that reinforced or attenuated their influence. Outcomes are historically contingent and thus cannot be reduced to presumed interests of the actors or to presumed, objective, functional needs of the system. Interests and needs themselves are constructed within institutional contexts and movement dynamics. Our approach is in contrast to many sociological explanations and working assumptions of historians, which tend to reduce the declining fortunes of religion to inevitable large-scale processes such as differentiation, to objective functional adaptations, or to powerful economic interests.

Throughout the nineteenth century, education was a national project of producing the participatory citizen. By 1876, educators, politicians, and the general public were calling for the modernization of education as the key institution for creating or constituting modern individuals and allocating them to functional positions, thereby solving the social problems of industrial society. In this context, Progressive movements revolutionized educational ideology at the national level and helped build bureaucratic school systems. They rationalized educational theory, administration, and pedagogy by couching them in abstract scientific knowledge (especially psychology) and pragmatic principles (especially business administration), and by professionalizing educators. They based educational reform in scientific, natural processes and thereby thoroughly secularized national educational ideology, marginalizing historic, "supernatural," religious discourse among elite educators.

The national Progressive educators pressed for change by applying nationally articulated models to local contexts, and they were associated with incorporating the local into national, rationalistic institutions. There was no central state or church that controlled education, so no palace coup could by fiat change local practices. There were, however, general legal mandates for modernizing mass education according to cultural imperatives and popular demands for efficiency. The mutually supporting legal and cultural imperatives devolved onto the superintendency, at the interface of the national and local. The superintendent had to contend with these forces in the context of local pressures and politics. The particular, historically contingent outcomes thus are not easily understood as objective functional adaptations to industrial society or as manipulations by economic elites.

In pressing their reform through these institutional arrangements, Progressives were supported by the cultural premium placed on modernization, efficiency, and science. The progressives gained powerful advantage by articulating with two other revolutionary movements: the creation of psychology and the research university. Psychology provided an independent, scientific legitimation of the Progressive agenda and a set of categories and measurements for efficiently ordering children and assessing school systems. The research university provided a place for the construction of abstract knowledge and the professionalization of educators. There was an

overlap among intellectuals: these educational elites held university positions, and many helped shape the new psychology. Moreover, while the
sources of reform were far removed from the local, both geographically and
in terms of abstract intellectual knowledge, this scientific knowledge and
authority "from a distance" made the reforms seem all the more natural and
authoritative.

The superintendency, at the interface of the national and local, was pivotal in the local diffusion of national movement influence. We can summarize these multiple forces *from the point of view of the superintendency.* (1) Superintendents attempted to conform to broad, legal-cultural and popular
demands for efficient mass education, and (2) they reacted to specific pressures and innovations brought to bear by Progressive reformers who drew
legitimacy and support from (a) the legal-cultural context and (b) revolutionary changes in psychology and higher education. Moreover, (3) they
acted in the context of local school boards, principals, teachers, and parents
who, while also demanding efficiency, generally insisted on preserving local
autonomy and practices, including religion.

During this period, national religious intellectuals and leaders attempted
to demonstrate consistency between new scientific knowledge and religion.
By early in the century, however, national educators had effectively excluded
religious articulations from their discourse. Religious groups responded to
national incorporation and Progressive reform by trying to keep particular
symbolic practices in the schools, notably Bible reading and prayer, or by
trying to legalize public monies for sectarian schools; these were Protestant
and Roman Catholic strategies, respectively. These issues were hotly contested in a three-way conflict among secular educators, Protestants, and
Catholics.

National political parties cast alternative policies as mutually exclusive.
At the local level, religious groups ended up dealing with superintendents
who were often in the position of mediating such conflicts. The overriding
concern of the superintendency was to maintain an orderly, efficient school
and to conform to Progressive, legal, and popular demands. They tended to
view religious conflict as archaic but were pragmatically open to compromise. The result was a pattern of formal adoption of Progressive elements,
but actual local practices often did not conform to—were decoupled
from—the formal structures. This explains the peculiar outcome of this
period: Nationally, educational ideology was thoroughly secularized, and
political conflict was polarized; locally, however, schools and conflicting religious groups negotiated compromises that often allowed practices reflecting a diffuse civil religion.

In the following sections, we describe the institutional context of education through 1875 and present an overview of educational reform during
the period 1876–1931, discussing theoretical approaches to secularization.

We then describe the national Progressive movements pressing for education reform, their goals, and how they influenced mass education. In the final section we draw out how these processes resulted in increased secularization.

INSTITUTIONAL DYNAMICS THROUGH 1875

Enlightenment-Protestant Culture:
The Most Religious and Most Secular Nation

The American people, according to their cultural narrative, were chosen to be special in history. They had freed themselves from corrupt, old-world institutions. Now, each individual citizen was authorized and obligated to associate to build new democratic institutions and thereby create progress and civilization. This narrative was an optimistic, post-millennialism that synthesized Enlightenment and Protestant traditions. In Protestant terms, the people were chosen by God to build the Kingdom of God—a thousand-year reign after which Christ would return (thus the label post-millennial). In Enlightenment terms, the people would use new scientific knowledge to take control of their own society and destiny, to create the new order of the ages.

To ensure progress, the individual citizen had to be constituted internally as rational and moral. Virtue, no longer assumed to be the result of conforming to traditional institutions, had to be instilled in autonomous individuals, who carried it into marketplace and public square. It was up to newly created democratic institutions to nurture the new citizen. The creation of the modern interior self went hand-in-hand with institution building; the techniques of self-creation were manifested in techniques of organization and mobilization. Institution building took the form of social control, but the more general process was that of discipline—of both self and other (Howe 1991).

The general consensus was that personal religion helped form morality. Evangelical ministers and churches after the Second Great Awakening were especially powerful in working on the individual self and directing collective action. The Enlightenment tradition held that reason compelled the enlightened individual to be virtuous in heartfelt appreciation of the Supreme Being. At the same time both traditions had an unquestioned faith in disestablishment: Religion breeds civilization only if it is of the heart and not imposed by state or church. In short, there was a strong belief both in disestablishment and in a natural integration of religion (Protestantism) and nation (Bellah 1975; Handy 1984).

Education was the primary institution through which reason and morality were to be instilled in the modern individual. Early in the nineteenth century diverse schools were established and run by private associations, Protestant denominations, and the Catholic Church. Education thus was in the hands of parents, a myriad of different schools, and enterprising "school keepers." After the second quarter of the century, social reform movements in different states attempted to build a common school system. Americans did not trust a central bureaucratic state or old-world church to control education. The common school movement, however, argued with evangelical fervor that education could no longer be left up to the whims of the family or to the special interests of religions. Whereas other schools represented the interests of their organizers, the common school, the impassioned leaders argued, embodied the interest of the whole community. In David Tyack's (1974) now classic phrase, they proclaimed it the "one best system." At the end of this episode of collective action, the public school emerged as the institution in which every child was to learn knowledge and "self-restraint through a common moral code" (McClellan 1999: 23).

Schools and the Religion Problem

Evangelical Protestant groups in general saw the common school as a major institution in building the new society (Meyer et al. 1979), but they had concerns. The common school shifted the institutional authority of the minister and church to the educator and school. Many thus were concerned about what religious content would be included. Out of the common school episode, four imperatives, almost ritual formulas, were negotiated for the one best system: (1) it is explicitly nonsectarian, (2) it encourages common religion, (3) it includes Bible reading "without commentary," and (4) no public money is to go to alternative sectarian schools.

The common school was to be nonsectarian by not teaching denominational doctrine. Religious groups, according to the long-standing view, are inherently in conflict, and this conflict must be excluded from political life (including schools), or it will fracture the nation. This view was reflected in a popular suspicion of doctrine and denominations (Tocqueville 1945; Lipset 1963). The principle of nonsectarian schools was further complicated by its coupling with the second principle: The public school would have a common religion representing the intrinsically religious nature of American identity. The common, or civil, religion (Bellah 1975; Bellah and Hammond 1980) was built by the strategy of excluding denominational doctrine but including what was asserted to be a common religious piety (Michaelson 1970). Religious revivalists supported this common religion because they were pressing for something similar in religion itself: Protestantism's core heartfelt piety (Thomas 1989).

There were many manifestations of the common religious piety or civil religion in the common schools (Marsden 1990): Judeo-Christian morality,

Biblical stories and themes, prayer, and histories claiming the superiority of Protestant civilization. Reading the Bible, though, was probably the most important practice, those in the Enlightenment tradition agreeing that it was the source of practical religion and morality. To make sure that its reading was nonsectarian, it had to be read "without commentary." The assumptions behind this imperative were that any interpretation would reflect sectarian opinion and that each individual hearer is able to interpret the Bible.

Much controversy arose over what was asserted to be common religion. Several Protestant groups discredited it as generic, liberal religion. The Catholic Church shared this concern and had others as well. The Church argued that the common school was in practice Protestant. Texts, for example, celebrated Protestant civilization, often by being explicitly anti-Catholic. Reading the Bible without commentary, moreover, was Protestant in a double sense. First, schools used the King James Bible, which was the received translation among Protestants but not Catholics. Second, the idea that lay individuals could interpret the Bible was a quintessential Protestant view. Many Protestants, including Henry Ward Beecher in 1869, suggested that for the sake of pluralism, Protestants should withdraw Bible reading from public schools because it obviously was not common (Michaelson 1970: 116). Nevertheless, "[b]y 1870 Protestants generally had arrived at the conclusion that the public school system was best for America, that sectarianism—as they understood it—had no place in that system, but that religion—'nonsectarian,' 'common' religion—was essential to the school. As the primary *modus operandi* of this nonsectarianism the Bible became a crucial rallying point for Protestants" (118).

The last pillar of the common school relationship to religion is that no public money should be given to religious schools. Early in the nineteenth century there were cases of public money going to religious schools for the poor. It seemed reasonable within conceptions of religious liberty to dispense money fairly to all viable school systems.[1] The emerging common school ideology, though, argued that support for alternative religious schools would mean that the public school was not in fact common, that there was no underlying religious, moral aspect of American identity that could be instilled in the child, and that religious factions would fight over public money. The unwavering faith in the religious nature of American character thus became embodied in the nonsectarian common school.

Controversy continued over this point as well. Several Protestant groups and the Catholic Church continued to press for financial support for their schools. The Catholic Church starkly argued that a common school either favors one religion over another, the current practice favoring Protestantism, or it is secular and thus anti-religious, which it would be if stripped of its Protestantism.[2] The Church's official national position was uncompromising: public money for its schools.

The common school episode, in summary, ended in a negotiated relationship between religion and public schools captured by the four directives. The public school was to be nonsectarian, which came to mean nondoctrinal, and there would be no state monies for religious schools. The public school was, however, to instill in the child a common religion, symbolized by Bible reading without commentary. Almost more important, the style of resolving religious conflict was set: Controversies over religion in the schools would be resolved at least in national discourse by "dropping any discussion of the particular and the distinctive" (Fraser 1999: 57).

The ending of this episode set the agenda for continued controversies, which, at the national level, came to focus on Bible reading and financial support for sectarian schools. While some Protestant groups dissented, these issues tended to divide along Catholic and Protestant lines. Nationally, Catholics clearly lost on Bible reading and the prohibition of public money for their schools. In the face of this, at the First Plenary Council of Baltimore in 1852, the Church encouraged Catholics to support Catholic schools. By the Second Plenary Council of Baltimore in 1866, it called for bishops to direct that schools be established in association with each church. Locally, there was room for compromise, but the national lines were drawn.

PROGRESSIVE EDUCATION REFORM AND PROFESSIONALIZATION

Education and Rationalistic Culture

The people embraced mass schooling well before bureaucratization and Progressive reform. In the North and West in 1880, the average state primary school enrollment as a proportion of school-age children was .75, reaching a rate of .84 by 1930. Individual-level data reveal that the national enrollment rates were even higher. Enrollments in rural areas were nearly the same as and possibly higher than those in urban ones. The southern states showed substantially lower rates: .45 until the 1910s (Meyer et al. 1979; NCES 1999). Secondary education during this period grew substantially. Secondary enrollments comprised only about 1 percent of all public school enrollments in 1880, reaching 17 percent by 1930. The number of children enrolled in high school in 1890 was .04 of the population aged 14–17. This proportion increased substantially in the 1910s reaching .51 by 1930. The number graduating from high school as a percentage of seventeen-year olds was 2.5 in 1880 and 6.4 by the turn of the century. Subsequent growth resulted in a percentage of 29 in 1930 (NCES 1999).

The growth of participation in the South and in secondary education thus was part of the bureaucratization and reform of an already established mass education. At the beginning of the Progressive episode, education and schools were viewed as paramount for creating the rational, moral citizen. Consider just two early examples from the *Journal of Education:* "The first and last aim of the American common school is to make American citizens of sufficient intelligence to apprehend, and sufficient moral stamina to perform the great duties of our common American public life" (1876: 4, no. 10: 110); and "The prime objective of State education is preparation for citizenship" (1881: 14, no 8: 137).

Progressive movements called for new scientific knowledge to reform the ideology, organization, and practice of education. Current theory and practices, according to Progressive reformers, were rural and traditional, having grown out of haphazard custom and nonscientific (i.e., religious) sources of knowledge. They were ineffective in coping with rapidly changing industrial society, inevitably leading to crisis. Progressives were confident that they could use science to discover the kind of individual needed for the new industrial democracy, and then apply to schools scientifically proven tools for creating that individual. Professionals must scientifically organize and administer schools and use psychological knowledge of the child to run classrooms. Only then could problems associated with industry, cities, and immigration be solved and a new society built. "Society would control its own evolution through schooling; professional management would replace politics, science would replace religion and custom as sources of authority; and experts would adapt education to the transformed conditions of modern corporate life" (Tyack and Hansot 1982: 107; see also Callahan 1962; Cremin 1962).

Progressive educational reform thus articulated thoroughly with the cultural models and imperatives of the day (Hays 1957). This was the era of corporate capitalism and increased involvement in industrial competition with Europe. Methods and principles of big business and industry, especially centralized bureaucratic administration and standardization, gained great trust for attaining coordination, progress, and efficiency in society. This period also witnessed astonishing innovations in the natural sciences, impressive claims by the new human sciences, and the ever-successful complex of science and industry. International scientific networks and the rise of the research university marked a new scientific infrastructure. It is difficult to overstate the degree to which science attained a general cultural authority.

A clear common culture prevailed that can be viewed as a rugged postmillennialism or, in Weber's terminology, practical or functional rationality. The source of knowledge was science, and it was proven in the rational administrative principles of big business (Wiebe 1962). Arguably, the post-millennial project at its most practical level consisted of the cult of efficiency and science (Callahan 1962).

The public, political parties, and government officials drew heavily on these rationalistic cultural models, especially as they theorized and grappled with problems of the cities, labor, and immigrants, all in the context of their place in the international system. Mass education, as ever, was the crux. Federal and state bodies increasingly set legal mandates that schools meet the needs of an industrial nation competing in the world economy and interstate system. By 1885 all states had a state superintendent and legislated teacher certification requirements, 71 percent had county superintendents, and 68 percent had state boards of education (Tyack, James, and Benavot 1987).

Rationalization/Differentiation, Social Movements, and Religion

Secularization is the process of differentiating historic religious organization and authority from public institutions and relegating them to private life. The historical model for this was laicization within Christendom. The fact that this was a period of differentiation thus would suggest a natural explanation for secularization. Theories of differentiation, however, have been overly abstract and deterministic (Martin 1978; Alexander and Colomy 1990; Lechner 1991; Smith, chap. 1 in this volume). As societies evolve, it is argued, the complexity of organization and coordination needs to increase, resulting in specialization and differentiation. In this view, religion naturally and inevitably gives place to science and technical rationality.

Social histories are replete with assumptions that Progressive reform was the functional adaptation to an increasingly complex industrial society. Many historians attempt to be more concrete, but they do so often by reducing changes such as secularization to the interests of particular groups. One prevailing argument, for example, is that industrial capitalism simultaneously weakened the Protestant elite and demanded social control over labor and new immigrants. Protestant elites forged a compromise with secular Progressives that decreased religion's presence in public schools but kept general values and morals as social control mechanisms (e.g., Apple 1979; Katz 1973; McClellan and Reese 1988). These historians accurately point to the ideological uses of culture and curriculum but reduce them to those uses and ultimately to objective actor interests and functional adaptations.

For these theories to work, differentiation must actually create greater coordination, efficiency, and control. Evidence, however, is to the contrary (e.g., Meyer and Scott 1983; Scott 1992). Specialization and standardized procedures are characteristics of formal organization, but actual practice is often kept separate from formal structures—everyday activity is "decoupled" from formal organization. Educational reformers, for example, long have noted the difficulty of affecting the classroom (Cuban 1993). The adoption of such reforms thus cannot be explained in terms of effects such as coordination and control.

The adoption of rationalistic reforms reflects cultural models of the efficient organization. Organizations adapt to their cultural environment: As cultural models come to emphasize rationalistic organizational forms, organizations adopt these forms even while decoupling their practices (Meyer and Rowan 1977). Professionalization, the creation of a bounded specialization of abstract knowledge and practice, thrives in a cultural context of rationalism (Abbot 1988). Thus, to explain differentiation, we must look to cultural models of organization: Differentiation is not an objective functional response to new needs but a principle of cultural rationalism.

Conceptualizing common cultural elements across modern differentiated society runs counter to common social science views, in which only small-scale traditional societies are integrated by overarching culture. This is a key assumption in the argument that religion inevitably loses force as an overarching "sacred canopy" (Bellah 1964; Berger 1969). Historic religions might be privatized but, we argue, not because of a lack of overarching culture. Rationalistic culture, itself functioning as a kind of naturalistic religion, displaces historic religions as the overarching canopy.[3]

The differentiation of knowledge and authority such that no single organization manages all of the others takes place in a cross-cutting culture marked by rationalistic principles, models, and styles. Differentiated institutions are rarely completely compartmentalized from each other (Douglas 1973). Modern organizations share formal elements of rationality because they imitate each other, professionals share common orientations, and states mandate accepted models of efficiency (Meyer and Rowan 1977; DiMaggio and Powell 1983; Abbott 1988). There is a routinized pattern in which some institutions are sources of knowledge and authority for others.

In fact, far from abstract knowledge of one institutional sphere being irrelevant to another, it can, by its very separateness, take on greater moral force. We refer to this as "distant knowledge," by which we mean locally applied knowledge the source of which is some authority external to the local situation. Such knowledge is reified in the sense that it is perceived and used as simply given, as factual, even though, or because, local actors lack access to any critical analysis of its genesis. Local resistance to "outsiders" is in part a response to the power of distant authority. Distant knowledge is a powerful weapon for those who are attempting to reform an institution because, as they pursue interests in conflict with those of other local actors, they are able to use distant knowledge that is taken to be beyond question.

Collective action is the mechanism by which rationalistic elements are elaborated and diffuse across organizational fields. Much of this process is routine; for example, factions in education use recent findings in developmental psychology, which they have learned from professional networks, to reform the curriculum. The process of creating new institutions as sources of authority takes the form of mobilizing social movements. In the Progressive episode, for example, the Progressives established psychology as the source of knowledge and authority for education. National intellectuals play an especially important role in elaborating rationalistic culture and stipulating the necessity of its application (Eisenstadt 1980). Strategic groups use intellectual models to push diverse interests and establish an institutional agenda (Colomy 1990).

These movements set into motion factions resisting such claims. The influence of the overarching rationalistic culture gives great advantage to reformers, but it by no means determines the outcomes, which are historically contingent on institutional arrangements and power relations. The Progressive reformers of public schools came into conflict with religious groups and with established educational groups. An inherent tension exists between rationalistic culture and religious "super-empirical" authority. One way historic religions and practical rationality can coexist is when they are said to have two different purposes and methods: Science pursues knowledge about how the material world works; religion reveals knowledge about personal meanings and ethics. This is an epistemological dualism in which someone such as an educator is oriented to two different accounts or discourses of action. The rationalistic set of accounts demands greater efficiency and scientific knowledge. The other is religious, locating the larger meaning of what the educator is doing as part of his or her calling to build a better society.

This tension becomes explicit when there is resistance. As Progressive movements rationalized the school system, they transformed religion and privatized historic religious accounts. Where historic religious discourse held sway, or when people mobilized to retain a historic religious presence, Progressive reformers took on more explicit anti-religious claims.

Progressive reformers also generated conflict because they claimed the power within their field to have their agendas established. This conflict within the field is highlighted by professionalization. An integral aspect of practical rationalism is the creation of expert authorities that have a monopoly over functionally specified practices and the abstract knowledge associated with them. Equally important is the process by which individuals are trained, certified, and allocated with sufficient resources to positions of expert authority. Professionalization movements call for the creation of relatively autonomous, bounded, rational actors with monopolistic control over professional practice and abstract knowledge (Abbott 1988). A group's claim to exclusive control over knowledge and practice exists within a field or system of professions and thus creates competition and conflict with other groups. Moreover, within a profession specialists engage in ongoing competition over subareas of knowledge and practice.

Progressive movements indeed focused on professionalizing educators, setting into motion complex patterns of conflict among teachers, principals, school boards, and superintendents. The process was driven by competition and by the models of medicine and law during this period (Bledstein 1976; Wiebe 1967).[4]

National Incorporation and the Superintendency

A major cleavage in education throughout the Progressive episode was between the national and local. The national intellectual movements actively pressed rationalistic ideology and administrative and pedagogical/curriculum reform downward into local areas. They made their influence felt throughout the educational field, in which different positions were competing for professional autonomy and control. State boards expanded their jurisdictions and bureaucracies, and town and city reforms resulted in centralization. Practice, nevertheless, remained in the hands of teachers, principals, superintendents, and local school boards. Any process that incorporated the local into the national provided further impetus for the application of Progressive reforms. National and local forces met and overlapped in the superintendency, which juggled and indeed was a product of these forces (Tyack 1988). In general, the superintendency gained autonomy and control by claiming an expertise embedded in the Progressive system and by demanding professionalization of the field.[5] It was the channel for national incorporation of the local and also the point at which the local decoupled from rationalistic pressures.

In the next sections, we first describe the national intellectual movement and its content, which shifted the source of authority from religion to science and professional experts. We then trace the movement's influence on the superintendency, making special note of its reliance on two other secularizing institutions: psychology and the university. Next we show how this episode ended with religion's marginalization and transformation.

In order to move below the national intellectual level toward the midlevel of the superintendency, we studied education journals of the period. We systematically sampled one, the weekly *Journal of Education* (*JE*). The *JE* reflected national ideology and agendas but also was geared to regional and local use; it included writings of well-known intellectual figures as well as items from lesser-known educators throughout the country.[6]

NATIONAL MOVEMENTS AND THEIR IMPACT

The National Progressive Intellectual Movements

The Progressive episode has three discernible subperiods. From 1876 through roughly the 1890s, diverse movements elaborated Progressive themes and built networks and infrastructures. While there are issues of definition (Buenker, Burnham, and Crunden 1977), these movements are identifiable by their imperative that institutions be based on scientific knowledge in order to solve social problems and build a new society. From the turn of the century to the end of World War I, Progressivism congealed into a coherent set of movements codified in scientific discourse and established in national associations, universities, and political parties. The new leaders of these movements criticized the "old guard" for not being truly Progressive. World War I marked the transition to the heyday of Progressivism. Progressives implemented programs, sharpened techniques in practice, manned the expanding educational bureaucracies, established professional associations, and elaborated more radical theories.[7]

The national educational movement built in the early period and consolidated in the second was referred to at the time as the educational trust.[8] It was a relatively small, elite group of educators largely with academic positions—a monopoly, as the term *trust* was meant to indicate. We focus on two of the most influential movements, the administrative and pedagogical/curriculum reformers. The former, referred to as "administrative Progressives" (Tyack 1974), emphasized scientific administration and business-proven principles. The latter elaborated scientific knowledge through psychology to design "child-centered" curricula and pedagogy.

The members of the educational trust knew that they were creating a movement. They exhibited all of the characteristics of a small, intensely networked generation of intellectuals that revolutionizes a field, as described by Randall Collins (1998) in his study of philosophies. They formed relationships in graduate schools, especially at places like Teachers College, and after taking academic positions they expanded their networks. They had frequent face-to-face interaction at national meetings, listened to each other give formal presentations, and talked informally in hotel lobbies and over dinners. They were intellectual entrepreneurs (Eisenstadt 1980), generating great energy and enterprise. They organized conferences, helped their students to obtain key jobs, actively appealed to foundations for research support, carried out surveys for school districts, and wrote prodigiously, from policy reports to textbooks. All of this brought individual success and wealth as they built an educational infrastructure. Tyack (1974: 128) summarizes by saying that the administrative Progressives "(1) were a movement with identifiable actors and coalitions; (2) had a common ideology and platform; and (3) gained substantive power over urban education."

Education Progressives had small-town, pietistic upbringings and thus shared Protestant American values (Tyack 1974; Tyack and Hansot 1982; Crunden 1982). They typically gravitated to liberal versions of Protestantism or claimed to be nonsectarian. Few publicly identified themselves as atheists, yet many openly rejected "supernatural" Christianity. Tyack and Hansot's description of Ellwood P. Cubberley is instructive. They use him to illustrate the administrative Progressives' implicit Protestant values, but they do not do justice to the differences between holding Protestant values (cultural Protestantism) and practicing the Protestant religion. "While he, like many others, turned away from the doctrinal content of Protestantism (diluted as it had become in the later nineteenth century) and rarely used explicitly religious language, the implicit values he took for granted as the basis of individual character and social morality were largely those he learned in his childhood and youth in pietist small-town America" (Tyack and Hansot 1982: 115).

The administrative professionals had been viewed as value-neutral, simply pushing efficient organization, and it is important to see that their agenda implicitly carried values informed by Protestantism (Apple 1979). It is, however, equally important that they had "turned away from the doctrinal content" of even the liberal (diluted) versions.[9] Consistent with their own biographies, the members of the educational trust viewed orthodox religion as a past, traditional source of knowledge. They viewed historic Christianity embodied in churches, doctrines, and creeds as part of the moral web of community and family in small-town, rural America. With the rise of industrial society, that small-town reality simply disappeared. In his brief *Changing Conceptions of Education* (1909), Ellwood Cubberley spent the first half describing "changes in the nature of our life," which concisely told the story of the passing of traditional small-town, rural America in the face of modern industrial society. The simplicity of the storytelling and the easy association of church religion with a bygone age make an eloquent example of this view.[10]

Progressives presented a veneer of harmony between nonsectarian religion and science. Epistemological dualism—espoused by liberal Protestants, social gospelers, and secularists—laid over privatization maintained the irrelevance of religion while assuring those for whom it was important that religion was nevertheless still valued.[11] This epistemological dualism would not have been sufficient if schools had to be wrested from church control, but it seemed effective in assuaging potentially offended, diffuse religious sensibilities. Moreover, it resonated with the particularly American style of religion, which had little tolerance for religious doctrines.

Other versions were more vitriolic. Many depicted historic, "supernatural" religion as superstition that had to be replaced by science as a source of knowledge.[12] Increasingly, the scientific ground was mapped by psychology and the social sciences. University-housed social scientists claiming to replace religion understandably could be more explicitly anti-religious (see Smith, chap. 2 in this volume).

Progressives saw "true" religion as the spiritual values intrinsic in human development. Progressives of all religious stripes, whether sincerely or disingenuously, used religious imagery to describe the higher nature of their careers and the professions they were building: Education was a religious calling to dispense the saving grace of knowledge, and the missionaries were teachers, trained and sent out by the schools of education.

The Movement's Influence through Institutional Arrangements: The Superintendency

The Progressives profoundly influenced public school ideology, organization, and policies. Because of the decentralized nature of education and the national-local cleavage, their influence was mediated through institutional arrangements, especially the superintendency. Superintendents, because of their social characteristics and training, and because of professional competition, were especially open to the Progressive agenda. Moreover, the Progressives' use of psychology and the university increased their influence.

Early in the period, superintendents were generally men who had held positions as teachers and principals, many moving back and forth between educator and pastor or businessman as they worked their way up. Increasingly, they pursued advanced training along the way to compete with those fresh out of education schools and graduate programs. By 1929 "more progressive boards of education will not 'look at' candidates" for superintendent without an M.A. degree, claimed *School Executive Magazine* (1929: 49, no. 3: 117). Surveys suggested that by 1923, 35 percent of superintendents had post-baccalaureate degrees and 60 percent did by 1933 (Tyack 1988: 187).

During this period and as late as the 1930s, superintendents, like the educational trust, for the most part grew up in pietistic Protestant families (Tyack 1988). Newlon (1934) reported a current survey of 850 superintendents nationwide. Over 90 percent reported that their fathers were in some way affiliated with a church, and only 12 percent said they were raised Roman Catholic. The same percentage reported that they were currently active members of a Protestant church, but, Newlon noted, "these churches are somewhat more liberal in their outlook than were those of their childhood" (129–30). Thus, superintendents seem to have remained somewhat more religious than the intellectual core of the trust but decidedly within a liberal Protestantism. Thus, by cultural background and professionalization, superintendents shared the liberal and cultural Protestant sensibilities about religion and epistemological dualism.

Progressive educators had direct effects on the superintendency because of their teaching positions in the universities. They obtained jobs for their students through an amazingly effective "old boy" network. There were several centers: Teachers College, Harvard, the University of Chicago, and Stanford (Clifford 1986). The networks were built around "barons" such as George Strayer at Teachers College, who at one point had former students in sixteen of eighteen superintendent positions that existed in the largest cities (Tyack and Hansot 1982: 135; Newlon 1930). Cubberley at Stanford placed students throughout California's administrative system. Other regional centers such as Ohio State University exhibited a similar pattern; for example, an alumnus from Teachers College had his own network and influence throughout Ohio.

All superintendents, even those not directly trained by the intellectual elite, were open to the Progressivist value placed on standardization, bureaucratization, and scientific efficiency. They were pursuing careers that depended on the institutionalization of these principles. The courses they picked up on their climb to the superintendency were by 1900 steeped in the science of administration, business principles, and psychology. Moreover, they faced demands from state legislatures and the public to run efficient schools. From the point of view of their everyday goal of maintaining order and meeting pressures to modernize, superintendents found it advantageous to adopt goals of professionalization and Progressive reform.

Superintendents also fueled the escalation of expert knowledge as they dealt with local tensions among school boards and teachers. Local school boards hired superintendents and, through the turn of the century, made minor budgetary decisions. Progressives pushed to professionalize the superintendency in large part to make it autonomous from the school board's micro-managing. Another Progressive goal was to reform the school board itself by basing membership on merit. Reformers saw the school board as the epitome of the local and stigmatized it as traditional, amateurish, and graft-ridden.[13] Professional knowledge was the key to elevating the superintendency's prestige, autonomy, and control. An article on improving rural schools, for example, argued that a superintendent must be someone "who by study is thoroughly versed in the science and art of pedagogy, the principles and methods of teaching, the philosophy of child-training, and the educational value of school subjects, in order that he may formulate a rational course of study for schools, and direct and systematize the work. . . . This is all professional, is an art, and needs preparation for as much as teaching" (*JE* 1896: 44, no. 10: 172).

While local superintendents often taught, they could control the practice of teaching only indirectly by setting policy and guidelines for principals. Progressives pressed for the professionalization of both superintendents and teachers, but unequally. The professional status of superintendents was elevated above that of teachers. The supervisor of schools from Boston, in a talk at the Maine superintendents meeting, stated that

> the nature and duties of the school superintendent . . . [are] . . . even higher than that of teaching. . . . Every impulse, every direction of the superintendent, not only shows itself in the work of the individual child as distinctly as the teacher's but showing itself through the work of a number of teachers, works into the lives not only of one child, but of a hundred children. (*JE* 1896: 44, no. 11: 198)

Superintendents in turn pressed the Progressive agenda for more teacher training, certification, and standards to professionalize them as practitioners. Teachers did not need to know the details of the science of education, only how to use practical applications. "Respect for the science of education and loyalty to the masters are desirable elements in every teacher" (*JE* 1891: 34, no. 9: 152). Thus, (female) teacher status was institutionalized as subordinate to that of other (male) education professionals (Herbst 1989; Warren 1989). This result is consistent with Abbott's (1988) description of how practitioners who administer treatment have lower professional status than those controlling abstract knowledge and diagnosis. The superintendent has the expertise to diagnose school problems and to prescribe science-based curriculum and pedagogy.[14]

Superintendents in towns and rural counties looked to the prestigious urban systems for administrative models. By formally adopting urban models often described as success stories by education journals, superintendents could demonstrate that they were meeting state and public mandates. At the same time, these models, couched in scientific discourse and proven in urban centers, gave the reformer great leverage over local resistance.

The administrative Progressives achieved direct local contact by using survey research to evaluate school systems. These studies proliferated rapidly in the second decade of the century and measured all aspects of schools, from administration to curriculum and pedagogy. The research organization brought together university researchers, national foundations and associations, and the school district, forging an infrastructure that oriented local educators to national standards and ideology. By claiming to measure success and efficiency objectively, survey researchers shaped the very definitions of successful education (Callahan 1962; Kliebard 1999; Tyack and Hansot 1982). Administrative Progressives used surveys to document problems and then prescribe the remedy of one or another program based on scientific and business principles. Local resistance arose often, at least initially, with complaints of outsiders taking over discourse and decision making. What is clear is that all players involved in education decision making after World War I learned to use the survey and its discourse.

The national intellectual movement and Progressive superintendents associated themselves and their reforms with two revolutionary developments: the formation of psychology and the research university. Educational intellectuals helped build a naturalistic psychology and held an advantage by virtue of their university positions. Psychology and the university helped Progressive educators shift the source of knowledge and authority from religious, local, and lay sources to experts in naturalistic, "distant knowledge."

Child-Centered Models and Psychology: Sources of Authority and Expertise

Progressive educators used child-centeredness and psychology to shift sources of authority from God and the super-empirical to nature, and from religion to science. They espoused themes of child-study and a science of child nature early and increasingly formalized them within psychology. Superintendents, moreover, used child-centeredness and psychology to establish their professional authority and to legitimate school reform. These changes were fueled by the relatively contradictory Progressive goals of adapting schools to individual needs while simultaneously constituting children to fit into an ordered society.

Child-Centeredness

Child-centeredness broadly refers to basing education on "child nature" and focusing on the child's interests, needs, and abilities (Cuban 1993). In the Enlightenment tradition illustrated by Rousseau's *Emile*, Progressives saw human nature as essentially good or neutral, rejecting the view of original sin. The child, in this view, develops naturally through reason and experience. Child-centeredness thus locates the source of authority in the self and human nature, rather than in God and the supernatural. Because human nature is good and because the child is innately programmed to develop naturally, education must nurture the intrinsic development and expression of child nature rather than break it or submit it to authority. "This conception lies at the basis of modern primary education. *The nature of the child:* here is the master-key to the whole mystery of education" (*JE* 1881: 14, no. 9: 153).

Progressives throughout the period, and especially after the turn of the century, used child-centeredness to critique current school practices.[15] They argued that traditional "school keeping" lacked child-centeredness, as manifested in its drilling information through rote memorizing into passive children sitting motionless facing the teacher in orderly rows. "[T]he purpose now is not to teach them a certain number of facts and rules, or to go through certain books within certain times, and be able to pass the examinations at the end of the term, but to acquire genuine strength and self-reliance" (*JE* 1901: 54, no. 10: 173). "Rote-memorizing, or second-hand thinking, has given way to rational thinking in all the common school subjects except grammar and arithmetic, and must very soon fly the white flag in this last trench also" (*JE* 1906: 64, no. 9: 260). An article making the same point at the end of the period quoted the current education commissioner of Massachusetts: "Our aims of education now place 'training' first and 'knowledge' second. . . . 'It is not the function of the public school to teach children what to think, it is the function of the public school to teach them how to think'" (*JE* 1931: 114, no. 4: 67).

Progressives elaborated the child-centered approach in two ways. First, they viewed the individual as developing in groups, and they thus defined individual development in terms of being able to fit into society. Self-development and social progress were reciprocal. Cooperation and learning to work productively in communities became a mark of the good citizen and an essential part of the school (Reuben 1997). Second, the Progressives' ultimate addition was that they wanted a science of child-nature and development that would replace custom and religious authority. They wanted to generate and use scientific knowledge of the self to engineer the self and the new society.

Actual implementation in the classroom was extremely difficult. Implementation required a curriculum that enabled students to make choices, that based the selection of topics on student interests, and that was constructed at least in part by the children. As Cuban (1993) shows, this indeed was more the discourse than the practice. A pattern of reform emerged in which an evaluation survey of a district ascertained that classrooms or administrative practices did not conform to the theoretical ideals and formal policies. They had to be reformed. Committees were formed and subsequent new programs modeled success stories from other cities. The cycle then would repeat, resulting in naturalistic child-centeredness becoming increasingly built into rationalized educational policy and organization, but with decoupled classroom practices.

Psychology in Education

The drive for a scientific base for child-centered pedagogy and curricula led Progressive intellectuals to help create and apply psychology. The institutionalization of psychology as a science and academic discipline and its impressive innovations in experimentation provided a powerful source of naturalistic abstract knowledge for professionalizing educators and grounding

Progressive agendas. Psychology broke with its natural philosophy roots late in the century, symbolized by Wilhelm Wundt's establishment of the first official research laboratory in Leipzig, Germany, in 1879. In the United States William James and G. Stanley Hall helped to formalize psychology. Together with Wundt in Germany, they trained nearly the entire first generation of Americans with doctorates in psychology from 1878 through 1900.

Early Progressive leaders such as W. T. Harris and Colonel Francis W. Parker used psychological paradigms to construct pedagogical theory that became the foundation of standardized professional knowledge for teachers and administrators. Several of the first generation psychologists such as James and Hall, and their students Edward L. Thorndike, John Dewey, and Charles H. Judd, promoted educational psychology with entrepreneurial, institution-building charisma. They saw the higher calling of education and also the opportunities for psychology. By 1920, prominent educator Ellwood Cubberley (1920) referred to psychology as the "master science" for education.

The early links between psychology and education were specialized and institutionalized during this period. Child study, later known as developmental psychology, and pedagogical or mental science were to improve instruction. In 1886 the *JE* normatively stated, "[E]very college has its department of mental science." By 1921 it reported that preservice teachers at most training schools were required to take at least one course in child psychology.

Curricula and instructional methods produced by the new pedagogical science created a demand for textbooks that was further stimulated by a capitalist textbook industry. Scholars produced thousands of courses of study. The educational trust took this opportunity to apply its models, writing prolifically, including textbooks, and establishing relationships with publishing houses. This was a major avenue by which intellectual elites directly influenced the classroom.

Educational psychology was also to develop scientific methods for measuring learners and learning. This emphasis led to the development of IQ tests, achievement tests, and graded report cards for assessing children's individual differences. IQ tests provided ostensibly hard scientific measurements as a basis for classifying children. The heyday of psychological measurement and testing began after World War I, although the *JE* reported that Binet's IQ classifications were being used by 1906.

Psychological measurements and tests were appealing to superintendents. Because it was accepted that IQ tests provided a classification system based on scientific measurement of the child, superintendents could claim that bureaucratic organization that used IQ classifications was efficiently meeting the needs of the child. IQ tests also provided a scientific basis for guidance. Schools used guidance, out of which counseling psychology eventually grew, to locate an individual in society. Vocationalism emerged as a general approach to the curriculum (Kliebard 1999). Vocationalism was defined in terms of fulfilling individual potential, but also it was explicitly geared to placing an individual in a job that was best for him or her and for industrial democracy.[16]

In summary, Progressive reformers used the paradigm of child-centeredness and psychology as a powerful frame for their agenda. This frame shifted authority from God and the super-empirical to nature, and from religion to science. Superintendents used this paradigm to claim that their reforms met state and public demands and to establish professional autonomy and control vis-à-vis school boards, principals, and teachers. Psychology, moreover, provided powerful tools for bureaucratic organization. Educators scientifically measuring individual potential could place children in the proper bureaucratic categories and guide them to the appropriate location in society.

Institutional Competition over Abstract Knowledge and Teacher Training

The creation of the research university during this period was itself a secularizing force, and the Progressive educational intellectuals were a part of that movement (Reuben 1996). The secular research university intensified institutional competition within higher education over the control of professional knowledge and teacher training. The result was an accelerated expansion of naturalistic abstract knowledge and degree requirements for teachers.

States established normal schools in the mid-1800s that typically were two-year schools admitting high school graduates for training as teachers. Their curriculum was organized around teaching methods. Normals promoted the professionalization of teachers and of themselves as professional schools, modeling professional degrees in law and medicine. By the late 1800s an increasing number of normals, especially in the Midwest and West, offered a general liberal arts curriculum, thereby competing with colleges and universities for students (Goodlad, Soder, and Sirotnik 1990). At the same time, colleges and universities created professorships, departments, and colleges of education. They argued that the normal school graduate might be able to teach elementary grades, but only their own graduates had the substantive knowledge to teach in the growing number of high schools. In 1896 the newly formed North Central Association of Colleges and Secondary Schools set a college degree as a qualification for high school teachers.

To avoid being excluded from training secondary school teachers, normal schools, especially in the Midwest and West, transformed themselves into four-year state teachers' colleges (Harper 1939: 130). The Department of Normal Schools within the National Education Association called for this transition in 1908 and resolved that normal schools should establish research departments (Harper: 138–39).

Education departments and schools in research universities had greater prestige and resources than state teachers colleges and normal schools, but within the university they were accorded low status, and some were even threatened with termination. Education faculty, to hold their place in the university, pressed the claim that there was a specialized science of education, and psychology was crucial to their claim. They also established links to the public school system, carrying out surveys, consulting, and giving talks. Through these two strategies, Progressive intellectuals increased the scientific nature of professional educational knowledge and the direct application of that knowledge to educational practice.

Competition among these institutions thus led to the spiraling growth of abstract, scientific knowledge and the location of that knowledge out of the hands of teachers, their associations, and institutions. Progressive superintendents used the most recent research in educational psychology and supported higher degree requirements for teaching positions. By doing so, they could demonstrate that they were meeting state standards and public demands. They also could use this distant knowledge and brand of professionalization to trump resistant school boards and teachers.

Overview: The School as Place, a Harbinger of the Millennium

Progressive education reformers used child-centered models to shift authority, and they used psychology and the research university to establish their agendas. Superintendents, faced with state and public mandates and professional competition, implemented Progressive reform in formal programs and organization. This was all framed in a secular post-millennialism. Despite the scholarly shortcomings of Cubberley's simple story of the passing of small-town America, Progressives enacted it religiously. The characteristics of the old were antitypes against which Progressive reform was opposed. During the period from 1876 to 1911 in the *JE*, for example, extremely negative language was reserved for the rural schools, amateur (women) teachers, graft-ridden school boards, and immigrants, the last viewed as products of even worse systems. There was at least a veneer of civility expressed regarding Catholicism and other religions. The message was no less clear, however, because contributors to the *JE* routinely grouped religions with the passing small-town institutions. The new urban, industrial society, of course, had its own ills depicted in the *JE:* dehumanization, poverty, delinquency and crime, capitalist greed, political corruption, and a host of other immoralities. Against the stagnation of the old and the swirling evils of the new stood the school. If factories and universities were the cathedrals of industry and knowledge, the public school was the local parish church around which the neighborhood huddled.

One is struck throughout the many education journals by the degree to which the ideal school as a physical place came to be viewed and experienced as progress. In the stagnant rural area or in the chaotic city, it stood as a special place embodying the future. It was a safe, clean, well-ventilated place. It was orderly and harmonious. Even the architecture of the school embodied orderliness and efficiency. If the school was, as the Progressive ideal prescribed, a functioning industrious democracy, a microcosm of progress, children would only have to conform to the school itself to be moral and rational, thereby guaranteeing the future.

The adults there were special, different from parents, clergy, and neighbors. They had a higher calling and were equipped with distant knowledge, techniques, and authority. They had the responsibility and mandate to protect the place from disorder. Each action of the Progressive superintendent—pursuing a career, competing for professional control, overcoming resistance, implementing new programs, and running an orderly school—was a dramatization of this grand narrative.

SECULARIZATION AND THE TRANSFORMATION OF RELIGION

No religious organization controlled either the practice of schooling or educational knowledge, reflecting the high degree to which the United States and schools already were secularized. For this reason, movements to build public schools run by secular government were not openly hostile to religion. If we look at nineteenth-century European education, we find that the overriding conflict was precisely over the organizational control of schools and education. Movements to make public schools autonomous from the church were therefore intensely anticlerical and anti-religious. In the United States, nevertheless, religious symbols and discourse articulated with national identity and citizenship. While the state and church were separated, nation and religion were not, as manifested in the common school system's civil religion. This became a point of conflict.

Frequently in the early period of the Progressive episode, people articulated Progressive themes with religion, but any success was short-lived. Progressive education intellectuals consistently rejected such syntheses and excluded them from their discourse. These intellectuals, moreover, became more explicitly anti-religious as they attempted to make education ideology and the sources of authoritative knowledge autonomous from religious discourse. Explicit anti-religion increased markedly after World War I with Progressivist successes and a more aggressive assertion of naturalism.

Local superintendents, in general even those who personally were liberal Protestants, used an epistemological dualism in their decision making: a personal, increasingly abstract religious calling and a practical rational concern for order. Increasingly during this period and especially after World War I religious issues became more conflictual in general, in part because intellectuals and the media asserted a more thoroughgoing naturalism and political parties politicized religious conflicts. Superintendents when mediating religious conflicts found themselves managing national secularizing pressures and local religious practices. The result was a secular formal organization within which administrators pragmatically accommodated local religious practices.

The Uneasy Relationship between Rationalism and Religion

Professionalization does not necessarily exclude religion, nor does the application of scientific knowledge to administration, curriculum, and pedagogy. The Catholic school system in the United States illustrates the coexistence of religion and rationalism. From at least 1905 it used scientific administration and rational planning principles, and Catholic high schools explicitly modeled public schools. The Catholic system was designed and implemented by "a newly established corps of professional Catholic educators, analogous to the professionals who were instrumental in controlling public schooling" (Baker 1992: 198). They integrated science-based curriculum and administration with a religious worldview administered by a religious bureaucracy.

Through the 1890s many educators articulated Progressive themes with Protestantism. They accepted whatever knowledge and methods scientists generated and defined them as part of a religious project of discovering truth about God's creation. In the 1870s and 1880s, many Progressives described themselves and all truly professional educators as using scientific tools to do God's work. In the following we see child-centeredness and the allusion to scientific methods subsumed under a religious canopy.

> Children are too often overwhelmed with quantity and variety of material, that makes [thought] formation impossible for them. And where shall we take the rule, if not from nature? We mortals can only imitate what the dear God has created, therefore we must make use of the same law according to which he creates. (*JE* 1876: 4, no. 8: 93)
>
> For we must remember that we can only teach well while we study the wondrous mystery of child-nature with open eye and receptive soul, and walk humbly along the path drawn by the finger of God in his providential training of his little ones. (*JE* 1881: 14, no. 8: 141)

These early Progressives asserted the consistency of practical rationality and historic religion. As these passages illustrate, however, they used an epistemological dualism. They derived meanings from a religious calling, but they based school organization and curriculum/pedagogy in scientific administration and psychology. They assumed the autonomy of practical decisions and policies from religion, even as they framed them in religious terms.

We found in the *JE* many articles making reference to religion and to God or a Supreme Being. In 1876 and 1881, 43 and 24 percent respectively of all coded items discussed religion. There was a substantial drop in 1886 to 13 percent. In 1891 only 9 percent of journal entries discussed religion, and this rate subsequently tapered off to nearly zero. The percentages of articles that mentioned God or a Supreme Being are 50 percent, 31 percent, and then 10 percent for 1876, 1881, and 1886, respectively. The substantial drop by 1886 was due, we think, to the transition of the *JE* from a regional to a nationally oriented journal in the early 1880s. We thus see attempts at articulating historic religion and Progressive themes at a local or regional level. When the journal moved to a more national orientation, the frequency of such attempts decreased.

The percentages of *JE* articles that addressed issues of morality and character were high in the early period through 1891 (46, 45, 44, and 34 percent). Subsequent percentages hovered around 20 through 1931. Unlike religion, morality was not excluded from educational ideology.

There were distinct qualitative changes in moral education and discourse in each of the three subperiods, culminating with Progressives scientizing and relativizing them in the 1920s (Hunter 2000). In the early period, educators spiritualized morality, distinguishing it from the rational. They talked about morality and character as the spiritual aspect of humanity, as the nonrational essential core of humanity that had to be nurtured in the midst of industrial society. Morality thus could not be taught, only lived. All hinged on the teacher's exemplary moral character. "So the teacher weaves around her pupils her personal interest and hopeful imaginings for the future, and thus, by a kind of divine alchemy, changes much of the dross to gold" (*JE* 1876: 4, no. 10: 113).

As schools expanded the space in the curriculum that was devoted to technical topics and as they demanded greater discipline, many critics expressed concern about ignoring the "whole person," the "soul." Educators addressed these concerns in part by developing programs for educating both the "mind and body" which came to focus on hygiene and eventually included athletics. By the turn of the century educators and the public called for explicit teaching of morality, in part because of a rising concern over delinquency and crime. At that time the major development in moral education was character education. In its simplest form it was a checklist of virtues or valued character traits formulated into codes. These were extremely popular, as exemplified in the Boy Scouts and 4-H Clubs, and similar codes proliferated after World War I. The Character Education Association, magazines such as *Colliers,* and many school boards and superintendents published innumerable character education programs. Many argued that the discipline of school itself taught the necessary character traits of "punctuality, silence, obedience, order, and industry" (*JE* 1911: 74, no. 9: 229).

Educators early in the century began developing child-centered pedagogical methods for character education, such as group discussion and co-operation (McClellan 1999). They claimed that the exemplary teacher was not enough: moral instruction had to be "purposed, regular, continuous, and systematic" (*JE* 1907: 66, no. 18: 481). In the late 1920s the *JE* ran a weekly "Character Chat," by Joseph B. Egan, comprised largely of moralistic stories. This was replaced in 1931 with "Character Workshop," by the same educator. It promised to give "insight into the underlying principles as well as the methods of character formation" and instruction on "the training of the emotions, arousing in the child the desire to do what is right, and developing in him a clearer sense of what he ought and ought not to do" (1931: 114, no. 6: 125). Repeatedly contributors echoed that a "new emphasis and a new technique in character formation seem to be required if the terrible failures represented in the crimes of youth are to be reduced in number" (*JE* 1931: 114, no. 7: 142). While many popular programs comprised little more than stories with morals, the sampling from *JE* suggests that educators applied to character education the Progressive approach of emphasizing child-centered pedagogy. God and civil religious elements were retained in character education, but as items on a checklist for fitting into modern society. Character education in a way completed the inversion begun in the nineteenth century: Morality was not an inherent worship of God; rather, God was used to create individuals who fit into society.

After World War I, Progressive education intellectuals developed a distinctive approach that was highly critical of character education. They criticized character education's methods as unscientific and ineffective. Their main criticism, though, was that it preserved traditional values, merely adapting them to industrial society. Progressive educators asserted, in contrast, that science showed morality to be relative to social life. Character training should not be based on a list of virtues but on the "seizing of the flashing current of the living will" (*Elementary School Principal* 1925: 5, no. 1: 7). What was required was a science-based curriculum that fostered a moral code that was functional for industrial society. They argued for relativity also from the point of view of the individual. Children should be taught to reason from experience about morality, not simply accept traditional values. This principle contradicted somewhat the idea of a scientifically discoverable morality for society. Progressives exhibited, however, a faith that child development would be consistent with social evolution if only a scientific pedagogy were used.

These Progressive educators rejected the nineteenth-century Enlightenment-Protestant view that Judeo-Christian morality was consistent with natural law and that therefore reason itself taught that it is good for society. In character education, Judeo-Christian morality was reduced to codes for fitting into society. In the later Progressive view, there is no one morality good for all societies, and reason in the form of science would discover what is good for society and the child. In this program, unlike in character education, Judeo-Christian morality is not even useful.

Progressive reformers had some success with relativistic moral education. Associations such as the National Education Association (NEA) in the early 1930s affirmed their approach. Practices reflected the pragmatic orientation of institutional arrangements. State boards and local schools tended to implement programs that were a bricolage of elements from both character education and relativistic approaches (McClellan 1999). Thus in the case of morality we again see the general pattern: thoroughly secularized national educational models with local schools somewhat decoupled.

Religious Conflict

By 1876 the dominant and official position was that the public school should provide a completely nonsectarian education that encouraged the religious nature of the individual and nation, which was necessary for adulthood and industrial democratic society. Conflict centered on how these imperatives were to be embodied in policy. As we have described, the policy mandating nonsectarian schools came to mean no public money for religious schools, and common religion meant generic prayer and Bible reading without commentary. Continuing through the Progressive episode, there was a three-cornered conflict over these principles among (1) secularists; (2) Protestant educators (liberal and Social Gospel) and mainline Protestant churches; and (3) proponents of sectarian schools (the Catholic Church being the most powerful).[17]

Progressive educators, even those who articulated Progressivism with Protestantism, were adamant about the principle of nonsectarian schools. Contributors and editors in the very first issues of the *JE* espoused the strict exclusion of religious instruction. For example in 1876, the *JE* proudly printed the report of a foreign correspondent who found no religious instruction in American schools because, he explained, Americans do not want to offend people of different creeds. Rev. A. D. Mayo, an early *JE* editor and prominent educator who articulated Progressive themes and Protestantism, was a strong advocate of excluding religious teaching. Referring to the work of public education, he wrote,

> The reason that we cannot give up this delicate work to the clergy is that they are, as a class, the representatives of religious sects and parties, and would ed-

ucate the children into such a zeal for theological and ecclesiastical partisan-
ship that the land would be rent with politico-religious feuds, exploding into
religious wars, as in every country where the experiment has been tried. (*JE*
1876: 4, no. 11: 122)

Mayo here expresses the prevalent view that historic, creedal denominations were motivated by sectarian or special group interest, and only the
public school embodied the common interest.

This ideology of a nonsectarian public school system was associated with
the melting-pot model of Americanization. This model both reflected and
channeled nativism and anti-Catholicism: children of immigrants and
Catholics had to be included to be remade. If these children, or those in
rural communities or of the urban laboring masses, did not enter the public schools, the argument went, they would not receive the training necessary to be American citizens, and America would fail.[18]

Before the turn of the century, most educators with Progressive sensibilities accepted American civil religion and supported the inclusion of prayer
and Bible reading as symbols of the common religion, although there were
some, such as liberal Protestant William T. Harris, who did not (see Beyerlein, chap. 3 in this volume). Public school proponents claimed it was easy
to accommodate all children. The *JE* in an 1876 issue (1876: 4, no. 11:
127), for example, printed seven letters written in response to its call for examples of how to conduct religious exercises. A subsequent issue (1876: 4,
no. 12: 139) included a long letter in support of the Bible's being read in
schools, over Catholic objections. The letters described what they considered appropriate and sufficient steps to ensure religious freedom, basically
allowing a child to not attend the exercise.

Proponents upheld the commonality of these practices in part by stigmatizing denominational religion. Rev. Mayo wrote extensively on the importance of nonsectarianism. In a passage immediately following the earlier
quotation stating that special religious interests must be excluded, he wrote,
"The reason why we cannot utterly ignore religion, as the basis of public
morals, and thrust the Bible and religious literature, music and art from our
schoolhouses, is, that our national ideal of morality is the logical outcome
of the Christian religion, in its most progressive state of modern development" (*JE* 1876: 4, no. 11: 122). It was well known that Christian religion
in its "most progressive state of modern development" meant ethical living
relatively denuded of supernaturalism, in contrast to the Christianity of
clergy and denominations.

Both secularists and Protestant educators were equally adamant about
not providing public monies for sectarian schools. This principle was reinforced by anti-Catholicism because the Catholic Church, while not the only
religious body claiming the right to state aid, was the largest and most pow-

erful. In 1876 (1876: 4, no. 12: 133), the *JE* printed a short history of the antebellum New York City conflicts over state funding of the Public School Society, Catholic schools, and the Bethel Baptist Church schools. It reported favorably the establishment by state law of a school board overseeing a single public school system and forbidding aid to sectarian ones. Five years later we found a similar item on schools in California with very telling language: "Until 1856, the different religious denominations were encouraged in their squabble over the school funds, and persistent efforts were made to establish the policy of the ecclesiastics. But the good sense of the people, instructed by a remarkably able body of leaders in educational affairs, fixed the policy of the State in favor of the American system in 1856" (*JE* 1881: 14, no. 9: 157). To allow these alternative systems would threaten the very idea of a national moral project. It would also undermine the "one best system," the professionalizing goal of exclusive jurisdiction, and the careers of Progressive administrators.

Many communities in practice negotiated accommodations. Many Catholic families and local priests worked with public schools, and many Protestant-dominated school boards agreed to remove Bible reading or other accommodations. One model worked out locally was known as the Poughkeepsie Plan. In 1873 the two Catholic schools in that city were forced to shut down, threatening to overwhelm the public school system. It was agreed that the public school would use Church buildings provided that no religious instruction would take place during school hours. In other cases, religious instruction was allowed in publicly owned buildings but before or after school hours and not at public expense. Many other plans and variations on plans were adopted across the country (Fraser 1999; Jorgenson 1987; McClellan 1999; Michaelson 1970).

At the national level, and of course in many local communities, positions on these issues increasingly were viewed as non-negotiable. The Catholic Church maintained its long-standing criticisms of the public system: The present public schools, the Church argued, were in fact Protestant, but if the solution was to rid them of Protestantism, then they would be completely secular. The Third Plenary Council of Baltimore in 1884 intensified the commitment to its own school system. It went beyond the first two councils by stipulating that a parish school must be built by every church within the next two years and that "all Catholic parents are bound to send their children to the parish school" (McCluskey 1964).

During the 1890s, many Americanist priests and bishops hoped to moderate the Church's stance toward accommodating American institutions, in part by making public schools more open to Catholic concerns. They appealed to national educators to shift commitments from a single public school system to a system of public support for private schools. They promoted local plans as examples. The conservative Catholic hierarchy harshly

criticized Americanists and their education proposals in particular. Ultimately the Pope, who was fighting worldwide against just such accommodations with nation-states, supported the hierarchy. Moreover, non-Catholic
educators were not responsive either (see Beyerlein, chap. 3 in this volume).

On the side of public school ideology, the Republican Party incorporated
public school issues into its post-Reconstruction national platform (McAfee
1998). The party pushed for a state-centered public school system following a Prussian model. It adamantly opposed state support for sectarian
schools, and especially through the early eighties used anti-Catholicism.
Since its formation in the 1850s and through the election of 1892, the Republican Party espoused moral reform politics, including temperance and
then prohibition (Thomas 1989). Consistent with its history, it fully supported moralism and civic religion in the schools, including Bible reading,
as essentially American. Other movements after 1890 lobbied state governments to pass laws explicitly requiring Bible reading in the schools and scientific temperance, and later outlawing the teaching of evolution (Tyack,
James, and Benavot 1987).

For Protestant leaders, the commitment to a nonsectarian public school
system infused with a common religion seemed absolute. Indeed, these
commitments even overrode the imperative of reading the Bible. Every now
and then, various prominent Protestants were willing to give up the practice
of Bible reading, as did local groups here and there. Given the prevalence
of anti-Catholicism, it is striking that many Protestants would be willing to
accommodate the Catholic Church's concerns over Bible reading. This in
itself suggests the absoluteness of the nonsectarian, civil religion ideal, and
in this case its ameliorating of anti-Catholicism effects. Protestant leaders,
however, generally were not willing to compromise on public support for
sectarian schools, despite the many available local models. The irony then
is that many Protestants contributed to secularization (being willing to remove the Bible and maintaining the ban on public monies for religious
schools) because they were committed to a nonsectarian religious national
identity socialized into children through one school system.[19]

Thus, by the end of the first period of the Progressive episode, national
intellectual and political actors polarized religious conflict. The local level
was not tightly controlled by the national, allowing for creative compromise.
Many of these accommodations failed, arguably because of national polar-
ization intensified by journalistic attention.

By the 1890s, the new Progressives shaped the frame in which these
conflicts played out. In their secular, post-millennial vision of using scientific knowledge to engineer a new cooperative society, they made one
public school system essential. This next generation of more rationalistic
Progressives, however, argued that the one system should exclude historic
religious symbols because historic religions, according to the binary narra-

tive, were part of the old order, nonscientific, and divisive.[20] The religious conflicts of the day were for them a vindication. This rationalistic frame shaped the floating coalitions in the three-cornered conflict. When the issue was giving public money for Catholic schools, secularists and mainline Protestants were opposed. If the issue was that Bible reading without commentary was offensive to a growing Catholic population, secularists and the Catholic Church supported the abolition of the practice.

The Progressive superintendents again were a channel of national ideological frames. Professional training, Progressive and professionalizing goals, career interests, accountability to state demands, vulnerability to journalistic claims, and simple bureaucratic logic all made the superintendent a carrier of practical rationalism and epistemological dualism. For the putatively neutral superintendent, even if personally a liberal Protestant, religion was simply irrelevant to objective rational decision making. More than this, however, superintendents carried the view that denominational religion and conflicts were hopelessly parochial, a leftover from a bygone era. They might have learned this from reading Cubberley's narrative of the decline of community, or at professional meetings, rubbing shoulders with administrators of large urban schools, or perhaps from reading education journals.

In this context, superintendents pragmatically looked for ways of making religious conflict go away, which often meant they were open to local compromise. Anything, such as state laws, professional imperatives, journalistic or popular concerns, that made it more difficult to be flexible caused the national discourse to be worked out locally and greater exclusion of religious practices and symbols.

The Transformation of Religion

Progressives thus excluded historic religion from education ideology and organization; more profoundly, however, they contested the very nature of religion. Progressives wanted not only to strip away the supernatural as mere superstition but to hold up the higher calling of human relationships and fulfillment as intrinsically religious.

This transformation is illustrated in a new approach to the Bible in schools. No matter how particular controversies over Bible reading were resolved, the increasing conflict made it problematic as the symbol of a common faith. The early common school principle had been to exclude religious organizational authority by excluding commentary. But the twentieth-century Progressive educators saw the Bible itself differently. They proposed retaining the study of the Bible, but as literature. The meaning of this was vague, but the principle was clear: the Bible would not be read devotionally, but it could be read as religious literature. The Bible now had value as an expression of humanity. If it were to be present in the school, it had to be denuded of the supernatural.

Institutionalizing the Bible as literature was part of a profound transformation of religion from being about the supernatural to being an intrinsic religiousness in human nature and relations. The idea of a new kind of religion usually was only implicit, such as in the idea that schools were to be new, special places of true education, free from parochial superstitions and conflicts. Educators overseeing this place were to be different from other people. The school administrators had a higher calling to rise above the historic religions. As Horace M. Rebok, superintendent in Santa Monica, California, claimed, "People do not know the problems a school administrator has to meet. He has to deal with many employees, he has to deal justly with the children of all the people of all religious faiths, of all sects and creeds, and of every political faith, but the law of our land says that these things must not cross the threshold of the public schools" (*JE* 1916: 84, no. 10: 264).

Educators were more explicit when they talked about their higher calling. Progressives framed that calling in terms of the intrinsic spirituality of child (human) nature and human society. It seems likely, moreover, that educators such as superintendents, when faced with managing religious conflict, would find speaking of the intrinsic religiousness of the child and America helpful for shifting the discursive frame from parochial interests to the higher calling of education while assuaging religious sensibilities. It certainly was common for educators to speak of public school's central role in fulfilling the human spirit. As President Flemley of Illinois State Normal University, stated,

> State and church, family and industrial life build for human perfection, each in its own narrow line. The school includes and supplements them all. Other institutions educate, but their education is partial and for their own ends; the school prepares for life in these institutions and for the life above and beyond them. It remains for the school to establish in the hearts of young people the true ideal of living, which our religious teaching calls oneness with God. In the phrase of the school, we call it the mastery of the thought and spirit of the world. This mastery of the thought and spirit of the world is true self-realization; it is the goal of humanity. (*JE* 1901: 54, no. 9: 151)

Michaelson (1970) describes this new common religion: "Life is one; life is all. Education is life; religion is life. Life is community. The individual emerges and develops in community" (136). In 1934, in *A Common Faith*, John Dewey wrote that the past years marked a transformation in the "seat of intellectual authority." This new authority was not religion, but it was a religiousness inherent in human experience in society and nature. Summarizing, he wrote, "I made a distinction between religion and the religious. I pointed out that religion—or religions—is charged with beliefs, practices and modes of organization that have accrued to and been loaded upon the religious element. . . . I urged that conditions are now ripe for emancipation of the religious quality from [these] accretions" (84). The religious is emancipated from religion by transferring the object of our "idealizing imagination" from the supernatural to "natural human relations" or the "comprehensive community."

Dewey thus elaborated a religion in which value and meaning did not flow from a transcendent reality but existed in humanity. True religion has humanity as its object and is self-realization, individual and collective, through civilization. Education was to nurture the child to develop in this ultimate Progressivism. Superintendents and other local educators were not necessarily as explicit as this. They were, nevertheless, in their practical rationality, building a world that bred this transformation. And this was powerful language when they communicated their higher calling to the public.

EPISODE'S END AND LEGACY

The Scopes trial in 1925 dramatized this episode's outcomes. Evolution was being used as a scientific foundation for a thoroughgoing naturalism. Intellectuals such as Julian Huxley and John Tyndall did this in England almost immediately after the publication of *The Origin of the Species*. In the United States it was not used in this way until the 1900s. An assertive naturalism entered education primarily as part of the growing secondary school system. Fraser (1999), for example, argues that high school biology textbooks after World War I were aggressively naturalistic. Religious groups mobilized for state laws prohibiting the teaching of evolutionism, and Tennessee was one of a few states in which they were successful.

Writing naturalism into textbooks, occasioned by the new high schools, constituted a tighter coupling of the local to the centers of abstract secular knowledge. The Scopes trial as media event was about just that: Journalists exposed the archaic, parochial, superstitious small town. They gave meaning to the synchronic distinction between the national and local, urban and rural, by imposing on it the diachronic evolution from traditional to modern society. Thus, although the case was decided in support of the law that outlawed teaching evolution, the larger cultural effect was to discredit historic religions. The local population's adamant rejection of extreme naturalism, however, was also communicated. Fraser (1999) argues that after the trial, textbook publishers substantially toned down their presentation of evolution and eschewed philosophical naturalism.

This episode of conflict over religion and schooling came to a close soon after the trial. By 1931, some version of Dewey's new common faith characterized the national intellectual elite. These intellectuals had mobilized to reform and secularize education and to transform religion. Given the institutional contexts, they were successful. Local communities and urban neighborhoods through decades of conflict had schools that were substantially more secular than a half century earlier, although they continued civil religious practices. School administrators, exemplified by the superintendents, were both the agents of Progressive national incorporation of the local and also the buffer allowing local practice not to be disrupted. Any structural change or collective action that would elaborate national ideology and incorporate the local into it would increase secularization.

Subsequently, groups mobilized to critique the now established public school system. People organized collective action, using individual rights and national ideology to purge more religion from local practices. Since then groups have attempted to replace the Protestant, middle-class, white/ Anglo values and melting-pot model that Progressives had built into the system with a more inclusive multiculturalism. Other groups have contested the monopoly of the one system, in part because it has diverged from the earlier models.

From the point of view of any particular actor, whether parent, child, cleric, teacher, or administrator, increased rationalism might seem inexorable and conflicts overwhelming. The changes appear to be generated somewhere else, and they seem to be everywhere. By focusing on a particular historical episode, we have attempted to understand better the dynamics between structure and collective action and to see outcomes as contingent. These outcomes in turn set the institutional frame and agendas for subsequent episodes.

NOTES

1. This is the model of religious liberty established in the Netherlands. The shift away from public monies for religious schools was a long, controversial process, intensifying in the second quarter of the century (for examples, see Cremin 1980 and Fraser 1999).

2. Two other factors came into play that intensified the emotional charge of these positions. First, nativism and anti-Catholicism made it extremely difficult to compromise by including Catholic symbols. Second, Roman Catholicism throughout the nineteenth century was "a deeply traditional religion with fundamental presuppositions that were radically different from the Protestant world view" (McClellan 1999: 37) and even more at odds with the Enlightenment world view, with which U.S. Protestants had forged an accommodation.

3. By historic religions we mean world and tribal religions oriented to a super-empirical reality. The term *supernatural,* used by the Progressives, is biased by depicting the religious as in some way not natural. We use the term *supernatural* because of its common currency but prefer the more neutral phrase *historic reli-*

gions. We distinguish these from "religiousness" or "humanistic religions," such as the "common faith" espoused by John Dewey, which do not recognize a super-empirical realm.

4. When professions are well established, professionals might resist reform, and reformers might criticize entrenched professional knowledge and practices. In early stages, however, professionalization shares with reform the goals of making knowledge and practice autonomous from prior authorities.

5. By focusing on the superintendency, we do not mean that it universally was the local progressive force. Young teachers fresh from state teachers colleges often were sources of Progressive classroom ideas. Our general argument is that anyone who pushed the Progressive agenda would be controversial but have particular advantages.

6. The *JE* was founded in 1875 from the merger of several state journals in the Northeast under the name *New England Journal of Education.* It absorbed an Indianapolis weekly in 1885, was sold to Rev. A. E. Winship in 1886, and was renamed the *Journal of Education: For School People in New England and Beyond.* A. E. Winship remained editor until his death in 1933. His biography reflected that of educators generally. He was a teacher from 1865 to 1868 and a principal of a grammar school from 1869 to 1872, along the way attending Bridgewater Normal School. He then studied at Andover Theological Seminary and became a pastor of a Congregational church in Massachusetts (1874–1883). He directed an education commission before taking over editorship. We selected the *JE* from a survey of twelve popular journals of the period. We read all issues in September every five years from 1876 through 1931, coding articles.

7. The war itself was an important catalyst. The revelation of high illiteracy among U.S. army-aged men, the recognition of interstate competition, and hopes for peace escalated demands for reform. "If, before the war, anyone doubted that education was to become the most effective instrument in man's development, certainly no one can doubt it now. In the coming years all social, economic, moral, civic, national and international problems will be brought finally for their solution to the school" (*JE* 1916: 84, no. 11: 289).

8. Progressive educators had international orientations and networks (Rohrs and Lenhart 1995). Leading national intellectuals and professors in normal schools studied in Europe. Progressives modeled German experimental psychology and Prussian school administration. The *JE* in its earliest issues from 1876 included a section called "The Kindergarten Messenger," which reported on European developments. Throughout the period each issue had a section on international educational news. Progressives used international science and industry exhibitions to call for educational reforms. A strong school system will, they argued, produce strong men and thus a strong, well-disciplined army. The principle was that the German schoolmaster won the Franco-Prussian war.

9. The Progressives largely were cultural or liberal Protestants. It is difficult in many cases to identify a particular figure as one or the other. In some sense it is not necessary, because both cultural and liberal Protestants tended to have a privatized, nonsupernatural religious sensibility. Many Progressives espoused the Social Gospel, a type of post-millennialism that infused progress with spirituality.

10. This was the period in which the concept of rural America was constructed

and reinforced by social science theories reifying the distinction between primitive/traditional and modern societies. Progressive intellectuals promoted this binary view. It had great rhetorical power to legitimate progressive goals and to stigmatize current practices and sources of knowledge.

11. The veneer of civility was sometimes exceedingly thin. The tone of many articles is illustrated by G. Stanley Hall, who, when arguing that religion should be minimized for early grades, added, "I would not say the child should be told no word of Jesus or of Santa Claus" (*JE* 1901: 54, no. 9: 151).

12. Religion itself was viewed as having evolved from magic and superstition to the ethics of the world religions. A particular belief of the intellectuals, aptly illustrated by Dewey, was that to leave behind "supernatural" religions in the pursuit of scientific truth is to be true to individual and human religiousness.

13. Charles Judd, for instance, a leading administrative Progressive and head of the University of Chicago's education school, called for the abolition of school boards (1934, quoted in Tyack and Cuban 1995). In a survey of the prior decade, the *JE* recommended, "When new school board members are elected, it should be ascertained whether or not they are secretly pledged to some mischievous anti-modern-education destructive policy" (1931: 114, no. 6: 116).

14. There was, however, an overall increase in the status of urban teachers over their rural counterparts, including pay and working conditions. The subordination of teachers to other professional educators was associated with feminization. Teachers organized in response to their management by scientific administration, voicing complaints that reforms were undemocratic, discriminated against female teachers, and separated management from classroom (Tyack and Hansot 1982: 114). Professionalization appears to have provided women with careers, but at the lower end of the educational hierarchy (MacDonald 1999). The official expectation was that the teacher show proper respect, and the pervasive tone was patronizing. In the 1929 September issue of the journal *Grade Teacher*, which was aimed at elementary school teachers, a "friendly talk" column ran an advice item entitled "How to talk with the superintendent," replete with suggestions for proper deference. In general, the teacher increasingly found everyday work populated with experts that carried greater expertise. For example, in the very next issue, the regular advice column, "Ask Florence Hale," in response to a letter asking about a second grade boy who could not read, suggested that the teacher consult the school psychologist.

15. They also started the kindergarten system, which, as a new system, was a model for child-centered schools.

16. Child guidance and mental hygiene, a precursor of clinical psychology, increasingly were preoccupied with solving problems of delinquency, reflecting the public demands that education solve social problems.

17. Scholars have reduced secularization to the interests of these groups. Some explain that secularists in alliance with liberal Protestants worked to exclude religion as an attempt to resist sectarian groups, especially Catholics (e.g., Glenn 1988; Monsma and Soper 1997). Others argue that conservative, nativist Protestants consumed with anti-Catholicism repeatedly undermined potential compromises between liberals and Catholics (e.g., Jorgenson 1987). These interpretations shed light on group interests, but they tend to focus almost exclusively on the national level. Several scholars have pointed to how political processes framed local religious

issues nationally as uncompromising positions (McAfee 1998) and how the different stances on issues reflected and drove different world views (Michaelson 1970). In a doctoral dissertation proposal, Justice (1999) gives a brief overview of these approaches.

18. These tensions were only partly fueled by actual competition with Catholic schools. Tensions with and attempts to incorporate Catholics occurred even in areas where there was little competition from Catholic schools (Baker 1992).

19. Another strategy was to incorporate Catholicism into the meaning of nonsectarian, for example by using the Catholic Bible. This strategy was not effective, in part because of anti-Catholicism and in part because the Catholic hierarchy rejected it.

20. Among educators who argued for the necessity of moral education, increasing numbers argued that even a generic civil religion was not necessary. For example a contributor in 1907, in an article entitled "Moral Training in the Public Schools," asserted that we must resist "any attempt to introduce into our public school system any item of instruction that could give offense in the least possible way to non-religious unbelief." He continued, "Morals can be taught entirely independently of religions or religious bias" (*JE* 1907: 66, no. 18: 482).

REFERENCES

Abbott, Andrew. 1988. *The System of Professions: An Essay on the Division of Expert Labor.* Chicago: University of Chicago Press.

Alexander, Jeffrey C., and Paul Colomy, eds. 1990. *Differentiation Theory and Social Change: Comparative and Historical Perspectives.* New York: Columbia University Press.

Apple, Michael. 1979. *Ideology and Curriculum.* New York: Routledge.

Baker, David P. 1992. "The Politics of American Catholic School Expansion, 1870–1930." In *The Political Construction of Education: The State, School Expansion, and Economic Change,* ed. Bruce Fuller and Richard Rubinson, 189–206. New York: Praeger.

Bellah, Robert N. 1964. "Religious Evolution." *American Sociological Review* 29: 358–74.

———. 1975. *The Broken Covenant.* New York: Seabury Press.

Bellah, Robert N., and Phillip E. Hammond. 1980. *Varieties of Civil Religion.* San Francisco: Harper & Row.

Berger, Peter. 1969. *The Sacred Canopy: Elements of a Sociological Theory of Religion.* Garden City, NY: Doubleday.

Bledstein, Burton J. 1976. *The Culture of Professionalism: The Middle Class and the Development of Higher Education in America.* New York: W. W. Norton.

Buenker, John D.; John C. Burnham; and Robert M. Crunden. 1977. *Progressivism.* Cambridge, MA: Schenkman.

Callahan, Raymond E. 1962. *Education and the Cult of Efficiency.* Chicago: University of Chicago Press.

Clifford, Geraldine J. 1986. "The Formative Years of Schools of Education in America: A Five-Institution Analysis." *American Journal of Education* 94, no. 4: 427–46.

Collins, Randall. 1998. *The Sociology of Philosophies: A Global Theory of Intellectual Change.* Cambridge, MA: Belknap Press.

Colomy, Paul. 1990. "Revisions and Progress in Differentiation Theory." In *Differentiation Theory and Social Change: Comparative and Historical Perspectives,* ed. Jeffrey C. Alexander and Paul Colomy, 465–95. New York: Columbia University Press.

Cremin, Lawrence A. 1962. *The Transformation of the School: Progressivism in American Education, 1876–1957.* New York: Alfred A. Knopf.

———. 1980. *American Education: The National Experience, 1783–1876.* New York: Harper & Row.

Crunden, Robert M. 1982. *Ministers of Reform: The Progressives' Achievement in American Civilization, 1889–1920.* New York: Basic Books.

Cuban, Larry. 1993. *How Teachers Taught: Constancy and Change in American Classrooms, 1890–1990,* 1–45. New York: Teachers College Press.

Cubberley, Ellwood P. 1909. *Changing Conceptions of Education.* New York: Houghton Mifflin.

———. 1920. *The History of Education.* Boston: Houghton Mifflin.

Dewey, John. 1934. *A Common Faith.* New Haven, CT: Yale University Press.

DiMaggio, Paul J., and Walter W. Powell. 1983. "The Iron Cage Revisited." *American Sociological Review* 48, no. 2: 147–60.

Douglas, Mary, ed. 1973. *Rules and Meanings: The Anthropology of Everyday Knowledge.* Baltimore, MD: Penguin Books.

Eisenstadt, S. N. 1980. "Cultural Orientation, Institutional Entrepreneurs, and Social Change: Comparative Analyses of Traditional Civilizations." *American Journal of Sociology* 85: 840–69.

Fraser, James W. 1999. *Between Church and State: Religion and Public Education in a Multicultural America.* New York: St. Martin's Press.

Glenn, Charles L. 1988. *The Myth of the Common School.* Amherst: University of Massachusetts Press.

Goodlad, John I.; R. Soder; and K. A. Sirotnik, eds. 1990. *Places Where Teachers Are Taught.* San Francisco: Jossey-Bass.

Handy, Robert T. 1984. *A Christian America.* Oxford: Oxford University Press.

Harper, Charles A. 1939. *A Century of Public Teacher Education.* Washington, DC: National Education Association.

Hays, Samuel P. 1957. *The Response to Industrialism, 1885–1914.* Chicago: University of Chicago Press.

Herbst, Jurgen. 1989. *And Sadly Teach: Teacher Education and Professionalization in American Culture.* Madison: University of Wisconsin Press.

Hilgard, Ernest R. 1987. *Psychology in America: A Historical Survey.* New York: Harcourt Brace Jovanovich.

Howe, Daniel Walker. 1991. "The Evangelical Movement and Political Culture in the North during the Second Party System." *Journal of American History* 77, no. 4: 1216–39.

Hunter, James Davison. 2000. *The Death of Character: Moral Education in an Age without Good or Evil.* New York: Basic Books.

Jorgenson, Lloyd P. 1987. *The State and the Non-Public School, 1825–1925.* Columbia: University of Missouri Press.

Judd, Charles H. 1934. "School Boards as an Obstruction to Good Administration." *The Nation's Schools* 13 (February): 13–15.

Justice, Ben. 1999. "Education, Religion, and the Empire State: Public Schools and

Religious Diversity in New York State, 1870–1900." Ph.D. diss. proposal. Stanford University.

Katz, Michael B., ed. 1973. *Education in American History: Readings on the Social Issues.* New York: Praeger.

Kliebard, Herbert M. 1999. *Schooled to Work: Vocationalism and the American Curriculum, 1876–1946.* New York: Teachers College.

Lechner, Frank J. 1991. "The Case against Secularization: A Rebuttal." *Social Forces* 69, no. 4: 1103–19.

Lipset, Seymour Martin. 1963. *The First New Nation.* Garden City, NY: Anchor Books.

MacDonald, Victoria-Maria. 1999. "The Paradox of Bureaucratization: New Views of Progressive Era Teachers and the Development of a Woman's Profession." *History of Education Quarterly* 39 (winter): 427–53.

Marsden, George M. 1990. *Religion and American Culture.* New York: Harcourt Brace Jovanovich.

Martin, David. 1978. *A General Theory of Secularization.* Oxford: Basil Blackwell.

McAfee, Ward M. 1998. *Religion, Race, and Reconstruction: The Public School in the Politics of the 1870s.* Albany: State University of New York Press.

McClellan, B. Edward. 1999. *Moral Education in America: Schools and the Shaping of Character from Colonial Times to the Present.* New York: Teachers College Press.

McClellan, B. Edward, and William J. Reese, eds. 1988. *The Social History of American Education.* Urbana: University of Illinois Press.

McCluskey, Neil G. 1964. *Catholic Education in America: A Documentary History.* New York: Teachers College Press.

Meyer, John W., and Brian Rowan. 1977. "Institutionalized Organizations: Formal Structure as Myth and Ceremony." *American Journal of Sociology* 83, no. 2: 340–63.

Meyer, John W., and W. Richard Scott. 1983. *Organizational Environments: Ritual and Rationality.* Newbury, CA: Sage.

Meyer, John W.; David Tyack; Joane Nagel; and Audri Gordon. 1979. "Public Education as Nation-Building in America: Enrollments and Bureaucratization in the American States, 1870–1930." *American Journal of Sociology* 85: 591–613.

Michaelson, Robert. 1970. *Piety in the Public School.* New York: Macmillan.

Monsma, Stephen V., and J. Christopher Soper. 1997. *The Challenge of Pluralism: Church and State in Five Democracies.* New York: Rowman & Littlefield.

National Center for Education Statistics (NCES). 1999. *The Digest of Education Statistics.* Washington, DC: NCES. <http://nces.ed.gov/>

Newlon, Jessie H. 1930. "George Strayer: An Appreciation." *School Executive Magazine* 49, no. 10: 451–53.

———. 1934. *Educational Administration as Social Policy.* New York: Charles Scribner's Sons.

Reuben, Julie. A. 1996. *The Making of the Modern University.* Chicago: University of Chicago Press.

———. 1997. "Beyond Politics: Community Civics and the Redefinition of Citizenship in the Progressive Era." *History of Education Journal* 37, no. 4: 399–420.

Rohrs, Hermann, and Volker Lenhart, eds. 1995. *Progressive Education across the Continents: A Handbook.* New York: P. Lang.

Scott, W. Richard. 1992. *Organizations: Rational, Natural, and Open Systems.* Englewood Cliffs, NJ: Prentice Hall.

Thomas, George M. 1989. *Revivalism and Cultural Change: Christianity, Nation Building, and the Market in the Nineteenth-Century United States.* Chicago: University of Chicago Press.

Tocqueville, Alex de. 1945. *Democracy in America.* New York: Vintage Books.

Tyack, David. 1974. *The One Best System: A History of American Urban Education.* Cambridge, MA: Harvard University Press.

————. 1988. "Pilgrim's Progress: Toward a Social History of the School Superintendency, 1860–1960." In *The Social History of American Education,* ed. B. Edward McClellan and William J. Reese, 165–208. Chicago: University of Illinois Press.

Tyack, David, and Larry Cuban. 1995. *Tinkering toward Utopia: A Century of Public School Reform.* Cambridge, MA: Harvard University Press.

Tyack, David, and Elisabeth Hansot. 1982. *Managers of Virtue: Public School Leadership in America, 1820–1980.* New York: Basic Books.

Tyack, David; Thomas James; and Aaron Benavot. 1987. *Law and the Shaping of Public Education, 1785–1954.* Madison: University of Wisconsin Press.

Warren, Donald. 1989. *American Teachers: Histories of a Profession at Work.* New York: Macmillan.

Wiebe, Robert H. 1962. *Businessmen and Reform: A Study of the Progressive Movement.* Cambridge, MA: Harvard University Press.

————. 1967. *The Search for Order, 1877–1920.* New York: Hill and Wang.

9

Promoting a Secular Standard

Secularization and Modern Journalism, 1870–1930

Richard W. Flory

What is to prevent a daily newspaper from being made the greatest organ of social life? Books have had their day—the theatres have had their day—the temple of religion has had its day. . . . A newspaper can send more souls to Heaven, and save more from hell, than all the churches or chapels in New York.

JAMES GORDON BENNETT, PUBLISHER, *New York Herald*, 1836

The journalist belongs to a sort of pariah caste, which is always estimated by "society" in terms of its ethically lowest representative.

MAX WEBER, 1918

Images of the press seem to remain fairly constant over time. Although it might be an overstatement to suggest that journalism can save one's soul from hell, or that journalists are the least ethical members of society, both the aspirations of journalists and the perceptions of the profession of journalism do still approximate these positions, at least on occasion. Much, in fact, has been written in recent years about the problems of the press, from how it misunderstands and misrepresents various religious perspectives, to how it may undermine American democracy and how a new model for journalism is needed (e.g., see Fallows 1997; Fuller 1996; Hoover 1998; Rosen 1999). Regardless of the problems identified or the solutions presented, it is generally accepted that a free press is essential to a free society, and that, despite its problems, the press and its limitations must be maintained.

Implicit within both critiques of and proposals for journalism is the power that the press has to influence large segments of the population. Michael Schudson (1995) has argued that although the news media should not be considered "responsible for directly and intentionally indoctrinating the public" (41), the media bestow "public legitimacy," on news items, and "amplify" their importance, by virtue of the fact that the items are published or otherwise presented in a professional journalistic forum (19). In this chapter, I focus on two limited areas of journalism history: changes in the presentation of traditional religion in the press—specifically the *New York Times*—and efforts to establish the "profession" of journalism, in particular, the efforts of what I call "journalism professionalizers," between 1870 and 1930, to establish a distinct identity for journalists and journalism, and the effects of these efforts in the changing conception of religion in the press and thus the role of journalism in promoting new ideas about religion.

The contribution of religion to the development of journalism in the United States has been largely marginalized, to the extent that it has been addressed at all, by journalism historians. In journalism textbooks throughout the twentieth century, religion was consistently dismissed in a paragraph or two as a form of journalism that simply couldn't compete in the marketplace of modern journalism. James Melvin Lee, who in the 1910s was the director of the Department of Journalism at New York University and authored the first general history of journalism published in the twentieth century (Olasky 1991: 136), provides a representative description of one religious newspaper:

> The *New York Daily Witness,* a "Christian, one-cent, afternoon newspaper," appeared . . . on July 1, 1871, and aimed not only to be religious in character, but also "to give the news of the day and much excellent family reading besides." It inserted no advertisement of "liquors, theaters, lotteries, or anything inconsistent with its character." It failed to receive the financial support it expected and was fittingly interred in the newspaper graveyard alongside its more secular companions. (Lee 1917: 332; for similar treatments, see Villard 1923; Kobre 1959; Emery and Emery 1988)

This approach to the role of religion in journalism history has persisted despite more recent research showing that various religious groups were at the forefront of both technological innovation in publishing and the development of regional and national distribution networks of various journalistic publications. These developments in mass media from religious sources were imitated and adopted by secular journalism organizations, which ultimately became the large corporate newspapers and magazines that dominated the journalistic landscape after the Civil War (Nord 2000; see also Sloan 2000).[1]

The few studies that have addressed the issue of the secularization of journalism have come to essentially opposite conclusions. Marvin Olasky (1988; 1991) has argued that journalism in the United States was a distinctly Christian enterprise prior to the rise of the penny press in the 1830s, the development of which effectively drove religious journalism from the marketplace. For Olasky, the secularization of the press was the result of a conflict of ideas in which secular ideas, promoted by powerful journalists and publishers, each of whom subscribed to some form of a materialist world view, simply won out over religious ideas (Olasky 1991). Mark Silk

(1995), on the other hand, has argued that journalism, although its practitioners may be personally inimical to religion, nonetheless have consistently presented religion in a positive light. In this, Silk argues that journalism has developed five *topoi*, which are "set pieces" or "simple and uncomplicated themes," that provide a news story about religion with a "familiar (social) context of meaning" (Silk 1995: 50). These *topoi*, Silk argues, find their source in religion; that is, journalists consistently frame religion in the same terms used by various religious groups to describe themselves. Ultimately then, the power of journalism over religion is circumscribed by the public itself, in that stories of religion rarely, if ever, go against common conceptions of religion.

In this chapter I present a different story than either Olasky or Silk; I argue that in pursuing their two primary interests—of establishing and expanding their journalistic enterprises, and establishing the profession of journalism—key persons within journalism (especially publishers and editors, and also journalism professionalizers from the ranks of the universities and the active press) actively sought to minimize and ultimately to undermine traditional religion. In this, traditional religion was presented as being too sectarian and lacking in modern understanding, and modern science was emphasized as the authoritative voice for modern life. Their motivation was twofold. First, economic concerns provided the context, especially as related to selling advertising space and establishing circulation, that led to reducing and ultimately eliminating different forms of advocacy journalism, including particularistic religious advocacy. Second, professionalization efforts that relied on scientific and legal models, for reasons of increased status and establishing jurisdiction over the news field (see Abbott 1988), ultimately privileged scientific authority over religious authority in reporting and in editorial content and, in the process, presented journalism as the profession best suited to succeed religion in the modern world.

Thus, journalism played a significant role in the secularization of American public life by spreading ideas adopted from other institutional spheres of knowledge-production to the general public, calling into question traditional religion and offering in its place, a modern, scientific perspective, appropriate to the age.

CHANGES IN RELIGION REPORTING

During the period 1870–1930, there was a general decline in both the space devoted to religion reporting and the positive presentation of traditional religion in journalistic accounts. Hornell Hart, reporting for the President's Research Committee on Recent Social Trends in 1933, argued that "the most fundamental change in the intellectual life of the United

TABLE 9.1 Trends in Religion Reporting, 1900–1930

	1900	1930
Magazine circulation (% of total periodicals)		
Popular scientific	1.02	3.73
Religious	4.69	0.83
	1905–1909	*1930–1931*
Articles dealing with religion (per 1,000 indexed in the *Reader's Guide*)	21.4	10.7
	1905	*1931*
Stories favorable to traditional religion (%)		
Popular magazines	78	33
	1912–1914	*1930*
Intellectual magazines	57	18

Source: Hart 1933.

States . . . is the apparent shift from Biblical authority and sanctions to scientific and factual authority and sanctions" (Hart 1933: 390). Among his findings were the following (see table 9.1): The circulation of religious periodicals declined, as a percentage of all periodicals, from 4.69 percent in 1900 to 0.83 percent in 1930, while "popular scientific" periodicals increased from 1.02 to 3.73 percent. In addition, articles emphasizing religion, as indexed in the *Reader's Guide,* dropped from an average of 21.4 stories per year between 1905 and 1909, to 10.7 stories per year, in the years 1930 and 1931 (398). Hart reported a similar pattern when these stories were analyzed for their content; in 1905, 78 percent were favorable to "traditional Christianity" on such measures as "the infallible Bible, traditional creeds, church organization and the propagation of organized Christianity," but this percentage had declined to 33 percent by 1931. These numbers showed an even greater decline when the magazines analyzed were what Hart termed, "intellectual" magazines such as the *Atlantic, World's Work,* and *Survey.* Between 1912 and 1914, traditional Christianity was written of approvingly 57 percent of the time, which declined to 18 percent in 1930 (405).

Similar patterns of decline in the number of religion stories were found in the *New York Times.* As reported by Robert B. Pettit (1986), coverage of religion by the *Times* declined in both frequency and prominence from the 1850s to the 1930s.[2] Among Pettit's findings are the following (see table 9.2): The percentage of news space devoted to religion coverage declined

TABLE 9.2 Trends in Religion Reporting, 1900–1930

Coverage of Religion	1875	1935
Percentage of total news space	6.85	2.13
Percentage of all stories	6.07	3.17
Percentage of page one stories	20.05	2.8
No. of mentions of religion per 1,000 cm of nonreligion advertising space	38.89	2.41

Source: Pettit 1986.

from 6.85 percent of the total news space in 1875 to 2.13 percent in 1935. In 1875, 6.07 percent of all *Times* stories were religion-oriented, but in 1935 this was only 3.17 percent. In 1875, 20.5 percent of all page one stories were religion-oriented stories; in 1935, only 2.8 percent of the page one stories dealt with religion. Finally, in 1875, religion was mentioned an average of 38.89 times per 1,000 centimeters of nonreligion advertising space, while in 1935, religion was mentioned only 2.41 times in the same amount of advertising space.[3]

In order to determine what the reduction in news space devoted to coverage of religion might mean in terms of how religion was treated on the pages of the *New York Times*, in particular asking whether there is any indication of secularizing tendencies, we need to analyze the content of the articles and editorials themselves. Does the content indicate a process of secularization? In particular, focusing on how conceptions of authority, whether religious or secular, were presented, we ask, Is religious authority represented as normative or preferable, or is a secular and/or scientific authority represented as normative or preferable to any religious authority? (see Chaves 1993, 1994). Finally, do the articles show evidence that such a decline is the result of different professionalization strategies of journalists?

I focus primarily on editorials published in the *New York Times* between 1870 and 1930, because the editorials, rather than the news stories, demonstrate in a more systematic way the more general position of the paper, in this case, regarding religion.[4] In addition, the editorial board of the *Times* maintained an amazing consistency of personnel between 1870 and the 1930s, consisting of three primary members: Charles Ransom Miller, Rollo Ogden, and John Huston Finley. This consistency over time of the *Times* editorial board, and the personal histories of the editors—which suggest that they each would be friendly to religion—thus provides a control on other factors, in particular new editors with different views of religion, which might in themselves contribute to a change in the treatment of religion in its editorials. Further, Adolph Ochs, owner and publisher of the *Times* (he purchased the paper in 1896), acted as the chair of the editorial board and regularly sat in on the editorial meetings, in part because of his concern with editorial content (Davis 1921; Berger 1951).

Ochs maintained an active presence in the editorial process, considering himself to be "the final word if there was a disagreement" over any particular editorial within what was widely considered to be a conservative editorial policy (Tifft and Jones 1999: 45). For example, Ochs, writing to his son-in-law and heir apparent, Arthur Hays Sulzberger in 1932, instructed that "[o]ur vocation should be more to inform and interpret. . . . It has been the policy of the *Times* to be conservative and cautious and not involve itself in all public clamor for a change, etc." (quoted in Shepard 1996: 105). This approach was apparently established in Ochs's first days as publisher in that he believed that "crusading editorials only alienated readers and advertisers," leading to a policy of editorials that were "largely drained of vehemence and advocacy, except on important questions such as the choice of a president" (Tifft and Jones 1999: 45).

Charles Miller, who first wrote for the editorial page of the *Times* in 1881, became the editor-in-chief in 1883 and remained in that position until just before his death in 1922, thus providing an important link from the pre-Ochs-owned *Times* and to its development into the "newspaper of record"[5] that it was to become in the early twentieth century. Miller was Dartmouth-educated and had worked only as a journalist, briefly for the *Springfield (Massachusetts) Republican,* and for the *Times* for the remainder of his career. Rollo Ogden, who had previously been the editor at the *New York Post,* came to the *Times* in 1920 and succeeded Miller as editor-in-chief in 1922. Ogden was the son of a minister and an ordained Presbyterian minister himself; he had served on the pastoral staff of two different churches and been a missionary in Mexico City. Ogden retired in 1937. John Finley's tenure at the *Times* can best be thought of as a capstone to a career that spanned higher education, both as a professor and college president, philanthropy, and journalism. Finley, like Ogden, was a Presbyterian, and was active both within that denomination and in more ecumenical endeavors, such as the Federal Council of Churches of Christ in America (forerunner of the National Council of Churches). He first came to the *Times* in 1921 as an associate editor and succeeded Ogden as editor-in-chief in 1937, retiring from the *Times* in 1938.

Religion in the Times

In the 1870s and the 1880s, the *New York Times* showed a notable tendency in its editorial content toward an explicitly pro-religion and, more specifically, pro-Protestant Christianity stance. In commenting on the efforts of Catholic leaders in Cincinnati, who were engaged in an effort to ban the reading of the Bible in public schools because the version of the Bible being used was Protestant, the *Times* argued for the importance of resisting "papal influence," and for the importance of maintaining Bible reading as a part of the school curriculum:

> [I]t is not so easy to understand how any Christian minister can reconcile it with his duty, to place the Bible under a papal interdict, so far as our common schools are concerned, and to assert the principle of the daily reading of the Scriptures is too unimportant a privilege to be worth contending for.
>
> It is not a question with us of introducing the Bible into schools, but of deliberately rejecting it. If it were the former, we should, in the highest interests of future generations, counsel the use of the Bible. But when we are asked to reverse a settled policy at the instigation of those who are irreconcilably opposed to our entire free school system, how can we hesitate about the answer we ought to return? (3/17/1870, 4)

Certainly a part of the *Times*'s position was its general opposition to Catholicism during this period, which continued at least through the 1890s. As evidenced by its response when the situation was reversed, the *Times* opposed Catholic efforts to introduce Bible reading for Catholic students, arguing against any "sectarian instruction" being forced upon the children whose parents were unwilling to have them receive such instruction. In this, the *Times* concluded that the only proper response was to make public schooling, "absolutely secular" (3/20/1890, 4). But this plea for secular schools was primarily a continuation of an anti-Catholic stance; the *Times*, on other religious issues, continued to argue for traditional religious values.

Especially illustrative in this regard is how the *Times* responded to the confrontation between science and religion that was just beginning to take shape in the 1870s and culminated in the Fundamentalist/Modernist controversy and the infamous Scopes trial of 1925. In editorials from the 1870s and 1880s, the *Times* argued for the importance of maintaining traditional religious understandings and opposed replacing them with more modern, scientific approaches. By the mid-1920s however, traditional religion was becoming an embarrassment, and by 1930 the *Times* was promoting what was essentially a new religion, compatible with modern science.

In a December 1875 editorial, the *Times*, using the Christmas season as an opportunity to "bring home to the mind the sacred associations" of the season, expressed its concern that science and its practitioners seemed to be working to undermine Christianity, rather than simply to expand the range of its own knowledge:

> Men of unquestionable learning and ability are everywhere striving to destroy the foundation of the Christian religion. They insist that God cannot and does not exist, but that the universe is governed by some unknown laws, which are the result of spontaneous evolution. . . . The belief in a wise and beneficent God, or in Eternal Wisdom ruling all things according to its own immutable

decrees, or in any dealings of the Creator with man, or in a life hereafter—all this is summarily rejected by the philosophers. It almost seems at times as though the present aim of science was not so much to enlarge its own boundaries and fields of knowledge, as to convince the world that Christianity is an imposture [*sic*] and that its founder was merely an amiable enthusiast. (12/26/1875, 6)

This support for traditional religion was still in evidence five years later, when the *Times* published an editorial entitled "The Religion of the Future," a pointed critique of a proposal by a Mr. Leslie Stephen, for a " 'Religion of All Sensible Men,' or, in other words, the religion which is to be adopted at some future time by men who have had the good sense to abandon Christianity" (5/2/1880, 6). Here the paper asked what foundation would remain for the religion of the future, after Christianity had been cleared away:

> Briefly summarized, the creed of the new religion will consist of three articles: 1st, There is no future life; 2d, Expediency is the only rule of conduct; and 3d, Perhaps there is, or has been, a personal God. In point of simplicity, this creed is vastly superior to the Thirty-nine Articles, and it affords no room for tiresome theological speculations. . . . The new religion will have neither priests nor churches, and the only trace of any cult will be confined to poets, who may occasionally write odes to the Great Probable First Cause, or may invoke the Possible God in company with the purely imaginative muses. (5/2/1880, 6)

Regarding the truths from this new religion upon which people might meditate, particularly in times of personal crisis, the *Times* continued that

> these will be, of course, the great truths of science and it is to be hoped that meditation upon them will purify the soul and strengthen the weak-hearted. The criminal who is approaching the gallows will endeavor to fit himself for death by meditating on the great and glorious truth of the binomial theorem [and] some scientific philanthropist will come to his cell and read him comforting extracts from Loomis's Algebra and soothe his way to annihilation by working out quadratic equations on a portable blackboard. (6)

Such critiques of efforts to replace traditional Christianity were not reserved for science and scientists per se—the *Times* was willing to take on even Protestant denominations that were, in the spirit of the times, looking to revise their articles of faith in order to make them more compatible with new scientific approaches to knowledge. Responding to a series of news articles run in the newspaper about the Presbyterian Church debating whether, and how, to revise its historic creeds, the *Times* editorialized that, while it seemed possible to "abandon some of the extreme Calvinistic doctrines and cease to demand a strict construction of the rest," it cautioned, "If the dogmas are taken away, Christianity ceases to exist, and if they are altered, it becomes something else than the Christian religion. Their effort is to preserve their creed intact, and not to make progress in the direction of improving it." The *Times* concluded, somewhat sarcastically, that this was "dreadfully narrow-minded and wholly unworthy of the age. . . . If progress in Christian thought means the rejection of Christian dogmas, progress in geometry must mean the rejection of geometrical axioms, and in their opposition to true progress there is little to choose between Christians and geometricians" (10/5/1880, 4).

By 1885 however, the *Times* had begun to moderate its views of traditional religious teachings and their relationship to modern scientific theory. Between 1885 and 1905, editorials in the *Times* were preoccupied with "heresy hunting" and "heresy trials," pitting conservatives in the Christian churches against the Progressive forces who were seeking, in various ways, to synthesize insights from evolutionary theory, and from the "higher criticism," with Christian theology.[6] In each case, the *Times* framed those on the Progressive side as representing advancement in Christian theology and teaching, and those on the conservative side as being an unnecessary impediment to progress.

In 1885, the *Times* wrote with some astonishment, about a "Rev. Dr. Woodrow," who had been forced to resign from his teaching position in a southern Presbyterian seminary because of his claim to be an evolutionist. The *Times* pointed out that "the trial will be interesting since it will decide whether a man can be at once a Presbyterian and an evolutionist," and argued that Woodrow could not correctly be found guilty of heresy unless evolution was shown to be in conflict with the "Presbyterian confession of faith." For the *Times,* the astonishing fact was that such a trial could be held at all: "The fact that such a trial could not this day be held at the North shows in a very striking way the difference between the North and the South in the respective attitudes toward modern religious thought" (4/5/1885, 8). In 1890, the *Times* wrote in support of an Episcopal priest from Ohio, a "Mr. MacQuery," who was the author of a book that attempted to "reconcile Christianity with evolution" and had been censured by the "Authorities of the Church Congress" for his views. The *Times* concluded that censuring Mr. MacQuery was tantamount to a conviction of heresy, and as such, was unfair. The *Times* argued that, instead, MacQuery should be treated as "one among many searchers after truth, who, though questioning old dogmas, are not opposing them with the desire to destroy the faith, but to make Christianity concordant with the dictates of plain common sense" (7/26/1890, 4).

The *Times* addressed yet another charge of heresy in 1895 when, in the space of four days, it published two editorials about the Episcopal minister "Rev. Heber Newton" of New York City. In his Sunday sermon—which had been published in the *Times*—Rev. Newton had included teachings that opposed the official position of the Episcopal Church regarding the "resurrection of the body" (4/24/1895, 4). In dealing with this issue, the *Times* took great pains to detail the historically different interpretations of this Christian doctrine, citing such sources as the Bible, the Athanasian creed, patristic literature, Tertullian, Justin Martyr, Chrysostom, and St. Augustine (4/28/1895, 4). In this, the *Times* argued that men of good faith throughout the history of the Christian church had presented different perspectives on this teaching, and that the issue regarding Rev. Newton, was not about theological issues but about whether Rev. Newton could hold his beliefs and teach them in opposition to the teachings of the Episcopal Church. The *Times* argued that for Newton to hold such beliefs in itself was not a problem, but because he was teaching them in opposition to the official position of the church, he could no longer be considered a minister in good standing of the Episcopal Church and should "leave the ministry of that Church." For the *Times,* the issue was not whether Newton held personal beliefs that were at odds with the Episcopal Church, or whether his views represented an advance for Christianity—which the *Times* implied that they did—rather, the issue was the moral position of holding a ministerial position in the Episcopal Church and teaching in direct opposition to the teachings of the church.

By the turn of the twentieth century, the *Times* had become more explicit in its acceptance and support of theological Progressives, and openly opposed to the "heresy hunters," whom the *Times* viewed as a disruptive force within the Protestant denominations. In an editorial about the role of the Westminster Confession in the Presbyterian Church, the *Times* suggested that the confession should not be considered as required beliefs for Presbyterian ministers; instead, ministers should simply be constrained from preaching in opposition to the teachings of the confession. The *Times* stated plainly that in its opinion, the "Deity of the Westminster confession has grown incredible . . . and has grown revolting to modern man," and that it was the "pernicious activity" of the "heresy hunters" that needed "to be repressed" (4/22/1900, 4). Similarly, in 1905 the *Times* wrote that the "forces of conservatism" in the churches were going too far in "opposition to everything that admits to classification under the name of 'higher criticism'" and was raising the distinct possibility that they were becoming "merely another name for dogged opposition to progress." The *Times* suggested that the conservative leaders were, as such, "no longer fit" to be "leaders of thought and teachers of doctrine." Responding to the efforts of the Progressives, the *Times* maintained that although adapting church teachings to modern thought could go too far, the benefit of the doubt should be given to the Progressives: "[N]one discovers this sooner than those who are themselves advanced thinkers, and such a tendency corrects itself easily, naturally, and quickly" (5/11/1905, sec. 8, 3).

By 1910, the *Times* wrote approvingly of a plan among Protestant ministers and Catholic priests in New York to cooperate in "promoting religion and morality," and argued, "The one secure basis of all religion is service. No matter what may be the form in which belief may be embodied, the essence of religion, as a social force, is to serve, to serve God and man, and God through man" (1/15/1910, 3). Thus not only were Catholic and Protestant alliances approved, but the *Times* now promoted a more general, functional conception of religion by suggesting that, regardless the particular form of belief, the potential for social good formed the core importance and essence of religion. These developments already seem a significant move away from its defense of traditional Christianity in the 1870s and 1880s to a perspective that placed "advancement" in "modern religious thought" above traditional religious teachings and reduced the claims of all religions to service, yet the *Times* would, over the next twenty years, continue to distance itself from even this conception of religion.

The conflict between science and traditional religion that had begun in the final decades of the nineteenth century reached its zenith in the public battles between so-called fundamentalist and modernist Protestants during the 1910s and 1920s (e.g., see Marsden 1980; Numbers 1993; Larson 1997). These issues not only were debated within the Protestant denominations but were regularly reported in the otherwise secular press, including the *Times*. News coverage in the *Times* was fairly even-handed, in general reporting developments on each side and often publishing articles by representatives from both the fundamentalist and the modernist positions. For example, in 1922, the *Times* published an article by William Jennings Bryan, in which he argued that no evidence of evolution had been produced, and one week later it published a response by Henry Fairfield Osborn, president of the American Museum of Natural History and a popular science author and lecturer, who argued that, contrary to Bryan's assertions, such evidence of evolution was "in the reach of every schoolboy" (quoted in Larson 1997: 31). Similarly, prior to the Scopes trial, the *Times* published what were intended as clear statements of what both fundamentalists and modernists believed, under the banner headline, "Both Sides: Fundamentalism, Evolution." This consisted of two articles: one, by J. Gresham Machen, a professor at Princeton Seminary and activist within the Presbyterian denomination, on the side of the fundamentalists, and the other, by Vernon Kellogg, who was listed as a "Zoologist and Permanent Secretary and Chairman of Educational Relations of the Natural Research Council," representing the modernist position (6/21/1925, sec. 9, 1, 12).

These apparently representative examples of the scientific and the fundamentalist positions notwithstanding, the *Times* editorial position regarding the relationship between science and religion was clearly on the side of science, seeking to distance itself from any religious beliefs that might be construed as sympathetic to the fundamentalist position. At the outset of the trial, the *Times* expressed its concern that the spectacle of religion calling into question modern science would bring "the whole nation under a reproach in the eyes of the world. We should be an object at once of astonishment and ridicule" (7/5/1925, part 2, 2). As the trial proceeded, and the scene in Dayton grew into an ever-larger spectacle—due mostly to the efforts of journalists who had descended on Dayton from across the nation—the *Times* laid the blame for the circus atmosphere not on its fellow journalists, nor even on the presence of Clarence Darrow, one of the most famous trial lawyers in America, who was defending John Scopes, but rather on Bryan:

> No one need be astonished to read of the influx of queer fish at Dayton, Tenn. It would seem that every freak and fanatic not already there is striving to arrive by the next train. It is a fine illustration of the attraction of the well advertised absurdities. . . . Mr. Bryan has given the signal to thousands of unregulated or ill-balanced minds that there is a chance for them at last. No one can yet measure the impulse and encouragement to erratic thinking which the Dayton trial is giving. It is a sort of notice, posted up so that the whole nation can read it, of the breakdown of the reasoning powers. . . . But the demonstrated immense attraction at Dayton for all sorts of half-baked creatures, is an indication of the mental and moral infection which has been let loose upon the land, with Mr. Bryan as its chief agent—let us hope, the unwitting agent. (7/13/1925, 16)

Thus, for the *Times,* the "unregulated," the "ill-balanced mind," "half-baked creatures," and a general lack of reasoning power were associated with the leader of the fundamentalist forces and, presumably, with the type of religious belief that would oppose certain forms of scientific knowledge. Indeed, as the trial neared its end, the *Times* concluded that two primary characteristics of the human mind had been exposed; on the one hand, the trial had "exhibited the tenacity of the mind in clinging to inherited ideas, in holding on to convictions acquired by association, or in defending atavistic inclinations," while on the other, it showed that the "unsatisfied mind," which pushed forward for knowledge, "in spite of all the weight of precedent, the clog of habit, the love of the familiar, the downward pull of passion and the peril of failure," was the reason for the "highest hope" for the future (7/19/1925, part 2, 6).

By 1930, the *Times* had moved well beyond simply being embarrassed by fundamentalist religion, to promoting a new, more "modern" religious perspective, enlisting in the effort such scientific luminaries as Albert Einstein and Nobel Prize winner Robert Millikan, and, on the religious side, G. K. Chesterton and Harry Emerson Fosdick. In the October 9, 1930, issue, the *Times* profiled Harry Emerson Fosdick on the occasion of the opening of the new Riverside Church in New York City. The description of Fosdick was unabashedly admiring, not for religious activities or service, per se, but for the way that he represented, in the words of the *Times* writer, a "new type of minister [that] is swift and strong and dynamic, and resembles the clergyman of old as much as the quick electric elevators that ascend this new edifice resemble the creaky winding stairs that lead through the dark of the tower of an ancient church" (10/9/1930, 5). Throughout the article, the *Times,* through the person of Fosdick, presented what it would later explicitly endorse, a religion that must change with the times, that "grows with the growth of human knowledge." Thus on Fosdick's desk was found not a Bible or other "dusty religious tomes," but only two books of modern detective stories. Indeed, the *Times* gushed, there was about Fosdick, "an air of modernity which pervades the very church itself . . . there is nothing of the recluse about this man. . . . The quickness of his walk and actions is a part of the city's streets, not of the cloister. There is nothing that reeks of old parchments or ancient books of creed. His God is a living God who moves through the life of this generation as evidently as through long-past centuries." Through such a presentation, the *Times* relegates traditional religion to the old, to the musty creedal books, and not to the living, vital activities of the modern man and the modern city.

Throughout the remainder of 1930, the *Times* devoted much space to the question of the relationship between religion and science, including the following: invited feature articles published in the *New York Times Magazine,* by Albert Einstein (11/9/1930) and G. K. Chesterton (12/28/1930); a front-page article on Robert Millikan's presidential address to the American Association for the Advancement of Science (AAAS), complete with the full text of his speech (12/30/1930), under the headline "Millikan Finds Creation Still Goes on While Creator Directs the Universe"; and several *Times* editorials that each argued for the harmony of religion and science, if only religion would change to incorporate the newest scientific discoveries.

Of particular importance here are not the specific arguments of Einstein, Millikan, or Chesterton, but how the *Times* used their arguments to promote its own version of what religion should look like. By way of summary, it is important to point out that neither Einstein nor Millikan wrote in a particularly supportive way about religion, nor did Chesterton write articles that fully supported modern scientific advancement. For example, Einstein's conception of the relationship between religion and science was an evolutionary conception of the development of religion—from primitive religions of fear to moral religions based on sympathetic understanding, which reached its zenith in a third level, "the cosmic religious sense." This level of religion was only available to "exceptionally gifted individuals or especially noble communities . . . and does not involve an anthropomorphic idea of God; the individual feels the vanity of human desires and aims, and the nobility and marvelous order which are revealed in nature and in the world of thought." Of course for Einstein, those most attuned to this cosmic religious sense were those who were working in modern scientific research, whose motivations he claimed, were based on this new religious sense. Millikan's AAAS speech barely mentioned religious themes, despite the *Times* headline. Millikan mentioned only that it had been "speculatively suggested [that radiant energy throughout space] allow[s] the Creator to be continually on His job." Similarly, despite the fact that the *Times* had subtitled Chesterton's article, "Religion, Mr. Chesterton asserts, is the one perfect example of Darwin's survival of the fittest, and great scientists lead the movement away from the camp of materialism," Chesterton merely used Darwin's ideas to argue for the survival of religion because it spoke to eternal human needs, something that he insisted science alone could not—not exactly acquiescing to the modern scientific age.

These articles, however, were used in fairly ingenious ways by the *Times*. In taking parts of the articles—and in the case of Millikan, adding some lines from one of his books and including parts of his personal history—the *Times* presented a conception of religion that was modern, rational, and scientific, in short, a more respectable religion, especially more respectable than its recent presentation by the fundamentalists at the Scopes trial. Following the article by Chesterton and the report on Millikan, a *Times* editorial argued for "a religion which grows with the growth of human knowledge." The editorial then quoted Millikan's book, with part of Chesterton's article woven in as further support. Millikan was quoted as saying, "I believe that essential religion is one of the world's supremest needs, and I believe that one of the greatest contributions that the United States ever can make to world progress will consist in furnishing an example to the world of how the religious life of a nation can evolve intelligently, wholesomely, inspiringly, reverently, completely divorced from all unreason, all superstition and all unwholesome emotionalism." To this the *Times* added Chesterton— only slightly out of context—who noted that "the man of science has come to the help of religion." In the end, it was Millikan the scientist, not Chesterton or even Fosdick, the religionists, to whom the *Times* gave the authority to speak in such terms about religion because, the editorial concluded, "he was born a minister's son; for he must have known religion 'pure and undefiled' as he has come to know pure science" (12/29/30, 20).

The *Times* wrote a similarly themed editorial the day following Einstein's article on religion and science. Recalling Einstein's three forms of religion, the *Times* editorialized, "Einstein called this the 'cosmic religious sense' which comes of contemplating the 'nobility and marvelous order revealed in nature and the world of thought.' It involved no 'God made in man's image,' but none the less recognizes an ancient of days, an antecedent power that set all things in motion and developed living, sentient beings." The *Times* concluded, "Certainly those who make researches into the very sources of existence should be profoundly religious, though it cannot be admitted that they are, as one of Einstein's contemporaries has said, 'the only deeply religious people'" (11/10/30, 20). In this then, not only has science become authoritative over religion, but it is the scientists, through their scientific work, whom the *Times* presents as having authority for genuine religious searching.

The *New York Times* editorial content shows a changing conception of religion over time. As science advanced, and as the battles over evolution, science, and religion heated up, the *Times*'s presentation of religion changed from reports and editorials generally supportive of the authority of traditional religion to, by 1930, an emphasis on religious progress and the harmony of science and religion, with science dominant over religion. Ultimately, the type of religion that was being promoted by the *Times* was a new religious expression in which science and rationality were authoritative, and it was only through them—and their foremost representatives like Einstein and Millikan—that religion would move forward.

Given these developments in the treatment of traditional religion in the *New York Times,* what developments within the larger culture and in the history of journalism itself can help account for these changes? In the sections that follow, I sketch out the historical development of journalism from the nineteenth to the twentieth centuries and then show how efforts to professionalize journalism led to a promotion of secular scientific values over traditional religious values both in the pages of the *New York Times* and within the profession of journalism more generally.

CONTEXT: JOURNALISM IN NINETEENTH-CENTURY AMERICA

The Rise of the Penny Press

Until the end of the 1830s, journalism in America consisted primarily of political party publications. Their content was unabashedly partisan, and they were funded by the political parties. What we would understand as "news" content was minimal, with political editorial content being the goal of the paper. By the 1830s however, the "penny press" emerged and brought with it several advances toward what can be called "modern" journalistic practice (Schudson 1978; 1988). These changes included a reduced price for the newspaper, from six cents to one cent per copy, thus making information more accessible to the masses, and the "nonsubscription" plan. Prior to the emergence of the penny press, newspapers were sold on a yearly subscription basis at a price that put them out of reach of most people; they were primarily oriented to the business and political classes. The nonsubscription plan, usually credited to James Gordon Bennett of the *New York Herald,* made newspapers available on a daily basis, at a reasonable price. Thus the news and views of a particular paper were more broadly accessible due to reduced cost and increased availability of the newspapers. Other changes the penny press brought were an officially nonpartisan stance in the reporting of news; an increase in the reporting of daily occurrences; and a switch from reliance on political patronage resources to advertising for revenues.

With these came changes in the content of the paper; as newspapers were established as nonpartisan publications, they were aimed in price and content at the mass of society and created a mass outlet for businesses to advertise on a daily or weekly basis to a wide segment of the city.

Journalism as a Commercial Enterprise

As newspapers became nonpartisan rather than partisan, editors and publishers had to find new patronage to support their efforts. Beginning in the penny press era, and extending across the nineteenth century, newspapers increasingly relied upon advertising for their revenues. As costs increased over time, this relationship became even more crucial—newspapers needed to establish high circulation numbers so that they could attract advertising dollars, and as circulation wars heated up, the nature of news was changed (Schudson 1978; Dicken-Garcia 1989; Baldasty 1992).

In this process, news became a managed, packaged commodity to be sold to consumers. Innovations such as society gossip columns, comics, jokes, human interest stories, and content tailored to specific segments of the population, whether women or the working class, were the result primarily of the conception of news as a commodity, and of a shift in the understanding of the news audience from that of voters, as in the politically partisan era, to that of consumers, for both the newspapers and the advertisers. Covert has observed that by the twentieth century, journalism had developed into a "massive inter-connected industry shaped by chain ownership and devoted to the sale of news, opinion and entertainment. These major products of the industry enticed buyers into the marketplace of its advertising columns, thus consolidating a major role for the daily press in the national system for distributing goods and services" (1975: 67).

Such commercialization brought about a significant change in how news was conceived, packaged, and created. On the one hand, this allowed journalists to, as they framed it, be more honest in their reports, in that they were no longer beholden to any vested political interest. On the other hand, they had simply shifted their obligation; that is, although it was not as blatantly partisan, journalism was dependent on advertisers for its primary stream of revenue, and so publishing stories that worked at cross purposes with the interests of advertisers was to be avoided. This was a form of self-censorship to be sure, but one motivated by the possibility of real threats from advertisers, who would withhold their advertising dollars if the content of stories did not meet their approval.[7]

Commenting on this relationship and its effects on journalism, John Macy, the Harvard-educated literary editor of the *Boston Herald,* observed that the content of newspapers was "amazingly uniform from Portland, Maine, to Portland, Oregon. It is . . . a . . . unified institution fed by the same news services and dominated by kindred financial interests" (Macy 1922: 36). The reason, he argued, was that "[n]o idea inimical to the advertiser's business or in general to the business system of which he is a dependent part must be allowed in the paper. Therefore all newspapers are controlled by the advertising department, that is, the counting-room" (45). Bourdieu (1998) has argued, similarly, that owing to its "permanent trial by market," journalism, through the competition between different journalism organizations over the "newest news," favors uniformity in the journalistic product rather than originality and diversity (71, 72). The practical result in newspapers was, as Bagdikian has argued, that they "neutralized information for fear that strong news and views pleasing to one part of the audience might offend another part and thus reduce the circulation on which advertising rates depend" (2000: 178). Bagdikian goes on to say that "socially sensitive material of interest to one segment of the population might offend those with different opinions who, regardless of their differences, might possess the relevant quality of interest to newspapers—money to spend on advertisers' products. News became neutralized both in selection of items and in the nature of writing" (179).

Yet as Benedict Anderson has argued, the consumption of this mass-produced, relatively uniform news product made it possible for readers to "think about themselves and relate themselves to others" (1991: 36). In this, newspapers ultimately served the interests of nation-building in the United States, showing through its various news items "that one is bound together with a multitude engaged in a steady, simultaneous activity, sharing a common culture and symbol" (Leonard 1995: 30). Thus, by providing similar stories, views, and opinions, newspapers, in response to an increasingly diverse population and emphasizing common cultural symbols, refrained from printing perspectives—either in editorials or otherwise in the news reports—that would serve to alienate segments of their customer base. With regard to religion reporting, as America increasingly became an urban instead of a rural nation, a nation of immigrants with increasingly diverse religious identities, newspapers would become less approving of sectarian religion, presenting instead a more generalized conception of religion that was compatible with a broader segment of the population.

Science and the Quest for Objectivity in Journalism

A final development, related to both the commercialization of journalism and its emerging professionalization, needs to be outlined: the rise of the ideal of objectivity in journalism. Michael Schudson (1978) and David Mindich (1998) each trace objectivity in journalism to the development of science and a more generalized infatuation with facts among the American public during the nineteenth century. It was in the context of new scientific discoveries, many leading, for example, to improved public health conditions, and others simply providing a wider view of the world, that journalists also became obsessed with fact-gathering. This was initially what Schudson has termed a "naive empiricism" on the part of journalists, which assumed that the facts could speak for themselves, if only enough facts were gathered and put together in the story. Mindich argues that the 1890s were the high point for the objectivity ideal, as evidenced by stirrings of professionalization within journalism, and by the "textbooks [that] told journalism students to 'chronicle, don't comment,' and newspapers and wire services . . . [that] embraced 'objectivity' and the idea that reality lies between competing truth claims" (1998: 14).

Yet some conflicting developments in journalism seemed to work at odds with a commitment to objectivity, in particular the encouragement in journalism textbooks, and on the part of some editors, to add "color" to news stories (Covert 1975; Schudson 1988).[8] In this, although objectivity was the normative ideal, reporters had developed "ways of evoking reader emotion, memory and identification with the universally appealing experiences they described. They knew how to appeal to both subjective and intuitional means of knowing, permitting readers to experience vicariously and to feel as well as think about the life that was reported" (Covert 1975: 67). Indeed, as Charles Merz, later the editor of the *New York Times,* wrote in 1925, an important strategy in this regard was to rely on conflict as the main ingredient in any successful news story. This, Merz argued, was especially true since conflict often included sex: "[I]n sex and crime, we have . . . [in] compact and vivid [form], the personal fight with the well-identified antagonists and the stage is set for suspense. If theology and religion envy sex and crime and sigh for first-page space, all that theology and religion need to do is produce a good personal encounter" (quoted in Covert 1975: 92).

As the ideals of objective reporting came into conflict with these more subjective aspects of reporting, journalists' conceptions of objectivity, and of their ability to impartially report the facts, also changed. Schudson has argued that journalists, in confronting the reality that true objectivity was indeed impossible, developed a greater ideology of objectivity than had existed before. He ultimately argues that journalists came to embrace the ideal of objectivity despite their conviction that it was impossible, because of the existential crisis that this had created: "Journalists came to believe in objectivity, to the extent that they did, because they wanted to, needed to, were forced by ordinary human aspiration to seek escape from their own deep convictions of doubt and drift" (1978: 159).

Whether or not journalists were facing such an existential crisis, there is broader explanation for their embrace of the objectivity ideal. If we place Schudson's claim within the context of the emerging ideals of professionalization to which journalism aspired, in particular its potential role in society, journalists were left with little choice; that is, if journalism and its approach to understanding the world was to have any value for journalists, they needed to embrace the objectivism ideal as a part of their work and life. Beyond this there were also practical interests at stake. Objectivity became and has remained a professional ideal, borrowed from science, because it served the ends of the profession more broadly, and the efforts of journalism professionalizers more specifically, in conferring on journalism a status similar to that enjoyed by science. This served the purpose of establishing jurisdiction over the news field for journalists and journalism organizations that made plausible claims to objectivity (Abbott 1988). The professional boundaries of journalism are porous; it follows therefore that the greater one's claims to objectivity, and thus to science, the greater one's claims to jurisdiction over the news field, and thus to the social status and societal influence that journalism professionalizers desired.

Within this context, important journalists were organizing to establish the "profession" of journalism and to elevate it to a status equal to that enjoyed by members of the legal and medical professions. The following section describes the efforts of journalism professionalizers to establish a journalistic profession and how, ultimately, they argued that journalism was the ideal successor to religion because it alone could provide the appropriate guidance for both individuals and society.

PROFESSIONALIZING JOURNALISM

Professionalization

Bruce A. Kimball has argued that the term *profession* has changed "episodically" in American history, and that those changes in meaning were directly related to the preeminent vocation to which the term referred. Thus, conceptions of the "ideal" profession have changed over time as one vocation has taken over another as the preeminent, or what Kimball calls the "architectonic," profession, meaning "the dominant science or discipline that gave systematic formalization to the highest values and ideals of the culture, the primary source of cultural validation" (Kimball 1992: 12). Kimball shows that different cultural ideals have characterized the professions at different periods in American history:

> In analyzing the development of the meaning of "profession" through the early twentieth century, I have found it helpful to think in terms of three eras, each identified with a primary source of cultural inspiration and validation, a

cultural ideal. These are "religion" through the mid-eighteenth century, "polity" through the mid-nineteenth century, and "science" through the 1910s. Each of these cultural ideals has special nuances conditioned by the context of the time, and is manifested in what I will call the "architectonic" of the era. (10)

By the twentieth century, Kimball argues, the "true professional ideal" had emerged and was characterized as "a dignified occupation espousing an ethic of service, organized into an association, and practicing functional science" (Kimball 1992: 16–17). Similarly, Abbott has argued that in order for groups to claim "jurisdiction" over specialized knowledge and its applications against competing professions, it must legitimate those claims by appealing to cultural values. Abbott identifies science and, more broadly, formal rationality as the "fundamental ground of the legitimacy of professional techniques" (Abbott 1988: 184–89).

Journalism professionalizers consistently presented two related rationales regarding the need for journalists to professionalize: (1) status, both as perception from the public and in economic terms, and (2) influence and power in society. The dominant reason given to develop journalism into a profession was to improve the status of the field. Organizers consistently compared professional ideals with an image of the old-time "newspaper man," who, although successful at getting the story, was not primarily motivated by any moral or ethical ideals other than getting a good story. As described by Eric W. Allen, the dean of the School of Journalism at the University of Oregon, the "old-timers" were

> able men, enthusiasts, and made a religion of newspaper work. . . . They were suspicious, cynical, unlettered, sharp as a knife, unscrupulous and at the same time idealistic. . . . [The newspaper man's] idea was to expose, attack, fight, excoriate, and then fight some more. His ambition was to dethrone "prominent citizens" and put them in the penitentiary if possible. For he believed that most of them were crooks, and could not have gotten their money as they did if they hadn't been. (Allen 1920: 3)

Allen acknowledged however, that these reporters were not the material out of which the profession of journalism could be built if it was ultimately to be recognized as the "most important of all professions to the success of civilization" (4).

Both Allen and Willard Bleyer, the founding director of the journalism program at the University of Wisconsin and a key journalism professionalizer, argued that in order to attract the best young people to the profession, several developments were required: first, salaries must be improved to levels comparable with those in business and advertising, and second, professional organizations and standards of admission and practice, comparable to those in the medical and legal professions, must be established (Bleyer

1925: 8; Allen 1920: 10). If such improvements were made, Allen believed, the public would more readily accept the journalistic product as professional, would pay more for it, and would eliminate the "cheap competition [that] we suffer from." He concluded that professional organization, looking to raise professional standards, must "serve society first, the paper second and ourselves third," and that it held the best future for journalism (Allen 1920: 10).

Implicit in their desire to elevate the status of journalism, and found more explicitly in the arguments of journalism professionalizers emphasizing the view that journalism should be considered the "educator" of society (see discussion below), is the desire for greater influence and power. The organizers believed that if journalists could be seen as competent, sober professionals, they would have a greater opportunity to influence society. This was often framed in terms of journalism's being the only institution capable of providing truthful facts, "the food of opinion," for the masses, who needed this food in order to form an adequate public opinion, which would guide society.

Beginning in the 1880s, efforts to professionalize journalism began on several different fronts, the most important of which were the publications intended for the journalism profession, the development of programs for journalism education, and the founding of professional organizations. These efforts, although complementary to each other, were not organized by any single segment within journalism but by a combination of educators, newspaper writers, publishers and editors, and even college students.

Journals

Beginning in March, 1884, a publication entitled the *Journalist,* billing itself as "A Weekly Publication Devoted to Newspaper Men and Publishers," began publication (3/22/1884). This journal remained in publication, though in somewhat different form, throughout the entire time period covered by this study and is still published today, under the name *Editor and Publisher.*[9] During the first years of its publication, the *Journalist* included news and information about journalists and newspapers from across the country in addition to a form of editorializing about what the editor believed to be bad developments within journalism, which included personal insult as an integral part of the argument. For example, Joseph Pulitzer was routinely referred to as "Jewseph Pulitzer," and William Randolph Hearst was called "a hoodlum Western newspaper editor who has more to learn about journalism than half the reporters in New York City" (see for example, 6/28/1884, 1; 7/5/1884, 1; 7/12/1884, 1). After the second year of publication however, a new editor dropped this approach, and the format included news of different aspects of journalism, ranging from information about small town and urban newspapers across the country and the "foreign press" to profiles of different newspaper publishers in the United States—especially when they had built an impressive new building—tips on different aspects of journalistic practice, and news of conventions and meetings of different journalistic associations.

A second journal, and the one I use for this analysis, was the *Quill*, which was published monthly beginning in 1912 by Sigma Delta Chi, the national journalism fraternity, and billed itself as "The Journalists' Journal." This journal differed from the *Journalist* in that most of its articles were contributed by editors, publishers, and other prominent figures from within journalism, who had memberships or other connections to Sigma Delta Chi, as well as addresses presented to meetings of journalism professionals. The topics addressed in the *Quill* ranged from rather mundane fraternity "chapter updates," to reports on developments within journalism, including many articles that specifically addressed issues related to the professionalization of journalism. Of particular importance here are the latter, which form what I call the "rhetorical strategies" of key journalism professionalizers, particularly as they articulated the perceived need to raise the level of journalistic practice from the popular conception of the "newspaper game," peopled by colorful but perhaps unsavory characters, to one that could actually carry the name "profession" of journalism.[10]

Journalism Education

Attempts in American colleges and universities to establish journalism programs date from immediately after the Civil War, when Robert E. Lee tried to establish such a program at Washington College (Virginia) in 1869. Although several additional efforts were attempted, and abandoned, between 1869 and 1905—including Joseph Pulitzer's initial proposal to endow a school of journalism at Columbia in 1892—the first permanent program was established at the University of Wisconsin in 1905, and within ten years, journalism departments and schools existed at eighteen universities (Bleyer 1934: 12). By 1926, this number had grown to fifty schools and departments of journalism, with 5,532 journalism students enrolled in these programs ("Journalism Education" 1926: 3). The importance placed on journalism education was addressed not only in different school publications such as school catalogs, where both course listings and program rationale were routinely published, but also by journalism educators and other organizers, in articles published in the *Quill* (Williams 1925; Bleyer 1934).

The course offerings of different programs and the rationale presented for journalism education, both from the universities and as published in the *Quill,* serve as important sources for determining the amount and type of education that was believed to be essential for professional journalists and, more generally, for understanding the values to which journalism was to aspire.

Journalism Associations

The first journalistic association to be organized was an undergraduate fraternity at DePauw University (Indiana), in 1909. Although originally a fraternity for journalism students, it was founded around somewhat broader ideals related to the journalism profession:

1. To associate college journalists of talent, truth, and energy into a more intimately organized unit of good fellowship.

2. To assist the members in acquiring the noblest principles of journalism and to co-operate with them in this field.

3. To advance the standards of the press by fostering a higher ethical code, thus increasing its value as an uplifting social agency (Sigma Delta Chi 1926).

By 1913, Sigma Delta Chi had become the official national fraternity for journalism, by vote of the American Conference of Teachers of Journalism, and ultimately became the Society for Professional Journalism, the main professional association for journalism. The importance of Sigma Delta Chi lay in its efforts to socialize college students into the norms and ideals of professional journalism, and to maintain continuing education for alumni who were working in the field of journalism, through the publication of the *Quill* and through its annual meetings, which routinely took up issues related to professional ideals and education. As one major report from the fraternity stated,

> Sigma Delta Chi . . . continues where the school of journalism leaves off. . . . It will send picked men, the cream of the journalism student bodies, trained in ethics and ideals, into the ranks of journalism practitioners. Sigma Delta Chi will . . . continue to influence these men. As they assume responsibility of making and directing the editorial policies of the publications which they serve, as they attain "the seats of the mighty," who can deny that Sigma Delta Chi will be serving the cause of better journalism? (Sigma Delta Chi 1926)

Other associations were also founded in this era with goals similar to those of Sigma Delta Chi, working toward a professional journalism: the American Association of Teachers of Journalism (AATJ) in 1912; the American Association of Schools and Departments of Journalism (AASDJ), a development from within the ranks of the AATJ, in 1917; and in 1923, the American Society of Newspaper Editors (ASNE). Most important for this analysis were the establishment and activities of the AATJ and AASDJ, in conjunction with Sigma Delta Chi. These organizations fostered a standardized journalism course of study for programs at American colleges and universities, and encouraged the professionalization of journalism, promoting the professional ideals to which those in journalism should aspire. Resolutions and program developments from each of these organizations were routinely published in the *Quill.*

Strategies

We can place the strategies employed by journalism professionalizers in two general categories, each intended to provide legitimacy for the professional status of journalism. First, *organizational strategies*—that is, the establishment of the associations, educational programs, and publications noted above— provided an organizational base from which journalism professionalizers operated. Second, *rhetorical strategies,* shaped the content and form of arguments used to articulate journalistic ideals and thus to legitimate a particular type of journalistic activity that they termed *professional.*

Organizational Strategies

Journalism professionalizers implemented several organizational strategies that provided an institutional base for their activities, which implied the same organization for journalism as had developed in the dominant—per Kimball, architectonic—professions of medicine and law. The successful strategies of the medical and legal professions were repeatedly referenced as models for the development of the journalistic profession; in particular, educational programs were developed for the adequate preparation of journalists and codes of ethics and standards of practice were created by the different professional organizations. Willard Bleyer, of Wisconsin, argued that journalism "must establish and maintain standards for admission and standards of practice, not unlike those of the older professions of law and medicine" (1925: 7). In this same article, Bleyer referenced the medical and legal professions as models for journalism to emulate a total of four times. Several other articles used the same comparison to argue for the development of these structures for journalism (e.g., see Getz 1916; Murphy 1922; Crawford 1925).

The establishment of departments and schools of journalism was an explicit effort to begin developing a professional infrastructure for the training and professionalization of new journalists, modeled after medical and law school programs. A typical rationale for the type of training the student was to receive emphasized the practical aspects of the coursework, in particular, the preparation for the journalism field. Indiana University presents a typical program description:

> The special courses in Journalism are planned to give the student a broad general idea of modern newspaper conditions and methods, together with

some helpful specific instruction to make his beginning easier and clearer in the field he is most likely to enter first—that of reporting. . . . Conditions [in journalism] are rapidly changing, but the importance of the subject is becoming more and more generally recognized, and it is receiving much study and investigation. In a course on "Principles and Methods of Journalism," this accumulating material is dealt with from the point of view of practical experience in newspaper work. (Indiana University 1911: 135–36)

In its curricular requirements, each program showed essentially the same pattern, beginning with a basic program and gradually expanding the course offerings and developing different specializations as the programs grew. Although schools varied in the way they put their programs together, the primary emphasis in each was on the more practical aspects of journalism: writing, newspaper history, legal issues, typesetting, and business issues. Eventually they offered other coursework in areas like advertising, illustration and artwork, and the teaching of journalism. In addition, coursework addressed basic journalistic principles like objectivity in reporting and the duty of the journalist to the profession and to the community. For example, on an examination dated June 5, 1917, for the class in editing at the University of Washington, the first question reads, "Discuss at some length the extent to which a newswriter's personality affects the stories he writes. To what extent should the newswriter consciously permit his stories thus to be affected? Do not make the sweeping negative answer frequently heard: that a news story never should bear the imprint of the author's individuality at all, which is neither practicable nor true" (University of Washington 1917).

In addition to the more practically oriented journalism curriculum, each program required students to be "broadly trained" by taking coursework in history, political science, economics, sociology, philosophy, psychology, and literature, which was usually framed as "fundamental" or "essential" to "journalistic work."[11] Such studies were viewed as essential because they would provide the student journalist with an appropriately broad context within which to interpret the information that was to be formed into "news." Of particular importance was an understanding of the "modern world" and the ability to interpret its events within the appropriate frame of reference. The course entitled "Problems of Contemporary Thought," offered in 1923–1924 at Northwestern University, provides an excellent example. Its description reads as follows:

This course is designed to give the student a unified idea of the world in which he lives. A survey of the sciences, the problems of social action and the appreciative and spiritual interests of the individual will be made with an aim to coordinate the student's knowledge and to help him to relate the fragments of his educational experience in an intelligible whole. Weekly lectures by authorities in natural science, biology, psychology, sociology, history, economics, art and philosophy will be given progressively, with a plan, not only to correlate these interests, but to suggest their tendencies of new growth and future changes. The lectures as a group are planned to present a survey of the field of modern thought. (Northwestern University 1923–1924: 447)

Thus, student journalists were trained to be generalists, with "authorities" from these disciplines instructing them in an overview of the latest findings and theories in these fields of modern thought. The appropriately "modern" context for the student journalist, then, was to be understood only through these perspectives, apparently excluding any discussions of religion.

Together, the establishment of schools, professional associations, and publications worked to provide not only such important things as training in journalistic skills and values, but a context in which journalists could, beginning in college, be socialized into the journalistic profession, be given an identity, and provided with support and community throughout their career in the professional organizations. In addition, these different structures provided the resources with which organizers could operate and work toward establishing the profession of journalism, through developing programs and organizations modeled on those of the legal and medical professions. This in turn helped them to begin promoting a more unified model of professional journalism to the public and thus gain some measure of respect for their work. As Andrew Abbott has argued, "In the last century, science, with the broader, related phenomenon of formal rationality, has become the fundamental ground for the legitimacy of professional techniques. In the value scheme on which modern professions draw, science stands for logic and rigor in diagnosis . . . it implies extensive academic research based on the highest standards of rationality" (Abbott 1988: 189). Thus, structures modeled on the medical and legal professions implied scientific rigor and allowed journalism to appeal, at least implicitly, to the dominant cultural value of science for the legitimation of its efforts. As I show below, this acceptance of a rational, scientific model ultimately resulted in the rejection of religion as a cultural authority and the simultaneous claim by journalism professionalizers that only journalism was suited to take the place in society formerly occupied by religion.

Rhetorical Strategies

The efforts of journalism professionalizers were not restricted to the organizational strategies detailed above; they included articles published in their newly established journals articulating their vision of professional journalism. These were intended to both educate and mobilize journalists toward their conception of journalism. Rhetorical strategies developed by professionalizers fall into five different patterns, which were often interwoven into single statements and were all intimately related. These patterns are as follows: (1) Journalism was essential to civilization, even more so than medicine and law. (2) The evolution of journalism from more primitive forms to "professional" status was assumed to be inevitable. (3) Journalism was to be the "educator" of the masses. (4) Traditional religion was dealt with in a way that abstracted religion to more general ethical and moral teachings, treating all religions as equivalent yet essentially powerless in the modern world. (5) Professional journalism was the functional equivalent and successor of religion.

Journalism as Essential to Civilization   The first pattern of rhetorical strategy presents journalism as the most essential profession to modern society because of its privileged position of gathering and disseminating knowledge to the masses. Accurate, truthful knowledge, as distributed through newspapers and other journalistic means, was presented as the most basic requirement for society, such that citizens could make appropriate decisions not only about public issues, but also about their own lives.

Herbert Swope, the founder of the American Society of Newspaper Editors, and the executive editor of the *New York World,* argued that "civilization is communication, for understanding flows from knowledge, which is primarily based on communication" (Swope 1924: 6) and that, ultimately, it is through this "understanding," that civilization will be advanced:

> [F]or its evolution civilization needs less sumptuary regulation and more education. It needs fewer laws of compulsion and more laws of reason. It needs less of enforced obedience and more of a free choice. In this adventure the Press takes a leading role. It offers in evidence a daily record of the thought and the action of man, a record that has a vast influence on behavior. (7)

Willard Bleyer went even further in stating the importance of journalism for society, elevating journalism to a position more important to the welfare of society than the medical and legal professions. He argued that while the actions of an incompetent doctor or lawyer would only result in "kill[ing] off prematurely [no] more than a few hundred persons," or might cost a client "loss of money, of freedom, or even of life itself," these would be insignificant in comparison to the damage that an "ignorant, incompetent reporter" could cause to society. Indeed, Bleyer argued, the very success of democracy, "is dependent on the competency and the character of our newspaper writers and editors, and I submit to you that the success of our democracy is more vital to the welfare of society than is the possible loss of lives, the money, or the freedom of a few of its members" (Bleyer 1925: 4).

The Inevitable Evolution of Journalism   The second pattern was framed in two different contexts, one in which modern journalism had naturally developed as society became more modern and complex, and another which presented journalism as developing because of the advances made in journalism education. H. F. Harrington, the dean of the journalism program at the University of Illinois, and later director of the Northwestern University journalism school, represented the view that journalism—specifically newspapers—had developed from being a "simple recorder of events" to a "compilation of every line of human activity." He further described the newspaper as the "moving-picture of today's passing show" and understood this development to be a result of the "complexity of city life" that had developed since the Civil War (Harrington 1919: 7). The complementary view held that, while in the past all professions had originally utilized an apprenticeship model for training new members, they had all developed "professional school" programs for training, so journalism was developing on the same path as had the legal, medical, and engineering professions (Bleyer 1925: 4).

Journalism as the Educator of the Masses   The third pattern emerged in several different accounts of the ideals of professional journalism. Professionalizers argued that journalism alone was positioned to provide the "facts" upon which public opinion, and thus action, could be based. It was journalism that would operate as the educator for life that would ensure an enlightened and moral public (e.g., see Cohen 1915; Bleyer 1925; Swope 1924; McKernon 1925; Williams 1924). The educative ideal of professional journalism was even memorialized in the official song of Sigma Delta Chi, the last verse of which reads, "We play the song of life upon a rattletrap machine, and daily sell the music for a sou, Our business is to brighten men, to frighten and enlighten men, To teach them what they should and shouldn't do" ("In Sigma Delta Chi" 1925: 20).

This does not seem to have been mere hyperbole on the part of the journalism fraternity; rather, this is how most of the organizers conceived of their task as well. Writing in the *Quill*, Mark Cohen, the editor of the *Evening Star* in Dunedin, New Zealand, wrote of the duty of the press as a "public educator"; Herbert Swope wrote of public opinion being "intelligenced by the Press," which in turn would have more effect on the morals of society than writing new laws; and James Williams, editor of the *Boston Transcript*, wrote of the "free press" as a "chronicle of the human race . . . [providing] the 'food of opinion.' To adulterate that food with the poison of untruth is a sin against the public" (Williams 1924: 8). The strongest statement about the educative task of journalism was made by Edward McKernon, superintendent of the Eastern Division of the Associated Press, who linked educating the public with the future of society:

> That is our mission. To know what is. To determine with industry and with cold-blooded exactness the facts of every happening significant of the society of today. To tell a bewildered world what is. To indicate what must be the start-

ing point of intelligent thinking if sanity is to rule. . . . If we don't think
straight, we are lost. We can't think straight unless we get straight information. . . . We must know what is. . . . To observe intelligently and reflect accurately is the profound responsibility of Modern Journalism. The future of society is in our keeping. (McKernon 1925: 19)

According to these professionalizers, the task of journalism was to find and
determine the truth, and then educate the public as to just what the truth
was, so that public opinion could be adequately formed and the future of
civilization ensured.

From Traditional to General Religion   The fourth pattern came from religious
as well as journalistic quarters. Rev. Lloyd C. Douglas, pastor of the Congregational Church in Ann Arbor, Michigan, and a former journalist, argued on the one hand that religion was one of the most basic instincts of
humans, that it was responsible for much of the development and civilization of the world, and that it still maintained a certain power for good in society. As such, Douglas encouraged journalists to recognize this fact and
court the support of the ministers in their own communities. On the other
hand, he suggested that, particularly in the wake of World War I, many ministers were disillusioned and discouraged with their visions of a "new heaven
and a new earth," now considered "unattainable." Journalists, by speaking a
positive word to these ministers, and perhaps writing them up in their newspapers, might buoy their confidence, which in turn would improve "civic
righteousness and morality," since the words of the ministers were "taken
into account by an aggregate of very many people" (Douglas 1919: 8, 10).
Thus, journalism had been elevated to the position of being able to positively influence the religious leaders of the community, rather than religion
having an influence on journalism.

Journalists who worked the "Church Department"—what we would call
the religion pages today—were told that the best way to fulfill their responsibilities toward religion was to "maintain a news ideal for religious news"
(Cameron 1925: 8). In other words, they were simply to report religion as
news; they should take no position on particular religious perspectives, but
be "governed by a spirit which will hasten the coming of the ideal church."
The author argued that "a secular newspaper church page cannot properly
be Protestant or Catholic or Jewish—it cannot be Fundamentalist or Modernist in a factional sense. Rather it must strive to give the fullest opportunity for spiritual self-expression to the Catholic, Protestant and Jewish and
other religious forces in the community" (8). Such an approach was understood as being no different than how other departments in the newspaper
approached their subject matter: "[I]t is merely general journalism applied
to the events connected with the battle against evil, just as police reporting
deals so much with events connected with the battle against good" (8).

Even editors from the *Christian Science Monitor,* which was founded in 1908 with the motto, "[T]o injure no man, but to bless all mankind" (Deland 1926: 3), took a notably neutral approach to religion reporting. Willis Abbott, editor of the *Monitor,* stated that the paper aimed simply to report the news of the day in a positive fashion, whether dealing with religion or not:

> No effort is made in the columns of the *Monitor* to emphasize its religious character. One brief metaphysical article daily, and the rigid exclusion of matters repugnant to the religious convictions of its readers, whatever their church or creed, are its chief manifestations of a religious purpose. The news of other churches is printed rather more fully than that of the church responsible for the paper. And yet in its whole policy the *Monitor* follows closely a text from Paul's Epistle to the Philippians. . . . "[W]hatsoever things are true . . . honest . . . just . . . pure . . . lovely . . . of good report; if there be any virtue . . . think on these things." (Abbot 1926: 6)

Religion then, even for a newspaper with specifically religious ownership, was treated as a general moral good, but without promoting any sectarian principles.

Professional Journalism as the Functional Equivalent of Religion   The final pattern is found throughout many of the sources analyzed, complete with a creed, martyrs, and heroes, and the language of truth-seeking and self-sacrifice to the ideals of journalism. Walter Williams, the founding dean of the School of Journalism at the University of Missouri,[12] wrote "The Journalists' Creed" in 1915, which is still used in promotional material by the school. This creed consists of eight articles, each beginning with "I believe . . . ," the first being, "I believe in the profession of journalism." This creed seems clearly to have been modeled after the historic confessions of the church, with which Williams would be familiar, in that he was an active Presbyterian who was the president of his local county Sunday School association, and had taught a large Sunday School class for many years. Most interesting, the last article of the creed reads rather like the Apostle Paul's chapter on the ideals of love, in which these journalistic ideals are presented as what should be aspired to, both for the profession and for individual journalists:

> I believe that the journalism which succeeds best—and which deserves success—fears God and honors man; is stoutly independent, unmoved by pride of opinion or greed of power, constructive, tolerant, but never careless, self-controlled, patient; always respectful of its readers, but always unafraid; is quickly indignant at injustice; is unswayed by the appeal of privilege or the clamor of the mob; seeks to give every man a chance and as far as law and honest wage recognition of human brotherhood can make it so, an equal chance;

is profoundly patriotic, while sincerely promoting the international good will and cementing world comradeship; is a journalism of humanity, of and for today's world. (Williams 1915: 12)

Other organizers spoke in similarly religious terms, of journalist-heroes standing against the powers of injustice and corruption, of journalist-martyrs who have been punished, even killed in journalistic service to humanity, and even of journalism as a pilgrimage from a lower to a higher ideal. H. F. Harrington, of Illinois and Northwestern, wrote of the heroic reporter who "shivers his lance against corruption high and low. Crime, money-lust, hypocrisy, vice, sin, stand within his confessional," which, once exposed, the reporter is rewarded by being "dubbed a muckraker, an underworld detective, a Paul Pry of sensations. The epithets bear witness to his thrift and to the sincerity of his purpose" (Harrington 1919: 7).

Similarly, the *New York World* editor, Herbert Swope, wrote of journalist martyrs, who gave their lives and fortunes as the price for liberty. Here, journalism "and its ministers have suffered themselves to be blamed, condemned, imprisoned, suffered themselves even to be hanged, but they have published their opinions and their versions of pivotal facts, regarding it not only as a right, but as a duty" (Swope 1924: 8). Swope further contended that journalism was always, in its ideals, "a priestly-mission," and as its practices have improved, there arose, "within its ranks, a divine dissatisfaction with its failure to be of even greater usefulness" (10).

Finally, Edward McKernon, of the Associated Press, candidly noted the state of the world, and the proper role of journalism:

> To put it bluntly, society is awakening to the realization that there "ain't no Santa Claus." To some the awakening is as gentle as the touch of a mother's hand. To others it is like falling out of bed. Do not misunderstand me. I do not refer to religion. This would be a sorry world without the spiritual. But we have just naturally stopped throwing salt over our shoulders. The intelligent are beginning to understand that this old world is pretty much what we make it. That if civilization is to endure we must mentally readjust ourselves to rapidly changing conditions—as the merchant would say, "take account of stock"—and, looking the facts squarely in the face, work out a philosophy of life that will stand up. (McKernon 1925: 19)

In this it was the responsibility of journalism to provide the information—truth—by which an adequate "philosophy of life" could be constructed. Ultimately, he contended, journalism was a "sacred trust" (19).

CONCLUSION

Both the decline in the number of religion stories in the *New York Times* and the shift in perspective on religion in the *Times,* from a stance in the 1880s in which traditional Christianity was upheld as authoritative, to a stance in the 1920s in which secular science was conceived as having authority over religion, as well as the treatment of religion more generally within journalism, can be explained by two related developments in the history of journalism. First, the larger context of change and development within journalism and, second, the specific activities—strategies—pursued by journalism professionalizers in the effort to elevate journalism to professional status.

Changes throughout the nineteenth century, in particular what journalism historians have termed the "commercialization of the news," set the context and lead to a partial explanation. For this discussion, the most important aspect of the commercialization process involves the shift from smaller independent news operations to large-scale corporate publishers. Of particular importance are the following: increased costs required either to maintain or to start a new journalistic enterprise that go along with such a corporate organization; increased competition between different journalistic enterprises—especially newspapers—competing in the same market; and a change from political patronage to a reliance on commercial advertising for revenues. These developments changed the way that news and opinion was conceived, packaged, and presented to the public (see Dicken-Garcia 1989: 56–62; Baldasty 1992: 85–94; also Schwarzlose 1989; 1990). In turn, the economic and commercial changes in the larger environment of journalism favored the larger, more established journalism firms, whose greater resources made them more able to compete in the news market.[13] This, on the one hand, favored a more uniform presentation of news and opinion (Bourdieu 1998; Bagdikian 2000); on the other hand, it encouraged "adding color" to news stories in order to provide a more vicarious reading experience—and a more marketable product—for the news consumer (Covert 1975). In producing a news product that would compete successfully in the market, journalists found that religion, particularly as a moral voice, didn't provide the "news hook" that they valued in other stories emphasizing, for example, crime and corruption. To the extent that religion was able to provide a good conflict story (per Charles Merz), it became front-page news—witness the Scopes trial and the battle between the fundamentalists and the evolutionists during the 1920s. While this provides a partial explanation in that it helps explain the decline in religion stories in the *New York Times,* as well as those developments reported by Hart (1933), it does not explain the antagonism toward traditional religion that developed throughout the 1920s in mass publications like the *New York Times,* and in professional journals like the *Quill.*

The efforts of journalism professionalizers to organize and establish ideals and otherwise develop the profession of journalism explain what became the opposition to traditional religion within journalism. Among journalism professionalizers, traditional religion was either ignored or alluded to in negative terms as some sort of quaint belief system from premodern society. To the extent that religion was presented as having any positive role, it was in purely functional terms, in the sense that moral precepts from religion might be a source of strength for some individuals, but had no authority for modern society. As a result of this perspective, professionalizers promoted secular scientific perspectives at the expense of traditional religious perspectives, in three ways.

First, these efforts began to emphasize such broadly construed secular and scientific values as an emphasis on rationality and empiricism for determining truth—the belief that humanity can only rely on itself for improvement—both of self and of society—and that answers to social problems can only be found through scientific work applied to the issues and problems of the day. These were assumed from other professional fields, and presented to the members of the journalism profession, as the ways to conceptualize their journalistic task.

Second, journalism professionalizers aligned themselves and the profession of journalism with science and scientific authority as its model for professionalization. Thus, journalism made its claim to professional status not only through the adoption of the objectivity ideal, but by pointing to its professional organization, ranging from university programs to journals and associations that gave a greater credibility to its status claims. If journalists could prove themselves to be sufficiently rigorous in their work, they would have some measure of control over journalistic practice and simultaneously increase their status and cultural authority.

Editorials in the *New York Times* expressed these status concerns, particularly during the Scopes trial. The overriding concern of the *Times* was how Americans appeared to Europeans, or how most Tennesseans might appear to the rest of America. As presented by the *Times,* the issue was one of the trial giving off the impression that American society was as ignorant and backward as the Bryan-led fundamentalists were made to appear. For the *Times* then, a scientific perspective conveyed a higher status than a backward religious perspective, and if a religious perspective was taken at all, it needed to be scientifically rigorous.

Third, journalism professionalizers presented journalism, and its objectively collected and presented news, as the profession to which the public should look for direction in working out various public—and perhaps private—issues. These efforts implicitly and explicitly emphasized the idea that although religion might in general be a good thing, it had seen its day, and modern society was in need of a new moral guide. Journalism was presented as the ideal successor to religion.

Journalism professionalizers consistently framed professional journalism in religious terms. Influential professionalizers such as Walter Williams wrote of "the calling of journalism," the "new kingdom of journalism," and of the "solidarity and spirit of journalism" (Williams 1925: 9, 13). Similarly, Herbert Swope wrote of "Journalism" (used as a proper noun), of the "sanctity" of facts, and of public opinion, once it was "intelligenced by the press" as being a more effective "resisting influence" by writing " 'ought' in the hearts of men, instead of placing 'must' in the statute books." The modern age was, according to Swope and other professionalizers, "the age of the reporter," with journalism and news "among the chief factors in the formulation of conduct" (Swope 1924: 7–8). Thus, journalism came to conceive of itself as the new moral voice for society. Journalists saw themselves as professionals of the same status as doctors and lawyers, who "wanted to dispense medicine, as a doctor would, for society's ills" (Thornton 1995: 39).

Embedded in this larger context, and as they organized toward professionalization, journalists ultimately came to organize their efforts toward unseating traditional religion from a place of cultural authority. Science had gained cultural authority, and, as Kimball has framed it, science embodied the "architechtonic" professional ideals of the time. As journalism moved toward professionalization and a higher status in society, such scientific values as empiricism ("fact" gathering and reporting), rationality, and rigor in method, were emphasized as being core elements of the journalism profession. As a part of this process religious authority was perceived as an enemy of modern science and was at first questioned and then overtly displaced by scientific authority both in mass publications like the *New York Times* and in professional journals like the *Quill* and the *Journalist*. This served the interests of journalism professionalizers in that journalism, by emphasizing the superior authority of science, by implication and through embracing scientific ideals, intended to gain status and power in society.

Beyond just embracing certain scientific ideals, journalism professionalizers argued that traditional religion had not solved the problems of the world and that "enlightened" people had simply come to realize that the world will only be what people make it to be, as Edward McKernon stated plainly, "[S]ociety is awakening to a realization that there 'ain't no Santa Claus.'" As such, and because of its faith in science, journalism presented itself as the successor to religion: Journalism was the bearer of truth (and sometimes "Truth"), and took on the task of working to improve society. Journalism professionalizers believed that "factual" knowledge was the key to solving social problems and that journalism alone was in the position to provide such knowledge to the mass of society. This placed journalism in an indispensable role between primary knowledge producers such as scientists and the rest of society. In this capacity, journalism could fulfill the role it had set for itself as the moral educator of modern society only if there were no other competitors. Thus, by debunking traditional religion as a relic from the past and elevating science—and by extension journalism—into the role of the primary authority in society, journalism could take its rightful place among the leading professions in modern society.

Journalism, as a profession that by definition "reported on" developments such as those that had been taking place in science and religion, and that explicitly patterned itself after the established scientific professions, thus sought the status associated with science. In the process, journalism, by promoting these ideas to a larger public, often at the expense of traditional religion, popularized these new conceptions of how science and religion related to each other and ultimately diminished the place of religion in society.

NOTES

1. The literature is unclear as to the processes that left the early innovators out, but I am pursuing this topic as a continuation of this research. As a partial answer, it seems that the increasingly fragmented nature of religions, including competing religious groups, weakened their ability to mount any sustained, unified efforts in journalism. That is, most of these publications were specialized by type and/or by theology or denomination, which made it easier for groups without these cleavages to organize and gain a larger market share for their journalistic product.

2. Pettit's study continues through 1975, and the patterns of decline in religion reporting held through that year.

3. These patterns can be understood as at least partial indicators of how journalism was promoting secular ideas at the expense of traditional religious ideas, yet they do not necessarily denote that secularization is taking place. That is, these changes might have been, at least in part, a function of the ever-increasing size of the *New York Times* over this time period. From its founding in 1851, the *Times* had consisted of four pages, which included two pages of advertisements, yet it had doubled its size by the 1890s to eight pages, and by the 1920s, the *Times* had grown to include several sections, including the *New York Times Magazine,* with more than twenty pages and more than forty in the Sunday edition. Thus, as much more news was being reported, some issues, including perhaps religion, may simply have gotten less space over time.

4. My examination of the *New York Times* was conducted in the following manner. Using the *New York Times Index* for the years 1870–1930, I selected all news articles and editorials listed under the headings "religion," "churches," "Protestantism," "Bible," "Fundamentalism," and so on, for each year, in five-year intervals (1870, 1875, 1880, through 1930). For this analysis, I have focused primarily on the editorials, although I have utilized news articles as well, insofar as they provided needed context for the editorials. Citations to the *Times* are given parenthetically in the text by date and page number.

5. Tifft and Jones (1999) suggest that this title was ultimately the result of the *Times* beginning, in 1913, to publish the *New York Times Index*.

6. The labels "fundamentalists" and "modernists" were not at this point in use. I have tried to keep the terminology of the *Times* in this regard.

7. Baldasty (1999) reports that E. W. Scripps was committed to decreasing advertising dollars as a source of revenue and increasing circulation as a source of

revenue, primarily so that his newspapers would not have to depend on advertising and thus not be the servants of corporate interests. Although this strategy worked for a while, it was ultimately unsuccessful in keeping most of his newspapers profitable.

8. Schudson points as well to the emergence of professional public relations personnel and the propaganda efforts in World War I as challenging the possibility of true objectivity in journalism (Schudson 1988: 151 ff.).

9. The *Journalist* was the earliest to be published (1884–1907). *Editor and Publisher* (founded 1901) had essentially the same look and content of the *Journalist,* and both names were actually on the masthead for several years, before the *Journalist* name was dropped from the publication, and the numbering of the editions was changed to reflect the longer history of the *Journalist.* Citations are by date and page number in the text.

10. I analyzed all *Quill* issues published between 1912 and 1930, focusing on articles that emphasized what the newly emerging profession of journalism should look like.

11. For this discussion I have relied on the catalog listings of the journalism programs at Wisconsin, Indiana, and Northwestern, in addition to the many schools who, in response to a call from the AASDJ in 1917, sent a listing of their curricular requirements to Willard Bleyer at Wisconsin, with the intention of standardizing journalism curricula at member schools. These schools are, the Universities of Washington, Oregon, Missouri, Kansas, and Ohio State University.

12. Whereas Wisconsin has the distinction of having established the first permanent "course," or department, of journalism in the United States, Missouri has the distinction of having established the first professional "school" of journalism. A subtle distinction perhaps, but one that is constantly pointed out in the sources.

13. Carroll (1987) and Carroll and Hannan (1989) have argued that the density, or number of journalism organizations in a population, is a function of the processes of legitimation and competition. At low levels of density, the legitimation process dominates, and there is a higher founding rate; at high density, competition dominates, resulting in a decline of founding rates and an increase in mortality rates. As applied here, the high number of journalism organizations, particularly in New York City, led to the dominance of competition, effectively restricting the founding of new journalism organizations while increasing the mortality rates of existing organizations.

REFERENCES

Abbott, Andrew. 1988. *The System of Professions: An Essay on the Division of Expert Labor.* Chicago: University of Chicago Press.

Abbot, Willis J. 1926. "A Force for Clean Journalism." *Quill* (January): 6.

Allen, Eric W. 1920. "Journalism as a Profession." *Quill* (April): 3–6, 10.

Anderson, Benedict. 1991. *Imagined Communities: Reflections on the Origins and Spread of Nationalism.* London: Verso.

Bagdikian, Ben H. 2000. *The Media Monopoly.* 6th ed. Boston: Beacon Press.

Baldasty, Gerald. 1992. *The Commercialization of the News.* Madison: University of Wisconsin Press.

————. 1999. *E. W. Scripps and the Business of Newspapers*. Urbana and Chicago: University of Illinois Press.

Berger, Meyer. 1951. *The Story of the New York Times, 1851–1951*. New York: Simon and Schuster.

Bleyer, Willard Grosvenor. 1925. "The Importance of High Editorial Standards." *Quill* (March): 3–7.

————. 1927. *Main Currents in the History of American Journalism*. Boston: Houghton Mifflin.

————. 1934. "The Rise of Education for Journalism." *Quill* (October): 12–13, 30, 32.

Bourdieu, Pierre. 1998. *On Television*. New York: The New Press.

Cameron, Charles D. 1925. "Church Department Calls for Service." *Quill* (September): 8.

Carroll, Glenn R. 1987. *Publish and Perish: The Organizational Ecology of Newspaper Industries*. Greenwich, CT: Jai Press.

Carroll, Glenn R., and Michael T. Hannan. 1989. "Density Dependence in the Evolution of Populations of Newspaper Organizations." *American Sociological Review* 54: 524–41.

Chaves, Mark. 1993. "Intraorganizational Power and Internal Secularization in Protestant Denominations." *American Journal of Sociology* 99, no 1: 1–48.

————. 1994. "Secularization as Declining Religious Authority." *Social Forces* 72: 749–74.

Cohen, Mark R. 1915. "Duty of the Press to the Reading Public: A Reply to William J. Bryan." *Quill* (October): 3.

Covert, Cathy. 1975. "A View of the Press in the Twenties." *Journalism History* 2: 66–67, 92–96.

Crawford, Nelson Antrim. 1925. "Professional Preparation for Journalism." *Quill* (January): 10–11.

Davis, Elmer. 1921. *History of the New York Times, 1851–1921*. New York: New York Times.

Deland, Paul S. 1926. "Helpfulness—Keynote of Christian Science Monitor." *Quill* (January): 3–4.

Dennis, Charles H. 1925. "What Schools of Journalism Might Do." *Quill* (January): 20.

Dicken-Garcia, Hazel. 1989. *Journalistic Standards in Nineteenth-Century America*. Madison: University of Wisconsin Press.

Douglas, Rev. Lloyd C. 1919. "The Press and the Pulpit." *Quill* (October): 7–8, 10.

Emery, Michael, and Edwin Emery. 1988. *The Press and America: An Interpretive History*. Englewood Cliffs, NJ: Prentice-Hall.

Fallows, James. 1997. *Breaking the News: How the Media Undermine American Democracy*. New York: Vintage.

Fuller, Jack. 1996. *News Values: Ideas for an Information Age*. Chicago: University of Chicago Press.

Getz, Carl H. 1916. "Standardization of Instruction in Journalism Proposed." *Quill* (July): 6, 12.

Harrington, H. F. 1919. "The Reporter as Story-Teller." *Quill* (July): 7–8.

Hart, Hornell. 1933. "Changing Social Attitudes and Interests." In *Recent Social*

Trends in the United States: Report of the President's Research Committee on Social Trends, 382–442. New York: McGraw-Hill.

Hoover, Stewart. 1998. *Religion in the News: Faith and Journalism in American Public Discourse*. Thousand Oaks, CA: Sage.

Indiana University. 1911. *Indiana University Catalog*. Bloomington: Indiana University Press.

"In Sigma Delta Chi." 1925. *Quill* (January): 20.

"Journalism Education in the United States." 1926. *Journalism Bulletin* 3, no. 3 (November): 3.

Kimball, Bruce A. 1992. *The "True Professional Ideal" in America: A History*. Cambridge, MA and Oxford, U.K.: Blackwell.

Kobre, Sidney. 1959. *Modern American Journalism*. Institute of Media Research, Tallahassee, Florida: Florida State University.

Larson, Edward J. 1997. *Summer for the Gods: The Scopes Trial and America's Continuing Debate over Science and Religion*. Cambridge, MA: Harvard University Press.

Lee, James Melvin. 1917. *History of American Journalism*. Garden City, NY: Garden City Publishing.

Leonard, Thomas C. 1995. *News for All: America's Coming-of-Age with the Press*. New York: Oxford University Press.

Macy, John. 1922. "Journalism." In *Civilization in the United States: An Inquiry by Thirty Americans*, ed. Harold E. Stearns, 35–51. New York: Harcourt, Brace and Company.

Marsden, George. 1980. *Fundamentalism and American Culture*. New York: Oxford University Press.

McKernon, Edward. 1925. "Journalism Defined." *Quill* (December): 18–20.

Mindich, David. 1998. *Just the Facts: How "Objectivity" Came to Define American Journalism*. New York: New York University Press.

Murphy, Lawrence W. 1922. "Schools of Journalism." *Quill* (April): 17–18.

Nord, David Paul. 2000. "The Evangelical Origins of Mass Media in America." In *Media and Religion in American History*, ed. William David Sloan, 68–93. Northport, AL: Vision Press.

Northwestern University. 1923–24. *Northwestern University Catalog*. Evanston, IL: Northwestern University Press.

Numbers, Ronald L. 1993. *The Creationists: The Evolution of Scientific Creationism*. Berkeley and Los Angeles: University of California Press.

Olasky, Marvin. 1988. *Prodigal Press: The Anti-Christian Bias of the American News Media*. Wheaton, IL: Crossway Books.

———. 1991. *Central Ideas in the Development of American Journalism: A Narrative History*. Hillsdale, NJ: Lawrence Erlbaum Associates.

Pettit, Robert. 1986. *Religion through the Times: An Examination of the Secularization Thesis through Content Analysis of the New York Times, 1855–1975*. Ph.D. diss. Columbia University.

Rosen, Jay. 1999. *What Are Journalists For?* New Haven, CT: Yale University Press.

Schudson, Michael. 1978. *Discovering the News: A Social History of American Newspapers*. New York: Basic Books.

———. 1988. "The Profession of Journalism in the United States." In *The Professions in American History,* ed. Nathan O. Hatch, 145–61. Notre Dame, IN: University of Notre Dame Press.

———. 1995. *The Power of News.* Cambridge, MA: Harvard University Press.

Schwarzlose, Richard A. 1989. *The Nation's Newsbrokers.* Vol. 1. *The Formative Years: From Pretelegraph to 1865.* Evanston, IL: Northwestern University Press.

———. 1990. *The Nation's Newsbrokers.* Vol. 2. *The Rush to Institution: From 1865 to 1920.* Evanston, IL: Northwestern University Press.

Shepard, Richard F. 1996. *The Paper's Papers: A Reporter's Journey through the Archives of the New York Times.* New York: Times Books/Random House.

Sigma Delta Chi. 1926 (May). "Sigma Delta Chi—Its Aims and Its Progress: A Statement by the Executive Council of the Fraternity." Sigma Delta Chi Archives, DePauw University, Greencastle, IN.

Silk, Mark. 1995. *Unsecular Media: Making News of Religion in America.* Urbana and Chicago: University of Illinois Press.

Sloan, William David, ed. 2000. *Media and Religion in American History.* Northport, AL: Vision Press.

Swope, Herbert Bayard. 1924. "Journalism: An Instrument of Civilization." *Quill* (December): 6–10.

Thornton, Brian. 1995. "Muckraking Journalists and Their Readers: Perceptions of Professionalization." *Journalism History* 21 (Spring): 1.

Tifft, Susan E., and Alex S. Jones. 1999. *The Trust: The Private and Powerful Family behind the New York Times.* Boston: Little, Brown.

Villard, Oswald Garrison. 1923. *Some Newspapers and Newspaper-men.* New York: Alfred A. Knopf.

Washington, University of. 1917. "Journalism Examination: Editing." AASDJ Files 1928–1939. Series 7/19/3 Box 13, Folder A. Archives, University of Wisconsin, Madison.

Williams, James T., Jr. 1924. "The Responsibility of the Press." *Quill* (May): 7–9.

Williams, Walter. 1915. "The Journalist's Creed." *Quill* (October): 12.

———. 1919. "The Barbed Entanglements of the Press." *Quill* (July): 6.

———. 1925. "Are Schools of Journalism Getting Anywhere?" *Quill* (January): 7–9, 13.

10

After the Fall

Attempts to Establish an Explicitly Theological Voice in Debates over Science and Medicine after 1960

John H. Evans

It is often quipped that what we think of as the "1960s"—with protests against establishments and the like—actually began in 1968. However, in discussions about the ethics of science and medicine, the questioning of the establishment actually *did* begin in 1960. The explosion in scientific research following World War II had begun to bear fruit, and scientists were now questioning its effects, as well as contemplating research that had earlier been incomprehensible. During the 1960s, what bioethicist Albert Jonsen has called the "decade of conferences," scientists had many meetings to discuss the Brave New World that beckoned before them. Science was seen as producing a number of side-effects with momentous implications, such as environmental pollution and overpopulation, which were seen as the result of improving agriculture and medicine. Technological improvements also suggested to scientists that humans would soon have a degree of control over themselves that had previously been the stuff of science fiction: mind-control, human cloning, human genetic engineering, test-tube babies, parthenogenesis, human/animal chimeras, artificial organs and body parts, and the transplantation of more symbolic body parts (such as the heart), which had not been accomplished as the decade began. As many noted at the time, scientists would have to make distinctions that they had not had to worry about before, such as when someone is "really" dead so that organs can be removed.

It was an era of questioning ends, not just means. "Where are we taking ourselves" with our new technological abilities was the central theme. As the dean of the Dartmouth Medical School stated at the opening of perhaps the first of these conferences in 1960, "Although [medicine's] foundations have become more rational, its practice . . . is said to have become more remote and indifferent to human values, and once again medicine has been forced to remind itself that it is often the human factors that are determinant." The point of the conference was "not simply question of the survival or the extinction of man, but *what kind* of survival? A future of what *nature?*" (cited in Jonsen 1998: 13).

Scientists during these early years kept the conversation limited to scientists. To use Abbott's terms, scientists had full jurisdiction over promulgating the ethics of their own work. Abbott's perspective in *The System of Professions* is a very useful one for studying macro-level secularization, at least in the past hundred years or so. I therefore highlight three particularly useful theoretical concepts from Abbott's book: jurisdiction, competition, and the ecological system (Abbott 1988).

First, he conceptualizes the central phenomena of interest in the study of professions as "jurisdiction," the link professionals make between themselves and a series of acts, their "work." For example, physicians have established the jurisdictional link between themselves and the acts of cutting into bodies with knives. A profession has jurisdiction if the audience for the jurisdictional evaluation thinks it should. In the case of physicians, the primary audience is public opinion—people are convinced that physicians should have jurisdiction over surgery and not some other profession (such as lawyers). More important, a profession obtains jurisdiction by having a "system of abstract knowledge" that legitimates its claim over certain acts and can be used to make jurisdictional claims over other acts. Medicine, for example, has medical science, which contains numerous theories about the reaction of the body to being cut by knives.

Professions do not simply take over and "professionalize" a task, but are in constant competition with each other for jurisdiction over acts. Medicine has been in competition with chiropractic care for years, and has faced recent challenges from acupuncture, aroma therapy, and the like. Medicine has been one of the most successful professions, competing for and winning jurisdiction over all sorts of acts formerly under the jurisdiction of other professions, such as alcoholism and obesity. Why agents who are members of professions compete with each other is left open in Abbott's work, but we can imagine that physicians compete with acupuncturists because they fear loss of income or because they fear that their patients will not be cured by them.

The final part of Abbott's work to raise up is that all of these competing professions and the acts they are competing over are considered to be in a large ecological system. Thus, the creation of a new series of acts (e.g., the production and use of MRI machines) leads to a vacuum in the system of professions, with professions competing for jurisdiction with the claim that these new acts are reducible to acts the profession already has jurisdiction over (e.g., physicians vs. X-ray technicians). Further, changes in the entire environment of the system, such as the rise of the state as the audience, can

lead to a reshuffling of the entire system of professions. Finally, other ecological metaphors can be helpful. For example, professions can concentrate
their energy on one task to protect themselves, or spread themselves thinly
in the interest of jurisdictional expansion.

So, to return to the 1960s using this new explanatory framework, the scientists had jurisdiction over promulgating the ethics of their work. The
"work" of ethics is a bit more abstract than the work of medical care itself, but
is work nonetheless, and many professions have competed to win jurisdiction over ethics for hundreds of years, including the theological profession.

As I discuss in more detail in my book (Evans 2002), many of the elite
scientists were attempting a jurisdictional expansion to go beyond simply
controlling the ethics of their own work toward controlling the ethics of
work that had been under the jurisdiction of the theological profession.
They thought that science should produce a sense of meaning and be a
source of ethics for human society—given that, in their view, religion had
been utterly discredited after Darwin. For example, C. H. Waddington and
Peter Medawar would imply, along with other biologists, that "the 'direction' of evolution, both biological and cultural, is the 'scientific' foundation
upon which to reestablish our system of ethics and to rest 'our most cherished hopes'" (Kaye 1997: 42). Similarly, population geneticist Theodosius
Dobzhansky believed that "restored to the 'Center of the Universe' by the
wisdom and beneficence of evolution, man is free to seek beauty, justice,
and self-transcendence and not 'mere survival'" (Kaye 1997: 42).

Robert Edwards, the first scientist to attempt in-vitro fertilization, was
also part of this expansionist project, complaining that "many non-scientists
see a more limited role for science, almost a fact-gathering exercise providing neither values, morals, nor standards. . . . My answer . . . is that moral
laws must be based on what man knows about himself, and that this knowledge inevitably comes largely from science." Given that science is the only
legitimate way of knowing, he concludes by agreeing with biologist Julian
Huxley that "[t]oday the God hypothesis has ceased to be scientifically ten-
able, has lost its explanatory value and is becoming an intellectual burden
to our thought" (Edwards 1989: 165–66).

The scientists were clear about who they defeated in this role and who
their primary challenger continued to be. As scientist Jacob Bronowski
would pronounce at one of these conferences in 1962, "I am, therefore, not
in the least ashamed to be told by somebody else that my values, because
they are grounded in my science, are relative, and his are given by God. My
values, in my opinion, come from as objective and definitive a source as any
god, namely the nature of the human being. . . . That makes my values
richer, I think; and it makes them no less objective, no less real, than any
values that can be read in the Testaments" (Wolstenholme 1963: 372). In
short, science was in a triumphalist mode; it needed to consult only itself to

determine what to do about these dilemmas. Scientists would decide where humans should go.

Perhaps surprisingly, it is here that theologians engaged in an attempt at regaining jurisdiction, a project which would counteract the long line of jurisdictions that had been taken from them by other professions. I will chart three short eras in this short-lived effort, focusing on the transition between the first two.[1]

An important distinction is required regarding the nature of the arguments that theologians made. Arguments, at their most basic, are about particular means—such as abortion—and the ends that these means advanced or were consistent with. With these terms in mind, the first era—when theologians made arguments that had theological ends—was short-lived, and scholars may want to debate whether it existed as a separate moment at all. An argument here might have been that we should accelerate the coming Kingdom of God on earth through science and medicine. This would have made the ethics of science and medicine rest on an explicitly theological base.

The second era began with the rapid retreat from this project, giving up on an *explicitly* theological language of ends, and fell back into having the ethics of science and medicine focus on secularly stated ends that were translations of theological ends. For example, a theologian could conclude that since we are all created in the image of God, we should pursue the end of ensuring the God-given sacredness of each person. This could be translated to the secular end of pursuing the autonomous decision-making power for individuals so that they can protect their own sacredness. Theologians were not arguing about the theology itself but about the various ends that they thought should be applied to medicine and science.

However, the theologians in this second era were conflicted. While some continued with the translation method, trying to convince the public to accept these ends, some began to search for ends that were already universally held by all people, regardless of their theological persuasion. This seed, planted by a faction of the theologians, ironically grew into a challenge to the jurisdiction of theology when the new profession of bioethics was born. As I describe in greater detail elsewhere (Evans 2002), the bioethics profession did not begin with theology and translate to secular language, resulting in a debate about various ends; rather, it started with a list of four ends portrayed as universally held by the citizens, from which one would derive what to do in the fields of science and medicine. As bioethicists gained strength the theological challenge slowly receded.

These three eras occurred in such rapid succession that it is difficult to consider them separately. Indeed, there is substantial overlap—even in the earliest era of explicit theological ends, the first theologians searching for secular universal ends were beginning to write. And even in the final era, some theologians went on arguing for explicitly theological ends. The three eras are like three bell-shaped curves on an axis with a high degree of over-lap, revealing three distinct humps, but with the majority of the area under the curve coinciding with the one next to it. In this chapter I examine the distinct humps, while simply acknowledging the more complicated picture described by the overlapping tails of the curves.

IN THE BEGINNING: EXPLICITLY THEOLOGICAL ENDS

The scientists in the 1950s and early 1960s were triumphant, but were suf-fering from a failure of nerve. A faction had created what could best be called a theology of science, and its members were ready to become the high priests of society. Scientists were also seemingly poised to engage in novel ex-periments such as merging two forms of life together by merging their DNA, suggesting that the new scientific vision could be used to shape humans themselves. Some scientists, perhaps not believing that scientists had an an-swer for everything, urged that the public be consulted. For scientists to "claim the right to decide alone" about the direction of scientific efforts, said viral geneticist Salvador Luria, would be "to advocate technocracy" (Luria 1965: 3, 17). By mid-decade, according to historian of science Susan Wright, "growing numbers of people—including many scientists—began finding the social role and impact of modern science and technology increasingly problematic.... Public confidence in technological development as the key to social progress gave way to disenchantment" (Wright 1994: 36–37).

Given how much ground theologians had lost in public life, one has to wonder why they began to challenge scientists for jurisdiction over the ethics of science and medicine. One reason was that the project of jurisdic-tional expansion by some scientists into the remaining jurisdiction of the-ology was perceived as a threat. Many elite scientists talked about scientific truth eliminating the need for the mental crutch of religion, and I argue that theologians saw their remaining jurisdiction over helping *individuals* determine the meaning and purpose of life as under threat.

Methodist theologian and Princeton Religion Professor Paul Ramsey (1913–1988) recognized that the scientists posed a challenge to theology's core jurisdiction.[2] As the scientists themselves had noted, theology has tra-ditionally had under its jurisdiction work such as helping people define the meaning and purpose of humanity, and now the scientists were impinging on that work. It was not simply that Ramsey was opposed to the emerging technologies, but throughout his work he stated that he was actually op-posed to what he called a "surrogate theology" of the "cult" of "messianic positivism" led by scientists. At a 1965 conference he used the phrase "play-ing God" to summarize the form of argumentation used by the scientists—what he called their worldview—saying that their goal was to provide the meaning of life:

taken as a whole, the proposals of the revolutionary biologists, the anatomy of their basic thought-forms, the ultimate context for acting on these proposals provides a propitious place for learning the meaning of "playing God"—in contrast to being men on earth.

[The scientists have] "a distinctive attitude toward the world," "a program for utterly transforming it," an "unshakable," nay even a "fanatical," confidence in a "worldview," a "faith" no less than a "program" for the reconstruction of mankind. These expressions rather exactly describe a religious cult, if there ever was one—a cult of men-gods, however otherwise humble. These are not the findings, or the projections, of an exact science as such, but a religious view of where and how ultimate human significance is to be found. It is a proposal concerning mankind's final hope. One is reminded of the words of Martin Luther to the effect that we have either God or an idol and "whatever your heart trusts in and relies on, that is properly your God." (Ramsey 1970a: 138–45)

There were many other conferences and controversies in science and medicine where theologians challenged scientists. Consider, for example, the conference that was held in reaction to the first heart transplant in 1967. This conference was to address the "clinical, moral, ethical, theological and psychological implications" of this technology, and despite the supposed range of topics, three of the six speakers were theologians (and one more was Jesuit Robert Drinan, a Catholic legal scholar). While not as explicit as Ramsey in naming the opponent, German theologian Helmut Thielicke, in discussing the ethics of deciding who should get a transplant, given the limited supply, spoke of a Christian perspective against what he sees as one secular alternative:

One possibility is to understand the value and dignity of man in terms of his "utility," for example, his capacity to function in the productive process, or his biological or historical potential. . . . The physician, for example, has to realize that in adopting this view of man he surrenders his healing ethos and becomes an engineer, a technician doing manipulations for a productive society. . . . There is an alternative, however, to this view of man in terms of his "utility." One can speak instead of his "infinite worth," a worth over which I have no control. And here I must say quite openly that I know of no place in the world where the inviolability of man is so expressly attested and defended as in the Bible. . . . The basis of human dignity is seen to reside not in any immanent quality of man whatsoever, but in the fact that God created him. Man is the apple of God's eye. He is "dear" because he has been bought with a price: Christ died for him. (Thielicke 1970: 169–70)

In sum, he was arguing that we should pursue as an end the idea that each human has an "infinite worth," as defined by the crucifixion.

The target for the re-sacralization project—science and medicine—was plausible because theology was really the only tradition outside of medicine and science that had a well-developed discourse to address these topics. Catholicism had of course a long history of explicitly Catholic medical ethics, and Protestants, while not having the same depth, nonetheless had a long tradition of discourse about suffering, the body and the purpose of human life. These early theologians knew that not all of the consumers of their texts would share their explicitly theological premises, but they seemed to feel that Christian theology was widely enough shared and dominant that it could serve as the basis for critique. For example, Ramsey, according to one of his critics, held "the conviction that Christianity had formed something called Western civilization, which continued to bear the marks of the Gospel" (Hauerwas 1997: 128).

Examination of Ramsey's work shows that he always seemed to insist upon the theological basis for his work, and while acknowledging that not all were Christians, he seemed to be writing for those he assumed were still within the orbit of Christian belief, urging them to come back into the fold. For example, in discussing the ethics of the giving of vital organs in 1969, Ramsey's reasoning included the following:

> From the standpoint of Christian ethics within the tradition of the Reformation, however, charity (agapé) is a free act of grace—first in God's gift of himself in love to man, and then in man's gift of himself in love to neighbor. . . .
>
> It is, therefore, important to mention a "counter argument" within the structure of Protestant ethics insofar as this has been more profoundly Biblical than past Catholic moralists. Biblical authors not only speak of love to God and Neighbor. They also hold a very realistic view of the life of man who is altogether flesh (sarx). God is in heaven, man is on earth. . . . No one who has been consciously formed by biblical perspectives is likely to be beguiled by notions of the person whose origin actually is a Cartesian dualism of mind and body; nor will he yield to the enchantment of mystical, spiritual notions of unearthly communion with God and fellow man. . . .
>
> From this point of view, one must ask of any Christian, who today without any hesitation flies into the wild blue yonder of transcendent human spiritual achievement while submitting the body unlimitedly to medical and other technologies, whether his outlook is not rather a product of Cartesian mentalism and dualism, and one that, for all its religious and personalistic terminology, has no longer any Biblical comprehension of joy in creaturely life and the acceptable death of all who are flesh. (Ramsey 1970b: 185–88)

Here we have fairly explicit theology. As in much of his work, he is writing for those scientists or physicians who, if not still Christian, had perhaps attended church as children—those who have "been consciously formed by biblical perspectives."

Ramsey was on the more conservative end of the theologians who engaged in this re-sacralization project. Although later scholars of this era have wondered why Ramsey became involved in the confrontation with science and medicine (Walters 1985), after writing extensively on topics such as peace and war, it seemed he was partially provoked by someone who would turn out to be his long-term sparring partner in theological debates—Joseph Fletcher.

Fletcher was probably the first American Protestant to enter debates about the ethics of medicine in modern times, writing a book in 1954 that was essentially an attempt to create a Protestant medical ethics in reaction to the long-standing Catholic medical ethics (Fletcher 1993). This was still a time when mainline Protestant theologians thought that they were the religious representatives of our culture, and that all good professionals fit into the Protestant-Catholic-Jew model of the 1950s articulated by Herberg. "Every doctor has loyalty, we may assume, to certain medical ideals [and] loyalty to religious convictions," begins the preface to Fletcher's book. "Dr. Fletcher has examined the ethical problems and the value systems of physicians, in the light of our Judaeo-Christian culture" (Fletcher 1954: vii–viii).

It was Fletcher's later role as the leading proponent of situation ethics, particularly in issues of medicine and science, that would raise Ramsey's ire (Attwood 1992: 29). The details of this debate between Fletcher and Ramsey are beyond the scope of this chapter, but suffice it to say they were arguing over how best to forward the Christian end of agape in the world— either through Ramsey's rules or Fletcher's utilitarian maximization of agape free of rules. The point is that they were both still forwarding explicitly Christian ends, assuming that the proponents of a "religion of science" were not the majority, that they were speaking to a more or less Christian scientist or physician.

THE BEGINNING OF THE DECLINE: PLURALISM AND SECULAR ENDS

As much as I have tried to raise the explicitly Christian ends forwarded in the writings of the theologians, they were already shifting toward the next era. What took place was a move from an explicitly theological set of ends to a translation of theological ends into a set of secular ends.

The general reason for this transition was, to put it colloquially, a heavy dose of realism as to how far the secularization project had already progressed, as described in other chapters in this volume. Faced with utter marginalization in the debate that they truly wanted to influence to further their theologically motivated beliefs, they took the risk of creating these secular ends so that they could continue in the debate. What was the environment at the time that suggested this compromise position? I will describe a number of features of the environment under the headings of characteristics of the jurisdiction-givers and characteristics of the theologians themselves.

Characteristics of the Jurisdiction-Givers

Who Needed to Be Convinced: The Strength of Scientists and the Hostility toward Theology

It is important to realize that in the struggle described here scientists and physicians were not in a weak position at this point. This public had not yet begun to question their jurisdiction. In this earliest period, the public had not really started paying attention, so it was scientists and other academics who would decide which scientific and medical acts were ethical. Among these elites, theology was in a very tenuous position, especially as it ventured into areas that had been labeled by previous efforts of the scientists as "scientific."

Consider a conference on "the sanctity of life" held in 1966 at Reed College. The organizers of the conference would later describe the reasoning behind their invitation list. Among the many threats to the sanctity of life in contemporary society, the organizers recognized a number "in the scientific area [which] were easily identified: contraception, abortion, eugenics, euthanasia, drug testing, and human experimentation." In light of this, "the biologists and medical scientists were absolutely essential [to invite]" (Labby 1968: ix).

"But the scientists could not be allowed to have the picnic all to themselves; they should be exposed to counterpoint from enlightened non-scientists," continued the organizers (Labby 1968: x). Contrary to the views of some scientists, the organizers felt that "values lie beyond the domain of science," seemingly a good sign for the theologians. Who, however, would be called upon to enlighten us about values? "Certainly law would be one discipline indispensable to the conference . . . [and] in light of contemporary moral concerns, an observer of man's social institutions and behavior—a sociologist—should be invited to comment on the relevance of this to the sanctity of life. Likewise, religion and philosophy could scarcely be overlooked" (Labby 1968: x–xi).

This last sentence may imply a field of equal competitors, but the next sentence belies this. "There is such uncertainty about the force of religious belief in face of modern scientific inquiry that one might reasonably ask what the role of religious principles will be in guiding human behavior." That comment is not followed up on, but is just allowed to dangle like an accusation. One gets the sense that the theologian was invited out of inertia, and that the organizers had wished to find a more plausible alternative. In a portentous comment for the future of these debates, the organizers thought that "since the entire discourse [of the conference] was well within the domain of philosophy" a philosopher was invited to comment at the end of the conference "in the hope that a final common path might be found, of reason, of arbitration (if necessary), and at least of common sense, if not pure logic" (Labby 1968: xi–xii). Perhaps the Ramseys of the world should have seen the writing on the wall, even at this early point.

The sociologist Edward Shils began the conference by summarizing the social conditions under which the question of the sanctity of life is to be examined. We must ask about the "sanctity of life" because of "the decline of Christian belief about the place of man in the divine scheme and the consequent diminution of its force as a criterion in the judgement of the work and permissibility of human actions" (Shils 1968: 2). Undeterred, the theologian at the conference, Ramsey, would make an argument for the immorality of abortion based almost exclusively on theological knowledge, using references to scripture and Protestant theologian Karl Barth (Ramsey 1968).

While not all scientists were advocates of the "religion of science" advocated by some scientists, neither were they willing to let explicit Christian ends determine what experiments they should and should not do. One of the great opponents of the theologians was one of the inventors of in-vitro fertilization, Robert Edwards. He was a forceful advocate of the idea of "scientific freedom," where scientists could set the ends of their research without the interference of the public. ("Scientific freedom," using my terminology, simply means exclusive jurisdiction by scientists over the ethics of their experiments.) In his autobiography Edwards gives an account of his first encounter with Ramsey at a conference on in-vitro fertilization in 1971. "He had to be seen and heard to be believed. I had to endure a denunciation of our work as if from some nineteenth-century pulpit. . . . He had uttered sentiments in his rhetorical way that would not have disgraced those directed against Charles Darwin one hundred years earlier" (Edwards and Steptoe 1980: 112).

What is more telling is not that Ramsey would have given a theologically based denunciation of Edwards's work, but Edwards's rendition of the response of the audience, which consisted of "senators, judges, doctors, scientists and writers" (Edwards and Steptoe 1980: 112). Of his response to Ramsey, he said, "I had hardly begun my second sentence—'Dogma that has entered biology either from Communist or from Christian sources has done nothing but harm . . .'—when I was interrupted by huge applause. The audience were on their feet clapping. . . . [Ramsey's] point of view had been shatteringly rejected by the audience. Indeed he made no further contribution to that symposium" (Edwards and Steptoe 1980: 114). In sum, it appeared that the audience that would give jurisdiction over promulgating the ethics of science and medicine was hostile to an explicitly theological message, suggesting that a change in strategy would be necessary.

The New Pluralism among Public Elites

The debates over the ethics of science and medicine did not remain restricted to academic scientists. Theologians and other critics of the scientists had been calling for the public—or at least the elite public—to pay attention to this debate, take away jurisdiction from the scientists, and (implicitly) give it to them. The public would increasingly be the group that would give jurisdiction over the ethics of science and medicine.

The reality of religious pluralism is that the United States has been extremely pluralistic almost from its founding. What matters in the case at hand is that pluralism among the general citizens did not come to be represented among societal elites until mid-way through the twentieth century. By the late 1960s it was clear that one could not assume that a generic mainline Protestant ethic was held among these elites.

Up until the 1950s there were still "Jewish quotas" at Ivy League schools, genteel discrimination against non-Protestant faculty, and Catholic and Jewish hospitals existed as separate institutions with Catholic and Jewish doctors. By the 1960s people of non-Protestant backgrounds were not unusual in the professions due to a decline in outright discrimination and expansions in availability of higher education. Simultaneously, in the 1960s, college enrollments were surging as government funding increased, making college and professional educations no longer the sole province of mainline Protestants (Wuthnow 1988: 86).

Ramsey, for example, came to experience this pluralism first hand as he moved into debates on science and medicine. In 1969 he was invited to give a prestigious series of lectures at Yale Divinity School, which were later published in his most influential work, *The Patient as Person*. He notes the long string of Protestant theologians who had been invited over the centuries to give these lectures—among the most recognizable are Henry Sloan Coffin, Harry Emerson Fosdick, and Reinhold Niebuhr—and notes that his lectures would be unique in the history of the series. They would be co-sponsored by the medical school, and "on each of the four nights, I would be joined by a panel of commentators, consisting of physicians and medical school professors and theologians—Protestant, Catholic and Jewish" (Ramsey 1970b: xix). Not only would he be confronted with this theological pluralism, but he also decided that he would do the theological equivalent of fieldwork. "I judged at once, of course, that I needed to know how medical men themselves discuss the questions they confront" (xix), and arranged to be tutored at Georgetown University hospital during the spring semesters in 1968 and 1969 on how doctors made decisions.

His invitation to observe physicians at work came from André Hellegers, an active Catholic obstetrician-gynecologist at the Catholic Georgetown University Hospital (Ramsey 1970b: xx). In the book that resulted from the lectures, he most effusively thanks for their reading of the chapters Hellegers and a Jewish physician/biologist/philosopher named Leon Kass. In an earlier time, Kass would not have been in his prestigious post at the National Academy of Sciences to encounter Ramsey, and Hellegers would not have expected a Protestant to be interested in the workings of a Catholic hospital. Yet, things had changed. Ramsey would state in the preface to *The Patient as Person* that "an increasing number of moralists—Catholic, Protestant, Jewish and unlabeled men—are manifesting interest, devoting their trained powers of ethical reasoning to questions of medical practice and technology" (Ramsey 1970b: xvi).

Characteristics of the Messengers

It was not simply the changing environment that resulted in the self-censoring of the theologians; forces internal to the theological movement itself led to its weakened state. Most notably, to necessarily oversimplify, theology was divided along a continuum of those on one end who only argued for explicitly theological ends from explicitly theological premises, through those who engaged in the translation to secular ends described above, to those who were committed to an almost entirely secular form of theology. This latter pole will probably sound strange to people unfamiliar with this era. However, in the 1960s there were movements in both liberal Protestant and Catholic theology toward a form of theology that was accessible to all people, whether they believed in God or not.

Among Protestants, I have already discussed the debate between "norm and context" or "rules and situations" represented by Ramsey and Fletcher, respectively. From the "situationist" wing also came what has become known as "death of God" theology. In Harvey Cox's influential version of this thesis, God had freed humans through secularization, and they must now live with the implications of this freedom (Laney 1970: 18). The "death of God" advocates and the "situationists" would both "eliminate any exclusively Christian conditions or terms" from what was also called "the new morality" (Laney 1970: 19). To slightly overstate the case, the claim was that there was nothing unique about Christian ethics that could not be obtained through secular sources.

Among Catholics, a similar strand of thinking had emerged. Reacting to neo-scholasticism, by the early 1970s a variant of natural law theology had emerged that Vincent MacNamara calls "an autonomous ethic" theology.[3] It is beyond the scope of this chapter to delve into the history of Catholic theology, but a quotation from Joseph Fuchs, one of the advocates, sums up the view of this new school well: "Christian morality . . . is basically and substantially a human morality, that is a morality of true manhood. That means that truth, honesty and fidelity, in their materiality, are not specifically

Christian but universally human values" (quoted in MacNamara 1985: 40). As Gustav Ermecke stated at the time (1972), "[W]hereas a few years previously theologians regarded it as natural to demand that the teaching of morality should be theological, i.e. 'Conceived in terms of scripture and of salvation history' things have been entirely reversed 'so that Christian morality is understood in rational, philosophical terms,' i.e. in terms of empirical human science" (quoted in MacNamara 1985: 55). The Catholic contributions to these debates were at their start approximately half-way between the types of arguments made in the second and third eras. In Gustafson's words, in natural law theology, "Ethical analysis and prescription was theological in principle; moralists were theologians by being moralists. Enough said about theology" (Gustafson 1978: 387).

In addition to the conflict in theology between theologians who translated to secular ends and those who started and ended with secular claims, there was substantive conflict about the religious nature of "scientific progress" itself. For example, a number of theologians of science and medicine were perceived, at least by the Ramseys of the world, as total apologists for a scientific and not a theological worldview. The divisions within the theological house were well articulated by Ramsey, who complained of Catholic theologian Karl Rahner, "Roman Catholic omega-pointers" (a reference to the omega-point theory of French Jesuit de Chardin), and Protestant theologians of secular, historical 'hope' who collapse the distinction between being men before God and being God before we have learned to be men" (Ramsey 1970a: 142). The gist of this new theology was that humans, created by God, had used their God-given powers to engage in Godlike activity, such as creating new life forms. An ally of Ramsey, Leon Kass, would call these theologians "theologians-turned-technocrats" who "sanctify the new freedoms: '[W]hat can be done, should be done'" (Kass 1972: 60).

Ramsey would have similar things to say about the situation ethics being promoted at the time by theologians such as Joseph Fletcher. Fletcher, who was personally beginning to secularize by this point (Fletcher 1993), would say that "if the greatest good of the greatest number . . . were served by it, it would be justifiable not only to specialize the capacities of people by cloning or by constructive genetic engineering, but also to bio-engineer or bio-design para-humans or 'modified men'" (Fletcher 1971: 779). As Ramsey would quip, this type of reasoning "sounds remarkably like a priestly blessing over everything, doing duty for ethics" (Ramsey 1970a: 139–40). Metaphorically, it is hard to win the battle when a portion of your soldiers are using the language of your enemy, seemingly blessing scientific activity as an end unto itself.

A second problem for the messengers was a lack of resources. The best resource for the theologians would have been access to the members of their respective traditions, but because of who these first activists were, this direct access was not open to them. These first critics of the scientists were mostly not employed by denominations but were academic theologians, public intellectuals, or lay activists. Among the Protestants, none of these issues, with the exception of abortion, were addressed by the denominations, and these Protestants were not theologians who wrote Sunday school materials but people who wrote scholarly journal articles.

Moreover, as already noted, these theologians were liberal Protestants, not evangelicals. Mainline Protestants are well known for deriving their beliefs from many sources beyond their religious experience, at least compared to evangelicals. For example, members of mainline faiths let their professional or educational background determine their beliefs, perhaps as much as their religion. This is the basic insight of the "strict" churches hypothesis (Kelley 1972; Iannaccone 1994), which claims that in "strict" traditions, such as evangelicalism, church teaching shapes beliefs. In traditions that are not so "strict," such as mainline Protestantism, beliefs are shaped by a wider range of forces. Therefore, even if mainline Protestants had had access to their denominations, they would have been less likely to influence the average member.

The reason the Catholic theological voice did not have access to the denominational machinery and the members is a bit more complex. First, many of the earliest theologically oriented critics of science and medicine were also involved with liberal politics in the Catholic church. The second Vatican Council met between 1962 and 1965, and in 1963 the Pope appointed a small group to review the Catholic position on contraception. One member of that group was Catholic lay-person and obstetrician-gynecologist André Hellegers (who would later invite Ramsey to study at Georgetown).

Watching the birth control debate was a Catholic public intellectual with a Ph.D. in philosophy named Daniel Callahan, who was an editor of the Catholic intellectual journal *Commonweal.* He, like Hellegers, was a liberal on the contraception debate, calling contraception "a test case for the contemporary renewal of the Church" (Walters 1985: 9). In 1968 the Pope, through the release of *Humanae Vitae,* rejected the recommendations of the Papal Commission and reiterated the traditional stance of the Roman Catholic church against contraception.

Hellegers was "deeply disappointed by the Pope's decision" (Walters 1985: 9). Callahan was "equally distressed by *Humanae Vitae,*" and the next year edited a book called *The Catholic Case for Contraception* for the "express purpose of supporting the moral arguments of couples who dissented from *Humane Vitae*" (Walters 1985: 10). He would also help to found the first institutional home for the growing movement challenging science and medicine—the Institute of Society, Ethics, and the Life Sciences (now called the Hastings Center).

In 1971, Hellegers founded the second institutional home for the growing movement—the Joseph and Rose Kennedy Institute for the Study of Human Reproduction and Bioethics at Georgetown University—and recruited an ecumenical group of Christian scholars to staff it. LeRoy Walters, interpreting these events, traces Hellegers's "determination to find a non-ecclesiastical forum for the ongoing exploration of problems at the interface of biology, medicine and moral theology" to his reaction to *Humanae Vitae* (Walters 1985: 10). Thus, in the Catholic component of the theological challenge, the institutions that began to solidify the movement after the "decade of conferences" were already committed to a separation of their theological approach from that of the institutional church.

A Debate about (Secularly Expressed) Ends

Theology was weak. It was weak among the scientists, and its particularism was out of touch with the growing pluralism of the professionals and elites who would actually make ethical decisions. It was also divided within itself and disconnected from traditional bases of resources. Neither theology in general nor any group of theologians was up to the challenge of removing jurisdiction from the scientists. The threats to humanity at the time seemed strong enough to justify some compromises in one's theological position in order to win the war. The compromise was that theologians would engage in a translation of their theological ends to secular ends, making them more suitable for widespread communication. It is important to note that, at least in the best cases, they started with theology and moved to secular ends, making their ends extremely diverse.

For example, Joseph Fletcher would move from a maximization of agape in the 1960s to a utilitarian maximization of happiness in the 1970s. Fletcher's 1966 *Situation Ethics* is essentially an argument that decisions in medicine and science should follow a consequentialist maximization of agape. There he states that the two principles to be maximized are from the apostle Paul: " 'The written code kills, but the Spirit gives life' (II Cor. 3:6), and 'For the whole law is fulfilled in one word, "You shall love your neighbor as yourself"' (Gal. 5: 14)" (Fletcher 1966: 30). By the 1970s he was maximizing utility, while the underlying theological motivations remained in place (albeit unstated, in Fletcher's case).

Ramsey provides another example. He was one of the first advocates in modern medical ethics of forwarding the end of autonomy in medical decision making by pursuing consent. For Ramsey this was a translation of his pursuit of the ends of agape and holding the covenant with God. According to one reviewer, he made use of consent because he "sought to find a language accessible to as many people as possible despite their theological convictions and 'consent' appeared to cross over communities and traditions" (Long 1993: 125–26).

This translation gave the appearance that theology was competing with science by asking the deep questions. Theologian James Gustafson, arguing for the approach used in this second era—and against the emerging third era we have yet to cover—gives the example of a debate between geneticists, where "what really divided the disputants were questions that traditionally have been judged to be religious in character." Some geneticists were essentially utopian, some were essentially apocalyptic, and "the whole discussion [was] a contest between competing eschatologies: prospects for a universal salvation pitted against prospects for eternal annihilation" through genetics. The dispute could not be settled by scientific facts but rested essentially on a secular faith. Gustafson related how he used his theological training to ferret out these secular theologies and pointed them out to the participants. "Theology might not provide answers you like to accept," he concluded, "but it can force questions you ought to be aware of" (Gustafson 1978: 389).

For example, consider Kass's remark about human cloning: "For man is the watershed which divides the world into those things that belong to nature and those that are made by men. To lay one's hands on human generation is to take a major step toward making man himself simply another of the man-made things" (Kass 1972: 54). Here is a conundrum that scientists do not usually like to think about, but it was *the* topic of conversation among theologians and fellow travelers, yet all without reference to explicit theology. For example, Callahan responded to Kass by asking "whether man's humanity can survive" new technologies such as in-vitro fertilization. He noted that scientists probably "believe that their work is both praiseworthy and intensively human. To seek knowledge is human. To improve man's lot is human. To make things, even human beings, is human." He is here helping the scientists onto his playing ground, because very few of them would engage issues in this depth. He calls for further debate over "some general, comprehensive, and universal norms for 'the human'" (Callahan 1972: 97–99).

So, during this middle period, theologians would debate the ends for which these technologies were the means. They would think through the question in their "first voice" of theology and argue for a secular end with their second. Scientists, while originally asking these big questions (at least in the human genetic engineering debate), were trying to back away from them now, realizing that if the debate took place on these topics, they were in trouble. I discuss this topic in more detail in the conclusion of this chapter, but I want to note here that this strategy of the theologians was not necessarily a bad one at the time. People truly felt that advances in science and medicine were threatening our humanity, even our human survival, and if translating their particularistic beliefs was required to win the battle, it probably seemed to be worth doing.

However, even this argument about theologically translated ends was not to last long. By the mid-1970s Gustafson would complain in print that he was unsure what made someone a "religious ethicist" in debates over science and medicine. He quipped that "an ethicist is a former theologian who does not have the professional credentials of a moral philosopher." The audience seemed to have the same perception. For example, an influential 1967 abortion conference, translated for a popular audience, listed the participants, and theology did not have its own category. Some were placed under the heading "ethics," and some under the social sciences (Cooke et al. 1968).

Gustafson was standing between the peaks of the second and third eras— he was writing out of concern for the lost theological voice of the first era and calling for a focus on the second, while witnessing the advent of the third. Many of the religious ethicists were beginning to ask thin little questions that did not call the scientific project into question: "Should one cut the power source to a respirator for patient *y* whose circumstances are *a*, *b* and *c*? [This] is not utterly dissimilar to asking whether $8.20 an hour or $8.55 an hour ought to be paid to carpenters' helpers in Kansas City" (Gustafson 1978: 387). The explicit theological challenge to science and medicine had lasted only a few years, and the second era of debating secular ends derived from theological ideas had lasted only a few more.

THEOLOGICAL DEFEAT: A DEBATE WITH ASSUMED ENDS

I discuss this final transition lightly because I have covered it in great detail elsewhere (Evans 2002). The theologians and their allies were essentially victims of their own success. They had started a movement that questioned where scientists were going with their technologies, and the public finally began to pay attention. In fact, they were paying so much attention that these issues soon caught the eye of elected officials, who began to suggest various legislative remedies to force scientists and physicians to adhere to the basic ethical insights that were being generated by the movement.

As early as 1968 Senator Walter Mondale had held hearings on setting up a government commission to oversee work in areas such as genetic engineering, organ transplantation, behavior control, experimentation on humans, and the financing of research. Like those in the movement to challenge the scientists, Mondale was interested in the deep questions. He started the hearings by saying, "Recent medical advances raise grave and fundamental ethical and legal questions for our society. Who shall live and who shall die? How long shall life be preserved and how should it be altered? Who will make decisions? How shall society be prepared?" (quoted in Jonsen 1998: 90–91).

Scientists were fearful that the cascade of money that had come their way since the 1950s would either slow to a trickle as the public became fearful of the fruit of scientific investigations, or that the money would come with strings attached if, for example, the Congress were to determine what experiments could and could not be done. They blamed this new attention not only on their scientific colleagues who were advocating utopian scientific visions that had scared the public, but also on the theologians and others that these visions had lured into the debate. Writing specifically about human genetic engineering, Harvard bacteriologist Bernard Davis stated in 1970 that the "exaggeration of the dangers from genetics will inevitably contribute to an already distorted public view, which increasingly blames science for our problems and ignores its contributions to our welfare." This "irresponsible hyperbole" of the previous generation of scientists "has already influenced the funding of research." He went on to say, "If, in panic, our society should curtail fundamental genetic research, we would pay a huge price" (Davis 1970: 1279, 1282). He finished by calling scientists to arms against those who use "unverifiable knowledge": "Genetics will surely survive the current attacks, just as it survived attacks from the Communist Party in Moscow and from fundamentalists in Tennessee. But meanwhile . . . we may have to defend vigorously the value of objective and verifiable knowledge, especially when it comes into conflict with political, theological or sociological dogmas" (Davis 1970: 1283).

When faced with a strong challenge, the best defense is a strong offence. Some scientists decided that they would suggest the setting up of various government advisory committees where the citizens could fulminate about their concerns but would be unable actually to constrain scientists. Edwards, the in-vitro fertilization pioneer introduced above, would say that biologists must "invent a method of taking counsel of mankind" or "society will thrust its advice on biologists . . . in a manner or form seriously hampering to science." What was needed was an organization "easily approached and consulted to advise and assist biologists and others to reach *their own* decisions" (Edwards and Sharpe 1971: 89, 90; my italics).

The issue of human experimentation finally made some sort of collective oversight of scientists inevitable. In 1972 it was revealed that the U.S. Public Health Service had for forty years been conducting an experiment in which the syphilis of a group of about six hundred poor and uneducated black men in Tuskegee, Alabama, was left untreated. The idea was to autopsy them when they died to see the effect of syphilis on the human body. This, combined with other revelations that physicians in hospitals had been experimenting on regular patients without their knowledge, made Congress feel compelled to respond; the result was the National Commission for the Protection of Human Subjects of Biomedical and Behavioral Research, which first met in 1974.

One of the mandated tasks of the commission was to "conduct a comprehensive investigation and study to identify the basic ethical principles which should underlie the conduct of biomedical and behavioral research involving human subjects" and "develop guidelines which should be followed in such research to assure that it is conducted in accord with such principles" (Jonsen 1994: xiv). That is, this state advisory commission was to determine the legitimate ends for arguments about research on human subjects—ends that would be applied to make ethical decisions by the members of institutional review boards throughout the country who, by accepting government money, were implicitly making decisions for the government.

The National Commission contained a few theologians among the physicians, social scientists, and others, and the group reduced the debate about ends to three ends that were "among those generally accepted in our cultural tradition": autonomy, beneficence and justice (National Commission 1978: 4). This alone was not a challenge to the theologians. Their own method had evolved to this point: one could search the Protestant tradition's debates on human research and certainly derive these ends as being consistent with the Protestant tradition. One could do the same for the Catholic tradition. While each tradition could have come up with additional ends, this path was not inherently destructive to the theologians.

The problem for theology came from a different angle. At the same time that the commission was trying to create its principles or ends, a group of philosophers and theologians at Georgetown University had been working on a principle-based approach to ethical problems that could be applied to public policy. The theologians in this new group were on the end of the spectrum described above where both the ends and the rationale for them were to be expressed in secular language. Under the influence of philosophical ethics, they were looking for principles that were not only universally held by the population but could be universally applied across problems.

The beginning of the end for theology occurred when this group successfully institutionalized the idea that autonomy, beneficence, and justice were not only universally held by all the citizens of the United States, but were *the* ends to pursue, not only for human experimentation but for all issues in science and medicine. Those who made such arguments came to be distinguished from those in other professions, and begin to refer to themselves as "bioethicists" rather than theologians or philosophers. The theologians had been examining each issue in its particularity, coming up with a theological conclusion, and translating this end into secular language. If we should pursue the same end for all issues, without this sort of theological reflection, of what use were the theologians? In turns out there would be no use for them, which was the beginning of the end. How had this happened?

The spread of this form of argumentation to other topics beyond human experimentation was due to a number of converging events. First, the state became involved with more and more debates considered to be bioethical. Reflecting on the birth of the bioethics profession, Warren Reich states that "there was a political urgency to many of the biomedical issues" at the time. "The media craved the biomedical controversies and federal and state policy makers wanted answers" (Reich 1995: 22). As I show elsewhere, the state bureaucratic authority requires calculable ethics, and a system claiming that three ends are universally applicable across problems, without requiring a reassessment of which ends are "among those generally accepted in our cultural tradition" makes for more efficient decision making.

Second, participants in these debates created a full-blown form of argumentation, applicable to all problems in science and medicine, that others could use to make arguments about issues other than human experimentation. The academics from Georgetown who had helped the National Commission were at the same time writing a textbook called the *Principles of Biomedical Ethics,* now in its fifth edition, which would further spread the form of argumentation (Beauchamp and Childress 2001). The form of argumentation in this text went beyond the problem of human experimentation to cover almost all problems related to ethical decisions in science, medicine, and society—abortion, euthanasia, medical rationing, and many more. Once the form of argumentation of bioethics was enshrined in public law for human experimentation and embodied in a popular textbook, it began to spread rapidly. There was an "enormous demand" for training in ethics, with the appearance of countless books, workshops, and courses to make "the theories and methods of ethics . . . readily available to more people in a shorter time" (Clouser and Gert 1990: 219). The "major strategy" in these educational events has been the approach embodied in the *Principles of Biomedical Ethics.*

According to observers of the profession, this book, more than anything else, has "shaped the teaching and practice of biomedical ethics in this country . . . [becoming] a standard text in courses and a virtual bible to some practitioners." The ethical framework provided by the book "shapes much of the discussion and debate about particular bioethical issues and policy, whether in the academy, the literature, the public forum or the clinic" (DuBose, Hamel, and O'Connell 1994: 1). The institutionalization of this form of argumentation for human experimentation and increasingly for other problems was so strong that one set of critics went so far as to begin their essay with the mocking claim that "throughout the land, arising from the throngs of converts to bioethics awareness, there can be heard a mantra . . . 'beneficence . . . autonomy . . . justice . . . ' " (Clouser and Gert 1990: 219).

The first jurisdictional expansion of the bioethics profession was from the ethics of medical research to the ethics of medical practice more generally. According to historian David Rothman, after being institutionalized in medical research, "the new rules for the laboratory permeated the examining room, circumscribing the discretionary authority of the individual physicians. The doctor-patient relationship was molded on the form of the researcher-subject; in therapy, as in experimentation, formal and informal mechanisms of control and a new language of patients' rights assumed unprecedented importance."[4] This was quickly followed by attempts at expansion into any area that could be metaphorically linked to either medicine or science, as long it somehow involved humans.

The institutionalization of this form of argumentation concerned some of the original advocates of broader public bioethical debates that would include theologians. As early as 1982 Daniel Callahan was warning about the new hegemony in ethical thinking in these debates. Calling this new hegemony "some kind of ultimate moral big bang theory" or an " 'engineering model' of applied ethics," he bemoaned the emphasis on one narrow form of argumentation. The broader approach that he had championed in the early days of the field had "the distinct advantage of leaving the way open for the insights of religion, of cultural observation and social analysis . . . and of concepts of human dignity and purpose that had a wider scope than mere autonomy." Opposing the creation of a separate profession of bioethics with its own form of argumentation, he hoped that "the other disciplines that are a part of applied ethics, will . . . shout and scream" when they detect the "diversion from what was intended to be a richer agenda" (Callahan 1982: 4).

Nonetheless, this new form of argumentation was found to be congenial "to the educational and policy making purposes being pursued" by bioethicists (Reich 1995: 22). That is, it was well suited for extracting resources from the new environment where the bureaucratic state was the primary decision maker. Reflecting on this success, a current Georgetown inhabitant reports that the first director of the Kennedy Institute at Georgetown was able to "promote the success of the Georgetown vision [by] marshall[ing] hitherto untapped federal and private funding and university resources for operating expenses and endowed chairs in bioethics. He fostered the need for medical bioethics in the government agencies and biomedical research and clinical centers that were seeking to develop ethical and regulative policies, and he supplied that need."[5]

To sum up, the rise of government commissions provided an exceptionally good environment for the growth of this form of argumentation used by the profession of bioethics, and the topic of the first bioethical concerns—which was also the topic of the first government commission—meant that the jurisdictional homeland of the bioethicist was the interaction between medical researcher and subject. That is, this is what their form of argumentation was originally designed to address. Yet, as bioethicists have moved beyond their home jurisdiction, they have used this same form of argumentation to address new problems, that is, to gain new jurisdictions.

THE DEBATE ABOUT SCIENCE AND MEDICINE
AT THE TURN OF THE NEW CENTURY

What was once a broad movement—epitomized by the early name of the Hastings Center, "the Institute of Society, Ethics, and the Life Sciences"— was now quite narrow. Theology is a much less influential contributor to these debates, but has been marginalized back into its own field. The new bioethics profession considers itself to have a neutral language that can adjudicate between the particularisms of different communities. It is worth quoting one of the leading bioethicists at length on the topic:

> The history of bioethics over the last two decades has been the story of the development of a secular ethic. Initially, individuals working from within particular religious traditions held the center of bioethical discussions. However, this focus was replaced by analyses that span traditions, including particular secular traditions. As a result, a special secular tradition that attempts to frame answers in terms of no particular tradition, but rather in ways open to rational individuals as such, has emerged. Bioethics is an element of a secular culture and the great-grandchild of the Enlightenment. Because the 1980s have been marked in Iran, the United States, and elsewhere by attempts to return to traditional values and the certainties of religious beliefs, one must wonder what this augurs for bioethics in this special secular sense. However, because the world does not appear on the brink of embracing a particular orthodoxy, and if an orthodoxy is not imposed, as say in Iran or the Soviet Union, bioethics will inevitably develop as a secular fabric of rationality in an era of uncertainty. That is, the existence of open peaceable discussion among divergent groups, such as atheists, Catholics, Jews, Protestants, Marxists, heterosexuals and homosexuals, about public policy issues bearing on health care, will press unavoidably for a neutral common language. Bioethics is developing as the lingua franca of a world concerned with health care, but not possessing a common ethical viewpoint. (Engelhardt 1986: 5)

Clearly, theology has no place in this vision. There were of course theologians who, along with Gustafson, resisted the secularization of the debates over science and medicine. Many resisted becoming bioethicists, although many did convert. Ramsey, while clearly trying to write in at least somewhat of a pluralist voice to have influence, was nonetheless made famous for declaring at various points that "I always write as the ethicist I am, namely a Christian ethicist, and not as some hypothetical common denominator" (quoted in Gustafson 1978: 386). Theologians such as Stanley Hauerwas would go on to write essays titled "Why I Am Neither a Communitarian Nor a Medical Ethicist" (Hauerwas 1993). The one institution ded-

icated to theological analysis of issues in medicine and science that had remained, the Park Ridge Center for the Study of Health, Faith, and Ethics,
was essentially disbanded in 2002. There remain some theologians whose
writing is as theological as such writing ever was. Yet most people who engage in debates about the ethics of science and medicine, unless part of this
smaller world, would be unaware of these authors.

In fact, when an explicitly theological voice does make an appearance in
mainstream debates, it is quickly surrounded and stamped out. For example, during the hearings in the late 1990s on human cloning the National Bioethics Advisory Commission found itself in a swirl of controversy
when a Scottish research team announced that they had cloned a sheep,
and President Clinton gave this commission a very short time to come to an
ethical conclusion. A panel of theologians was invited to the hearing, and
some of them did indeed make very theological statements—including a
Ramseyesque statement by one of Ramsey's former students who, when
asked to translate his theology into a secular form, said that he was a Christian theologian and insisted on speaking as one.

The input of the theologians was registered but appeared to have no impact on the conclusions. A consultant to the commission who wrote a paper
on religious perspectives on cloning would later claim that "the contributions of the religious perspectives were deemed politically important and
ethically insignificant" (Campbell 1997). To put it somewhat more bluntly,
theologians were no longer to be taken as serious contributors to the debate
itself, but only as spokespersons for communities within a pluralistic public
that was watching the cloning debate closely.

CONCLUSIONS

Some scholars, particularly the card-carrying members of the theological
remnant, have traversed this history. They have talked about how the "renaissance of medical ethics" was quickly followed by its "enlightenment,"
where "interest in religious traditions moved from the center to the margins
of scholarly attention" (Verhey and Lammers 1993: 3). Reasons for the "enlightenment" remain unexamined, except through reference to recognition of the pluralism of American society. I have tried to sketch the more detailed causes of the "enlightenment" here.

I have told this history in three stages, while most observers of the secularization of bioethics simply talk about the religious time and the irreligious time. I have described three overlapping phases: first, when theologians, challenged by scientists who seemed to be attempting to determine
the meaning and purpose of humanity through science, entered these debates using theological ends. Assuming a more or less Christian class of

elites, they attempted to appeal to the Christian consciences of the scientists and physicians.

This attempt at having theological ends determine what science and medicine should do was extremely short-lived. For a number of reasons having to do with the audience of the theologians and the internal nature of the theological camp itself, theologians during what I call the second period turned to theological reflection that resulted in ends that could be expressed in a secular language. This debate was a debate about ends—and with each particularistic group using its own tradition to determine ends, there were many to debate. Even this debate about ends was not to last, because the rise of bureaucratic authority over matters in science and medicine required a simple, universal system of ethics that theologians were unwilling to participate in. During the third period, the new profession of bioethics rose to the challenge and has been in control to this day.

This chapter is different from the others in this volume because it describes such a recent process, undertaken at a time when theology had already been severely weakened by the processes described in the other chapters. For example, the secularization of the American university was basically complete by this time, making the re-sacralization project of the theologians that much more difficult. The theologians never had designs on directly controlling science or medicine—that effort was lost in the Middle Ages. They instead simply wanted theological insights to be used in deciding what activities scientists and physicians would focus on. They started this project on incredibly weak terms, almost immediately deciding that they needed to express their theological conclusions with secular ends.

Yet inevitability is one of the features of the secularization narrative that this volume is dedicated to questioning. By reinserting agency into these investigations and by looking in fine detail, we hope to gain greater understanding of secularization processes. This narrative above includes one of the great, inevitable, impersonal mechanisms often gestured to in secularization studies—the rise of the state and the decline of the lifeworld (Habermas 1987)—and the subsequent decline in debate about ends. Does it contribute to our understanding of the influence of the state on secularization to analyze events at this more detailed level? That is, does it help to name the particular bioethicist who became the chair of a government bioethics commission because he used ethical arguments useful to the state and to name the theologian who did not get the nod because of his unwillingness to compromise in his arguments?

I believe that such detailed examination does matter to secularization theory. It reveals that the strategy of trying to speak to a collective public by translating to secular ends was probably the beginning of the end for the theologians' influence in this debate. Their use of this strategy was not inevitable; they could, for example, have tried to speak the language of their home communities to their home communities—Methodists, in Ramsey's case—and these Methodists could have influenced Methodist scientists and doctors, and written letters to Congress based upon their Methodist views. Ethics could have been enacted through interest-group practices, as in the abortion debate and, to a lesser extent, in the euthanasia debate.

Looking at the detail of this particular case shows us that the forces of secularization do not sweep through society, transforming all in their path. Rather, these forces are like the sirens on the shore—tempting the theologians who advocate participation in public debate into various deals with the devil that ultimately undermine their sacralizing strategy. In this case, the temptation was the ability to influence directly and rapidly the actions of elites, as well as the need to appeal to a broader audience outside one's own tradition. However, looking at the details continues to remind us of the power of the macro forces. The growing responsibility of the state after World War II in America was a powerful resource that some participants in the debate could tap into to defeat the others. Resistance is not impossible, yet those who are aligned on the side of the enlightenment rationalism promoted by the state have many advantages (Ezrahi 1990).

I end with an interesting note. Theologians, writing fairly explicit theology, are still attempting to influence science and medicine. In addition to the ranks of the unrepentant theologians, some denominations have been trying to educate their members about issues in medicine and science. For example, the United Methodist Church has distributed a number of educational documents on human genetic engineering. They use interest-group methods, which do not require translation of the theological message. Perhaps more interesting, some theologians are trying to undercut the epistemological foundations of the bioethics profession. Relying upon the insights of Alasdair MacIntyre that there is nowhere to stand above the fray to evaluate truth claims, they are trying to show that the arguments based on the three universal ends of the bioethics profession are just another discourse that has no more legitimacy than theology.

Whether or not the theologians will succeed in this second attempt to bring theology back into discussions of medicine and science remains to be seen. Even some people in the debate who have gone through a personal secularization experience bemoan the loss of religion to these debates. Callahan employs a personal metaphor to describe the problem with the secularization of bioethics: "Those of us who have lost our religious faith may be glad that we have discovered what we take to be the reality of things, but we can still recognize that we have also lost something of great value as well: the faith, vision, insights, and experience of whole peoples and traditions who, no less than we unbelievers, struggled to make sense of things. That those goods are part of a garment we no longer want to wear does not make their loss anything other than still a loss; and it is not a negligible one" (Callahan 1990: 2).

NOTES

1. The data for this chapter come from three sources. First, the limited secondary literature on these debates. Second, the data on influential texts gathered for my book on one of the issues under debate—human genetic engineering (Evans 2002). Third, what could be called the "overflow" from the previously described data source. In this earliest era, theologians and their competitors did not separate out issues in their debates but tended to talk about them all simultaneously. Therefore, many of the sources that my method in my book identified as influential also contain data about broader debates. If there is any bias, it is toward the debates over human genetic engineering, but I believe that this issue was representative of debates more broadly during this era. This chapter is essentially a description of the early theological movement in greater detail then was necessary for the purposes of the book. There, I described what I am calling eras one and two as a single era, focusing on the transition to what I call era three in this chapter.

2. Before turning to medical issues, Ramsey was well known for basic theology and just-war theory. Many summaries of Ramsey's work exist; see Long 1993; Attwood 1992; Smith 1993; Tubbs 1996; Hauerwas 1997: chap. 8.

3. Neo-scholasticism in Catholic ethics produced a stream of moral manuals that have, according to one account, "a great air of security and certainty," reflecting "a confident understanding of the identity of Christian morality." Oversimplifying, the whole point is to make sure you get to heaven (MacNamara 1985: 9, 10).

4. See Rothman 1991: 89, 107. "Patients' rights" are derived from autonomy or respect for persons.

5. See Reich 1995: 23. Clearly, Reich also believes that the charisma of this first director was partially responsible for this success, and not simply that the principles were particularly well suited for the state and other bureaucratic forms.

REFERENCES

Abbott, Andrew. 1988. *The System of Professions: An Essay on the Division of Expert Labor.* Chicago: University of Chicago Press.

Attwood, David. 1992. *Paul Ramsey's Political Ethics.* Lanham, MD: Rowman and Littlefield.

Beauchamp, Tom L., and James F. Childress. 2001. *Principles of Biomedical Ethics.* 5th ed. New York: Oxford University Press.

Callahan, Daniel. 1972. "New Beginnings in Life: A Philosopher's Response." In *The New Genetics and the Future of Man,* ed. Michael P. Hamilton, 90–106. Grand Rapids, MI: Eerdmans.

———. 1982. "At the Center." *Hastings Center Report* (June): 4.

———. 1990. *What Kind of Life? The Limits of Medical Progress.* New York: Simon and Schuster.

Campbell, Courtney S. 1997. "Prophecy and Policy." *Hastings Center Report* 27, no. 5: 15–17.

Clouser, K. Danner, and Bernard Gert. 1990. "A Critique of Principlism." *Journal of Medicine and Philosophy* 15: 219–36.

Cooke, Robert E.; André Hellegers; Robert G. Hoyt; and Herbert W. Richardson. 1968. *The Terrible Choice: The Abortion Dilemma.* New York: Bantam Books.

Davis, Bernard D. 1970. "Prospects for Genetic Intervention in Man." *Science* 170: 1279–83.

DuBose, Edwin R.; Ronald P. Hamel; and Laurence J. O'Connell. 1994. "Introduction." In *A Matter of Principles? Ferment in U.S. Bioethics,* ed. Edwin R. DuBose, Ronald P. Hamel, and Laurence J. O'Connell, 1–17. Valley Forge, PA: Trinity Press International.

Edwards, Robert. 1989. *Life before Birth: Reflections on the Embryo Debate.* New York: Basic Books.

Edwards, Robert G., and David J. Sharpe. 1971. "Social Values and Research in Human Embryology." *Nature* 231: 87–91.

Edwards, Robert, and Patrick Steptoe. 1980. *A Matter of Life: The Story of a Medical Breakthrough.* London: Hutchinson.

Engelhardt, H. Tristram. 1986. *The Foundations of Bioethics.* New York: Oxford University Press.

Evans, John H. 2002. *Playing God? Human Genetic Engineering and the Rationalization of Public Bioethical Debate.* Chicago: University of Chicago Press.

Ezrahi, Yaron. 1990. *The Descent of Icarus: Science and the Transformation of Contemporary Democracy.* Cambridge, MA: Harvard University Press.

Fletcher, Joseph. 1954. *Morals and Medicine.* Princeton, NJ: Princeton University Press.

———. 1966. *Situation Ethics: The New Morality.* Philadelphia, PA: Westminster Press.

———. 1971. "Ethical Aspects of Genetic Controls." *New England Journal of Medicine* 285, no. 14: 776–83.

———. 1993. "Memoir of an Ex-Radical." In *Joseph Fletcher: Memoir of an Ex-Radical,* ed. Kenneth Vaux, 55–92. Louisville, KY: Westminster/John Knox.

Gustafson, James M. 1978. "Theology Confronts Technology and the Life Sciences." *Commonweal* 105: 386–92.

Habermas, Jürgen. 1987. *The Theory of Communicative Action.* Vol. 2. *Lifeworld and System: A Critique of Functionalist Reason.* Boston: Beacon Press.

Hauerwas, Stanley M. 1993. "Why I Am Neither a Communitarian Nor a Medical Ethicist." *Hastings Center Report* (November–December): S9–S10.

———. 1997. *Wilderness Wanderings: Probing Twentieth-Century Theology and Philosophy.* Boulder, CO: Westview Press.

Iannaccone, Laurence R. 1994. "Why Strict Churches Are Strong." *American Journal of Sociology* 99, no. 5: 1180–211.

Jonsen, Albert R. 1994. "Foreword." In *A Matter of Principles? Ferment in U.S. Bioethics,* ed. Edwin R. DuBose, Ronald P. Hamel, and Laurence J. O'Connell, ix–xvii. Valley Forge, PA: Trinity Press International.

———. 1998. *The Birth of Bioethics.* New York: Oxford University Press.

Kass, Leon R. 1972. "New Beginnings in Life." In *The New Genetics and the Future of Man,* ed. Michael Hamilton, 15–63. Grand Rapids, MI: Eerdmans.

Kaye, Howard L. 1997. *The Social Meaning of Modern Biology: From Social Darwinism to Sociobiology.* New Brunswick, NJ: Transaction Publishers.

Kelley, Dean M. 1972. *Why Conservative Churches Are Growing.* New York: Harper & Row.

Labby, Daniel H. 1968. "Introduction." In *Life or Death: Ethics and Options,* ed. Daniel H. Labby, viii–xxiii. Seattle, WA: University of Washington Press.

Laney, James T. 1970. "The New Morality and the Religious Communities." *Annals of the American Academy of Political and Social Science* 387: 14–21.

Long, D. Stephen. 1993. *Tragedy, Tradition, Transformism: The Ethics of Paul Ramsey.* Boulder, CO: Westview Press.

Luria, S. E. 1965. "Directed Genetic Change: Perspectives from Molecular Genetics." In *The Control of Human Heredity and Evolution,* ed, T. M. Sonneborn, 1–19. New York: Macmillan.

MacNamara, Vincent. 1985. *Faith and Ethics: Recent Roman Catholicism.* Washington, DC: Georgetown University Press.

National Commission for the Protection of Human Subjects of Biomedical and Behavioral Research. 1978. *The Belmont Report: Ethical Principles and Guidelines for the Protection of Human Subjects of Research.* Washington, DC: Government Printing Office.

Ramsey, Paul. 1968. "The Morality of Abortion." In *Life or Death: Ethics and Options,* ed. Daniel H. Labby, 60–93. Seattle: University of Washington Press.

———. 1970a. *Fabricated Man: The Ethics of Genetic Control.* New Haven, CT: Yale University Press.

———. 1970b. *The Patient as Person.* New Haven, CT: Yale University Press.

Reich, Warren Thomas. 1995. "The Word 'Bioethics': The Struggle over Its Earliest Meanings." *Kennedy Institute of Ethics Journal* 5, no. 1: 19–34.

Rothman, David J. 1991. *Strangers by the Bedside: A History of How Law and Bioethics Transformed Medical Decision Making.* New York: Basic Books.

Shils, Edward. 1968. "The Sanctity of Life." In *Life or Death: Ethics and Options,* ed. Daniel H. Labby, 2–39. Seattle: University of Washington Press.

Smith, David H. 1993. "On Paul Ramsey: A Covenant-Centered Ethic for Medicine." In *Theological Voices in Medical Ethics,* ed. Allen Verhey and Stephen E. Lammers, 7–29. Grand Rapids, MI: Eerdmans.

Thielicke, Helmut. 1970. "Ethics in Modern Medicine." In *Who Shall Live? Medicine, Technology, Ethics,* ed. Kenneth Vaux. Philadelphia, PA: Fortress Press.

Tubbs, James B. 1996. *Christian Theology and Medical Ethics.* Dordrecht: Kluwer Academic Publishers.

Verhey, Allen, and Stephen E. Lammers. 1993. *Theological Voices in Bioethics.* Grand Rapids, MI: Eerdmans.

Walters, LeRoy. 1985. "Religion and the Renaissance of Medical Ethics in the United States." In *Theology and Bioethics,* ed. E. E. Shelp, 3–16. Boston: D. Reidel.

Wolstenholme, Gordon, ed. 1963. *Man and His Future.* London: J. & A. Churchill.

Wright, Susan. 1994. *Molecular Politics: Developing American and British Regulatory Policy for Genetic Engineering, 1972–1982.* Chicago: University of Chicago Press.

Wuthnow, Robert. 1988. *The Restructuring of American Religion.* Princeton, NJ: Princeton University Press.

CONTRIBUTORS

Kraig Beyerlein is a doctoral candidate in sociology at the University of North Carolina at Chapel Hill. His areas of interest include sociology of religion, political sociology, social movements, and moral philosophy and epistemology.

Channin G. De Haan is a doctoral candidate in sociology at Arizona State University. Her dissertation studies cultural constructions of leadership, authority, and self and how they are formalized in religious organization. She also is interested in how teachers' personal definitions of religious liberty influence their classroom discussion of religion.

John H. Evans is Assistant Professor of Sociology at the University of California, San Diego. His research focuses on debates in the public sphere—specifically on religious involvement in politics, health policy, and public bioethics. He is the author of *Playing God? Human Genetic Engineering and the Rationalization of Public Bioethical Debate* (University of Chicago Press, 2002), and coeditor (with Robert Wuthnow) of *The Quiet Hand of God: Faith-Based Activism and the Public Role of Mainline Protestantism* (University of California Press, 2002).

Richard W. Flory is Associate Professor of Sociology at Biola University, La Mirada, California. His areas of interest are historical sociology and the sociology of religion, and he is currently researching post–baby boomer religion in the United States.

Eva Marie Garroutte received her Ph.D. from the Department of Sociology at Princeton University in 1993. Her main research interests include religion, science, race, ethnicity, health, and Native American Studies. She teaches in the sociology department at Boston College.

P. C. Kemeny is Assistant Professor of Religion and Humanities at Grove City College. He is the author of *Princeton in the Nation's Service: Religious Ideals and Educational Practice, 1868–1928* (Oxford University Press, 1998), and he is currently working on *The First Moral Majority: The New England Watch and Ward Society and Moral Reform Politics in Late Nineteenth and Early Twentieth-Century America* (forthcoming, Rutgers University Press).

Keith G. Meador is Professor of the Practice of Pastoral Theology and Medicine at Duke University's Divinity School, where he directs the Theology and Medicine Program and also serves as Clinical Professor of Psychiatry in the Duke University School of Medicine. Dr. Meador is a physician and board-certified psychiatrist and served on the faculty at the Vanderbilt University School of Medicine prior to coming to Duke. He received his B.A. from Vanderbilt University, his M.D. from the University of Louisville, his Th.M. from Duke University, and his M.P.H. from the University of North Carolina at Chapel Hill. He is coauthor (with Joel Shuman) of *Heal Thyself: Spirituality, Medicine, and the Distortion of Christianity* (Oxford University Press, 2002).

Lisa R. Peck is a doctoral candidate in the Division of Psychology in Education at Arizona State University. She is interested in person-environment fit; specifically, how institutionalized environments are related to individuals' cognitive and epistemological development. Her current projects include an analysis of discourse surrounding education policy reform and a dissertation study of how parents' values are related to their decisions about children's schooling.

David Sikkink is Assistant Professor of Sociology at the University of Notre Dame and a Fellow in the Center for Research on Educational Opportunity. He received a doctorate in sociology from the University of North Carolina at Chapel Hill in 1998. His dissertation, *Public Schooling and Its Discontents,* funded by the National Science Foundation, examined the relationship of religion, schooling choices for children, and civic participation. Sikkink's areas of interest include the politics of education, religion and public life, private schooling and civil society, and quantitative methodology. His publications include a *Social Forces* (1999) article on the cultural and religious sources of disaffection from public schools. His other historical essays include a thesis on the Taiping Rebellion in nineteenth-century China and a paper on the role of religion in the rise of National Socialism in Germany.

Christian Smith is Professor of Sociology at the University of North Carolina at Chapel Hill. His interests are in sociology of religion, cultural sociology, and social movements. Smith is the author of *Christian America? What Evangelicals Really Want* (University of California Press, 2000), *American Evangelicalism: Embattled and Thriving* (University of Chicago Press, 1998), *Resisting Reagan: The U.S. Central America Peace Movement* (University of Chicago Press, 1996), *The Emergence of Liberation Theology: Radical Religion and Social Movement Theory* (University of Chicago Press, 1991), coauthor (with Michael O. Emerson) of *Divided by Faith: Evangelical Religion and the Problem of Race in America* (Oxford University Press, 2000), editor of *Disruptive Religion: The Force of Faith in Social Movement Activism* (Routledge, 1996), and coeditor (with Joshua Prokopy) of *Latin American Religion in Motion* (Routledge, 1999).

George M. Thomas is Professor of Sociology at Arizona State University. His interests are in emerging world culture, international organization, and issues of global governance. He studies how religions engage global processes with a focus on conflicts over education. He is the author of *Revivalism and Cultural Change* (University of Chicago Press) and coeditor of *Constructing World Culture* (Stanford University Press).

High Lights :
Intro - pgs 2, 3, 4, 5, 7, 8

universalism, *viii*, 46, 103, 136
universities, 2, 28, 32, 48, 97, 316, 328, 351, 357, 367, 372, 376; German, 56–57, 85n44. *See also* higher education
University of Berlin, 56, 113
University of California at Berkeley, 9, 153
University of Chicago, 8, 75, 112, 150–151, 273–274, 277–278, 283, 294; Divinity School, 294, 301, 370, 390n13
University of Florida, 151
University of Göttingen, 56, 112
University of Halle, 187
University of Illinois, 188, 422, 425
University of Indiana, 241, 430n11
University of Kansas, 430n11
University of Michigan, 294
University of Minnesota, 151, 176
University of Missouri School of Journalism, 424, 430nn11,12
University of Oregon School of Journalism, 414, 430n11
University of Washington, 419, 430n11
University of Wisconsin, 9, 113, 151, 176, 414, 416, 418, 430nn11,12
urbanization, 13, 17, 22, 86n46, 376, 385, 387, 411
U.S. Commissioner of Education, 187
U.S. Congress, 49, 318, 451, 458
U.S. Constitution, 26, 51, 63, 322, 345, 348
U.S. Department of Justice, 335
U.S. Library of Congress, 154n5
U.S. Post Office, 237, 335
U.S. Public Health Service, 451
U.S. Supreme Court, 26, 86n45, 220, 310–311, 317–322, 329–330, 333–334, 338–339, 341–349, 350, 350n2
Utah, 260, 321
utilitarianism, 128

Valley Forge, 337
Vanderbilt, Cornelius, 75
Vanderbilt University, 50
Van Dyke, Henry, 220, 234
Vanzetti, Bartolomeo, 249, 252
Vatican Council, second, 447
Veblen, Thorstein, 78
"Velvet Revolution" (Czechoslovakia), 4
Vermont, 293
Victorian era, 27–28, 49–50, 52, 83n33, 121, 129–130, 220–221, 227–232, 234, 241–243, 260, 317, 319, 322, 326, 328, 339
Viking Press, 229
Villard, Oswald Garrison, 224, 247
Vincent, George, 110, 116, 122–123, 125–126, 133, 135, 138, 148
Vincent, John, 109–110
Virginia, 416
Vocationalism, 375
Voltaire, 34–35, 111, 235

Waddington, C. H., 436
Wagar, W. Warren, 18
Walker, Samuel, 231
Wallace, Anthony, 16, 24
Walters, LeRoy, 448
Ward, Lester, 34, 111, 113, 115–124, 126–131, 134, 137–140, 143, 145, 150, 153, 154n7, 337
"warfare" view of science and religion, 10, 197
Warren, William F., 226
Washington, DC, 226, 276
Washington, George, 3
Washington College (Virginia), 416
Washington University, 151, 338
Watch and Ward Society, 216–220, 222–232, 234–253, 255–261, 263n65
Watchman-Examiner, 250
Wayland, Francis, 99
Weber, Max, 6, 12, 19, 40, 42, 80n6, 81n15, 82n16, 362, 395
Webster, Noah, 283
Weeks, Edward, 247, 256, 258
welfare, 13; states, 80n6; workers, 36
Wellesley College, 257
Wells, Herbert George, 35, 60
Wesley, John, 292
Wesleyan College, 76
Western College of Professional Teachers, 162
Westminster, 128
Westminster Confession, 404
Whewell, William, 198
White, Andrew Dickson, 9, 33, 100, 103, 197, 200–201
White, Emerson Elbridge, 167–168, 171, 173, 177–179, 182, 189, 191
White, Joseph, 167–168, 173
Whitehead, Alfred North, 333

Compositor: G & S Typesetters, Inc.
Text: 10/12 Baskerville
Display: Baskerville
Printer and Binder: Thomson-Shore, Inc.